France

Perfect places to stay, eat & explore

Published by Time Out Guides Ltd, a wholly owned subsidiary of Time Out Group Ltd.
Time Out and the Time Out logo are trademarks of Time Out Group Ltd.

© **Time Out Group Ltd 2009**

10 9 8 7 6 5 4 3 2 1

This edition first published in Great Britain in 2009 by Ebury Publishing
A Random House Group Company
20 Vauxhall Bridge Road, London SW1V 2SA

Random House Australia Pty Limited 20 Alfred Street, Milsons Point, Sydney, New South Wales 2061, Australia
Random House New Zealand Limited 18 Poland Road, Glenfield, Auckland 10, New Zealand
Random House South Africa (Pty) Limited Isle of Houghton, Corner Boundary, Road & Carse O'Gowrie,
Houghton 2198, South Africa

Random House UK Limited Reg. No. 954009

Distributed in USA by Publishers Group West
1700 Fourth Street, Berkeley, California 94710

Distributed in Canada by Publishers Group Canada
250A Carlton Street, Toronto, Ontario M5A 2L1

For further distribution details, see www.timeout.com

ISBN: 978-1-84670-118-4

A CIP catalogue record for this book is available from the British Library

Printed and bound by Firmengruppe APPL, aprinta druck, Wemding, Germany

The Random House Group Limited supports The Forest Stewardship Council (FSC), the leading international
forest certification organisation. All our titles that are printed on Greenpeace approved FSC certified paper carry
the FSC logo. Our paper procurement policy can be found at http://www.rbooks.co.uk/environment.

Time Out carbon-offsets all its flights with Trees for Cities (www.treesforcities.org).

Introduction

Welcome to *Time Out France: Perfect places to stay, eat & explore*, one in a new series of guidebooks that picks out the very best of a country. We've chosen France's most inspiring destinations, with compelling sights and landscapes, and singled out the most appealing hotels, shops and places to eat and drink in all price brackets. We hope that our selection will provide exactly what you need both for planning a visit and then for enjoying it.

France is a wonderfully diverse country, and many of its riches are familiar – plenty of visitors will have treasured memories of waving goodbye to the White Cliffs of Dover on Channel crossings, spending lost weekends on Paris's Left Bank, banging in pegs on sizzling summer camping holidays along the Côte d'Azur or trying in vain to heed ski instructors' pleas to 'bend ze knees' on the slopes of Méribel or La Plagne. And while these classic nostalgia trips have all naturally made it into our selection, we have also tried to delve a little deeper and stray a little further from the well-trodden holiday path – not too hard in a country twice the size of the UK but with a similar population. And if your memories of France also consist of infuriatingly lumpy bolsters, overly rich sauces and surly service, then you'll be pleased to discover that, like the rest of Europe, the French have smartened up their act, and as far as accommodation and – especially – food is concerned, things are improving all the time, as restaurants concentrate more and more on sourcing quality raw ingredients and chefs open up to influences from around the world, although you're still likely to sense a whiff of disdain if you ask for your steak cooked any more than '*saignant*'.

Our team of writers – mostly locals, others with local knowledge – have explored everywhere from the wild, weather-beaten Cévennes to the stunning Atlantic beaches of the Vendée and Charente-Maritime; from the dramatic peaks of the Hautes Pyrénées to the gently green, rolling *ballons* of the Volcans d'Auvergne. We have picked distinctive cities, such as Toulouse and Lille, packed with cultural interest as well as fascinating architecture; and small towns that are big draws, like Montpellier, a perfect mix of medieval and modern just minutes from the Med, and emerging Metz, a rising star of France's cultural scene and soon to be home to a brand new Pompidou Centre. We hope you find some inspiration amid the diversity.

Contents

Rural Idylls

Cities

292

335

379

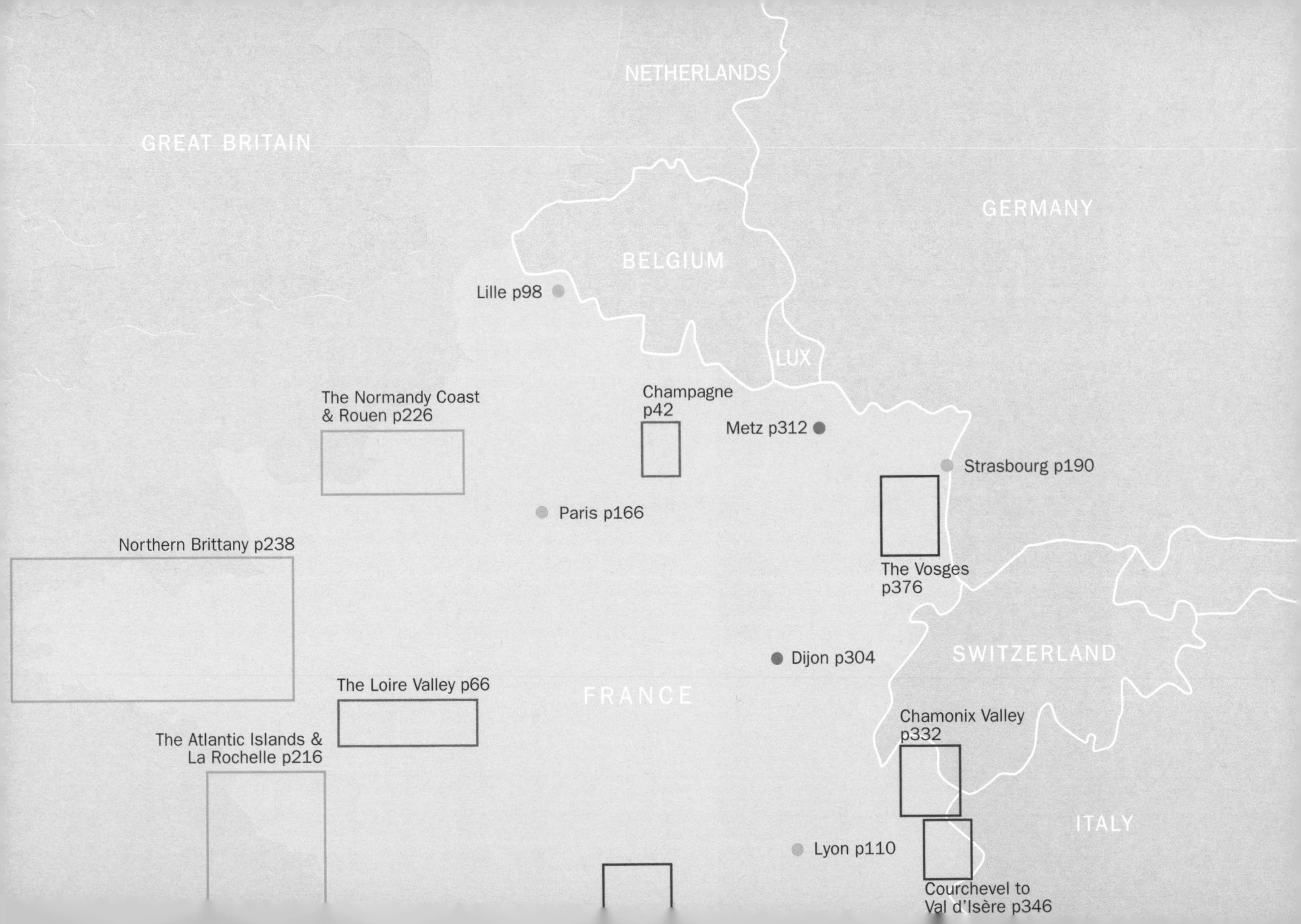

GREAT BRITAIN

NETHERLANDS

GERMANY

BELGIUM

LUX

SWITZERLAND

ITALY

FRANCE

Lille p98

Strasbourg p190

The Vosges p376

Metz p312

Champagne p42

Paris p166

Dijon p304

Chamonix Valley p332

Lyon p110

Courchevel to Val d'Isère p346

The Normandy Coast & Rouen p226

The Loire Valley p66

Northern Brittany p238

The Atlantic Islands & La Rochelle p216

France

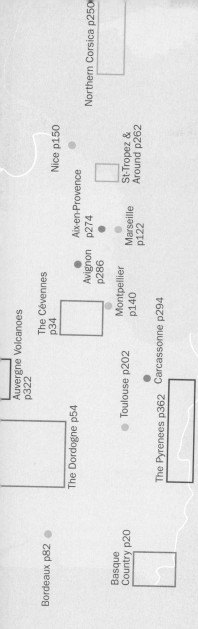

Northern Corsica p250

Nice p150

Aix-en-Provence
p274

St-Tropez &
Around p262

Marseille
p122

Avignon
p286

Montpellier
p140

The Cévennes
p34

Auvergne Volcanoes
p322

Toulouse p202

Carcassonne p294

The Dordogne p54

The Pyrenees p362

Bordeaux p82

Basque
Country p20

SPAIN

0   100km

- Rural Idylls pp18-79
- Cities pp80-213
- Coast pp214-271
- Small Gems pp272-319
- Mountains pp320-385

Editor's Picks

STAR DESTINATIONS

Each destination in the book is rated in a series of categories. Here are the best performers in each:

ART & ARCHITECTURE

EATING & DRINKING

HISTORIC SITES

HOTELS

NIGHTLIFE

OUTDOOR ACTIVITIES

Chez Michel, Marseille p135

Le Ciel d'Or, The Pyrenees p370

Emile, Toulouse p207

Le Parc Franck Putelat, Carcassonne p300

Le Pirate, Northern Corsica p257

Restaurant Richard et Christopher Coutanceau, Atlantic Islands & La Rochelle p222

MID-RANGE
L'Ardoise, Paris p183

Le Bistrot Paul Bert, Paris p184

Café Bastide du Cours, Aix-en-Provence p284

Le Colysée, Lille p104

L'Etude, Metz p315

La Feuillantine, Basque Country p29

L'Impossible, Chamonix p341

Le Jarrousset, Auvergne Volcanoes p326

Les Ménestrels, The Loire Valley p76

La Table du Domaine, The Vosges p382

Tentation, The Pyrenees p372

BUDGET
Bistro Pizay, Lyon p118

Brasserie Georges, Lyon p118

Les Caves Jean Jaurès, Montpellier p144

Chez Yvonne, Strasbourg p196

La Merenda, Nice p159

ART

Atelier Cézanne, Aix-en-Provence p281

Centre Pompidou, Paris p175

Grotte de Niaux, The Pyrenees p368

Horizons Festival, Auvergne Volcanoes p329

Musée des Beaux Arts, Lyon p113

Musée Fabre, Montpellier p142

Musée Granet, Aix-en-Provence p281

Musée du Louvre, Paris p171

Musée Matisse, Nice p157

Musée d'Orsay, Paris p183

Palais des Beaux-Arts, Lille p103

La Piscine, Musée de l'Art de l'Industrie, Lille p104

Pompidou Metz, Metz p318

Vallée de l'Homme, The Dordogne p58

BUILDINGS

CHATEAUX & PALACES
Azay-le-Rideau, The Loire Valley p69

Château du Haut-Koenigsbourg, The Vosges p381

Château de Milandes, The Dordogne p58

Palais des Papes, Avignon p290

Château Royal d'Amboise, The Loire Valley p68

CHURCHES & CATHEDRALS
Abbaye de St-Guilhem, The Cévennes p37

Abbaye Royale de Fontevraud, The Loire Valley p72

Basilique Notre-Dame de Fourvière, Lyon p113

Basilique Notre-Dame-de-la-Garde,Marseille p125

Basilique St-Sernin, Toulouse p204

Cathédrale Notre-Dame, Reims, Champagne p46

Cathédrale Notre-Dame de Paris, Paris p168

Cathédrale de Notre-Dame, Strasbourg p192

Cathédrale St-Etienne de Metz, Metz p314

Eglise St-Germain-des-Prés, Paris p178

Eglise St-Jean-Baptiste, Basque Country p26

GARDENS

Château de Marqueyssac, The Dordogne p56

Jardin Botanique de la Bastide, Bordeaux p89

this is my **P&O**

I like to travel with someone I trust

If you're thinking of heading over to France for your holiday, you can rely on P&O Ferries to get you there. It's not just that we have a proud maritime heritage stretching back over 150 years we also have more sailings to France than anyone else. That means that you get to travel at a time that suits you.

It's quick too. Drive onto one of our spacious, comfortable ferries at Dover, and in less than 90 minutes – just enough time to enjoy our great restaurants, bars and shopping – you'll be in Calais and on your way. Then there's the price. A car and up to nine people are all covered by one great value ticket. So if want to get away from it all, we've made sure you can still afford to

Check out our best prices and book online now.

POferries.com
08716 64 64 64

P&O Ferrie

dover calais • **hull** zeebrugge / rotterdam • **portsmouth** bilbao • **cairnryan / troon** larne • **liverpool** dublin

ABOUT THE GUIDE

The € symbols in the area chapters indicate the price bracket of a venue: €=budget, €€=moderate, €€€=expensive and €€€€=luxury. Unless otherwise stated, all venues accept Visa and MasterCard credit cards. Some restaurants and hotels are hidden away deep in the countryside. In these cases we've indicated a location relative to a nearby town or village, but do check venues' websites for detailed directions. All our listings are double-checked, but businesses do sometimes close or change their hours and prices, so we recommend that you check particulars by phone or online before visiting.

www.hammond-villas.co.uk

Hammond Villas offers some of the most beautiful villas with pools in France and Italy. Our expert staff has a combined experience of over 50 years in the holiday letting market, and we know all the owners of our villas personally. We know how important your holiday is to you, and we will love to help you find the perfect villa.

Online booking

We have a number of exclusive villas in Southwest France. Now it is easier than ever to book your preferred dates; simply click on the "book online" button on our main page, and you will see the list of **beautiful villas that you won't find anywhere else**. You can book any available dates at your convenience.

Posta Di Guardia, Italy

La Bergeronière, Charente, France

More Italian villas

Our updated selection of Italian villas is simply outstanding. We have added twenty new villas and taken new photos of the whole lot. During our visit we became more familiar with what this gorgeous country can offer – and we would love for you to **discover it too**.

Les Gueybauds, Dordogne, France

Financial protection

In 2008 we became a member of the Travel Trust Association. This means that every holiday at Hammond Villas is now financially guaranteed.

• Katrina Hammond Villas Limited •
• Registered in England Number 5448816 •
• Registered Office: 2-6 Cannon Street, London EC4M 6YH •
• Mailing Address: Domaine de la Bergère 33420 Moulon France •
• www.hammond-villas.co.uk • katrina@ hammond-villas.co.uk •

Contributors

Anna Brooke lives in Paris and frequently contributes to Time Out's Paris publications. She is also the author of several guidebooks and writes features for a variety of UK newspapers. For this book she happily ate and drank too much in the Loire Valley and Champagne.

Simon Cropper is a former staff writer at Time Out's Paris office. He has edited and written for a variety of Time Out books on travel and the arts, and fulfilled his passion for planes with a trip to Toulouse for this book.

Alison Culliford moved to France in 2001 to work in Time Out's Paris office and contributes regularly to Time Out's Paris guides. For this book she conquered her fear of hairpins to report on the Auvergne and the Pyrenees, as well as the gentler Dordogne.

Dominic Earle is a freelance travel journalist and confirmed Francophile. In addition to editing Time Out guides to Paris, Copenhagen, Stockholm and European skiing, he has also contributed to publications including the *Guardian* and *Independent*.

Natasha Edwards has lived in Paris for over 15 years, exploring France and writing about design, food and culture. She is a regular contributor to and former editor of the *Time Out Paris* and *Time Out South of France* guides.

Tristan Rutherford has been a freelance travel writer and Riviera resident since 2002. One of his first guidebook assignments was in Corsica, and the island has had an irresistible pull ever since. He recently returned on his red scooter to complete this chapter. His writing appears in the *Independent* and *Guardian*.

Cyrus Shahrad is a musician, writer and former snowboard magazine editor living and working in London. He has been travelling annually to Chamonix since 2001, and every year finds something new to inspire and intimidate in equal measure.

Paul Sullivan has been a freelance travel writer and photographer since 2000, and was a previous contributor to Time Out's *Perfect Places Italy*. For this book he covered Metz and Dijon, two of France's most charming cities.

Kathryn Tomasetti formed a teenage crush on the South of France during an Interrail trip in the early '90s and moved to Nice in 2005. She produces features and photographs from all over Provence, Turkey and her own native Italy.

Rich Woodruff is a Paris-based journalist and video producer specialising in cinema, culture, sport and travel. For this book he wrote about two of his favourite places in northern France – Strasbourg and the Vosges.

Contributors by chapter

Basque Country Natasha Edwards. **The Cévennes** Dominic Earle. **Champagne** Anna Brooke. **The Dordogne** Alison Culliford. **The Loire Valley** Anna Brooke. **Bordeaux** Natasha Edwards. **Lille** Natasha Edwards. **Lyon** Dominic Earle. **Marseille** Natasha Edwards. **Montpellier** Dominic Earle. **Nice** Elizabeth Winding, Tristan Rutherford & Kathryn Tomasetti. **Paris** Dominic Earle. **Strasbourg** Rich Woodruff. **Toulouse** Simon Cropper. **The Atlantic Islands & La Rochelle** Simon Cropper. **The Normandy Coast & Rouen** Simon Cropper. **Northern Brittany** Simon Cropper. **Northern Corsica** Tristan Rutherford & Kathryn Tomasetti. **St-Tropez & Around** Tristan Rutherford & Kathryn Tomasetti. **Aix-en-Provence** Natasha Edwards. **Avignon** Stephen Mudge. **Carcassonne** Simon Cropper. **Dijon** Paul Sullivan. **Metz** Paul Sullivan. **Auvergne Volcanoes** Alison Culliford. **Chamonix Valley** Cyrus Shahrad. **Courchevel to Val d'Isère** Dominic Earle. **The Pyrenees** Alison Culliford. **The Vosges** Rich Woodruff.

THE LUXURY
DEPARTMENT STORE
DESTINATION

PRINTEMPS.COM

PRINTEMPS

PARIS

Time Out Guides Limited
Universal House
251 Tottenham Court Road
London W1T 7AB
Tel + 44 (0)20 7813 3000
Fax + 44 (0)20 7813 6001
Email guides@timeout.com
www.timeout.com

Maps Kei Ishimaru. Street maps by JS Graphics Ltd (john@jsgraphics.co.uk). Maps of Lyon and Toulouse are based on material supplied by Netmaps.

Cover photography Lavender field by village, Provence © Getty Images

Photography: pages 4 (left), 20, 23, 27, 28, 31, 32, 34, 39, 40, 57, 59, 62, 202, 206, 211, 212, 362, 365, 366, 369, 371, 373 Jonathan Perugia; pages 4 (middle), 5, 42, 47, 51, 52, 150 (bottom), 158 (bottom), 161, 163, 190, 193, 194, 197, 200, 262 (top, left), 262 (middle, right), 266, 269, 274, 276, 279, 280, 283, 286, 292, 304, 307, 310, 312, 317, 332, 339, 343, 344, 346, 349, 352, 355, 359, 360, 376, 378, 381, 383, 384 Charlie Pinder; page 4 (right), 173 (bottom, left), 262 Karl Blackwell; page 24 Courtesy of Le Petit Train De La Rhune; page 59 Akim Benbrahim/Pays du Périgor; pages 66, 70, 77, 78, 166, 169, 173(top, right), 173 (bottom, right), 175, 179 (middle, right), 179 (bottom, right), 181, 182, 185, 186, 226 Olivia Rutherford; page 66 (middle, right) JF Le Sc; pages 75, 90 [http://www.france-balloons.com]www.france-balloons.com; pages 80, 81 Getty Images; pages 82, 92, 95 [http://www.bordeaux-tourisme.com]www.bordeaux-tourisme.com; page 86 Thomas Sanson/Mairie de Bordeaux; page 98 (top) Frederic Lovino; pages 98 (bottom left), 102 OT Lille /Don Muschter; pages 98 (bottom, right), 98 (middle, left) OT Lille/Maxime Dufour Photographies; pages 110 (top), 110 (bottom right) Marie Perrin Lyon Tourism; page 110 Jacques Leone; page 110 Francesco Dazzi/Shutterstock; page 150 (top, left) Franck Follet; page 150 (top, right) Asasirov/Shutterstock; page 158 (top) Hugues Lagarde; pages 173 (top, left), 173 (middle) Heloise Bergman; page 179 (top) Oliver Knight; page 179 (bottom, left) Jean-Christophe Godet; pages 226 (top), 226 (bottom right), 233, 236, 238, 243, 244, 247, 248 Olivia Rutherford; page 226 (bottom left), 230 Sofron/Shutterstock; page 229 (middle, right), 299 Xavier MARCHANT/Shutterstock; page 229 Pack-Shot/Shutterstock; page 229 Alexey Seleznev/Shutterstock; page 294 (top), 294 (top), 229 (left) Walid Nohra/Shutterstock; page 294 (bottom) Javier Gill/Shutterstock; page 294 (middle, left) Jerome Scholler/Shutterstock; page 297 (top) Philippe Benoist; page 297 (bottom, right) Alexander Studentschnig/Shutter; page 297 (bottom, left) Karoline Cullen/Shutterstock; pages 318 © CA2M/Shigeru Ban Architects Europe & Jean de Gastines/Artefactory; page 332 Monica Dalmasso; page 362 (bottom, left) Alison Culliford.

The following images were provided by the featured establishments/artists: page 66, 70, 72 (bottom, left), 94, 97, 105, 108, 116, 119, 164, 235, 270, 302, 335, 371 (bottom, right), 209, 374.

The editor would like to thank Rail Europe (www.raileurope.co.uk) and Maison de la France.

Rural Idylls

Top and below: Pyrenees.
Below left: St-Jean-de-Luz.

Basque Country

Where France meets Spain, and the mountains meet the sea.

Red peppers, oxblood farmhouses, crashing breakers, spicy food and a language that seems to consist almost entirely of Xs, Zs and Vs all contribute to making the Basque Country one of the most exotic corners of France. This is a place where age-old traditions mix with lively nightlife, palace hotels and a laid-back surf lifestyle; where towering mountains mix with the rugged Atlantic coast; and where a sporty lifestyle of pelote, *force basque* (highland games-style tests of strength), rugby, golf, mountain walking and world-class surfing mixes with a spiritual lifeblood of galleried churches, choirs and oral story-telling tradition.

Of the seven historic Basque provinces, the French Basque Country encompasses the three northern provinces (Labourd, Basse-Navarre and Soule), which after oscillating between French, Spanish and English domination were finally absorbed into France in the 16th century. All the same, with their shared language cross-border exchanges with Spain remain important – old smugglers' routes between the two have been replaced by the more official Eurocité Basque Bayonne San Sebastian trading agreement. The French head to Spain for frontier *ventas*, source of cheap petrol, alcohol, cigarettes and tacky souvenirs, and the tapas bars of San Sebastian; the Spanish come to France for the sandy beaches and the boutiques of Biarritz.

In this chapter we concentrate on the coastal strip, where fortified Bayonne, royal St-Jean-de-Luz and French surf capital Biarritz give an idea of how the region has evolved over the centuries; on the western end of the Pyrenees, with the Rhune mountain and the picturesque villages of the southern Labourd; and inland on the isolated Aldudes Valley and the historic town and hikers' halt of St-Jean-Pied-de-Port.

Explore

BAYONNE

Situated at the confluence of the Adour and Nive rivers, the historic port of Bayonne is the rough diamond to elegant Biarritz. Birthplace of the bayonnet and still a garrison town, Bayonne has the year-round appeal of a living, working place that is fiercely attached to Basque culture, notably during the riotous Fêtes de Bayonne each August. The historic centre divides roughly into the Grand Bayonne on the left bank of the Nive, with its ramparts, quayside tapas bars and restaurants, chocolate shops along arcaded rue du Pont Neuf and narrow streets climbing up to the cathedral; the Petit Bayonne on the right bank, home to the area's two main museums; and the Quartier St-Esprit around the station.

Cathédrale Ste-Marie

Pl Monseigneur Vansteenberghe (05.59.59.17.82). Open Cathedral 10-11.45am, 3-5.45pm Mon-Sat; 3.30-6pm Sun. Cloister (05.59.46.11.43) May, Oct 9.30am-12.30pm, 2-6pm daily. June-Sept 9am-6pm daily. Nov-Apr 9.30am-12.30pm, 2-5pm daily. Admission free.
The twin spires of the Gothic Ste-Marie cathedral dominate Bayonne. The broad, triple-naved interior is famous for its rib vaulting and painted, sculpted ceiling bosses, including a battleship and the arms of England. The beautiful UNESCO-listed cloister (reached around the back on place Pasteur) has three sides of finely carved trefoil arcading.

Musée Basque et de l'Histoire de Bayonne

Maison Dagourette, 37 quai des Corsaires (05.59.59.08.98/www.musee-basque.com). Open May-Oct 10am-6.30pm Tue-Sun; Nov-Apr 10am-12.30pm, 2-6pm Tue-Sun. Admission €5.50; €3 reductions.
This vast collection, displayed across a beautifully restored early 17th-century mansion, presents the history and folk traditions of Bayonne and the Basque Country, from costumes and faïence to religious festivals, the symbolism of the Basque farmhouse and the still active craft of making *chisteras* (wicker gloves) for the game of pelote. The museum uses imaginative presentation techniques, with items and archive photos brought to life by documentary film footage and sound recordings.

Musée Bonnat

5 rue Jacques Laffitte (05.59.59.08.52/www.musee-bonnat.com). Open May, June, Sept, Oct 10am-6.30pm Mon, Wed-Sun; July, Aug 10am-6.30pm daily (until 9.30pm Wed); Nov-Apr 10am-12.30pm, 2-6pm Mon, Wed-Sun. Admission €5.50; free-€3 reductions.
Bayonne owes its impressive fine art museum to Léon Bonnat, local art teacher and successful society portraitist, who donated his personal collection to be presented in specially conceived galleries built around a glazed atrium. The display is strong on Spanish paintings, including El Greco, Goya and Ribera, and English portraiture by Reynolds and Lawrence, while the 19th-century French school includes Bonnat's own sugary fare, portraits by Degas and the sensual *Baigneuse* by Ingres, which has become the museum's mascot.

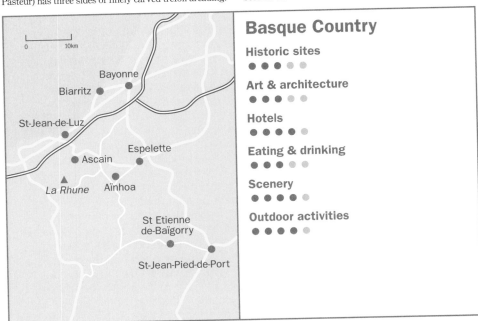

Basque Country

Historic sites
● ● ● ● ●

Art & architecture
● ● ● ● ○

Hotels
● ● ● ● ○

Eating & drinking
● ● ● ○ ○

Scenery
● ● ● ● ○

Outdoor activities
● ● ● ● ○

St-Jean-de-Luz.

La Rhune.

BIARRITZ

The most glamorous resort on France's Atlantic coast grew up when a tiny former whaling village became a fashionable bathing spot, its success sealed by the arrival in the 1850s of the Spanish-born Empress Eugénie and Napoléon III, who built what is now the Hôtel du Palais and the Hispano-Romano-Mauresque Chapelle Impériale. The cream of European royalty and aristocracy followed in their wake, leaving a legacy of eccentric belle époque villas, mock castles and neo-Basque architecture. The resort thrived in the 1920s and '30s, when it gained its art deco casino and town hall. It was reborn in the 1950s thanks to the new sport of surfing, supposedly brought here from California by Hollywood scriptwriter Peter Viertel during the filming of Hemingway's The Sun Also Rises.

Today this makes for a fascinating mix of well-bred families, the odd showbiz star and a young sporty set, reflected in the town's shops where designer labels (it's no coincidence that Coco Chanel had her first boutique here), Basque table linens and chocolates vie with surfwear and streetwear. The Grande Plage dominates the town centre with its stripy tents, seafront promenade and the spectacle of surfers riding the waves. Another focus is Les Halles covered market, both for its superb fresh produce and for the bistros and tapas bars in the surrounding streets. The former Anglican church on rue Broquedis (spot the memorial to British troops who took on Napoleon) is now a dusty museum of local history with whalebone spoons, early bathing costumes and royal memorabilia.

For majestic sea vistas, head for the top of the lighthouse at the northern edge of town or south from the Grande Plage on the footpaths that wind around the rocky headland to the tiny Port des Pêcheurs. For surfers, the legendary spot is the Plage de la Côte des Basques, used for the women's longboard world championship in July.

Casino de Biarritz

1 av Edouard VII (05.59.22.77.77/www.lucien barriere.com). Open Slot machines 10am-3am daily; gaming tables 8pm-3am daily; restaurant 8pm-midnight daily; club midnight-5am Thur-Sat.

Biarritz's art deco casino sits in a splendid position along the Grande Plage but there's much more than gambling here, with gaming tables and slot machines complemented by a theatre, restaurant, beachside café/tearoom and brasserie (Maison Dodin is the place for ice-creams and snacks, the Café de la Grande Plage for more formal meals), surf shops under the arcades, and the municipal swimming pool. Over-21s only allowed in the gaming rooms (bring ID).

La Gare de Midi – Ballet Biarritz

23 av du Maréchal Foch (05.59.59.23.79/www. entractes-organisations.com/www.balletbiarritz.com). Open times vary.

This converted art nouveau train station has become one of the prime dance venues in southern France thanks to choreographer Thierry Malandrain's acclaimed Ballet Biarritz, renowned for its imaginative interpretations of classic works. Visiting dance companies also perform here, especially during September's Le Temps d'Aimer la Danse festival, which also features pop concerts and theatre.

Musée de la Mer

Esplanade du Rocher de la Vierge (05.59.22.33.34/ www.museedelamer.com). Open Apr, May, Oct 9.30am-12.30pm, 2-6pm daily; June, Sept 9.30am-7pm daily; July, Aug 9.30am-midnight daily; Nov-Mar 9.30am-12.30pm, 2-6pm Tue-Sun. Closed 2 weeks mid Jan. Admission €7.80; €5 reductions.

The art deco maritime museum is enormously popular for its basement aquariums of the fish and marine invertebrates found in the Bay of Biscay. Up above are displays about the fishing industry and a collection of the region's stuffed birds, but there's no doubt that the stars of the show are the seals (feeding time 10.30am & 5pm daily). The museum is currently undergoing expansion with the addition of a new Caribbean lagoon.

LA RHUNE & THE INLAND LABOURD VILLAGES

Straddling the Franco-Spanish border, the 900-metre (2,950 feet) Rhune is not the highest mountain in the Pyrenees. But its pyramidal form is an alluring presence, dominating the western end of the range for miles around. The Petit Train (www.rhune.com, open Mar-Nov), a vintage rack-and-pinion railway that crawls to the summit from the Col de St-Ignace, takes the effort out of the climb and you'll be rewarded by the sight of birds of prey, long-haired manech sheep and wild pottok ponies.

The gorgeous inland villages of Aïnhoa, Ascain, Espelette and Sare epitomise the Basque Country at its most picture-perfect, with half-timbered red and white farmhouses, salmon-coloured pelote *frontons* (walled courts) and sober churches against a backdrop of rolling farmland and lush green mountains. Aïnhoa, a *bastide* founded by the Premonstration Order, essentially consists of one street of fine houses mostly dating from the 17th century, when the village was rebuilt after the Thirty Years War, as reflected in the dates and inscriptions carved into stone door lintels. Lively Sare, centred on the quintessential trio of pelote *fronton*, church and *mairie* – and busy bar next door – remains authentic, despite a tradition of illustrious visitors, with fine houses reflecting fortunes made from contraband with the town of Zugarramurdi across the mountains in Spain. The main village is surrounded by a series of outlying hamlets and tiny roadside chapels. Larger Espelette, built up around the medieval Château des Barons d'Ezpeleta (now the town hall and tourist office) owes its notoriety and tourists to the spicy red espelette peppers, grown only here and in a handful of nearby villages, which hang in picturesque strings on the façades of the houses, where they gradually turn from scarlet when picked to a dark maroon when dry.

Grottes de Sare

6km SE of Sare (05.59.54.21.88/www.sare.fr). Open July, Aug 10am-7pm daily; Apr-June, Sept 10am-6pm daily; Oct 10am-5pm daily; Nov-Mar 2-5pm daily. Closed Jan. Admission €6.50; €3.50 reductions.
Since flooding a couple of years ago, this prehistoric cave complex, inhabited some 20,000 years ago, has reopened with a multimedia sound and light show – you are led around the caves by a Lamin, a sort of Basque pixie. Outside, the surrounding park contains dolmens, primitive huts and other features of prehistoric life.

Villa Arnaga Musée Edmond Rostand

Rte du Dr Camino, Cambo-les-Bains (05.59.29.83.92/ www.arnaga.com). Open times vary. Admission €6.20; free-€3.20 reductions.
Sitting in manicured formal gardens, this former home of playwright Edmond Rostand, built when he moved to this rural spa town for health reasons, is a sort of Arts and Crafts take on a Basque house, with murals depicting fairytales in his children's bedroom, marquetry and furniture made by local craftsmen, as well as a collection of memorabilia.

ST-ETIENNE-DE-BAIGORRY & THE ALDUDES VALLEY

Sprawled beneath the turreted Château d'Etchauz, the village of St-Etienne-de-Baïgorry marks the entrance to the isolated Aldudes Valley, a forgotten slice of rural France jutting into Spain, with vineyards, flocks of sheep, trout farms and not much else. At the end of the valley at Aldudes is the farm of Pierre Oteiza (05.59.37.56.11/www.pierreoteiza.com), the farmer and *charcutier* who saved the small, hairy pink and black Basque pig from extinction (by turning it into excellent ham). A circuit can be followed on foot, with a donkey or in a four-wheel-drive from the pregnant sows in the nursery in the valley, through beech and oak woods where young pigs are introduced to nature, and up on to the open mountainsides above.

ST-JEAN-DE-LUZ TO THE SPANISH FRONTIER

St-Jean-de-Luz is both an important fishing port, where colourful smacks bob in the mouth of the Nivelle, and an elegant beach resort with a long, sheltered Grande Plage – more child-friendly than the roaring surf of Biarritz – and tree-lined avenues of neo-Basque villas. The town packs in an old-fashioned, innocent charm, along with traces of its aristocratic heyday – Louis XIV and Maria Theresa, the Spanish Infanta, were married here in 1660 as part of the Treaty of the Pyrenees, bringing peace between France and Spain. The Maison Louis XIV (guided visits

Easter-Sept) and the Maison de l'Infante (open mid June-mid Oct), the two fine 17th-century mansions where the future couple stayed in the days leading up to the marriage, are both open to visitors. Town life focuses on the café terraces of place Louis XIV and shop-filled rue Gambetta.

The *criée* or wholesale fish market takes place at Ciboure, St-Jean-de-Luz's quieter twin across the estuary, which has some fine old houses and its own pleasant small beach by the Socoa fort, a castle built successively by the French and Spanish; in summer a small ferry potters between the Socoa and St-Jean's Grande Plage. The Ciboure tourist office at 27 quai Maurice Ravel occupies a 17th-century shipowner's house where composer Maurice Ravel was born in 1875.

West of here the scenic Corniche Basque (D912) follows the coast, or you can walk it along the Sentier du Littoral footpath (allow a minimum of three hours from St-Jean-de-Luz to Hendaye; seven-and-a-half hours if starting at Bidart on the edge of Biarritz). Unless you're a surf fanatic, you probably won't want to spend much time in down-at-heel Hendaye, except to visit the eccentric Château d'Abbadie and its clifftop grounds.

Château d'Abbadie

D912, rte de la Corniche, Hendaye (05.59.20.04.51/ www.academie-sciences.fr/abbadia.htm). Open June-Sept 12.30-2pm Mon-Fri; 2-6pm Sat, Sun (gided visits Feb-May, Oct-mid Dec 2-5pm Tue-Sat; June-Sept 10-11.30am, 2.30-6pm Mon-Fri). Admission €5.50; free-€2.70 reductions. Guided visits €6.60; free-€3.30 reductions.
If you appreciate 19th-century excess, then this mock castle built between 1864 and 1879 for astronomer and explorer Antoine d'Abbadie is for you. True to form, Gothic Revivalist Viollet-le-Duc made it more medieval than medieval, full of turrets, gargoyles, carved frogs and crocodiles. Admission includes a visit to Abbadie's library and private observatory with its impressive vintage telescopes.

Eglise St-Jean-Baptiste

Rue Gambetta, St-Jean-de-Luz (05.59.26.08.81). Open 8.30am-noon, 2-7pm daily. Admission free.
This is perhaps the finest of all the Basque Country's churches. The simple exterior conceals a richly decorated interior with three tiers of turned wood galleries along the sides reserved for the men while women sat below, an ornate pulpit and a Baroque altarpiece with rows of carved gilded statues of saints. Louis XIV and the Spanish Infanta were married here on 9 June 1660, although the doorway used by the royal couple was subsequently walled up.

ST-JEAN-PIED-DE-PORT

The former capital of Basse Navarre was long a pawn in power games between Gascon-controlled Bayonne and Navarre-controlled Pamplona, hence the handsome set of pink stone ramparts that ring the old town, and the sturdy Citadelle reinforced by Vauban at the top. At its liveliest

The chocolate coast

One of Bayonne's lesser-known claims to fame is as the birthplace of French chocolate, and it's still big business here. Many Jews who were expelled from Spain and Portugal during the Inquisition in 1609 subsequently settled in the St-Esprit quarter of the town, and they brought with them the know-how to transform the cocoa bean discovered by the Conquistadores in Latin America. Before long hot chocolate had become a fashionable drink and was introduced into court circles by Anne of Austria, consort of Louis XIII.

Today Bayonne, along with Biarritz and St-Jean-de-Luz, is still home to a vast number of *chocolatiers*. Cazenave (19 rue du Port Neuf, Bayonne, 05.59.59.03.16) has been using the same machinery to make chocolates since 1850 and keeps up the tradition of hot drinking chocolate, served under a mound of hand-whipped froth in rose-sprigged Limoges porcelain at its period tearoom. Daranatz (15 rue du Port Neuf, Bayonne, 05.59.59.59.03, www.chocolat-bayonne-daranatz.fr), which was founded in 1890, is the source of chocolate bars in numerous plain and flavoured varieties (including, of course, the inevitable espelette pepper version).

Century-old Pariès (14 rue du Port Neuf, Bayonne, 05.59.59.06.29, www.paries.fr) is renowned for its prize-winning chocolate ganaches, as well as *kanougas* (toffees) and marzipan *tourons* (nougats). Maison Adam in Biarritz (27 pl Clémenceau, Biarritz, 05.59.26.03.54. www.macarons-adam.com), although famed for its macaroons, also creates some spectacular chocolate window displays in its glamorous new boutique.

If all those sweet treats have left you hungry for a bit of background, you can learn more about the history of chocolate, from the Mayas to the present day, at the excellent Planète Musée du Chocolat (14 av Beaurivage, Biarritz, 05.59.23.27.72, www.planetemuseeduchocolat.com), which has a huge collection of chocolate moulds, advertising memorabilia and weird chocolate sculptures on display. Alternatively, the Atelier du Chocolat de Bayonne (17 allée du Gibéleou, Bayonne, 05.59.55.70.23, www.atelierduchocolat.fr) allows you to drool as you watch chocolates being made on the spot.

And if that's still not enough to satisfy your cravings, you can go for total body immersion with a skin-softening Modelage Hot Chocolate at the Sofitel Thalassa Miramar (13 rue Louison Bobet, Biarritz, www.sofitel.com).

Sissinou.

during the big produce and general market on Mondays, St-Jean-Pied-de-Port is a meeting point of the GR10 and GR65 long-distance footpaths and still an important halt on the pilgrimage route to Santiago de Compostela – the town is sprinkled with pilgrims' hostels and rooms, which are often indicated by a cockleshell sign or hiking boot. The route goes through the town and the attractive nearby villages of Caro and St-Martin. At 41 rue de la Citadelle, the vaulted medieval rooms of the so-called Prison des Evêques (open Apr-Oct) contain a display about the pilgrimage routes.

Eat

The Basque Country's distinctive cuisine reflects its land-sea mix: Basque ham and pork, lamb, sheep's cheese and pigeon from the Pyrenees; tuna, hake, sardines, anchovies and squid from the sea. Red espelette pepper seasons countless dishes such as *ttoro* (fish soup), *piperade* (a sort of scrambled egg mixed with peppers, tomatoes, onions and Bayonne ham) and *axoa* (finely diced veal cooked with garlic).

Ahizpak

Biarritz *13 av de Verdun (05.59.22.09.26). Open 7.30-10pm Mon; noon-2pm, 7.30-10pm Tue-Sat; noon-2pm Sun. €€€.*
Ahizpak (pronounced like icepack) is Basque for 'sisters' and refers to Yenufa in the kitchen and her two siblings in the dining room. It is a fine example of the new breed of affordable gourmet bistro, drawing Biarritz's chattering classes with a suave beige interior and a blackboard menu that adds a personal touch to fresh local ingredients – perhaps seafood risotto, cod with white haricot beans and sorrel or a delicate fruit gratin.

Arcé

St-Etienne-de-Baïgorry *(05.59.37.40.14/www.hotel-arce.com). Open Sept-15 July 7-9pm Mon; noon-2pm, 7-9pm Tue, Thur-Sun. 15 July-end Aug noon-2pm, 7-9pm daily. Closed mid Nov-mid Mar. €€€.*
This big Basque-style restaurant with a terrace overhanging the river has in the same family ever since Jean Arcé built a *trinquet* court here (now the dining room) in 1865. Although the restaurant is part of a hotel (doubles from €125), it is very definitely a place where locals come for a celebratory meal out. Chef Pascal Arcé is dedicated to using local seasonal produce, including mountain lamb and home-smoked river trout.

Auberge Basque

Inland Labourd *St-Pée-sur-Nivelle, Helbarron, on the D307 old road to St-Jean-de-Luz (05.59.51.70.00/ www.aubergebasque.com). Open term time 8-9.30pm Tue, Fri, Sat; 12.30-1.45pm, 8-9.30pm Wed, Thur, Sun; school hols 8-9.30pm Tue, 12.30-1.45pm, 8-9.30pm Wed-Sun. Closed Feb. €€€€.*

Since it opened in 2007, the Auberge Basque has become one of the area's most prized gastronomic destinations for the inspired modern cooking of young chef Cédric Bechade, whose imaginative dishes make use of the finest local ingredients. The very strong wine list is yet more reason to make the trip here. After training at the Hôtel du Palais in Biarritz and Plaza Athénée in Paris, Bechade bought up a simple country inn and added a sophisticated modern extension, which offers views of the open kitchen in one direction and across open countryside in the other.

Le Bar Basque

Biarritz *1 rue du Port Vieux (05.59.24.60.92). Open Summer 9am-2am daily; Winter 9am-2am Wed-Sun. Closed 3wks Dec. €€.*
This convivial, rustic-looking Basque tavern with its dark wood and zinc bar is the place to come for sophisticated tapas and *pinxos*, mini salads, plates of Spanish ham, sheep's cheese with quince jelly, tempting desserts and an international selection of wines of the month. Eat around the bar, at small candlelit tables or on the outside terrace.

Bodega Chez Gilles

Bayonne *23 quai Jaureguiberry (05.59.25.40.13). Open noon-2.30pm, 7.30-11pm daily. €€.*
One of the best addresses on Bayonne's lively riverside drag, both for its reliable cooking and for the friendly welcome of Gilles himself. Sit on the riverside terrace or in the rustic interior with big wooden tables, long bar and view of the chefs at work. Feast on excellent steak, sea bass with serrano ham, a *parillada* of mixed grilled fish or shared plates of marinated anchovies, stuffed peppers and other tapas. Good Spanish wines on offer too.

Le Caritz

Biarritz *Pl du Port Vieux (05.59.24.41.84/www. lecaritz-biarritz.com). Open noon-midnight daily. €€.*
Long serving hours make Le Caritz a popular option. Add to this some funky decor, much better than average brasserie fare and a genuine welcome from former rugby international Pascal Ondarts, as well as prized sea views from the roof terrace in fine weather, and you'll see why it draws an eclectic mix of locals and visitors. As well as the expected steaks, tartares and shellfish, more original dishes include grilled fish in red pepper sauce or sheep's milk ice-cream. There are also 12 stylish bedrooms.

Le Feuillantine

Bayonne *21-23 quai Amiral Dubourdieu (05.59.46.14.94/www.lafeuillantine-bayonne.com). Open 12.30-2pm, 7.30-9.30pm Mon, Tue, Thur-Sat; 12.30-2pm Wed. Closed 1wk Dec & 2wks Feb. €€€.*
Hidden in a cluster of touristy brasseries, this unassuming-looking restaurant is a welcome discovery for the refined cooking and earnest welcome of young couple Virginie and Nicolas Borteyru – she's front of house, he's an haute cuisine-trained chef. The daily lunch menu is a bargain, with offerings such as an accomplished tomato *tarte fine* and the catch of the day, but the chef shows his prowess in more ambitious creations, such as sea urchin soufflé served with soldiers.

Olatua

St-Jean-de-Luz *30 bd Thiers (05.59.51.05.22/www. olatua.fr). Open 12.15-1.30pm, 7.45-9pm daily. €€€.*
This spacious bistro in a converted perfume shop is one of St-Jean-de-Luz's recent success stories. Chef Olivier Lataste clearly has plenty of ideas and a love for fashionable offal, but if you can't cope with pig's ears and veal brawn, then there are also plenty of less daunting options, such as excellent fish soup or duck confit.

Paxkal Oillarburu

St-Jean-Pied-de-Port *8 rue de l'Eglise (05.59.37.06.44). Open Sept-June noon-2pm, 7-9.30pm Mon, Wed-Sun. July, Aug noon-2pm, 7-9.30pm daily. Closed 1wk Jan. €€.*
This simple restaurant virtually built into the side of the ramparts is unpretentious, animated and very good value, with a friendly waitress who manages to remain cheerful while serving an entire dining room. Go for regional faves, such as *piperade* or *gâteau basque*, on one of the inexpensive menus or order up a generous plate of fried Iraty *truitelles* (baby trout).

Sissinou

Biarritz *5 av du Maréchal Foch (05.59.22.51.50). Open July, Aug 8-10pm Tue-Sat. Sept-June noon-1.30pm, 8-10pm Tue-Sat. Closed Feb. €€€€.*
Sissinou is a sleek, chic shopfront dining room where chef Michel Cassou Debat does some of the best modern cooking in town, though prices have unfortunately shot up since he was discovered by the *beau monde*. His style mixes rusticity and sophistication: think millefeuille of rabbit and vegetables, lamb sweetbreads crowned with pea sauce, and a must-have *russe d'oloron* for dessert.

Stay

Grand Hôtel Loreamar Thalasso Spa

St-Jean-de-Luz *43 bd Thiers (05.59.26.35.36/ www.luzgrandhotel.fr). €€€.*
This pink and white *gâteau* of a hotel swans it over St-Jean-de-Luz's Grande Plage. Opened in 1909, it was totally redone a couple of years ago by decorator Pierre-Yves Rochon in Victorian spirit with lots of flowers, canopied beds and flouncy touches; a couple of rooms even share their own private pool. Complete your pampering at the high-tech thalassotherapy spa, a luxury haven for seawater and beauty treatments, with heated indoor seawater pool as well as direct access to the beach. There's also a cosy bar and two restaurants, one gastronomic, the other a simpler *rôtisserie*.

Hôtel Arraya

Inland Labourd *Sare (05.59.54.20.46/www. arraya.com). Closed Nov-Mar. €€.*
This gorgeous village hotel, once a pilgrims' halt on the route to Compostela, has been an inn for centuries, with wooden banisters polished by the years, old oak settles, and a narrow staircase that climbs to a secret raised garden. Bedrooms are compact but pretty, with antique furniture,

old blue and white tiles and stylish fabrics, with a more contemporary touch in the attics. The reliably good restaurant serves regional classics in a large beamed dining room or under the plane trees.

Hôtel Beaumanoir

Biarritz *10 av de Tamames (05.59.24.89.29/ www.lebeaumanoir.com). Closed mid Nov-Mar. €€€€.*
The Beaumanoir, which gives the impression of being part of an intimate country house party yet within the confines of residential Biarritz, is in fact the former stable block of a now demolished late 19th-century villa. The conservatory-style breakfast room is an *Alice in Wonderland*-style play on scales: a long table stretching into infinity, giant vases that almost touch the ceiling. Then there's the champagne bar, salon-cum-library and a mini vineyard alongside the swimming pool. The eight salubrious suites and bedrooms are a tongue-in-cheek take on the Baroque.

Hôtel La Devinière

St-Jean-de-Luz *5 rue Loquin (05.59.26.05.51/ www.hotel-la-deviniere.com). €€.*
Tucked between the beach and busy rue Gambetta, intimate La Devinière still feels like a private home, decorated with plenty of taste by its collector owners with 18th-century portraits, antique furniture, and a parlour-style breakfast room. The ethos is deliberately low-tech: no TV, internet downstairs only. Instead there's a drawing room lined with books to read, a grand piano to play and ten pretty bedrooms, some with balconies overlooking a shady garden.

Hôtel du Palais

Biarritz *1 av de l'Impératrice (05.59.41.64.00/ www.hotel-du-palais.com). €€€€.*
Jutting out on a promontory at one end of the Grande Plage, the Hôtel du Palais pretty much encapsulates the history of Biarritz: originally a summer residence built by Napoléon III for the Empress Eugénie (on an E for Eugénie-shaped plan), it became a hotel in 1893, attracting royalty and aristocrats from across Europe. Curiously it now belongs to the municipality, which had the sense to preserve it when many of the town's other grand hotels were being demolished or converted into flats, perhaps explaining why it is less stuffy than many palace hotels. Yet there is still something awesome about the heavily gilded furniture, imperial bees, N and E monograms, extravagant chandeliers and sheer acres of space. Many of the 152 rooms, especially the rotunda suites, have mesmerising sea views. There's an outdoor saltwater swimming pool, luxurious Guerlain spa with indoor pool and two restaurants.

Hôtel Restaurant Lastiry

Inland Labourd *Pl du Village, Sare (05.59.54.20.07/ www.hotel-lastiry.com). €€.*
This friendly village hotel, set behind an 18th-century red and white checkerboard façade on the main street of Sare, has reopened after being beautifully refurbished in a spirit of modern Basque chic. The 11 rooms, named after Luis Mariano, Pierre Loti and other personalities who stayed here in the past, feature wood floors, specially made wood and leather furniture, exposed stone in the older wing, and

Hôtel du Palais.

Maison du Lierre.

sparkling new tiled bathrooms. Some have gorgeous views of the Rhune, the church or the village square – but a couple have no view at all. The restaurant aims ambitiously upmarket too, with excellent foie gras and seasonal game.

Hôtel Windsor
Biarritz *10 bd Général de Gaulle (05.59.24.08.52/ www.hotelwindsorbiarritz.com). €€€.*
This classic seafront hotel had been looking distinctly shabby. But it has been going through a metamorphosis of late that is going to once again make it one of the best addresses in town, as frumpy 'Classique' rooms are gradually replaced by sexy new 'Harmonie' rooms, with a neo-1960s feel, slinky white finishes, stripy bed throws and sophisticated lighting. There's a bar and tearoom, as well as the Galion restaurant next door. Various spa, surf and golf packages are available.

Maison Biscaya
3km S of St-Jean-Pied-de-Port *Caro (06.21.16.94.04/www.biscaya.fr). €.*
Patrick and his artist wife Adeline escaped the rag-trade rat race to convert this old farmhouse into a comfortable, boho *chambre d'hôte*. Set in a tiny village surrounded by mountains, it's a place for those after rural calm, hiking (the GR10 crosses the village) and chilling out in the garden or around the log fire. Rooms are spacious and colourful with comfortable beds, and a spa and massages are available *in situ*, as is dinner prepared by Patrick if ordered in advance.

Maison du Lierre
Biarritz *3 av du Jardin Public (05.59.24.06.00/ www.maisondulierre.com). €.*
This used to be a rather ordinary *pension de famille* until decorator Hélène Devèze bought it a couple of years ago and restored the beautiful staircase, wooden wainscotting and creaky parquet, to transform it into a charming, tranquil retreat in the centre of Biarritz. Bedrooms are spacious, with colour-washed walls, quilts and colonial-style ceiling fans. Breakfast is served on the terrace in summer.

Mercure Biarritz Centre Plaza
Biarritz *10 av Edouard VII (05.59.24.74.00/ www.mercure.com). €€€.*
This art deco gem just back from the beach has been brought into the present while respecting the spirit of its age. The hotel was built in 1928, with a flurry of mosaic and angled windows to maximise sea views, and the renovations have preserved the listed lift, stained-glass stairwell and much of the original walnut furniture. The downstairs bar (also open to non-residents) offers some of the best cocktails in town, along with light meals and occasional live jazz

Factfile

When to go
From early July to mid August, Biarritz and St-Jean-de-Luz get packed to the gills with mega traffic jams along the coast, but it can also be a good time to visit the interior; late August is calmer but often wet, with very high tides during the late summer equinox. Indeed one of the features of the Basque Country weather is its unpredictability: it can pour at any moment but also change to bright sunshine within minutes. September, early autumn and spring are often lovely and see the cultural calendar in full swing. Winters are mild and Biarritz and St-Jean-de-Luz are very popular Christmas destinations, but many of the inland villages pretty much hibernate between November and March.

Getting there
Aéroport Biarritz-Anglet-Bayonne
(05.59.43.83.83/www.biarritz.aeroport.fr) is served by direct flights from the UK with Ryanair and Easyjet. High-speed TGV trains from Paris Montparnasse follow the coast, stopping at Bayonne (about six hours), Biarritz, St-Jean-de-Luz and Hendaye along the way; there are also direct trains from Lille Europe (handy for Eurostar passengers) and Paris Charles de Gaulle airport.

Getting around
There's a good local bus network and regular buses along the coast. More limited bus services run from St-Jean-de-Luz inland to Ascain, Sare, Espelette and Cambo-les-Bains, as well as occasional local trains from Bayonne to Cambo-les-Bains and St-Jean-Pied-de-Port, but a car is really necessary to visit the inland areas. The A63 motorway and N10 main road roughly follow the coast, while the D918 runs inland from St-Jean-de-Luz and the D932 inland from Bayonne. Cars can be hired at the airport and at Bayonne station.

Tourist information
For information on the area as a whole, visit www.tourisme64.com.
Bayonne Pl des Basques (08.20.42.64.64/ www.bayonne-tourisme.com).
Biarritz Sq d'Ixelles (05.59.22.37.10/ www.biarritz.fr).
St-Jean-de-Luz 20 bd Victor Hugo (05.59.26.03.16/www.saint-jean-de-luz.com).
St-Jean-Pied-de-Port 14 pl Charles de Gaulle (05.59.37.03.57/www.pyrenees-basques.com).

Internet access
Formatic 64 15 av de la Marne, Biarritz (05.59.22.12.79/www.formatic64.fr). Open 10am-8pm daily.

Top left: Abbaye de St-Guilhem. Top right: La Couvertoirade. Bottom: St-Guilhem-le-Désert.

The Cévennes

A weather-beaten wilderness in sight of the Med.

'I have been after an adventure all my life, a pure dispassionate adventure, such as befell early and heroic voyagers; and thus to be found by morning in a random woodside nook in Gevaudan – not knowing north from south, as strange to my surroundings as the first man upon the earth, an inland castaway – was to find a fraction of my daydreams realised.'

The Cévennes is one of the most diverse wildernesses left in France, and this extract from Robert Louis Stevenson's 1789 travelogue *Travels with a Donkey*, about his 12-day solo journey through the area with only a stubborn donkey, Modestine, for company, is as relevant today as it was more than 200 years ago.

To enter into the vast, empty spaces of the Cévennes is truly to become an 'inland castaway', and one feels a million miles (and several centuries) removed from the buzzing modern metropolis of Montpellier just some 50 kilometres (30 miles) to the south. This land that time forgot, depopulated to within an inch of its life in parts, survives today on tourism alone. But this is no mass tourism – rather this is a greener tourism of rustic gîtes, mountain rambles and heritage trails, all protected by the green boundaries of the Parc National des Cévennes, one of only six such parks in mainland France. The park contains the highest density of long distance footpaths in France and has a height difference of some 1,500 metres (5,000 feet) from top to bottom.

Stevenson referred to the area as 'that undecipherable labyrinth of hills' as he made his pioneering way along what is now the GR70, from Le Monastier southwards to St-Jean-du-Gard. His route has now been immortalised as the Stevenson Trail, and following it in the 21st century shows just what little has changed in this wonderfully diverse land of granite mountains, deep river valleys and dramatic limestone gorges.

Explore

MONT AIGOUAL

The drive up the Col des Miniers from the pretty market town of Le Vigan towards the domineering peak of Mont Aigoual is stunning, passing sweet chestnut forests, terraces of sweet Cévenol onions, dramatic waterfalls and little human life as you pull up high into the Cévennes. Make a brief stop at the Belvedere de la Cravate, some 15 kilometres (ten miles) shy of the summit, to get your bearings from the observation table as you soak up the sublime panorama of the surrounding mountains, the town of Le Vigan several thousand feet below, and, in the distance, the hazy blue of the Mediterranean.

Once over the 1,264-metre (4,150 feet) Col du Minier – from where numerous, well-marked walks set off into the surrounding forest – the road begins to level out a little as it crosses the limestone plateau of the high Cévennes, a truly other-worldly place. Up here sights include the Abime de Bramabiau, an underground river that slices through the *causse noir* (black limestone), and of course Mont Aigoual itself, which stands at a height of 1,567 metres (5,150 feet) and whose bald head is crowned by a weather station, built in 1887 and still occupied by Météo France. There can't be many better places to get the hearts of a gaggle of meteorologists racing. Mont Aigoual forms part of the watershed between the Atlantic and the Mediterranean and the weather can be highly unpredictable, to say the least, with wild extremes and, almost inevitably, the whistle of the *tramuntana* wind blowing through. The highest wind speed ever recorded at the summit station was 360km/h (225mph) in 1966, while the lowest temperature ever recorded was -28°C. If that isn't enough to contend with, average annual rainfall is around 2,000 millimetres (79 inches), making it the wettest place in France. If you happen to chance on the summit on a clear day, though, it is possible to see as far as the Mediterranean, the Pyrenees and Mont Blanc from its summit.

The lower approaches are dotted with a few chalets here and there (this is a popular spot for cross-country skiing in winter), and then about eight kilometres (five miles) below the summit as you approach from Le Vigan is an excellent tourist office with multimedia exhibitions on the area and a boutique selling all manner of local goodies – honeys, cheeses, juices and the like. A little further on towards the summit is the ski resort of Prat Peyrot. This is no alpine mega-resort, with 14 runs, 13 lifts and a meagre 200 metres (650 feet) of vertical descent, but a half-day lift pass costs just €10, pretty much the price of a drink in some of France's swankier resorts.

Heading back down the lower slopes towards the A75 motorway, the countryside is thick with beautiful forests, and the occasional isolated village such as Trèves, seemingly forgotten in the

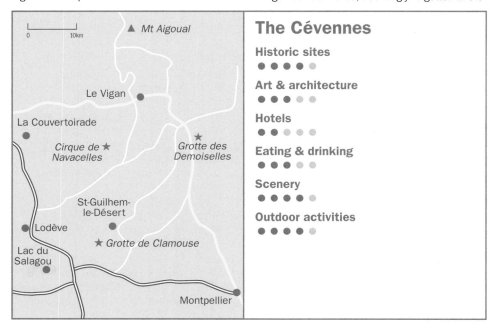

The Cévennes

Historic sites
● ● ● ● ○

Art & architecture
● ● ● ○ ○

Hotels
● ● ○ ○ ○

Eating & drinking
● ● ● ○ ○

Scenery
● ● ● ● ○

Outdoor activities
● ● ● ● ○

deep valleys that typify the area, with rivers such as the Dourbie and Trévezel shooting down the steep slopes towards the Tarn.

Abime de Bramabiau

Camprieu (04.67.82.60.78/www.abime-de-bramabiau.com). Open Apr-June, Sept 10am-5.30pm daily. July, Aug 9.30am-6.30pm daily. Oct, Nov 10.30am-4.30pm daily. Admission €7.50; €3.50-€5 reductions.

The Abime de Bramabiau is often cited as the birthplace of modern caving, as it was here in June 1888 that explorer Édouard Martel first traversed the 500m (1,650ft) Bramabiau underground river from top to bottom. Nowadays things are a little easier, and a path leads visitors down to where the river emerges into the open and then heads a short distance inside the cave, where the temperature is a constant 10°C. Bramabiau is local dialect for 'roaring ox', although you will need to come out of high summer to experience the full effect of the river in spate.

LA COUVERTOIRADE

Just a few kilometres short of the A75 motorway, atop the Larzac plateau, lies one of the most stunning sights in the region. La Couvertoirade is a wonderfully well preserved medieval town, which grew up around a 12th-century château built by the Knights Templar as a stopping-off point on the way to the Crusades. It was subsequently fortified in the 15th century and the ramparts remain virtually intact. Most of the houses within the castle walls are also perfectly preserved, with exterior stone staircases leading to the upstairs living quarters, and on the ground floor a vaulted roof sheltering what was once a sheep's pen and today is more likely to shelter an artisan shop. Come out of season if you can, as the narrow streets and tourist hordes can become oppressive in high summer.

ST-GUILHEM-LE-DESERT

St-Guilhem-le-Désert, perched high up the Gorges de l'Hérault, is almost too good to be true. The village was an important stopping-off point on the route to Compostela, and the little lanes are lined with fountains marked with *coquilles St-Jacques* to sate the thirst of pilgrims on their long trek south. Nowadays there are a multitude of places to assuage the thirst of modern-day pilgrims, and during summer the village is unsurprisingly rammed with tourists keen to explore the beautiful narrow alleyways, vast abbey and numerous craft shops on a day away from the Med beaches. But even in August it's easy enough to escape the crowds – simply walk to the top of the village and follow one of the paths that lead up the surrounding hillside. After 20 minutes of fairly strenuous uphill through the sweet-scented shrubs and flowers, you'll reach the ridge along which the old castle ruins sit in a seemingly impregnable rocky eyrie. From up here the views of the village and surrounding countryside are stupendous, and the peace and quiet is worth every step.

Back down towards the A75 is the Grotte de Clamouse and, a little further on, the Pont du Diable, a handsome old stone bridge constructed by Benedictine monks in the first half of the 11th century. This is the oldest Romanesque bridge in France. Cars are catered for by a newer bridge, from which there are splendid views of the original bridge and an aqueduct that takes water to the vineyards of St-Jean-de-Fos. The bridge has been listed as a UNESCO World Heritage Site, though that doesn't stop daredevil kids from leaping off into the river some 18 metres (60 feet) below – follow them at your peril. Just below the bridge is a popular stony beach and a canoe hire firm for a paddle up the Hérault.

Abbaye de St-Guilhem

Admission free.

This Benedictine abbey, now a UNESCO World Heritage site, was founded in 804 by Guilhem (Guillaume) au Court-Nez, duke of Aquitaine and a member of Charlemagne's court. By the 12th century, the abbey had been named in honour of its founder and had become an important site on the pilgrimage roads that ran through France to Santiago de Compostela. Like other French monasteries, St-Guilhem suffered greatly in the religious wars following the Reformation and during the French Revolution, and also suffered somewhat at the hands of an American collector, who in the early 1900s bought part of the cloister and shipped it home – it now resides at the Metropolitan Museum of Art in New York. Fortunately parts remain in place, and the walk through the cloisters is wonderfully tranquil, with exquisite stonework to admire. At the far end of the cloisters is a well-stocked bookshop for modern-day pilgrims to stock up on religious souvenirs.

Grotte de Clamouse

3km S of St-Guilhem-le-Désert, off the D25 (04.67.57.71.05/www.grottedeclamouse.com). Open Feb-May, Oct, Nov 10am-5pm daily. June, Sept 10am-6pm daily. July, Aug 10am-7pm daily. Admission €8.70; free-€7.40 reductions.

Caving is big business in the Cévennes, and a few minutes south of St-Guilhem-le-Désert is one of France's finest *grottes*. Discovered by a Montpellier caving club in 1945, the spring and cave owe their name to the Occitan word *'lamousa'* (a woman who shouts or screams) because of the noise the underground river makes when in flood. The cave stretches for about 4km (2.5 miles) in total, of which almost a quarter is open to the public and includes a series of dramatically lit chambers and stalactites galore.

LODEVE

Lodève is a pretty market town, once set in an idyllic position but now somewhat blighted by the domineering presence of the A75 motorway flyover, which bypasses the town and has sucked some of the life out of the area.

Nevertheless the centre is still charming, and if you visit on market day (Saturday morning) the whole town comes to life with a wonderful array of cheeses, charcuterie, fruit, fish and dodgy string vests.

The town was a stopping-off point on the pilgrimage to Santiago de Compostela. It was also a centre for textile production under Louis XV and was home to one of only two royal tapestry manufacturers, the other being the Gobelins in Paris. More recently, the area was the centre of firm resistance against the Nazi occupation during World War II. At the heart of the town is the imposing Cathédrale St-Fulcran, a clear sign of Lodève's glory days, with its imposing 57-metre (187 feet) square bell tower. Parts of the cathedral, which was the former seat of the Bishop of Lodève, date from as far back as the sixth century, and there is plenty to admire, particularly the dramatic stained glass windows behind the apse.

> "Take a brief stop to admire the view and gather your nerves, as from here the road winds its way down, zig-zagging along the almost sheer cliffs."

A few kilometres from Lodève, and well worth the diversion, is the handsome medieval village of Soubès. Wander round the ancient streets below the château and then eat in the café on the shaded main square or pack a picnic and head out for a *petite randonnée* in the surrounding countryside. While you're here, don't miss out on a trip to see rising viticulture star and boutique winery Mas Fabregous (1772 chemin d'Aubaygues, 04.67.44.31.75), run by Philippe and Corinne Gros. The vineyards cover some ten hectares and have been in Philippe's family since 1610. Over the last 20 years he has replanted most of the vines and has been bottling his own wines since 2004.

A few miles north of Lodève, just off the A75 motorway as it climbs steeply away from the coast, is the pretty little hamlet of Peyguirolles de l'Escalletes, with a wine cooperative, a château and, if you head out the back of the village and park at the cemetery, then walk up the track that runs alongside the river, some lovely secluded bathing pools that you can have virtually to yourself. The Lergue river has carved out holes in the rock that make for great swimming pools far from the madding crowds on the coast.

CIRQUE DE NAVACELLES

This vast geological marvel is a truly awesome sight, not least because it is so unexpected. After driving across miles of scrubland, with the roads getting narrower and narrower, you finally reach the lip of the vast hollow. The surrounding area is very isolated, with only a few small village communities, and the nearest notable settlement is Millau, a two-hour drive away.

Formed some three million years ago, when the Vis river cut through the limestone plateau of Larzac, this fantastic natural canyon is now classified as a Grand Site Naturel. Right at the bottom, in the midst of a green oasis, lies the tiny village of Navacelles in an abandoned meander of the river, overshadowed for most of the day by the dizzying heights of the limestone canyon. At the top of the Cirque is La Baume Auriol, an information centre, shop and restaurant with a vast terrace. Take a brief stop to admire the view and gather your nerves, as from here the road winds its way down some 500 metres (1,650 feet), zig-zagging along the almost sheer cliffs. There are no barriers and only occasional passing places, so keep your eyes on the road.

LAC DU SALAGOU

If you're looking for somewhere to cool off but can't face the seaside crowds or traffic, then this is the place to head. Situated halfway between the Larzac plateau and the Mediterranean, the man-made Lac du Salagou was created in 1968 as a reservoir for irrigation purposes; it quickly became popular with locals looking to swim, fish, windsurf and canoe. The vast stretch of water also has a few camping spots dotted around the shoreline.

Eat & Stay

Château du Rey
5km E of Le Vigan *Le Rey (04.67.82.40.06/ www.chateau-du-rey.com). €€.*
Open from April to the end of September, this imposing château sits on the road between Le Vigan and Ganges. Although built in the 13th century, it was bashed about during the Revolution and rehashed in the 19th century by Viollet-le-Duc. The Cazalis de Fondouce family has lived here for 750 years, and the present incumbent opened the château as a hotel in 1967. There are Aubusson tapestries in reception, family heirlooms in the salon and, in one suite, not only an antique library, but also a baby grand piano. The restaurant (open Tue-Sat, €€) is housed in a handsome converted stable, and you can walk off your feast with a stroll through the gardens. There's also a swimming pool.

Pont du Diable.

Top: Le Guilhaume d'Orange. Bottom: Hôtel du Nord.

Gîte de la Tour

St-Guilhem-le-Désert *38 rue Font du Portal (04.67.57.34.00). €.*
A number of gîtes in and around St-Guilhem can put you up for the night, including the English-speaking Gîte de la Tour, located in a medieval tower set down a beautiful little alley just a stone's throw from the tourist office. It can sleep 17 people in two, four and five-bedded rooms, with shared facilities. Rooms are pretty basic, but at €15 a night it's an absolute bargain for St-Guilhem. Book well in advance during high season.

Le Guilhaume d'Orange

St-Guilhem-le-Désert *2 av Guilhaume d'Orange (04.67.57.24.53/www.guilhaume dorange.com). €€.*
This is the only hotel option in St-Guilhem-le-Désert, and is consequently rammed between July and September. Located at the bottom end of the village, it's a few minutes' walk from the main village square but next to the road up from the Pont du Diable. Owner Aurore opened the hotel in 2005 in an old village house, and there are now ten spacious, carefully restored en suite rooms, with handsome tiled floors and *toile de jouy* furnishings. Outside there is a pretty dining terrace overlooking the river and shaded by plane trees.

Hôtel du Nord

Lodève *18 bd de la Liberté (04.67.44.10.08/ www.hotellodeve.com). €.*

The two-star Hôtel du Nord is a decent budget option, located on one of Lodève's main streets. There are 25 basic but comfortable en-suite bedrooms surrounding a large, shaded terrace, where a buffet breakfast is served during the summer months. Georges Auric, the composer, was born here in 1899. The hotel has garage parking and free Wi-Fi.

Hôtel de la Paix

Lodève *11 bd Montalangue (04.67.44.07.46/ www.hotel-dela-paix.com). €.*
At the heart of Lodève, this converted former coaching inn has been run as a hotel and restaurant by the Escudié family since 1876. The 23 individually designed rooms are all done out with a bright provençal vibe. The mellow walled patio terrace, complete with Moorish mosaics and palm tree, has a small swimming pool and is a great spot to kick back and escape the afternoon heat.

Le Logis du Pénitent

St-Guilhem-le-Désert *Pl de la Liberté (04.67.57.48.63). Open lunch & dinner daily. €€.*
Situated plum on St-Guilhem's beautiful main square, with outside seating under a giant plane tree planted in 1855, Le Logis is the pick of the numerous eating options. In winter the dishes are based on classic mountain fare, such as *cassoulet de canard* and wonderfully rich *boeuf bourguignon*, while in the summer the menu switches to pizzas and hearty salads to satisfy the hordes of day-trippers streaming in from the coast. Even at peak times, though, service manages to remain friendly.

Factfile

When to go

Although the region is only 50km (30 miles) north of the Mediterranean, the climate in the mountainous Cévennes is far more extreme than the coast, with cold, snowy winters and hot, dry summers. There's also plenty of rain in the area (Mont Aigoual is the wettest place in France). There's cross-country and limited downhill skiing in the winter on Mont Aigoual, and walking throughout the year.

Getting there

Montpellier is the nearest airport to the region. There are 12 buses a day Mon-Sat (www.cg34.fr/ herault-transport) from Montpellier to Lodève (lines 301/381), and two buses a day on Sundays. There is also one bus a day from Montpellier to St-Guilhem-le-Désert (line 308). Buses leave from Montpellier bus station. To get to the bus station from the airport, either catch a taxi or take the shuttle bus (line 120) to the centre. Montpellier is easily accessible by train from Paris (and therefore from the UK via Eurostar). There are approx 15 trains a day, and the journey takes just over three hours. The bus station is located right next to the train station.

Getting around

There are infrequent buses between the various Cévennes villages, but a car is essential to enjoy the area to the full, unless you want to follow in Robert Louis Stevenson's footsteps and travel by donkey. On the subject of RLS, there are several trekking companies offering tours that follow the Robert Louis Stevenson trail (GR70).

Tourist information

Lodève Maison du Tourisme, 7 pl de la République (04.67.88.86.44/www.lodeve.com).
Mont Aigoual Maison de l'Aigoual, L'Espérou (04.67.82.64.67/www.causses-aigoual-cevennes.org).
St-Guilhem-le-Désert 2 rue Font du Portal (04.67.57.44.33/www.saintguilhem-valleeherault.fr).
Le Vigan Maison du Parc du Vigan, bd des Châtaigniers (04.67.81.20.06/ www.cevennes-parcnational.fr).

Internet access

Most of the hotels listed in this chapter, such as the Hôtel du Nord (*see p38*), offer either free or paid internet access.

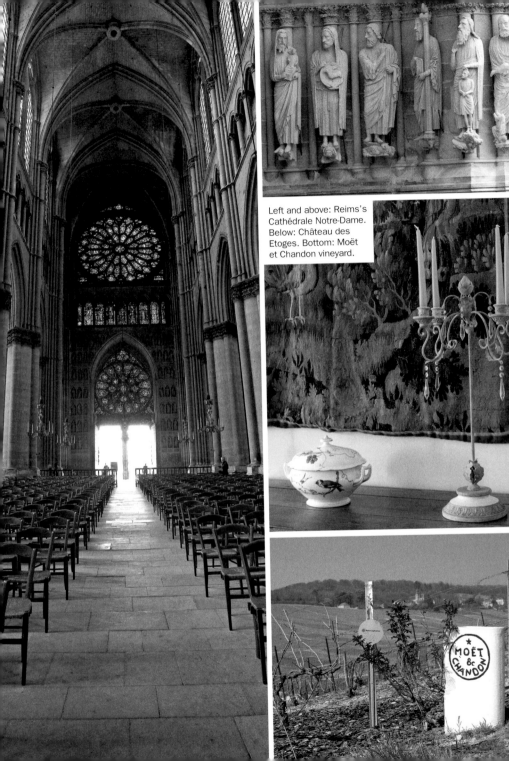

Left and above: Reims's Cathédrale Notre-Dame. Below: Château des Etoges. Bottom: Moët et Chandon vineyard.

Champagne

Popping corks and picturesque hills less than an hour from Paris.

The Champagne region is full of delicious contrasts. On the one hand there's the drink; that gold-hued, sparkling elixir eternally associated with decadence, whose luxurious image is carefully managed by the marketing teams of the renowned champagne houses in Reims and Epernay. Then there's the countryside; 86,000 acres of sleepy, undulating hills striped with low-slung trestled vines of pinot noir, pinot meunier and chardonnay grapes, all tended to by families whose members are far more likely to greet you with fresh mud on their boots than adhere to the glamour their champagnes inspire.

Away from the limelight of giants like Moët et Chandon, Pommery and Mercier, the Route du Champagne in the so-called 'Sacred Triangle' between Reims, Epernay and Châlons-en-Champagne wends its way through plains and villages littered with lesser-known family-run wineries where you can experience champagne in the company of those who made it – and at lower prices. Visits nearly always include a tour of the cellars, an explanation about how champagne is made and the grapes used. Each vintner has his own secret blending techniques, but the best bottles usually come from the chalky slopes of the Montagne de Reims south of Reims, and the Côte des Blancs south of Epernay. Together they form the territory of the 'Grands Crus' where the quality of the grapes assures top-end prices.

This chapter concentrates on the Sacred Triangle, taking you round the best of the *petits producteurs* (family-run producers), as well as into the beautiful cathedral city of Reims – a gastronomic capital with a fabulous architectural heritage, and down Epernay's avenue de Champagne, a *grand boulevard* of fizz production.

TimeOut

timeout.com/travel
Get the local experience

Lifeguards keep watch over Lummus Park beach, **Miami**

© Chris Tomlinson

Explore

Champagne is a perfect short-break destination (two to four days should do it). The TGV, which now runs between Reims and Paris in just 45 minutes, has put some life back into the local tourist industry: the champagne houses here (along with those further south around Troyes) – which are responsible for producing every single one of the 300 million bottles sold across the world each year – usually offer in-depth tours of their cellars throughout the year (some by appointment only). Several family-run houses on the Route du Champagne encourage visitors to sign up for the *vendanges* (grape harvest) in September, and an increasing number offer excellent on-site accommodation.

REIMS

As home to several major champagne houses (mostly set around the Musée St-Rémi) and some excellent restaurants, the city of Reims (pronounced rahns) is definitely a place in which to indulge your inner epicurean. However, it is also a magnet for architecture and history fans, with noteworthy attractions that stretch from Roman times to the 1930s: the awe-inspiring Gothic Cathédrale Notre-Dame, in which every single French king was crowned from the 11th century onwards; the triumphal Corinthian arch known as the Porte de Mars (in the middle of the busy roundabout at the top of rue de Mars); and the wonderful Gallo-Roman Cryptoportique (grain galleries) built around 200 AD (place du Forum, 03.26.77.75.16) are just some of the highlights. These and all the following sites can be reached on foot (although the Champagne houses lie a little further out and justify catching a bus, taxi or driving). The tourist office can also provide audio-guides for you to follow.

Art deco fans are also in for a particular treat as Reims offers a collection of art deco structures unrivalled in France. After losing 80 per cent of its buildings during World War I, the city was rebuilt in the 1920s and '30s. Today there are over 33 structures such as the Carnigie library (2 place Carnigie, 03.26.77.81.41), characterised by its psychedelic green and white circular-patterned ceiling in the entrance hall; the first cubic house in Reims (1 rue des Tournelles); the imposing post office built entirely of reinforced concrete (2-4 rue Cérès); and the airy interior of the Grand Théâtre, modelled on Paris's Théâtre des Champs-Elysées (1 rue de Vesle, 03.26.50.03.92). For maps consult www.reimsartdeco.fr or go to the tourist office.

Ancien Collège des Jésuites

1 pl Museux (03.26.35.34.71). Open 2-6pm daily. Admission free; planetarium €3.

Set around a pretty, secluded garden, this former Jesuit chapel, founded in 1606 and used as a hospital in the 18th century, contains a 300-year-old vine brought from Palestine

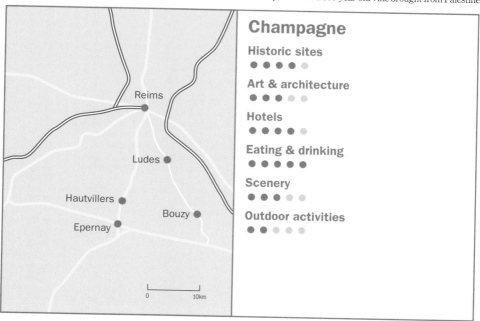

Champagne

Historic sites
● ● ● ● ○

Art & architecture
● ● ● ○ ○

Hotels
● ● ● ● ○

Eating & drinking
● ● ● ● ●

Scenery
● ● ● ○ ○

Outdoor activities
● ● ○ ○ ○

by one of the Jesuit fathers that still bears fruit. The grand refectory is full of intricate 17th-century wooden carvings that depict the lives of St Ignace de Loyola and St François-Xavier, and you can also visit an atmospheric old library containing over 18,000 books that were evacuated to Paris during World War I. If you're travelling with kids, try the on-site planetarium.

Basilique & Musée St-Rémi
53 rue St-Simon (03.26.85.23.36). Open 2-6.30pm Mon-Fri; 2-7pm Sat, Sun. Admission €3; free-€1.50 reductions.
This former Benedictine abbey still contains the tomb of St Rémi (who was the guardian of the holy ampula used to anoint the kings of France), a Romanesque nave leading to a magnificent choir crowned with pointed arches, and an early 16th-century Flamboyant Gothic transept. The main attraction today, however, is its museum focusing on the history of Reims and local military history.

"Pommery's spectacular cellars house millions of fermenting bottles and display works by contemporary artists. Exhibits have included a chamber of chaffinches that play music when they land on upturned electric guitars."

Cathédrale Notre-Dame
3 rue Guillaume de Machault (03.26.47.55.34/ www.cathedrale-reims.com). Open 7.30am-7.15pm daily. Admission free.
Clovis, first king of the Franks, was baptised in Reims's original cathedral in the fifth century AD by St Rémi. Thanks to painstaking restorations, financed by John Rockefeller after World War I (like the rest of Reims it escaped World War II relatively unscathed), the present cathedral, which was begun in 1211, still has rich Gothic decoration that includes thousands of well-preserved figures on the portals – look out especially for the large angels that have earned it the nickname 'Cathedral of Angels'. The jewel in the cathedral's crown is the set of intense blue stained-glass windows designed by Chagall that depict biblical scenes such as the Sacrifice of Abraham, the Cross, and Clovis's baptism. Statues damaged during World War I are on show next door in the Palais du Tau (place du Cardinal-Luçon, 03.26.47.81.79, www.palais-

du-tau.fr), built in 1690 as the residence of the bishops of Reims. Also on display are holy relics including a talisman supposedly containing part of the True Cross originally worn by Charlemagne.

Foujita Chapel
33 rue du Champ de Mars (03.26.40.06.96). Open May-Oct 2-6pm Mon, Tue, Thur-Sun; Nov-Apr by appointment only. Admission €3; free-€1.50 reductions.
In 1964 the head of Mumm champagnes, Réné Lalou, invited his friend, the Japanese painter Leonard Foujita, to build and design the walls of the Chapel of Notre-Dame de la Paix in the Mumm gardens. The result is one of the most visited sights in town – a spectacular, Romanesque-style church with intricate frescoes of blue, gold, green and yellow that depict primitive Christian art.

Mumm
34 rue du Champ de Mars (03.26.49.59.69/ www.mumm.com). Reservations required for tours. Open Mar-Oct 9-11am, 2-5pm daily. Nov-Apr By appointment only. Admission €8-€20.
Mumm's tour isn't the most exciting of the lot, but if you love the famous Cordon Rouge label it's a must. The visit is pleasantly informative, with an educational video on champagne production and a guided tour of the labyrinthine tunnels and storage cellars, capped off with a traditional tasting of one, two or three types of champagne.

Musée des Beaux-Arts
8 rue Chanzy (03.26.35.36.00). Open 10am-noon, 2-6pm Mon, Wed-Sun. Admission €3; free-€1.50 reductions.
Set in the former 18th-century Abbaye St-Denis, this is one of the best fine arts museums outside Paris, featuring sculptures, paintings, drawings, furniture and *objets d'art* from Europe's most prominent artistic movements from the 16th to the 20th centuries. Look out also for beautiful 15th- and 16th-century religious *toiles peintes* (light painting on rough linen) and an excellent series of 27 of Corot's tree-shaded walks.

Pommery
Pl du Général-Gouraud (03.26.61.62.55/www. pommery.com). Reservations required for tours. Open Apr-Nov 9.30am-7pm daily; Dec-Mar 10am-6pm daily. Admission varies.
Even if you don't visit any other cellars don't miss Pommery's, which are the most spectacular of the lot. An eerie 116-step stairway leads to an 18km (11-mile) maze of underground tunnels that date back to the Gallo-Roman era. The tunnels serve the triple purpose of explaining the champagne-making process, housing the company's millions of fermenting bottles and displaying works by contemporary artists. Pommery's owner, Mr Vranken, is mad keen on art and set up the Expérience Pommery five years ago, a rotating, year-long exhibition by young artists who fill the cellars with wacky creations. Previous exhibits have included a chamber full of chaffinches that inadvertently play music when they land on upturned electric guitars, and a huge 3D graph laid out like a hilly carpet evoking the crime rates in Greater Manchester.

Château des Etoges.

Discover the city from your back pocket

Essential for your weekend break, 25 top cities available.

POCKET SIZED *from £6.99*

TIME OUT GUIDES
WRITTEN BY
LOCAL EXPERTS
visit timeout.com/shop

Salle de Reddition
12 rue Franklin Roosevelt (03.26.47.84.19). Open 10am-noon, 2-6pm Mon, Wed-Sun. Admission €3; free-€1.50 reductions.
On 7 May 1945, the Germans surrendered to General Eisenhower inside this former schoolhouse near the railroad tracks behind the station. Since then, the room has been kept exactly as it was on the day of surrender, maps and all still on the walls. You'll find an insightful World War II exhibition in the attached museum.

Taittinger
9 pl St-Nicaise (03.26.85.84.33/www.taittinger.fr). Open Apr-Oct 9.30am-1pm, 2-5.30pm daily. Nov-Mar 9.30am-1pm, 2-5.30pm Mon-Fri. Admission €10.
The formula here is pretty much the same as it is at the other major *caves*: explore the Romanesque cellars dug from Gallo-Roman chalk mines, learn about the Taittinger family lore and the history of Reims, then finish it all off with a slurp of champers and a trip around the shop. Taittinger produces some of the world's most popular champagnes, and exports two-thirds of its production to over 100 countries.

EPERNAY
Take the N51 south from Reims and you get to this sleepy town on the left (south) bank of the Marne river. In sharp contrast to the rest of the area, Epernay is no beauty. In fact, heavy bombing in both World Wars has left it scarred with ugly 1960s flats and factories. However, it keeps excellent company in the east of town on the avenue de Champagne, one of Epernay's few intact streets, filled with intricately sculpted champagne palaces that look like 18th- and 19th-century follies. This is where you'll find the big champagne houses of Mercier, Moët et Chandon and De Castellane, whose chalky cellars contain the liquid cash that paid for the lavish architecture overhead. Epernay might have only one sixth of the population of Reims, but it produces almost as much champagne, and it is thought that if all the houses on the avenue were to lay their tunnels out end to end they would measure more than 300km (190 miles).

De Castellane
63 av de Champagne (03.26.51.19.11/www.castellane. com). Open Apr-Nov 10am-noon, 2-6pm daily. Jan-Mar by appointment only. Admission €8.
If you want to see a working champagne house, Castellane is for you. As well as a guided tour of the cellars, and a small museum that explains the traditional champagne-making process, your ticket also includes a trip into the ultra-modern assembly rooms where labels are put on to the bottles and wine ferments in gargantuan stainless steel barrels. Perhaps even more fascinating is how the barrels are cleaned: an agile, thin man has to climb inside the tiny opening on the front. It's hard to imagine, but apparently nobody has ever got stuck inside. A highlight of the visit is a climb to the top of De Castellane's emblematic tower.

The 66m (216ft) tower is an exact copy of Paris's Gare de Lyon clock tower (also designed by the architect Marius Toudoire) and offers an excellent panorama over Epernay and the surrounding vineyards.

Mercier
68 av de Champagne (03.26.51.22.22/www.champagne-mercier.fr). Open Mid Mar-mid Dec 9.30-11.30am, 2-4.30pm daily. Mid Feb-mid Mar 9.30-11.30am, 2-4.30pm Mon, Thur-Sun. Closed 15 Dec-17 Feb. Admission €8.50.
The history of Mercier champagne is fascinating: a rags-to-riches tale involving universal exhibitions, hot-air balloons, the world's first ever filmed advert (made by the Lumière brothers) and the world's largest champagne barrel, still on display when you enter the building today. The visit starts inside a glass lift that descends 30m (100ft) underground. From here a train takes you through a vast network of tunnels where over 15 million bottles lie fermenting. Look out for the highly protected *glacière* (cave) that contains Mercier's finest vintages from 1923 onwards. The visit naturally finishes up with a glass of bubbly.

Moët et Chandon
20 av de Champagne (03.26.51.20.20/www.moet.com). Open Apr-mid Nov 9.30-11.30am, 2-4.30pm daily. Mid-Nov-Dec, Feb, Mar 9.30-11.30am, 2-4.30pm Mon-Fri. Closed Jan. Admission €14-€26.
You can feel the wealth bounce out of every single nook and cranny in this place. Founded by Jean-Rémy Moët in 1743, the champagne was favoured by Napoleon who, legend has it, used to lug cases of the stuff around to drink before battle. If you survive the mental indigestion brought on by the initial video presentation you have earned the right to partake in the fascinating tour around the 28km (17 miles) of spooky tunnels, followed by a glass of Moët's finest.

Eat
In a region so wholly attached to the art of champagne making, it's no surprise that the Champenois folk are also a dab hand in the kitchen – although unlike champagne's delicate bubbles, the cuisine tends to be heavy and belly-filling fare that was substantial enough to satisfy the workers after a long day in the fields. Look out for local favourites such as game (mainly venison, wild boar, hare or rabbit), *salade de crétons* (dandelion leaves with cubes of bacon), *boudin blanc* (white sausage), *andouillette* (tripe sausage), *potée à la champenoise* (cabbage, gammon and sausage hotpot), and *cacasse* (a rich gratin of potatoes and bacon). Reims is also famed for its mustard and ham as well as pink, sugary finger-shaped biscuits called *biscuits de Reims* (best dunked in champagne), and champagne-filled cork-shaped chocolates

christened *bouchons de champagne*. To wash all that down, head to Epernay's hippest champagne bar, C Comme Champagne (8 rue Gambetta, 03.26.32.09.55/www.c-comme.fr), a real discovery: here you can taste over 250 champagnes from the surrounding family-run houses and explore the swish modern cellars downstairs.

"Thierry Sidan prides himself on his rustic chic cuisine that might include foie gras rolled in speck with onion chutney or a surprising but utterly delicious magret of duck sprinkled with sugared almonds."

Le Bocal
Reims *27 rue de Mars (03.26.47.02.51). Open 11.30am-2.30pm, 7-10pm Tue, Thur-Sat; 11.30am-2.30pm Wed.* €€.
Set just behind the fishmonger's stand in Reims's Marché des Halles, Le Bocal is a new concept eaterie with a menu made up entirely of the catches of the day. Don't expect luxury – this a market after all – but everything is wonderfully simple and fresh. Look out for occasional exhibitions by local artists on the walls.

Brasserie du Boulingrin
Reims *48 rue de Mars (03.26.40.96.22/www.boulingrin.fr). Open 9am-1am Mon-Sat.* €€.
Art deco frescoes and 1930s furniture decorate this traditional brasserie, which turns out classics such as snails, foie gras, lamb with creamy gratin, and crème brûlée. The service is a great spectacle – a ballet of black-and-white clad waiters dancing in and out of the tables. Order a bottle of Buzet (the only red wine grown in Champagne) then sit back and enjoy the show.

Le Café du Palais
Reims *14 pl Myron-Herrich (03.26.47.52.54/www.cafedupalais.fr). Open 10am-3pm Mon; 10am-3pm, 7-9pm Tue-Sat.* €€€.
This handsome 1930s-era café is packed to the gunnels with art collected by the family over the years: paintings, sketches (including a Chagall) and arty photos cover every inch of wall, and the back section contains a stunning art deco cupola crafted by Jacques Simon. In fact the only free space is at the tables, and even they tend to fill up faster

than you can pop a cork. Dishes include a giant plate of Reims ham, potato gratin and cheese; foie gras and morel mushroom pasta; and *potée champenoise*. But whatever you do, leave room for the biggest home-made desserts you have ever seen, including a rum baba that can easily feed four.

Château des Etoges
22km S of Epernay *4 rue Richebourg, Etoges (03.26.59.30.08/www.chateau-etoges.com). Open 12.30-2pm, 7.30-9.30pm Mon-Fri; 7.30-9.30pm Sat, Sun. Closed end Jan-mid Feb.* €€€€.
You'd have to search far and wide to find somewhere more idyllic than this gorgeous 17th-century château surrounded by a moat (*see also p53*). The restaurant is in a lovely orangery, which in summer opens its doors out on to the lawn so that you can enjoy the sunshine. The dining room is a modern, stately affair, with a huge stone fireplace, high ceilings and bright silky fabrics. Expect top-end cuisine such as a starter of red mullet and mussel roulade in saffron sauce, followed by sage-infused rabbit and exotic fruit mousse with coconut meringue; and, of course, an excellent champagne list.

Les Crayères
Reims *64 bd Henry Vasnier (03.26.82.80.80/www.lescrayeres.com). Open noon-2pm, 7-9.30pm Wed-Sun.* €€€€.
Les Crayères is the finest place to dine in the Champagne region. This astonishing palace hotel (*see also p53*), set in a 17-acre park, is worth every euro – and you'll be spending plenty of them inside the elegant, wood-panelled restaurant, where chef Didier Elena (a Ducasse disciple) creates fantastic dishes such as Bresse chicken en croute stuffed with truffles; oyster, lobster and langoustine ravioli; and sublime black forest gâteau. If you're on a budget, book the business lunch menu (Wed-Fri).

La Table Kobus
Epernay *3 rue Dr Rousseau (03.26.51.53.53/www.latablekobus.com). Open noon-2pm, 7-9pm Tue, Wed, Fri, Sat; noon-2pm Thur, Sun. Closed 2wks Dec, 3wks Aug & 1wk Apr.* €€€.
Enjoy some of the best cooking in Epernay at this belle époque-style brasserie where ex-Crillon chef Thierry Sidan prides himself on his rustic chic cuisine that might include foie gras rolled in speck with onion chutney, a surprising but utterly delicious magret of duck sprinkled with sugared almonds, and a splendidly runny chocolate *moelleux*. The dining room is also rather appealing, adorned with beautiful 19th-century paintings.

Stay

Champagne Ployez-Jacquemart
13km S of Reims *8 rue Astoin, Ludes (03.26.61.11.87/www.ployez-jacquemart.fr).* €€.
At this hotel in the middle of the Montagne de Reims vineyards, owners Gérard and Claude like to share their passion for champagne and open their arms to guests

Follow the fizz

As you drive along the Route du Champagne between Reims and Epernay, keep in mind that champagne tasting is about swallowing rather than spitting, and go steady behind the wheel. There are three classic circuits to discover. The Montagne de Reims and Côte des Blancs circuits are renowned for the quality of their champagnes, including several 'Grands Crus'. The nearby Vallée de la Marne circuit is where you'll find the best prices and some of the fruitiest champagnes.

The circuits are all well signposted from Epernay and Reims and you can also download maps from www.tourisme-en-champagne.com. The sheer number of champagne houses is astonishing, but these are our favourites:

Champagne Barnaut (Montagne de Reims)

Bouzy *1 pl André Collard (03.26.57.01.54/ www.champagne-barnaut.com).*
Champagne Barnaut is one of the few houses to make red wines as well as fizz, and it makes an equally good job of both in the heart of the tiny village of Bouzy.

Champagne Charlier (Vallée de la Marne)

20km (12 miles) W of Epernay off the D24, follow signs to Châtillon *4 rue des Pervenches, Montigny-sous-Châtillon (03.26.58.35.18/ www.champagne-charlier.com).*
A flower-clad *domaine* (best appreciated in spring and summer) that uses traditional methods to grow, press and assemble its own champagnes. Charlier's champagnes are light and fruity, including some delicious party-pink rosés, and start at around €12.70 a bottle.

Champagne Milan (Côtes des Blancs)

11km (7 miles) S of Epernay on the D10 *6 rue d'Avize, Oger (03.26.57.50.09/ www.champagne-milan.com).*
If you fancy a day picking grapes during the *vendanges* (harvest) or a real grape-picking job, Milan is for you (enquire from July onwards). The production methods here haven't changed since 1864 and the champagnes (all Grands Crus) are mostly woody with hints of lemon.

Champagne Ployez-Jacquemart (Montagne de Reims)

13km (8 miles) SE of Reims on the D9 *8 rue Astoin, Ludes (03.26.61.11.87/ www.ployez-jacquemart.fr).*
As well as being a great place to sleep off all the tastings (*see Stay*), Ployez-Jacquemart's champagnes are among the most prestigious of the smaller producers. The pinot noir and pinot meunier grapes give the champagnes an almost nutty bouquet.

Tribaut (Vallée de la Marne)

7km (4.5 miles) N of Epernay on the D386 *88 rue d'Eguisheim, Hautvillers (03.26.59.40.57/www.champagne. g.tribaut.com).*
Set in a chocolate-box village where Dom Pérignon created champagne as we know it, Tribaut offers panoramic views, friendly faces and a lip-smacking Grande Cuvée Spéciale (€19), plus five other top-end champagnes.

La Villa Eugène.

looking to learn about the champagne-making process and experience staying on a working winery. Choose between five rooms: Azur (white and duck-egg blue with 18th-century style furniture), Baroque (red in a boudoir style), Nature (light and airy with pale woods), Provence (yellow and oranges) and Savane (colonial). Meals can be served on request.

Château des Etoges
22km S of Epernay *4 rue Richebourg, Etoges (03.26.59.30.08/www.chateau-etoges.com).* €€€.
What strikes you most at this former 17th-century staging post for monarchs is the silence, broken only by the sprinkling of the natural fountains that pour into the moat surrounding the château. The 28 rooms conjure up images of palatial country living with high ceilings, ancient furniture and stone staircases; all have lovely views out on to the gardens or over the moat towards the orangery restaurant. It's a listed building, so there's no lift, but the receptionists will help you carry your bags up and down the stairs.

Les Crayères
Reims *64 bd Henry Vasnier (03.26.82.80.80/ www.lescrayeres.com).* €€€€.
This opulent hideaway is easily one of the finest châteaux in eastern France. Happily located opposite the Pommery champagne house, the 20 luxurious rooms make for a truly unforgettable stay. Rooms overlooking the landscaped park (several with balconies) have fine views of Reims cathedral thanks to former owner Madame Pommery, who ordered a gap to be made in the trees. Service is five-star, the bathrooms are sumptuous and the breakfast is a lesson in fine dining itself. If you can't afford to stay here, you can still stop by for a lavish afternoon tea or champagne in the 19th-century conservatory.

Les Grappes d'Or
7km S of Epernay *350 rue des Grappes d'Or, Cramant (03.26.57.54.96/www.champagne-eric-isselee.com).* €.
Closed during grape harvest (early-mid Sept).
In the tiny village of Cramant, surrounded by nothing but the prestigious Grand Cru vines, Eric and Carole Isselée welcome you into their home with a smile and a trip around the cellars. Three sunny rooms, named after the champagne they produce, feature tasteful French country furniture with quilted bedspreads, and all have wonderful views across the vines. Breakfast, which is served in your room, is included in the price.

La Villa Eugène
Epernay *82-84 av de Champagne (03.26.32.44.76/ www.villa-eugene.com).* €€€.
After years of lying derelict, the old Mercier champagne family house has finally been smartened up and can now stand proud as one of the best hotels Epernay has to offer. Rooms range in style from classical and airy with light colours, traditional fireplaces and antiques, to neo-colonial with dark woods and earthy tones. Even in winter you might need your sunglasses to eat breakfast in the restored conservatory – a veritable well of light that overlooks the garden and heated outdoor pool.

Factfile

When to go
Thanks to its roaring fizz industry, Champagne is a year-round destination, with the exclusion of November to January when some champagne houses open by appointment only – an exception is made on 22 January or the Saturday before, when Champenois folk celebrate St Vincent's day (the patron saint of champagne) with a boozy parade through Epernay and surrounding villages. Other festivals to look out for are Reims's Flaneries Musicales (June-Aug, www.flaneries reims.com) when classical music concerts take place in some of the city's oldest and loveliest buildings; the biennial Fête Ay (Montagne de Reims, every even year), when the village opens its cellars for a champagne-fuelled celebration; and Hautvillers' Festival BD (cartoon festival) on the second or third weekend in April, when artists from far and wide come together to show off their work and drink a bottle or two of champers.

Getting there
Trains connecting Paris to Reims (45mins) and Epernay (1hr 20mins) leave several times a day from Gare de l'Est (www.sncf.com) in Paris. Hire cars can be picked up in both cities. The nearest airports are Paris Charles de Gaulle and Paris Orly.

Getting around
If you want to discover the Route du Champagne you will need a set of wheels. It is possible to attack the route by bike. Promenades en France (03.80.26.22.12/www.promenades-en-france. com) organises circuits around the Montagne de Reims or you can pick up a cycle map and bike hire information from the local tourist offices.

Tourist information
Epernay 7 av de Champagne (03.26.53.33.00/ www.ot-epernay.fr).
Reims 12 bd Général Leclerc (03.26.77.45.00/ www.reims-tourisme.com).

Internet access
Reims Clique et Croque, 19 rue Chanzy (03.26.86.93.92/www.cliqueetcroque.com). Open 10am-midnight Mon-Sat; 2-8pm Sun.

Top: La Roque-Gageac.
Bottom: Sarlat.

The Dordogne

Cave paintings, foie gras and expats aplenty in the Pays de l'Homme.

With its gorgeous rolling countryside, village markets and slow pace of life, the Dordogne has been a favourite destination for Brits for a long time. This means that you won't have any problems travelling around if you don't speak French, but the search for authentic France can be marred by the prevalence of spoken English and an undercurrent of anti-English feeling in the very touristy area around Sarlat, though the worst that might happen is someone accuses you of being a 'rosbif'. Maybe it all goes back to the Hundred Years War, when for most of the 13th and 14th centuries Aquitaine was English and many local barons supported the English cause.

Head off the beaten track, however, and things are quite different. There are still plenty of villages in Périgord (the ancient name for the Dordogne still used by the French) where English is not the lingua franca and plenty of Périgordins who will extend you a hearty welcome, especially if you share their passion for fine food and terroir. Plus the incredible density of châteaux (more than 1,000) and prehistoric sites makes this one of the most rewarding areas of France to visit. The region has branded itself 'Pays de l'Homme' (Country of Mankind) and visiting the cave paintings in the Dordogne river valley is a humbling experience that shows modern civilisation has much to learn from its distant past.

Referring to the different parts of Périgord, with their varied landscapes, as Noir (black), Blanc (white) and Vert (green) goes back centuries, with Pourpre (purple) added in the 1970s. Périgord Noir, the area around Sarlat with the biggest concentration of cave paintings and châteaux, is named for its deep oak forests and the truffles that grow there. Périgord Blanc, around the capital, Périgueux, is a country of limestone plateaux and green valleys through which the Auvézère and Isle rivers flow. In the north, Périgord Vert is a green land that includes the pretty villages of Brantôme ('the Venice of the Dordogne') and Aubeterre. And Périgord Pourpre is named for the grape, as it encompasses the wine region centred on Bergerac. For the purposes of this chapter we also go upstream, following the Dordogne river into the Lot département, where the châteaux, rock villages and caves continue.

Explore

PERIGORD NOIR

The medieval town of Sarlat is the gateway to the Dordogne river valley's fairytale landscape of castles and cliffs in the south, and the Vézère valley's prehistoric caves to the east. Such is the concentration of historic sites that this area is often referred to as the 'golden triangle', an apt description given the beautiful ochre glow of the local stone. Sarlat was the first town centre to be preserved by the Malraux Law (which also saved Paris's Marais), which protected 77 buildings, including the birthplace of Montaigne's friend Etienne de la Boëtie.

The town is built in a kind of basin, with narrow cobbled alleyways running down to attractive place de la Liberté, where the Wednesday and Saturday morning market is one of the best in the area. Otherwise a covered market in the converted church of Ste-Marie and some chi-chi food boutiques will enable you to stock up on the Sarladaise specialities of foie gras, *confit de canard*, walnuts and honey.

Food is the main attraction in Sarlat, as it doesn't have much to offer culturally, with the exception of its festivals: the Périgord Noir Festival (www.festivalduperigordnoir.com) with classical music in historic buildings all around the area; the Sarlat Theatre Festival (www.festival-theatre-sarlat.com); and the Sarlat Film Festival (www.ville-sarlat.fr/festival), which has been going for almost two decades and grew out of the fact that the town and its surrounding area was almost perpetually being used as a shoot location. If you want relief from the film-set perfection, head out to nearby Gorodka (05.53.31.02.00, www.gorodka.com), the artistic folly of Pierre Shasmoukine; the house and garden are filled with wonderfully kitsch art brut sculptures and light installations.

In the loop of the Dordogne below Sarlat every bend of the road seems to reveal another astonishing edifice perched high on the rocks. Castelnaud and Beynac eye each other across the river, rivals since the Hundred Years War when the former was on the English side and the latter on the French. For further enchantment, visit the gardens of the Château de Marqueyssac (05.53.31.36.36, www.marqueyssac.com), perched on a promontory high above the river. Even if you hate French formal gardens, this one can't fail to delight with its paths winding between rounded topiary to the belvedere. On Thursday nights in July and August the whole garden is lit up by candles.

Also in this loop of the Dordogne are the villages of La Roque-Gageac and Domme, both best avoided in high summer as their picture-postcard fame has led to a traffic nightmare that will mar any pleasure you get from the mellow

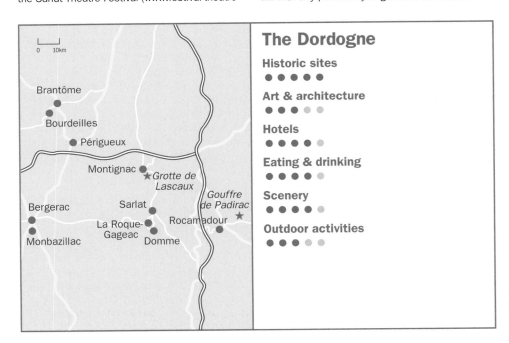

The Dordogne

Historic sites
● ● ● ● ●

Art & architecture
● ● ● ○ ○

Hotels
● ● ● ● ○

Eating & drinking
● ● ● ● ○

Scenery
● ● ● ● ○

Outdoor activities
● ● ● ○ ○

Château de Marqueyssac.

stone of the towering rock-face architecture. At La Roque-Gageac, you can escape the riverfront hotels and restaurants by heading up the village's steep lanes lined with terraced houses. If you're not afraid of vertigo, the troglodyte fort at the top is worth a visit for its views. Another way to escape the crowds is on a replica *gabare* – the sailing boats that plied the Dordogne delivering goods in the 18th century (Gabares Norbert, 05.53.29.40.44, www.norbert.fr). The hour-long trip takes in five châteaux. On the south bank of the river, Domme is a magnificent 13th-century *bastide* (fortified village) with a breathtaking view from its chestnut-shaded esplanade. A group of Knights Templar was imprisoned in the Porte des Tours for 11 years, and you can see their medieval graffiti by making an appointment with the tourist office (05.53.31.71.00).

"The Vallée de l'Homme is home to Europe's greatest concentration of prehistoric sites."

Château de Beynac
10km S of Sarlat *Beynac-et-Cazenac (05.53.29.50.40). Open Mar-May 10am-6pm daily. June-Sept 10am-6.30pm daily. Oct-Feb 10am-dusk daily. Admission €7; free-€3 reductions.*
Across the river from Castelnaud, the château of Beynac towers austerely over the village of Beynac-et-Cazenac. Though it doesn't go in for re-enactments, the château has been used for several costume dramas, including *The Visitors, D'Artagnan's Daughter* and Luc Besson's *Joan of Arc*. It has been beautifully restored, and there are sumptuous tapestries, a chapel with frescoes and the dungeon where Richard the Lionheart took refuge with his army.

Château de Castelnaud
12km S of Sarlat *Castelnaud-la-Chapelle (05.53.31.30.00/www.castelnaud.com). Open Feb, Mar, Oct-11 Nov 10am-6pm daily. Apr-June, Sept 10am-7pm daily. July, Aug 9am-8pm daily. 12 Nov-Jan 2-5pm daily. Admission €7.80; free-€3.90 reductions.*
Castelnaud is the most visited château in the region, not only for its dramatic views of Beynac, Marquessac and La Roque-Gageac, but also because it holds an impressive collection of medieval warfare. In July and August costumed actors entertain visitors with swordfighting displays.

Château de Milandes
12km S of Sarlat *Castelnaud-la-Chapelle (05.53.59.31.21/www.milandes.com). Open Apr, Oct 10am-6.15pm Mon-Fri, Sun. May, June, Sept 10am-6.30pm Mon-Fri, Sun. July, Aug 9.30am-7.30pm daily. Admission €8; free-€5.50 reductions.*

Josephine Baker's Neverland was where the Folies Bergère star and wartime *résistante* lived with a troupe of adopted children from 1947 to 1968. The stunning Renaissance château was fitted out with luxury art deco bathrooms inspired by her favourite perfumes, and a fantasy garden. A Josephine soundtrack helps you drift dreamily from room to room, where you can see her risqué banana costume and photos that recount the poignant story of her eventual eviction from the château.

Jardins d'Eyrignac
10km NE of Sarlat *Salignac (05.53.28.99.71/www.eyrignac.com). Open Apr 10am-7pm daily. May-Sept 9.30am-7pm daily. Oct-Mar 10.30am-12.30pm, 2.30pm-dusk daily. Admission €9.50; free-€4 reductions.*
Garden-lovers should not miss the Jardins d'Eyrignac, located 10km (six miles) north-east of Sarlat. It is a beautifully restored masterpiece of 18th-century garden design, and every Monday night from mid July to mid August visitors can take part in a 'picnic in white' in the white rose garden with live music – a great excuse to buy a hamper of gourmet goodies in Sarlat.

THE VEZERE VALLEY
Along the Vezère river between Montignac and La Bugue is the Vallée de l'Homme (Valley of Mankind), home to the greatest concentration of prehistoric sites in Europe and a UNESCO World Heritage winner. Also in the valley, you can visit the troglodyte cities of La Roque St-Christophe (05.53.50.70.45, www.roque-st-christophe.com) and La Madeleine (05.53.46.36.88, www.village-la-madeleine.com), both inhabited until very recently. La Madeleine was not deserted until the 1920s, and was last used by *résistants* in World War II.

Musée National de Préhistoire
20km W of Sarlat *1 rue du Musée, Les Eyzies (05.53.06.45.45/www.musee-prehistoire-eyzies.fr). Open June, Sept 9.30am-6pm Mon, Wed-Sun. July, Aug 9.30am-6.30pm daily. Oct-May 9.30am-12.30pm, 2-5.30pm Mon, Wed-Sun. Admission €5; free-€3.50 reductions.*
The pretty village of Les Eyzies is home to the impressive Musée National de Préhistoire (National Museum of Prehistory), a modern structure designed by Jean-Pierre Buffi and cleverly built into the rock to make it almost invisible from afar. Covering some 400,000 years of human history, it examines the lifestyle, art and rituals of prehistoric man through the many artefacts dug up in the surrounding area.

Vallée de l'Homme
20km NW of Sarlat *Guided tours only. Book through Sarlat Tourist Office, 3 rue de Tourny, Sarlat (05.53.31.45.45/www.sarlat-tourisme.com) or Les Eyzies Tourist Office, 19 av de la Préhistoire, Les Eyzies (05.53.06.97.05/www.leseyzies.com). Open times vary.*
Lascaux, the area's most famous cave, was discovered in 1940 by four teenagers out looking for their dog. It has been closed since 1963 and its iconic Great Hall of the Bulls and

Château de la Treyne.

Painted Gallery have been reproduced at Lascaux II, an artificial cave created in the same hillside. Of the other sites, the Grotte de Font-de-Gaume, the Grotte des Combarelles with over 800 drawings and engravings, the Abri de Cap-Blanc with a monumental sculpture of horses, bison and deer, and the Abri du Poisson with its clear representation of a fish, are the best. Admission to some of these sites is very limited, and you will have to book well in advance for visits from April to September (preferably in January of the year you want to visit).

PERIGORD BLANC

White Périgord is carved through by the Dordogne's other major river, the Isle, which merges with the Auvézère a few kilometres before Périgueux, the capital of the *département*. While it's tempting to rush through Périgueux en route for Brantôme and the pretty villages of Périgord Vert, the city is worth a stop for its Roman remains, and medieval and Renaissance old town. The mainly pedestrianised centre is dominated by the Cathédrale de St-Front, a Byzantine-style edifice that was badly tinkered with by Paul Abadie, the architect of Paris's Sacré-Coeur. South of the cathedral are the cobbled alleys and ancient merchants' houses of the medieval Le Puy-St-Front quarter; to the north are some magnificent carvings and the attractive place St-Louis. The tourist office offers some excellent historical tours.

The road north to Brantôme is a picturesque one, but you could also take a detour via Sorges, known as the truffle capital of the Dordogne. The limestone plateau around here is particularly rich in truffles, and the local mayor, an enthusiast, has created the Eco-Musée de la Truffe (05.53.05.90.11) to unearth some of its mysteries – all translated into English. There's a truffle-centric nature trail too, and you can feast on the beauties at the Auberge de la Truffe (*see p63*). Sorges' annual truffle market is held on the Sunday nearest 20 January.

Vesunna

Parc de Vésone, 20 rue du 26ème Régiment d'Infanterie, Périgueux (05.53.53.00.92/www.vesunna.fr). Open Apr-June, Sept 9.30am-5.30pm Tue-Fri; 10am-12.30pm, 2.30-6pm Sat, Sun. July, Aug 10am-7pm daily. Oct-Mar 9.30am-12.30pm, 1.30-5pm Tue-Fri; 10am-12.30pm, 2.30-6pm Sat, Sun. Admission free-€5.50.

Vesunna, the Roman city of 20,000 inhabitants, had a forum, basilica, baths, amphitheatre and 7km (four-mile) viaduct, though most of this was destroyed by Germanic tribes who ransacked the Romans' monuments to build defensive walls. You can see the remains of the amphitheatre in the Jardin des Arènes, and other fragments jumbled up in the Porte Normande, part of the defensive wall. The best-preserved monument is the Tour Vésone, the sanctuary of the goddess Vesunna's temple, and beside it is the new Vesunna Gallo-Roman Museum, which is built around the remains of a large Roman villa.

PERIGORD VERT

Brantôme's nickname, 'the Venice of Périgord', might lead you to expect something rather grander, but this little town on an island created by monks on the Dronne river is undeniably lovely, especially outside of high summer. There's a Benedictine abbey supposedly founded by Charlemagne and caves where troglodytic monks once lived. Other highlights include walks along the river, boat trips and simply lingering on the café terraces. The Sunday morning market and winter truffle markets in the village hall are fantastic, and on Friday nights in July and August there is water jousting on the river.

Meandering around the nearby villages by car – or better, bicycle – is enjoyable, taking in St-Jean-de-Côle, one of the 'Plus Beaux Villages de France', and Bourdeilles with its château. Several other châteaux are scattered around, including the eccentric Jumilhac and small Renaissance Puyguilhem with walks through the nut woods.

Heading north from Brantôme, the stunning cross-border Regional Natural Park of Périgord-Limousin stretches out with its forests, limestone valleys and fast flowing rivers. The Saut du Chalard and Roc Branlant are two natural beauty spots. In the far west of Périgord Vert, just over the border into Charente, don't miss Aubeterre-sur-Dronne, another stunning village, which is home to the incredible Eglise Monolithe de St-Jean (05.45.98.65.06), a 12th-century church carved into the rock face.

PERIGORD POURPRE

Bergerac built its wealth on wine and river transport, and the main reason to visit this part of Périgord is to taste its wines and enjoy fine food. The city has an attractive old town spreading out from the former port, whose half-timbered cottages and bourgeois houses have been handsomely restored. One of the latter contains the Musée du Tabac (05.53.63.04.13/www. france-tabac.com), covering the history of tobacco growing in Dordogne (still a major industry), and all manner of artefacts connected with smoking and snuff-taking. Nearby, the Cloître des Récollets, a former monastery, hosts the Maison des Vins (05.53.63.57.57/www.vins-bergerac.fr), with free tastings and weekly classes (€8). Here you can pick up the Route des Vins de Bergerac guide for visiting the vineyards.

Of the 13 Bergerac *appellations*, Monbazillac and Pécharmant are the most interesting. The Pécharmant vineyards, centred on the eponymous village six kilometres (3.75 miles) north-east of Bergerac, produce the best of the Bergerac reds – always a good choice in any Dordogne restaurant and often offered by the glass. Vineyards such as the family-run Domaine du Haut-Pécharmant (05.53.37.29.50) will be only too happy to give you a tasting.

History of art

Most people are familiar with prehistoric cave paintings, if only from the Lascaux-themed waste-paper bins popular in the 1970s. But to actually see the paintings and carvings in the 15 UNESCO World Heritage sites of the Vezère valley in the flesh fills you with a sense of wonder that makes you question whether evolution really is a forward not a backward step. As Picasso commented after visiting the Lascaux caves: 'We have learned nothing in 12,000 years'.

The reason that seeing them with your own eyes (you can't touch) is so different from a photographic representation is that the paintings were designed to be viewed in a flickering light. Those done in the Magdalene era (17,000 to 10,000 years ago) were accomplished by the light of tallow candles made from refined reindeer fat, engraved with flint and coloured using brushes with dyes made from charcoal, manganese dioxide and red ochre. Though the caves are now lit using dim electric lights, the excellent guides encourage visitors to imagine the flickering light that made the paintings live and move. Photos also don't reveal the 3D aspect, as the artists made use of the natural folds and hollows of the rock to form the belly or hind quarters of the animals.

Mystery still surrounds the purpose of the paintings. Were they associated with hunting rites, shamanistic dreams or fertility beliefs? Were the artists men or women? Contrary to expectations, there is no violence, no killing in the cave art. Instead they celebrate living animals, sometimes with scenes of great tenderness such as a reindeer licking the forehead of another at the Grotte de Fond-de-Gaume. What does seem to have been agreed on by prehistorians, though, is that they were done by accomplished artists, selected from their tribe, who may have practised in more ephemeral ways such as drawing in sand with a stick. There was no margin for error in the work, as the outlines are engraved and perfect every time.

Hôtel de France. Below:
Les Frères Charbonnel.

Château de Monbazillac

3km S of Bergerac *Rte de Mont-de-Marsan, Monbazillac (05.53.63.65.00/www.chateau-monbazillac.com). Château-museum open Apr, May, Oct 10am-noon, 2-6pm daily. June-Sept 10am-7pm daily. Nov-Mar 10am-noon, 2-5pm Tue-Sun. Admission €6.30. Cave-cooperative open Jan, Feb 10am-12.30pm, 2-6pm Mon-Sat; Mar-June, Sept-Dec 10am-12.30pm, 1.30-7pm Mon-Sat. July, Aug 9am-7pm Mon-Sat.*

Based around the village and château of Monbazillac, a few kilometres south of Bergerac, the Monbazillac vineyards profit from the botrytis fungus ('noble rot') to produce their famous sweet white wine that goes so wonderfully with foie gras. The château contains a wine museum and a *cave-cooperative*, offering tastings and wine for sale.

INTO THE LOT

Following the river from Sarlat towards Souillac, you'll pass the Cingle de Montfort, a tight bend in the river overlooked by the Château de Montfort (not open to the public) and Fénélon (05.53.29.88.99), a grand feudal château that was the birthplace of Louis XIV's tutor. Then the Dordogne descends for a few kilometres into the Lot *département*, where the magical Château de la Treyne (*see p64*) offers the chance to stay the night in what must be the most romantic of all French châteaux.

It's only a few kilometres from here to Rocamadour, a village clinging to the rock. This famed tourist and religious site is impressive as you first glimpse it from the hairpin bends of the approach. A lift from inside the walled village takes pilgrims halfway up, followed by several hundred steps to the complex of chapels carved into the rock that form a station on the road to Compostella. Like La Roque-Gageac, it's best avoided in high summer. The nearby Gouffre de Padirac (05.65.33.64.56/www.gouffre-de-padirac.com), is a cave with an underground river and some spectacular stalactites. The visit is by boat, followed by a walk through the caves.

Eat

Périgord is the most gastronomic region in France. Large swathes of it are given over to foie gras production and apiculture, its rivers are rich with pike-perch, and the forests give walnuts and, in season, that most prized ingredient: the black truffle.

Auberge de la Truffe

Périgord Blanc *Sorges, 18km NE of Perigueux (05.53.05.02.05/www.auberge-de-la-truffe.com). Open 7.30-9.30pm Mon; noon-2pm, 7.30-9.30pm Tue-Sun (closed Sun eve Nov-Easter). €€€€.*

Set in the truffle capital of the Dordogne, this unpretentious hotel and restaurant is all about what's on the plate. The

terrace chairs may be plastic, but who cares when you're in the company of a chef who is passionate about the tuber melanosporum. The black diamonds first make an appearance on the €44 menu (two courses with an alcoholic sorbet in the middle) in the form of a truffle omelette. Go the whole hog and they feature in all five courses, including the dessert. Pierre Corre also runs truffle cooking courses.

Aux Berges de la Vézère

Périgord Blanc *Pl Tourny, Montignac (05.53.50.56.31). Open noon-2pm, 7-9pm Mon, Thur-Sun; noon-2pm Tue, Wed. €€.*

On the banks of the Vézère, just as the name says, this gourmet pizzeria defies you to drive on by with its glorious terrace view over the river. The charming French owners have sourced only the best products from Italy, including the oils and balsamic vinegar on sale inside. Perfect pillowy pizza crusts and unusual fresh toppings give you a welcome break from heavy Périgord fare. Inside is a contemporary space decorated in Tuscan colours, with picture windows to enjoy the view in all weathers.

Bistro de l'Octroi

Périgord Noir *111 av de Selve, Sarlat (05.53.30.83.40/www.lebistrodeloctroi.fr). Open noon-2pm, 7.30-9.30pm daily. €€.*

Gérard Lasserre's bistro is the best reasonably priced restaurant in Sarlat by a mile, as any local will tell you. Housed in an 1830s building where the 'octroi' tax used to be collected, it has a garden with a summer terrace and stone walls with simple bistro furniture inside. As well as the expected *magret* and *confit de canard* (the former with ceps in season), you'll find wonderful Limousin steaks, venison, and scallops. Starters cost around the same price as the mains as most of them revolve around foie gras.

Les Frères Charbonnel

Périgord Vert *Hôtel Chabrol, 57 rue Gambetta, Brantôme (05.53.05.70.15/www.lesfreres charbonnel.com). Open noon-1.30pm, 7.30-9pm Tue-Sun (closed Sun eve Oct-July). Closed mid Nov-mid Dec & Feb. €€€.*

Long-standing stars of the Brantôme restaurant scene, the Charbonnel brothers do the right thing with foie gras, ceps, duck, pike-perch and truffles, accompanied by an impressive wine list with a large choice of Bordeaux. Their many ways of combining the quintessential Périgordian ingredients include a superb *pigeon façon Rossini* and truffle-stuffed pike-perch. The dining room is a bit dated, though the terrace overlooking the river is an enchanting place to be in fine weather.

Les Jardins de Brantôme

Périgord Vert *33 rue de Mareuil, Brantôme (05.53.05.88.16/www.lesjardins-brantome.com). Open noon-2pm, 7.30-9pm Mon, Tue, Fri-Sun (also open Thur eve July & Aug). Closed Jan. €€.*

Young, friendly owners Florence and Christophe have made the most of their flower-filled garden, which provides summer dining and also inspires a menu of flavoursome, aromatic and refreshingly light dishes. The speciality is a starter of thyme-marinated rabbit in a salad with pine nuts – a variation on an old country dish that you won't find elsewhere. In winter there is a cosy room inside with an open fire.

Les Truffières

Périgord Noir *Bosredon, Trémolat, 35km E of Bergerac (05.53.27.30.44). Open 7.30-9.30pm Tue; noon-2pm, 7.30-9.30pm Wed-Sun. Closed Jan, Feb.* €€.
We ran into the owner of Les Truffières, Yanick Legoff, while sampling the wine at the Domaine du Haut-Pécharmant. It was an apt way to find out about this *auberge à la ferme*, a working farm that offers meals using home-grown produce in the converted old tobacco shed. Yanick was an architect before leaving the city to live the good life. With his son Aurélien he raises free-range geese and chickens, and everything on the farm is organic. Dishes include the likes of home-made *foie gras poêlée* or *magret de canard*. Good news travels fast, so make sure you book.

> ## "At Château de la Treyne your senses are heightened by the loveliest little touches: fresh flowers everywhere, an aperitif in a crystal decanter and a walnut cake complete with its recipe on a parchment."

Le Vieux Logis

Périgord Noir *Trémolat, 35km E of Bergerac (05.53.22.80.06/www.vieux-logis.com). Open noon-1.30pm, 7-9.30pm daily.* €€€.
Prize-winning chef Vincent Arnould draws gourmands from miles around to taste his seasonal, inventive cuisine, which includes dishes such as monkfish with ginger-infused carrot juice, saffron and lime or lamb with roasted tomatoes and peppers. You can dine in the old tobacco-drying room, the cosy wood-lined winter dining room or on the lime-shaded terrace with a view of the French formal garden.

Stay

La Couleuvrine

Périgord Noir *1 pl de la Bouquerie, Sarlat (05.53.59.27.80/www.la-couleuvrine.com).* €.
La Couleuvrine is brilliantly placed in the centre of the old town, with oodles of character that belies its two-star status. Part of the building is in the last remaining tower from the medieval town wall, and a warren of corridors lead to the 28 rooms, which feature antique desks and wardrobes. No.22 with its view over the square is particularly charming, but the manager will let you take the key to several before you make your choice. Downstairs is an attractive restaurant with a fireplace and gallery serving decent, well-priced Périgord specialities. There is also a lunchtime bistro that becomes a wine bar in the evening.

Château Les Merles

Périgord Pourpre *Tuilières, Mouleydier, 10km E of Bergerac (05.53.63.13.42/www.lesmerles.com).* €€€.
Ten kilometres (six miles) along the Dordogne east of Bergerac, Les Merles describes itself as a 'design château' and its daring black and white decor certainly gives it the hip hotel stamp. Aside from the simple beauty of the surroundings, there are two points to coming here: gastronomy and golf. It has its own nine-hole course and resident pro. As for the food, Dutch chef Albert Kooy cooks up wonderful seasonal dishes using local produce and organic vegetables from the kitchen garden. Wine lovers can taste vintages from the seven Bergerac regions.

Château des Reynats

Périgord Blanc *15 av des Reynats, Chancelade, 2km W of Périgueux (05.53.03.53.59/www.chateau-hotel-perigord.com).* €€€.
Just five minutes from Périgueux by car is this lovely 19th-century château run by friendly owners, with a large choice of rooms ranging from functional to exquisitely romantic. The latter are those inside the château itself, including the Monbazillac suite in the tower, with raspberry brocade and a fresco of the god of love; the former are in the Orangerie annexe, allowing guests on a smaller budget to enjoy the inviting swimming pool, tennis court, nearby golf course and gastronomic restaurant (menus €35-€65).

Château de la Treyne

Into the Lot *Lacave, 10km N of Rocamadour (05.65.27.60.60/www.chateaudelatreyne.com).* €€€.
Château de la Treyne, with its 17th-century round tower perched on a cliff overhanging the Dordogne, is a fairytale castle. From the minute you drive up the gravel path your senses are heightened by the loveliest little touches: sweet-smelling fresh flowers everywhere, an aperitif in a crystal decanter in the room and a walnut cake complete with its recipe on a parchment. Every room is charming, but the Dordogne apartment is particularly special, with its private terrace over the river where you can look down on swans gliding by. You might feel like dressing for dinner to match Stéphane Andrieux's divine cuisine, but the general atmosphere is relaxed, with Stephanie Gombert greeting guests on first-name terms. Along with a French formal garden, there are tennis courts and a forest to explore.

Hôtel de France

Périgord Vert *Pl Trarieux, Aubeterre-sur-Dronne (05.45.98.50.43/www.hoteldefrance-aubeterre.com).* €.
With its striped awning on Aubeterre's market square, the Hôtel de France is the very picture of a French provincial hotel. The delightful Dutch family who took it over 15 years

ago have taken the place's history to heart and added quirky touches – bric-a-brac furniture, a rogue's gallery of paintings and brightly coloured curtains. The ten rooms include some with views, some with en suite showers, and five in the roof that share bathrooms. The first two floors are taken up by the cosy bistro, which is a real village gathering place.

Maison Fleurie
Périgord Vert *54 rue Gambetta, Brantôme (05.53.35.17.04/www.maison-fleurie.net). €€.*
Carol Robinson has been running this B&B for nearly two decades, and one of the great things about staying here is the chance to benefit from her local knowledge: she'll point you in the direction of pretty detours, off-the-beaten track châteaux and great places to eat, tell you about truffle auctions, farmers' dances and why the conker world championships are now held in the Dordogne. The townhouse has five bedrooms; the finest is the four-poster Rose. The bathrooms could do with a revamp, but the flower-filled garden, small swimming pool and delicious breakfast with hot croissants and home-made jams more than make up for it.

Manoir de la Brunie
Périgord Noir *Le Coux et Bigaroque, 30km W of Sarlat (05.53.31.95.62/www.manoirdelabrunie.com). €€.*
Just about equidistant from Sarlat, Périgueux and Bergerac, with the Vézère valley less than half an hour away, the Manoir de la Brunie makes a good base for day trips. On the other hand, you may feel like not moving at all from this 15th-century *maison forte* set in three hectares of parkland

overlooking rolling countryside. Aside from its own swimming pool, there is a riverside beach on the Dordogne nearby. The manor has been decorated sparingly to make the most of its ancient stone walls: five large, airy rooms with wooden floors, white curtains over the beds and a few carefully chosen antiques. The hosts will serve a candlelit meal on request (€28), and also offer themed weekends such as cooking with foie gras or well-being with massages and reflexology. There is also a beautiful beamed house for rent by the week.

Mercure Perigueux Centre
Périgord Blanc *7 pl Francheville, Perigueux (05.53.06.65.00/www.accorhotels.com). €€.*
Medieval Périgueux is let down by its lack of charming hotels, but if you want to be in the city centre you could do worse than the comfortable new Mercure. The 66 air-conditioned rooms feature contemporary two-tone decor and gleaming bathrooms. There is free Wi-Fi in the lobby.

Moulin de l'Abbaye
Périgord Vert *1 rte de Bourdeilles, Brantôme (05.53.05.80.22/www.moulinabbaye.com). Closed Dec-Mar. €€€.*
This ivy-clad mill offers bucolic heaven in the centre of Brantôme. A member of Relais & Châteaux, it is family-run and features 19 rooms across three historic buildings – the Moulin, the Maison de Meunier and Maison de l'Abbaye – all decorated in impeccable taste with toile de jouy, original prints and antiques. During summer the gastronomic restaurant expands outwards on to a riverside terrace.

Factfile

When to go
In July and August the Dordogne is heaving with tourists, bringing traffic jams, queues and frayed nerves. May, June, September and October are far more relaxing. Many hotels, restaurants and attractions close from November to Easter and winters are wet and cold.

Getting there
Ryanair and Flybe fly to Bergerac. Trains to Périgueux from Paris (change at Limoges) take approx 4hrs 15mins; you can also get right through to Les Eyzies on this line. Trains to Bergerac or Sarlat from Paris (change at Bordeaux) take approx 4hrs 15mins (Bergerac) or 5hrs 45mins (Sarlat).

Getting around
Several railway lines run through the Dordogne: from Périgueux west to Bordeaux and north-east to Limoges; from Brive south to Gourdon via Souillac; and along the Dordogne river from Bergerac to Sarlat. The line from Périgueux to Les Eyzies cuts through the centre, and several bus services are run by SNCF to connect towns

and villages. Pick up printed timetables from the station or ask at tourist offices. Outside high summer a car is a great way to potter around, as is a bicycle.

Tourist information
Bergerac 43 bd Maine de Biran (05.53.27.30.18/www.pays-de-bergerac.com).
Les Eyzies 19 av de la Préhistoire (05.53.06.97.05/www.leseyzies.com).
Périgueux 26 pl Francheville (05.53.53.10.63/ www.tourisme-perigueux.fr).
Sarlat 3 rue de Tourny (05.53.31.45.45/ www.sarlat-tourisme.com).

Internet access
Bergerac Forum Espace Culture, 5-9 rue de la Résistance. Open 2-7pm Mon; 10am-7pm Tue-Sat.
Périgueux Net Runner, 11 rue Victor-Hugo. Open 10am-midnight Mon, Wed, Fri; noon-midnight Tue, Thur; 2pm-midnight Sat, Sun.
Sarlat Easy Planet, 16 av Gambetta. Open 10am-7pm Mon-Thur; 10am-midnight Fri, Sat; 6pm-midnight Sun.

Clockwise from top: Saumur; Château de Brézé; Château Royal d'Amboise; Clos Lucé.

LEONARDO DA VINCI

The Loire Valley

Majestic châteaux, mellow villages and food fit for a king.

Resplendently lush and supremely regal, France's Loire Valley is a fairytale land of medieval and Renaissance châteaux, strung out like cream-coloured pearls along the sweeping Loire, Maine, Vienne and Indre rivers. It is a UNESCO-protected national park of hunting forests, vineyards and landscaped gardens, a place where sleepy hamlets and Romanesque churches sit alongside troglodyte dwellings whose interiors are carved into the pale tufa rock. Then, of course, there's the wine and food: with dozens of *appellations* – including some highly quaffable sparkling vouvrays and well-rounded saumur-champignys – and local specialities such as pike-perch in butter, this is a gastronomic heaven.

For over 250 years it was the seat of power of the Valois kings, who preferred to rule from towns like Amboise than Paris. Then under François I (1494-1547) it became the wellspring of the French Renaissance, as architects and artists from Italy were brought in to design and build royal palaces. The trail of crowd-pleasers left behind from this era is arguably one of the best in the world.

This chapter focuses on the Loire's central regions of Touraine and Anjou, which contain the main historical towns of Amboise, Chinon, Saumur and Angers, each with their own castle and chocolate-box town centre. They make ideal springboards from which to launch yourself into the surrounding countryside, but you will need a set of wheels: the Loire's heritage is so vast and varied that a car is essential. On the way you'll see fishing boats tethered to riverbanks, wineries coaxing you in for a tasting, troglodyte dwellings, and châteaux quite literally fit for a king.

Explore

In the Loire, it's more a question of where to start than what to see. Between Amboise and Angers, it is no exaggeration to say that there is something worth visiting every few kilometres, so be prepared for some hard decision-making – you'd need a lifetime to do it all. Although not covered here, Tours, the capital of the Touraine, is a pleasant city just an hour from Paris by TGV and an ideal spot in which to pick up a hire car. Tours' tourist office also organises minibus excursions to several of the sites listed below, should you decide to sit back and let someone else do the driving.

AMBOISE & AROUND

A leisurely 20-minute drive east from Tours along the D952, Amboise is a good place to start. Overlooking the Loire river, it is a small town of narrow streets and quaint residences whose pretty contours are best appreciated when seen from the north bank of the river. You can easily spend a whole day here, sharing your time between two star sites: the imposing Château Royal d'Amboise, set on a rocky spur and one of the most historically important buildings in the region; and Leonardo da Vinci's former home, the Clos Lucé, an exquisitely restored manor house with landscaped gardens and a museum of da Vinci's inventions.

Château Royal d'Amboise

Pl Michel Debré, Amboise (02.47.57.00.98/www. chateau-amboise.com). Open Jan, 16 Nov-31 Dec 9am-12.30pm, 2-4.45pm daily. Feb 9am-12.30pm, 1.30-5pm daily. Mar, 1-15 Nov 9am-5pm daily. Apr-June 9am-6.30pm daily. July, Aug 9am-7pm daily. Sept-1 Nov 9am-6pm daily. Admission €9.50; free-€8 reductions.

Amboise was favoured by Louis XI and Charles VIII, who grew up behind the safety of the ramparts away from the squalour of the town. In the early 19th century, much of the castle was demolished by its owner Roger Ducos – after receiving it as a gift from Napoleon, he couldn't afford the upkeep. But the remaining parts, spanning several styles from vaulted Gothic to Renaissance and Empire, are fascinating and include Charles VIII's and François I's living quarters, as well as a complex network of underground tunnels leading to the curious Tour des Minimes (open April-Sept only), a breathtaking 15th-century helter skelter-like tower that looks like a medieval predecessor of New York's Guggenheim museum. Outside, the jewel in the crown is the tiny Flamboyant Gothic Chapelle St-Hubert, thought to house Leonardo da Vinci's remains.

Chenonceau

Chenonceaux, 12km SE of Amboise (02.47.23.90.07/ www.chenonceau.com). Open 5 Nov-6 Feb 9.30am-5pm daily. 7 Feb-15 Mar 9.30am-6pm daily. 16-31 Mar 9.30am-7pm daily. June, Sept 9am-7.30pm daily. July, Aug 9am-8pm daily. 1-23 Oct 9am-6.30pm daily. 24 Oct-4 Nov 9am-6pm daily. Admission €10; free-€8 reductions.

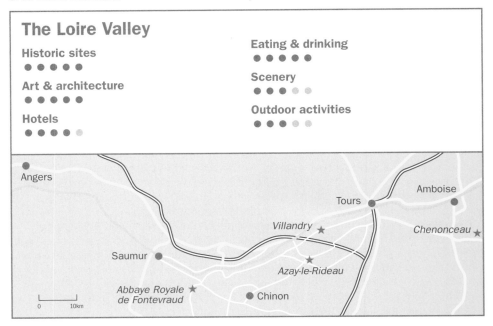

The Loire Valley

Historic sites
● ● ● ● ●

Art & architecture
● ● ● ● ●

Hotels
● ● ● ● ○

Eating & drinking
● ● ● ● ●

Scenery
● ● ● ● ○

Outdoor activities
● ● ● ○ ○

Angers

Tours

Amboise

Villandry ★

Chenonceau ★

Saumur ●

Azay-le-Rideau ★

Abbaye Royale ★
de Fontevraud

● Chinon

0   10km

Shrouded in aristocratic grace and spanning the Cher river, the château of Chenonceau is all about girl power: Catherine Briçonnet (the first owner's wife) built the turreted pavilion and France's first ever straight staircase; Henri II's mistress Diane de Poitiers added the formal gardens and arched bridge before his jealous wife, Catherine de Medici, evicted Diane and converted the bridge into an Italian-style gallery; and in the 18th century owner Madame Dupin, a high-society tax collector's wife, was so popular with the villagers that the château survived the Revolution unscathed. Nowadays, Chenonceau's beauty is world-famous, so try not to be put off by the jam-packed car park and coachloads of visitors. Its original ceilings, fireplaces, tapestries and paintings (many by 16th- and 17th-century masters like Van Loo and Rubens) are all worth seeing (the black-and-white bedchamber where the bereaved wife of Henri III, Louise de Lorraine, spent most of her days is particularly haunting); and the gardens – from Diane de Poitiers' *Jardin Italien* to the surrounding shaded alleys – offer welcome refuge. The only part you should skip is the cheesy waxwork museum (Musée de Cire).

Clos Lucé

Amboise (02.47.57.00.73/www.vinci-closluce.com). Open Jan 10am-6pm daily. Feb-June, Sept, Oct 9am-7pm daily. July, Aug 9am-8pm daily. Nov-Dec 9am-6pm daily. Admission Mar-15 Nov €12.50; free-€7 reductions; 16 Nov-Feb €9.50; free-€6 reductions.
A short walk up a well signposted hill takes you to Clos Lucé, the only Renaissance château built entirely from red brick and white tufa. It served as a retreat for Anne de Bretagne. Then, in 1516, François I invited Leonardo da Vinci to Amboise, giving him this house so that he could be 'free to think, dream and work'. He resided here for three years until his death in 1519. Now the house has been painstakingly restored to its former Renaissance glory, both inside and out, including the chapel whose frescoes were painted by da Vinci's pupils. There's also a gallery with sketches and 40 models of da Vinci's machines, featuring the world's first car, paddle steamer and metric counter. For nine months of the year, from March to mid November, a trail of 16 of da Vinci's giant working machines dot the landscaped park.

Pagode de Chanteloup

3km SW of Amboise on D31 (02.47.57.20.97/ www.pagode-chanteloup.com). Open Apr 10am-6pm daily. May-Sept 10am-6.30pm daily (until 7pm June, 7.30pm July, Aug). Feb half-term 2-5pm Mon-Fri; noon-5pm Sat, Sun. Closed 15 Nov-Apr (except Feb half-term). Admission €8; free-€6 reductions.
If you're into architectural oddities don't miss this 18th-century Chinese pagoda on the outskirts of Amboise. It is the only remaining part of the Duc de Choiseul's (Louis XV's finance minister) Versailles-inspired château, which was sinfully bulldozed by estate agents in 1823. It's a hairy climb up the seven storeys (only six people at a time), each narrower than the other, but the balcony views from the top hint at the Château de Chanteloup's former grandeur. On a fine day, the surrounding expanses are prime spots for a picnic.

CHINON & AROUND

Medieval Chinon is best described like its famous wines: full of local flavour with a hint of sophistication. Its dinky town centre looks like the set of a period movie, with remarkably preserved half-timbered medieval houses (plus a few 17th-century ones thrown in for good measure) and a majestic medieval fortress ruin, perched precariously above the streets. It was here that Joan of Arc pleaded with Charles le Dauphin (the future Charles VII) to take action against the English during the Hundred Years' War. After the 15th century, however, the court moved away and the fortress gradually fell into a state of disrepair. A huge restoration project is finally nearing completion.

Before you visit the ruin, the prettiest views are to be had from quai Danton across the Vienne river, which affords sweeping vistas of the town and the river. Once over the bridge, rue Voltaire represents a cross-section of Chinon's history with its fine 15th- and 16th-century houses, including a quaintly old-fashioned automated wine museum at No.12. If you fancy a DIY walking tour, the tourist office provides a map of the main historic monuments and churches. It's a circuit worth following, and by surreptitiously sneaking behind closed doors you can often glimpse at Chinon's pretty hidden courtyards.

The Renaissance writer François Rabelais (1494-1553), author of the burlesque adventures of two giants, Pantagruel and his father Gargantua, grew up in Chinon (on rue de la Lamproie) and his legacy is carried on in the utopian gardens at the nearby Château du Rivau. From here it's just a hop, skip and jump to the picture-perfect boxed flowerbeds at the Château de Villandry and, queen of all Renaissance châteaux, Azay-le-Rideau.

Azay-le-Rideau

Azay-le-Rideau, 21km NE of Chinon (02.47.45.42.04/ http://azay-le-rideau.monuments-nationaux.fr) Open Oct-Mar 10am-12.30pm, 2-5pm daily. Apr-June, Sept 9.30am-6pm daily. July, Aug 9.30am-7pm daily. Admission €8; free-€5 reductions.
Compared with Villandry, Azay-le-Rideau feels positively bite-sized with its compact pleasure moat (actually the Indre river) and neat proportions. Its architecture epitomises the qualities of Renaissance château-building, with its high roofs, tall watch turrets and long rows of windows. Upon seeing Azay-le-Rideau, King François I accused its builder, his finance minister Gilles Berthelot, of misappropriating funds and took it into royal possession. Enter the castle through the ticket office on rue Pinceau, then watch a succession of wonderfully preserved chambers unfurl inside two main wings set around the château's gorgeous staircase. Some rooms are decorated with magnificent pieces, including a late 15th-century oak canopy throne and a huge collection of 16th- and 17th-century tapestries from Antwerp, Brussels and Paris.

Clockwise from
top: Azay-le-Rideau;
Château de Brézé;
Château Royal d'Amboise;
Château de Brézé.

Château du Rivau

Le Coudray, Lémeré, 13km SE of Chinon on the D749 (02.47.95.77.47/www.chateaudurivau.com). Open Easter-May, Oct-8 Nov 10am-12.30pm, 2-7pm Mon, Wed-Sun. June-Sept 10am-7pm Mon, Wed-Sun. Closed 9 Nov-Easter. Admission €8; free-€6 reductions.

Little-known Rivau is a beautiful hybrid of medieval heritage and cutting-edge modern art, woven together by colourful gardens and one of the biggest collections of roses in Europe (over 400 varieties). Built in the 13th century and fortified in the 15th century by Charles VII's chamberlain, Pierre de Beauvau, it is a fairytale castle with a working drawbridge, *donjon*, turreted towers, archers' slits and a trophy room, all painstakingly restored by the current owners. As you arrive you'll notice the vaulted Renaissance-era stables on your left. This is where Joan of Arc gathered her horses for her crusade against England. Rabelais is also linked to the castle – his character Gargantua the Giant granted Rivau as a prize to one of his knights after the Picrocholine war. The gardens pay homage to Rabelais' giants and the world of fairy stories with wonderful themed sections (Rapunzel, Tom Thumb, Alice in Wonderland and Gargantua's vegetable patch) strewn with oversized pieces of contemporary art. Giant wellington boots and a watering can by Lilian Bourgeat; huge running legs by Basserode (symbolising the forest running away from human destruction); a massive nipple piercing for the garden's oldest oak tree by Philippe Ramette; and Nicole Tran Va Bang's goliath saké cup that displays a naked lady in the bottom when it rains. If you come to Rivau between June and September, when Gargantua's vegetable patch has produced its giant organic vegetables, drop into the castle's café, La Table des Fées, which serves excellent regional dishes made from Rivau's rich harvest.

> # "As you arrive you'll notice the vaulted Renaissance-era stables. This is where Joan of Arc gathered her horses for her crusade against England."

La Forteresse Royale

Chinon (02.47.93.13.45/www.monuments-touraine.fr). Open Oct-Mar 9.30am-5pm daily; Apr-Sept 9am-7pm daily. Admission free-€3.

For years no one could decide what to do with Chinon's castle: sustain it as a ruin or rebuild the rubble? It was finally decided that it would be criminal not to repair such an important example of medieval military architecture, and in 2003 archaeological digs marked the beginning of a €14.5m restoration project. By 2010 the work should be finished, revealing three 'new' sections: the commanding Château du Milieu, with its clock tower and keep; the Fort du Coudray, a showcase for understanding medieval military defence; and the showpiece Fort St-Georges.

Villandry

Villandry, 32km NE of Chinon (02.47.50.02.09/ www.chateauvillandry.com). Open Gardens 9am-5pm daily (until 6pm Mar, Oct; 7pm June-Sept). Castle 7 Feb-15 Nov & Xmas hols 9am-5pm daily (until 6pm Mar-Oct). Admission Castle & gardens €9; free-€5 reductions; Gardens only €6; free-€3.50 reductions.

Villandry is possibly the only château in the Loire whose gardens are more famous than the building itself – and for good reason. They're France's most complete example of the formal Renaissance style adopted in the 16th century, with majestic patchwork flowerbeds best appreciated from the castle's upper terrace. From here you get a bird's-eye view over the first ornamental garden's topiary hedges, symbolising the faces of love – tender, tragic, passionate and lustful. In the centre lies the ornamental vegetable patch whose 40 varieties of 16th-century vegetables (excluding the potato which hadn't yet arrived in France) are rotated with the seasons. The castle itself was built in typical Renaissance style by François I's secretary of state, Jean Le Breton, and the building owes its longevity to the Spanish physician Joachim Carvallo, who acquired Villandry in 1906 and devoted his life to its restoration. You'll notice that unlike other sites Villandry's interior is mainly in Empire style, having been decorated by the Carvallos. Madame Carvallo's bedroom commands a particularly pretty view over the gardens, on to the church and village. Don't miss the well-furnished picture gallery displaying Spanish religious art and a gruesome severed head by Goya.

SAUMUR & AROUND

It's a pretty drive along the D947 into Saumur, with the expanses of the Loire river on one side and a succession of bucolic villages on the other. This was the Plantagenets' favourite country and even in death their presence is all-pervading at Fontevraud Abbey, where Henry II of England and Richard the Lionheart are entombed. The area also has a particularly large concentration of cave dwellings, such as the quirky Château de Brézé, a veritable underground village within a castle.

Saumur lies on the banks of the Loire, and unlike at Amboise or Chinon, it feels like it has a life outside of the tourist season: it's larger for a start, with more shops (especially on rue St-Jean), including familiar chains that can add a refreshing sense of normality after a few days of château-hopping. There are also over 62 listed historic monuments dotted among its 18th-century mansions and narrow, twisting streets, which climb up to a turreted, fairytale fortress.

Saumur's other highlights are its Cadre Noir cavalry school, and its wines. All around the town, the riverbanks of the Loire rise gently to meet vine-covered slopes. The Maison des Vins (quai Lucien Gautier, 02.41.38.45.83) next door to the tourist office offers tastings of 30 official Anjou and Saumur AOC wines; and the D947, on the way into Saumur, is lined with enticing private wine cellars (mainly rosés).

Abbaye Royale de Fontevraud

Fontevraud, 16km SE of Saumur (02.41.51.73.52/ www.abbaye-fontevraud.com). Open 2 Nov-Mar 10am-5pm daily. Apr-June, Sept, Oct 10am-6pm daily. July, Aug 10am-7pm daily. Admission Jan-Apr, Nov, Dec €7; free-€4.50-reductions. May-Oct €8.40; free-€5.90 reductions.

This is the largest, most intact medieval abbey in the whole of France – a miracle considering that it was desecrated by Huguenots in 1561, attacked during the Revolution and turned into a prison under Napoleon III in 1804 that wasn't decommissioned until 1963. The visit starts inside the stark 12th-century Romanesque abbey church (the old prison). The focal point is four painted royal tombs belonging to Henry II, his wife Eleanor of Aquitaine, Richard the Lionheart and Isabelle d'Angoulême, widow of Richard's infamous brother King John. From here a wooden door leads to the nuns' Renaissance cloisters; this was once one of the largest nunneries in France and the adjacent chambers contain breathtaking biblical frescoes and underground tunnels. A door from one of the refectories leads out into the garden, which contains a fabulous piece of rare secular architecture – the octagonal Romanesque Tour d'Evraud, a circular kitchen with half-moon fireplaces crowned by a conical turret, all capped with a pyramidal lantern tower pierced with lancets. The adjacent former St-Lazare Priory is now a quirky hotel with a gourmet restaurant in the cloisters (02.41.51.73.16/www.hotels-francepatrimoine.com)

Le Cadre Noir – L'Ecole Nationale d'Equitation

Terrefort-Saumur (02.41.53.50.60/www.cadrenoir.fr). Open Apr-early Oct 2-4pm Mon; 9.30-11.30am, 2-4pm Tue-Fri; 9.30-11.30am Sat. Closed early Oct-Mar. Admission €7.50; free-€5 reductions.

Saumur has been the capital of classical French horse riding since the 17th century, and the world-famous resident Cadre Noir (Black Squad) are fine exponents of equestrian choreography and jumping (several riders are Olympic gold medallists). Based just outside the town centre, the Black Squad frequently giddy up in the Grand Manège (arena), showing off French riding techniques to the general public. In May, July and October, there are special public galas with displays set to music (check website for dates).

Château de Brézé

Brézé, 10km SE of Saumur (02.41.51.60.15/www. chateaudebreze.com). Open Feb-Mar 2-6pm Mon-Fri; 10am-6pm Sat, Sun. Apr-Sept 10am-6pm daily. Closed Oct-Jan. Admission Underground only €8.55; free-€6.20 reductions. Castle & underground €14.45; free-€10.30 reductions.

Upon approaching Brézé you are struck first by its typical Renaissance contours surrounded by the oldest vines in the Loire. Then you notice that some parts date from the early 19th century and there's a rather pretty arcaded gallery,

above which sit the castle's classy apartments (open for visits). Nothing, however, prepares you for what lies behind a discreet wooden door, just off the main courtyard – an underground troglodyte village set in Europe's deepest dried moat, invisible to all but those standing on top of it. Count Gilles Maillé-Brézé dug out a vast complex of passageways when he built the castle in 1448, using much of the stone as brickwork for the structure. The chambers he carved into the new dry moat contributed to Brézé's affluence, serving as a grape press and wine store (the château still produces excellent wine and offers tastings), a working bakery (last used by the occupying Germans in World War II) and a silkworm farm. Also don't miss the Cathedral of Images audio-visual experience, where the walls of the cellars are painted with medieval images, accompanied by patterns of light and haunting music.

ANGERS

Angers, the former capital of Anjou on the Maine river, is a year-round city with a thriving student population, decent museums, a direct TGV link to Paris and a tradition for the arts that comes to a head during July's Festival d'Anjou (www. festivaldanjou.com), a month-long celebration of drama, music and poetry. It is also home to the famous medieval Apocalypse tapestry (inside Good King René's formidable 13th-century château) and a modern replica, Le Chant du Monde, inside the Musée Jean-Lurçat et de la Tapisserie Contemporaine, sealing the city's reputation as an international centre for modern tapestry-making. After driving around the Loire, Angers provides a fine opportunity to do some exploring on foot. The prettiest parts are in the old town between the château, the Cathédrale St-Maurice – a majestic medieval edifice with vivid 13th-century blue and red stained glass and an 18th-century organ propped up by four muscley telamones – and the Logis Barrault, which houses the interesting Musée des Beaux Arts (32 rue Lenepveu, 02.41.05.38.00, www.musees.angers.fr).

One of the funkiest buildings in town is the Galerie David d'Angers, a glass-covered ruin of a 13th-century church that now displays plastercasts of the 19th-century Angers-born sculptor's works (37 rue Toussaint, 02.41.05.38.90, www.musees.angers.fr). If it's panoramas you're after, cross over to the north bank and walk along the water's edge between the Pont de la Haute-Chaîne and Pont de la Basse-Chaîne for fine views of the château.

Château d'Angers

2 promenade du Bout-du-Monde (02.41.86.48.77/ http://angers.monuments-nationaux.fr). Open 2 May-4 Sept 9.30am-6.30pm daily. 5 Sept-30 Apr 10am-5.30pm daily. Admission €8; free-€5 reductions.

Built by Louis IX between 1230 and 1240 with 17 daunting defence towers, Angers' stripy slate and tufa château was one of the most formidable military constructions in the

Château Royal d'Amboise.

whole of France. In the 14th and 15th centuries the Dukes of Anjou moved their court here, then Good King René introduced the first elements of Renaissance architecture in the 15th century, visible in the royal apartments (a fire tragically swept through here in January 2009 so some rooms may still be closed to the public). After René, the castle was used mainly as a prison, for defence and arms storage. Today you can see one of the world's longest and oldest medieval tapestries, known as the Apocalypse. Displayed inside a dimly lit gallery specially designed to preserve the ageing fibres, 76 scenes of the Apocalypse are recounted as per the Revelation of John (the last book of the New Testament).

Musée Jean Lurçat et de la Tapisserie Contemporaine

4 bd Arago (02.41.24.18.48/www.musees.angers.fr). Open Oct-May 10am-noon, 2-6pm Tue-Sun. June-Sept 10am-6.30pm daily. Admission €4.

You get two attractions for the price of one here: the stunning, vaulted medieval Hôpital St-Jean (a hospital for the poor from 1174 to 1854), and a load of textile art from the 1950s to the present day. Since 1967 the hospital has housed the *Chant du Monde* (Song of the World) tapestry (1957-66) by Jean Lurçat, an artist profoundly impressed by the Apocalypse tapestry, and considered to be largely responsible for reviving the art of tapestry making in Angers. His work is a ten-part symbolic humanist vision of the 20th century that deliberately restricts the use of colour and perspective to evoke the joys and pains of life and death.

Eat

Les Alchimistes

Saumur *6 rue de Lorraine (02.41.67.65.18). Open 12.15-1.30pm, 7.30-9pm Mon, Tue, Thur-Sat; 12.15-1.30pm Sun. €€.*

As the restaurant's name suggests, chef François Deplagne and his wife Lydie are culinary alchemists, serving delicious gourmet food at unbeatable prices. The €17.50 three-course set menu is a feast of local dishes reworked with a modern twist – pike-perch with beetroot butter, hare in red wine sauce, bitter chocolate mousse with orange sorbet – all made with seasonal ingredients fresh from the market. A la carte dishes might include terrine of foie gras and langoustines served with curried apple chutney, grilled Charolais beef with walnuts, and caramelised fruit tiramisu.

Les Années 30

Chinon *8 rue Haute Saint Maurice (02.47.93.37.18/ www.lesannees30.com). Open 12.15-1.30pm, 7.30-9pm Mon, Thur-Sun; 7.30-9pm Tue. €€€.*

This restaurant gets progressively more contemporary the further you go in: medieval on the outside, 1930s in the small inside dining room and contemporary cuisine on the table. Three increasingly gourmet menus (€28, €37 and €43) feature dishes such as foie gras with cider and camembert cream, peppered duckling with Jerusalem artichokes or orange and ginger cod with fennel purée. Desserts include

treats such as calvados toffee apples or caramelised lemon meringue pie. During summer ask for a table outside on the shady terrace.

Au Chapeau Rouge

Chinon *49 pl du Général de Gaulle (02.47.98.08.08/ www.auchapeaurouge.fr). Open noon-1.15pm, 7.30-9pm Tue-Sat; noon-1.15pm Sun. Closed 3wks Nov & 3wks Feb. €€€€.*

The Red Hat (named after the hats worn by the royal post carriage drivers) is one of Chinon's finest restaurants. Chef Christophe Duguin gives pride of place to locally grown, seasonal produce, and the menu might include starters like duo of home-smoked, Loire-caught fish served with lime cream, followed by mains like lamb steak roasted with dried fruits and served with wine-soaked *rillons*. To finish, maybe fondant of chocolate with red wine jelly and saffron ice cream. The wine list is excellent.

La Croix Blanche – Le Plantagenêt

14km E of Saumur *Pl Plantagenêts, Fontevraud (02.41.51.71.11/www.fontevraud.net). Open May-Oct noon-2pm, 7-9pm daily. Nov-Apr 7-9pm Mon; noon-2pm, 7-9pm Tue-Sat; noon-2pm Sun. €€€.*

This friendly inn in a prime spot opposite the entrance to the abbey covers the needs of all hungry punters by offering three eating options – a café serving all-day snacks and crêpes; the Fontaine d'Evraud brasserie; and the fabulous Le Plantagenêt restaurant where young chef Emmanuel Vincent concocts innovative dishes using what he calls 'forgotten' flowers, herbs, spices and root vegetables. On the plate this might translate as frog's legs with garlic butter and a fricassée of Jerusalem artichokes, sea bream with lemon salt and crunchy purple carrots, or dried fruit risotto with Earl Grey tea and home-made ice-cream.

L'Etape Gourmande

25km NE of Chinon *La Giraudière, Villandry (02.47.50.08.60/www.letapegourmande.com). Open 15 Mar-15 Nov noon-2.30pm, 7.30-9pm daily. €€.*

This 17th-century farm's idyllic pastoral setting – replete with black pigs, chickens, goats and fluffy bunnies – is reason alone to come here, but the backdrop is matched by the food and the friendly owners' cheery welcome. Menus are great value, starting at €16.50 (for a starter plus cheese or dessert) and ending at just €34.50 for what could turn into your most memorable four-course meal in the Loire. Starters might include succulent scallops with puy lentils, followed by rabbit in mustard sauce, goat's cheese from a nearby farm and a Villandry – chocolate cake layered with biscuit, red fruits, white chocolate mousse and hot melted chocolate.

Le Favre d'Anne

Angers *18 quai des Carmes (02.41.36.12.12/ www.lefavredanne.fr). Open noon-2pm, 7-9.30pm Tue-Sat. €€€€.*

In a prime spot overlooking the Maine river and Château d'Angers, this classy one Michelin-starred restaurant has a wonderfully original menu which might include the likes of fillet of beef with bacon and peanuts, fennel *tatin* with giant langoustines or strawberry and verbena *vacherin*. Chef

A view from above

It seems unreal, drifting like a bird on a warm breeze above the pepperpot-towered châteaux of the Loire, but that's exactly what Montgolfières d'Anjou (02.41.40.48.04/ www.montgolfieres.com, flights €190-€320) do between Easter and October, when six of its balloons ship a lucky few up, up and away into the air above the Loire. The castles are impressive enough from the ground, but nothing can prepare you for the delights of their dramatic proportions when seen from above. Then there's the countryside: quilts of green expanding into the horizon, interrupted only by roads, towns, rivers and, of course, the magnificent châteaux themselves.

Montgolfières d'Anjou's balloons take off from four sites in the region. The first site is the Château de Brissac, France's tallest castle (15km/8 miles south of Angers, www.chateau-brissac.fr), with its own vineyard and richly clad apartments. The owners are hot-air balloon fanatics and frequently open their gardens to host the European hot-air ballooning championships. There are also four princely *chambres d'hôte* (doubles from €390), should you decide to splurge. The second site is the delightful Château de Pignerolle (just east of Angers, www.musee-communication.com), whose interior houses a quaint communications museum. The third site, the Île de Gennes, is a sandy island in the middle of the Loire west of Saumur (www.cc-gennois.fr), used mainly for early morning flights; and the fourth site is the Gratien & Meyer vineyard just outside Saumur (www.gratienmeyer.com).

If you do decide to take a flight, you need to allow at least three hours for the whole trip, wear sturdy shoes and bring a jumper along in case it gets nippy. Children under eight and pregnant women are not allowed to fly.

Pascal Favre d'Anne takes great pride in using local produce but his heart lies in his native Haute Savoie, from where he ships in ripe reblochons and tommes.

La Licorne
14km E of Saumur *Allée Sainte-Catherine, Fontevraud (02.41.51.72.49/www.la-licorne-restaurant.com). Open Apr-Sept noon-2pm, 7-9pm daily. Oct-Mar noon-2pm, 7-9pm Tue, Thur-Sat; noon-2pm Wed, Sun. €€€€.*
One of the most charming things about this temple of gastronomy is its setting inside a picture-perfect townhouse with a flower-filled garden that doubles as a terrace in the summer and has its own resident cat. But the stuff going on in the kitchen is worth the detour too. Much of the menu is sourced locally (they even grow their own fruit and vegetables in an allotment just outside the village), and includes dishes such as turbot *à l'orange* with parsnip gratin or pears poached in chinon wine.

"Try to come for one of the truffle-hunting weekends when the owners take you and a lovely Labrador out to hunt the black diamonds of the Loire."

Les Ménestrels
Saumur *11 rue Raspail (02.41.67.71.10/www. restaurant-les-menestrels.com). Open 7-9.30pm Mon; 12.15-1.30pm, 7-9.30pm Tue-Sat. €€€.*
It's official: chef Christophe Hosselet is a culinary genius, inventing what could be some of the most flavoursome dishes in the region – rabbit and chorizo ravioli; succulent scallops with a delicious orange, artichoke and parmesan sauce; lobster consommé served with a straw; and a sinfully creamy profiterole stack. Wash it all down with a 2006 saumur-champigny from the Clos Cristal *domaine*.

Le Pavillon des Lys
Amboise *9 rue d'Orange (02.47.30.01.01/ www.pavillondeslys.com). Open 7-9pm Wed-Sat; noon-2pm Sun. €€€.*
Sébastien Bégouin, the owner of this smart guesthouse and restaurant, is a one-man miracle, somehow managing to welcome guests, prepare and serve breakfast, act as concierge, tidy rooms and also cook lip-smacking gourmet cuisine worthy of a larger establishment. The two menus (including one vegetarian) might feature confit of duck in a spiced bread crust; mushroom ravioli in a cappuccino of ceps, parmesan and cream; and a velvety seasonal fruit mousse to finish.

Le Prieuré
3km W of Saumur *Chênhutte-les-Tuffeaux (02.41.67.90.14/www.grandesetapes.fr). Open noon-3pm, 7.15-9pm daily. €€€.*
The old Prieuré hotel, set high on a rocky spur, boasts some the best views in the Loire, overlooking the river's sandy expanses and surrounding villages. Food is top notch too, served in a bottle-green 19th-century dining room by impeccable waiters in traditional black and white attire. Expect elaborate gourmet cuisine such as salad of *rillauds* with an egg poached in red wine, cod with mustardy potatoes and lobster cream, and gooey chocolate soufflé with a hint of citrus fruits.

Le Relais Chenonceaux
12km SE of Amboise *10 rue du Docteur Bretonneau, Chenonceaux (02.47.23.98.11/www.chenonceaux.com). Open noon-2.30pm, 7-9pm daily. Closed mid Nov-early Feb. €.*
Great galettes filled to the brim with ham, cheese, egg and mushrooms, washed down with a glass of local wine, make this place a hit with locals and tourists alike. For something more substantial, the menu includes hearty *steak-frites* and *moules-frites* too. Don't leave without saying hello to Charlie, the well-loved parrot in the courtyard outside.

Stay

Château des Briottières
24km N of Angers *Rte de Marigné, Champigné (02.41.42.00.02/www.briottieres.com). €€€.*
The frustration of seeing so many glorious châteaux but never being able to stay in one is solved at this gorgeous, family-run 16th-century castle, which oozes history and romance from every nook and cranny. In fact the whole place is so lovely, with its ancient park, swimming pool and sumptuous period decor, that you might never want to leave. The 11 rooms all feature antique furniture, thick floral fabrics and bathrooms big enough to live in. All in all, a superlative, princely experience.

Château de Verrières
Saumur *53 rue d'Alsace (02.41.38.05.15/ www.chateau-verrieres.com). €€€.*
Uno the dog bounds out to greet you, Andrew the English handyman waves hello, and Thierry and Yolaine, the welcoming owners, take your bags inside their sumptuous belle époque home, built by one of the Louvre's architects. Thus begins one of the most memorable stays in the Loire Valley. This is the perfect hideaway, brimming with antique furniture, sculpted wood panelling and views to die for over Saumur's castle.

La Croix Blanche
14km E of Saumur *7 pl Plantagenêts, Fontevraud (02.41.51.71.11/www.fontevraud.net). €€.*
The Croix Blanche coach house has been around since medieval times and couldn't be in a better location, right next door to Fontevraud Abbey. Until a few years ago it

Top: Château de Verrières. Bottom: Hôtel La Marine de Loire.

Le Pavillon des Lys.

was the main port of call for coach trips, but the passionate new owners have put a stop to that by revamping most of the bedrooms in bright, art deco style. Dining here is an experience in itself, and if you plan to visit in the winter try to come for one of the truffle-hunting weekends when the owners take you and a lovely Labrador out to hunt the black diamonds of the Loire.

Le Diderot
Chinon *4 rue de Buffon (02.47.93.18.87/ www.hoteldiderot.com). €.*
With ancient beams, 19th-century furniture, warm-toned fabrics and a flower-filled terrace, the ivy-clad Diderot is one of those cutesy, olde-worlde hotels that makes you feel snug as soon as you step through the door. In summer breakfast is served on the terrace, but it's almost worth coming in winter just to take advantage of the roaring fire.

Hôtel d'Anjou
Angers *1 bd Foch (02.41.21.12.11/ www.hoteldanjou.fr). €€.*
Angers has surprisingly few decent places to stay in the city centre, but this place is an exception to the rule, with 53 bedrooms all individually decorated in plush fabrics with traditional French furniture. Its restaurant, La Salamandre, is a François I-style dining room serving traditional cuisine, and for those in search of pampering in-room massages with essential oils can be organised.

Hôtel La Marine de Loire
10km E of Saumur *9 quai de la Loire, Montsoreau (02.41.50.18.21/www.hotel-lamarinedeloire.com). €€€.*

This tasteful hotel is in a great location at the foot of the Château de Montsoreau, between Fontevraud Abbey and Saumur. The beautifully furnished rooms are decorated in airy pastels, and there's a peaceful garden for lounging and a small outhouse containing a spa. The 'Sous la Lune' suite, which sleeps four, overlooks the Loire and re-creates the night sky with encased lights above the bed. Stargazers can also use the in-room telescope.

Le Pavillon des Lys
Amboise *9 rue d'Orange (02.47.30.01.01/www.pavillondeslys.com). €€.*
A street away from Amboise's royal castle, this wonderful 18th-century townhouse has seven luxurious rooms, decorated in classy art deco style with fine pieces of furniture, modern art and bright fabrics. Breakfast is served outside in the pretty courtyard or in the art-filled drawing room by owner Sébastien, fresh as a daisy despite having cooked all evening in the hotel's gastronomic restaurant.

Troglododo
18km NE of Chinon *9 chemin des Caves, Azay-le-Rideau (02.47.45.31.25/http://troglododo.fr). €.*
This is your chance to sleep inside a real troglodyte dwelling. Troglododo used to be a hamlet of cave dwellings inhabited by local farm workers, before friendly owners Cathy and Alain Sarrazin (who grew up in the village) put much sweat and tears into turning the cliffside into self-contained grottoes. The results are appealing: four rooms with exposed stone, a colourful feature wall and a bathroom entirely dug into the rock. The fifth room isn't troglodyte, but it makes up for it by having its own private terrace.

Factfile

When to go
The region is very busy during the summer holidays, and several sites are closed between November and Easter, so either check before you come or visit in the spring and autumn, when everywhere is open and crowds are less dense. That said, lovers of French theatre should brave the crowds in June and July for the month-long Festival d'Anjou, France's second most important theatre festival after Avignon, which is held at various locations across the Loire.

Getting there
Easiest by far is to take the TGV from Paris to either Tours (57mins) or Angers (1hr 30mins), then hire a car. The nearest airport is Tours.

Getting around
A car is the easiest option for exploring the region, but one of the best ways to escape the crowds (between sites at least) is to cycle. Over 800km (500 miles) of cycle paths cover the area between Sancerre in the east and the Atlantic

Ocean beyond Nantes. Route and bike hire information can be found on www.loire-a-velo.fr.

Tourist offices
Amboise Quai du Général de Gaulle (02.47.57.09.28/www.amboise-valdeloire.com).
Angers 7 pl Kennedy (02.41.23.50.00/ www.angersloiretourisme.com).
Azay-le-Rideau 4 rue du Château (02.47.45.44.40/www.ot-paysazaylerideau.com).
Chinon Pl Hofheim (02.47.93.30.44/ www.chinon.com).
Fontevraud Pl St-Michel (02.41.51.79.45/ www.saumur-tourisme.com).
Saumur Pl de la Bilange (02.41.40.20.60/ www.ot-saumur.fr).
Tours 78-82 rue Bernard Palissy (02.47.70.37.37/www.ligeris.com).

Internet access
Most hotels in this chapter offer free Wi-Fi. If not, try Cyber Espace in Angers (25 rue de la Roë, 02.41.24.92.71/www.angersweb.com).

Central Bordeaux.

Bordeaux

Vintage wines and venerable architecture on the banks of the Garonne.

Bordeaux has undergone a remarkable transformation during the past few years. France's sixth city has always been beautiful, but for long it was a mystery why much of it was so shabby. Now decades of grime have been cleaned off, derelict warehouses that cluttered the waterfront have been knocked down and a new landscaped riverside promenade has been created, drawing attention to the wealth of gorgeous 18th-century architecture.

Much of this urban renewal is due to the arrival of former prime minister Alain Juppé in 1995 in his new role as mayor and eco-warrior, and a vast swathe (roughly half) of the city has now been granted World Heritage status by UNESCO. The cosmetic work has also brought about a change of mood: the tramway has reduced traffic and pulled disparate *quartiers* together, new districts are developing and a sense of adventure has been breathed into this traditionally conservative city, from the monthly Sunday without cars to new outdoor art festival Evento in October. Bordeaux still has to adapt to this new-found attention – it is more used to visitors coming here for the wine than to visit the city itself, which has its plus and minus sides. On the one hand, restaurants and shops are largely frequented by the *bordelais* and there is little tourist tat; on the other, some of the finest churches are rarely open to the public and you'll be hard pushed to find a brochure in English in the city's museums.

Capital of Aquitaine and the first bridging point on the Garonne river, Bordeaux was the jewel in the dowry brought by Eleanor of Aquitaine with her marriage to Henry II of England in 1152, creating a period of English rule that lasted until the end of the Hundred Years War 300 years later. Bordeaux saw its glory age in the 18th century, as the port boomed thanks to burgeoning wine exports, the triangular slave and spice trade with Africa and the Caribbean, and the urban planning ambitions of the powerful royal intendants Boucher and Tourny, laying out squares and avenues and leaving the city with an unmatched legacy of creamy stone façades, lacy wrought iron and grimacing mascarons, some of them clearly portraits. While there are plenty of things to see in Bordeaux, the true delight is simply wandering the streets.

Bags packed, milk cancelled, house raised on stilts.

You've packed the suntan lotion, the snorkel set, the stay-pressed shirts. Just one more thing left to do – your bit for climate change. In some of the world's poorest countries, changing weather patterns are destroying lives.

You can help people to deal with the extreme effects of climate change. Raising houses in flood-prone regions is just one life-saving solution.

**Climate change costs lives.
Give £5 and let's sort it *Here & Now***

www.oxfam.org.uk/climate-change

Be Humankind Oxfam

Explore

VIEUX BORDEAUX

Central Bordeaux grew up along the crescent moon-shaped curve of the Garonne river that gave the town its nickname 'Port de la Lune'. The quaysides on either side of the semi-circular place de la Bourse, Bordeaux's finest square, still provide an almost non-stop array of fine 18th-century façades. The square itself was designed in the 1730s by Jacques Ange Gabriel, architect of place de la Concorde in Paris, and its neo-classical façades are now cleverly reflected in the 'water mirror' that forms the centrepiece of the new riverside gardens. Behind here, in the heart of Vieux Bordeaux, elegant 18th-century façades are punctuated by some unexpected fortified medieval gateways and Gothic churches. Further north, the esplanade des Quinconces, a vast open space with columns at the river end and the Monument aux Girondins, a fountain full of thrashing half-fish, half-horse sea beasts at the other, is used for all sorts of festivities, from funfairs to the biennial summer wine festival.

The Grand Théâtre, used for opera and ballet, is at one tip of the 'golden triangle' formed by allées de Tourny, cours Georges Clémenceau and cours de l'Intendance, home to Bordeaux's smartest shops and some lively brasseries. Parallel to cours de l'Intendance, rue de la Porte Dijeaux leads to restaurant-packed place du Parlement and place St-Pierre with its Gothic church. Pedestrianised rue Ste-Catherine, which cuts through the old town on the trace of the ancient Roman *cardo*, is busy with clothes stores.

Around the Gothic cathedral, which curiously has its main portal on the north side, you'll find Bordeaux's town hall in the elegant former bishop's palace, as well as most of the city's museums. On rue des Frères Bonie, a fragment of the Hâ, the city's 15th-century fortifications, makes an unlikely contrast with the modernity of Sir Richard Rogers' Tribunal de Grand Instance (law courts), whose conical wooden turrets were apparently inspired by wine bottles in a rack.

South of cours Victor Hugo, the shops of rue Ste-Catherine head dramatically downmarket. Here, life centres on the studenty bars on place de la Victoire and the Gothic church of St-Michel, with its cluster of junk dealers and Sunday flea market. Further towards the station, through the neo-classical Porte de la Monnaie, is a bohemian district that's home to ancient houses, the Romanesque church of Ste-Croix, the art school and the Théâtre National Bordeaux Aquitaine.

Musée d'Aquitaine

20 cours Pasteur (05.56.01.51.00/www.bordeaux.fr). Open 11am-6pm Tue-Sun. Admission free; temporary exhibitions €5.

The most substantial of Bordeaux's museums spans the archaeology, history and ethnography of the Aquitaine region from prehistoric times to the 20th century. A broadly

Bordeaux

Historic sites

Art & architecture

Hotels

Eating & drinking

Nightlife

Shopping

Bordeaux

0   100km

Jardin Botanique
de la Bastide.

chronological route begins with cave life, flint arrowheads, pottery and Gaulish jewellery, before taking in statues and mosaic floors from Bordeaux's Roman forebear Burdigala, medieval sculpture, Renaissance tombs and sections on the wine trade and oyster production. A new display devoted to the city's 18th-century role in the slave trade opened in 2009. The 20th-century section includes film footage and memorabilia of figures who have marked local history, including Marcel Dassault (of Falcon planes fame, still manufactured nearby) and writer François Mauriac.

Musée des Arts Décoratifs

39 rue Bouffard (05.56.10.14.00/www.bordeaux.fr). Open 2-6pm Mon, Wed-Sun. Admission free; temporary exhibitions €5.

The decorative arts museum, housed in the handsome 18th-century Hôtel de Lalande, still has the intimate appeal of a private residence with its panelled period rooms and creaking parquet. Along with furniture, glass, fans, a large array of faïence from manufacturers all over France and art deco items, highlights include several gorgeous old harpsichords and spinets, plus a selection of curios from the royal restoration.

Musée des Beaux-Arts

20 cours d'Albret (05.56.10.20.56/www.bordeaux.fr). Open 11am-6pm Mon, Wed-Sun. Admission free; temporary exhibitions €5.

Languishing in a vast building behind the town hall, Bordeaux's fine art museum feels a little unloved. Works are stacked high on the walls and poorly labelled, but it merits a look for the fine altarpiece by Perugino, Titian's dramatic *Tarquin and Lucretia*, lots of Dutch and Flemish landscapes, and Delacroix's scary *Greece on the Ruins of Missolonghi*, as well as pastels and prints by Bordeaux visionary Odilon Redon. Temporary exhibitions are put on in a second wing across the garden and in the Galerie des Beaux-Arts up the street (place du Colonel Raynal).

Tour Pey-Berland

Place Pey-Berland (05.56.81.26.25/www.monuments-nationaux.fr). Open June-Sept 10am-1.15pm, 2-6pm daily; Oct-May 10am-12.30pm, 2-5.30pm Tue-Sun. Admission €5; €3.50 reductions.

This 15th-century Gothic belfry was built separately from the medieval cathedral so its tolling didn't shake the foundations, but it didn't actually have any bells until 1869; in the event it was converted first into dwellings and then into a bullet factory. The very narrow, 231-step spiral staircase leads to two viewing platforms at the top: the first signposts the principal buildings of Bordeaux, the second sits up amid the Gothic pinnacles just beneath the gilt copper statue of the Virgin that surmounts the spire.

LES CHARTRONS & BACALAN

North of the esplanade des Quinconces lies the Chartrons, the district built up in the 18th century by the *négociants*, Bordeaux's powerful wine merchants, a few of whom still have headquarters here today. The merchants' houses, typically containing residential and business premises and long cellars where wine was aged, alternate with humbler dockworkers' cottages. The main sight here is the CAPC contemporary art museum, but the waterside promenade, with its skate park and organic food market on Thursdays (6am-4pm), is also a growing attraction. A street back from the quays, antiques dealers congregate along rue Notre-Dame on either side of the Marché des Chartrons. Further downstream, the warehouses of quai de Bacalan now contain a cluster of discount factory outlets. Beyond here, there are still a few boats and ship chandlers in the Bassins à Flots, along with a growing nightlife hub and the Base Sous Marine, the vast concrete wet docks where German U-boats were berthed during the Occupation; today the space is used for exhibitions and performances.

CAPC Musée d'Art Contemporain

7 rue Ferrère (05.56.00.81.50/www.bordeaux.fr). Open 11am-6pm Tue, Thur-Sun; 11am-8pm Wed. Admission free; temporary exhibitions €5.

The imposing Entrepôt Lainé, built in the early 19th century to stock coffee, spices and rum from trade with the colonies, was brilliantly converted in the 1980s into the city's contemporary art museum. The lofty central nave is used for a dynamic programme of temporary exhibitions, while the permanent collection is particularly strong on arte povera, minimalism and land art, including works by Janis Kounellis and a Richard Long slate line up on the roof. There's also an excellent restaurant at the top for lunch or Sunday brunch.

Musée du Vin et du Négoce de Bordeaux

41 rue Borie (05.56.90.19.13/www.mvnb.fr). Open Apr-Oct 10am-6pm Mon-Wed, Fri-Sun; 10am-10pm Thur. Nov-Mar 10am-6pm Tue-Sat; 2-6pm Sun. Admission €7.

Appropriately housed in the long, barrel-vaulted cellars of the wine house founded by Irishman Francis Burke in 1720, the wine trade museum differs from most wine museums in that the emphasis is not on cultivating and making wines but on the role of the *négociants*, the wine merchants who shaped both the character of Bordeaux wines for export and this district of Bordeaux. Displays make ample use of high-tech gadgetry and, needless to say, visits finish with a tasting in the former barrelling room.

LA BASTIDE

Long a poor industrial suburb, the Bastide district on the right bank of the Garonne was only connected to the city by the Pont de Pierre, Bordeaux's oldest bridge, in 1822. Today, helped by the arrival of the tramway, it is going through a resurgence, with rehabilitated industrial buildings, an adventurous modern botanical garden, swish riverside apartments, university faculties and the Mégarama multiplex cinema, housed in a converted train station.

Whatever your carbon footprint, we can reduce it

For over a decade we've been leading the way in carbon offsetting and carbon management.

In that time we've purchased carbon credits from over 200 projects spread across 6 continents. We work with over 300 major commercial clients and thousands of small and medium sized businesses, which rely upon our market-leading quality assurance programme, our experience and absolute commitment to deliver the right solution for each client.

Why not give us a call?

T: London (020) 7833 6000

Jardin Botanique de la Bastide
Quai des Queyries or esplanade Linné (05.56.52.18.77/ www.bordeaux.fr). Open Gardens Apr-Oct 8am-8pm daily; Nov-Mar 8am-6pm daily. Glasshouses/exhibitions 11am-6pm Tue-Sun. Admission free.

The brilliant modern botanical gardens manage to be both highly conceptual and great fun. Catherine Mosbach, a rising star of landscape design, has created scaled-down slices of 11 different Aquitaine habitats – Landes forest, grass meadow, chalk hill – plus a jigsaw-like water garden full of stepping stones, community gardens and giant fake boulders dotted around the park that serve as information points, café, offices and workshops. The glasshouses continue where the park leaves off, with tropical and desert species imaginatively planted alongside their end products, from tinned pineapple to rubber.

GREATER BORDEAUX

Beyond the centre of Bordeaux itself, Le Grand Bordeaux, a conurbation of some 750,000 inhabitants, is largely contained within the ring road. This varied area incorporates the unloved 1970s shopping centre, chain hotels and the administrative complex of Mériadeck; residential and industrial suburbs; the modern convention centre and trade fair site of Bordeaux Lac; and former wine villages, such as Pessac and Talence, where vines, among them the prestigious Château Haut-Brion, continue to be cultivated well within the city's fringes.

Maison Frugès – Le Corbusier
4 rue Le Corbusier, Pessac (05.56.36.56.46/ www.mairie-pessac.fr). Open 2-6pm Wed, Fri; 10am-noon, 2-6pm Thur; 2-6.30pm Sat, Sun.

Le Corbusier's first large-scale project was conceived as a laboratory of social housing by local industrialist Henry Frugès, who called in the modernist architect in the 1920s to create an ideal garden city for his factory workers. Le Corbusier came up with six different geometrical modules of terraced and detached houses, in a rhythmic scheme of rust, green, pale blue and white. Despite some subsequent alterations, you can still spot typical features, such as roof terraces, patios and sculptural staircases, and visit the Maison Frugès which has been bought by the local council and contains a permanent exhibition.

Stade Chaban-Delmas
Place Johnston (www.bordeaux.fr/www.girondins.com).

The city's 1930s reinforced concrete stadium, inspired by antique amphitheatres, is named after the late prime minister Jacques Chaban-Delmas, who was mayor of Bordeaux for 48 years. It is home to FC Bordeaux (Les Girondins).

Eat

Bordelaise cuisine used to be characterised by generous helpings of local fish and meat (Pauillac lamb, duck), simply prepared so as not to distract from its grand wines, and was typified by brasseries serving oysters (here often curiously accompanied by chipolata sausages) and grilled steaks, rather than elaborate haute cuisine temples. But the restaurant scene is evolving, with trendy designer haunts, cosmopolitan touches and adventurous bistros. Note that *à la bordelaise* often denotes a red wine and shallot sauce, and look out for Aquitaine caviar, now farmed in the region.

Le Chapon Fin
Vieux Bordeaux 5 rue Montesquieu (05.56.79.10.10/ www.chapon-fin.com). Open noon-2pm, 8-9.30pm Tue-Sat. Closed Aug. €€€.

Opened in 1825, Bordeaux's oldest restaurant acquired its OTT fake grotto interior in the early 1900s when it was the fashionable haunt of politicians and actresses. But it took the arrival of young chef Nicolas Frion, former second to Thierry Marx at Château Cordeillan Bages, in 2003 to bring it back into the gastronomic top league. Frion likes to marry exotic spices with the best of the region's seasonal produce, in sometimes daring combinations such as red mullet, smoked eel and black radish, or spiced tuna and foie gras. The bargain lunch menu is a great way to sample his style.

Chez Greg Le Grand Théâtre
Vieux Bordeaux 29 rue Esprit des Lois (05.56.31.30.30/www.chezgreg.fr). Open noon-2.30pm, 7.30-11.30pm daily. Closed mid-end Aug. €€€.

Chez Greg is the place to come for a buzzy night out, with its chic location by the opera and striking modern decor: white tables, leather chairs, video monitors behind the bar and stainless steel bottle racks lining the walls. The menu mixes south-western favourites – foie gras, oysters, duck or a vast T-bone steak for two cooked on an open fire, accompanied by a mound of chips – with Asian fusion dishes, such as sushi or Thai curry. Despite its reputation as one of Bordeaux's hippest spots, the crowd is varied and service is friendly. There are some first-rate Bordeaux wines to discover, so ask the waiter for advice.

L'Estaquade
La Bastide Quai de Queyries (05.57.54.02.50/www. lestaquade.com). Open noon-2pm, 7.30-10pm daily. €€€.

From its glass-sided hut jutting out on stilts over the river, L'Estaquade has what must be the most stunning view in the city as the panorama of place de la Bourse and the fine façades along the Garonne stretch out across the river before you – as well as of the coypu who play in the water below. High prices reflect the view, but the food – a creatively cosmopolitan take on brasserie cooking by Ducasse-trained Frédéric Montemont – is taken seriously too.

Gravelier
Chartrons & Bacalan 114 cours de Verdun (05.56.48.17.15). Open noon-2pm Mon; noon-2pm, 7.30-9.30pm Tue-Fri. Closed Aug & 1wk Feb. €€€.

This is just the sort of example of France's new generation of good-value, chef-owned bistros that Bordeaux needs. The beige dining room has a window offering glimpses of what's

Place de la Bourse.

going on in the kitchen as Yves Gravelier reinvents bistro cooking with precise preparations and flavours inspired by his travels, combined with a knack for perfect seasoning.

Jean-Marie Amat

Greater Bordeaux *Château du Prince Noir, 26 rue Raymond Lis, Lormont (05.56.06.12.52/ www.jm-amat.com). Open noon-2pm, 8-10pm Tue-Fri; 8-10pm Sat. €€€€.*

Jean-Marie Amat was credited by many as the founder of modern Bordelaise cuisine at the Hauterive Saint James before being somewhat unceremoniously ousted. He made his comeback in 2007 with this stylish restaurant located within the Black Prince's medieval castle. The cooking is adventurous and beautifully presented, with intense flavours. Note that the castle is easy to spot from the ring road, but very complicated to reach through the one-way system.

Le Noailles

Vieux Bordeaux *12 allées de Tourny (05.56.81.94.45). Open noon-11.30pm daily. €€€.*

A classic upmarket 1930s brasserie for feasting on oysters and steaks amid globe lights, big mirrors and waiters in long white aprons; an institution for observing Bordeaux's haute bourgeoisie.

Le Petit Commerce

Vieux Bordeaux *22 rue du Parlement St-Pierre (05.56.79.76.58/www.le-petit-commerce.info). Open 9am-2am Mon-Sat; 6pm-midnight Sun. €€.*

Le Petit Commerce, nestled down a narrow pedestrianised street, is all about superb fresh fish and shellfish delivered daily from the ports of Arcachon and Royan and served without frills. It likes to call itself a 'fish canteen' rather than a restaurant, which gives an idea of the casual atmosphere, where you can just as easily snack at the Formica bar over a plate of whelks while watching sports on TV as feast on turbot at one of the tables.

Le Pressoir d'Argent

Vieux Bordeaux *Regent Grand Hotel, 2-5 pl de la Comédie (05.57.30.44.44/www.pressoir-argent.com). Open noon-2pm, 7.30-10pm Tue-Sat. Closed Aug & 1wk Nov. €€€€.*

Set within a splendid first-floor dining room, decked out with chandeliers and plush orange and purple velvet love seats, the Pressoir is the most upmarket of the Grand's three restaurants and has serious gastronomic ambitions in the hands of chef Pascal Nibaudeau. The menu is bursting with luxury ingredients – turbot, scallops, truffles, pigeon and Aquitaine caviar – with an emphasis on fish and place of honour to the *pressoir d'argent* (silver lobster press).

Quai West

Chartrons & Bacalan *Hangar H19, quai des Bacalans (05.57.87.13.57). Open 9am-11pm daily. €€.*

This lively restaurant and bar in a refurbished riverside hangar draws a young crowd to newly happening Bacalan. Inside there's an industrial vibe with exposed brick and a metal mezzanine, while the outdoor terrace is a good place for sunning it over pizzas and south-western duck dishes.

La Terrasse Saint Pierre

Vieux Bordeaux *7 pl St-Pierre (05.57.85.89.17). Open noon-2.30pm, 7-11.30pm daily. €€.*

With tables inside an 18th-century building or under the trees in front of a Gothic church, this is a reliable Vieux Bordeaux address for unpretentious regional cooking and a huge choice of wines. Specialities include fish and steak tartares, calf's liver or the catch of the day. Be sure to finish up with the individual tarte tatin cooked in its own mini frying pan.

La Tupina

Vieux Bordeaux *6 rue Porte de la Monnaie (05.56.91.56.37/www.latupina.com). Open noon-2pm, 7-11pm daily. €€€€.*

The bubbling cauldron, wooden crates of shallots and ceps, and strings of garlic and espelette peppers may look rustic, but the international foodies who crowd into La Tupina's series of small dining rooms are anything but. Owner Jean-Pierre Xiradakis is a Bordeaux personality dedicated to authentic south-western cooking based on first-rate produce (Landes chicken, Bigorre pork, lampreys) and simple recipes. Up the street at No.34, offshoot Bar Cave de la Monnaie is a more casual wine bar.

Villa Tourny

Vieux Bordeaux *20 allées de Tourny (05.56.44.60.48). Open 8am-2am Mon-Fri; 10am-2am Sat. €€.*

With its tongue-in-cheek, neo-baroque setting replete with sultry lighting and claret-coloured banquettes, this new generation brasserie is a current favourite with Bordeaux's beautiful people. The menu features vast helpings of meat, sautéed squid and bowls of pasta, plus a help-yourself pâtisserie tray for dessert or afternoon tea.

Shop

Designer fashion labels are concentrated in the golden triangle. More mainstream clothes labels can be found on rue de la Porte Dijeaux, rue Ste-Catherine and in the St-Christoly shopping centre, with smaller individual boutiques on the side streets of Vieux Bordeaux. Look for discount factory outlets on the quai de Bacalan, and antiques and collectibles on rue Bouffard, in passage St-Michel, on place Canteloup by the Eglise St-Michel and the Village Notre-Dame on rue Notre-Dame in the Chartrons district.

Baillardran

Vieux Bordeaux *111 rue de la Porte Dijeaux (05.56.51.02.09/www.baillardran.com). Open 8am-7.30pm daily.*

The sticky, fluted *canelé*, made with a batter-like mixture flavoured with vanilla and rum, is emblematic of Bordeaux, and should be moist in the interior and slightly caramelised at the base. Baillardran has several outlets around town – this one includes a coffee bar.

Bradley's Bookshop

Vieux Bordeaux *8 cours d'Albret (05.56.52.10.57/ www.bradleys-bookshop.com). Open 2-7pm Mon, 9.30am-7pm Tue-Sat.*

A useful shop if you're hungry for some English-language reading matter, stocking fiction and non-fiction, children's books and a large section devoted to English-language teaching materials.

L'Intendant

Vieux Bordeaux *2 allées de Tourny (05.56.48.01.29). Open 10am-7.30pm Mon-Sat.*

Bottles arranged around a stunning spiral staircase plus a Dubuffet painting hanging behind the counter make this wine shop worth a visit for its beauty alone, but that's not counting the vast choice from all the Bordeaux *appellations*. Prices rise as you climb.

La Vinothèque de Bordeaux

Vieux Bordeaux *8 cours du XXX Juillet (05.56.52.32.05/www.la-vinotheque.com). Open 10am-7.30pm Mon-Sat.*

This double boutique – reds on one side, whites on the other – has an enormous choice of Bordeaux, although the rest of France does kindly get a look in, too. The staff are helpful and there are frequent wine tastings.

Arts

Opéra National de Bordeaux

Vieux Bordeaux *Grand Théâtre, pl de la Comédie (05.56.00.85.95/www.opera-bordeaux.com). Tickets €8-€110.*

With its colonnaded classical exterior topped by statues of muses and goddesses, grand staircase – said to have inspired Charles Garnier for the Palais Garnier in Paris – and frescoed auditorium, the opera house, designed in the 1770s by architect Victor Louis, provides a splendid setting for some first-rate opera and ballet. The acoustics are excellent, although the small stage can be a limitation for large-scale productions.

TnBA (Théâtre National Bordeaux Aquitaine)

Vieux Bordeaux *Square Jean Vauthier (05.56.33.36.80/www.tnba.org). Tickets prices vary.*

Bordeaux's main subsidised theatre occupies an old sugar warehouse in the Sainte-Croix district and contains assorted performance spaces, rehearsal studios and a drama school. Under resident director Dominique Pitoiset, the repertoire goes from French classics to new drama.

Nightlife

There are countless bars in the old town clustered around place du Parlement and place St-Pierre. Later on the action shifts south to quai du Paludate, and north to a new nightlife focus in the docks of Bacalan. Student central is place de la Victoire and adjoining streets.

La Dame de Shanghai

Chartrons & Bacalan *Quai Armand Lalande (05.57.10.20.50/www.damedeshanghai.com). Open times vary.*

Students from the city's huge university give a festive vibe to many of the city's central bars, but for something more clubby head to this Bacalan hangout – a floating nightclub, bar and fusion restaurant all rolled into one.

El Bodegon

Vieux Bordeaux *14 pl de la Victoire (05.56.94.74.02). Open 7am-2am Mon-Sat; 1pm-2am Sun.*

Themed club nights, live music and tapas keep El Bodegon at the heart of the place de la Victoire scene and it's also a popular student haunt at lunchtime.

Stay

Hôtel Continental

Vieux Bordeaux *10 rue Montesquieu (05.56.52.66.00/www.hotel-le-continental.com). €€.*

There's nothing particularly swish about this hotel, but it's a friendly, practical option on a pedestrianised street in the heart of shopping territory. Behind the 18th-century façade, the functional bedrooms are done out in predominantly natural tones with plenty of light. There's a welcoming reception area and a duplex suite at the top with roof terrace.

Hôtel des 4 Soeurs

Vieux Bordeaux *6 cours du XXX Juillet (05.57.81.19.20). €€.*

Its prime position by the Grand Théâtre and low prices make the venerable Four Sisters one of the best-loved hotels in Bordeaux, ever proud that Richard Wagner stayed here in 1850. Bedrooms are bright and clean, and the bathrooms have all recently been redone. The spacious family rooms at the front are the pick of the bunch, with high ceilings and a great view. The owner is a wonderful source of local gossip.

Hôtel de la Tour d'Intendance

Vieux Bordeaux *16 rue de la Vieille Tour (05.56.44.56.56/www.hotel-tour-intendance). €€.*

This place is a well-kept secret located on a narrow side street just off the upmarket Cours de l'Intendance. The exposed stone of an 18th-century building meets flatscreen TVs, comfortable beds and modern bathrooms, with a whiff of the Cap Ferrat seaside bringing a personal touch and charm often lacking in bigger hotels.

Maison Bord'eaux

Chartrons & Bacalan *113 rue du Dr Albert Barraud (05.56.44.00.45/www.lamaisonbord-eaux.com). €€€.*

Hidden behind a curtain of ivy, this gorgeous mini hotel a short walk from the centre was masterminded by Bridget Lurton, a member of one of Bordeaux's great wine dynasties.

Monument aux Girondins.

Jean-Marie Amat.

All a matter of tasting

With thousands of châteaux, 57 *appellations*, 800 million bottles a year and everything from the greatest, priciest wines in the world to inexpensive plonk, discovering the vineyards of Bordeaux can seem a mind-boggling prospect. There are few easy brand names to help you wade through the wine lists; rather you have to learn to play a memory game of *appellations*, châteaux, first and second growths, and good and bad vintages.

A drive through the vineyards helps to give an image of the different landscapes that make up the Bordelais – the chalky hills of St-Emilion, gravelly Graves and Pessac-Léognan, the sloping estuarine vineyards of the Côtes de Blaye – and understand the concept of *terroir*: the idea that wine-making is not just about grape varieties but also about the land the wine comes from, its soils, aspect, climate, history and know-how.

The celebrated Route des Châteaux follows the D2 up the Rive Gauche (Left Bank) of the Gironde, through the Médoc and its prestigious *appellations* – Margaux, St-Julien, Pauillac and St-Estèphe – passing such legendary names as Château Margaux, Beychevelle, Latour and Mouton-Rothschild, some of them beautiful historic buildings in their own right.

The CIVB (Conseil Interprofessionnel du Vin de Bordeaux) in Bordeaux and the Maison du Vin of each *appellation* can provide information on which châteaux accept visitors, often by appointment only. However, if you're not in the wine trade, getting past the threshold of many of the grandest names is nigh on impossible, and you have a much better chance if you join a wine tour or holiday.

An easy starting point are the full-day coach tours organised by the Bordeaux tourist office. Different tours each day of the week by area or by theme include 'art and wine', 'Graves and the home of Montesquieu' and the grandiose '1855 Médoc classification'. Most run from mid May to October; reserve at least five days ahead at the tourist office or by internet (€30-€90). In St-Emilion, the tourist office (05.57.55.28.28, www.saint-emilion-tourisme.com) runs bilingual 'Friday with a Winemaker' and 'Saturday as an Oenologist' tours (€70-€75), combining wine tasting, vineyard tour, lunch and a tour of the town.

Wine schools will take your appreciation a step further. The CIVB's own Ecole de Vin (3 cours du XXX Juillet, 05.56.00.22.85, www.bordeaux.fr) runs assorted tasting courses, from a two-hour 'summer express'

introduction to the serious, intensive two-day 'Wine Tasting from A to Z' and three-day 'Grands Crus', visiting the Médoc, Sauternes, Graves and St-Emilion. The Ecole du Bordeaux (05.56.73.19.31, www.bordeauxsaveurs.com) is based at the prestigious Château Lynch-Bages in Pauillac. The two-hour introductory course (€60-€75) teaches how to look at colour and limpidity, sniff out those mushroom, spice or blackberry flavours, swirl and finally taste, complemented by a visit to the Lynch-Bages cellars. Up in the pedestrianised upper town of St-Emilion, the two-hour class at L'Ecole du Vin de St-Emilion (4 rue de Clocher, 05.57.24.61.01, www.vignobleschateaux.com, in English at 3pm Mon-Sat, €29), above the Vignobles et Châteaux wine shop, aims to provide an enjoyable introduction, ending with a blind tasting of a St-Emilion, a Médoc and one other Bordeaux.

For something less conventional, the Winery (Arsac-en-Médoc, 05.56.39.04.90, www.winery.fr) takes a novel approach with its *signe oenologique*, a sort of wine horoscope to determine the style of wines you like, as you zap a choice on a scale from 'I love' to 'I hate' in a blind tasting of six wines. It helps to know the basics, but you learn a lot as you taste, and to trust your instincts: you are what you drink.

The five rooms, each in a different colour, are sleekly minimalist with Jean Nouvel furniture. Wine tastings and dinners can be organised, as can tours of the vineyards.

Maison du Lierre

Vieux Bordeaux *57 rue Huguerie (05.56.51.92.71/ www.maisondulierre.com). €€.*

Feeling more like a friendly B&B than a hotel, the 12-room Maison de Lierre is the stand-out address on this street of budget hotels. The 18th-century building, with beautiful stone staircase (no lift), has been attractively done up by its interior decorator owner. Bedrooms feature subtle lime-washed walls, old furniture and quilted bedspreads, and there's a courtyard patio for relaxing in summer.

Pavillon du Château Raba

Greater Bordeaux *35 rue Rémi Belleau, Talence (05.56.37.48.12/www.lepavillonderaba.com). €€€.*

Although it has been engulfed by suburban housing and the university's architecture faculty, the golden stone Pavillon, built to put up guests of the prestigious Château Raba (now sadly gutted) that stands next door, is an oasis of country house calm only a tram ride into the centre. There are romantic gardens dotted with statues, a pond with swans, an indoor spa and pool, plus just 11 beautifully decorated rooms, each named after a wine château, where soothing tones meet old parquet, fireplaces and four-posters. The restaurant offers a daily changing gourmet menu.

Regent Grand Hôtel

Vieux Bordeaux *2-5 pl de la Comédie (05.57.30.44.44/www.theregentbordeaux.com). €€€€.*

With the reopening of the Grand in 2008, Bordeaux at last has the luxury hotel it had been lacking, only much bigger and blinger than before. It has kept its elegant main façade designed by Victor Louis, architect of the Grand Théâtre across the square, and colonised seven adjacent buildings. The result is a sort of urban resort. Hallways are decked out with chandeliers, while the bedrooms are a lavish exercise in revisited Napoléon III by Jacques Garcia, suitably laden in stripes and swirls. Three restaurants, a wine bar and a glitzy arcade of designer fashion shops complete the picture, for now – a spa, indoor pool and nightclub are still to come.

Seeko'o Hôtel

Chartrons & Bacalan *54 quai de Bacalan (05.56.39.07.07/www.seekoo-hotel.com). €€€.*

Definitely the hippest hotel to have hit Bordeaux in centuries, this gleaming white iceberg (seeko'o in Inuit) stands out in pearly splendour in the newly happening Bacalan warehouse district – the tram stop almost opposite the hotel is useful for reaching the town centre. Inside is a black and white style exercise with lots of dark wood and slate, floor to ceiling windows, supremely comfortable beds, and witty touches such as shiny black lacquered ceilings that act as mirrors and chenille curtains into the bathroom. Other pluses include the excellent buffet breakfast.

Les Sources de Caudalie

Greater Bordeaux *Chemin de Smith Haut-Lafitte, Martillac (05.57.83.83.83/www.sources-caudalie.com). €€€€.*

This supremely romantic getaway is set amid the vineyards of Château Smith Haut-Lafitte, a few kilometres outside the city. Bedrooms are spread over five different buildings, ranging in style from the cosy trad Bastide and neo-colonial Comptoir des Indes to the lakeside Ile aux Oiseaux. The USP here is the pioneering vinotherapy spa, where you can be pampered with beauty treatments based on grape juice, seeds, wine must and the hotel's own thermal spring.

Factfile

When to go

Spring, early summer and autumn are particularly good times to visit. July and August can be very hot, the cultural season slows down and some of the best restaurants close as residents leave town for the beach. Winter is generally wet but mild. Note that during the annual trade-only Vinexpo wine fair in June, hotels get fully booked up for miles around.

Getting there

There are plenty of direct flights from the UK to Bordeaux-Mérignac airport (05.56.34.50.50, www.bordeaux.aeroport.fr), which is located 11km (8 miles) from the centre. A Jet'bus runs from the airport to the city centre every 45mins (€12 return) – the journey takes approx 45mins. The city is also served by frequent high-speed TGV trains from Paris Gare Montparnasse (3hrs) to Gare St-Jean (08.00.87.28.72/www.sncf.fr).

Getting around

Central Bordeaux is easily walked and semi-pedestrianised, but the sleek, modern tramway (www.infotbc.com) is useful for reaching the Gare St-Jean train station, as well as Bacalan and the Rive Droite. Tickets (€1.40/1hr, €4.10/1 day) are valid on both trams and buses. On the first Sunday of the month (Dimanche sans voiture), the city centre is closed to cars and reserved for pedestrians, cyclists and Rollerbladers, accompanied by special events ranging from outdoor fitness classes to tours in the art bus.

Tourist information

Tourist office 12 cours du XXX Juillet (05.56.00.66.00/www.bordeaux-tourisme.com).

Internet access

La Cyb 23 cours Pasteur (05.56.01.15.15). Open 11am-2am daily.

Top: Regent Grand Hôtel.
Bottom: Seeko'o Hôtel.

Clockwise from top:
Opéra de Lille; Vieille
Bourse; Grand' Place;
Marché de Wazemmes.

Lille

Culture is king in this former wool town just over an hour from London.

With its gabled brick houses, tall belfries, beer culture, and mussels and chips, Lille is a fascinating historic blend of French and Flemish. But it is also a dynamic city with a young student population, an adventurous year-round cultural scene, and plenty of lively bars and *estaminets* (a bistro-pub crossover).

While the population of Lille itself is only 220,000, it is the pulsing heart of Lille Métropole, an association of 85 *communes* that make up a densely populated conurbation of almost 1.1 million inhabitants – and closer to 1.8 million if you include Mons, Ypres, Kortrijk and Tournai across the Belgian frontier.

Long before it was finally integrated into France under Louis XIV in 1667, Lille was one of the powerful Flemish wool towns, where Countess Jeanne of Flanders ruled the roost while her husband was away on crusade. Later the town came into the hands of the Habsburgs as part of the vast Austro-Spanish empire, a period that left the city with much of its finest heritage – painters such as Rubens worked for the city's monasteries, and powerful merchants outdid each other to show off their wealth with ornately carved façades.

The locals are rightly proud of their city, but it took Lille's year as European City of Culture in 2004 to put it firmly on the cultural map with the establishment of the Maisons Folies, a dozen cultural centres in rehabilitated factories, fortresses and farmhouses in the region and across the Belgian frontier. And the city has cleverly kept up the impetus with Lille 3000, a biennial multidisciplinary cultural season.

Lille is its craziest on the first weekend of September for the Grande Braderie, the jumble sale to end all jumble sales in a tradition going back to the Middle Ages, when vassals were allowed to clear out their lords' attics. Starting at noon on Saturday and finishing at midnight on Sunday, antiques dealers and locals selling off their junk set up stands on the pavements and two million visitors throng the streets, accompanied by beer galore and a prize for the restaurant with the biggest pile of mussel shells outside its door.

Explore

If you're planning extensive sightseeing, the Lille Métropole City Pass, available from the tourist office in one-, two- and three-day options, can be a good deal, offering free entry to numerous sights and museums, an hour-long minibus city tour, free public transport and assorted extra discounts.

VIEUX LILLE & LES GARES

The heart of Lille is its beautiful Grand' Place (officially named place Charles de Gaulle), once the medieval market place and still a popular gathering spot, with its decorative brick houses, ornate Vieille Bourse and pavement brasseries around the fountain of the Déesse – the goddess said to have saved the town when it was besieged by Austria in 1792. At one end the Grand Garde, now the Théâtre du Nord, once housed the royal guardsmen and bears the sun motif of Louis XIV. Behind the Vieille Bourse, on place du Théâtre, you'll find Lille's belle époque opera house, the neo-vernacular Chambre de Commerce and the Rang de Beauregard, an elegant terrace of tall decorative houses.

Beyond here a tangle of narrow streets form the heart of Vieux Lille, the oldest part of the city, which narrowly escaped demolition in the 1970s to become Lille's trendiest district, packed with bars, restaurants and upmarket shops. Many

buildings along streets like rue des Chats Bossus, rue de la Monnaie, rue Lepelletier and place Louise de Bettignies have been beautifully restored. Broad avenue du Peuple Belge was once one of the town's many canals until it was filled in during the 19th century, hence the bridge that crosses it halfway down. Beyond here, restaurant-packed rue de Gand leads to the Porte de Gand, one of the city's old fortified gateways.

North-west of Vieux Lille, the Quartier Royal was laid out in the 17th century under Louis XIV, with regular terraces of brick houses. The southern end of rue Royale is a popular early evening bar crawl, while further down are some grand 18th-century *hôtels particuliers*, built according to the Parisian fashion with a mansion set at the back of an entrance courtyard. The domed Baroque church of Ste-Marie Madeleine is now used for unusual art installations. To the north-west lies the Citadelle, the massive star-shaped fortress built by Louis XIV's military engineer Vauban as one of a line of frontier defences. It is still used by the army, but is now surrounded by Lille's very popular small zoo (open daily mid Feb-mid Dec) and a park.

East of the Grand' Place, semi-pedestrianised rue de Béthune is marked by several art deco façades reflecting the reconstruction after World War I, while busy rue Faidherbe leads to the 19th-century Gare Lille Flandres and a typical train station hinterland of brasseries and cheap hotels, where you'll also find the medieval Eglise

Lille

Historic sites
● ● ● ● ○

Art & architecture
● ● ● ● ●

Hotels
● ● ● ● ○

Eating & drinking
● ● ● ● ○

Nightlife
● ● ● ● ○

Shopping
● ● ● ● ○

St-Maurice. Just seconds away, the mood changes entirely with the glass and steel Gare Lille Europe, which forms the frontispiece of Euralille, a brash new district of office space, vast shopping mall and conference facilities begun in the 1990s. New housing, offices and a casino are still going up in a second phase of construction, although the district's most recognisable landmark is the L-shaped Crédit Lyonnais building designed by Christian de Portzamparc, nicknamed the 'ski boot'.

Cathédrale Notre-Dame de la Treille
Place Gilleson (03.20.55.28.72/www.cathedralelille.com). Open 10am-noon, 2-6.30pm Mon-Sat; 10am-1pm, 3-6pm Sun. Admission free.
Lille's cathedral is an architectural curiosity. Begun in 1854 on what was probably the site of the medieval castle mound, it remained unfinished until the 1990s, when a stark grey marble west end was added on to the neo-Gothic apse and transept. Although the exterior looks forbidding, go inside on a sunny day and you'll appreciate the orange glow of the translucent marble façade and the rose window designed by artist Ladislas Kijno. The crypt contains the Centre d'Art Sacré Contemporain (2-5pm Thur, Fri; 2-6pm Sat), a surprising collection of modern religious works by artists including Baselitz, Combas and Warhol.

Eglise St-Maurice
Parvis St-Maurice, rue de Paris (03.20.06.07.21). Open 2-6pm Mon; 10am-noon, 2-6pm Tue-Sat; 3-8pm Sun. Admission free.
Behind its ornate west front, this lofty, light-filled Gothic church begun in the 14th century is a fine example of a northern *hallekerke*, built on an almost square plan with a forest of tall columns intended to spread the load on marshy land, and a ring of spiky chapels around the apse.

Maison Natale Charles de Gaulle
9 rue Princesse (03.28.38.12.05/www.maison-natale-de-gaulle.com). Open 10am-noon, 2-6pm Wed-Sat; 1.30-5.30pm Sun. Closed Sun in July & Aug. Admission €6.
This house, where France's World War II liberation hero and president was born in 1890, is now a museum and study centre. Furnished rooms present the bourgeois lifestyle of the time, along with memorabilia including the general's cradle and christening robe. Across the courtyard, the former industrial premises contain a multimedia centre.

Musée de l'Hospice Comtesse
32 rue de la Monnaie (03.28.36.84.00/www.musenor. com). Open 2-6pm Mon; 10am-12.30pm, 2-6pm Wed-Sun. Admission €2.30; free-€1.50 reductions.
This lovely, intimate museum is housed in a former charity hospice founded in 1237 by Countess Jeanne de Flandre. Downstairs rooms, furnished with religious paintings, *ex voto* portraits and richly carved oak buffets, give a good idea of the workings of the charity hospital – the pretty kitchen covered in blue and white glazed tiles, the nuns' refectory, the prioress's parlour, pharmacy and linen room,

as well as the 15th-century chapel and sick ward, now used for exhibitions. Upstairs in the nuns' dormitory a local history collection contains wood carvings, puzzle jugs and antique globes, as well as some fascinatingly detailed paintings by Louis Watteau (nephew of Jean-Antoine Watteau) and his son François.

Vieille Bourse
Place du Théâtre. Open 1-7pm Tue-Sun. Admission free.
Widely considered to be Lille's finest building and a summit of the northern Renaissance style, the Vieille Bourse is in fact a block of 24 identical houses, designed in 1652-53 by Julien Destrée as a mercantile stock exchange with shops on the ground floor constructed around an arcaded central cloister. Façades feature carved stone masks, swags of fruit and caryatids. The central court is home to second-hand booksellers and chess players in the afternoon.

REPUBLIQUE & WAZEMMES

South of the Grand' Place, Lille takes on a different mood, with the broad boulevards and official buildings that marked the city's 19th-century transformation centred on place de la République, home to the neoclassical Préfecture and massive Palais des Beaux-Arts. Boulevard de la Liberté is lined with pompous bourgeois residences, while parallel rue de Solférino and neighbouring streets are home to university faculties, the eccentric Théâtre Sébastopol, student bars and vast churches.

Beside the Baroque Porte de Paris, an extravagantly sculpted gateway-cum-triumphal arch celebrating Louis XIV's conquest of the town, is the Hôtel de Ville, the sprawling town hall built in the 1920s in an unusual mix of Modernist and vernacular styles in the then insalubrious St-Sauveur district. At the foot of its soaring belfry (reserve at the tourist office for visits) are sculptures of Lille's mythical founding giants Lydéric and Phinaert. Around here modern housing developments alternate with a few fragments of medieval Lille in the Noble Tour and the Hermitage Gantois, another old charity hospice that is now a chic hotel.

Further south, the former villages of Wazemmes and Moulins were absorbed into the growing city in 1858. Today, terraced housing alternates with old textile factories and breweries. Focus of the *quartier*, especially on Sunday mornings, is the animated Marché de Wazemmes on place de la Nouvelle Aventure. The iron-framed covered market (open Tue-Sun) contains some excellent food stalls but the true draw here is the frenetic, North African-flavoured outdoor market that takes over the square outside on Tuesday, Thursday and Sunday mornings in a sprawling hotchpotch of fruit, veg and flower stalls, ethnic snacks, bric-a-brac, job lots of make-up and toiletries, kitchenwares and acres and acres of dirt cheap clothing.

Grand' Place.

Maison Folie de Wazemmes

70 rue des Sarrazins (03.20.78.20.30). Open 2-7pm Wed-Sat; 10am-7pm Sun. Admission free.

Probably the most successful of the Maisons Folies created for the 2004 City of Culture celebrations, and certainly the most spectacular. The Maison Folie de Wazemmes is a daring marriage between a converted 19th-century spinning factory and a radical cloudlike extension made of steel mesh, designed by Dutch architect Lars Spuybroek of NOX. Within you'll find exhibitions, concerts, a café and a Moroccan-style hammam spa.

Palais des Beaux-Arts

Place de la République (03.20.06.78.00/www.pba-lille.fr). Open 2-6pm Mon; 10am-6pm Wed-Sun. Admission €6; free-€4 reductions.

Lille's extensive fine art collection, housed in a monumental 19th-century building, is one of the best in France thanks to its Flemish heritage and presents from Napoleon. Highlights include Rubens' *Descent from the Cross*, originally painted for a monastery in Lille, Veronese's study for a never executed *Paradise for the Doge's Palace in Venice*, Delacroix's menacing *Furious Medea*, and Goya's unmissable allegorical portraits of old age in *Les Vieilles* and youth in *La Lettre*. The basement galleries house medieval and Renaissance works, and an unusual set of 18th-century *plans reliefs* (detailed scale models) of northern towns fortified by Vauban. The museum's modern glass extension is used for temporary exhibitions.

> "The Maison Folie de Wazemmes is a daring marriage between a converted 19th-century spinning factory and a cloudlike extension of steel mesh."

LILLE METROPOLE

On the outskirts of Lille, former industrial textile towns like Roubaix and Tourcoing alternate with smart suburbs, such as Marcq-en-Baroeul and Bondues, the new town of Villeneuve d'Ascq and remnants of rural villages like Hem, where old farmhouses and patches of agricultural land survive amid the urban sprawl. Whether travelling by tram or car, the best route to Roubaix and Tourcoing is not by the motorway but along the 'Grand Boulevard', laid out in the late 19th century and lined with the fanciful houses of self-made textile barons. Roubaix was another of Flanders' medieval wool towns, of which few traces remain except the impressive *hallekerke*

facing the ornate 19th-century town hall on the Grande Place. The town boomed with the arrival of steam power, and the skyline is still peppered with red factory chimneys. Although noticeably poorer than Lille, Roubaix has been a pioneer in rehabilitating its industrial heritage, whether as cultural venues or discount factory shops.

Distillerie de Wambrechies

1 rue de la Distillerie, Wambrechies (03.20.14.91.91/www.wambrechies.com). Open Guided tours 10am-6pm daily (reserve three days in advance). Admission €6; free-€4 reductions.

The Distillerie Claeyssens is Lille's last remaining distillery, where genièvre, once the staple drink of textile workers and miners, is still made on vintage machinery according to traditional methods. Although flavoured like gin with juniper berries, it is closer to whisky in taste and fieriness, drunk straight or lacing coffee. The tour of the listed canalside buildings takes in different stages, from sifting the rye and malt barley via cooking and fermentation to the double distillation process in impressive brass columns. It is possible to take a boat trip here from Lille.

Le Fresnoy Studio National des Arts Contemporains

22 rue du Fresnoy (03.20.28.38.00/www.lefresnoy.net). Open 1-7pm Wed, Thur; 2-9pm Fri, Sat; 2-7pm Sun. Admission varies.

Le Fresnoy is a unique combination of art and film school and audio-visual production centre directed by artist Alain Fleisher, drawing postgraduate students from all over the world and putting on film- and video-based exhibitions. The premises constructed by Bernard Tschumi around and over a former *guinguette* dance hall also contain an arthouse cinema.

Hospice d'Havré

100 rue de Tournai, Tourcoing (03.59.63.43.53). Open 1.30-6pm Mon, Wed-Sun. Closed Aug. Admission free.

This medieval charity hospice and subsequent monastery of Notre-Dame des Anges was reborn as one of the Maisons Folies for Lille 2004, creating temporary exhibition spaces around the peaceful cloister and herb garden, and restoring the Baroque chapel.

Musée d'Art Moderne de Lille Métropole Villeneuve d'Ascq

1 allée du Musée, Villeneuve d'Ascq (03.20.19.68.68/http://mamlm.fr). Due to reopen spring 2010.

This low red-brick building, which was designed by Roland Simounet, is home to a first-rate collection of modern and contemporary art that includes Modigliani, Léger and Picasso, the Fauves, a *cabanon* by Daniel Buren and younger artists such as Thomas Hirschhorn. It is due to reopen in 2010 after the addition of a new wing by young architect Manuelle Gautrand to house the recently donated Aracine collection of *art brut*. In the meantime sculptures by Calder, Dodeign, Deacon and others can still be seen in the surrounding park.

Musée des Beaux-Arts de Tourcoing

2 rue Paul Doumer, Tourcoing (03.20.28.91.60).
Open 1.30-6pm Mon, Wed-Sun. Admission free.
Tourcoing's fine art museum takes the unusual stance of presenting historic paintings and drawings – mainly Dutch and Flemish old masters – alongside contemporary works, making interesting thematic and stylistic links. Thus you might find an Aurélie Nemours monochrome next to a 17th-century flower painting, a Eugène Leroy abstract painting beside a Mannerist landscape, or a Raymond Hains oil next to a Guercino drawing. Upstairs, a Sol LeWitt wall painting reflects the adventurous commissioning policy.

La Piscine, Musée de l'Art de l'Industrie

23 rue de l'Espérance, Roubaix (03.20.69.23.60/
www.roubaix-lapiscine.com). Open 11am-6pm Tue-
Thur; 11am-8pm Fri; 1-6pm Sat, Sun. Admission
€4.50; €3.50 reductions.
Roubaix's old swimming pool has been imaginatively converted into an inspiring museum. Sculptures line up on either side of the former pool beneath art deco stained glass sunbursts and water still gushes out of Neptune's mouth, and textiles, drawings and ceramics are displayed in the old changing cubicles. While the building is a major attraction in its own right, there is also some worthwhile art from the mid 19th to mid 20th century, including Ingres's *Angélique*, Orientalist paintings, Camille Claudel's sculpture *La Petite Châtelaine*, Remy Cogghe's *The Cockfight*, society portraits by Tamara de Lempicka and thickly encrusted 1950s abstraction by the post-war Groupe de Roubaix (Marc Rouet, Eugène Leroy and Dodin).

Eat

Northern cuisine is one of the most underrated in France. Mussels, cooking in beer, *houblon* (hops) and chicory reflect the dual Franco-Flemish heritage. Typical dishes include *carbonnade de boeuf* (beef stewed with beer), *coq à la bière*, *waterzoi* (fish or chicken cooked with cream and vegetables), rabbit with prunes and the unpronounceable *potjevleesch* (a layered meat and vegetable terrine), along with excellent fish and shellfish from the nearby ports of Boulogne-sur-Mer and Dunkerque. Pungent maroilles cheese – not as strong as its smell would have you believe – gets into all sorts of things, from savoury tarts to sauces.

L'Assiette du Marché

Vieux Lille *61 rue de la Monnaie (03.20.06.83.61/*
www.assiettedumarche.com). Open noon-2.30pm,
7-10.30pm Mon-Thur; noon-2.30pm, 7-11pm Fri,
Sat. €€.
Set at the rear of a cobbled courtyard, the historic former city mint provides a stylish setting for an evening out, with its high ceilings, fireplaces, well-spaced tables and civilised service. Cuisine puts a modern spin on classic dishes from all over France and the market-inspired weekly changing menu is a bargain, although success means that cooking sometimes falls down on precision when the kitchen is stretched. Tables outside in summer.

La Cave aux Fioles

Vieux Lille *39 rue de Gand (03.20.55.18.43/*
www.lacaveauxfioles.com). Open noon-2pm Tue;
noon-2pm, 7.30-10pm Wed-Fri; 7.30-10.30pm
Sat. €€€.
This cosy, dimly lit old-town address, set in a series of small rooms furnished with antiques, is the perfect spot for a romantic dinner. Traditional bistro favourites include a good steak, skate with capers, and duck confit, and the wine list is excellent.

La Chicorée

Vieux Lille *15 pl Rihour (03.20.54.81.52/www.*
chicoree.restaurantsdelille.com). Open 10am-6am
daily. €€.
The scarlet-coloured Chicorée is a well-known standby for night owls with food served till dawn, but its huge, heated pavement terrace also fills up fast as soon as the sun is out. Brasserie and regional standards are decently prepared, including oysters, mussels, steaks and *carbonnade*, although service can be slow when the place is busy. Prices rise by 20 per cent after midnight.

Le Colysée

Lille Métropole *201 av du Colisée, Lambersart*
(03.20.45.90.00/www.le-colysee.com). Open noon-
2pm Mon; noon-2pm, 8-10pm Tue-Thur; noon-2pm,
8-11pm Fri; 8-11pm Sat. Closed mid-end Aug & 1wk
Jan. €€€.
Young chef Benjamin Bajeux is one of the bright young talents of northern cuisine, drawing the occasional celeb among the well-dressed locals, and he conveys his enthusiasm with a genuine welcome. After working for Alain Ducasse in New York and Monaco, he returned home to take over this restaurant on the ground floor of the Colysée Maison Folie. Distressed concrete, bronze leather and modern art provide a suitable background for Bajeux's light, modern dishes, such as foie gras with apple chutney, scrambled egg in a crab emulsion or pork fillet cooked in beer. Desserts include a fabulous chocolate mousse layered with crispy caramel and fizzy sugar.

La Ducasse

République & Wazemmes *95 rue de Solférino*
(03.20.57.34.10). Open noon-2pm, 7.30-11pm Mon-
Thur; noon-2pm, 7.30pm-midnight Fri; 8pm-midnight
Sat. Closed 1-15 Aug. €€.
This characterful corner bistro with scarlet walls, old posters, wooden banquettes and a piano by the entrance provides a wonderfully convivial experience. Locals and students pile in at lunchtime for the inexpensive *plat du jour* (perhaps steak and chips or sautéed veal), while the more extensive menu includes regional dishes and lots of offal. Staff are laid-back and friendly even to first-timers, and the place doesn't take itself too seriously: menus are slotted inside comic-strip books.

Top: Le Colysée. Bottom:
L'Assiette du Marché.

Estaminet Chez la Vieille

Vieux Lille *60 rue de Gand (03.28.36.40.06).*
Open noon-2.30pm, 7.30-10.30pm Tue-Sat. €€.
Chez la Vieille is a thriving example of the *estaminet* revival
with a setting that is almost too good to be true: exposed
bricks, tightly packed tables, a collection of old advertising
plaques and prints, bar games and miscellaneous bric-a-
brac. Hearty traditional regional specialities include leek
tart, chicken with maroilles cheese, and even chicory- and
beetroot-flavoured ice-creams, preferably accompanied by
one of the wide choice of beers.

A la Huitrière

Vieux Lille *3 rue des Chats Bossus (03.20.55.43.41/*
www.huitriere.fr). Open noon-2pm, 7-9.30pm Mon-Sat;
noon-2pm Sun. Closed Aug. €€€€.
Lille's luxury gastronomic treat occupies a dressy dining
room above a gorgeous art deco fishmonger and deli, run
by the same family since the 1930s. Although there are meat
options, the emphasis is on the fish delivered daily
downstairs. Think lobster, langoustines in foie gras sauce,
turbot, sole and decorative desserts, prepared by a brigade
of chefs. In 2008 a more casual oyster bar opened inside the
downstairs fishmonger.

La Terrasse des Remparts

Vieux Lille *Logis de la Porte de Gand, rue de Gand*
(03.20.06.74.74/www.terrassedesremparts.fr). Open
noon-2pm, 7-11pm Mon-Sat; noon-2pm Sun. €€€.
This contemporary dining room, set inside the fortified
Porte de Gand that formed part of the city's new defences
in 1620, provides a chic setting for a flexible mix and match
menu, where you'll find local ingredients such as endives
and maroilles cheese alongside distinctly Mediterranean
flavours in modishly presented modern dishes.

Tous les Jours Dimanche

Vieux Lille *13 rue Masurel (03.28.36.05.92).*
Open Summer noon-6.30pm Tue-Sat. Winter noon-
6.30pm Tue-Sat; 11.30am-5pm Sun. Closed mid July-
mid Aug. €.
TJD is an insiders' address on the increasingly trendy
streets around the cathedral. Sit amid eclectic furniture,
lamps and knick-knacks picked up at jumble sales and
antiques fairs, with the prospect of buying your cups and
plates or even the chair you are sitting on if you wish.
Quiches, salads and the lasagne of the day are served at
lunch, with home-made cakes and fruit tarts all afternoon.

"Vintage *pâtissier* Meert
is famous for its *gauffres
fourrés*, stuffed with
vanilla cream, which
have been made on the
premises since 1849."

Aux Moules

Vieux Lille *34 rue de Béthune (03.20.57.12.46/*
www.auxmoules.com). Open noon-3.30pm, 6.30-11pm
Mon-Sat; noon-3.30pm Sun. €€.
The name leaves no doubt as to the speciality at this popular
1930s brasserie, nor do the cheerful tiled scenes depicting
mussel fishermen around the walls, so opt for a casserole of
moules marinières served with delicious chips. This place
is always one of the contenders for the mussel shell award
at the Grande Braderie.

Le Square d'Aramis

Vieux Lille *52 rue Basse (03.20.74.16.17/*
www.lesquaredaramis.com). Open noon-
11.30pm daily. €€.
Occupying an excellent people-watching corner in old
Lille, the Square d'Aramis is a relaxed modern brasserie
that draws a trendy young clientele. The cuisine has a
cosmopolitan edge, with a menu that goes from ever-so-trad
northern faves like maroilles tart and *carbonnade de boeuf*
to savoury crumbles and tartares. Crêpes and pâtisseries
are served all afternoon.

Shop

Lille's prime shopping area is concentrated in
picturesque Vieux Lille. The city's big, hectic
market experience is the Marché de Wazemmes,
athough there is also a smaller, more chic affair
on place du Concert in Vieux Lille on Wednesday,
Friday and Sunday mornings.

L'Abbaye des Saveurs

Vieux Lille *13 rue des Vieux Murs (03.28.07.70.06/*
www.abbayedessaveurs.com). Open 2-7.30pm Tue;
11am-7.30pm Wed-Sat; 10.30am-1.30pm Sun.
This tiny shop on a pedestrianised street near the place aux
Oignons is stacked high with bottled beers from small
northern French and Belgian breweries – plus the right-
shaped glasses to drink them from – along with other
regional specialities, such as chicory conserves, terrines, jars
of *carbonnade* and bétise de Cambrai sweets.

Bleu Natier

Vieux Lille *26, 26bis & 40 rue Basse (03.20.74.04.54).*
Open 2-7pm Mon; 10.30am-7pm Tue-Sat.
Three neighbouring outlets are dedicated to adventurous
fashion labels (Jérôme Dreyfuss, Celine, Notify, Citizens of
Humanity), a selection of young independent clothes and
jewellery designers, and sophisticated interior decoration.

Le Furet du Nord

Vieux Lille *Pl Charles de Gaulle (03.20.78.43.43/*
www.furet.com). Open 9.30am-7.30pm Mon-Sat.
Behind its modest shopfront, the ferret, named after a furrier
that used to occupy the premises, conceals one of the largest
bookshops and stationers in Europe, in an enjoyable maze
of levels and stairways.

Meert
Vieux Lille *27 rue Esquermoise (03.20.57.07.44/ www.meert.fr). Open 9.30am-7.30pm Tue-Fri; 9am-7.30pm Sat; 9am-1pm, 3-7pm Sun.*
Vintage *pâtissier* and *chocolatier* Meert is famous for its wonderful *gauffres fourrés*, waffles stuffed with vanilla cream, which have been made on the premises since 1849, although others also rave about the stripy *tigrés* and bitter chocolate tart. An elegant tearoom at the rear serves full-scale meals at lunchtime, and tea and cakes all afternoon.

Arts

Lille's dynamic arts scene ranges from classical music to clowning and fringe theatre at Le Prato (www.leprato.fr). Tickets for many events can be bought at the Fnac store (www.fnac.com) on the Grand' Place.

Le Nouveau Siècle
Vieux Lille *30 pl Mendès France (03.20.12.82.40/ www.onlille.com). Tickets €18-€30.*
You could easily be forgiven for thinking that this circular 1960s building is a multi-storey car park. In part it is, but it is also home to the Orchestre National de Lille, one of France's most respected regional symphony orchestras, which performs here when its founder and principal conductor Jean-Claude Casedeseus is not carrying out his mission of bringing classical music to the people in community halls and cultural centres around the region.

Opéra de Lille
Vieux Lille *Pl du Théâtre (03.28.38.40.50/ 08.20.48.90.00/www.opera-lille.fr). Tickets €5-€62.*
Lille's opera house is an old-fashioned feast of gilding, marble and chandeliers, curiously designed in the 1920s by Louis-Marie Cordonnier, who was also responsible for the very different-looking Chamber of Commerce next door. Beautifully restored in 2003, it puts on opera ranging from Mozart and Puccini faves to Kurt Weill, plus big names in contemporary dance.

Tri Postal
Vieux Lille *Av Willy Brandt (03.20.14.47.60/ www.mairie-lille.fr). Tickets prices vary.*
Ever since Lille 2004, the monster-sized former postal sorting office squeezed between the city's two train stations has become a focus for cutting-edge contemporary art and video exhibitions, often complemented by lively debates and DJ sessions.

Nightlife

Rue Royale, rue Thiers and the studenty area around the former covered market on rue de Solférino are good places to check out Lille's bar culture, with many venues staying open late.

Aéronef
Vieux Lille *Centre Commercial 168, av Willy Brandt (08.92.56.01.50/www.aeronef-spectacles. com). Tickets prices vary.*
The pillar of Lille's live music scene for 20 years has a slightly incongruous location in one of the towers of the Euralille shopping centre. The choice ranges from up-and-coming local bands and international indie outfits to big-name comebacks and even afternoon *goûter-concerts* for five- to 12-year-olds.

Le Biplan
République & Wazemmes *19 rue Colbert (03.20.12.91.11/www.biplan.org). Tickets prices vary.*
This dynamic, shabby-looking music venue in Wazemmes has two halls putting on an almost nightly programme of live music, including monthly jazz and folk jam sessions, along with stand-up comedy and *café-théâtre*.

Stay

Many of Lille's hotels offer lower rates at the weekends, particularly if you reserve on the internet. If you intend to come for the Grande Braderie in September be prepared to book several months ahead.

All Seasons Lille Centre Gare Beffroi
République & Wazemmes *172 rue de Paris (03.20.30.00.54/www.accor.com). €€.*
The former Ibis near the town hall has re-emerged as a young, fun experience, revamped in neo-'70s pop colours, with an open-plan lobby bar and Perspex chairs. The 140 rooms boast 'anti-stress' pillows and quilts (something to do with carbon fibre) plus all you need to plant iPods and video games, although they are decidedly boxy and some bathrooms verge on the minuscule. Prices include breakfast and all-day serve-yourself tea and coffee.

Alliance Lille Couvent des Minimes
Vieux Lille *17 quai de Wault (03.20.30.46.08/ www.alliance-lille.com). €€€.*
Located a little out of the centre on a peaceful quayside towards the Citadelle, the centrepiece of this listed 17th-century monastery is its stunning rib-vaulted red brick cloister, its courtyard now glazed over as a slightly glitzy bar and restaurant. The traditionally furnished bedrooms are a little tired-looking in comparison, though most cleverly open off galleries above the cloister.

Grand Hôtel Bellevue
Vieux Lille *5 rue Jean Roisin (03.20.57.45.64/ www.grandhotelbellevue.com). €€.*
The old-fashioned Hôtel Bellevue has lived for too long on its reputation as the place where Mozart stayed as a child in 1765, but things are now finally changing. The Empire-style chandeliers in the entrance and antique furniture remain, but the beds are being replaced throughout,

Hermitage Gantois.
Bottom right: Alliance Lille
Couvent des Minimes.

corridors are being spruced up and tired old fabrics are making way for sumptuous new wallpaper. The whole place should be redone by early 2010.

Hermitage Gantois

République & Wazemmes *224 rue de Paris (03.20.85.30.30/www.hotelhermitagegantois.com). €€€€.*

Lille's most luxurious lodgings occupy a gorgeous Flemish charity hospice founded in 1460 by merchant Jean de Gambe for the old and decrepit. It was still in use until the 1990s, before being cleverly converted. The hotel's charm lies in its series of garden courtyards, and the clever mix of historic features and sophisticated modern design in the bedrooms, where oak panelling and exposed beams meet steel desks and Philippe Starck chairs. There are two restaurants, one gastronomic, the other the inexpensive Estaminet Gantois specialising in regional fare.

Hôtel Brueghel

Vieux Lille *5 parvis St-Maurice (03.20.06.06.69/ www.hotel-brueghel.com). €€.*

The quirkily eccentric Brueghel has soul, from its cheerful downstairs clutter of pot plants, knick-knacks and squashy sofas to the charmingly antiquated lift. The smallish bedrooms are freshly painted in pretty colour schemes and have attractive wrought-iron lamps, though the streetside ones overlooking Eglise St-Maurice can be noisy at night.

Hôtel Kanaï

Vieux Lille *10 rue de Béthune (03.20.57.14.78/ www.hotelkanai.com). €.*

In a building that was revamped just two years ago, the Hôtel Kanaï offers a sleek design experience at bargain prices, featuring a polished concrete hallway, modern art, neat mosaic bathrooms and plummy shades. There's air-conditioning but no lift.

Hôtel des Tours

Vieux Lille *27 rue des Tours (03.59.57.47.00/ www.hotel-des-tours.com). €€.*

On a quiet side street off restaurant-packed rue de Gand, the Hôtel des Tours integrates an old brick façade on one side with a modern extension on the other. Although the reception spells '80s business modern, staff are helpful and rooms are pleasant, decked out in warm colours, with white tiled bathrooms. The high-ceilinged mezzanine duplexes sleeping up to four are ideal for families. There's a downstairs bar and outdoor tables in a small courtyard.

Hôtel de la Treille

Vieux Lille *7-9 pl Louise de Bettignies (03.20.55.45.46/www.hoteldelatreille.fr). €€.*

This smart, modern take on a tall Flemish townhouse, slotted into the heart of Vieux Lille, has views over the square at the front or cathedral at the rear (avoid rooms that overlook the courtyard). Rooms are clean and practical.

Novotel Lille Centre Grand' Place

Vieux Lille *116 rue de l'Hôpital Militaire (03.28.38.53.53/www.accor.com). €€€.*

This decidedly upmarket Novotel, well placed near the Nouveau Siècle, is one of the best surprises in Lille. The decent-sized bedrooms are bright and comfortable with natural wood detailing, sofa and well-conceived lighting. There's a fitness room and airy lobby lounge, plus meals are served from noon to midnight. Look out for good deals on the internet.

Factfile

When to go

Lille is rarely sweltering in summer and relatively mild in winter, though it can be foggy. The main arts season runs from mid September to June, while the first weekend in September sees the Grande Braderie, an extraordinary event for antiques enthusiasts and collectors, though not the time for quiet sightseeing.

Getting there

There are frequent Eurostar trains direct to Lille from London St Pancras (1hr 20mins). Lille's two train stations, Lille Flandres and Lille Europe, are only a couple of minutes apart, with high-speed services to Paris and the rest of France, Belgium, the Netherlands and northern Germany. The nearest international airports are Paris CDG and Brussels, both served by direct trains. By car, the nearest Channel ports are Dunkerque (71km/45 miles), Calais (110km/70 miles) and Boulogne-sur-Mer (118km/74 miles).

Getting around

Vieux Lille is easy to walk around, while the driverless métro system, two tramlines and a network of local buses, all run by Transpole (www.transpole.fr), can be useful for outer districts such as Wazemmes and Moulins or the assorted towns of Lille Métropole. Bikes can be hired from Ch'ti Vélo (www.chti-velo.fr), on av Willy Brandt, beside Gare Lille Flandres.

Tourist information

Tourist office Pl Rihour (08.91.56.20.04/ www.lilletourisme.com). Open 9.30am-6.30pm Mon-Sat; 10am-noon, 2-5pm Sun. See also www.mairie-lille.fr, www.lillemetropole.fr and www.tourisme-nordpasdecalais.fr.

Internet access

Atlanteam 93 rue Solférino (03.20.10.05.15/ www.atlanteam.com). Open 10.30am-midnight Mon-Sat; 2-11pm Sun.

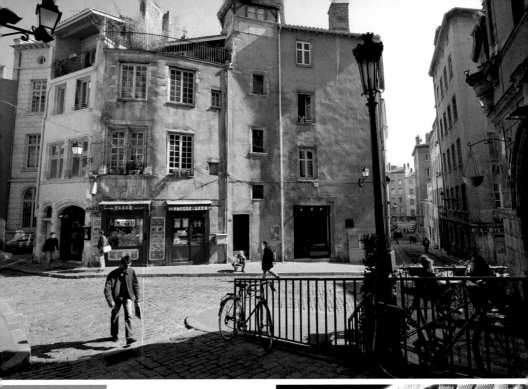

Clockwise from top: Vieux Lyon; ferris wheel on place Bellecour; the Saône; Fourvière hill.

Lyon

Fall back in love with France's second largest city.

For Brits, Lyon was too often seen as somewhere to avoid, to circumnavigate, to bypass on long family journeys south or to the mountains, and its reputation for suburban rioting did little to improve its image as a weekend break destination. The only time most people got a view of Lyon's centre was from a traffic jam as they crawled through the city, by which time it was more a desire to see the back of rather than see Lyon. But since the construction of a motorway ring road, this handsome city has finally had the chance to flourish and is now a perfect weekend destination, just two hours from Paris on the TGV.

Lyon has its beautiful parts – what better place to build a city than at the confluence of two of France's most graceful rivers, the Rhône and the Saône – and its history stretches back to Roman times, but France's second largest city is best loved for the here and now: for food, fashion and culture. In addition to its Renaissance architecture, Lyon has a thriving arts scene, a fine opera house, a slew of museums and monuments, superb shopping and, best of all, some of the country's true gourmet tables.

Unfortunately for such a grand stage, arriving by train at Gare Perrache is a thoroughly unglamorous experience. Having raced seamlessly through the Burgundy countryside, the final few minutes of the journey entails a trawl through Lyon's grimier suburbs. As you step off the super-sleek TGV, you enter a rather seedy shopping arcade as you stroll towards place Carnot. Fortunately, though, this polytunnel torture doesn't last long, and the majestic open spaces of place Bellecour soon hove into view.

Explore

Although Lyon is ordered into numbered *arrondissements*, and subdivided into *quartiers*, the city and its two rivers, 28 bridges and numerous hills can be difficult to navigate. The centre, or Presqu'île, is a thin strip of land where the Saône and the Rhône meet. To the west lies Vieux Lyon, to the east the Rive Gauche and the new business districts.

PRESQU'ILE

Most of commercial Lyon is based on the long, thin strip of the Presqu'île. From Gare Perrache to the Opera House, along rue Victor Hugo and rue de la République, stretches what is essentially a six-kilometre (four-mile) high street. But this is no ordinary high street, with handsome 19th-century Haussmanian buildings forming the backbone to this shopping artery between two of France's greatest rivers. After a walk down rue Victor Hugo from Gare Perrache, you eventually emerge on to the vast expanse of place Bellecour. This is one of the largest squares in Europe and stretches pretty much the width of the Presqu'île. In the middle sits a statue of King Louis XIV on horseback, made by François-Frédéric Lemot in 1825. Apart from the tourist office and a café tucked away in one corner, the square is one big parade ground, attracting everything from political rallies to antiques fairs.

To the side of the main square are some interesting public monuments, the most stunning and thought-provoking of which is the Mémorial du Génocide Arménien in adjoining place Antonin-Poncet, which was erected in 2006 and has been cloaked in controversy since its inception. It is made up of 36 simple concrete plinths, which are lit up dramatically at night. Further along place Antonin-Poncet is a rather less grave piece of public art – a giant flower sculpture and fountain. But perhaps the most appealing thing about place Bellecour is the uninterrupted views it offers up towards the lofty treasures of Fourvière above Vieux Lyon, especially at night when the famous basilica is lit up like a Christmas tree.

From place Bellecour, rue de la République heads north in a sea of chain stores and fast-food signs, although this low-grade commerce heads upmarket the further you escape from the main square. By the time you reach handsome place de la République, with its stunning water feature and vintage merry-go-round, Lyon's reputation as a serious shopping rival to Paris can start to be taken slightly more seriously. Side streets off here are lively, with a lot of bar action near the Lycée, unsurprisingly.

Towards the top of the Presqu'île sits the wonderfully dramatic place des Terreaux, hemmed in on two sides by the Musée des Beaux Arts and the Hôtel de Ville. At its centre is a 19th-century fountain constructed from

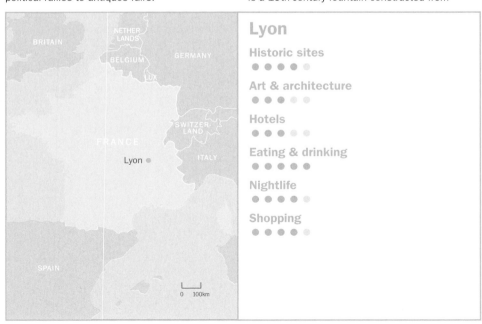

Lyon

Historic sites
● ● ● ● ○

Art & architecture
● ● ● ● ○

Hotels
● ● ● ○ ○

Eating & drinking
● ● ● ● ●

Nightlife
● ● ● ● ○

Shopping
● ● ● ● ○

21 tonnes of lead and sculpted by Frédéric Bartholdi, who was also responsible for the Statue of Liberty.

Musée des Beaux Arts

20 pl des Terreaux, 1st (04.72.10.17.40/www.mba-lyon.fr). Open 10am-6pm Mon, Wed, Thur, Sat, Sun; 10.30am-6pm Fri. Admission €6; free-€4 reductions.
Set plum on grand place des Terreaux, the Museum of Fine Arts occupies a former Benedictine abbey dating from the 17th century. The building was renovated in the 1990s and now offers a wonderfully uncluttered showcase for its excellent collection. The 70 rooms are divided into five sections – antiquities, objets d'art, paintings, graphic arts and sculpture, with acres of white space and plenty of natural light. At the heart of the building is a sculpture garden encircled by a cloister. Highlights on the ground floor include Rodin sculptures, while upstairs features big hitters such as Matisse, Rubens, Picasso and Monet. There is also a handsome café terrace on the first floor overlooking the sculpture garden and a well stocked bookshop. This is probably the finest French collection of sculptures and paintings outside Paris.

Musée de l'Imprimerie

13 rue de la Poulaillerie, 2nd (04.78.37.65.98/ www.imprimerie.lyon.fr). Open 9.30am-noon, 2-6pm Wed-Sun. Admission €3.80; free-€2 reductions.
Lyon was one of the main centres for book production during the 15th and 16th centuries, and this museum, set in a beautiful 15th-century building near the place de la Bourse, takes visitors through the history of printing and its changing techniques. If you fancy getting stuck in yourself, the museum also runs plenty of short courses, including a day learning all about paper (€35), which involves talks on the history of paper making and the chance to create a few sheets of your own.

Musée des Tissus et des Arts Décoratifs

34 rue de la Charité, 2nd (04.78.38.42.00/www.musee-des-tissus.com). Open 10am-5.30pm Tue-Sun. Admission €6; free-€3.50 reductions.
Originally created as the Arts & Industry Museum in the 19th century, today the Musée des Tissus' comprehensive collection covers some 2,000 years of textiles and costumes, and is a fitting tribute to Lyon's long-held dominance of the French fabric trade. Highlights include Coptic tapestries, Persian textiles, Byzantine and Muslim fabrics, as well as some local weaving heroes, such as Pillement, Philippe de Lasalle and Dugourc. The Musée des Arts Décoratifs next door puts it all into context, with a mock-up of textiles displayed in an 18th-century private residence.

VIEUX LYON & FOURVIERE

A few minutes' walk west from place Bellecour and you find yourself in the heart of Vieux Lyon, tucked in tight beneath the Fourvière hill. Claustrophobia increases as you delve further into the network of narrow alleys and tightly woven streets that make up the district. Sadly, the tourist potential is not lost on the area and there is a surfeit of tat shops and multilingual menus around, so best save shopping and eating until you're safely back on the Presqu'île. But in terms of atmosphere there's little to beat it, especially if you come equipped with a free tourist map of the *traboules*, a network of ancient alleyways that run between the area's main streets.

The first *traboules* are thought to have been built in Lyon in the fourth century. The layout of the old town was such that there were very few connecting streets running down towards the Saône, and the *traboules* allowed easy acess to the river. Nowadays, these 'secret' passageways are tourist attractions, and over 40 are open to the public. Most are on private property, though, and serve as entrances to local apartments, so a map is essential.

The dramatic Fourvière basilica sits atop a steep hill immediately west of Vieux Lyon. The area is also the site of the original Roman settlement of Lugdunum.

Basilique Notre-Dame de Fourvière

8 pl de Fourvière, 5th (04.78.25.13.01/www.fourviere. org). Open 8am-noon, 2-6pm daily. Admission free.
Don't miss a funicular ride up to the basilica. Visible from all over the city, it rises fortress-like on a hill with four octagonal towers and crenellated walls. Its austere and imposing exterior contrasts strongly with the richly decorated interior. The cathedral, built between 1872 and 1876 by architect Pierre Bossan, is Baroque with a capital B and was decorated to display the full wealth and might of the Catholic Church at the end of the 19th century. Inside there is gilt aplenty and downstairs is a wonderfully vast, airy crypt. For the best view of all, head up to the roof on a guided tour for a panorama across the city – and onwards to the Alps on a clear day.

Cathédrale St-Jean

Pl St-Jean, 5th (http://cathedrale-lyon.cef.fr). Open 8.15am-12.05pm, 1.45-7.30pm Mon-Fri; 8.15am-12.05pm, 1.45-7pm Sat, Sun. Admission free.
Sitting proudly on the banks of the Saône, in the heart of Vieux Lyon, the cathedral is the seat of Lyon's 135th bishop and was constructed between the 11th and 16th centuries. The two towers overlooking the river are topped with a dramatic four-metre oak cross. The Flamboyant Gothic façade was finished in 1480 and is decorated with 280 square stone medallions. Don't miss the Astronomical Clock in the north transept – built during the 14th century, it chimes at noon, 2pm, 3pm and 4pm. On the opposite wall from the clock is the painting of *The Visitation* by 17th-century French artist Noêl Coypel.

Musée de la Civilisation Gallo-Romaine & Théâtre Gallo Romain

17 rue Cléberg, 5th (04.72.38.49.30). Open 10am-6pm Tue-Sun. Admission Museum €4; free-€2.50 reductions. Theatre free.

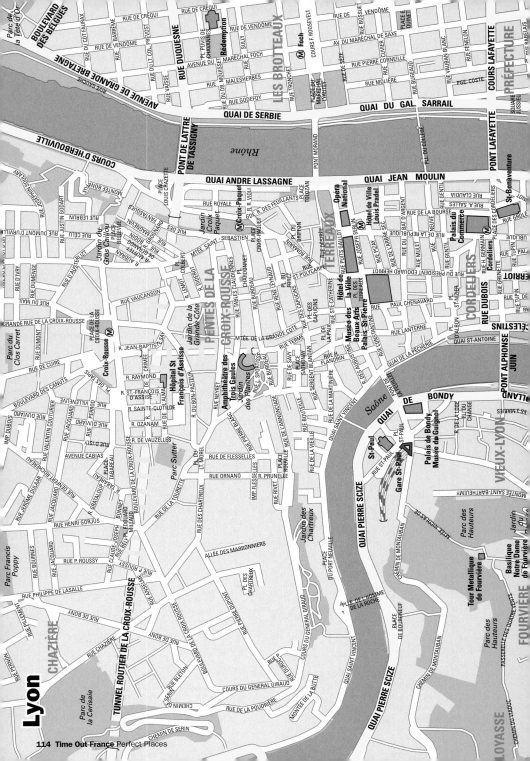

Lyon

Musée Lumière.

A few minutes' walk downhill from the basilica stands the classical Théâtre Gallo Romain, the oldest Gallo-Roman theatre in France and a truly dramatic sight, especially in the context of its grey urban surroundings. Built around 15 BC and enlarged in AD 120 with the addition of the smaller Odéon, the main theatre sat some 11,000 spectators and gives splendid views from its hillside position down over the centre of Lyon. The site has been handsomely preserved and in summer plays host to the annual Nuits de Fourvière arts festival (www.nuits-de-fourviere.org), which in 2009 included performances by the likes of Blur, Tracey Chapman and Pete Doherty. Adjoining the site is the Musée de la Civilisation Gallo-Romaine. Built in 1975, it retraces the history of Lyon from the end of the prehistoric age to the seventh century AD. Highlights include some splendid mosaics and the Claudien Tablet, which was discovered at the beginning of the 16th century and records a speech that Emperor Claudius, born in Lyon, gave in AD 48 in Rome in favour of the Gauls.

Musée des Miniatures et Décors de Cinéma

60 rue St-Jean, 5th (04.72.00.24.77/www.mimlyon. com). Open 10am-6.30pm daily. Admission €7; free-€5.50 reductions.
This museum, housed in a beautiful 16th-century building on the main tourist drag through Vieux Lyon, is a truly bizarre cultural experience. The visit begins in the dingy basement with a display of original stage sets from the film *Perfume* – in which Jean-Baptiste Grenouille, born with a superior olfactory sense, creates the world's finest perfume – replete with micro detailing from Grenouille's laboratory. The second half of the museum features some 120 miniature mock-ups of buildings, from Maxim's to Lyon's St-Paul prison, created by the man behind the miniatures, Dan Ohlmann. His current work in progress is Brasserie Georges, the famous restaurant near Perrache, and you can glimpse its development in the *atelier*. On the way out all manner of mini mementoes are for sale, from Evian bottles to dolls. Weird but also rather wonderful.

RIVE GAUCHE

The Left Bank is home to much of Lyon's sprawling new development, especially around the Gare de la Part Dieu, but there are definitely a few sights worth crossing the Rhône for, including the green lungs of the 290-acre Parc de la Tête d'Or, replete with ornamental lake, botanical garden and zoo, plus boats to hire, pony rides, the Musée d'Art Contemporain (www.mac-lyon.com) and the HQ of Interpol, the international police agency. To the south-east is the Musée Urbain Tony Garnier, an outdoor mural museum based around the buildings of early 20th-century Lyon architect Tony Garnier.

Centre d'Histoire de la Résistance et de la Déportation

14 av Berthelot, 7th (04.78.72.23.11/www.chrd. lyon.fr). Open 9am-5.30pm Tue-Sat. Admission €4; free-€2 reductions.

Housed in the former Military School of Medecine, which was occupied by the Gestapo between 1943 and 1944 and whose cellars housed many of its victims, this is a hugely thought-provoking museum, full of brooding lighting and evocative tableaux (all translated excellently into English). On top of this, there are some 700 filmed first person accounts, as well as video extracts of the trial of Klaus Barbie, the 'butcher of Lyon'. Lyon was declared by De Gaulle as the 'Capital of the Resistance' and this is a fitting tribute to its inhabitants.

Musée Lumière

25 rue du Premier-Film, 8th (04.78.78.18.95/ www.institut-lumiere.org). Open 11am-6.30pm Tue-Sun. Admission €6; €5 reductions.
The Musée Lumière, five minutes from the centre of Lyon by métro, is a film buff's nirvana and the birthplace of cinematography. At the end of the 19th century, Antoine Lumière, father of Louis and Auguste, built a grand villa in the then rural neighbourhood of Monplaisir, and 'Château Lumière' became home to the Lumière Company until the late 1960s. It was here, in March 1895, that Louis and Auguste filmed the world's first ever motion picture, *La Sortie des Usines Lumière* (Workers leaving the Lumière Factory). The four-floor villa is packed with Lumière memorabilia, from cameras to film projections, and next door stands the last surviving building from the great film factory, which today houses a 270-seat cinema.

CROIX ROUSSE

Set high up on a hill north of the centre of Lyon is the Croix Rousse district, a classic working man's neighbourhood turned chi-chi hangout, which retains a village atmosphere with wonderful views down over the presqu'île. It is accessed by a very steep métro ride which brings you out on to place de la Croix Rousse, the main square, with a busy thoroughfare on one side and little streets leading off the other into a warren of cafés, restaurants and boutiques. The area was originally home to Lyon's silk trade, and this heritage path is well trodden nowadays by tourists.

The district is divided into two areas, the *pentes* in the first *arrondissement* and the *plateau* du the fourth *arrondissement*. The hill, which reaches some 250 metres (820 feet) at its summit, is nicknamed 'la colline qui travaille' (the hill that works), in contrast to Fourvière which is known as 'the hill that prays'. The district grew up around the silk workshops, which moved here from Vieux Lyon during the 18th century. The *canuts* (silk workers) were subjected to extremely poor working conditions and staged many worker uprisings, known as the *canut* revolts. The first of these revolts, in 1831, is considered to be one of the very first worker uprisings.

Maison des Canuts

10-12 rue d'Ivry, 4th (04.78.28.62.04/www.maison descanuts.com). Open Guided tours 11am & 3.30pm Tue-Sat. Tours €6; free-€3 reductions.

This back room introduction to the art and toil of silk weaving in 19th-century Lyon (*canut* is a local word for silk weaver) makes fairly grim listening, with plenty of stories of underage weavers struggling away amid low pay and appalling working conditions, which eventually led to the famous *canut* uprising in 1831. The tour also gives a demonstration of an old Jacquard loom. Afterwards you can offload a few euros in the attached silk shop next door.

Eat

L'Amphitryon
Vieux Lyon *33 rue St-Jean, 5th (04.78.37.23.68). Open noon-midnight daily. €€.*
Culinary pickings are generally pretty poor around Vieux Lyon, with a surfeit of *menus anglais*, but this traditional Lyonnais restaurant (or *bouchon*) manages to hold its form. The ambience is cosy, with tables crammed in and trinkets hanging from every inch of the ceiling. On the table you'll find all the usual *bouchon* suspects, from *andouillette* to *saucisson brioché à la beaujolaise*, plus some good wines by the bottle. Don't miss the towering *fondant au chocolat*.

"Starters of charcuterie are followed by breaded, fried stomach, with a squishy st-marcellin and apple tart to round things off."

Le Bistro Autrement
Rive Gauche *12 pl Ambroise Courtois, 8th (04.78.01.00.11). Open 7am-midnight daily. No credit cards. €€.*
After a stroll round the busy food market on place Ambroise Courtois or a trip to the Lumière museum a few doors away, make for this handsome old bistro with a big wooden bar, large picture windows and oodles of cinema relics, from projectors to cine-8s, hanging from the walls. *Plats du jour* such as *pierrade* (meat or fish cooked on a hot stone) and *tartiflette* (a baked potato dish with Reblochon cheese) are simple but satisfying, and there's an attractive terrace at the front for summer evenings.

Bistro Pizay
Presqu'île *4 rue Verdi, 1st (04.78.28.37.26). Open noon-2.30pm, 7-11.30pm daily. €€.*
This very attractive bistro is scattered among several others on this small street close to the opera house. Inside the atmosphere is wonderfully cosy with exposed stone walls, wooden bar, tightly packed tables, low lighting and good food. The €18.90 menu might include an earthy paté de campagne simply served with green salad, followed by flavoursome confit of duck served *en cocotte* with dauphinoise potatoes. Forget about buying a bottle of wine and instead do as everyone else does and order a '*pot*' (carafe) of Côtes du Rhone (€5.50 for 25cl). A real find.

Brasserie Georges
Presqu'île *30 cours de Verdun, 2nd (04.72.56.54.54/ www.brasseriegeorges.com). Open 11.30am-11.15pm Mon-Thur, Sun; 11.30am-12.15am Fri, Sat. €€.*
This place is as classic as they come, having sated the appetites of Rodin, Zola and Piaf over the years. It's set in the rather dowdy surroundings of Gare Perrache, but once through the doors you are transported back to a far more civilised age (1836 to be precise). The splendid art deco room is vast and serves up to 2,000 people a day. Brasserie fare rules, from sauerkraut to seafood platters, daily specials and a menu lyonnais incude *andouillette* and st-marcellin cheese (€22-€25). There's also house-made Georges beer on tap, with the copper tanks on show behind the bar to prove it.

Brasserie Léon de Lyon
Presqu'île *1 rue Pleney, 1st (04.72.10.11.12/ www.bistrotsdecuisiniers.com). Open noon-2.30pm, 7-11pm daily. €€€.*
In 2008, Lyon masterchef Jean-Paul Lacombe transformed his seriously swanky Michelin-starred restaurant Léon de Lyon, halving the prices and trebling the capacity in the process. The stained glass, woodwork and parquet floor remain, but prices are now on a par with other brasseries in the area. Quality still shines through in dishes such as duck breast with caramelised pears, and the old wine list is available with a 25 per cent reduction on prices.

Café des Fédérations
Presqu'île *8-10 rue Major Martin, 1st (04.78.28.26.00/www.lesfedeslyon.com). Open noon-2pm, 7-9.30pm Mon-Sat. €€.*
This supremely quaint *bouchon* is one of the city's most famous restaurants, replete with curtained windows, wood panels, red-checked tablecloths and seriously carnivorous treats – a real chance to literally pig out. Starters of charcuterie are followed by one of 11 *bouchon* classics – *tête de veau sauce ravigote*, maybe, or *tablier de sapeur* (breaded, fried stomach) – with a squishy st-marcellin and apple tart to round things off, all for the bargain price of €25.50. *Bonne bouffe* indeed. Be sure to reserve well in advance.

Plato
Croix Rousse *1 rue Villeneuve, 4th (04.72.00.01.30/ www.leplato.com). Open 12.30-2.30pm, 8-11.30pm Mon-Sat. €€€.*
A few minutes' walk from place de la Croix Rousse is this handsome restaurant with elegant decor and plenty of natural light flooding in through the glass roof. The food is smart too. Main courses come in at around €25 to €30 (confit of pork with honey and ginger, for example), so if you're on a budget come at lunchtime and enjoy the *menu du marché* (€19.50 for two courses), which might feature dishes such as roast lamb with aubergine. The place is full of local business types at lunch, but evenings are cooler and cosier.

Top: Brasserie Georges. Left: Le Royal Hôtel. Right: Cour des Loges.

Shop

Bouillet

Croix Rousse *15 pl de la Croix Rousse, 4th (04.78.28.90.89/www.chocolatier-bouillet.com). Open 8.30am-7.15pm Tue-Sat; 8am-1pm Sun.*
Bouillet has been wowing sweet-toothed locals since the opening of this first shop in 1977. The master *chocolatier* now has three branches in Lyon and one in Tokyo, and serves up sumptuous chocolate and macaroon creations. As well as the classics, don't miss out on the *macarons sucré-salés*, such as guacamole or tapenade. If you want to learn how to do it yourself, there are now three-hour *pâtisserie* courses available (€65).

Didier Galland

Croix Rousse *8 rue Austerlitz, 4th (04.78.39.98.84). Open 8am-12.30pm, 3.30-7.30pm Tue-Sat; 8.30am-1pm Sun.*
This highly recommended cheese shop, located in the heart of the pretty Croix Rousse district, is worth the effort of a trip up the hill. The wonderfully smelly selection includes classic comtés, tommes and st-marcellins, plus a few more curious concoctions such as camembert infused with calvados.

Nature et Découvertes

Presqu'île *58 rue de la République, 2nd (04.78.38.38.74/www.natureetdecouvertes.com). Open 10am-7.30pm Mon-Sat.*
This ethical chain stocks a great range of kit for junior and grown-up gadgeteers and outdoor types, from infrared night vision equipment and high-tech weather stations to more mainstream (but still high-tech) camping equipment, as well as an eclectic collection of music from all over the world. Ten per cent of all profits go to the Fondation Nature et Découvertes, which supports environmental causes in Europe and Africa.

Olympique Lyonnais

Presqu'île *Corner rue Grolée & rue Jussieu, 2nd (04.78.37.49.49/www.olweb.fr). Open 10am-7pm Tue-Sat.*
Lyon is a huge footballing town and Olympique Lyonnais come out top in the French first division with predictable regularity, having been champions for seven years on the trot. So it's no surprise to come across this footballing treasure trove over two floors in the centre of town, stocking everything from mugs to replica shirts. The 40,000-seater Stade Gerland, in the south of the city, is usually sold out for home games.

Pagès Védrenne

Presqu'île *5 pl Bellecour, 2nd (04.72.77.55.28/www.vedrenne.fr). Open 10am-1pm, 2-7pm Tue-Sat.*
Founded in 1923 in Nuits-St-Georges, Pagès Védrenne is one of France's largest liqueur producers and this delightful shop on Lyon's main square sells liqueurs infused with everything from prunes to apricots in all shapes and sizes, from bottles to jars of flavoured mustard. If you're feeling particularly fruity, you can even visit their quirky museum, Cassisium, in Nuits-St-Georges, and learn everything there is to know about the humble blackcurrant.

Printemps

Presqu'île *42 rue de la République, 2nd (04.26.03.44.29/www.printemps.com). Open 9.30am-7pm Mon-Sat.*
The Lyon outpost of the Paris department store is slap bang in the middle of the city's main shopping street and has four floors of well-sourced treats. But fashion is where it really excels, along with an excellent beauty and shoe department. Printemps de la Maison stocks everything from everyday tableware to design classics.

Arts

Opéra de Lyon

Presqu'île *1 pl de la Comédie, 1st (www.opera-lyon.com). Open times vary. Admission varies.*
Lyon's opera house is a real focal point for the city and its cultural nerve centre, with opera, ballet and classical recitals in the main auditorium, plus live jazz and world music gigs happening in the cool basement Amphi bar. The original building was constructed in 1832, but the theatre tripled in size after Jean Nouvel's dramatic 1980s renovation, when he added a huge glass drum roof to the existing structure and excavated new rehearsal space below ground. The results are a dramatic blend of old and new, with the original foyer leading to metal staircases up to the higher balconies. You can get a restricted view ticket for as little as €13, although the top tiers are not recommended for vertigo sufferers.

Nightlife

Le Bar

Presqu'île *10bis rue de la Bourse, 1st (04.78.39.51.08). Open 10am-3am Mon-Fri; 4pm-3am Sat, Sun.*
This place is seriously trendy (so trendy it's hard to find the name), but Le Bar delivers in the style stakes, with striking chandeliers, black awnings and thick velvet drapes, plus some of the city's chicest cocktails. If it's too busy, you could try the Comptoir de la Bourse opposite – a little more laid-back with mellow outdoor seating and 'real' fires on the flatscreen TVs inside.

Café 203

Presqu'île *9 rue Garet, 1st (04.78.28.66.65). Open 7am-2am daily. €.*
Café 203 is a hub of laid-back café-bar action just behind the opera house in the heart of student land, with wood-panelled walls, old-style bar and lots of trendy young Lyonnais tucking into a chilled *verre* or *plat du jour*. Staff are friendly, drinks are cheap and the place is buzzing into the early hours. There's limited outdoor seating on the little terrace if you need a drag.

Ninkasi
Presqu'île *267 rue Marcel Mérieux, 7th (04.72.76.89.00/www.ninkasi.fr). Open 10am-1am Mon-Wed; 10am-2am Thur; 10am-3am Fri; 10am-4am Sat; 4pm-midnight Sun.*
This microbrewery out near the Olympique Lyonnais stadium attracts a young, up-for-it crowd for decent beer on tap, live music and DJs. It pulls in some pretty decent acts and in summer the action moves outside on to the terrace.

Stay

College Hôtel
Presqu'île *5 pl St-Paul, 5th (04.72.10.05.05/ www.college-hotel.com). €€.*
Forget School Disco, this is a whole School Sleepover. From the gymnasium horse serving as a reception desk to the vintage TV running cult classics and the leather benches in the breakfast room, this hotel is definitely too cool for school. The 39 bedrooms, with flatscreen TVs, gym lockers for cupboards and panoramic city views, are painted pure white and bathrooms are supremely stylish. Prices range from undergraduate to postgraduate, but it's top marks all round.

Cour des Loges
Vieux Lyon *2, 4, 6, 8 rue du Boeuf, 5th (04.72.77.44.44/www.courdesloges.com). €€€€.*
Set in a peaceful back street in the heart of the Old Town, the Cour des Loges hotel sprawls across four stunning Renaissance buildings set around a tranquil, glass-covered inner courtyard that serves as the lobby. The 62 individually designed rooms are decked out in velvet, taffeta and antique Lyon silks, with bathroom fittings by Philippe Starck. There's also a small indoor pool, sauna and rooftop gardens.

Hôtel des Célestins
Presqu'île *4 rue des Archers, 2nd (04.72.56.08.98/ www.hotelcelestins.com). €€.*
Located opposite the handsome Théâtre des Célestins, this simple but well presented hotel is perfectly placed for checking out Lyon's smarter shops and restaurants. The best rooms look across the square, but all have double glazing, internet access and cable TV. The buffet breakfast goes on as late as you want but there's no restaurant, although you're spoiled for choice in the area.

Le Royal Hôtel
Presqu'île *20 pl Bellecour, 2nd (04.78.37.57.31/ www.lyonhotel-leroyal.com). €€€.*
Lyon's grandest hotel, set plum on its largest square, is a smart, well run and characterful four-star, now part of the Accor group. The 76 rooms, decked out with *toile de jouy* fabrics, are handsomely decorated and some have views across the main square. But the real winner here is the public areas, from the sleekly sexy Côté Bellecour lounge to the all-day Côté Cuisine, a fresh, relaxed eat-in kitchen area, with service by students of the Institut Paul Bocuse hotel school. As you can imagine, they're only too eager to please.

La Tour Rose
Vieux Lyon *22 rue du Boeuf, 5th (04.78.92.69.10/ www.latourrose.fr). €€€€.*
Situated on the same street as the Cour des Loges, the four-star Tour Rose (pink tower) is set within three buildings dating from the 16th to the 17th century. With just 12 rooms named after and decorated by the city's most prestigious silk houses, this is Lyon's best stab at boutique chic. If you want to push the boat out, opt for the grand suite, replete with open fire, grand piano and private garden. From May to October, the main courtyard transforms into a handsome cobbled dining area.

Factfile

When to go
Weather-wise, May to September is the best time to visit the city – in winter you'll often have to contend with sub-zero temperatures. The impressive Nuits de Fourvière arts festival (www.nuitsdefourviere.fr) takes place during July and August, before the city empties out for the summer holidays.

Getting there
Lyon-Saint Exupéry Airport, served by BA and Easyjet from the UK, is located approximately 20km (12 miles) east of the city centre and is also home to the Santiago Calatrava-designed TGV station (08.26.80.08.26/www.lyon airport.com). Trains from Paris to the city centre take approx 2hrs. A Satobus runs from the airport to the city centre every 20mins (€15.80 return) – the ticket desk is on the first

floor of the airport's main hall (open 7am-10pm). A taxi to the city centre will cost around €45-€65.

Getting around
The centre of Lyon is fairly walkable, although to visit Fourvière, Croix Rousse or the Rive Gauche it is best to hop on the fast, clean métro network. There are four lines and tickets are €1.60 single or €13.30 for a 10-ticket carnet.

Tourist information
Tourist office Pl Bellecour, 1st (04.72.77.69.69/ www.lyon-france.com). Open 9am-6pm daily. A LyonCityCard provides free and discounted access to various sights and costs €18.

Internet access
Café 203 9 rue Garet, 1st (04.78.28.66.65). Open 7am-2am daily. Free Wi-Fi.

Clockwise from top left:
Vieux Port; Cité Radieuse;
Le Panier; Cité Radieuse;
Vieux Port.

THEATRE

Marseille

Take the rough with the smooth in this passionate port.

In France's oldest city, medieval churches, Roman remains, 19th-century palaces and tiny cottages on hilly streets jostle with huge housing estates, louche cafés and avant-garde architecture. There may be glorious sea views at every turn, but Marseille is proudly, defiantly urban: not a seaside resort out to fleece tourists, but a year-round working city with a lively cultural scene, where you might just happen to join the locals for a swim on the beach.

If the *French Connection* movies and, more recently, Robert Guédiguian's *La Ville est Tranquille* haven't exactly painted a pretty bouillabaisse-suffused picture of the city, other images capture its upbeat energy: the omnipresent blue and white of football team Olympique de Marseille (OM); Luc Besson's *Taxi* films, packed with local humour and colour; and the nationwide success of France's most popular soap opera, *Plus Belle la Vie*. Of late, Marseille has been undergoing an ambitious programme of urban renewal, which has brought a sleek new tramway; what's more, it has been chosen as the European City of Culture for 2013.

This is a city of fascinating contradictions. The sun almost always shines, but the ferocious winds of the Mistral chill the bones in winter. The architecture can be stunning but, despite much restoration in hand, many buildings are crumbling and Marseille has its share of modern eyesores. Yuppies dine in the Vieux Port's smart restaurants, while boy racers charge around in souped-up cars late at night. Some of the neighbourhoods behind the Vieux Port remain relatively poor, while the Corniche coastal road to the south is peppered with grand stucco villas. A dangerous reputation lingers, but the crime rate is no higher than in other major French cities and continues to drop.

Bouillabaisse, *méchoui* (roasted lamb), pizza and *nems* (spring rolls) illustrate the ethnic mix, but France's second city offers so much more. Loud-mouthed and welcoming to those who appreciate their city, its citizens first and foremost consider themselves Marseillais.

Time Out
Travel Guides

France

Written by local experts

**Available at all good bookshops
and at timeout.com/shop**

PHOTO CREDIT: HÉLOISE BERGMAN

Time Out
Guides

Explore

Marseille takes in 57 kilometres (35 miles) of seafront, from L'Estaque in the north to the Calanques in the south. The city is laid out in 16 *arrondissements*, moving clockwise from the Vieux Port, then anticlockwise in an outer semi-circle.

AROUND THE VIEUX PORT

The Vieux Port remains the centre of Marseille life, as it has been for the past 26 centuries. It's a favourite place for a stroll, scene of the 14 July fireworks and somewhere for jubilant OM fans to celebrate after a victory. Fashionable bars and avant-garde theatres rub shoulders with ship's chandlers, while luxury yachts bob alongside the tiny fishing boats that deliver the day's catch to the market at quai des Belges (officially renamed quai de la Fraternité). This eastern quay, bordered by cafés, stately hotels and the Baroque church of St-Ferréol, is the departure point for ferries to Château d'If, the Iles de Frioul and Calanques.

Abbaye de St-Victor

3 rue de l'Abbaye, 7th (04.96.11.22.60). Open 9am-7pm daily. Admission free. Crypt €2; free under-12s. No credit cards.

Looking more like a castle than a place of worship, this medieval church was built on the remains of an ancient necropolis. The earlier church, founded in the fifth century by St-Jean Cassian, was the city's first basilica and the heart of a powerful abbey complex. Destroyed by Saracens in the 11th century, it was rebuilt in the 13th in a simple, massive Gothic style and fortified in the 14th century. On either side of the main altar, alcoves contain ornate reliquaries, witness to the medieval passion for collecting bones and other saintly memorabilia. Chunks of the earlier church remain in the convoluted crypt, part of it dug directly out of the rock, where finely carved sarcophagi include the tomb of St-Victor, ground to death between two millstones by the Romans.

Basilique Notre-Dame-de-la-Garde

Montée de la Bonne Mère, 6th (04.91.13.40.80). Open 7am-7pm daily. Admission free.

Topped by a massive gilded statue of the Virgin Mary and Child, this 19th-century basilica is the emblem of Marseille, and the most visited tourist site in Provence. Known locally as 'La Bonne Mère' ('the good mother'), it is deeply loved by Marseillais. The Byzantine-style interior is filled with remarkable ex votos, including thanks for those saved from shipwreck and one for Olympique de Marseille. The mosaic floors were made in Venice, while alternating red and white marble pillars add to the richness of the surprisingly intimate chapel. Outside, the esplanade offers wonderful vistas in all directions.

Fort St-Jean

Quai du Port, 2nd (04.96.13.80.90/www.musee-europemediterranee.org). Open (during exhibitions) 10am-noon, 2-7pm Mon, Wed-Sun. Admission €2; free-€1.50 reductions. No credit cards.

Marseille

Historic sites
● ● ● ● ○

Art & architecture
● ● ● ● ○

Hotels
● ● ● ○ ○

Eating & drinking
● ● ● ● ○

Nightlife
● ● ● ○ ○

Shopping
● ● ● ● ○

Marseille

0   200 m
0   200 yds

© Copyright Time Out Group 2009

Docks de
la Joliette

Ferry to Château d'If & Iles de Frioul

QUAI DE LA TOURETTE

RUE SCHUMAN

Cathédrale
de la Major

Ancienne-
Major

RUE DE L'EVÊCHE

AVENUE VAUDOYER

RUE ST FRANÇOISE

RUE BAUSSENQUE

AVENUE DE LA TOURETTE

MONTÉE DES ACCOULES

RUE CAISSERIE

Fort St-Jean

St-Laurent

RUE ST LAURENT

Mémorial des
Camps de la Mort

AVENUE ST JEAN

Musée des
Docks Romains

RUE DE LA LOGE

PLACE
VIVAUX

QUAI DU PORT

Jardin du
Pharo

Anse de
la Reserve

V i e u x

Ferry Boat

Club
Nautique

Fort
St-Nicolas

RUE DES CATALANS

BOULEVARD CHARLES LIVON

Basin de
Carénage

Théâtre
de la Criée

AVENUE PASTEUR

RUE E DUCHESNE

CORNICHE

LE PHARO

ST MAURICE

ST VICTOR

RUE NEUVE SAINTE CATHERINE

PLACE
ST VICTOR

RUE D'ENDOUME

RUE ROBERT

RUE SAINTE

RUE DE LA CROIX

Abbaye de
St-Victor

AVENUE DE LA CORSE

BD DE LA CORDERIE

RUE DES LICES

Jardin Puget

RUE CRINAS

RUE J RECHER

RUE SAUVEUR TOBELEM

PLACE
J. ETIENNE

RUE ABBE DASSY

RUE D'ENDOUME

BOULEVARD TELLENE

AVENUE VAUDENARGUES

MONTÉE DE L'ORATOIRE

BOULEVARD

LAMBERT

ST VICTOR

RUE DAVID

RUE SCUDERY

Stade

Basilique Notre-Dame-
de-la-Garde

Inset map

500m

14

15

La Friche

13

Docks
de la
Joliette

Gare St-
Charles

3

4

1

La Canebière

2

Vieux
Port

12

7

6

5

8

Corniche

Avenue du Prado

11

10

9

Stade
Vélodrome

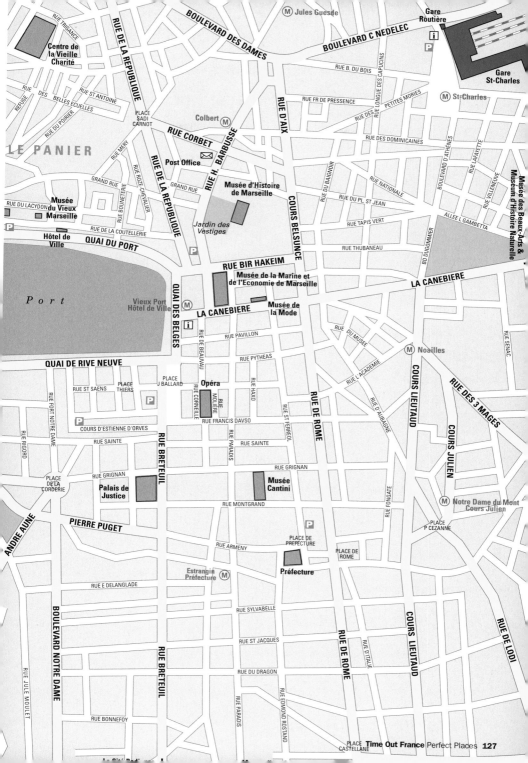

There's been a fortress on this site for centuries, although the oldest remaining part is the square tower built in the 15th century by Good King René. The fortress is currently used for temporary exhibitions, which prefigure the Musée National des Civilisations de l'Europe et de la Méditerranée. Due to open some time in 2012, with a modern extension designed by Rudy Ricciotti, the new museum will be based around the folk art and ethnographic collection of the former Musée National des Arts et Traditions Populaires in Paris.

Jardins des Vestiges/
Musée d'Histoire de Marseille

Centre Bourse, 1 sq Belsunce, 1st (04.91.90.42.22). Open noon-7pm Mon-Sat. Admission €2.50; free-€1 reductions. No credit cards.
While the foundations for the Centre Bourse shopping centre were being dug in the 1970s, remains of Marseille's original Greek walls and a corner of the Roman port were unearthed, and are now preserved here in a sheltered garden. The splendid collection at the adjoining Musée d'Histoire ranges from vintage promotional posters to historical models of the city.

"Le Panier has been the traditional first stop for successive waves of immigrants. It's hard to resist the charm of its narrow streets, steep stairways and pastel-coloured houses – think Italy meets Tunisia."

Mémorial des Camps de la Mort

Esplanade de la Tourette, 2nd (04.91.90.73.15). Open June-Sept 11am-6pm Tue-Sun. Oct-May 10am-5pm Tue-Sun. Admission free.
In January 1943, following orders from Hitler, Karl Oberg, head of the Gestapo in France, declared: 'Marseille is the cancer of Europe. And Europe can't be alive as long as Marseille isn't purified... That is why the German authorities want to cleanse the old districts and destroy them with mines and fire.' These chilling words resonate in a series of haunting and fascinating pictures that capture subsequent events, on display in a former bunker.

Musée des Docks Romains

Pl Vivaux, 2nd (04.91.91.24.62). Open June-Sept 11am-6pm Tue-Sun. Oct-May 10am-5pm Tue-Sun. Admission €2; free-€1 reductions. No credit cards.

During post-war reconstruction in 1947, the remains of a first century AD Roman shipping warehouse were discovered. This museum preserves the site intact and documents maritime trade through an impressive collection of terracotta jars, amphorae and coins.

Musée du Vieux Marseille
(Maison Diamantée)

2 rue de la Prison, 2nd (04.91.55.28.68). Open June-Sept 11am-6pm Tue-Sun. Oct-May 10am-5pm Tue-Sun. Admission €3; free-€1.50 reductions. No credit cards.
Reopened following painstaking renovation, the Maison Diamantée, so named thanks to its diamond-faceted Renaissance façade, was built in the late 16th century, probably for a wealthy merchant. Exhibitions focus on daily life in Marseille since the 18th century, with furniture, photographs and provençal costumes.

LE PANIER & LA JOLIETTE

Le Panier, rising between quai du Port and rue de la République, has been the traditional first stop for successive waves of immigrants. Today, it's at the top of the tourist itinerary. It's hard to resist the charm of its narrow, hilly streets, steep stairways and pastel-coloured houses – think Italy meets Tunisia. Behind Le Panier, the up-and-coming La Joliette area, centred on the 1860s Docks de la Joliette, is the focus of the Euroméditerranée redevelopment project. The bold plans embrace public housing, a museum and aquarium, restaurants, a theatre, offices and two hotels.

Cathédrale de la Major

Pl de la Major, 2nd (04.91.90.53.57). Open 10am-noon, 2-5.30pm Tue-Sun. Admission free.
The largest cathedral built in France since the Middle Ages, the neo-Byzantine Nouvelle Major was started in 1852 and completed in 1893, with oriental-style cupolas and a lustrous mosaic. The remains of the 11th-century Ancienne Major, parts of which date back to Roman times, lie in a state of disrepair.

Centre de la Vieille Charité

2 rue de la Charité, 2nd (04.91.14.58.80). Open June-Sept 11am-6pm Tue-Sun. Oct-May 10am-5pm Tue-Sun. Admission Each museum €2; free-€1 reductions. Exhibitions €3; free reductions. No credit cards.
Constructed from 1671 to 1749 as a poorhouse to round up 'poor natives and errants', this ensemble was designed by Marseille-born architect and sculptor Pierre Puget, and eventually completed by his son François. Open loggias surround a courtyard which his dominated by its magnificent domed chapel. The building was reopened as a cultural complex in 1986, housing temporary exhibitions in the former chapel, along with the Musée d'Archéologie Méditerranéenne and the Musée des Arts Africains, Océaniens and Amerindiens (MAAOA). The former has a superb collection of archaeological finds, and the most

Clockwise from top left: Cité Radieuse; Vieux Port; Le Panier; Vieux Port; Le Panier.

important Egyptian collection in France outside Paris. MAAOA displays tribal art and artefacts from Africa, the Pacific and the Americas.

Docks de la Joliette

10 pl de la Joliette, 2nd (04.91.14.45.00/www.euro mediterranee.fr). Open 9am-6pm Mon-Sat. Admission free.

The handsome warehouses of this 19th-century port run along the waterfront for almost a mile, and were modelled on St Katharine Docks in London. They were state of the art in 1866, but as traffic declined and cargo shifted to containers, the buildings fell into disuse and there were plans to demolish them. Now brilliantly renovated by architect Eric Castaldi, they form the centrepiece of the Euroméditerranée redevelopment. The warehouses are occupied by a diverse mix of companies, bars and restaurants: in atrium 10.2, an information centre displays designs and models of the entire scheme.

LA CANEBIERE & AROUND

Running inland from the Vieux Port, La Canebière marked the expansion of the city under Louis XIV and long served as the dividing line between the 'poor' north and the 'rich' south of Marseille. In its 19th-century heyday it was lined with grand hotels and smart department stores; now rather shabby in parts, it's dominated by chain stores. Nonetheless, its faded wedding cake façades and lively multicultural atmosphere still make for an interesting walk. At the Vieux Port end, by the Office du Tourisme, rue Beauvau leads to the colonnaded façade of the Opéra de Marseille. Behind here is Marseille's smartest shopping area, around rue Francis Davso, rue Paradis and rue St-Férreol.

Around broad cours Belsunce stretches the predominantly North African neighbourhood of Belsunce, known for its handsome 18th-century residences and considered the most likely place to be mugged in the city. This may be unfair, but best be wary of loitering lads in quiet backstreets. It's also home to the tremendous modern municipal library designed by Adrien Fainsilber, constructed around the old entrance of the Alcazar music hall. The streets east of the cours offer a vibrant snapshot of modern-day Marseille: corner-shop mosques, boutiques selling cheap fabrics and gadgets, and sweetmeats of every kind. It's minutes from the Vieux Port, but so different in mood you might have spent 24 hours on a ferry.

Eglise des Réformés

1 rue Barbaroux, 1st (04.91.48.57.45). Open 4-6pm daily. Admission free.

This handsome neo-Gothic church got its nickname from an order of reformed Augustine monks whose chapel stood on this site; its actual name is St-Vincent-de-Paul. Founded in 1852, it wasn't consecrated until 1888. The two spires, one housing four bells, are 69m (226ft) high.

Musée Cantini

19 rue Grignan, 6th (04.91.54.77.75). Open June-Sept 11am-6pm Tue-Sun. Oct-May 10am-5pm Tue-Sun. Admission €3; free-€1.50 reductions. No credit cards.

In an elegant 17th-century mansion, Musée Cantini houses one of France's foremost collections of Fauve and Surrealist art, along with some fine post-war works. Highlights include a Signac of the port, Dufy from his early Cézannesque neo-Cubist phase and paintings by Camoin, Kupka, Kandinsky, Léger and Ernst. Upstairs the collection focuses on Surrealist and abstract artists, including Arp, Brauner and Picabia, along with works by Dubuffet and Bacon.

Musée de la Marine et de l'Economie de Marseille

9 La Canebière, 1st (04.91.39.33.33). Open 10am-6pm daily. Admission €3; free-€1.50 reductions.

This grandiose former stock exchange, housing the city's Chamber of Commerce, was inaugurated by Napoléon III in 1860. The museum charts the maritime history of Marseille, with paintings, models, old maps and engravings, as well as a global celebration of different ports around the world, from Liverpool to Montevideo.

Musée de la Mode de Marseille

11 La Canebière, 1st (04.96.17.06.00/www.espacemode mediterranee.com). Open June-Sept 11am-6pm Tue-Sun. Oct-May 10am-5pm Tue-Sun. Admission €3; free-€1.50 reductions. No credit cards.

Adjoining the Espace Mode Méditerranée and housed in a grand Haussmanian building, the fashion museum's vaults contain more than 6,000 accessories and outfits, from the 1940s to the present day. Selected pieces are displayed in regular themed exhibitions. Also on site is a wonderful collection of style and fashion magazines to browse (by appointment only).

ST-CHARLES & THE BELLE DE MAI

One look around the Gare St-Charles when you step off the train is enough to get an idea of the transformation this district is undergoing. Alongside the fine 19th-century train station, with its majestic entrance and imposing glazed train shed, is a gleaming new glass shopping mall with marble floors, cafés, shops and the bus station ticket office. At the far end, landscaped with fountains and palm trees, a square leads to part of the University of Provence Marseille.

Beyond is the old industrial neighbourhood of Belle de Mai, which grew up in the 19th century with the arrival of the railway. Here, a former tobacco factory has become the thriving cultural centre La Friche la Belle de Mai. The surrounding area is hardly appealing on foot, although a former maternity hospital is set to be converted into a university arts faculty, and the south-east corner of Belle de Mai is to become the central focus of a new media park as part of the Euroméditerranée project.

La Friche la Belle de Mai

41 rue Jobin, 3rd (04.95.04.95.04/www.lafriche.org).
Open 3-6pm Mon-Sat. Admission free.
A disused tobacco factory in the increasingly trendy Belle de Mai quarter, La Friche started life as an artists' squat. These days its vast concrete halls are home to numerous artistic, musical, theatrical, dance and media outfits, that are often open to the public for performances, workshops and exhibitions. Names to look out for include Aide aux Musiques Innovatrices, Théâtre Massalia, Triangle France, Radio Grenouille and Georges Appaix's La Liseuse dance company.

Musée des Beaux-Arts & Muséum d'Histoire Naturelle

Palais Longchamp, bd de Longchamp, 4th
(04.91.14.59.50/www.museum-marseille.org). Open
Musée des Beaux-Arts closed for renovation. Muséum
d'Historie Naturelle 10am-5pm Tue-Sun. Admission
Muséum d'Histoire Naturelle €4; free-€2 reductions.
No credit cards.
No monument better expresses the ebullience of 19th-century Marseille than the Palais Longchamp. This ostentatious complex, inaugurated in 1869, was built to celebrate the completion of an 84km (52-mile) aqueduct bringing the waters of the Durance to the drought-prone port. A massive horseshoe-shaped classical colonnade, with a triumphal arch at its centre and museums in either wing, crowns the hill. On the ground floor are works by sculptor and architect Pierre Puget, while the upper floors contain French, Italian and Flemish paintings from the 16th to 19th centuries. The natural history museum has zoological and prehistoric artefacts.

Musée Grobet-Labadié

140 bd de Longchamp, 1st (04.91.62.21.82).
Open June-Sept 11am-6pm Tue-Sun. Oct-May 10am-5pm Tue-Sun. Admission €2; free-€1 reductions.
No credit cards.
This 1873 mansion houses the private art collection of a wealthy 19th-century couple. Scrupulously renovated, it offers an intriguing glimpse into cultivated tastes of the time, its collection ranging from 15th- and 16th-century Italian and Flemish paintings to Fragonard and Millet, medieval tapestries and 17th- and 18th-century provençal furniture and faïence.

LA CORNICHE, PRADO & THE SOUTH-WEST

The Corniche Président JF Kennedy – known simply as La Corniche – carves along the coast from just beyond the Vieux Port to where the 8th begins near the Centre de Voile. Vantage points, craggy coves and little beaches along the way offer stunning views of the rocky coastline, offshore islands and spooky Château d'If. The sheltered, sandy plage des Catalans, encircled by cafés and restaurants, is the closest beach to the city centre. Along the top of the hill, past the rond-point du Prado on boulevard Michelet, stands the Stade Vélodrome, proud home to the

city's beloved Olympique de Marseille. Further along, you can stop for a meal or spend the night at Le Corbusier's landmark Cité Radieuse. Heading south-west between Ste-Anne and Mazargues on avenue d'Haïfa – just before César's gigantic bronze sculpture of a thumb – the Musée d'Art Contemporain contains an adventurous collection of contemporary art.

The avenue du Prado ends at the plage du Prado in front of a bold marble copy of Michelangelo's *David*. Along this broad stretch of beach, you'll see David-like windsurfers being tossed about on the waves as they brave Marseille's fearsome Mistral. Across the road is the handsome 42-acre Parc Borély, with its horseracing track, botanical gardens and 18th-century château.

La Cité Radieuse

280 bd Michelet, 8th (hotel 04.91.16.78.00). Open
for guided tours, ask at the hotel reception or at the
tourist office.
La maison de fada ('the madman's house') is the locals' once-scornful but now affectionate name for Le Corbusier's hugely influential 1952 reinforced concrete apartment block, where the architect tried out his prototype for mass housing. Perched on stilts, the Cité Radieuse complex contains 340 flats, plus a hotel, restaurant, shops and nursery school, all arranged over 12 storeys.

Musée d'Art Contemporain (MAC)

69 av d'Haïfa, 8th (04.91.25.01.07). Open June-Sept 11am-6pm Tue-Sun. Oct-May 10am-5pm Tue-Sun. Admission €3; free-€1.50 reductions.
No credit cards.
Marseille's contemporary art museum, dedicated to post-1950s art, is located in a hangar-like space. Displays change regularly, mixing temporary exhibitions with selections from the permanent collection, which include Fluxus, *arte povera* and *nouveau réalisme*; recent acquisitions include works by Carsten Höller, Jimmie Durham and Nan Goldin. The garden is dotted with sculptures by the likes of César (born in Le Panier), Absalon and Dietman.

Stade Vélodrome (Olympique de Marseille)

3 bd Michelet, 8th. Club office: 25 rue Negresco, 8th (04.91.76.56.09/www.om.net). Open Shop & museum 10am-1pm, 2-6pm Mon-Sat. Admission free.
This isn't a football stadium, it's a place of worship. L'Olympique de Marseille commands the sort of fervour that separatist movements might elsewhere. OM has had a rollercoaster ride since winning the UEFA Champions League in 1993, but came a respectable third in the French premier division in the 2007-08 season. The second largest stadium in France, Stade Vélodrome can hold 60,000 seated spectators: the best seats are in the Jean-Bouin stand, but the Ganay also offers a relatively quiet viewpoint. Tickets can be bought from the stadium on match day, in advance from L'OM Café (3 quai des Belges, Vieux Port) or by ringing 32 29 Allo OM.

Left: La Caravelle.
Right: L'Epuisette.

Cité Radieuse: high rise, middle class

Children splash in the rooftop paddling pool, while a few feet away two Japanese tourists take photos of a concrete funnel, silhouetted like a sculpture against the sky. It's a curious dichotomy – but the Cité Radieuse (*see p132*) is no ordinary apartment block.

Commissioned in 1945, it was the first of Le Corbusier's forays into mass housing. A 'vertical garden city', it was designed to create a model for social living – so as well as flats, the building encompassed shops, a crèche, a nursery school, a gym and a rooftop amphitheatre and paddling pool.

The ingeniously interlocking design means that while every apartment opens off a convivial central corridor or 'street', each then has another level, above or below, that spans the width of the building, giving every resident a sea and a mountain view. Inside, it's the attention to detail that impresses. The fitted kitchens, designed by Charlotte Perriand, were way ahead of their time, incorporating everything from extractor fans to saucepan racks. Downstairs, a pivoting bookcase has shoe storage hidden behind it, while a blackboard serves as a sliding door between two kids' rooms.

Locals once dubbed the Cité 'la maison de fada' ('the madman's house') – but over 50 years on, attitudes have changed, with duplexes selling for prices that few Marseillais can afford. 'It has become very middle class,' says one of its residents, Jocelyne Gamus – a design aficionado who cherishes her flat's original features and has furnished it with Mouille lights and Perriand bookshelves.

'Fortunately, though, the school has an intake from the whole district, so a social mix still takes place among the children.'

'It has become a bit of a sect, with architects, people working in culture, English and Parisians,' confirms Dominique Gerberin, owner of the Hôtel Le Corbusier. 'But then it always was; before, there were lots of teachers. It has gone from being the fief of the communist gauche to the fief of the bobo (shorthand for bourgeois bohemian) gauche.'

An architectural bookshop, design gallery, architectural practice and accountancy firm have replaced the grocery shops on the indoor 'rue commerçante' – although the bakery remains, and residents are battling for the return of the mini-supermarket, which was closed down in 2008.

The hotel was part of the concept from the outset – and its carefully restored studios and budget-priced *cabines* offer visitors a unique opportunity to experience the Le Corbusier lifestyle. The hotel's guests, says Gerberin, fall into two camps. 'There are architecture students, architects and those in love with design, and there are those who arrive by chance. Either they run away immediately or they let themselves be guided; I take them around almost literally by the hand, so that they gradually understand the place. I take them up to the rooftop and say, "Look, this is the most wonderful view in the world…"'

Guided visits are organised by the Office de Tourisme; alternatively, ask at Hôtel Le Corbusier (*see p138*).

ILE D'IF & ILES DE FRIOUL

The Ile d'If, a tiny islet of sun-bleached white stone 20 minutes from the Vieux Port, is today inhabited by salamanders and seagulls. Its two most famous residents, though, are Edmond Dantès and Abbé Faria, the main characters of Alexandre Dumas' *The Count of Monte Cristo*.

To keep Marseille under control, François I had a fortress built here in 1524 – so formidable that it never saw combat and was eventually converted into a prison. Thousands of Protestants met grisly ends here after the Edict of Nantes was revoked in 1685, but it was Dumas who put If on the map by making it the prison from which Dantès escaped. The château is quickly visited, so bring a picnic and enjoy the clean seawater before catching the boat back.

"Chez Michel has been a failsafe choice for bouillabaisse and *bourride* since it opened in 1946. The fresh fish is expertly de-boned by sea-weathered waiters, and served up with garlicky rouille."

It's easy to combine a visit to the Ile d'If with the Iles de Frioul, a collection of small islands. Aside from a few holiday flats by the marina, they consist largely of windswept rock, wonderfully isolated beaches and fragrant clumps of thyme and rosemary. Ile Ratonneau is also home to the impressive Hôpital Caroline, constructed in the 1820s as a quarantine hospital to protect Marseille from epidemics. Today, it is a curious historic site with terrific views, well worth the slog up the hill. In June and July, it hosts the Nuits Caroline – a series of events ranging from live jazz to open-air theatre (04.96.11.04.61).

Château d'If

Ile d'If, 1st (04.91.59.02.30). Open May-Sept 9.30am-6.30pm daily. Oct-Apr 9am-5pm Tue-Sun. Admission €8; free-€3.10 reductions.
GACM (04.91.55.50.09, www.answeb.net/gacm) runs regular crossings (Tue-Sun, less frequent Oct-May), many of which stop at Ile d'If and Iles de Frioul. A return ticket for one island costs €10, with €5 reductions; both islands costs €15, with €6.50 reductions. Under-threes go free, and credit cards aren't accepted.

Eat

Les Arcenaulx

Vieux Port *25 cours d'Estienne d'Orves, 1st (04.91.59.80.30/www.les-arcenaulx.com). Open noon-2pm, 8-11pm Mon-Sat. Closed 1wk Aug. €€€.*
Set within a strikingly converted former arsenal building, this chic dinner rendezvous shares its interesting space with an antiquarian bookshop, publishers and kitchen shop-cum-*épicerie*. With elevated prices and a prime Vieux Port position, Les Arcenaulx is popular with Marseille's chattering classes, and the modern southern Mediterranean cooking (pan-fried pork with rosemary, chorizo and caponata, for instance) doesn't disappoint.

Baie des Singes

La Corniche *Cap Croisette, Les Goudes, 8th (04.91.73.68.87). Open Mon-Sat (phone for details). Closed Sept-mid Apr. €€€.*
Even though getting a table at the Baie des Singes involves arriving by boat or scrabbling over a rocky promontory, you won't be the first: ex-president Chirac and a host of TV personalities have already made the journey. And you can see why – with the bare white rock and blue seas, you could easily be on a remote Greek island. The speciality here is supremely fresh, grilled fish, presented in a basket for you to choose from.

Le Café des Epices

Le Panier *4 rue du Lacydon, 2nd (04.91.91.22.69). Open noon-3pm, 8-11pm Tue-Fri; 8-11pm Sat. €€.*
You can expect deft spicing and inventive takes on traditional favourites by haute cuisine-trained young chef Arnaud de Grammont at the highly rated Café des Epices – although beware that prices have shot up since the place first opened. You'll need to reserve well ahead, as there are just a handful of tables in the slick interior and on the terrace.

La Caravelle

Vieux Port *34 quai du Port, 2nd (08.26.10.09.47). Open 7am-2am daily. €€.*
Hidden up a flight of stairs inside the historic Hôtel Bellevue, La Caravelle serves breakfast and lunch but is above all a boho cocktail bar, with occasional live music at the weekends. If you get the chance, grab one of the handful of coveted tables on the narrow balcony, which offer an idyllic view of the Vieux Port.

Chez Michel

La Corniche *6 rue des Catalans, 7th (04.91.52.30.63/ www.restaurant-michel.com). Open noon-2pm, 7.30-9.30pm daily. Closed mid Feb-2 Mar. €€€€.*
This Marseille institution, looking across the Anse des Catalans, has been a failsafe choice for bouillabaisse or *bourride* (€60 a head) since it opened in 1946. The fresh fish is expertly de-boned by sea-weathered waiters, and served up with garlicky rouille. Other options on the menu include Marennes oysters and fish soup.

La Côte de Boeuf

Vieux Port *35 cours d'Estienne d'Orves, 1st (04.91.54.89.08). Open noon-2pm, 7.30-11.15pm Mon-Sat. €€€€.*

This two-storey bistro in a converted warehouse behind the port makes a welcome change from Marseille's many fishy treats. Go for the namesake house speciality: a vast *côte de boeuf* for two, served sliced and deliciously rare in the middle. The other draw is the legendary wine list – one of the most extensive in France.

Cup of Tea

Le Panier *1 rue Caisserie, 2nd (04.91.90.84.02). Open 8.30am-7pm Mon-Fri; 9.30am-7pm Sat. €.*

One part tearoom, one part bookshop and one part exhibition space, this fabulous little café in Le Panier is one of the best pit stops in town. All manner of teas and coffees are available, plus various pastries, quiches and huge, garden-fresh salads. If the sun's out, grab a table on the pretty terrace overlooking place du Mazau.

L'Epuisette

La Corniche *156 rue de Vallon des Auffes, 7th (04.91.52.17.82/www.l-epuisette.com). Open 12.15-2pm, 7.45-10pm Tue-Sat. Closed 4 Aug-2 Sept. €€€€.*

Young wonder-chef Guillaume Sourrieu continues to impress at this blow-the-budget seafood restaurant, dramatically set on a craggy stone finger surrounded by the Med and with wonderful views of the offshore islands. Starters include the likes of lobster ravioli and spring vegetables with a tarragon mousse, followed by mains of skewered king prawns with dressed crab and avocado in ginger sauce or goat's cheese-stuffed lamb medallions. Among the desserts, chocolate brownie with pistachios, rose ice-cream and wild strawberries is heavenly.

Le Jardin d'à Côté

La Canebière *65 cours Julien, 6th (04.91.94.15.51). Open noon-2.30pm Mon-Sat. €€. No credit cards.*

The nicest restaurant on 'cours Ju', this traditional bistro offers a warm welcome, tasty, well-priced food, and a terrace that's perfect for people-watching. Typical mains might include a rich, hearty *daube de boeuf* with creamy polenta to soak up the juices. Quaffable house wine is served in handy, lunchtime-sized carafes.

La Kahena

Vieux Port *2 Rue de la République, 1st (04.91.90.61.93). Open noon-2.30pm, 7-10.30pm. €€.*

This is one of the best North African restaurants in the city centre, as evidenced by its popularity (you'll need to book at the weekend), and you'll struggle to eat three courses. To start, try the *chorba* (spicy chickpea broth), calamares or a substantial salad. The merguez are also good, as is the fish couscous.

Le Miramar

Vieux Port *12 quai du Port, 2nd (04.91.91.10.40/ www.bouillabaisse.com). Open noon-2pm, 7-10pm Tue-Sat. Closed 2wks Jan, 3wks Aug. €€€€.*

A legendary address for bouillabaisse, this Vieux Port restaurant has Christophe Buffa in the kitchen, and has recently been expanded to add a few extra tables. Sample the fishy delicacy in the '50s-vintage portside dining room or out on the busy terrace, or alternatively enrol on one of the bouillabaisse cooking courses.

La Table à Denise

Vieux Port *63 rue Sainte, 1st (04.91.54.19.74). Open 11.30am-2.30pm Mon-Fri; 7.30-10.30pm Sat. Closed mid July-mid Aug. €€.*

With its brick walls, wooden tables and fado music playing in the background, this tiny, convivial local haunt is full of twangy Marseille accents. This is the place to come to experience some true southern hospitality and home cooking, with dishes such as lamb simmered with aubergine purée, veal with artichokes or duck *magret* with figs and honey.

Une Table au Sud

Vieux Port *2 quai du Port, 2nd (04.91.90.63.53/ www.unetableausud.com). Open noon-2pm, 7.30-10.30pm Tue-Thur; noon-2pm, 7.30pm-midnight Fri, Sat. €€€€.*

After working for Alain Ducasse, chef Lionel Lévy opened this relaxed gourmet restaurant (incongruously located above a Häagen-Dazs café) and has quickly won a fine reputation – and a Michelin star – for his modern French cooking. Specialities include *foie gras brûlée, milkshake de bouillabaisse* and amazing squid dishes. The wine list is impressive too.

Shop

La Compagnie de Provence

Le Panier *1 rue Caisserie, 2nd (04.91.56.20.94). Open 10.30am-7.30pm Mon-Sat.*

Set just back from the Vieux Port, the delightful Compagnie de Provence shop is the perfect place to stock up on cubes of traditional Marseille soap. The classic is non-perfumed olive-oil green, but vanilla, jasmine and honey varieties are also on sale.

G Bataille

La Canebière *25 pl Notre-Dame-du-Mont, 6th (04.91.47.06.23). Open 10am-7pm Mon-Sat.*

G Bataille is a magnificent old *traiteur* (deli) and the ideal place to shop for local wines and olive oils to take home, or to pick up a picnic of delicious cheeses, tapenades, salads, cold meats and pastries.

Marianne Cat

Vieux Port *53 rue Grignan, 6th (04.91.55.05.25). Open 2-7pm Mon; 10am-7pm Tue-Sat.*

Several designer boutiques have sprung up on rue Francis Davso and rue Grignan during the last few years. The latter is home to the likes of Cartier and Louis Vuitton, along with this chic concept store in an 18th-century townhouse where hip clothes and accessories are mixed

Hôtel Hermès.

with 1930s and '40s furniture and modern design *objets* by local designer Marianne Cat.

Pâtisserie d'Aix
St-Charles *2 rue d'Aix, 1st (04.91.90.12.50). Open 9am-6pm Tue-Sun.*
This tiny pâtisserie is famed for its wonderful Tunisian pastries and its shelves are stacked high with pyramids of honey-drenched delights. Don't miss out on a mint tea with your sweet treat.

Rive Neuve
Vieux Port *30 cours d'Estienne d'Orves, 1st (04.96.11.01.01). Open 10.30am-7.30pm Mon-Sat.*
Seriously cool Rive Neuve is indicative of the influx of designer boutiques now colonising Marseille's trendier *quartiers*, with a cutting-edge selection of labels on show, including the likes of Alberta Ferretti, Camarlinghi, Paul Smith and Coast.

Arts

For details of arts events in the city, you should pick up a copy of weekly freebie *Marseille Hebdo*, Provence-wide *César* or the Marseille edition of *Métro*. In summer, the Festival de Marseille programmes some first-rate contemporary dance and music.

Opéra de Marseille
Vieux Port *2 rue Molière, 1st (04.91.55.11.10). Open Box office 10am-5.30pm Tue-Sat. Tickets €8-€60. No credit cards.*
The original opera house was one of the city's great 18th-century buildings. Partially burnt down in 1919, it was rebuilt in art deco style, preserving the original façade. Today, it holds performances of opera under the watchful eye of new artistic director Maurice Xiberras, as well as dance from the Ballet National de Marseille.

Théâtre du Gymnase
La Canebière *4 rue du Théâtre Français, 1st (04.91.24.35.24/box office 08.20.00.04.22/ www.lestheatres.net). Open Box office 11am-6pm (in person noon-6pm) Tue-Sat. Tickets €20-€30.*
This candy-box of a theatre, dating from 1834, was restored in 1986. Directed by Dominique Bluzet, it's one of the best-attended, most innovative theatres in France, staging its own fascinating take on everything from classics to contemporary drama.

Nightlife

Espace Julien
La Canebière *39 cours Julien, 6th (04.91.24.34.10/ infoline 04.91.24.34.19/www.espace-julien.com). Open times vary. Admission free-€21.*

This long-standing, very active venue on the boho 'cours Ju' offers a packed musical programme, which ranges from international pop and blues to local electro; smaller bands and DJs play in the Café Julien.

L'Intermédiaire
La Canebière *63 pl Jean Jaurès (04.91.47.01.25). Open 6.30pm-2am Mon, Tue; 5.30pm-2am Wed-Sat; 6.30am-2am 1st Sun of the mth. Admission free. No credit cards.*
This hip jazz, blues and rock venue is crowded but friendly. Gigs are held at 10.30pm, Wednesday to Saturday, with jam sessions on Tuesdays and jazz on the first Sunday of the month.

Le Trolleybus
La Corniche *24 quai de Rive Neuve, 7th (04.91.54.30.45/www.letrolley.com). Open 11pm-dawn Wed-Sat. Admission free Wed-Fri; €10 Sat.*
This sprawling harbourside bar and club has been a major Marseille hit since the late 1980s and continues to pack in the punters (into its 17th-century cavern-like arsenal building), with different themed rooms offering techno, salsa, funk… and *pétanque*. An equally heterogeneous crowd runs the gamut from well-heeled young bankers to rappers in tracksuits.

Le Warm'Up
La Corniche *8 bd Mireille Jourdan Barry, 8th (04.96.14.06.30/www.warmup-marseille.fr). Open 8pm-2am Tue-Sat. Admission free Tue, Fri; €8-€12 Wed, Thur, Sat.*
Marseille's answer to the super-club, Warm'Up has everything from a state-of-the-art sound system and heaving dancefloor to an oriental chill-out room and terrace bar, with a swimming pool and views of the distant hills. DJs spin diverse sets, from straight-ahead house through electro bleeps to spirited salsa.

Stay

Hôtel Le Corbusier
La Corniche *280 bd Michelet, 8th (04.91.16.78.00/ www.hotellecorbusier.com). €€.*
Modern architecture aficionados won't want to miss the chance to stay in this iconic building. The Le Corbusier spirit is lovingly preserved, although the cheapest rooms, with a shared loo, resemble the monks' cells on which they were modelled. Pricier rooms are large and there are two studios with terraces, sea views and original Le Corbusier kitchens (not for use).

Hôtel Hermès
Vieux Port *2 rue Bonneterie, 2nd (04.96.11.63.63/ www.hotelmarseille.com). €.*
Though its rooms are rather on the small side, this simple two-star hotel, which was renovated in 2006, is just a few steps away from the main Vieux Port action and offers good value for money. The three rooms on the top

floor have small terraces with superb views of the harbour and the Basilique Notre-Dame-de-la-Garde, and there's a rooftop sundeck too.

Hôtel Résidence du Vieux Port
Vieux Port *18 quai du Port, 2nd (04.91.91.91.22/ www.hotelmarseille.com). €€.*
The three-star Résidence du Vieux Port is one of the most sought-after places to stay in town. The 1950s building features balconies (except on the second floor) and unbeatable views across the Vieux Port to Notre-Dame-de-la-Garde. Some of the rooms are decorated in traditional provençal style, while others have been refurbished to keep up the '50s feel.

Hôtel Richelieu
La Corniche *52 Corniche JF Kennedy, 7th (04.91.31.01.92/www.lerichelieu-marseille.com). €.*
Clinging perilously on to the seashore by the popular plage des Catalans, this charming hotel has bright paintings in the lobby and colourful murals of seagulls and sailing boats in the 21 bedrooms. Rooms at the rear have incredible sea views, and some have mini-balconies – though a few share a loo on the landing. There's free Wi-Fi available.

Mercure Grand Hôtel Beauvau Vieux Port
Vieux Port *4 rue Beauvau, 1st (04.91.54.91.00/ www.mercure.com). €€€.*

This historic hotel, where Chopin and George Sand once stayed, has a wonderful position overlooking the Vieux Port and has been luxuriously renovated. The 73 bedrooms feature Napoléon III furniture and traditional provençal textiles in abundance; the duplexes are a particularly good option for families.

New Hôtel Bompard
La Corniche *2 rue des Flots-Bleus, 7th (04.91.99.22.22/www.new-hotel.com). €€.*
Tucked away in a quiet residential area near the Corniche, the Bompard offers a tranquil retreat from the bustle of city centre. Accommodation features air-conditioned rooms in the old wing and extension, family apartments with kitchens, and four sumptuous provençal-style mas (€170-€200). There's a nice swimming pool and handsomely tended gardens, along with a guests-only restaurant. Free car parking on site.

Radisson Vieux Port
Vieux Port *38-40 quai de Rive Neuve, 7th (04.89.61.90.05/www.marseille.radissonsas.com). €€€€.*
The pick of the new bunch of business hotels is also a good holiday option, with a prime position on the Vieux Port. Spacious guestrooms have provençal or African-inspired decor, and are spread over two buildings with a rooftop swimming pool between the two. A generous breakfast buffet, colourful bar, gym and restaurant complete the facilities.

Factfile

When to go
The weather is pretty mild and dry all year round, except for late autumn which can be blustery, cold and wet. Beware summer temperatures, which can become oppressive during the middle of the day. The annual Festival de Marseille (www.festivaldemarseille.com), with international contemporary dance, theatre and music, takes place over three weeks in July.

Getting there
Aéroport Marseille-Provence (04.42.14.14.14) is 25km (15.5 miles) north-west of Marseille near Marignane. It has two terminals, one for the main international airlines (www.marseille.aeroport.fr), the second (www.mp2.aeroport.fr) for low-cost carriers. 'La Navette' coaches (04.42.14.31.27) run every 20mins 6.15am-10.50pm to Gare St-Charles, and from the station to the airport 5.30am-9.50pm; the trip takes about 25mins and costs €8.50. A taxi to the Vieux Port costs around €40. The main station is Gare St-Charles (08.10.87.94.79, www.sncf.com), with frequent high-speed TGV trains from Paris (3hrs). The bus station adjoins the train station (08.91.02.40.25).

Getting around
RTM (04.91.91.92.10, www.rtm.fr) runs a comprehensive network of bus routes, two métro lines and two tramlines. The same tickets can be used on all three and can be bought in métro stations, on the bus (singles only, have the right change) and also at tabacs and newsagents displaying the RTM sign. A single ticket costs €1.70 and entitles the user to one hour's travel. There are cab ranks on most main squares; alternatively, call Marseille Taxi (04.91.02.20.20), Taxi Plus (04.91.03.60.03) or Taxi Radio Tupp (04.91.05.80.80). The city's municipal bike hire scheme, Le Vélo (www.levelo-mpm.fr), is a great way to see the sights, with pick-up stations dotted around the city.

Tourist information
Tourist office 4 La Canebière, 1st (04.91.13.89.00/www.marseille-tourisme.com). Open 9am-7pm Mon-Sat; 10am-5pm Sun.

Internet access
Info-Café 1 quai Rive Neuve, 1st (04.91.33.74.98/www.info-cafe.com). Open 9am-10pm Mon-Sat; 2.30-7.30pm Sun.

Clockwise from top: Antigone;
Opéra Comédie; Arc de Triomphe.

Montpellier

Medieval meets ultra modern just a bike ride from the beach.

A long-term programme of renovation and innovation – including a new tramway, Ricardo Bofill's postmodern Antigone quarter by the river Lez, and the Corum concert and conference complex – has helped transform Montpellier into France's fastest-growing city, leaping up the urban league table in the last 20 years from 20th to eighth. Located just a few miles inland from the sea, it has been transformed from a sleepy university city into the powerhouse of Mediterranean France – and the new darling of the international party set. But it's not all about technology and transformation: Montpellier is also an ancient academic centre with handsome historic buildings, abundant gardens and an impressively vast central square.

It's also a young city, with the under-25s making up nearly 40 per cent of the 230,000 population. The student quota has quadrupled in the last 20 years, maybe helped by the fact that it's within a bike ride of the Med, enough to pull in any sensible 18-year-old. Talking of two wheels, bikes are a big thing in Montpellier, which now has nearly 160 kilometres (100 miles) of cycle paths linking the historic old town and the blindingly modern new town (Polygone and Odysseum), and onwards towards the seaside at Palavas. What's more, this development is coupled with a brilliant municipal bike hire scheme, which is cheap (€2 per day), very easy to use and more sustainable than Paris's big city Vélib scheme.

The smoothest way to arrive is by train (less than two hours from Lyon) – a supremely civilised experience as the TGV pulls into Gare St-Roche and you are faced with a simple five-minute stroll up rue de Maguelone to the heart of Vieux Montpellier. This is one of the best places in France to be right now – a city teetering on the edge of global recognition, with the perfect combination of urban sophistication and Mediterranean relaxation.

Explore

City life centres on the vast, pedestrianised and attractive place de la Comédie, dominated by the opera house, which owes its ornate look to Charles Garnier of Paris Opéra fame. At the opposite end, the landscaped esplanade Charles de Gaulle, where there's a market most mornings, leads to the modern and much maligned Corum concert hall and conference centre. At the market you can try a wonderful variety of local delicacies produced by the city's position between mountain and Med – such as pélardon goat's cheese, savoury olive and bacon *fougasse* breads, and oysters from Bouzigues. The square is buzzing at any time of day, and is also home to Montpellier's one really world-class museum, the Musée Fabre, which recently reopened after a massive renovation project.

The city's main shopping street, rue de la Loge, runs directly off place de la Comédie and leads up through Vieux Montpellier, with its wealth of elegant private mansions and courtyards dating from the 15th to the 18th centuries. At the top of the town sits the ornate 17th-century Arc de Triomphe, from where the terraced promenade de Peyrou provides views as far as the Med and Cévennes National Park. Nearby lie the peaceful Jardin des Plantes, one of Europe's oldest botanical gardens, and bulky St-Pierre cathedral, a hotch-potch of architectural styles.

Jardin des Plantes

Bd Henri IV (04.67.63.43.22). Open June-Sept noon-8pm Tue-Sun; Oct-May noon-6pm Tue-Sun. Admission free.

Montpellier's botanical garden is one of the oldest in Europe and is a wonderfully peaceful spot just a few minutes' walk from place de la Comédie. It was originally created in 1593 for Pierre Richer de Belleval and served as a model for Paris's Jardin des Plantes, which was built some 40 years later. The handsome orangery was designed by Claude-Mathieu Delagardette and completed in 1804, while the English Garden, complete with pool and greenhouse, dates from 1859. The garden now belongs to the university and is classified as a historical monument.

Musée Atger

2 rue Ecole de Médecine (04.67.41.76.40). Open 1.30-5.45pm Mon, Wed, Fri. Closed 17 July-24 Aug. Admission free.

Montpellier's faculty of medicine was founded at the end of the 13th century and is the oldest medical school in Europe. This museum is tucked in among its buildings and consists of a surprisingly fine collection of drawings from the Flemish, Italian, Dutch, German and French schools, patiently assembled by skilled art enthusiast Xavier Atger, who left it to the school during the last century.

Musée Fabre

39 bd Bonne-Nouvelle (04.67.14.83.00/www. montpellier-agglo.com). Open 10am-6pm Tue, Thur, Fri, Sun; 1-9pm Wed; 11am-6pm Sat. Admission €6; €4 reductions.

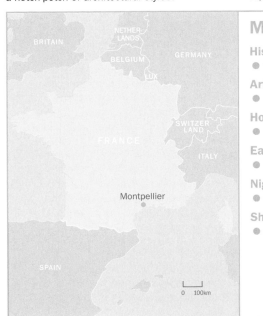

Montpellier

Historic sites
● ● ● ● ○

Art & architecture
● ● ● ● ○

Hotels
● ● ● ○ ○

Eating & drinking
● ● ● ● ○

Nightlife
● ● ● ● ○

Shopping
● ● ● ○ ○

The Musée Fabre was founded by local painter François-Xavier Fabre in 1825. The museum recently underwent a €60 million renovation, which was completed in January 2007, and the visit now begins with Daniel Buren's *La Portée*, a dramatic black-and-white granite and Carrara marble pathway up to the main entrance. The museum is housed in a maze of galleries within a 17th-century Jesuit college, an 18th-century *hôtel de ville* and 19th-century extensions, plus a brand new contemporary art wing. The collections of 15th- to 19th-century painting and sculpture fall into three major groups, beginning with 17th-century Flemish and Dutch painting, followed by European painting from the 14th century to the mid-18th century, and ending with neoclassical works. Other galleries pay tribute to the museum's great 19th-century donors, Fabre and Valedau. The collection may not hold many big hitters, but highlights include Courbet's *Bonjour Monsieur Courbet* and Benouville's *The Wrath of Achilles*, plus a series of 20 painting by Pierre Soulages covering a 50-year period from 1951 to 2005.

"Odysseum is the future of Montpellier in action, a city that is growing faster than any other in France and is absolutely determined to remain at the forefront of modern urban planning."

Musée de l'Histoire de Montpellier
Pl Jean-Jaures, in the crypt of Notre Dame des Tables (04.67.54.33.16). Open 10.30am-12.30pm, 1.30-6pm Tue-Sat. Admission €1.60.
The Montpellier History Museum is situated in a Romanesque crypt, which is part of the Ste-Marie church built in the tenth century, and offers a virtual tour of Montpellier's past, with the use of light projection, and video and audio commentaries.

Musée Languedocien
7 rue Jacques Coeur (04.67.52.93.03/www.musee-languedocien.com). Open 2.30-5.30pm Mon-Sat. Admission €6; €3 reductions.
This museum of art, history and archaeology, which is housed in Montpellier's first private historic mansion, contains rich collections of Gallo-Roman art, Greek ceramics and decorative arts from the 16th century to the 19th century, unearthed during various archaeological digs in the surrounding region.

La Serre Amazonienne
50 av Agropolis (04.67.54.45.23). Open 10am-7pm Tue-Sat. Admission €6; free-€4 reductions.
La Serre Amazonienne, opened in 2007 in the grounds of Montpellier zoo on the outskirts of town, is the largest tropical greenhouse in France. Inside you can come face to face with alligators, anacondas, tarantulas and piranhas, plus a display of some 3,500 plants, as you walk through the mangrove swamps and dense forests. There's even an artificial rainstorm every half an hour to simulate the rain forest environment.

ANTIGONE
If you head east from place de la Comédie and struggle through the deeply depressing 1970s Polygone shopping centre, you will emerge at the other side and feel like you've been transported to some ill-conceived historical film set. For before you stretches the neo-Grecian suburb of Antigone, a wonderfully over-the-top housing and office development from the 1980s by Catalan architect Ricardo Bofill. Built on the grounds of the former Joffre barracks, the complex is designed in a grand neoclassical way, blowing up classical motifs such as pediments and pilasters to a gigantic scale. The effects are actually pretty impressive, stretching all the way from the back door of the Polygone shopping centre to the banks of the Lez river, a distance of about one kilometre. In among the triumphal arches and grand agoras are a host of decent places to eat, busy at lunch with the business crowd, or alternatively take a stroll down to the Esplanade de l'Europe at sunset for a drink on one of the many terraces overlooking the river, whose source provides the city with drinking water.

ODYSSEUM
There is plenty to dislike about Odysseum, a vast leisure-retail complex awash with theme restaurants and hangar-like superstores under construction in the south-east of the city. But this is the future of Montpellier in action, a city that is growing faster than any other in France and is absolutely determined to remain at the forefront of modern urban planning. The development has a lot to live up to after Antigone's dramatic appearance on the 1980s cityscape, but it also has plenty in its favour – this is no white elephant, with tram lines already up and running, the imminent arrival of the TGV, and enough ice skating, go-karting, bowling and eating opportunities to keep the city's 80,000-strong student population happy. The complex is already home to the Mare Nostrum aquarium with more than 300 species on display, a vast cinema multiplex, and a state-of-the-art climbing wall (www.altissimo.fr, €11.50). A great way to visit is to pick up a Vélomagg bike in the Old Town and cycle the half an hour or so out of town.

This way you can experience the embryonic stages of the city, from medieval Montpellier, through the Antigone complex and ending at the futuristic Odysseum.

Château de Flaugergues
1744 av Albert Einstein (04.99.52.66.37/ www.flaugergues.com). Open Château June, July, Sept 2.30-6.30pm Tue-Sun. Gardens Oct-May, Aug 9.30-12.30pm, 2.30-7pm Mon-Sat. June, July, Sept 9.30-12.30pm, 2.30-7pm Mon-Sat; 2.30-7pm Sun. Admission €8; free-€5.50 reductions.
Starting at the end of the 17th century, the city's leading dignitaries began to build country pads outside the city surrounded by magnificent gardens to serve as summer retreats, and several of these *folies* still stand today. One of the finest is this château, now dwarfed by the rising edifice of near neighbour Odysseum. Highlights include a rare collection of 17th-century Flemish tapestries and a Louis XV zograscope. Outside, the ornamental gardens are wonderful for a stroll, and there's also the chance to taste the estate's own wine.

Eat & Drink

Café Bibal
Rue Jacques Coeur (04.67.60.61.42/www.cafes-bibal.fr). Open 8.30am-7pm Mon; 7.30am-7pm Tue-Sat. €.
This café, tucked away down a shady street in the heart of pedestrianised Vieux Montpellier, just a few steps away from the bustle of place de la Comédie, is a welcoming place, with free Wi-Fi and a vast choice of coffees on offer. The inside is cosy going on cramped, but the place to be is outside on the mellow pavement terrace area, with a box of blankets for the winter months. Food is mostly traditional café favourites; better to order a thick hot chocolate and pose on the pavement.

Les Caves Jean Jaurès
3 rue Collot (04.67.60.27.33). Open 7-9.30pm Mon; noon-2pm, 7-9.30pm Tue, Thur-Sat. €€.
This is a lovely place to eat, just a couple of minutes downhill from busy place Jean Jaurès. Order a *plat du jour* from the blackboard menu – dishes might include cassoulet or lamb shanks glazed in honey and orange – and then head up to the vast wine rack in the middle of the room and choose your wine by the glass or bottle, with a sommelier on hand to lend tips. The food is excellent and pretty good value at around €13 for a main. The room is also a treat and service is friendly. In summer, try to bag one of the tables in the courtyard out the back.

Comptoir de l'Arc
Pl de la Canourgue (04.67.60.30.79). Open 7am-1am Mon-Sat; 10am-1am Sun. €€.
Situated on place de la Canourgue, one of the most beautiful squares in Montpellier, this mellow bar-restaurant is just a few steps away from the main drag of rue Foch, but you could easily be in a provençal village – the buildings all around are stunning and the outside seating backs on to a small park. There's a pretty covered terrace too and the food is pretty good, although dieters should probably steer clear of the foie gras burger.

Grand Café Riche
8 pl de la Comédie (04.67.54.71.44). Open 7am-9pm daily. €€.
This iconic, two-tier brasserie has sat plum on place de la Comédie for more than 100 years, and while the interior is nothing to get excited about, it's the suntrap terrace that pulls in the punters. The salads are surprisingly good for such a honey trap establishment, but the wait can be long and the high prices match the prime position. But for a brew with a view it's pretty hard to beat – just don't forget to pack your shades.

Jardin des Sens
11 av St-Lazare (04.99.58.38.38/www.jardin dessens.com). Open 7-10pm Tue, Wed; noon-3pm, 7-10pm Thur-Sat. €€€€.
The Pourcel twins' empire now stretches as far as Bangkok and Tokyo, but this was the original, opened back in 1988. This is Montpellier's gastronomic high point, with artful Mediterranean dishes such as lobster tail salad, ravioli of pineapple with sichuan pepper, marinated turnip, vinaigrette with carrot juice and ham shavings or pan-fried slice of foie gras, puréed rhubarb in a spicy wine syrup. The Sens & Découvertes menu weighs in at a hefty €190, but come at lunch for the more accessible but equally divine €50 prix fixe. The smart, spacious dining room has views out on to a Mediterranean herb-scented garden – a true feast for the senses. If you want to take some of the magic home with you, sign up for one of the cookery courses that take place next door.

Pain et Compagnie
4 pl Jean Jaurès (04.67.60.24.35/www.pain etcompagnie.fr). Open 8.30am-11pm Mon-Sat; 10am-4pm Sun. €€.
This southern French mini-chain is open all day for breakfast, lunch and dinner. The decor – wooden floors, tables and chairs and exposed brick – feels more Seattle than Montpellier. But the food is unreservedly French – snails in roquefort sauce, roast lamb shanks, tarte tatin. The wine list is short but sweet, with delicious faugères at €3.50 a glass. The room also doubles as a deli and the shelves are lined with all manner of syrups, vinegars and juices. Handsomely done and a refreshing change from the standard bistro-brasserie formula.

Le Petit Nice
1 pl Jean Jaurès (04.99.58.12.63). Open 9am-1am Mon-Sat; 9am-10pm Sun. €.
This is probably the pick of a busy bunch of cafés on central place Jean Jaures, especially during happy hour (7-8pm) when pints are cut to a bargain basement €2.50. The surrounding square is handsome enough with a statue of the man himself plonked squarely in the middle. The vibe feels all very South of France, with director's chairs and a

Top: Le Rebuffy Pub.
Bottom: Les Caves
Jean Jaurès.

vast terrace out the front (heated in winter). The interior is less inspiring, with TV sports blaring, so better stay outside and watch the locals stroll by.

Restaurant La Suite
Pl du Nombre d'Or (04.67.64.87.87). Open 9am-1am Mon-Sat. €€.
This buzzing restaurant, at the heart of Ricardo Bofill's neo-Greco Antigone development, is a good lunch option as you enter the complex from the Polygone shopping centre. The *plats du jour* – such as lamb, chicken and merquez couscous or *thon à la plancha* – are an excellent deal, and there's a handsome heated terrace on the main square. Unsurprisingly, most fellow diners are suited and booted at lunchtime, but the overall vibe remains resolutely relaxed. Inside things are a touch grander, with drapes, chandeliers and a smarter feel.

"Leave plenty of room for dessert, as Chapon is a *double champion de France de dessert*, and turns out puds such as foie gras fried with chocolate."

Tamarillos
2 pl Marché aux Fleurs (04.67.60.06.00/www.tamarillos.biz). Open noon-2.30pm, 7.30-10pm daily. €€€€.
The motto of this upmarket eaterie on place Marché aux Fleurs is fruit and flower power, and all the dishes have fruit as an ingredient, as does the decor, all primary colours and palm fronds. If the colours are too intense, there's a pretty terrace as well. Chef Philippe Chapon spent many years learning his craft under Guy Savoy and his talent shines through in dishes such as langoustines with lime, scallops and warm baby spinach with pistachio nuts, or sea bass with purée of herbs, vanilla and lime sauce. Leave plenty of room for dessert, as Chapon is a *double champion de France de dessert*, and turns out puds such as foie gras fried with chocolate or vanilla millefeuille with pear coulis. Prices are not cheap – the tasting menu comes in at a fairly hefty €90 – but for cooking of this quality it's worth every cent.

Welcomedia
Pl de la Comédie (04.67.02.82.65/www.welcomedia.fr). Open noon-2.30pm Mon-Wed, Sat; noon-2.30pm, 7-10pm Thur, Fri. €€.
This trendy newcomer, tucked alongside the handsome opera house on place de la Comédie, is a stylish bar-bistro with a smart terrace that occupies a prime spot overlooking the square. The place attracts plenty of lunchtime suits for the reasonable *plats du jour* and excellent desserts, plus a decent selection of wines by the glass. Come evening, though, unless there's a performance on at the opera house, there are plenty of other livelier bars nearby.

Shop

Rue de la Loge is the place for serious shopping, but its tributaries are worth exploring for quirkier finds. The big names (C&A, Galeries Lafayette) can be found in the vast Polygone mall linking place de la Comédie to the Antigone quarter. The Med offshoot of Lafayette has prime position right at the end of the Polygone shopping centre. The first floor is dedicated to menswear and womenswear, the ground floor contains yet more clothes but also make-up, beauty and lingerie. Finally, the basement level houses books and stationery as well as a range of kitchen utensils and crockery. The recently renovated Halles Castellane, just off rue de la Loge, is a handsome covered market selling a wide range of food and drink.

Agnès B
14 rue Foch (04.67.57.80.94/www.agnesb.com). Open 10am-7pm Mon-Sat.
Agnès B rarely wavers from her classic design vision: pure lines in fine quality cotton, merino wool and silk. Best buys are shirts, pullovers and cardigans that keep their shape for years. The Montpellier branch is at the heart of rue Foch, the chicest shopping street in town.

Book In Bar
8 rue du Bras de Fer (04.67.66.22.90/www.bookinbar.com). Open 1-7pm Mon; 10am-7pm Tue-Sat.
This excellent, two-level English bookshop is packed to the rafters with a wide range of new and second-hand reads to mull over in mellow surroundings. The shop also runs an English–French conversation exchange most Fridays, and there's a café where you can grab a coffee and browse the UK newspapers.

Les Cinqs Continents
20 rue Jacques Coeur (04.67.66.46.70/www.les cinqcontinents.com). Open 1-7pm Mon; 10am-7pm Tue-Sat.
Having travelled the globe, Alain Londmer and Christine Guérard came home to open this excellent travel bookshop. It's a veritable treasure trove of useful information, with a collection of some 7,000 titles, including maps, guide books, photo books and travel journals, as well as a section selling travel essentials such as mosquito nets, water purifiers and money belts.

Fnac
Centre Polygone (08.25.02.00.20/www.fnac.com). Open 10am-8pm Mon-Fri; 9.30am-8pm Sat.

Fnac, which is located deep in the bowels of the rather unprepossessing Centre Polygone shopping mall, is a real supermarket of high-tech culture: there are two floors of books, DVDs, CDs, audio kit, computers and photographic equipment to peruse, as well as concert tickets for sale.

Nature et Découvertes

Centre Polygone (04.67.20.20.03/www.nature etdecouvertes.com). Open 10am-8pm Mon-Fri; 9.30am-8pm Sat.

This commendably ethical store stocks a great range of stuff for junior and grown-up gadgeteers, from infrared parent detectors to high-tech weather stations. It's also worth remembering that ten per cent of all the group's profits go to the Fondation Nature et Découvertes, which supports environmental causes in Europe and Africa. Souvenirs with a conscience.

Arts

The excellent Montpellier Danse season runs for a couple of weeks during June and July (www.montpellierdanse.com), followed by Montpellier Skateboard (www.montpellier skateboard.fr) in September, which draws young people for an urban festival of hip hop, graffiti and skateboarding.

Opéra Comédie

Pl de la Comédie (04.67.60.19.99/www.opera-montpellier.com). Tickets €8-€60.

The Opéra Comédie, which dominates Montpellier's main square, has had a chequered past. The first theatre on this site was built in 1755 but was destroyed by fire and replaced by an exact replica in 1788. The second theatre was also destroyed by fire, in 1881. The current opera house was completed in 1888 and can seat 1,200 spectators. The programming tends to stick with the classics – the 2008-09 season headlined with the likes of *Falstaff*, *Faust* and *Aïda*. There's a second, smaller auditorium, the Salle Molière, at the rear of the building, where recitals are held. In 1990, the city built a second opera house at the other end of place de la Comédie. The Berlioz Opera House in the controversial Corum conference centre was designed by architect Claude Vasconi and seats 2,000 people.

Nightlife

Bar Foch

2 pl Rebuffy (04.67.63.30.76). Open 10am-2am Mon-Sat; 2pm-2am Sun.

This place is bang next door to the student-heavy Rebuffy Pub, but the vibe is a world away. Foch is definitely more upmarket wine bar than scruffy beer den, but it still shares the same charming square and, unlike at the Rebuffy, you might actually stand a chance of getting a seat on the terrace on a summer's evening.

Le Rebuffy Pub

2 rue Rebuffy (04.67.66.32.76). Open 10am-2am daily.

If you need convincing that Montpellier is a student town, then make a beeline for this incredibly popular, laid-back drinking spot, situated just off the main shopping drag in a cute little *endroit* with a buzzing terrace under the trees and fairy lights. Pints are decently priced at €4.20 a pop, plus the bar has loads of board games and information about the city's club nights.

Rockstore

20 rue Verdun (04.67.06.80.00/www.rockstore.fr). Open 10am-1am daily.

This legendary concert venue, which has welcomed the likes of Radiohead, Pulp and Faith No More since it opened back in 1986, also doubles as an after-gig disco, with big-name French and international DJs spinning for a young, up-for-it crowd. If you're having any trouble finding the address, there's the rear end of a Cadillac sticking out the front of the building.

Stay

Hôtel des Etuves

24 rue des Etuves (04.67.60.78.19/ www.hoteldesetuves.fr). €.

The recently renovated, family-run Etuves, situated just off the place de la Comédie, is a good bet for budgeteers who want to be close to the action. The hotel has 15 pretty basic en-suite rooms, half of which overlook the peaceful pedestrianised rue des Etuves, accessed by a cosy but cramped spiral staircase.

Hôtel Le Guilhem

18 rue Jean Jacques Rousseau (04.67.52.90.90/ www.leguilhem.com). €€.

This charming little 16th-century hotel is located on a peaceful street at the top of the Old Town, just a few steps away from the tranquil Jardin des Plantes, and a few minutes downhill to the place de la Comédie. The 36 individually designed bedrooms look out over gardens or the prestigious School of Medicine, founded in the 12th century. Room 100 is a vaulted suite with its own little terrace and garden. Breakfast is served on the terrace in summer. There's no restaurant, but there are plenty of decent options on the doorstep.

Hôtel du Palais

3 rue du Palais (04.67.60.47.38/www.hoteldupalais-montpellier.fr). €.

The Palais' USP is not its interior, which is simple two-star fare, but its position on one of Montpellier's most charming squares, seconds away from rue Foch's shopping opportunities, but peacefully tucked away under the welcome shade of a vast plane tree. Some of the 26 air-conditioned rooms lead on to handsome metal balconies overlooking the square, while those at the back are quieter. Breakfast is served downstairs, or during summer there are a few tables on the pavement out the front.

Left: New Hôtel du Midi.
Right: Jardin des Sens.

Hôtel du Parc

8 rue Achille Bège (04.67.41.16.49/www.hotelduparc-montpellier.com). €.

This former 18th-century Languedoc manor house, once home to the grandly titled Count Vivier de Châtelard, is now a charmingly restored two-star hotel, with plenty of period detailing and furniture, plus a handsome breakfast terrace. The 19 individually designed, air-conditioned rooms are all en suite and have free Wi-Fi. There's also free parking on site and a very friendly welcome. Location is a bit out of town, about a 15-minute walk to the centre, but the free parking is invaluable.

Jardin des Sens

11 av Saint Lazare (04.99.58.38.38/ www.jardindessens.com). €€€.

This four-star Relais & Châteaux property in the suburbs is Montpellier's stand-out hotel, with a fancy price tag to match, but for that you get designer luxury – mahogany floors, stunning bathrooms, and walls decorated with works from owners the Pourcel twins' thoroughly contemporary art collection, plus a wonderful terrace with swimming pool. If you really want to indulge, then book into the Terrace Suite, replete with a large lounge opening on to a private terrace with plunge pool – a snip at €480 a night. The other advantage to bedding down here, of course, is that you'll get first dibs on a table at the twins' two Michelin-starred restaurant (*see p144*). And if you like the vibe of the hotel, the twins have even opened an on-site boutique so you can take a slice away with you.

New Hôtel du Midi

22 bd Victor Hugo (04.67.92.69.61/www.new-hotel.com). €€€.

The renovated New Hôtel du Midi's USP is its position, set just off the main place de la Comédie and featuring some rooms with balconies looking straight across at the heart of the city action. On the downside, the welcome could be a little warmer and the breakfast is poor – skip it and head out to one of the multitudinous cafés on the main square instead. The 44 air-conditioned rooms are simple but comfortable, with decent-sized bathrooms, and the central staircase and old-style cage lift is handsome. Check the website for deals.

SuiteHôtel Montpellier Antigone

45 av du Pirée (04.67.20.57.57/www.suitehotel.com). €€.

If you find it hard to switch off, then head for the SuiteHôtel, a newish Accor chain firmly aimed at the business market that provides 116 suites, or 'flexible living spaces' in marketing speak, complete with bed, bath, desk, mini kitchen (kettle, microwave, fridge, sink) and suitebox – basically an all-in-one multimedia package with internet, unlimited landline calls within France, TV, music and films on demand, and computer games. Breakfast is a DIY affair, and there's also a small outdoor pool on site. The location is the only downer if you're not on business, at the river end of the vast Antigone business park and a good 15-minute walk to the centre of town or a tram stop away – but that's assuming you can ever tear yourself away from your multimedia experience.

Factfile

When to go

Montpellier is a big university town, with students making up a large part of the population, so it's busiest during term time. Weather-wise, the climate is mild all year round, although it can get oppressively hot during July and August. June to September sees the city's biggest music and dance festivals take place.

Getting there

Montpellier airport (www.montpellier.aeroport.fr) is just a few kilometres from the city centre. To get to the centre from the airport, either catch a taxi or take the shuttle bus (line 120) to the centre. Easyjet flies to Montpellier from London Gatwick, Ryanair has flights from London Stansted. Montpellier is easily accessible by train from Paris (and therefore from the UK via Eurostar). There are approx 15 trains a day, and the journey takes just over three hours. The bus station is located right next to the train station.

Getting around

The centre of Montpellier is pretty compact, so walking is the best way to explore most of the sights, from Antigone all the way up the hill through the old town to the Arc de Triomphe. In fact, much of the city centre is pedestrianised. The city also has two very efficient tram lines to access outlying areas, such as Odysseum. Vélomagg, the city's excellent municipal bike hire scheme, has 50 *stations* in and around Montpellier, and bikes cost just €2 a day to hire. The city has an extensive network of cycle paths, often separated from traffic for added safety. There is also a bike path running all the way to the beaches at Palavas-les-Flots and Carnon. The ride from the city centre to the beach takes about an hour.

Tourist information

Tourist office Pl de la Comédie (04.67.60.60.60/ www.ot-montpellier.fr). Open 9am-6.30pm Mon-Wed, Fri; 10am-6.30pm Thur; 10am-6pm Sat; 10am-1pm, 2-5pm Sun.

Internet access

Café Bibal 4 rue Jacques Coeur (04.67.60.61.42/www.cafes-bibal.fr). Open 8.30am-7pm Mon; 7.30am-7pm Tue-Sat.

Clockwise from top left: Promenade des Anglais; Cours Saleya; New Town.

Nice

This belle époque darling still rules the Riviera.

Roman Abramovich drops anchor off the Cap de Nice, Angelina and Brad's twins were introduced to the world in a hospital on the Promenade and Elton John lords it over the Baie des Anges, installed in his pad atop Mont Alban. Long the perennial favourite of pampered aristocrats, these days the French Riviera reeks of celebrity status with more than a whiff of crude new money. Yet while visitors flock here from every corner of the globe, Nice itself – less glossy than its counterparts along the Côte d'Azur – remains remarkably unfazed by all the attention.

Wealthy British travellers seeking mild winters stumbled upon this obscure seaside village during the early 19th century. In 1822, they raised funds for the building of the seafront promenade, with smart hotels springing up to cater to the demand. Queen Victoria graced the city with her presence during the 1890s. Three decades later, the exclusively first-class Train Bleu ferreted an affluent slipstream of travellers from Calais to Nice. With artists and socialites digging in year round, Nice's role on the international stage was assured.

Nice was part of the Kingdom of Savoy until 1860, when a fiddled local vote cast the region's lot in with Gallic fortunes. In stark contrast to the rest of the country, Italian tastes have played a heavy hand in Nice's art and architecture. The Old Town's ochre-hued buildings, pretty churches and gallery-filled alleys are almost indistinguishable from those peppering town centres across the border, 40 kilometres (25 miles) to the east. The foundations of Niçois cuisine – summer vegetables, olive oil, wild herbs – are more pan-Mediterranean than Picardy.

The promenade des Anglais is the city's star. Europe's glitterati, from Isadora Duncan to The Beatles, have strutted their stuff on this seaside esplanade. Curving between the Old Town and a turquoise bay, it's crowned by the flamboyant Hôtel Negresco and flanked with sun-drenched palm trees. Base yourself nearby and you'll find everything you need a few steps away. The intrepid visitor would do better, however, to cast an eye a little further. Part of what makes Nice so likeable is that it's a working city. Dive into the clamour of the Old Town's back streets, shop at the Marché de la Libération north of the train station or explore Cimiez's belle époque neighbourhood behind boulevard Carabacel.

Explore

The city's neighbourhoods range from the lively Vieux Nice, between the Baie des Anges and orderly New Town, to the Vieux Port, teeming with glitzy yachts and traditional wooden fishing boats year round. West of the Old Town, the seafront quai des Etats-Unis segues into the promenade des Anglais, 19th-century Nice's most famous landmark. Hilltop Cimiez, founded by Romans, lies inland, a bus ride north of the city centre.

VIEUX NICE

Faded, pastel-painted buildings line the Old Town's labyrinthine alleys, opening up into café-filled squares. Its heart lies just back from the seafront, along cours Saleya, this ancient quarter's main drag and home of its morning market. Marking the Old Town's northern boundary is the elegantly arcaded place Garibaldi, laid out in the 18th century and later named in honour of the hero of Italian unification, born nearby in 1807.

Cathédrale de Ste-Réparate

Pl Rossetti (04.93.62.34.40). Open 8.30am-noon, 2-6pm daily. Admission free.
With its stucco façade and ceramic-tiled dome, this 17th-century cathedral dominates the Old Town. It's named after Saint Réparate, the city's patron saint. The decapitated body of this 15-year-old girl, martyred in the Holy Land in 250 AD, washed up in the Baie des Anges in a flower-laden boat.

Colline du Château

Open June-Aug 9am-8pm daily. Apr-May, Sept 9am-7pm daily. Oct-Mar 10am-5.30pm daily. Admission free.
East of the Old Town looms the Colline du Château, a craggy, pine-shaded hill and park. Two ancient cemeteries occupy its northern reaches; one Christian, one Jewish. The park itself is a tranquil spot to escape the Old Town's tourist crush, with terrific views across the bay. Steps ascend from rue du Château or rue Ste-Claire, but if you don't fancy the slog, there's a lift (8am-6pm daily, €1.10) by the 19th-century Tour Bellanda.

Palais Lascaris

15 rue Droite (04.93.62.05.54). Open 10am-6pm Mon, Wed-Sun. Admission free.
Exhibits at this magnificent Genoese-style villa include an 18th-century pharmacy, preserved in its entirety, as well as a collection of antique musical instruments. Simply wandering through the still, dimly lit second-floor rooms is a delight, as ornate Baroque furniture, heavy Flemish tapestries and frescoed mythological scenes evoke the gilded opulence of the villa's heyday.

VIEUX PORT

Following the curve of quai Rauba Capeu from the promenade des Anglais takes you past the imposing War Memorial on place Guynemar. Keep walking around the headland to reach the Vieux Port. Lined with tall, multicoloured houses, it has plenty of cafés where you can watch ferries leaving for Corsica or snack on *pan bagnat* (a local classic that's effectively salade niçoise in a bun).

Nice

Historic sites
● ● ● ● ●

Art & architecture
● ● ● ● ●

Hotels
● ● ● ● ●

Eating & drinking
● ● ● ● ●

Nightlife
● ● ● ● ●

Shopping
● ● ● ● ●

PROMENADE DES ANGLAIS & THE BEACHES

A chaotic parade of in-line skaters, joggers, street performers and sun-worshippers, the promenade des Anglais is busy from dawn until dusk, when families dawdle over last ice-creams and couples watch the sun setting over the bay. The promenade is lined with grandiose belle époque and art deco palaces, including the domed Hôtel Negresco and the Musée Masséna. The beach below is a broad expanse of sun-bleached pebbles, curving around the bay. While stretches are open to anyone, the rest is carved up into private beaches, where you'll pay €10 to €15 for a sun lounger for the day.

Musée Masséna

65 rue de France/35 promenade des Anglais (04.93.91.19.10). Open 10am-6pm Mon, Wed-Sun. Admission free.

Reopened in 2008 after a massive renovation operation, the Musée Masséna occupies a sumptuous late 19th-century Italianate villa, built as a winter residence for the aristocratic Victor Masséna. Elaborate mosaics and friezes, ornate carvings and marble pillars evoke its owner's life of moneyed ease in a series of carefully restored rooms. Upstairs, exhibits and paintings recount Nice's colourful history, with particular emphasis on the early 20th century; all signs are in French.

THE NEW TOWN

Laid out in the 18th and 19th centuries, the New Town's orderly grid of streets and stuccoed apartments seem a world away from the crowded alleys of Nice's old quarters. In reality, it's just a hop, skip and jump across the Jardins Albert 1er and place Masséna – crossing the city's sleek new tramline as you go.

Cathédrale St-Nicolas (Eglise Russe)

Av Nicolas II (04.93.96.88.02/www.acor-nice.com). Open May-Sept 9am-noon, 2.30-6pm daily. Oct-Apr 9.30am-noon, 2.30-5pm daily. Admission €3; free under-12s. No credit cards.

Built between 1903 and 1912, this beautiful pink and grey marble and brick and tile Russian Orthodox cathedral is Nice's most visited venue. The five brilliantly hued onion-dome cupolas are a wonderfully incongruous addition to the city's skyline; inside, the visual feast continues with various intricate carvings and frescoes, and a marvellous iconostasis. Note that a strict dress code bans shorts, short skirts and T-shirts.

MAMAC (Musée d'Art Moderne et d'Art Contemporain)

Promenade des Arts (04.97.13.42.01/www.mamac-nice.org). Open 10am-6pm Tue-Sun. Admission free.

In the early 1960s, Nice became a cutting-edge artistic hub, thanks to the impetus of New Realists Yves Klein and Arman. This colossus of a museum is devoted to European and American art from the 1960s onwards,

with particular emphasis on the Nice School, including pieces by Venet, César and Ben, as well as a room full of Niki de Saint Phalle's flamboyant works. The roof terrace, dotted with Klein's minimalist sculptures, offers panoramic views of the city.

Musée des Arts Asiatiques

405 promenade des Anglais (04.92.29.37.00/ www.arts-asiatiques.com). Open May-mid Oct 10am-6pm Mon, Wed-Sun. Mid Oct-Apr 10am-5pm Mon, Wed-Sun. Admission free.

Influential Japanese architect Kenzo Tange designed this coolly minimalist white marble and glass structure, whose select collection of rare pieces ranges from a 12th-century Japanese Buddha to the latest in Asian high-tech design. Don't miss the tea ceremonies under the gingko trees (3pm Sun, €10; for reservations call 04.92.29.37.02).

Musée des Beaux-Arts

33 av des Baumettes (04.92.15.28.28/www.musee-beaux-arts-nice.org). Open 10am-6pm Tue-Sun. Admission free.

A steep climb up avenue des Baumettes, this picturesque museum is housed in a grand, Genoese-style villa, built for a Ukrainian princess in 1878. In summer 2007, its impressive collection of 15th- to early 20th-century art made it a target for thieves who escaped with works by Monet, Brueghel and Sisley. Still left are pieces by Raoul Dufy, Pierre Bonnard and Jules Cheret. Lesser-known Niçois symbolist Gustav-Adolf Mossa's watercolours are not to be missed; scenes of death and corruption, presided over by languid, darkly erotic sirens.

Villa Arson

20 av Stephen Liégeard (04.92.07.73.73/www.villa-arson.org). Open July-Aug 2-7pm Mon, Wed-Sun. Sept-June 2-6pm Mon, Wed-Sun. Admission free.

Set in sprawling parkland, 18th-century villa Villa Arson is at the cutting edge of avant-garde art, and one of the few places in Nice to hold refreshingly contemporary shows. As well as the exhibition space, there's an art school on site: after looking round, you can listen to heated discussions in the café (closed Aug & Sept).

CIMIEZ

Perched on a hillside to the north of the city centre, lofty Cimiez is Nice's most affluent neighbourhood, swathed in large villas, Roman ruins and sweeping belle époque apartments. The walk from Vieux Nice or place Masséna takes half an hour; alternatively, take bus no.15 from place Masséna towards Cimiez.

Musée Archéologique de Nice-Cimiez

160 av des Arènes (04.93.81.59.57/www.musee-archeologique-nice.org). Open 10am-6pm Mon, Wed-Sun. Admission free. No credit cards.

This smart archaeological museum charts Nice's history from 1100 BC up to the Middle Ages through an impressive array of ceramics, sculpture, jewellery and tools. Outside are the first- to fourth-century remains of the Roman city of

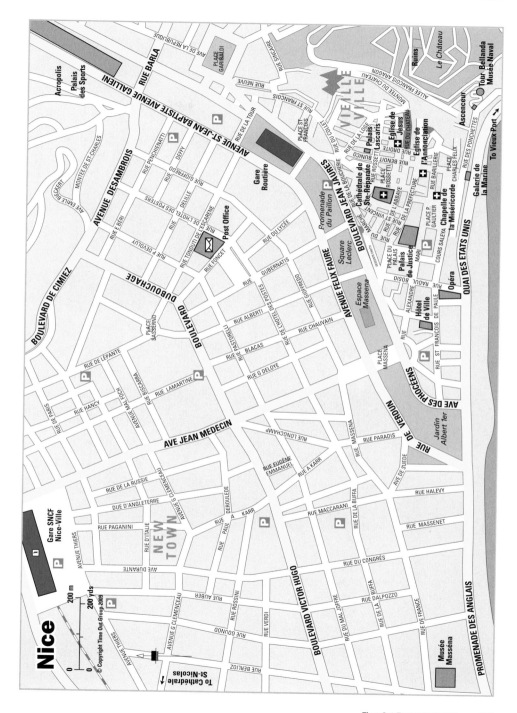

Nice

Get the local experience

Over 50 of the world's top destinations available.

Cemenelum, with vestiges of the public baths, paved streets and a 4,000-seat amphitheatre – now used as a venue during the Nice Jazz Festival.

Musée Matisse

164 av des Arènes (04.93.81.08.08/www.musee-matisse-nice.org). Open 10am-6pm Mon, Wed-Sun. Admission free.

This 17th-century Italianate villa (and its modern extension) houses a collection of Henri Matisse's work, including paintings, drawings, engravings and sculptures. The long-time Riviera resident credited his stylistic development to the French Riviera's unique light: from dark, brooding early works through to the famed colourful paper cut-outs, they're all on display.

Musée National Message Biblique Marc Chagall

Av du Dr Ménard (04.93.53.87.20/www.musee-chagall.fr). Open May-Oct 10am-6pm Mon, Wed-Sun. Nov-Apr 10am-5pm Mon, Wed-Sun. Admission €6.50-€8.50; free-€6.50 reductions.

Designed by the artist himself in co-operation with the Niçois municipality, the Musée Chagall displays a complete set of canvases interpreting episodes from the Old Testament, notably the Song of Songs. Chagall provided mosaics, sketches and stained glass for the gallery, which also hosts temporary exhibitions and small-scale acoustic concerts in its lovely amphitheatre.

Eat

Along the Côte d'Azur heavy sauces are a rarity. In this coastal region, meat was long considered a luxury and is still frequently used in small quantities, stuffing local delights like *petits farcis*, rather than acting as the star itself. Expect plenty of fresh summer vegetables, especially tomatoes, aubergines and courgettes, as well as garlic and olive oil, fresh cheeses and fish.

Au Petit Gari

Vieux Nice *2 pl Garibaldi (04.93.26.89.09/www.aupetitgari.com). Open noon-2pm, 7-10pm Mon-Fri. €€.*

Restaurants huddle beneath the arches in place Garibaldi, but this sweetly old-fashioned bistro is the ace in the pack. You can't go wrong with the lunchtime *plat du jour*, served up at one of the ten or so tables. A mere €13, with a glass of wine and a coffee thrown in, it might be anything from a piled-high plate of mussels to fresh fish. Regulars still remember the glorious day when truffle-stuffed chicken breast was served.

Le Bistrot d'Antoine

Vieux Nice *27 rue de la Préfecture (04.93.85.29.57). Open noon-2pm, 8-10pm daily. €€.*

Tucked in as it is among a *tabac*, clothing store and scores of mediocre restaurants, it's no surprise that most tourists give Bistrot d'Antoine a miss. But how much they are

missing. Succulent grilled meats such as *magret de canard*, lentils with *saucisson* and the occasional pasta dish provide a perfect foil for wines selected from small producers and sold at reasonable prices, starting at around €13 a bottle. Note that this spot is a meat-lover's paradise; veggie dishes are outstanding but the chalkboard menu rarely includes more than one.

Le Chantecler

Promenade *Hôtel Negresco, 37 promenade des Anglais (04.93.16.64.00). Open 12.30-2pm, 7.30-10pm Wed-Sat. Closed Jan. €€€€.*

For those longing to bask among ornate tapestries and a slew of 16th-century antiques, the Negresco's classy restaurant is the only place to dine. Having taken the helm in this Michelin-starred kitchen, young wonderchef Jean-Denis Rieubland has introduced some modern touches to its menu. The foie gras is served with pineapple, pomegranate jelly and chutney, for example, with hazelnut- and mushroom-stuffed sole to follow. Go at lunchtime for the bargain €50 *menu plaisir* – an outstanding three-course sampler of Rieubland's latest creations.

Fenocchio

Vieux Nice *2 pl Rossetti (04.93.80.72.52/www.fenocchio.fr). Open 9am-midnight daily. Closed Dec & Jan. €*

The legendary Fenocchio ice-cream parlour, which has been open since 1966 on place Rossetti, offers no fewer than 90 different flavours, making for much last-minute indecision as you near the front of the queue. There are 59 ice-creams and 35 sorbets to choose from, with avocado, black olive, thyme, rosemary and chewing gum among the more *outré* scoops.

Le Grand Café de Turin

Vieux Nice *5 pl Garibaldi (04.93.62.29.52/www.cafedeturin.com). Open 8am-11pm Mon, Tue, Thur-Sun. €€€.*

At the northern tip of the Old Town, this classic seafood brasserie rounds the corner under the colonnades of place Garibaldi, where it expanded in 2008 to include an additional two rooms. Since its opening 100 years ago, Café de Turin has been jammed with locals slurping oysters and devouring towering plates of mussels, langoustine, crab and sea urchins. Service can be testy, but the atmosphere is the real thing.

Keisuke Matsushima

New Town *22ter rue de France (04.93.82.26.06/www.keisukematsushima.com). Open 7.30-10pm Mon, Sat; noon-2pm, 7.30-10pm Tue-Fri. €€€€.*

One of the most respected chefs in town, Japanese-born Kei Matsushima is going from strength to Michelin-starred strength. His minimalist dining room is a mecca for gastronomes and expense-accounters, while the Mediterranean cuisine combines innovative flavours with artful presentation: try the wild turbot, served with fava beans, squid, rocket and tapenade. At lunchtime, Kei offers a weekly menu for €35; if you're feeling brave, splash out on the surprise tasting menu (€100) instead.

Top: Cours Saleya market.
Bottom: Cathédrale St-Nicolas.

Lou Pistou

Vieux Nice *4A rue Raoul Bosio (04.93.62.21.82).
Open noon-2pm, 7-10pm Mon-Fri. €€.*
With its sweet lace curtains, diminutive premises and
strictly regional menu, Lou Pistou is a splendid place
to sample local recipes: *farcis niçois*, perhaps, or *tripes à
la niçoise* with chunky strips of deep-fried chickpea *panisse*.
Next door is the equally good – and equally small –
La Merenda.

La Merenda

Vieux Nice *4B rue Raoul Bosio (no phone). Open
noon-2pm, 7-10pm Mon-Fri. Closed 3wks Aug.
No credit cards. €€.*
Shoebox-sized and invariably packed, the legendary La
Merenda has just two rows of tables and a barrage of tiny
stools. If you come alone, expect to share: the focus here is
on the food, not the seating plan. For months, chef
Dominique Le Stanc (previously at the Negresco's Michelin-
starred Le Chantecler) trained up with the bistro's original
owners, mastering (and later exceeding) the ultimate version
of every Niçois classic. Try the slowly stewed *daube de
boeuf*, *petits farcis* (stuffed vegetables) or perfect little pizzas.
To reserve, stop by in person.

La Part des Anges

New Town *17 rue Gubernatis (04.93.62.69.80). Open
noon-8pm Mon-Thur; noon-2pm, 7-10pm Fri, Sat. €€.*
Part shop, part wine bar, La Part des Anges puts many of
the country's best natural wine producers on display: look
for names such as Gramenon, Breton, Richaud and Lapierre.
Take advantage of the lack of corkage fee to indulge in an
exceptional bottle of Burgundy, or try something more
unusual such as vin de pays from the Ardèche; at
lunchtimes and on Friday and Saturday nights you can
nibble on cheese and charcuterie or choose from a handful
of delicious hot dishes.

Les Pêcheurs

Vieux Port *18 quai des Docks (04.93.89.59.61/
www.lespecheurs.com). Open Apr-Sept 12.15-2.15pm,
7.15-10.15pm Mon, Tue, Fri-Sun; 7.15-10.15pm Thur.
Oct-Mar 12.15-2.15pm, 7.15-10.15pm Wed-Sun. €€€.*
You'll find all the usual Mediterranean seafood (sardines,
octopus, sea bream) at this accomplished portside brasserie,
but often with an Asian or Creole touch – prawns are
fried with ginger and lemongrass and served with curry-
spiked courgette purée; tuna is seared in a sesame crust.
Fish soup, a Niçois classic, is prepared with just the right
mix of rockfish and plenty of saffron. The spacious
west-facing terrace makes Les Pêcheurs a sunny pick for a
leisurely Sunday lunch.

L'Univers de Christian Plumail

Vieux Nice *54 bd Jean Jaurès (04.93.62.32.22/
www.christian-plumail.com). Open noon-2pm,
7.30-10pm Mon-Fri; 7.30-10pm Sat. €€€€.*
This smart Old Town address remains a destination dining
spot, thanks to renowned Niçois chef Christian Plumail. His
simple but beautifully executed Mediterranean cuisine has
won him a Michelin star. Try the sardine tempura served

with a salad of violet artichokes, or foie gras cappuccino
and woodland mushrooms; there's also a cracking wine list.
Those on a budget can still sample the cellar's finest: for an
extra €5, add a glass of red, rosé or white to the affordable
lunchtime menu (two courses for €22).

20/Vin

New Town *18bis rue Biscarra (04.93.92.93.20/
www.restaurant-20survin.com). Open noon-2.30pm,
7-10.30pm Mon-Sat. €€.*
This knowledgeably staffed *bistro à vins* with a terrace
is on a semi-pedestrianised street in the New Town. Wines
are stored in a temperature-controlled 'cellar' in the back
of the dining room, which you can visit with the sommelier
to select your bottle. Organic wines are available, as are
an excellent selection of wines by the glass. The menu
changes with the seasons – if you can, make sure you try
the boned sea bream, stuffed with a mix of courgettes and
sun-dried tomatoes.

La Zucca Magica

Vieux Port *4bis quai Papacino (04.93.56.25.27/
www.lazuccamagica.com). Open noon-2.45pm,
7pm-midnight Tue-Sat. No credit cards. €€.*
Pumpkin plays a starring role on the menu – and in the
eccentric decor – at this portside vegetarian restaurant. The
Piedmontese chef serves up a no-choice five-course menu
(lunch €17, dinner €27), along with a choice of three house
wines; one white, one red, one rosé. Dishes are seasonal, and
include a mix of Italian and French influenced recipes:
ricotta and baby spinach in a clear, truffle-infused soup, or
saffron rice wrapped in beet leaves. Italian cheeses do
generally feature heavily, so make sure you arrive hungry.

Shop

The city's main shopping street is named after
former mayor Jean Médecin (father of long-time
mayor Jacques, who ended up fleeing a trail of
shady financial shenanigans to Uruguay). Major
chains (department store Galeries Lafayette,
book and record shop Fnac et al) are all present
here, along with the multi-level Etoile shopping
mall. Luxury labels congregate in the nearby
zone piétonne, a pedestrianised shopping area
that covers rue Paradis, avenue de Suède and
avenue de Verdun. In general, if you're a diehard
shopper, Nice won't fulfil your wildest dreams.
That said, there are plenty of markets and
speciality food shops that sell directly from
producers and at a fraction of the price abroad.

Bellet wines

8km (5 miles) NW of Nice *(www.vinsdebellet.com).*
On the western side of town, the pretty little vineyard
enclave of Bellet, France's smallest AOC (appellation
d'origine contrôlée), lies on the steep slopes in the alpine
foothills, and is easily explored in a morning trip. Made
from little-known grape varieties such as folle noire

and braquet, Bellet's rosés and reds are quite hard to find outside this local area. A trio of producers worth hunting down are Château de Crémat (442 chemin de Crémat, 04.92.15.12.15, www.chateau-cremat.com), Château de Bellet (chemin de Saquier, Les Séoules, 04.93.37.81.57) and Clos Saint Vincent (collet des Fourniers, 04.92.15.12.69, www.clos-st-vincent.fr). Almost all of Nice's wine shops stock wines from Bellet producers: try the long-established Cave Bianchi (7 rue Raul Bosio, 04.93.85.65.79).

Cours Saleya market
Vieux Nice *Cours Saleya. Open 7.30am-12.30pm, vegetables & flowers Tue-Sun, antiques & brocante Mon.*
Cut flowers perfume the air, and fruit and vegetable stalls operate from dawn until lunchtime every day except Monday; head to place Gautier, in the centre, to purchase primarily organic produce (it's an ideal supply spot for picnics on the beach) directly from local farmers. On Mondays, *brocanteurs* take over, selling a jumble of antiques, junk and second-hand clothes.

Marché de la Libération
New Town *Av Malaussena, bd Joseph Garnier. Open 7.30am-12.30pm Tue-Sun.*
North of the train station and centred on place du Général de Gaulle is the Marché de la Libération, its stalls piled high with courgette flowers, yellow-fleshed peaches and Cavaillon melons. It's more down-to-earth than cours Saleya, and locals with tartan wheelie shoppers far outnumber snap-happy tourists.

Oliviera
Vieux Nice *8bis rue du Collet (04.93.13.06.45/ www.oliviera.com). Open 12.30-9.30pm Tue-Sat; 12.30-2.30pm Sun.*
Much loved by local foodies, Nadim Beyrouti's shop and restaurant is lined with gleaming vats of local olive oil. A tiny kitchen at the back serves up freshly made dishes at mealtimes; Nadim douses each one liberally with an olive oil to match. Feel free to try before you buy – bottles are carefully corked and swathed in bubble wrap for your journey home.

Arts

For music and theatre listings, buy the weekly French-language *Semaine des Spectacles* or pick up *Le Pitchoun*, a free French-language guide to what's on.

Cinémathèque de Nice
New Town *3 esplanade Kennedy (04.92.04.06.66/ www.cinematheque-nice.com). Open times vary. Tickets €2; €18 10-film pass. No credit cards.*
Located in a side entrance of the Acropolis centre, Nice's *cinémathèque* puts on an international selection of classic films and recent releases, all screened in the *version originale* with French subtitles. Recent programmes have been

dedicated to such Hollywood greats as Alfred Hitchcock, Audrey Hepburn and Woody Allen. A membership card (€1) is necessary to attend screenings.

Opéra de Nice
Vieux Nice *4-6 rue St-François-de-Paule (04.92.17.40.00/www.opera-nice.org). Open Box office 9am-6pm Mon-Thur; 9am-8pm Fri; 9am-5pm Sat. Tickets €8-€85.*
This 19th-century gem of an opera house, on the edge of Vieux Nice, is decked out in sumptuous red velvet, with crystal chandeliers and lashings of gilt. First-rate visiting artists perform symphonies and ballet as well as opera. There's also an 'Opera Junior' programme, with 50-minute operatic performances targeted at a younger audience. On a budget? Matinée tickets are a steal at €5 each.

Théâtre National de Nice
New Town *Promenade des Arts (04.93.13.90.90/ www.tnn.fr). Open Box office 2-7pm Tue-Sat. Tickets Grande Salle €7.50-€30. Petite Salle €16-€20.*
If your French is up to scratch, the Théâtre National de Nice stages some high-profile productions of both French and foreign classics (in French), along with a robust programme of contemporary drama. Built in 1989, it's next to MAMAC on the promenade des Arts and mirrors the former's octagonal shape.

Nightlife

Le Bar des Oiseaux
Vieux Nice *5 rue St-Vincent (04.93.80.27.33/ www.bardesoiseaux.com). Open noon-2pm Mon; noon-2pm, 7.30-11pm Tue-Fri; 7.30-11pm Sat.*
The Bar des Oiseaux, just behind rue de la Préfecture, is the Old Town's only restaurant-bar-theatre combo and has been serving up heaps of local atmosphere since 1961. The venue is packed from evening onwards; there are live bands, snippets of theatre and comic sketches (in French).

Bliss Bar
Vieux Nice *12 rue de l'Abbaye (04.93.16.82.38/ www.myspace.com/blissbar06). Open 8pm-2am Tue-Sat.*
A large but amiable doorman selects who steps through the sliding glass doors at this sleekly appointed bar; don't make the painful mistake of trying to saunter in before he's pressed the button. Inside, Nice's beautiful crowd quaff mojitos, flirt and party in air-conditioned comfort, while DJs spin funk and soul from Wednesday to Saturday.

Hi Beach
Promenade *47 promenade des Anglais (04.97.14.00.83/ www.hi-beach.net). Open 9am-midnight daily.*
Opened in summer 2008, Hi Hotel's beach bar and restaurant immediately became the place to be seen. The menu, masterminded by none other than Kei Matsushima (*see p157*), is on the pricey side, but the drinks aren't too steep – and it's a lovely spot to sip a caipirinha as the sun sets over the bay.

Hôtel Negresco.

Le Klub

New Town *6 rue Halevy (04.93.16.87.26/ www.leklub.net). Open midnight-5am Wed-Sun.*
The most popular gay nightspot in Nice, Le Klub throws open its doors to clubbers of all orientations. Its line-up of DJs is one of the best on the Riviera, mixing local talent with global big-hitters; look out, too, for quirky regular nights like the cabaret evening. Turning up between 11.30pm and midnight often gets you in for free.

Odace

New Town *29 rue Alphonse Karr (04.93.82.37.66/ www.odaceclub.com). Open 11pm-5am Tue-Sat.*
The sleek, oriental-inspired decor at Odace oozes opulence, and attracts a champagne-sipping clientele. There's a decent restaurant, but most people come here for the decadent party atmosphere that cooks up later on as DJs take to the decks. The upstairs Golden Club, with balconies overlooking the main dancefloor, is VIPs only.

Stay

Aside from high summer – and of course the Cannes Film Festival or Monaco Grand Prix – finding a hotel is Nice is hardly tricky. Rates taper off in winter, even though this working city does not. Beware of the business hotels advertised as 'five minutes from the Old Town' that offer tempting summer rates. Many are further out than they mention, meaning you'll fritter away any savings on taxi rides.

Hi Hôtel

New Town *3 av des Fleurs (04.97.07.26.26/ www.hi-hotel.net). €€€.*
With its experimental living spaces in jellybean colours, this place remains the funkiest place to stay in Nice. The tiny rooftop pool has a lovely view and there are DJ soirées in the funky gardens at weekends. Guests can pick from nine far-out concept rooms, including Indoor Terrasse (with a Balinese beach hut vibe), Rendezvous (with a bathtub in the middle of the room) and the slick White & White (complete with custom-made transformable four-poster bed-to-bathtub). Non-guests can drop into the Hi for breakfast, Saturday morning yoga or an indulgent massage session, as well as hitting the brand new Hi Beach (*see p160*).

Hôtel Beau Rivage

Vieux Nice *24 rue St-François-de-Paule (04.92.47.82.82/ www.nicebeaurivage.com). €€€€.*
Matisse began his 30-year love affair with Nice at the Beau Rivage in 1917, but he probably wouldn't recognise his former home in its sleek, modern reincarnation. Rooms are kitted out with neutral colour schemes, plasma TVs and crisp linen, along with light switches that can lead to confusion after one too many drinks from the minibar. The hotel also has its own cool beach club. Day passes (for guests and non-guests) are €17, including sunlounger,

umbrella and beach towel. The more indulgent can relax on the beach bar's deckchairs, where crisp Bandol rosé starts at €25 a bottle.

Hôtel Ellington

New Town *25 bd Dubouchage (04.92.47.79.79/ www.ellington-nice.com). €€€.*
An elegant newcomer on the city's hotel scene, the Hôtel Ellington opened at the end of 2006. Its lofty, chandelier-lit lobby and lounge evoke the glamour of a bygone age, while the bar is a stylish spot for a snifter. The well-equipped guestrooms are more modern in style (and less chic), and tend to be on the small side. A minute from Nice's tramway and avenue Jean Médecin, the leafy boulevard Dubouchage couldn't be more cocooned from the nearby high street buzz. Guests can also find solace on the Ellington's patio and Mediterranean courtyard garden.

Hôtel Negresco

Promenade *37 promenade des Anglais (04.93.16.64.00/ www.hotel-negresco-nice.com). €€€€.*
Nothing succeeds like excess, as this domed, pink and white icon proves. The sumptuous bedrooms and suites are a visual feast, with themes ranging from art deco to Louis XIV pomp, while public spaces are dotted with artworks from the owner's impressive private collection. The giant Baccarat crystal chandelier in the lobby was originally commissioned by Czar Nicholas II. He was sadly knocked off by the Bolsheviks before he could take delivery, and a sister copy still hangs in the Kremlin. A meal at the famed Chantecler (*see p157*) is a must, while the nightly piano sessions in Le Relais bar are best soaked up with a negroni in hand.

Hôtel du Petit Palais

Cimiez *17 av Emile Bieckiert (04.93.62.19.11/ www.petitpalaisnice.com). €€.*
Formerly the home of Russo-French actor and director Sacha Guitry, the belle époque Petit Palais has spacious rooms, panoramic views and plenty of character. Located amid the mansions of Cimiez, it's ideally stationed for those visitors who are keen to spend afternoons at the hilltop cluster of museums. Guestrooms are a 1970s Waldorf Astoria lookalike: club chairs, heavy wooden furniture, fine linen and carpets. Some have terraces that overlook Nice and the Mediterranean beyond, and are not much more pricey than those without. The hotel may be a steep walk from the centre of town, but the reward is glorious tranquillity: you're more likely to be woken by birdsong than urban bustle.

Hôtel Suisse

Vieux Nice *15 quai Rauba Capeu (04.92.17.39.00/ www.hotels-ocre-azur.com). €€.*
Standing on the headland of the Baie des Anges, where it basks in the late afternoon sun, the Hôtel Suisse is perfectly positioned for easy access to both the beach and Old Town. Its rooms are kitted out in a subtle, modern style; some are small-ish, but magnificent panoramas across the bay more than compensate. For those with a terrace, breakfasting outside is de rigueur. During the off-season, the hotel's rates

Top: Fenocchio. Bottom: Lou Pistou.

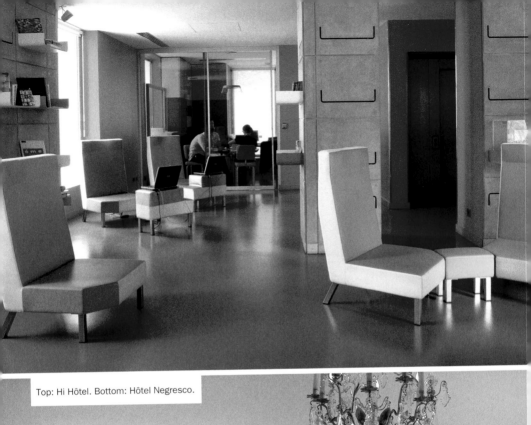

Top: Hi Hôtel. Bottom: Hôtel Negresco.

drop like a stone, although it's definitely worth spending the extra to secure a sea-facing room. Guests receive a concessionary rate for use of sunloungers and parasols at the Castel Plage beach club below.

Hôtel Windsor
New Town *11 rue Dalpozzo (04.93.88.59.35/ www.hotelwindsornice.com). €€.*
Unassuming on the outside, the Hôtel Windsor is a cult address for bohemian types. Avoid the cheaper 'standard' rooms and check into one of the 25 artist-decorated ones instead: from the stripped-down simplicity of Oliver Mosset's design to the primary-coloured scribbles of Niçois artist Ben. There's also a chic fitness suite complete with a hammam and sauna. Best of all is the walled tropical garden, a rarity in this bourgeois quarter of town. Bordered by jasmine and hibiscus is a swimming pool. It's not the biggest, but the overhanging palm tree adds a certain desert island feel.

Le Palais de la Méditerranée
Promenade *13-15 promenade des Anglais (04.92.14.77.00/www.concorde-hotels.com). €€€.*
The imposing Palais de la Méditerranée is another of the strip's architectural icons. Built by American millionaire Frank Jay Gould in 1929, it stood abandoned for two decades before it was shamefully gutted in the 1990s, preserving only its original art deco façade. The Palais was reborn as a luxury hotel and casino in 2004, and has been popular with high rollers ever since. The sea views are

extraordinary, as is the heated open-air pool on the third floor. Locally inspired haute cuisine comes courtesy of chef Philippe Thomas in the hotel's restaurant, Le Padouk.

Riviera Pebbles
(09.52.78.27.65, www.rivierapebbles.com). €€.
Dotted across the Riviera, the apartments on the books of this holiday lets company are a cut above the average – and there's a particularly chic cache in Nice. Properties range from gracious, antique-filled hideaways to sleek, architect-designed renovations with home cinema systems, custom-built showers and palatial kitchens; handily, you can book for one or two nights as well as longer lets. The pick of the bunch in Nice include Katja (a hip mix of ultra-modern design and flea market finds) and Vincent – an opulent Old Town pad that's equipped with every conceivable luxury, from built-in KEF wall speakers to a Philippe Starck bath.

Villa de la Tour
Vieux Nice *4 rue de la Tour (04.93.80.08.15/ www.villa-la-tour.com). €-€€.*
Small and perfectly formed, Villa de la Tour is just off the pedestrianised place Garibaldi; the airport bus, beach, cours Saleya and port are all five minutes away. It's a hike up several flights of stairs, but the 14 petite bedrooms are well worth it. Within a portion of an 18th-century convent, several of the rooms have a small balcony or view over the old town and all are welcome to use the rooftop garden. Best of all, the hotel is sheltered from the noise of the Old Town, despite being the only hotel actually inside it.

Factfile

When to go
May, June and September are the best months to visit Nice. Days are sunny and the sea is warm. During July and August, Vieux Nice and the promenade throng with tourists, and the crowds can be a little overwhelming. What little rain the region gets normaily arrives in March and October.

Getting there
Nice Airport is 8km (5 miles) west of the city centre, along the promenade des Anglais (08.20.42.33.33/www.nice.aeroport.fr). From here, Bus No.98 runs past Vieux Nice to the gare routière (bus station), while No.99 stops in the New Town and at the main SNCF station (every 20mins Mon-Sat, every 30mins Sun) (www.lignedazur.com; tickets €4; pay on bus). A taxi to the city centre will cost about €35.

Getting around
The main SNCF railway station (3 av Thiers, www.sncf.com) is served by frequent trains from Paris and Marseille. Local services to Menton also stop at Gare Riquier, north of the port. The

Gare St-Augustin station is near the airport. The private Gare de Provence (4bis rue Alfred Binet, 04.97.03.80.80), just north of the main station, is the departure point for the narrow-gauge Train des Pignes, which heads into the Alps.

The A8 connects Nice with Aix-en-Provence to the west and the Italian border to the east. You can take exits 50 (promenade des Anglais) or 55 (Nice east, to the port), but for visiting nearby towns it's more scenic to drive the D6098 (basse corniche) along the coast (though expect traffic jams in summer and during rush hour).

Tourist information
Tourist office 5 promenade des Anglais (08.92.70.74.07/www.nicetourisme.com). Open 8am-8pm Mon-Sat; 9am-7pm Sun. Office de Tourisme Gare SNCF, av Thiers (04.93.87.07.07). Open June-Sept 8am-8pm Mon-Sat; 9am-7pm Sun. Oct-May 8am-7pm Mon-Sat; 10am-5pm Sun.

Internet access
Email Café 8 rue St-Vincent (04.93.62.68.86). Open 10am-7pm Mon, Sun; 7.30am-7pm Tue-Sat.

Clockwise from top:
Cimetière de Montmartre;
Cathédrale Notre-Dame;
Jardin du Luxembourg;
Arc de Triomphe.

Paris

A city where flânerie will get you everywhere.

No city in the world has the same weight of fable and history as Paris, much less the same wealth and complexity of association and influence. Royal and republican, religious and secular, French and foreign, artistic and monumental – Paris has lived up to all these contradictions. Although it's older than Christianity, it's a city with a forward-thinking administration that crafts 21st-century urban refinements, which are subsequently copied across Europe and beyond. And it's the capital of a country that regards it with jealousy and disdain, whose residents are supposed to be standoffish with outsiders – especially those who don't speak the lingo.

You only have to look at any view of the city painted in the 17th century to realise, with a pleasurable shock, that Paris is a city of no fixed abode. Three centuries ago, nearly all its roofs were terracotta, as though it were in Provence. And you need only explore the multi-ethnic north-eastern quarters to see that its population is as changeable as its fabric. Paris is fascinating not because it's so reassuringly itself. Rather, Paris is dizzyingly exciting because it's a city you can never really know.

The best way to approach Paris is with a blend of open-mindedness and scepticism; a blend that, as it happens, is one of the many admirable characteristics of Parisians themselves. The periphery is not necessarily more 'authentic' than the main attractions, and there's much of interest hidden in plain view – above second-storey level, say, where hundreds of stone faces watch passers-by with rarely an answering gaze. When you visit the famous sights and museums, more numerous and better all the time, try to do so early in the morning – or, if they open late, at the end of the day. Get out of the centre. Explore on foot as much as you can. Go out after midnight, or set the alarm clock and depart at dawn. And finally, speak to the locals in their own language, even if it's just a couple of words. Not the least unfamiliar thing about Paris is how easily defrosted most Parisians are.

Explore

Neatly contained within the Périphérique ring road and divided by the Seine, Paris is a compact city. The city's 20 *arrondissements* (districts) spiral out, clockwise and in ascending order, from the Louvre.

THE SEINE & ISLANDS

The Seine is at its best in summer. Port de Javel and Jardin Tino-Rossi become open-air dancehalls; and there's the jamboree of Paris-Plage, Mayor Delanoë's city beach that brings sand, palm trees, loungers and entertainment to both sides of the river. Come on Sundays, and stretches of roads will be closed for the benefit of cyclists and rollerskaters. And, of course, there's a wealth of boat tours.

The Ile de la Cité is where Paris was born around 250 BC, when the Parisii, a tribe of Celtic Gauls, founded a settlement on this convenient bridging point of the Seine. Perhaps the most charming spot on the island is the western tip, where Pont Neuf spans the Seine. Despite its name, it is in fact the oldest bridge in Paris. In the centre of the bridge is an equestrian statue of Henri IV; the original went up in 1635, was melted down to make cannons during the Revolution, and replaced in 1818.

The Ile St-Louis is one of the most exclusive residential addresses in the city. Delightfully unspoiled, it has fine architecture, narrow streets and pretty views from the tree-lined quays, and still retains the air of a tranquil backwater. Rue St-Louis-en-l'Ile – lined with fine historic buildings that now house gift shops and gourmet food stores, quaint tearooms, stone-walled bars, restaurants and hotels – runs the length of the island. At the western end there are great views of the flying buttresses of Notre-Dame.

Cathédrale Notre-Dame de Paris

Pl du Parvis-Notre-Dame, 4th (01.42.34.56.10/ www.cathedraledeparis.com). Open 8am-6.45pm Mon-Fri; 8am-7.15pm Sat, Sun. Towers Apr-Sept 10am-6.30pm daily (June, Aug until 11pm Sat, Sun). Oct-Mar 10am-5.30pm daily. Admission free. Towers €7.50; free-€4.80 reductions.

Notre-Dame was constructed between 1163 and 1334, and the amount of time and money spent on it reflected the city's growing prestige. The west front remains a high point of Gothic art for the balanced proportions of its twin towers and rose window, and the three doorways with their rows of saints and sculpted tympanums: the *Last Judgement* (centre), *Life of the Virgin* (left) and *Life of St Anne* (right). Inside, take a moment to admire the long nave with its solid foliate capitals and high altar with a marble *Pietà* by Coustou. To truly appreciate the masonry, climb up the towers. The route runs up the north tower and down the south. Between the two you get a close-up view of the gallery of chimeras – the fantastic birds and hybrid beasts designed by Viollet-le-Duc along the balustrade. After a detour to see the Bourdon (the massive bell), a staircase leads to the top of the south tower.

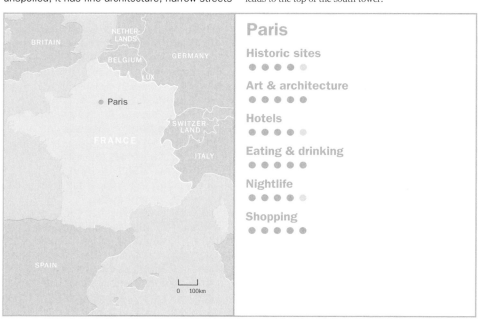

Paris

Historic sites
● ● ● ● ○

Art & architecture
● ● ● ● ●

Hotels
● ● ● ● ○

Eating & drinking
● ● ● ● ●

Nightlife
● ● ● ● ○

Shopping
● ● ● ● ●

BRITAIN NETHER-LANDS BELGIUM GERMANY LUX
● Paris SWITZER-LAND FRANCE ITALY SPAIN

0   100km

Top: Cathédrale
Notre-Dame. Bottom:
Les Catacombes;
La Goutte d'Or.

120 ans et toujours dans le vent !

MOULIN ROUGE

Discover Féerie, the Show of the Most Famous Cabaret in the World !

Dinner & Show at 7pm from €150 • Show at 9pm : €102, 11pm : €92

Montmartre - 82, boulevard de Clichy - 75018 Paris
Reservations : 33 (0)1 53 09 82 82 • www.moulin-rouge.com

La Conciergerie

2 bd du Palais, 1st (01.53.40.60.80). Open Mar-Oct 9.30am-6pm daily. Nov-Feb 9am-5pm daily. Admission €6.50; free-€4.50 reductions.

The Conciergerie looks every inch the forbidding medieval fortress. However, much of the façade was added in the 1850s, long after Marie-Antoinette, Danton and Robespierre had been imprisoned here. The visit takes you through the Salle des Gardes, the medieval kitchens with their four huge chimneys, and the Salle des Gens d'Armes, an impressive vaulted Gothic hall built between 1301 and 1315 for Philippe 'le Bel'. After the royals moved to the Louvre, the fortress became a prison under the watch of the Concierge. The wealthy had private cells with their own furniture, which they paid for; others made do on beds of straw. A list of Revolutionary prisoners, including a hairdresser, shows that not all victims were nobles. In Marie-Antoinette's cell, the Chapelle des Girondins, are her crucifix, some portraits and a guillotine blade.

Sainte-Chapelle

6 bd du Palais, 1st (01.53.40.60.97). Open Mar-Oct 9.30am-6pm daily. Nov-Feb 9am-5pm daily. Admission €7.50; free-€4.80 reductions.

Devout King Louis IX (St Louis, 1226-70) had a hobby of accumulating holy relics (and children: he fathered 11). In the 1240s he bought what was advertised as the Crown of Thorns, and ordered Pierre de Montreuil to design a suitable shrine. The result was the exquisite Flamboyant Gothic Sainte-Chapelle. With 15m (49ft) windows, the upper level, intended for the royal family and the canons, appears to consist almost entirely of stained glass. The windows depict hundreds of scenes from the Old and New Testaments, culminating with the Apocalypse in the rose window.

OPERA TO LES HALLES

The swathe of the Right Bank between the Grands Boulevards and the Seine is, and has been for centuries, a commercial powerhouse. The two stock exchanges and the Banque de France are here, and so was the city's wholesale food market – until 1969, when it moved from Les Halles to the suburbs. For many observers, French and foreign, the soulless shopping centre that took its place was no compensation for the loss of local colour and tradition that the market sellers had built up over centuries.

A short distance west of Les Halles is the Louvre, no longer the centre of French power though it still exerts considerable influence: first as a grandiose architectural ensemble, a palace within the city; and, second, as a symbol of the capital's cultural pre-eminence. Across rue de Rivoli from the Louvre stands the elegant Palais-Royal. After a stroll in its quiet gardens, it's hard to believe this was the starting point of the French Revolution. Today, its arcades house a mix of antiques dealers, philatelists and fashion showcases. The city's business district is squeezed between the elegant calm of the Palais-Royal and shopping hub the Grands Boulevards.

Jardin des Tuileries

Rue de Rivoli, 1st. Open 7.30am-7pm daily.

Between the Louvre and place de la Concorde, the gravelled alleyways of these gardens have been a chic promenade ever since they opened to the public in the 16th century; and the popular mood persists with the funfair that sets up along the rue de Rivoli side in summer. André Le Nôtre created the prototypical French garden with terraces and central vista running down the Grand Axe through circular and hexagonal ponds. As part of Mitterrand's Grand Louvre project, sculptures such as Coysevox's winged horses were transferred to the Louvre and replaced by copies, and the Maillol sculptures were returned to the Jardins du Carrousel; a handful of modern sculptures have been added, including bronzes by Moore, Ernst, Giacometti, and Dubuffet's *Le Bel Costumé*. There's a specialist gardeners' bookshop by place de la Concorde.

Musée des Arts Décoratifs

107 rue de Rivoli, 1st (01.44.55.57.50/www. lesartsdecoratifs.fr). Open 11am-6pm Tue, Wed, Fri; 10am-6pm Sat, Sun. Admission (with Musée de la Mode & Musée de la Publicité) €8; free-€6.50 reductions.

Taken as a whole along with the Musée de la Mode et du Textile and Musée de la Publicité, this is one of the world's major collections of design and the decorative arts. Located in the west wing of the Louvre since its opening a century ago, the venue reopened in 2006 after a decade-long, €35-million restoration of the building and of 6,000 of the 150,000 items donated mainly by private collectors. The major focus here is French furniture and tableware, from extravagant carpets to delicate crystal and porcelain. Of most obvious attraction to the layman are the reconstructed period rooms, ten in all, showing how the other half lived from the late 1400s to the early 20th century.

Musée du Louvre

Rue de Rivoli, 1st (01.40.20.50.50/www.louvre.fr). Open 9am-6pm Mon, Thur, Sat, Sun; 9am-10pm Wed, Fri. Admission €9; free-€6 reductions.

Some 35,000 works of art and artefacts are on show, divided into eight departments and housed in three wings: Denon, Sully and Richelieu. Treasures from the Egyptians, Etruscans, Greeks and Romans each have their own galleries in the Denon and Sully wings, as do Middle Eastern and Islamic works of art. The first floor of Richelieu is taken up with European decorative arts from the Middle Ages up to the 19th century. The main draw, though, is the painting and sculpture. Two glass-roofed sculpture courts contain the Marly horses on the ground floor of Richelieu, with French sculpture below and Italian Renaissance pieces in the Denon wing. The Grand Galerie and Salle de la Joconde (home to the *Mona Lisa*) run the length of Denon's first floor with French Romantic painting alongside. Dutch and French painting occupies the second floor of Richelieu and Sully. Laminated panels found throughout provide a lively commentary, and the superb website is a technological feat unsurpassed by that of any of the world's major museums. Work continues on the new Islamic Arts department, which should open in 2010.

Paris

AVE DES TERNES

AVE CARNOT

AV. MAC MAHON

AVENUE DE WAGRAM

BOULEVARD DE COURCELLES

Parc Monceau

BOULEVARD

Museé Jacquemart André

RUE DE COURCELLES

AVENUE DE MESSINE

BOULEVARD HAUSSMANN

Eglise St Augustin

Gare St Lazare

RUE SAINT LAZARE

AVENUE HOCHE

8

BOULEVARD HAUSSMANN

BOULEVARD HAUSSMANN

AVENUE DE FRIEDLAND

Arc de Triomphe

PLACE CHARLES
DE GAULLE

Chambre de Commerce

AVENUE DE

Chapelle Expiatoire

BOULEVARD MALESHERBES

Eglise de la Madeleine

BD. DES CAPUCINES

AVENUE KLEBER

AVENUE D'IENA

AVENUE MARCEAU

CHAMPS

ELYSEES

Ministère de l'Intérieur

LA MADELEINE

American Cathedral

Palais Galliera

Museé Guimet

AVENUE D'IENA

AVENUE DU PRESIDENT WILSON

Franklin D. Roosevelt

Th. Marigny

AVENUE DES CHAMPS ELYSEES

Grand Palais

Petit Palais

Palais de l'Elysée

CHAMPS ELYSEES

Espace P. Cardin

Concorde

RUE ROYALE

Min. de la Justice

AVENUE DE NEW YORK

Palais de Tokyo

PONT DE L'ALMA

Palais de la Découverte

W. CHURCHILL

Obélisque

PLACE DE LA CONCORDE

Jeu de Paume

RUE DE RIVOLI

Orangerie

Jardin des Tuileries

Musée des Arts Décor

Jardin Carrous

COURS ALBERT 1ER

COURS LA REINE

PONT DE LA CONCORDE

Seine

QUAI BRANLY

Musée du Quai Branly

QUAI D'ORSAY

Invalides

Assemblée Nationale

QUAI DES TUILERIES

Seine

Tour Eiffel

AVENUE RAPP

AVENUE BOSQUET

AVENUE DE LA BOURDONNAIS

Assemblée Nationale

Min. du Commerce

BOULEVARD

ANATOLE FRANCE

Musée d'Orsay

Musée d'Orsay

Q. VOLTA

Ministère de la Défense

SAINT

Parc du Champ de Mars

Ecole Militaire

BOULEVARD DES INVALIDES

Hôtel des Invalides

Min. du Travail

Min. de l'Education

Ministère des Transports

Université Paris V

AVENUE DE LA MOTTE

AVENUE DE SUFFREN

Ecole Militaire

AVENUE DE TOURVILLE

Musée Rodin

Min. de l'Industrie

RUE DE BELLECHASSE

RUE DE VARENNE

Musée Maillol

BOULEVARD RASPAIL

ST GERMAI DES PRÈS

SÈGUR

PLACE DE FONTENOY

St François Xavier

Sèvres

UNESCO

Min. de la Santé

AVENUE DE SAXE

BD. DES INVALIDES

RUE VANEAU

Hôpital Laennec

RUE DE SÈVRES

RUE DE RENNES

BOULEVARD DE GRENELLE

RUE FRÉMICOURT

AVENUE DE SUFFREN

UNESCO Annexe

15

BOULEVARD GARIBALDI

SÈVRES-Lecourbe

BOULEVARD DU MONTPARNASSE

6

Hôpital Necker

BOULEVARD PASTEUR

BOULEVARD DE VAUGIRARD

Musée Bourdelle

Montparnasse Bienvenüe

RUE LECOURBE

0   500 m

0   500 yds

Top: Le Train Bleu.
Bottom: Bread & Roses.

Musée de l'Orangerie

Jardin des Tuileries, 1st (01.44.77.80.07/www.musee-
orangerie.fr). Open 12.30-7pm Mon, Wed, Thur,
Sat, Sun; 12.30-9pm Fri. Admission €6.50; free-
€4.50 reductions.

The long-delayed reopening of this Monet showcase finally took place a few years ago, and the new look is utilitarian and fuss-free, with the museum's eight, tapestry-sized *Nymphéas* (water lilies) paintings housed in two plain oval rooms. They provide a simple backdrop for the ethereal romanticism of Monet's works, painted late in his life. Downstairs, the Jean Walter and Paul Guillaume collection of Impressionism and the Ecole de Paris is a mixed bag of sweet-toothed Cézanne and Renoir portraits, with works by Modigliani, Rousseau, Matisse, Picasso and Derain.

Palais-Royal

Pl du Palais-Royal, 1st. Open Gardens 7.30am-
8.30pm daily. Admission free.

Built for Cardinal Richelieu by Jacques Lemercier, the building was once known as Palais Cardinal. Richelieu left it to Louis XIII, whose widow Anne d'Autriche preferred it to the Louvre and rechristened it when she moved in with her son, the young Louis XIV. In the 1780s the Duc d'Orléans enclosed the gardens in a three-storey peristyle and filled it with cafés, shops, theatres, sideshows and accommodation to raise money for rebuilding the burned-down opera. Daniel Buren's controversial striped columns grace the main courtyard.

CHAMPS-ELYSEES & WESTERN PARIS

The eighth *arrondissement* is all wealth and grandeur, and those qualities spill over into much of the 16th and the nearer parts of the 17th. Through the heart of this district runs the Champs-Elysées, the city's most iconic thoroughfare. For all its historic associations, the 'Elysian Fields' underperformed for years, offering little other than fast-food joints and drab shops. But the area is now jumping again with new hotels and restaurants, luxury and concept stores, and renovations of old landmarks.

The western end of the Champs-Elysées is dominated by the Arc de Triomphe towering above place Charles-de-Gaulle, also known as L'Etoile. Built by Napoleon, the arch was modified to celebrate the Revolutionary armies. From the top, visitors can gaze over the square (commissioned later by Haussmann), with 12 avenues radiating out in all directions. South of the arch, avenue Kléber leads to the monumental buildings of the panoramic Trocadéro.

Arc de Triomphe

Pl Charles-de-Gaulle, 8th (01.55.37.73.77). Open Oct-
Mar 10am-10.30pm daily. Apr-Sept 10am-11pm daily.
Admission €9; free-€5 reductions.

Napoleon ordered the Arc de Triomphe's construction in 1809 as a monument to the achievements of his armies, but his empire began to collapse almost immediately; the arch was completed only in 1836. Still, it bears the names of

Napoleon's victories, and is decorated on its flanks with a frieze of battle scenes and sculptures, including Rude's famous *Le Départ des Volontaires* (aka La Marseillaise). French troops finally got their victory march through it at the end of World War I; the annual Bastille Day military procession now starts here. Climb the stairs for wonderful views, a fully renovated interior and a new museum, which opened in 2008 with interactive displays.

Musée Marmottan – Claude Monet

2 rue Louis-Boilly, 16th (01.44.96.50.33/www.
marmottan.com). Open 10am-6pm Mon, Wed-Sun
(last entry 5.30pm); 11am-9pm Tue (last entry 8.30pm).
Admission €9; free-€5 reductions.

This old hunting pavilion has become a famed holder of Impressionist art thanks to two bequests: the first by the daughter of the doctor of Manet, Monet, Pissarro, Sisley and Renoir; the second by Monet's son Michel. Its Monet collection, the largest in the world, numbers 165 works, plus sketchbooks, palette and photos. A special circular room was created for the stunning late water lily canvases; upstairs are works by Renoir, Manet, Gauguin, Caillebotte and Berthe Morisot, 15th-century primitives, a Sèvres clock and a collection of First Empire furniture.

Palais de Tokyo: Site de Création Contemporaine

13 av du Président-Wilson, 16th (01.47.23.54.01/
www.palaisdetokyo.com). Open noon-midnight
Tue-Sun. Admission €6; free-€4.50 reductions.

When it opened in 2002, many thought the Palais' stripped-back interior was a design statement. In fact, it was a practical answer to tight finances. The 1937 building has now come into its own as an open-plan space with a skylit central hall, hosting exhibitions, shows and performances. Extended hours and a funky café have succeeded in drawing a younger audience, and the roll-call of artists is impressive (Pierre Joseph, Wang Du and others).

MONTMARTRE & PIGALLE

For such a young part of Paris – it was only annexed by the city in 1860 – Montmartre has astonishing renown, among foreigners as much as Frenchmen. It doesn't take much exploring before you realise that the fame and affection are deserved: the steep streets and staircases spiralling round the mound below the dome of Sacré-Coeur, the ghosts of some of the 19th and 20th centuries' greatest artists, and the present-day buzz of hip cafés and bars all produce a charm that even mass tourism can't obscure. The same can't be said of louche Pigalle at the bottom of the hill, with its sex shops and grime. Still, these days, many of the red lights are attached not to brothels but to hot music venues and nightspots.

La Goutte d'Or, north of Barbès Rochechouart métro station, is primarily an African and Arab neighbourhood, and can seem like a colourful slice of the Middle East or a state under perpetual siege due to the frequent police raids.

www.parisaddress.com

Short term apartment rentals in Paris

Live in Paris like a true Parisian!
You wish to live Paris from "within", like a true Parisian?
Saint-Germain-des-Prés, the Latin Quarter, the Marais...

Paris Address invites you to discover picturesque and lively central apartments.

Prices all included, instant availability and easy-booking on the website.

A market sets up under the métro tracks along boulevard de la Chapelle on Monday, Wednesday and Saturday mornings, with stalls of exotic vegetables and African fabrics. Further north, at porte de Clignancourt, is the city's largest flea market, the Marché aux Puces de Clignancourt (open 7am-7.30pm Mon, Sat, Sun).

Cimetière de Montmartre
20 av Rachel, access by staircase from rue Caulaincourt, 18th (01.53.42.36.30). Open 6 Nov-15 Mar 8am-5.30pm Mon-Sat; 9am-5.30pm Sun. 16 Mar-5 Nov 8am-6pm Mon-Sat; 9am-6pm Sun. Admission free.
Truffaut, Nijinsky, Berlioz, Degas, Offenbach and German poet Heine are all buried here. So, too, are La Goulue, the first great cancan star and model for Toulouse-Lautrec, celebrated local beauty Mme Récamier, and consumptive heroine Alphonsine Plessis, inspiration for Dumas's *La Dame aux Camélias* and Verdi's *La Traviata*. Flowers are still left on the grave of pop diva and gay icon Dalida.

Sacré-Coeur
35 rue du Chevalier-de-la-Barre, 18th (01.53.41.89.00/ www.sacre-coeur-montmartre.com). Open Basilica 6am-10.30pm daily. Crypt & dome Winter 10am-5.45pm daily. Summer 9am-6.45pm daily. Admission free. Crypt & dome €5.
Work on this enormous mock Romano-Byzantine edifice began in 1877. It was commissioned after the nation's defeat by Prussia in 1870, voted for by the Assemblée Nationale and built from public subscription. Finally completed in 1914, it was consecrated in 1919 – by which time a jumble of architects had succeeded Paul Abadie, winner of the original competition. The interior boasts lavish mosaics.

THE MARAIS & EASTERN PARIS
Beaubourg and its eastern neighbour the Marais are a chunk of town largely untouched by Haussmann, which means lots of small streets in which to get lost and – to a degree – a sense of old Paris. The clean-up operation begun in the Marais in the 1960s by culture minister André Malraux did much to primp and preserve the old buildings. However, although much of the fabric is ancient, the people and the activities are resolutely fashionable and exuberant. This, famously, is the city's gay quarter, but it's just as popular with other inclinations – museums, boutiques, bars and restaurants abound, and the crowds, particularly at the weekends, can be oppressive. Come with time, and money, to spare. A little further east is the edgy Oberkampf district, home to some of the city's best bars.

Centre Pompidou
(Musée National d'Art Moderne)
Rue St-Martin, 4th (01.44.78.12.33/www.centre pompidou.fr). Open 11am-9pm (last entry 8pm) Mon, Wed, Fri-Sun (until 11pm some exhibitions); 11am-11pm Thur. Admission Museum & exhibitions €10-€12; free-€8 reductions.

The primary colours, exposed pipes and air ducts make this one of the best-known sights in Paris. The Centre Pompidou (or 'Beaubourg') holds the largest collection of modern art in Europe, rivalled in its breadth and quality only by MoMA in New York. For the main collection, buy tickets on the ground floor and take the escalators to level four for post-1960s art. Level five spans 1905 to 1960. Masterful ensembles let you see the span of Matisse's career on canvas and in bronze, the variety of Picasso's invention, and the development of cubic orphism by Sonia and Robert Delaunay. Others on the hits list include Braque, Duchamp, Mondrian, Kandinsky, Dali, Giacometti, Ernst, Miró, Calder, Magritte, Rothko and Pollock. Video art and installations by the likes of Mathieu Mercier and Dominique Gonzalez-Foerster are in a room given over to *nouvelle création*.

Musée d'Art et d'Histoire du Judaïsme
Hôtel de St-Aignan, 71 rue du Temple, 3rd (01.53.01.86.60/www.mahj.org). Open 11am-6pm Mon-Fri; 10am-6pm Sun. Closed Jewish hols. Admission €6.80; free-€4.50 reductions.
Set in a Marais mansion, this museum sprang from the collection of a private association formed in 1948 to safeguard Jewish heritage after the Holocaust. Displays illustrate ceremonies, rites and learning, and show how styles were adapted around the globe through examples of Jewish decorative arts. Photographic portraits of modern French Jews, each of whom tells his or her own story on the audio soundtrack, bring a contemporary edge. The Holocaust is marked by Boris Taslitzky's stark sketches from Buchenwald and Christian Boltanski's courtyard memorial to the Jews who lived in the building in 1939, 13 of whom died in the camps.

Musée Carnavalet
23 rue de Sévigné, 3rd (01.44.59.58.58/www.carnavalet. paris.fr). Open 10am-6pm Tue-Sun. Admission free. Exhibitions €7; free-€5.50 reductions.
Here, 140 rooms depict the history of Paris, from pre-Roman Gaul to the 20th century. Original 16th-century rooms house Renaissance collections, with portraits by Clouet and furniture and pictures relating to the Wars of Religion. The first floor covers the period up to 1789 and neighbouring Hôtel Le Peletier de St-Fargeau covers the period from 1789 onwards. Displays relating to 1789 detail that year's convoluted politics and bloodshed, with prints and memorabilia, including a chunk of the Bastille. There are items belonging to Napoleon, a cradle given by the city to Napoleon III, and a reconstruction of Proust's bedroom.

Musée National Picasso
Hôtel Salé, 5 rue de Thorigny, 3rd (01.42.71.25.21/ www.musee-picasso.fr). Open Oct-Mar 9.30am-5.30pm Mon, Wed-Sun. Apr-Sept 9.30am-6pm Mon, Wed-Sun. Admission €6.50; free-€4.50 reductions. Exhibitions vary.
Picasso's paintings, sculptures, collages, drawings and ceramics are shown off in style here. Many of the 'greatest hits' hang in other state-owned Paris museums, but to get a feeling for Picasso's artistic development this is the best resource in the city. From a haunting, blue-period self-

portrait and rough studies for the *Demoiselles d'Avignon*, the collection moves to Picasso's cubist and classical phases, the surreal *Nude in an Armchair* and portraits of his abundant lovers, in particular Marie-Thérèse and Dora Maar. A covered sculpture garden displays pieces that sat around Picasso's studio until his death.

NORTH-EAST PARIS

Traditionally, the area north and north-east of place de la République was a proletarian district, shot through by the Canal St-Martin that brought raw goods and rough barges into the city. Many streets around here are still tatty, but others, especially near the canal, have been fashionable for at least ten years. Gentrification as such is not much in evidence – unless you take the rise in rents as an index, in which case it's rampant. But to the visitor, unconcerned by property prices, this part of Paris has much to offer: there's a palpable buzz and strong sense of authenticity on streets such as rue du Fbg-St-Denis – and any number of side streets that take you into a completely different world. Still further north-east are the manifold delights of La Villette, with its science and music museums, performance venues and landscaped gardens, and a new arts space in the former city undertaker's.

104

104 rue d'Aubervilliers, 19th (01.53.35.50.00/ www.104.fr). Open 11am-8pm Mon, Sun; 11am-11pm Tue-Sat. Admission free. Exhibitions €5; €3 reductions.
104, described as a 'space for artistic creation', occupies a 19th-century building on the rue d'Aubervilliers that used to house Paris's municipal undertakers. The site was saved from developers by Roger Madec, the mayor of the 19th, who's made its renovation the centrepiece of a massive project of cultural and urban renewal. There aren't any constraints on the kind of work the resident artists do – 104 is open to 'all the arts' – but they're expected to show finished pieces in one of four annual 'festivals'. And they're also required to get involved in projects with the public.

Cimetière du Père-Lachaise

Bd de Ménilmontant, 20th (01.55.25.82.10). Open 6 Nov-15 Mar 8am-5.30pm Mon-Fri; 8.30am-5.30pm Sat; 9am-5.30pm Sun. 16 Mar-5 Nov 8am-6pm Mon-Fri; 8.30am-6pm Sat; 9am-6pm Sun. Admission free.
Père-Lachaise has almost anyone French, talented and dead that you care to mention. Not even French, for that matter. Creed and nationality have never prevented entry: you just had to have lived or died in Paris or have an allotted space in a family tomb. Finding a particular grave can be tricky, so buy a €2 map from the hawkers at the Père-Lachaise métro entrance or from shops nearby. Highlights include Chopin's medallion portrait and the muse of Music, famous neighbours La Fontaine and Molière, who knew each other in life and now share the same fenced-off plot, and Victor Noir. This journalist, shot by Napoleon's cousin Prince Pierre, rests underneath a bronze likeness, its groin rubbed so often by women hoping to conceive that it gleams.

La Cité des Sciences et de l'Industrie

La Villette, 30 av Corentin-Cariou, 19th (01.40.05.70.00/ www.cite-sciences.fr). Open 10am-6pm Tue-Sat; 10am-7pm Sun. Admission €8; free-€6 reductions.
This ultra-modern science museum pulls in five million visitors a year. Explora, the permanent show, occupies the upper two floors, whisking visitors through 30,000sq m (320,000sq ft) of space, life, matter and communication: scale models of satellites including the Ariane space shuttle, planes and robots, plus the chance to experience weightlessness, make for an exciting journey. In the Espace Images, try the delayed camera and other optical illusions, draw 3D images on a computer or lend your voice to the *Mona Lisa*. The hothouse garden investigates developments in agriculture and bio-technology.

Musée de la Musique

Cité de la Musique, 221 av Jean-Jaurès, 19th (01.44.84.45.00/www.cite-musique.fr). Open noon-6pm Tue-Sat; 10am-6pm Sun. Admission €8; free-€6.40 reductions.
Alongside the concert hall, this innovative music museum houses a gleamingly restored collection of instruments from the old Conservatoire, interactive computers and scale models of opera houses and concert halls. Visitors are supplied with an audio guide in a choice of languages, and the musical commentary is a joy, playing the appropriate instrument as you approach each exhibit. Alongside the trumpeting brass, curly woodwind instruments and precious strings are some more unusual items, such as the Indonesian gamelan orchestra, whose sounds influenced the work of Debussy and Ravel.

THE LATIN QUARTER & THE 13TH

The Latin Quarter holds a considerable mystique for many foreign visitors, thanks to the historical presence of Hemingway, Orwell and Miller and the seedbed of the 1968 revolt. However, traces of those fabled eras are harder to find: property in the Latin Quarter is now among the dearest in Paris, and every year another relic is renovated out of existence. To cite just one example, the removal of the ancient wooden 'Vieux Chêne' sign from a building in rue Mouffetard in 2005 went almost wholly unnoticed and unlamented. The 'Latin' in the area's name probably derives from the fact that it has been the university quarter since medieval times, when Latin was the language of instruction. The corner of the 13th known as the ZAC Rive Gauche has seen plenty of development in the last 15 years: a new library, a new bridge, a floating pool, and a vast cultural centre, the Cité de la Mode et du Design.

Institut du Monde Arabe

1 rue des Fossés-St-Bernard, 5th (01.40.51.38.38/ www.imarabe.org). Open Museum 10am-6pm Tue-Sun. Library 1-8pm Tue-Sat. Café noon-6pm Tue-Sun. Tours 3pm Tue-Fri; 3pm, 4.30pm Sat, Sun. Admission Roof terrace, library free. Museum €5; free-€4 reductions. Exhibitions prices vary. Tours €8.

Top: Diptyque.
Bottom left: Fromagerie
Quatrehomme.
Bottom right: LE66.

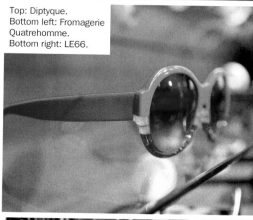

A clever blend of high-tech and Arab influences, this Seine-side *grand projet* was constructed between 1980 and 1987 to a design by Jean Nouvel. Shuttered windows, inspired by the screens of Moorish palaces, act as camera apertures, contracting or expanding according to the amount of sunlight. A museum covering the history and archaeology of the Islamic Arab world occupies the upper floors: start at the seventh with Classical-era finds and work down via early Islamic dynasties to the present day. There's an excellent Middle East bookshop on the ground floor, and the views from the roof terrace (access is free) are fabulous.

Jardin des Plantes
36 rue Geoffroy-St-Hilaire, 2 rue Bouffon, pl Valhubert or 57 rue Cuvier, 5th. Open Main garden Winter 8am-dusk daily. Summer 7.30am-8pm daily. Alpine garden Apr-Sept 8am-4.30pm Mon-Fri; 1-5pm Sat, Sun. Closed Oct-Mar. Ménagerie Apr-Sept 9am-5pm daily. Admission Alpine Garden free Mon-Fri; €1 Sat, Sun. Jardin des Plantes free. Ménagerie €7; free-€5 reductions.
Although small and slightly dishevelled, the Paris botanical garden – which contains more than 10,000 species and includes tropical greenhouses and rose, winter and Alpine gardens – is an enchanting place. Begun by Louis XIII's doctor as the royal medicinal plant garden in 1626, it opened to the public in 1640. The formal garden, which runs between two avenues of trees, is like something out of *Alice in Wonderland*. Ancient trees on view include a false acacia planted in 1636 and a cedar from 1734. A plaque on the old laboratory declares that this is where Henri Becquerel discovered radioactivity in 1896.

Musée National du Moyen Age – Thermes de Cluny
6 pl Paul-Painlevé, 5th (01.53.73.78.00/www.musee-moyenage.fr). Open 9.15am-5.45pm Mon, Wed-Sun. Admission €7.50; free-€5.50 reductions.
The national museum of medieval art is best known for the beautiful, allegorical *Lady and the Unicorn* tapestry cycle, but it also has important collections of medieval sculpture and enamels. The building itself, commonly known as Cluny, is also a rare example of 15th-century secular Gothic architecture, with its foliate Gothic doorways, hexagonal staircase jutting out of the façade and vaulted chapel. It was built from 1485 to 1498 – on top of a Gallo-Roman baths complex. The baths, built in characteristic Roman bands of stone and brick masonry, are the finest Roman remains in Paris. A themed garden fronts the whole complex.

Le Panthéon
Pl du Panthéon, 5th (01.44.32.18.00). Open 10am-6pm (until 6.30pm summer) daily. Admission €7.50; free-€4.80 reductions.
Soufflot's neoclassical megastructure was the architectural *grand projet* of its day, commissioned by a grateful Louis XV to thank St Geneviève for his recovery from illness. But by the time it was ready in 1790, a lot had changed; during the Revolution, the Panthéon was rededicated as a 'temple of reason' and the resting place of the nation's great men. The austere barrel-vaulted crypt now houses Voltaire, Rousseau, Hugo and Zola. New heroes are installed but

rarely: Pierre and Marie Curie's remains were transferred here in 1995; Alexandre Dumas in 2002. Inside are Greek columns and domes, and 19th-century murals of Geneviève's life by Symbolist painter Puvis de Chavannes, a formative influence on Picasso during the latter's blue period. Mount the steep spiral stairs to the colonnade encircling the dome for superb views.

ST-GERMAIN-DES-PRES
In the first half of the 20th century, St-Germain-des-Prés was prime arts and literature territory. Writers and painters swapped concepts and girlfriends on its café terraces before World War II, and former GIs jammed in its cellars when the fighting was over. The heart of the Paris jazz boom and haunt of Camus, Prévert, Picasso and Giacometti epitomised – and to a large extent coined – a very Parisian amalgam of carefree living and audacious thinking. Some of that intellectual and hedonistic lore still clings to this small part of the Left Bank, but for decades the main concern here has been more sartorial than Sartrian. St-Germain-des-Prés is now serious fashion territory, and has some of the most expensive property – and cafés – in the city.

Eglise St-Germain-des-Prés
3 pl St-Germain-des-Prés, 6th (01.55.42.81.33/ www.eglise-sgp.org). Open 8am-7.45pm Mon-Sat; 9am-8pm Sun. Admission free.
This is the oldest church in Paris. On the advice of Germain (later Bishop of Paris), Childebert, son of Clovis, had a basilica and monastery built here around 543. It was first dedicated to St Vincent, and came to be known as St-Germain-le-Doré ('the gilded') because of its copper roof, then later as St-Germain-des-Prés ('of the fields'). During the Revolution the abbey was burned and a saltpetre refinery installed; the spire was added in a clumsy 19th-century restoration. Still, most of the present structure is 12th century, and ornate carved capitals and the tower remain from the 11th. Tombs include those of Jean-Casimir, the deposed King of Poland who became Abbot of St-Germain in 1669, and of Scots nobleman William Douglas.

Jardin & Palais du Luxembourg
Pl Auguste-Comte, pl Edmond-Rostand or rue de Vaugirard, 6th (01.44.54.19.49/www.senat.fr/visite). Open Jardin summer 7.30am-dusk daily; winter 8am-dusk daily.
The palace itself was built in the 1620s for Marie de Médicis, widow of Henri IV, by Salomon de Brosse on the site of the former mansion of the Duke of Luxembourg. Its Italianate style was intended to remind her of the Pitti Palace in her native Florence. The palace now houses the French parliament's upper house, the Sénat. The mansion next door (Le Petit Luxembourg) is the residence of the Sénat's president. The gardens, though, are the real draw: part formal (terraces and gravel paths), part 'English garden' (lawns and mature trees), they are the quintessential Paris park. The garden is crowded with sculptures: a looming Cyclops (on the 1624 Fontaine de Médicis), queens of

Open house

Claude Berri, who died in January 2009, was for many years best known as one of France's most successful film directors and producers – he directed the international art-house hit *Jean de Florette* and produced France's second biggest box office success, *Bienvenue chez les Ch'tis*. But in 2008 the 74-year-old made a name for himself in another field, the world of contemporary art, when he opened the Espace Claude Berri (8 rue Rambuteau, 3rd, 01.44.54.88.50, www.espace-claudeberri.com) – a showcase for exhibitions by up-and-coming talent and Berri's own impressive collection.

The film mogul had been buying paintings and sculptures since the 1970s and by the time of his death boasted one of France's biggest collections. His first purchase was a Magritte, followed by works by Picasso, Dalí, Giacometti and Fernand Léger, but the bulk of Berri's collection is made up of living artists. Robert Ryman was a favourite, while other contemporary luminaries in the collection

include Richard Serra, Bruce Nauman, Dan Flavin, Daniel Buren, Jeff Wall, Christian Boltanski and Paul McCarthy.

Berri had long wanted to share his collection with the public. Back in 1991, he opened a small gallery space in Paris, which featured exhibitions by Ryman, Buren and Yves Klein. This time around, he invested in premises in the Marais, a stronghold for art galleries and dealers. Dominated by a high, sloping skylight, the luminous interiors were redesigned by Jean Nouvel, architect of both the Fondation Cartier and the Musée Quai Branly. The aim of the new space is to alternate themed exhibitions of works from Berri's private collection with solo shows organised around artists, critics or gallery owners. For the opening event, the whole ground floor was filled with giant, irreverent installations by Frenchman Gilles Barbier. Other exhibitions have been dedicated to Indian artists, and to trees in contemporary art.

L'Hôtel.

France, a miniature Statue of Liberty, wild animals, busts of Flaubert and Baudelaire, and a monument to Delacroix. There are orchards (300 varieties of apples and pears) and an apiary. The Musée National du Luxembourg hosts prestigious exhibitions. Most interesting, though, are the people: an international mixture of *flâneurs* and *dragueurs*, chess players and martial-arts practitioners, as well as children on ponies, in sandpits, on roundabouts and playing with the sailing boats on the pond.

MONTPARNASSE

Picasso, Léger and Soutine fled to 'Mount Parnassus' in the early 1900s to escape the rising rents of Montmartre. They were soon joined by Chagall, Zadkine and other refugees from the Russian Revolution, along with Americans such as Man Ray, Henry Miller, Ezra Pound and Gertrude Stein. Between the wars, the neighbourhood was the epitome of modernity: studios with large windows were built by avant-garde architects; artists, writers and intellectuals drank and debated in the quarter's showy bars; and naughty pastimes – including the then risqué tango – flourished. Sadly, the Montparnasse of today has lost much of its former soul, dominated as it is by the lofty Tour Montparnasse, the first skyscraper in central Paris. The dismay with which its construction was greeted prompted a change in building regulations. For those with a head for heights, there are fabulous panoramic views to be had from the café on the 56th floor.

Les Catacombes

1 av du Colonel-Henri-Rol-Tanguy, 14th (01.43.22.47.63/ www.catacombes-de-paris.fr). Open 10am-5pm Tue-Sun. Admission €7; free-€5.50 reductions.

This is the official entrance to the 3,000km (1,864-mile) tunnel network that runs under much of the city. With public burial pits overflowing in the era of the Revolutionary Terror, the bones of six million people were transferred to the catacombs. The bones of Marat, Robespierre and their cronies are packed in with wall upon wall of their fellow citizens. It's not a journey for the faint-hearted: an 85-step spiral staircase takes visitors some 20m (66ft) below ground level to a mass of bones and carvings. Carry a torch.

Cimetière du Montparnasse

3 bd Edgar-Quinet, 14th (01.44.10.86.50). Open 16 Mar-5 Nov 8am-6pm Mon-Fri; 8.30am-6pm Sat; 9am-6pm Sun. 6 Nov-15 Mar 8am-5.30pm Mon-Fri; 8.30am-5.30pm Sat; 9.30am-5.30pm Sun. Admission free.

This huge cemetery was formed by commandeering three farms (you can still see the ruins of a windmill by rue Froidevaux) in 1824. As with much of the Left Bank, the Montparnasse boneyard has literary clout: Beckett, Baudelaire, Sartre, de Beauvoir, Maupassant, Ionesco and Tristan Tzara all rest here. There are also artists, including Brancusi, Henri Laurens, Frédéric Bartholdi (sculptor of the Statue of Liberty) and Man Ray. The celebrity roll-call continues with Serge Gainsbourg, André Citroën, comedian Coluche and actress Jean Seberg.

THE 7TH & WESTERN PARIS

The seventh arrondissement is the Paris of the establishment: home to the French parliament, the Assemblée Nationale, to several French ministries and foreign embassies, to the army's training establishment, the Ecole Militaire, and to the headquarters of UNESCO. Much of it is rather formal and lacking in soul, with few visitor-friendly cultural and historic attractions. However, the attractions that do occupy this lofty district are big hitters: the Musée d'Orsay, Les Invalides and the Eiffel Tower. Near to St-Germain-des-Prés is the cosy Faubourg St-Germain, with its historic mansions and upmarket shops. Further west is the 15th arrondissement, with its predominantly residential buildings done in a suprisingly broad array of styles.

Chapelle de la Médaille Miraculeuse

Couvent des Soeurs de St-Vincent-de-Paul, 140 rue du Bac, 7th (01.49.54.78.88). Open 7.45am-1pm, 2.30-7pm daily. Admission free.

In 1830, saintly Catherine Labouré was said to have been visited by the Virgin, who gave her a medal that performed miracles. This kitsch chapel – murals, mosaics, statues and the embalmed bodies of Catherine and her mother superior – is one of France's most visited sites, attracting two million pilgrims every year. Reliefs in the courtyard tell the nun's story, and slot machines sell medals.

Eiffel Tower

Champ de Mars, 7th (01.44.11.23.45/recorded information 01.44.11.23.23/www.tour-eiffel.fr). Open 13 June-Aug 9am-12.45am daily. Sept-12 June 9.30am-11.45pm daily. Admission By stairs (1st & 2nd levels, Sept-mid June 9.30am-6pm, mid June-Aug 9am-midnight) €4; free-€3.10 reductions. By lift (1st level) €4.80; free-€2.50 reductions; (2nd level) €7.80; free-€4.30 reductions; (3rd level) €12; free-€6.70 reductions.

No building better symbolises Paris than the Tour Eiffel. The radical cast-iron tower was built for the 1889 World Fair and the centenary of the 1789 Revolution by engineer Gustave Eiffel. Eiffel made use of new technology that was already popular in iron-framed buildings. Construction took more than two years and used some 18,000 pieces of metal and 2,500,000 rivets. The 300m (984ft) tower stands on four massive concrete piles; it was the tallest structure in the world until overtaken by New York's Empire State Building in the 1930s. Vintage double-decker lifts ply their way up and down; you can walk as far as the second level. There are souvenir shops, an exhibition space, café and even a post office on the first and second levels. At the top (third level), there's Eiffel's cosy salon and a viewing platform. Views can reach 65km (40 miles) on a good day.

Les Invalides & Musée de l'Armée

Esplanade des Invalides, 7th (01.44.42.38.77/museum 08.10.11.33.99/www.invalides.org). Open Apr-Sept 10am-6pm daily. Oct-Mar 10am-5pm daily. Closed 1st Mon of mth. Admission Courtyard free. Musée de l'Armée & Eglise du Dôme €8; free-€6 reductions.

Its imposing gilded dome is misleading: the Hôtel des Invalides was (and in part still is) a hospital. Commissioned by Louis XIV for wounded soldiers, it once housed as many as 6,000 invalids. Behind lines of topiaried yews and cannons, the main (northern) façade has a relief of Louis XIV and the Sun King's sunburst. Wander through the main courtyard and you'll see grandiose two-storey arcades, sundials on three sides and a statue of Napoleon glaring out. The complex contains two churches: the Eglise St-Louis was for the soldiers, the Eglise du Dôme for the king. You'll find an opening behind the altar that connects the two. Since 1840, the Eglise du Dôme has been solely dedicated to the worship of Napoleon. Included in the entry price is the impressive Musée de l'Armée, which is in effect several museums in one. The Plans-Reliefs section is a collection of gorgeous 18th- and 19th-century scale models of French cities, used for military strategy; also here is a stunning 17th-century model of Mont St-Michel, made by a monk from playing cards. The World War I rooms are moving, with the conflict brought into focus by uniforms, paintings, a scale model of a trench on the western front and, most sobering of all, white plastercasts of the hideously mutilated faces of two soldiers.

Musée National Rodin

Hôtel Biron, 79 rue de Varenne, 7th (01.44.18.61.10/ www.musee-rodin.fr). Open Apr-Sept 9.30am-5.45pm Tue-Sun (gardens until 6.45pm). Oct-Mar 9.30am-4.45pm Tue-Sun (gardens until 5pm). Admission €6; free-€4 reductions. Exhibitions €7; €5 reductions. Gardens €1.

The Rodin museum occupies the *hôtel particulier* where the sculptor lived in the final years of his life. The *Kiss*, the *Cathedral*, the *Walking Man*, portrait busts and terracottas are exhibited indoors. Rodin's works are accompanied by several pieces by his mistress and pupil, Camille Claudel. The walls are hung with paintings by Van Gogh, Monet, Renoir, Carrière and Rodin himself. Most visitors have greatest affection for the gardens: look out for the *Burghers of Calais*, the elaborate *Gates of Hell*, and the *Thinker*.

Musée d'Orsay

1 rue de la Légion-d'Honneur, 7th (01.40.49.48.14/ recorded information 01.45.49.11.11/www.musee-orsay.fr). Open 9.30am-6pm Tue, Wed, Fri-Sun; 9.30am-9.45pm Thur. Admission €9.50; free-€7 reductions.

The building was originally a train station, designed by Victor Laloux to coincide with the Exposition Universelle in 1900. Now it's a huge museum spanning the fertile art period between 1848 and 1914. It follows a chronological route, from the ground floor to the upper level and then to the mezzanine, showing links between Impressionist painters and their forerunners: here you'll find a profusion of paintings by Delacroix, Corot, Manet, Renoir, Pissarro, Gauguin, Monet, Caillebotte, Cézanne, Van Gogh, Toulouse-Lautrec and others. A central sculpture aisle takes in monuments and maidens by Rude, Barrye and Carrier-Belleuse, but the outstanding pieces are by Carpeaux, including his controversial *La Danse* for the façade of the Palais Garnier. The sculpture terraces include busts by Rodin, heads by Rosso and bronzes by Bourdelle and Maillol.

Musée du Quai Branly

37-55 quai Branly, 7th (01.56.61.70.00/www. quaibranly.fr). Open 11am-7pm Tue, Wed, Sun; 11am-9pm Thur-Sat. Admission €8.50; free-€6 reductions.

Surrounded by trees on the banks of the Seine, this museum, housed in an extraordinary building by Jean Nouvel, is a vast showcase for non-European cultures. Dedicated to the ethnic art of Africa, Oceania, Asia and the Americas, it joins together the collections of the Musée des Arts d'Afrique et d'Océanie and the Laboratoire d'Ethnologie du Musée de l'Homme, as well as indigenous art. Treasures include a tenth-century anthropomorphic Dogon statue from Mali, Vietnamese costumes, Gabonese masks, Aztec statues, Peruvian feather tunics, and rare frescoes from Ethiopia.

Eat

L'Ambassade d'Auvergne

The Marais & Eastern Paris *22 rue du Grenier-St-Lazare, 3rd (01.42.72.31.22/www.ambassade-auvergne.com). Open noon-2pm, 7.30-10pm daily. €€€.*

This rustic *auberge* is a fitting embassy for the hearty fare of central France. An order of cured ham comes as two hefty, plate-filling slices, and the salad bowl is chock-full of green lentils cooked in goose fat, studded with bacon and shallots. The *rôti d'agneau* arrives as a pot of melting chunks of lamb in a rich, meaty sauce with a helping of tender white beans. Dishes arrive with the flagship *aligot*, the creamy, elastic mash-and-cheese concoction. Of the regional wines (Chanturgue, Boudes, Madargues), the fruity AOC Marcillac makes a worthy partner.

L'Ardoise

Opera to Les Halles *28 rue du Mont-Thabor, 1st (01.42.96.28.18/www.lardoise-paris.com). Open noon-2.30pm, 6.30-11pm Tue-Sat; 6.30-11pm Sun. Closed 1st 3wks Aug. €€€.*

One of the city's finest modern bistros, L'Ardoise is regularly packed with gourmets eager to sample Pierre Jay's delicious cooking. A wise choice might be six oysters with warm chipolatas and a pungent shallot dressing; equally attractive are a hare pie with an escalope of foie gras nestling in its centre. A lightly chilled, raspberry-scented Chinon, from a wine list arranged by price, is a perfect complement. Unusually, it's open on Sundays.

A la Bière

North-east Paris *104 av Simon-Bolivar, 19th (01.42.39.83.25). Open noon-3pm, 7pm-1.30am daily. €.*

A la Bière looks like one of those nondescript corner brasseries, but what makes it stand out is an amazingly good-value €13.40 prix fixe full of fine bistro favourites. White tablecloths and fine kirs set the tone; starters of thinly sliced pig's cheek with a nice French dressing on the salad, and a home-made rabbit terrine exceed expectations. The mains live up to what's served before: charcoal-grilled entrecôte with hand-cut chips, and juicy Lyonnais sausages with potatoes drenched in olive oil, garlic and parsley.

Hôtel Particulier
Montmartre.

Le Bistrot Paul Bert

The Marais & Eastern Paris *18 rue Paul-Bert, 11th (01.43.72.24.01). Open noon-2pm, 7.30-11pm Tue-Thur; noon-2pm, 7.30-11.30pm Fri, Sat. Closed Aug. €€€.*
This heart-warming bistro gets it right almost down to the last crumb. A starter salad of *ris de veau* illustrates the point, with lightly browned veal sweetbreads perched on a bed of green beans and baby carrots with a sauce of sherry vinegar and deglazed cooking juices. A roast shoulder of suckling pig and a thick steak with a raft of golden, thick-cut *frites* look inviting indeed. Desserts are superb too, including what may well be the best *île flottante* in Paris.

Au Bon Accueil

The 7th & Western Paris *14 rue de Monttessuy, 7th (01.47.05.46.11). Open noon-2.30pm, 7.30-10.30pm Mon-Fri. Closed 2wks Aug. €€€.*
Jacques Lacipière runs Au Bon Accueil, and Naobuni Sasaki turns out the beautiful food. Perhaps most impressive is his elegant use of little-known fish such as grey mullet and meagre (maigre), rather than the usual endangered species. The €27 lunch menu might highlight such posh ingredients as *suprême de poulet noir du Cros de la Géline*, free-range chicken raised on a farm run by two former cabaret singers. But the biggest surprise comes with desserts, worthy of the finest Paris pastry shops. In summer book a table out on the pavement terrace with its view of the Eiffel Tower.

Bread & Roses

St-Germain-des-Prés *7 rue de Fleurus, 6th (01.42.22.06.06). Open 8am-8pm Mon-Sat. Closed Aug & 1wk Dec. €€€.*
Giant wedges of cheesecake sit alongside French pastries, and huge savoury puff-pastry tarts are perched on the counter. Attention to detail shows even in the authentically pale taramasalata, which is matched with buckwheat-and-seaweed bread. Prices reflect the quality of the often organic ingredients, but that doesn't seem to deter any of the moneyed locals, who order towering birthday cakes here for their snappily dressed offspring.

Chez Miki

Opéra to Les Halles *5 rue de Louvois, 2nd (01.42.96.04.88). Open noon-10pm Tue-Sat; 6-10pm Sun. €€.*
There are plenty of Japanese restaurants to choose from along nearby rue Ste-Anne, but none is as original – nor as friendly – as this tiny bistro run entirely by women, next to the square Louvois. The speciality here is bento boxes, which you compose yourself from a scribbled blackboard list (in Japanese and French). For €15 you can choose two small dishes – marinated sardines and fried chicken wings are especially popular – and a larger dish, such as grilled pork with ginger. Don't miss the inventive desserts, which might include lime jelly spiked with alcohol.

Granterroirs

Champs-Elysées & Western Paris *30 rue de Miromesnil, 8th (01.47.42.18.18/www.granterroirs. com). Open 9am-8pm Mon-Fri. Food served noon-3pm Mon-Fri. Closed 3wks Aug. €€€.*

This *épicerie* with a difference is the perfect remedy for anyone for whom the word '*terroir*' conjures up visions of grease-soaked peasant food. Here, the walls heave with more than 600 enticing specialities from southern France, including Périgord foie gras, charcuterie from Aubrac and a fine selection of wines. Great gift ideas – but why not sample some of the goodies by enjoying the midday *table d'hôte* feast? Come in early to ensure that you can choose from the five succulent *plats du jour* (such as marinated salmon with dill on a bed of warm potatoes).

Mon Vieil Ami

The Seine & Islands *69 rue St-Louis-en-l'Ile, 4th (01.40.46.01.35/www.mon-vieil-ami.com). Open noon-2.30pm, 7-11.30pm Wed-Sun. Closed 3wks Jan & 1st 3wks Aug. €€€.*
Antoine Westermann from the Buerehiesel in Strasbourg has created a true foodie destination here. Starters such as tartare of finely diced raw vegetables with sautéed baby squid on top impress with their deft seasoning. Typical of the mains is a cast-iron casserole of roast duck with caramelised turnips and couscous. Even the classic room has been successfully refreshed with black beams, white Perspex panels and a long *table d'hôte* down one side.

Pétrelle

Montmartre & Pigalle *34 rue Pétrelle, 9th (01.42.82.11.02). Open 8-10pm Tue-Sat. Closed 4wks July/Aug & 1wk Dec. €€€.*
Jean-Luc André is as inspired a decorator as he is a cook, and the quirky charm of his dining room has made it popular with fashion designers and film stars. But behind the style is some serious substance. André seeks out the best ingredients from local producers, and the quality shines through. The €29 no-choice menu is huge value for money (marinated sardines with tomato relish, rosemary-scented rabbit with roasted vegetables, deep purple poached figs) – or you can splash out with à la carte dishes such as tournedos Rossini.

Le Train Bleu

The Marais & Eastern Paris *Gare de Lyon, pl Louis-Armand, 12th (01.43.43.09.06/www.le-train-bleu.com). Open 11.30am-3pm, 7-11pm daily. €€€€.*
This listed dining room – with vintage frescoes and big oak benches – exudes a pleasant air of expectation. Don't expect cutting-edge cooking, but rather fine renderings of French classics. Lobster served on walnut oil-dressed salad leaves is a beautifully prepared starter, as is the pistachio-studded saucisson de Lyon with a warm salad of ratte potatoes. Mains of veal chop topped with a cap of cheese, and *sandre* (pike-perch) with a 'risotto' of *crozettes* are also pleasant.

Shop

Shopping in Paris is a sensual pleasure. Whether you're trying on clothes behind the velvet curtains or tasting cheeses at an open-air market, the joy is in experiencing the pursuit of perfection for which the French are famous. Whereas we have window-shopping, they have window-licking (*lèche-vitrine*). Big department stores and global chains have their roles to play, but there are also plenty of small independent boutiques, which combine to make shopping here a unique experience.

Diptyque
The Latin Quarter & the 13th *34 bd St-Germain, 5th (01.43.26.45.27/www.diptyqueparis.com). Open 10am-7pm Mon-Sat.*
Diptyque's divinely scented candles are the quintessential gift from Paris. They come in 48 varieties, with scents such as *feu de bois*, *figuier* and *jasmin*, and are probably the best you'll ever find.

Fromagerie Quatrehomme
The 7th & Western Paris *62 rue de Sèvres, 7th (01.47.34.33.45). Open 8.45am-1pm, 4-7.45pm Tue-Thur; 8.45am-7.45pm Fri, Sat.*
The award-winning Marie Quatrehomme runs this delightful Left Bank *fromagerie*. Justly famous for her comté fruité, beaufort and st-marcellin, she also sells specialities such as goat's cheese with pesto. The perfect place to stock up for a picnic in the park.

Lanvin
Opéra to Les Halles *22 rue du Fbg St-Honoré, 8th (01.44.71.31.73/www.lanvin.com). Open 10am-7pm Mon-Sat.*
The couture house that began in the 1920s with Jeanne Lanvin has been reinvented by the talented Albert Elbaz. In October 2007 he unveiled this, the revamped showroom that set new aesthetic standards for luxury fashion retailing. Lanvin has an exhibition room devoted to her in the Musée des Arts Décoratifs, and this apartment-boutique comes close, incorporating original furniture from the Lanvin archive that has been restored. All this would be nothing, of course, if the clothes were not exquisite.

Lavinia
Opéra to Les Halles *3 bd de la Madeleine, 1st (01.42.97.20.20/www.lavinia.fr). Open 10am-8pm Mon-Fri; 9am-8pm Sat.*
Lavinia is a thoroughly contemporary emporium that stocks a broad selection of French alongside many non-French wines; its glassed-in *cave* has everything from a 1945 Mouton-Rothschild at €22,000 to trendy and 'fragile' wines for under €10. Have fun tasting wine with the *dégustation* machines on the ground floor, which allow customers a sip of up to ten different wines each week for €10.

LE66
Champs-Elysées & Western Paris *66 av des Champs-Elysées, 8th (01.53.53.33.96/www.myspace.com/lesoixantesix).Open 11am-8pm daily.*
Eschewing the glass cabinet approach of Colette, this fashion concept store is youthful and accessible, with an ever-changing selection of hip brands including Puma Black Label. Assistants, who are also the buyers and designers, make for a motivated team. The store takes the form of three transparent modules, the first a book and magazine store run by Black Book, and the second two devoted to fashion. It even has its own vintage store, in collaboration with Come On Eline and Kiliwatch.

Maison Fabre
Opéra to Les Halles *128 galerie de Valois, 1st (01.42.60.75.88/www.maisonfabre.com). Open 11am-7pm Mon-Sat.*
This glovemaker from Millau, which was founded in 1924, has capitalised on its racy designs from the sports car eras of the 1920s and '60s, opening a sexy little boutique. Classic gloves made from the softest leather (€100) come in 20 wild colours. Then there are the variations: crocodile, python, coyote, fur-trimmed, fingerless. But the ultimate lust object is the patent leather 'Auto' glove fastened with a massive button – somewhere between the cool of *The Avengers* and the kook of *Austin Powers*.

Shakespeare & Co
The Latin Quarter & the 13th *37 rue de la Bûcherie, 5th (01.43.25.40.93/www.shakespeareandcompany.com). Open 10am-11pm Mon-Sat; 11am-11pm Sun.*
Unequivocally the best bookshop in Paris, the historic and ramshackle Shakespeare & Co is always packed with expat and tourist book-lovers. Aside from permanent staff there is a selection of bookish travellers who live in the store's upper rooms in exchange for working there. There is a large second-hand section, antiquarian books next door, and just about anything you could ask for new.

Arts

La Cinémathèque Française
The Marais & Eastern Paris *51 rue de Bercy, 12th (01.71.19.33.33/www.cinematheque.fr). Admission Exhibitions €2.50-€9. Films €6; €3-€5 reductions; free for members. Membership €10/month.*
Relocated to Frank Gehry's striking, spacious cubist building, the Cinémathèque Française now boasts four screens, a bookshop, a restaurant, exhibition space and the Musée du Cinéma, where it displays a fraction of its huge collection of movie memorabilia. In the spirit of its founder Henri Langlois, the Cinémathèque hosts retrospectives, cult movies, classics, experimental cinema and Q&A sessions.

Comédie Française
www.comedie-francaise.fr.
Opéra to Les Halles *Salle Richelieu, 2 rue Richelieu, 1st (08.25.10.16.80/01.44.58.15.15). Box office 11am-6.30pm daily. Admission €11-€37.*
Opéra to Les Halles *Studio-Théâtre, Galerie du Carrousel du Louvre, 99 rue de Rivoli, 1st (01.44.58.98.54). Box office 2-5pm on performance day. Admission €13-€17; €8-€13 reductions.*
St-Germain-des-Prés *Théâtre du Vieux Colombier, 21 rue du Vieux Colombier, 6th (01.44.39.87.00). Box office 1-6pm Mon, Sun; 11am-6pm Tue-Sat. Admission €28. 45mins before show €13 under-28s.*

The gilded mother of French theatres, the Comédie Française turns out season after season of classics, as well as lofty new productions. The red velvet and gold-flecked Salle Richelieu is located right by the Palais-Royal; under the same management are the Studio-Théâtre, a black box inside the Carrousel du Louvre, and the Théâtre du Vieux Colombier on the Left Bank.

Opéra National de Paris, Palais Garnier
Opéra to Les Halles *Pl de l'Opéra, 9th (08.92.89.90.90/www.operadeparis.fr). Box office 10.30am-6.30pm Mon-Sat. By phone 9am-6pm Mon-Fri; 9am-1pm Sat. Admission €7-€172.*
The Palais Garnier, with its ornate, extravagant decor and ceiling by Marc Chagall, is the jewel in the crown of Paris music-making, as well as a glistening focal point for the Right Bank. The Opéra National often favours the high-tech Bastille for new productions, but the matchless acoustics of the Palais Garnier are superior to the new house.

Nightlife

Bateau Concorde Atlantique
The 7th & Western Paris *Port de Solférino, 25 quai Anatole-France, 7th (01.47.05.71.03/www.concorde-atlantique.com). Open 11pm-5am Mon-Fri; 5pm-5am Sat; 6pm-5am Sun. Closed mid Sept-mid June. Admission free-€10.*
With its terrace and voluminous dancefloor, this two-level boat is a clubbing paradise in the summer. The celebrated Respect crew held a fondly remembered Wednesday night here, and are still involved in putting on parties at the venue, alongside other cool crews like Ed Banger.

Crazy Horse Saloon
Champs-Elysées & Western Paris *12 av George V, 8th (01.47.23.32.32/www.crazyhorse.fr). Shows 8.30pm, 11pm Mon-Fri, Sun; 7.30pm, 9.45pm, 11.50pm Sat. Admission Show (incl 2 drinks) €70. Show (incl champagne) €100-€120; €50-€60 reductions.*
More risqué than the other cabarets, the Horse, whose art du nu was invented in 1951 by Alain Bernadin, is an ode to feminine beauty: 13 lookalike dancers with identical body statistics (when standing, the girls' nipples and hips are all the same height) move around the stage, clad only in rainbow light and strategic strips of black tape. The girls put on some tantalising numbers, with titles such as 'God Save Our Bare Skin' (a sexy take on the Changing of the Guard) and 'Va Va Voom'.

Point Ephémère
North-East Paris *200 quai de Valmy, 10th (01.40.34.02.48/www.pointephemere.org). Open 10am-2am daily. Admission varies.*
This hunk of Berlin in Paris was meant to be temporary, but thankfully it's still around. An uncompromising programming policy delivers some of the best electronic music in town; there's also a restaurant and bar with decks and a gallery, and terrace space by the canal in summer.

Rex
Opéra to Les Halles *5 bd Poissonnière, 2nd (01.42.36.10.96/www.rexclub.com). Open 11.30pm-6am Wed-Sat. Admission free-€15.*
The Rex's new sound system puts over 40 different sound configurations at the DJ's fingertips, and has proved to be a magnet for top turntable stars. Once associated with iconic techno pioneer Laurent Garnier, the Rex has stayed at the top of the Paris techno scene, and occupies an unassailable position as the city's serious club music venue.

Stay

L'Hôtel
St-Germain-des-Prés *13 rue des Beaux-Arts, 6th (01.44.41.99.00/www.l-hotel.com). €€€€.*
Guests at the sumptuously decorated L'Hôtel are more likely to be models and film stars than the starving writers who frequented it during Oscar Wilde's last days (the playwright died in a room on the ground floor in November 1900). Under Jacques Garcia's careful restoration, each room has its own special theme: Mistinguett's chambre retains its art deco mirror bed, and Oscar's tribute room is clad in green peacock murals. In the basement is a small pool.

Hôtel Amour
Opéra to Les Halles *8 rue Navarin, 9th (01.48.78.31.80/www.hotelamour.com). €€.*
This boutique hotel is a real hit with the in crowd. Each of the 20 rooms (with free Wi-Fi) is unique, decorated on the theme of love or eroticism by a coterie of contemporary artists and designers such as Marc Newson, M&M, Stak, Pierre Le Tan and Sophie Calle. Seven of the rooms contain artists' installations, and two others have their own private bar and a large terrace on which to hold your own party. The late-night brasserie has a coveted outdoor garden.

Hôtel les Degrés de Notre-Dame
The Latin Quarter & the 13th *10 rue des Grands-Degrés, 5th (01.55.42.88.88/www.les degreshotel.com). €€.*
On a tiny street across the river from Notre-Dame, this vintage hotel is an absolute gem. Its ten rooms are full of character, with original paintings, antique furniture and exposed wooden beams (nos.47 and 501 have views of the cathedral). It has an adorable restaurant and, a few streets away, two studio apartments that the owner rents to preferred customers only.

Hôtel Particulier Montmartre
Montmartre & Pigalle *23 av Junot, 18th (01.42.58.00.87/www.hotel-particulier-montmartre. com). €€€€.*
Visitors lucky (and wealthy) enough to manage to book a suite at the Hôtel Particulier Montmartre will find themselves in one of the city's hidden gems. Nestled in a quiet passage off rue Lepic, this sumptuous Directoire-style house is dedicated to art, with each of the five luxurious suites personalised by an avant-garde artist. Free Wi-Fi.

Hôtel du Petit Moulin
The Marais & Eastern Paris *29-31 rue de Poitou, 3rd (01.42.74.10.10/www.hoteldupetitmoulin.com). €€€.*
Within striking distance of the Musée Picasso and the hip shops situated on and around rue Charlot, this listed, turn-of-the-century façade masks what was once the oldest *boulangerie* in Paris, lovingly restored as a boutique hotel by Nadia Murano and Denis Nourry. The couple recruited fashion designer Christian Lacroix for the decor, and the result is a riot of colour, trompe l'oeil effects and a savvy mix of old and new. Each of its 17 exquisitely appointed rooms is unique, and the walls in rooms 202, 204 and 205 feature swirling, extravagant drawings and scribbles taken from Lacroix's sketchbook. Free parking.

Mama Shelter
North-east Paris *109 rue de Bagnolet, 20th (01.43.48.48.48/www.mamashelter.com). €€.*
Mam Shelter is Philippe Starck's latest design commission. It's set a stone's throw east of Père Lachaise, and its decor appeals to the young-at-heart with Batman and Incredible Hulk light fittings, dark walls, polished wood and splashes of bright fabrics. Every room comes with an iMac computer, TV, free internet access and a CD and DVD player; and when hunger strikes, there's a brasserie. If you're sure of dates, book online and take advantage of the saver's rate.

Le Meurice
Opéra to Les Halles *228 rue de Rivoli, 1st (01.44.58.10.10/www.lemeurice.com). €€€€.*
With its extravagant Louis XVI decor, intricate mosaic tiled floors and clever, modish restyling by Philippe Starck, Le Meurice is looking grander than ever. All 160 rooms are done up in distinct historical styles; the Belle Etoile suite on the seventh floor provides 360-degree panoramic views. You can relax in the Winter Garden to the strains of jazz; for more intensive intervention, head over to the lavishly appointed spa. The hotel's three Michelin-starred restaurant has chef Yannick Alléno at the helm.

Le Montalembert
The 7th & Western Paris *3 rue Montalembert, 7th (01.45.49.68.68/www.montalembert.com). €€€€.*
Grace Leo-Andrieu's boutique hotel is a benchmark of quality and service. It has everything that *mode* maniacs (who flock here for Fashion Week) could want: bathrooms stuffed with Molton Brown toiletries, a set of digital scales and plenty of mirrors with which to keep an eye on their figure. Decorated in pale lilac, cinnamon and olive tones, the entire hotel has Wi-Fi access, and each room is equipped with a flatscreen TV. Clattery two-person stairwell lifts are a nice nod to old-fashioned ways in a hotel that is otherwise *tout moderne.*

Factfile

When to go
Spring and autumn are the best times to visit Paris. In July and August there are often cheap deals on hotels and a good range of free events (such as Paris-Plage), but many family-run restaurants and shops close as the locals go *en vacances.* Avoid October, with its fashion weeks and trade shows.

Getting there
Paris has two main airports, with decent transport links: Roissy-Charles-de-Gaulle (01.70.36.39.50/www.adp.fr) and Orly (01.70.36.39.50/www.adp.fr). Budget hub Paris Beauvais (08.92.68.20.66/www.aeroport beauvais.com) is 70km (44 miles) from the city. Eurostar trains (www.eurostar.com) to Paris depart from London's St Pancras. The journey to Paris takes 2hrs 15mins direct. Check-in is at least 30mins before departure time. Eurostar trains arrive at Gare du Nord (08.92.35.35.39, www.sncf.fr), with easy access to public transport and taxi ranks.

Getting around
The Paris métro is the fastest and cheapest way of getting around. Trains run 5.30am-12.40am Mon-Thur, 5.30am-1.30am Fri-Sun. Batobus (08.25.05.01.01/www.batobus.com) runs river

buses stop every 15-25mins via the Eiffel Tower, Musée d'Orsay, St-Germain-des-Prés (quai Malaquais), Notre-Dame, Jardin des Plantes, Hôtel de Ville, Louvre and Champs-Elysées (Pont Alexandre III). Taxis can be hard to find. Your best bet is to find a taxi rank (*station de taxis*, marked with a blue sign) on major roads, crossroads and at stations. A white light on a taxi's roof indicates the car is free; an orange light means the cab is busy. In 2007, the mayor launched a municipal bike hire scheme – Vélib (www.velib.paris.fr). There are now over 20,000 bicycles available 24 hours a day, at nearly 1,500 'stations' across the city. The Vélib scheme is complemented by 372km (231 miles) of bike lanes.

Tourist information
Espace du Tourisme d'Ile de France
Carrousel du Louvre, 99 rue de Rivoli, 1st (08.26.16.66.66/www.paris-ile-de-france.com). Open 8.30am-7pm Mon-Fri.

Internet access
Many hotels and cafés offer Wi-Fi access, and an increasing number of public spaces are setting themselves up as free Wi-Fi hotspots. Otherwise try the following:
Milk 31 bd de Sébastopol, 1st (08.20.00.10.00/www.milklub.com). Open 24hrs daily.

Top: Palais des Droits de l'Homme. Bottom: La Petite France.

Strasbourg

A European union of party politics and picture-book streets.

Strasbourg is both an immaculately preserved medieval town and a dynamic European capital. Its crisp pink sandstone cathedral is a defining landmark in Gothic architecture, and the cobbled roads and waterways around its centre spill over with brightly coloured, higgledy-piggledy half-timbered houses, their tidy window boxes brimming with vibrant geraniums. This is a picture-book city that stands at the crossroads of Europe, just over two hours from Paris and three kilometres (two miles) from Germany.

Over the centuries, the Franco-German border has constantly been redrawn either side of Strasbourg, and it only takes a short wander around its clean, prosperous streets to discern the Teutonic influence. Grandiose Imperial architecture dominates the area north of the centre, and hearty meat and sauerkraut dishes are staples on any traditional menu. Food is a high point here. You can eat well and inexpensively in any number of cosy Alsatian *winstubs*, while virtuoso chefs in gastronomic restaurants are renowned for their uncompromising standards and creative flair. The region's wines are internationally acclaimed, and Kronenbourg is the local brewery.

The Strasbourgeois are proud of their traditions, and none brings more visitors than the month-long Christmas market in December. Dating back to 1570, the market stretches out across the whole of the Grande Ile, the island that makes up the city's historic centre. You only have to stroll through the garland-bedecked stalls in the fairytale streets of La Petite France to understand its worldwide appeal.

While Strasbourg's cultural heritage is an integral part of its identity, the city has today reshaped itself as a cosmopolitan capital of Europe. The banks of the river Ill house three major EU institutions, including the European Parliament. This has bred a multiculturalism that finds expression in all facets of city life, from nightlife to the arts. The influential architect Le Corbusier once commented that Strasbourg 'is a city that has grown up well'. It would be hard to disagree.

Explore

Strasbourg's historic centre is an island, the Grande Ile, surrounded by the river Ill. It is extensively pedestrianised and easily covered on foot. If you're planning on visiting more than one museum, consider buying a pass for the day (€8; €4 reductions) or for three days (€10). These are available at all museums.

CATHEDRAL AREA

The magnificent Gothic Cathédrale de Notre-Dame dominates Strasbourg's centre, its fragile-looking spire towering above the medieval neighbourhood's narrow cobbled streets. At the edge of place de la Cathédrale is the Maison Kammerzell, a 16th-century house adorned with wooden beams and intricately sculpted figures. Its classic top-heavy design is the result of a medieval tax dodge: payments were calculated according to the surface area of the ground floor.

Immediately south of the cathedral on place du Château is the imposing 18th-century Palais Rohan, which today hosts a trio of museums. Make your way towards the river from here and you'll hit place du Marché-des-Cochons-de-Lait, surrounded by crooked, half-timbered houses. Along the quayside, steeply gabled roofs and protruding oriel windows are further reminders of the city's architectural heritage.

The central place Gutenberg is named after the Strasbourg resident who invented the printing press in the 15th century. Just north, place Kléber is the commercial hub, while tree-lined place Broglie is home to the city's opera house. It's here that you'll find the heart of the city's Christmas Market (www.noel-strasbourg.com) in December. Expansive alleys of kiosks proffer mulled wine, pretzels, gingerbread, spiced sausage and handicrafts, and stalls spill out across the old town, including the cathedral, where regular concerts are held. It may sound kitsch, but there's no finer Yuletide setting than Strasbourg's story-book streets – and it takes only a modicum of festive cheer to be won over.

Cathédrale de Notre-Dame

28 pl de la Cathédrale (www.cathedrale-strasbourg.fr). Open 7-11.20am, 12.35-7pm daily. Admission free.
Sculpted in vivid pink Vosges sandstone, the cathedral's main façade is a testimony to the peerless skills of its 13th-century masons. The tympana of the three portals depict the life of Christ and the Last Judgement. High above, the characterful steeple, completed in 1439, offers unrivalled panoramas from its viewing platform. The cathedral's crowning glory, however, is its astronomical clock. Located in the south transept, alongside the stone-carved Pillar of Angels, the colourful 16th-century clock was given a makeover in 1842, and now performs a spectacular show at 12.30pm every day (€2, access via the southern door from noon), during which figures of the Apostles parade in front of Christ while a cock crows and beats its wings.

Strasbourg

Historic sites
●●●●○

Art & architecture
●●●●○

Hotels
●●●○○

Eating & drinking
●●●●○

Nightlife
●●●●○

Shopping
●●●●○

European Parliament.

Buerehiesel.

Musée Historique

*2 rue du Vieux Marché aux Poissons (03.88.52.50.00/
www.musees-strasbourg.org). Open noon-6pm
Tue-Fri; 10am-6pm Sat, Sun. Admission €5;
free-€2.50 reductions.*

Refurbished and rethought in 2007, this is perhaps the city's most attractive museum. It traces the history of Strasbourg with the aid of an audioguide (available in English), which automatically springs into life whenever you approach a new section of the exhibition. There are cannons and armour from the Middle Ages, a selection of 15th-century books celebrating Gutenberg's innovations in printing, and monuments to General Kléber, a leading post-Revolution military figure. A lot of thought has gone into making the experience interactive: visitors can take electronic multiple choice quizzes and try on period headwear, and kids can design stained-glassed windows. There's also a superb scale model of the city c1725.

Musée de l'Oeuvre Notre-Dame

*3 pl du Château (03.88.52.50.00/www.musees-
strasbourg.org). Open noon-6pm Tue-Fri; 10am-6pm
Sat, Sun. Admission €5; free-€2.50 reductions.*

During the Revolution, the statues decorating Strasbourg cathedral's façade were removed (and eventually replaced with facsimiles). Many of the original sculptures are today preserved in this museum, set in the former stonemasons' lodge, offering a chance to see their intricate details up close and personal. The rest of the collection focuses on medieval religious and decorative artefacts, the highlight being the 11th-century Tête de Christ – one of the earliest depictions of man in stained glass.

Palais Rohan

*2 pl du Château (03.88.52.50.00/www.musees-
strasbourg.org). Open noon-6pm Mon, Wed-Fri;
10am-6pm Sat, Sun. Admission (per museum) €5;
free-€2.50 reductions.*

Completed in 1742, this immense palace was inhabited by four successive Rohan Cardinals during the 18th century and subsequently served as an Imperial palace. It now houses three museums. In the basement, the Musée Archéologique exhibits findings from digs in Strasbourg from neolithic mammoths to Roman remains. On the second floor, the unexceptional Musée des Beaux-Arts showcases European paintings up to the middle of the 19th century. Most interesting is the Musée des Arts Décoratifs on the first floor, mainly for its grandiose palatial rooms, which have been reconstituted with original furniture belonging to the Rohan Cardinals and Napoleon I. In a separate wing, the decorative arts collection itself features an intriguing collection of 20th-century toys donated by Tomi Ungerer.

LA PETITE FRANCE

Undoubtedly Strasbourg's most postcard-friendly area, the idyllic Petite France is a 15-minute walk from the cathedral at the western tip of the Grande Ile. The area owes its name to a hospital (since destroyed) that catered for patients with the 'French disease' (venereal diseases) in the

16th century, but thanks to its network of canals it is best remembered as the district of millers, fishermen and tanners. The narrow streets are crammed with fairytale-like half-timbered houses, many built with multi-tiered roofs for drying animal hides. The Maison des Tanneurs (42 rue du Bain aux Plantes), which today houses a restaurant, is one of the oldest.

The edge of the district is marked by four watchtowers united by the Ponts Couverts, the sole remnants of the city's 14th-century ramparts. Beyond here is the Barrage Vauban, a dam built to protect Strasbourg from waterborne attacks. Its panoramic terrace is closed for work until 2011, but the Musée d'Art Moderne et Contemporain, located just behind the dam, offers a similarly spectacular view.

Musée d'Art Moderne et Contemporain

*1 pl Hans Jean Arp (03.88.23.31.31/www.musees-
strasbourg.org). Open noon-7pm Tue, Wed, Fri;
noon-9pm Thur; 10am-6pm Sat, Sun. Admission
€6; free-€3 reductions.*

On the ground floor of this striking glass-fronted museum, flagship works represent the major schools of early modern art: Monet and Sisley head up Impressionism, Signac Pointillism, and Picasso and Braque Cubism. The centrepiece, though, is a high-ceilinged room given over to Strasbourg-born Gustav Doré and dominated by *Le Christ quittant le prétoire* (1871-72), an immaculately restored painting depicting a luminous and resolutely calm Christ on his way to the cross, while Roman soldiers hold back crowds of hysterical Christians. If you don't suffer from vertigo, you can admire the work from an overhanging balcony on the first floor, where the focus is late 20th-century conceptual art from the likes of Buren, Hains and Arman.

GERMAN QUARTER

Over the river from place Broglie, the grandiose architecture of place de la République is a vestige of the city's time under Imperial Germany from 1870 up until World War I. The area's Gothic-Renaissance buildings were intended to celebrate Strasbourg's new status as capital of Reichsland. Famed for its magnolias in spring, the square houses the twin domes of the Bibliothèque Nationale and the Palais du Rhin, as well as the Théâtre National. Follow the river east and you'll arrive at the city's university, in front of which is a statue of former student Goethe. Behind here are the botanical gardens, home to some 6,000 plant varieties.

Musée Tomi Ungerer

*2 av de la Marseillaise (03.69.06.37.27/www.
musees-strasbourg.org). Open noon-6pm Mon,
Wed-Fri; 10am-6pm Sat, Sun. Admission €5;
free-€2.50 reductions.*

Opened in 2007, this stylish museum pays homage to famed Strasbourg illustrator Tomi Ungerer. Best known for his children's books, for which he won the prestigious Hans

Christian Andersen Award in 1998, Ungerer spent many years in America working on advertising posters and has also dabbled with political satire and erotica. The museum traces these different preoccupations over three floors in rooms featuring striking whitewashed walls and ceilings. Insightful explanatory texts (in English, French and German) put the works in context, so that even the uninitiated can enjoy the experience.

EUROPEAN DISTRICT

Thanks to its chequered ownership history and strategic location, Strasbourg was chosen as a capital for Europe after World War II. Thirty minutes' walk north-east of the cathedral, the banks of the river Ill are home to three major European institutions. The circle-and-ellipse design of the European Parliament elegantly follows the curve of the river. It houses a chamber for 750 Euro MPs, and can be visited by appointment only (03.88.17.20.07). On the opposite bank is the Palais de l'Europe, seat of the Council of Europe, and across the way sits Richard Rogers' Palais des Droits de l'Homme, the human rights court designed to resemble a curved ship.

Nearby, the Parc de l'Orangerie is Strasbourg's largest green area. Its mini zoo is most well known for its part in a region-wide initiative to repopulate Alsace with storks, and the birds can be seen nesting atop nearby trees all year round. Another park, the Jardin des Deux Rives, situated some three kilometres (two miles) south-east, is a reminder that Strasbourg is a frontier city. Its footbridge over the Rhine takes you straight into Germany.

Eat

Meaty Alsatian dishes can be found in traditional *winstubs* (think French bistro meets country pub), as well as more elegant establishments. Specialities include *choucroute garnie*, sauerkraut heaped with a generous selection of pork charcuterie, and *baeckeoffe*, a marinated lamb, beef and pork stew. But, as you'd expect from such a cosmopolitan city, there is also a healthy world cuisine scene. Rue des Tonneliers near the cathedral is packed with restaurants of all kinds. In summer, head for the terraces of the place du Marché Gayot and La Petite France.

Art Café

La Petite France *1 pl Hans Jean Arp (03.88.22.18.88/ www.musees-strasbourg.org). Open May-Sept 11am-10pm Tue-Sat; 10am-6pm Sun. Oct-Apr 11am-7pm Tue, Wed, Fri; 11am-9pm Thur; 11am-6pm Sat, Sun. €€.*
There's no need to visit the modern art museum to sample its café, which boasts the best terrace view in Strasbourg. From here, you can sip coffee or eat a light bite while gazing

down on the Barrage Vauban, La Petite France and the cathedral beyond. If it's too cold to go alfresco, the Yves Taralon-designed interior affords the same panorama thanks to its huge bay windows. The salads are excellent and there's a decent brunch on weekends.

Les Brasseurs

Cathedral *22 rue des Veaux (03.88.36.12.13). Open 11.30am-1am Mon-Sat; 11.30am-midnight Sun. €.*
This popular student hangout is famed for its home-brew beer and cheap, tasty *flammekueche* (*tarte flambée* in French), a pizza-like Alsatian speciality that consists of bread dough traditionally topped with crème fraîche, onions and lardons. At Les Brasseurs, there's a variety of alternative toppings on offer: cheese, mushrooms and *choucroute*. The early evening happy hour and all-you-can-eat menu provide excellent value, although be warned that peak-hour crowds result in slow service. In summer, the festive *winstub* atmosphere spills out on to the terrace.

Buerehiesel

European District *4 parc de l'Orangerie (03.88.45.56.65/www.buerehiesel.fr). Open noon-2pm, 6-10pm Tue-Sat. Closed 3wks Jan & 3wks Aug. €€€€.*
The Buerehiesel may have forfeited its three Michelin stars when chef Antoine Westermann handed over the reins to his son Eric in 2007, but it remains the city's most prestigious restaurant. Mixing traditional Alsatian and French cuisine with elegant innovation, Eric Westermann has maintained his father's impeccably high gastronomic standards while significantly reducing prices. The *cuisses de grenouille* slide straight off the bone and melt in the mouth, while the *brioche caramelisée à la bière* makes dessert a near obligation. Ask for a seat on the veranda with a view over the Parc de l'Orangerie when you reserve. Note that there is a special €68 menu for under-35s.

Chez Yvonne

Cathedral *10 rue du Sanglier (03.88.32.84.15/ www.chez-yvonne.net). Open noon-2.15pm, 6pm-midnight daily. €€.*
This Strasbourg institution attracts the country's rich and famous, from President Sarkozy to legendary actress Jeanne Moreau, as the signed photos in the staircase attest. The classic Alsatian decor, right down to the red-and-white checked tablecloths, smacks of class rather than kitsch – and the cuisine follows suit. Regional specialities, all made from local produce, include the *coq au riesling* with *spaetzle* and *maennerstolz*, a smoked sausage served with sauerkraut. For dessert, don't miss the *granité de gewürztraminer vendanges tardives*, a finely sliced, frozen mound of the wine that has all the characteristic richness of its liquid form.

L'Epicerie

Cathedral *6 rue du Vieux Seigle (www.lepicerie-strasbourg.com). Open 11.30am-1.30am daily. €.*
Always packed, this cosy, laid-back café attracts a young crowd. The decor is that of an old-fashioned corner shop, with enamel advertising signs on the walls and a bar counter

Chez Yvonne.

littered with sweet jars, old scales and other bric-a-brac. The home-style cooking includes salads, large bowls of soup and the house speciality, *tartines* – large slabs of dark bread heaped with all manner of savoury goodies.

HK
Cathedral *12 rue Vieux Marché aux Grains (03.88.32.11.05). Open (meals) noon-3pm, 6.30-10pm Tue-Sat. €€.*
In the midst of the high-street stores, this colourful, laid-back restaurant-café makes for a great retreat from shopping. Outside meal times, it proffers tempting hot drink and cake combinations (try the latte with cookies). During lunchtimes and weekend evenings, it serves up simple, original fusion dishes such as kangaroo curry or vegetable and goat's cheese lasagne. The assiette HK lets you choose four mini main courses from a list of 12.

Il Girasole
Cathedral *12 quai Saint Nicolas (03.88.37.16.76/ www.ilgirasole.fr). Open 11.30am-2.30pm, 6.30-10.30pm daily. €€.*
Decorated with large sunflowers (*girasole*) and warm colours, this family-run Italian restaurant offers copious portions in a stylish, modern setting. The speciality of Matteo and Anna, originally from Puglia, is their creamy cheese-filled gnocchi, while the *tris di pasta* – a selection of three stuffed pasta in three different sauces – is also a delight. For a starter, try the *antipasto sotto olio primavera*, an assortment of flavoursome vegetables soaked in rich olive oil. And should you have any room left, make straight for the home-made tiramisu, which thankfully is light. The pizzas are also excellent, and there is a good selection of Italian wine.

Mooze
Cathedral *1 rue Demi Lune (03.88.22.68.46/www. mooze.fr). Open noon-2pm, 7-10.30pm Mon-Sat; 6-10pm Sun. €€.*
A huge conveyer belt winds back and forth around this open-plan Japanese restaurant, proffering varied dishes of sushi, maki, tempura and oddball deserts. Centre stage is the chef, while on the other side are the punters. From your bar stool or table, just reach over and pull off any dish you fancy. Plates are colour-coded for price, and there's a great range of green and black teas. The decor is funky, and a trip to the toilets proves distinctly zen: the floor is lined with small paving stones over a bed of pebbles that lead right into the cubicle.

Shop

The streets around place Kléber house high-street shops aplenty, with upper-end stores concentrated around rue de la Haute Montée. Just north of the river, Place des Halles (24 place des Halles) is the city's largest shopping centre. For designer clothes, try rue des Hallebardes by the cathedral.

La Boutique du Gourmet
Cathedral *26 rue des Orfèvres (03.88.32.00.04/ www.bruck-foiegras.com). Open Apr-Dec 2-7pm Mon; 9.30am-12.30pm, 2-7pm Tue-Thur; 9am-7pm Fri, Sat. Jan-Mar 9am-noon, 2.30-6.30pm Tue-Sat.*
The Bruck family from Strasbourg has been making foie gras since 1852, and you'll find it here in myriad forms: fresh, preserved, in pastry, with truffles. Of course, foie gras needs to be washed down with the right tipple, and you can take your pick from local wines and spirits. For eaux-de-vie, try the prize-winning marc de gewürztraminer (a grape-based spirit like Italian grappa) from the Lehmann distillery in Obernai, or the excellent mirabelle d'Alsace, made from local mirabelle plums.

I.T.O
Cathedral *18 rue des Soeurs (03.88.35.55.93). Open 1-7pm Tue-Thur; noon-7pm Wed; 10am-12.30pm, 2-7pm Fri, Sat.*
I.T.O stands for Idées – Textiles et Objets, and this small boutique is crammed with unusual ideas for interior design and women's fashion. Clothes, shoes and accessories are carefully selected for the subtle touches that make the design unique. Some brands are well established (Blink shoes, St Martins clothes), but there is also a choice offering of lesser-known young designers.

Kirn
La Petite France *17-19 rue du 22 novembre (03.88.32.16.10/www.kirn-traiteur.fr). Open 9am-7pm Mon; 8am-7pm Tue-Thur; 7.30am-7pm Fri, Sat.*
The Kirns have been creating top-quality charcuterie since 1904, and today their city centre boutique has become a benchmark for all things gourmand. The extensive selection is sublime, from foie gras and *bierwurscht* (beer sausage) to pre-prepared *choucroute* and Alsatian black pudding. The food-fest doesn't stop at the meat, though; the boulangerie boasts elaborate house concoctions, and there's a wonderful cheese counter (including several stinky munsters). For instant gratification, head to the restaurant upstairs.

Un Nöel en Alsace
La Petite France *10 rue des Dentelles (03.88.32.32.32/www.noelenalsace.fr). Open 10.30am-12.30pm, 1.30-6pm Mon-Sat (daily in Dec).*
Christmas is such a big deal in Strasbourg that it can sustain an entire boutique all year round. The focus is handmade decorations of yore, including hand-painted wooden cut-outs of Father Christmas, old-fashioned pewter storks and delicate lace Christmas trees. For a splurge, check out the traditional Germanic tiered candleholders that turn on their own axis when the candles are lit.

L'Occase de l'Oncle Tom
Cathedral *119 Grand'Rue (03.88.37.33.60/www. oncletom.com). Open 1-7pm Mon; 10.30am-7pm Tue-Fri; 10am-7pm Sat.*
Rare and second-hand CDs, vinyl and DVDs are bought and sold here. On the ground floor, there's a wealth of CDs of all styles – including a bargain basement where prices range

from €1 to €6. Upstairs, vinyl is king. Some shelf space is also given over to second-hand music-related books and old Airfix models and toy cars.

L'Oeillade

La Petite France *16 Grand'Rue (no phone).*
Open 2-7pm Mon; 10am-7pm Tue-Sat.
There's no better place than L'Oeillade to find original gifts for children. Anke and Vincent Meurice take pride in stocking lovingly crafted, traditional toys from all over Europe, with an emphasis on quality. Wooden toys, baby rattles and cuddly teddy bears sit on the shelves alongside music boxes and colourful mobiles.

Pain d'épices – Mireille Oster

La Petite France *14 rue des Dentelles*
(03.88.32.33.34/www.mireille-oster.com).
Open 9am-7pm daily.
Alsace has a long tradition of gingerbread (*pain d'épices*), and Mireille Oster is one of the region's finest exponents. The family recipes, handed down from her grandparents, have today spawned some 40 different varieties of gingerbread, as well as chocolates and confectionary eggs, in this small, homely boutique. Of the *pain d'épices*, the *aphrodisiaque* variety, made with ginger, coriander, pepper and cumin, is excellent – but it's the melt-in-your-mouth cinnamon stars that really blow the taste buds.

Poterie d'Alsace

Cathedral *3 rue des Frères (03.88.32.23.21/*
www.poterie-alsace-strasbourg.eu). Open 2-7pm
Mon; 10am-7pm Tue-Sat.
This store, crammed with Alsatian pottery in all its many forms, uses 20 suppliers from two local villages – Betschdorf, known for its hardy grey and blue sandstone; and Soufflenheim, which produces colourful floral and spotted terracotta. You'll find moulds for *kugelhopf* (a local cake) in every size, oval *baeckeoffe* tureens, dishes, jugs, eggcups and decorative hearts. In the glassware section, look out for the classic green-stemmed wineglass of the region.

Arts

For information about Strasboug's upcoming concerts, shows and films, head to Boutique Culture (10 place de la Cathédrale, 03.88.23.84.65).

Opéra National du Rhin

Cathedral *19 pl Broglie (03.88.75.48.00/bookings*
08.25.84.14.84/www.operanationaldurhin.fr).
Tickets prices vary.
Awarded 'national' status in 1997, the Opéra National du Rhin is a partnership between the region's three biggest towns: Strasbourg, Colmar and Mulhouse. The Strasbourg wing focuses on opera, but the venue also stages regular world-class ballet. Marc Clémeur recently took over as director and promises to continue a varied programme, with a particular focus on contemporary works.

Palais de la Musique et des Congrès

European District *Pl de Bordeaux (03.88.37.67.67/*
www.strasbourgmeeting.com). Tickets prices vary.
This vast complex is home to Strasbourg's philharmonic orchestra, which has been conducted by such luminaries as Strauss, Berlioz and Brahms since its creation in 1855. Today, director Marc Albrecht is famed for his interpretation of Germanic classics from the likes of Wagner and Strauss.

Nightlife

L'Abattoir

La Petite France *1 quai Charles Altorffer*
(03.88.32.28.12). Open noon-2am Mon-Thur;
noon-3am Fri; 3pm-3am Sat; 3pm-1am Sun.
During afternoons and weekday evenings, this is a popular, laid-back bar. There's a good selection of teas and cocktails, and artsy events are organised regularly. At weekends, the oriental feel is transformed into a party vibe by DJs.

Les Frères Berthom

Cathedral *18 rue des Tonneliers (03.88.32.81.18/*
www.lesberthom.fr). Open 5pm-1am Mon, Sun;
5pm-1.30am Tue, Wed; 5pm-2.30am Thur-Sat.
Wood-panelled walls and low beams make this a snug, lively pub smack bang in the city centre. There's a huge selection of Belgian beers, including Kriek on tap, as well as a decent selection of cocktails – and prices are slashed during happy hour. The groovy rock music is never too loud to talk.

La Laiterie

La Petite France *13 rue du Hohwald (03.88.23.72.37/*
www.laiterie.artefact.org). Open times vary.
Although the Zénith, opened in 2008, is now the city's biggest concert hall, La Laiterie, with its capacity of 1,000, remains a more intimate venue for up-and-coming or cult artists of every style. Every autumn it organises Osophère, a digital arts and electro music festival with international groups and DJs.

La Passerelle

Cathedral *38 quai des Bateliers (03.88.36.19.95).*
Open 6pm-1.30am Tue-Sun.
One of the city's trendiest hangouts, La Passerelle serves up flamboyant cocktails in a designer decor that's all velvets and purples lined with bar stools and plush sofas. The DJs tend towards cool electro, culminating in dancy house by the end of the night. A small courtyard acts as a chill zone.

Stay

Best Western – Hôtel de L'Europe

La Petite France *38 rue du Fossé des Tanneurs*
(03.88.32.17.88/www.hotel-europe.com). €€.
This brightly coloured half-timbered building used to be a posthouse and previous guests have included Voltaire, Goethe and Schiller. Today, its comfortable guestrooms are

Top: Regent Petite France.
Bottom: Hôtel Cathédrale.

kitted out with cable TV, air-conditioning and free Wi-Fi. Many rooms include period furniture and exposed beams, while some are also equipped with a whirlpool tub. The hotel is situated just a minute's walk from the canals of La Petite France. Look out in the lobby for the intricate 1:50 scale model of Strasbourg Cathedral, sculpted from the same pink sandstone as the original.

Hôtel Beaucour Baumann

Cathedral *5 rue des Bouchers (03.88.76.72.00/ www.hotel-beaucour.com). €€€.*
When you step under the arched gateway and into the courtyard of the Beaucour, it's like you've arrived in a sort of mini-Alsace. On all sides, brightly coloured half-timbered houses are tidily lined with geranium-filled window boxes. Five adjoining buildings house the hotel's 49 rooms, which all come with air-conditioning, TV and whirlpool bathtub. The interior of each, however, has been individually designed in styles somewhere between modern and kitsch.

Hôtel Cathédrale

Cathedral *12-13 pl de la Cathédrale (03.88.22.12.12/ www.hotel-cathedrale.fr). €€.*
The Hôtel Cathédrale is a good mid-range option with a very central location. The rooms on the square boast a picture-postcard view of the cathedral and Maison Kemmerzell, although light sleepers be warned that the bell tower starts chiming early. The view can also be admired from the first-floor breakfast room, where the spread includes a choice of eggs, cheese, ham and salamis. There's a bar open till midnight, and Wi-Fi and bike hire are offered free to guests.

Hôtel du Dragon

La Petite France *2 rue de l'Ecarlate (03.88.35.79.80/ www.dragon.fr). €€.*
Situated just the other side of the river from La Petite France, the Hôtel du Dragon offers quiet, moderately priced rooms in a 17th-century setting. It once welcomed Louis XIV, but today the 32 bedrooms are somewhat more modest. Simple and comfortable, they come with en suite bathrooms and cable TV – and many have views of the river and cathedral. When the weather allows, you can enjoy the excellent sweet-and-savoury buffet breakfast in the garden. Drivers should note that there is no car park. But if you leave your car on the street, the staff will keep the parking meter topped up.

Hôtel Villa Novarina

European District *11 rue Westercamp (03.90.41.18.28/www.villanovarina.com). €€€.*
Located in the embassy district next to the calm of the Parc de l'Orangerie, Villa Novarina combines the mod cons of a top-class hotel with the homely attention of hostess Christine Claus. The spacious rooms are decorated with an elegant mix of modern and antique furniture, and light floods in through large bay windows that overlook the garden. The little extras include remote-controlled electric blinds, swimming pool, and home-made pâtisseries at breakfast. Suites are available, as well as an apartment that sleeps up to four. The hotel is a half-hour walk or quick tram ride from the city's historic centre.

Regent Petite France

La Petite France *5 rue des Moulins (03.88.76.43.43/ www.regent-petite-france.com). €€€€.*
Converted from an old ice factory, this top-of-the-range hotel boasts a premium location in the heart of Strasbourg's prettiest area. While the dominant feel is elegant modernity, there are occasional signs of the building's past: many of the rooms feature original wooden beams and the classy champagne bar is tastefully decorated with old machinery. The rooms all come with air-conditioning, satellite TV and a view over the canal, while many of the suites feature large tubs with jacuzzi water jets. There's also a garage and sauna/gym. In the warmer months, the Pont Tournant restaurant spills out on to the waterside terrace.

Factfile

When to go

Winter often brings sub-zero temperatures, but December's Christmas market makes it the busiest time. Summer can be extremely hot and stuffy, while spring and autumn bring the most temperate weather.

Getting there

Strasbourg Airport is south-west of the city in Entzheim (03.88.64.67.67/www.strasbourg. aeroport.fr). A shuttle train (08.91.67.00.27) runs two to five times an hour to the main train station. The nine-minute journey costs €3.50 and includes a connecting tram journey. Arriving from Paris by TGV (2hrs 15mins), you also come into the main station, which is located just west of the city centre.

Getting around

CTS (03.88.77.70.70/www.cts-strasbourg.fr) runs the city's five tram lines and bus services. Tickets (€1.40 or €12 for ten) can be bought from vending machines at tram stations and used on both trams and buses. Validate your ticket by inserting it in the quayside machines or on board the bus.

Tourist information

Tourist office 17 pl de la Cathédrale (03.88.52.28.28/www.otstrasbourg.fr). Open 9am-7pm daily.

Internet access

L'Utopie 21 rue du Fossé des Tanneurs (03.88.23.89.21). Open 6.30am-11.30pm daily.

Clockwise from top: Le Capitole; Grand Hôtel de l'Opéra; Pont Neuf.

Toulouse

The dynamic capital of the Midi-Pyrénées is pretty in pink.

To say that Toulouse is a colourful city would be a sizeable understatement. Set halfway between the Mediterranean and the Atlantic, and enjoying over 2,000 hours of sunshine a year, the capital of the Midi-Pyrénées region is known in France as '*la ville rose*', a nickname it acquired by its abundance of buildings in reddish-pink brick; the predominance of this warm-hued construction material makes for a historic centre of great elegance and harmony. 'Colourful' also describes the people who live here, with their outgoing attitude and the distinctive singsong twang of the local accent. They are people who love food, festivity and sport, especially rugby (Toulouse is the spiritual home of French *ovalie*); if you share an interest in any of the above, you'll find it easy to fall into conversation.

This good-time town has art, gastronomy and history in spades – but unlike every French city other than Paris, it also has a pronounced technological slant that even the visitor can sample and enjoy. For Toulouse has a long and illustrious history of aviation achievement, and is now a powerhouse of Europe's aerospace industry; good news for dads and sons, who can gorge on museums devoted to classic and cutting-edge flying machines and spacecraft. The city also boasts some impressive aquatic attractions, being cradled by the Garonne river and the historic Canal du Midi – and, following the growing fashion for city beaches, the municipal Toulouse Plage initiative strews tonnes of soft white sand on the banks of the Ile du Ramier for most of July and August.

With all of the above, plus a hot bar and nightlife scene, dozens of good shops and one of the busiest cultural calendars anywhere in the country, Toulouse really does seem to have it all. There's clearly more than civic piety in the Occitan motto '*Per Tolosa totjorn mai*' – For Toulouse, Always More.

Explore

Toulouse is the fourth largest city in France, but its historic heart, which contains nearly all of the main visitor attractions and most of the shops, restaurants and hotels, is a compact district bounded by boulevard Lascrosses to the north, boulevard de Strasbourg to the north-east, and allées Jules-Guesde to the south.

The site has been inhabited since the eighth century BC, and from the start was a key trading post; but it was only when it earned the favour of Julius Caesar that it really flourished, to the point where 'Tolosa' was one of the major cities of the Roman empire. With the decline of the Romans it became the domain of the Visigoths, then the Franks, remaining independent until the 13th century, when it became the property of the French crown. Much of the city burned down in 1453, and during the subsequent reconstruction several local merchants built themselves elaborate *hôtels particuliers* (private mansions) in the new Renaissance style. The Hôtel de Bernuy on rue Gambetta and the glorious Hôtel d'Assézat on place d'Assézat were once such homes.

The focal point of the city is the arcaded place du Capitole, a huge pedestrianised square with the Occitan cross, emblem of the city flag, outlined in the paving in the middle. The monumental Capitole building on the east side functions as the seat of local government;

municipal events permitting, it's worth looking inside if only to see the wall-to-ceiling 19th-century paintings, including Henri Martin's depiction of Toulouse life. The renowned Théâtre du Capitole, on the south side, was renovated in 2004 and still looks stunning; and behind the Capitole building itself, the Donjon du Capitole now operates as the city's tourist office.

To the south lies medieval Toulouse; to the north, up rue du Taur, stands the city's finest building, the Basilique St-Sernin. The historic quarter is dotted with a bizarre assortment of churches, including the Gothic Les Jacobins on rue Lakanal where the Dominican order was founded, and Notre-Dame-de-la-Daurade, a hotchpotch of styles presided over by a black statue of the Virgin. Across the Pont Neuf, modern art has a stylish home in Les Abattoirs (76 allée Charles-de-Fitte, 05.62.48.58.00, www.lesabattoirs.org). The show-stopper here is Picasso's 1936 stage curtain *La Dépouille du Minotaure en costume d'arlequin* – but it's on display for just three months of the year.

A number of companies organise cruises on the wide Garonne or the UNESCO-rated Canal du Midi, to the west and north of the city centre.

Basilique St-Sernin
13 pl St-Sernin (05.61.21.70.18/www.basilique-st-sernin-toulouse.fr). Open Oct-June 8.30am-noon, 2-6pm Mon-Sat; 8.30am-noon, 2-7.30pm Sun. July-Sept 8.30am-6.30pm daily. Admission free.

Toulouse

Historic sites
● ● ● ● ●

Art & architecture
● ● ● ● ○

Hotels
● ● ● ● ○

Eating & drinking
● ● ● ● ●

Nightlife
● ● ● ● ●

Shopping
● ● ● ● ○

0   100km

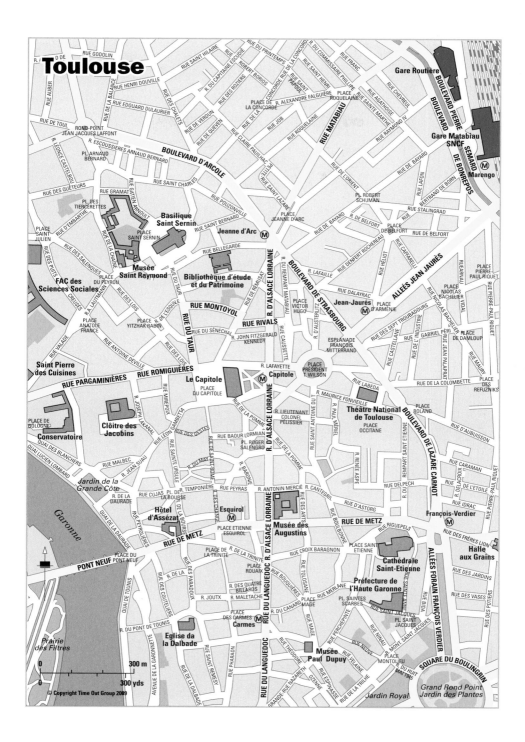

Top: Brasserie des Beaux-Arts.
Bottom: Emile.

This is the largest Romanesque church in Europe, with an awe-inspiring octagonal wedding-cake spire. It became a stop for pilgrims after Charlemagne donated a collection of holy relics (many of which are on display), and it contains the tomb of Saturnin, the city's patron saint, who was dragged to his death by a bull in 257. The basilica also has an astounding 1889 Cavaillé-Coll pipe organ, which is considered to be one of the most important in the country; it's played in regular free recitals on Sunday afternoons.

Fondation Bemberg

Hôtel d'Assézat, pl d'Assézat (05.61.12.06.89/ www.fondation-bemberg.fr). Open 10am-12.30pm, 1.30-6pm Tue, Wed, Fri-Sun; 10am-12.30pm, 1.30-9pm Thur. Admission €5; free-€3 reductions.
The 16th-century Hôtel d'Assézat is one of the architectural marvels of Toulouse, with a glorious inner courtyard surrounded by three storeys of brick and stone that constituted one of the earliest examples of French Classicism. As well as providing a base for various scientific societies, it's home to the Fondation Bemberg, an art museum that holds paintings by Monet, Matisse and Pissarro, and 30 major works by Pierre Bonnard. The collection was assembled by Argentine art lover George Bemberg.

Musée des Augustins

21 rue de Metz (05.61.22.21.82/www.augustins.org). Open 10am-6pm Mon, Tue, Thur-Sun; 10am-9pm Wed. Admission €3; free-€1.50 reductions.
This 14th-century convent is impressively atmospheric. It was appropriated by the revolutionaries in 1793, and became a museum two years later; today it houses a large collection of sculpture and paintings from the Middle Ages to the 20th century. Highlights include works by local artist Edouard Debat-Ponsan, Delacroix's vast *Sultan Moulay Abd Al-Rhaman*, and Courbet's *Anacréon, Bacchus et l'Amour*. The sculpture collection is particularly rich in Romanesque works, and also includes several busts by Rodin and another by Camille Claudel.

Musée St-Raymond

Pl St-Sernin (05.61.22.31.44/www.museesaintraymond. toulouse.fr). Open 10am-6pm daily. Admission €3; free-€1.50 reductions.
Occupying the walls of a 16th-century hospital, the Musée St-Raymond gathers together the city's archaeological remains. The building has been used for this purpose since the 1950s, but in the early 1990s someone had the idea of excavating part of the building's own footprint, which proved to have been a burial ground in the fourth and fifth centuries AD; the resulting basement space is now used to exhibit the stone sarcophagi and personal items that were dug up. Elsewhere in the museum there are dozens of Roman sculptures, including busts of the emperors, and a regular programme of temporary exhibitions brings other items out of the vast reserve.

Muséum de Toulouse

35 allées Jules-Guesde (05.67.73.84.84/www.museum. toulouse.fr). Open 10am-6pm Tue-Sun. Admission €5; free-€3.50 reductions.

The second largest natural history museum in France (the largest is in Paris) reopened in 2007, after a mammoth eight-year enlargement and improvement programme. It's now an absorbing, faultlessly modern museum with a large botanical garden. The exhibition spaces are arranged by theme – 'natural forces', 'breaking down hierarchy', 'vastness' and so on – and explore every aspect of life on Earth. Interactive features abound, and some of the exhibits, like the suspended skeleton of a blue whale, are guaranteed to inspire wonder.

Eat

Local specialities include sausages, foie gras and cassoulet, as well as Fronton and Gaillac wines. A good selection of cheap eats can be found on rue des Filatiers.

Le 19

19 descente de la Halle aux Poissons (05.34.31.94.84/ www.restaurantle19.com). Open 12.30-1.30pm Mon; 12.30-1.30pm, 7.30-8.30pm Tue-Fri; 7.30-8.30pm Sat. Closed 2wks Aug. €€€.
A dramatically deep, brick-walled staircase takes you down to the basement of this 16th-century fish storehouse that gave the narrow street its name. Although subterranean, this is one of the highest-profile restaurants in Toulouse – and little wonder. The vaulted dining room is carpet underfoot, but pink brick from the skirting boards upwards, and it looks fantastic. The seasonal menu includes faultlessly prepared dishes such as cream of watercress soup with warm oysters, roasted shoulder of rabbit with polenta, and a saffron-scented *sabayon* with ice-cream. There's a very swanky bar, sparkling with glasses, bottles and mirrors, and an original wine cellar – still used for its first purpose – visible from the dining room.

Brasserie des Beaux-Arts

1 quai de la Daurade (05.61.21.12.12/www.brasserie lesbeauxarts.com). Open noon-2.30pm, 7.30-10.30pm daily. €€.
Attached to the Hôtel des Beaux-Arts at the eastern end of the Pont-Neuf, this award-winning brasserie is run by France's upmarket Flo restaurant group, so standards are reliably high. It's a lovely-looking place, all belle époque trimmings, wooden panels, large mirrors and soft lighting; Ingres and Matisse supped here in the days when it was the Café Bellevue. The seasonal food is light and refined: an aubergine *papeton* served with tomato marmalade, perhaps, followed by tartare of avocado and Mediterranean prawns or melting beef carpaccio dressed with olive oil and flakes of fragrant parmesan.

Emile

13 pl St-Georges (05.61.21.05.56/www.restaurant-emile.com). Open noon-1.45pm, 7-9.45pm Tue-Sat. €€€€.
When Airbus launched its latest airliner, the A380 superjumbo, the assembled heads of state were brought for dinner to this renowned local address – and clues to a

restaurant's quality don't get much stronger than that. Emile has been run by the same family for nearly 50 years, earning a golden reputation for its fish and, in particular, its cassoulet. Inside, it's the picture of a classic French diner, with old-fashioned wooden chairs, homely red or floral napery and small lamps on tables. The menu is reassuringly traditional: as well as the signature dishes, you'll find the likes of oysters, smoked salmon, *magret de canard*, steak and Grand Marnier soufflé, all wonderfully fresh and attractively served; a wildly popular terrace completes the picture.

En Marge

8 rue Mage (05.61.53.07.24/www.restaurantenmarge. com). Open noon-1.30pm, 8-9.15 pm Wed-Sat. Closed 3wks Aug & 1st 2wks Sept. €€€€.
This new, pocket-sized restaurant has gone for the cool, contemporary approach, and its monochrome colour scheme won't be to everyone's taste. Fortunately, the mood is friendly and relaxed to the point of playful: each table has a silver chair, whose occupant is designated MC for the duration of the meal, and some dishes come in disguise – like the chocolate tube made up to look like a lit cigar. Still, you don't get a Michelin star for presentation alone, and local boy Frank Renimel's food is fresh and inventive, riffing on produce such as truffles, guinea fowl, squid and even flowers. Portions are on the modest side, but the flavours are out of this world.

La Faim des Haricots

3 rue du Puits-Vert (05.61.22.49.25/www.lafaimdes haricots.fr). Open noon-2.30pm, 7-9.30pm Mon-Sat. €€.
Eyebrows were raised when the first branch of this three-restaurant mini chain opened in 1996, when vegetarian restaurants were rare enough in carnivorous southern France to be news. They're still not exactly legion, but this outfit at least is well established and well thought of. The Toulouse branch applies the formula of the other two: a cheerfully painted dining room, a large buffet bar of salads, and daily quiches (feta, tomato and basil, perhaps), soups and main courses such as a Mexican casserole of peppers, sweetcorn, red beans and bulgur wheat. It's cheap, cheerful and fun – and you can eat as much as you like.

Les Jardins de l'Opéra

1 pl du Capitole (05.61.23.07.76/www.lesjardins delopera.com). Open noon-2pm, 8-10pm Tue-Sat. €€€€.
Even if you're not staying at the Grand Hôtel de l'Opéra, it's worth booking for a meal at its very elegant restaurant – thought of by many as the best table in the city. The dining area consists of a series of salons, some set under a fan-shaped glass roof with views of a 'Florentine' inner courtyard complete with Canova-style lions and pond (dedicated to Neptune, we were told); some salons can be set aside for private parties. The upmarket south-western cuisine includes dishes such as sea bass with cauliflower cream and preserved kumquats, fillet of beef with black olives and a tomato gâteau or the signature foie gras ravioli drizzled with a truffle reduction. It's certainly not cheap, but the three-course lunchtime menu, which includes wine and coffee, is good value at €44.

Le Louchebem

Marché Victor-Hugo, Loge 3-5 (05.61.12.12.52/www. lelouchebem.com). Open noon-2.30pm Tue-Sun. €€.
Louchebem is a tasty form of back slang specific to French butchers – or, in this case, a tasty restaurant run by a former butcher in an enormous, recently renovated indoor food market. It's a carnivore's paradise: owner Jean-Philippe Deschamps knows all the market's butchers personally, so the meat is first class: meltingly soft fillet steak, veal kidneys, steak tartare, rack of lamb and some 20 other types of fleshy fare, all served in a clean and simple dining area with tiled floor and cow-print tablecloths (in case you were forgetting what you came for).

Michel Sarran

21 bd Armand-Duportal (05.61.12.32.32/www.michel-sarran.com). Open noon-1.45pm, 8-9.45pm Mon, Tue, Thur, Fri; noon-1.45pm Wed. Closed Aug. €€€€.
Although this restaurant has two Michelin stars, the atmosphere in the attractive 19th-century building is surprisingly homely and welcoming. There are three dining areas: a modern room on the ground floor, a more domestic-looking space on the first floor, and an attractive terrace. While wife Françoise looks after the diners, chef Sarran works in the kitchen with the best local and seasonal produce, sending out fantastic dishes such as poached sea bass served with polenta and lobster sauce, wild salmon cooked and raw with green curry emulsion, or a light mousse of Tarbais beans scented with vintage rum and coconut milk.

Le Valentin

21 rue Perchepinte (05.61.53.11.15/www.valentin-restaurant.fr). Open 8-11pm Tue-Sun. €€€.
Valentin Neraudau was the youngest chef in Toulouse when he opened his eponymous restaurant in 2006, and the venture was successful enough to encourage him to launch sister establishment Le Carré Rouge (05.62.88.07.21, www.lecarrerouge-restaurant.fr) just over a year later. Once past its glazed frontage, diners at Le Valentin are seated in a gorgeous 17th-century cellar – all bare brick, gilt-framed mirrors and candlelight – and served refined and creative modern takes on classic southern French cuisine: *langoustine croustillante* on a bed of fennel and artichokes, followed perhaps by fat oxtail ravioli with preserved sucrine lettuce. Le Carré Rouge is more contemporary.

Shop

Streets with a good variety of independent shops include rue des Filatiers, rue de la Colombette and rue Cujas, which organises its own festival in September; the lively Marché des Carmes covered food market, on rue du Languedoc, is a good source of local produce (closed Mon).

La Fleurée de Pastel

Hôtel Pierre-Delfau, 20 pl de la Bourse (05.61.12.05.94/ www.bleu-de-lectoure.com). Open 10am-12.30pm, 2-6.30pm Mon-Sat.

Flying visit

Visiting a factory doesn't, on the face of it, sound like the kind of activity dream holidays are made of – unless you're spending the holiday in *la ville rose* and have even the slightest interest in aeroplanes. Toulouse has been an aviation city for nearly as long as man has been airborne, making its reputation back in the 1920s when pioneering pilots took off from here for dangerous flights to Casablanca, Dakar and beyond. To a plane buff, Toulouse means Aéropostale, Latécoère, St-Exupéry and Mermoz – names evocative of an era when flying was risky, romantic, and almost a spiritual endeavour.

It also means Airbus. The European airliner giant, maker of the world's largest passenger aircraft, the A380, has its main assembly plant at Toulouse-Blagnac airport, and the colossal facility is open to the public on guided tours. It's a factory visit unlike any other. The scale alone of the operation is worth seeing for yourself, because no photo can do justice to the awe-inspiring dimensions and complexity of the equipment involved. This is where wings made in Britain, fuselage sections made in Germany, tail sections made in Spain and nose sections made on site are mated together with the help of monstrous gantry cranes; you don't have to be an aircraft anorak to be thrilled by what is undeniably one of the pinnacles of human industrial achievement.

The visits are run exclusively by Taxiway (05.34.39.42.00/www.taxiway.fr), an outfit that specialises in industrial tourism in the south-west. Some of the tours are held in English, but all require booking well in advance, ideally before you come to Toulouse. On the day, you'll need to bring your passport – but, sadly, not your camera: Airbus wouldn't want spies from Boeing snapping away at its work. Prices vary according to the size of the aircraft you want to see being made: the flagship A380 costs more than the smaller A330 and A340; and these can be seen on their own or, for an extra fee, in combination with one or both Concordes on static display.

Cutting-edge aeronautical technology is one thing; but where, you may ask, is the history, the glamour, the romance? Right next door to the Airbus factory, as it happens, in a fine collection of vintage flying machines assembled and restored by preservation group Ailes Anciennes (05.61.21.70.01/www.aatlse.org): historic planes like the Caudron Phalène, Douglas DC3 and De Havilland Vampire. For now, they're only visible to the public on guided Saturday morning tours (you'll need ID for these, too), but a new, multimillion-euro, full-time museum to house them, the two Concordes, an Airbus and a Super Guppy is due to open by 2011. Spending hours at the airport will finally seem like a good thing.

Derived from the woad plant, blue pastel was a major pillar of the Toulouse economy in the 15th and 16th centuries. This rather gorgeous, Gothic-vaulted boutique sells latter-day derivatives: silk and cotton clothing (including the 'Napoleon shirt', a modern copy of a Napoleonic military shirt), artist's materials and decorative items for the home. There's also the very classy Graine de Pastel cosmetics range, which contains some excellent gift items.

La Maison de la Violette
2 boulevard Bonrepos (05.61.99.01.30/www.lamaison delaviolette.fr). Open 10am-12.30pm, 2-7pm Mon-Sat.
Violets are to Toulouse what lemons are to Capri; there's even a festival sponsored by the city council in February, the Journées Violettes, when visitors flock to marvel at 80 different varieties. The connection was forged when Napoleon's soldiers brought the flower back from Italy, and today it's the key ingredient in a wide range of local products. The most comprehensive stockist is this barge moored on the Canal du Midi just across and down from the train station. Violet liqueur, violet cosmetics, violet jam, violet sugar, sugared violets, bathroom linens with violet motifs – you name it, they have it.

Arts

La Halle aux Grains
pl Dupuy (05.61.63.13.13/www.onct.mairie-toulouse.fr). Open times vary. Admission €14-€44.
The Halle aux Grains is the city's main live music venue, and one of the most distinctive performance spaces in Europe. The striking brick and terracotta building began life as the city's grain market in the mid 19th century, became a sports venue in the 1950s, and was converted to concert duty 20 years later. A revamp in 1988 greatly improved the acoustics and seating, and the octagonal auditorium can now seat 2,500 people. As well as providing a permanent home for the Orchestre National du Capitole de Toulouse, it also hosts solo recitals; Chuck Berry played here in 2009.

Nightlife

The nightlife scene here is exuberant; you'll find plenty of late-opening bars and clubs on and around place St-Pierre, place Wilson and place St-Georges. Toulouse is a university city, so there are always plenty of students around, especially in the venues on and near place Arnaud-Bernard and rue de la Colombette.

La Cale Sèche
41 rue Gambetta (no phone). Open 6pm-1.30am Tue-Sun.
The Dry Dock has nothing dry about it: behind an unprepossessing entrance just off place du Capitole, this funky little bar does a roaring trade in rum, with some

25 varieties on offer and a starting price of €2 a glass. The bar staff whisk up a mean mojito, and there are bands several nights a week. It's hardly surprising that come late evening, the Dry Dock is absolutely chock-a-block.

Le Purple
2 rue Castellane (05.62.73.04.67/05.34.41.81.20/ www.le-purple.com). Open midnight-5am Tue-Sat. Admission varies.
Purple by name, purple-tinged by decor. This is considered to be the hippest nightclub in town, and consequently has the longest queues outside the door; dress to impress if you want to get in. There are several spaces for dancing, a good bar, and a lounge area kitted out with faux Louis XVI chairs; the music policy leans heavily towards electro or funk, and things don't get cooking until after 11pm. Le Purple is more grown-up than studenty, yet for all its big-name reputation the vibe is friendly.

Stay

High season is from July to August; outside those months, it's well worth checking hotel websites for cut-price deals.

Le Clos des Potiers
12 rue des Potiers (05.61.47.15.15/www.le-clos-des-potiers.com). €€.
This lovely, recently opened three-star address is small – just eight rooms and two junior suites housed in a grand Second Empire townhouse with its own garden, just a stone's throw from St-Etienne cathedral. No two rooms are alike, but all are very elegantly kitted out with antique furniture and old-fashioned linens; some even have exposed wooden beams and fireplaces. The modern exception is the chalet-style room with furniture by Philippe Starck. There's a cosy drawing room with open fire and wide settees, and one of the suites has a disabled-adapted bathroom.

Garonne
22 descente de la Halle aux Poissons (05.34.31.94.80/www.hotelgaronne.com). €€€.
The former Hôtel des Capitouls has changed its name, but not its allure. This bijou hotel (just 14 rooms) occupies an old warehouse, and has its entrance on a tranquil narrow former market street a stone's throw from the Pont-Neuf. The bedrooms are sumptuously appointed, and done out largely in a judicious palette of browns that chime with the dark wood floors. If your budget allows, try to book room 27, a junior suite from which you can see the Garonne. Breakfasts are served in the rooms, but hotel guests can eat main meals at Le 19 just across the street.

Grand Hôtel de l'Opéra
1 pl du Capitole (05.61.21.82.66/www.grand-hotel-opera.com). €€€.
The doyen of Toulouse lodgings is this four-star hotel housed in a 17th-century convent. It's right on the place du Capitole, so enjoys some pretty impressive views, and the

Grand Hôtel
de l'Opéra.

Hôtel des
Beaux-Arts.

whole place oozes quiet luxury. Rooms and suites are decorated in rich, deep colours – dark reds predominate; a few in the upper categories are partially wood-panelled. All are air-conditioned and, as you'd expect, have internet access. If you're feeling peckish, the hotel has its own brasserie as well as upmarket restaurant Les Jardins de l'Opéra, and the bar is a marvel of dark wood, deep carpets, mirrors and velvet armchairs, all set beneath an impressive glass ceiling. There's also a spa and hammam.

Hôtel les Bains-Douches
4 rue du Pont-Guilheméry (05.62.72.52.52/ www.hotel-bainsdouches.com). €€€.
The exterior is art deco, but the interior, designed by the hotel's owner Françoise Henriette, is 21st-century modish to its fingertips: minimalist Italian furniture, corridors lit by pink or blue fluorescent tubes. Your room might have a purple fur rug on a shiny tiled floor, or floor-to-ceiling windows on either side of your bed; all have flatscreen TV, free high-speed internet and semi-open bathroom separated from the sleeping area by a printed glass screen – leopard spots, say, or a crashing ocean wave. There's a pleasant inner courtyard where you can eat tapas or sip a cool glass of white wine, and a couple of lounge areas.

Hôtel des Beaux-Arts
1 pl du Pont-Neuf (05.34.45.42.42/www.hotel desbeauxarts.com). €€.
Right beside the Pont-Neuf, this charming three-star hotel has a welcoming red-brick façade, superb views of the Garonne, and individually decorated rooms that have been recently revamped. The colour schemes are resolutely modern – dark brown, mauve, olive – but there are wilder touches here and there to save it from soullessness. Try to book No.42, which has a high ceiling, walls covered with

toile de Jouy and its own terrace looking over the river. For relaxation and refreshment there's a raffish 'English-style' salon, and the upmarket Brasserie des Beaux-Arts adjoins the hotel. Extras include free Wi-Fi.

Hôtel le Grand Balcon
8 rue Romiguières (05.34.25.44.09/www.grand balconhotel.com). €€€.
Like its website, Toulouse's newest four-star hotel is very cool indeed. The wedge-shaped, all-brick building just off place du Capitole has been a hotel for decades, but its current owners have had the whole place restyled with a discreet aviation theme: it was a popular stopping-off point for professional pilots in the 1920s, including Antoine de Saint-Exupéry. His room, with iron-framed bed, old-fashioned clock and modern bathroom is a characteristic example of the blend of old and new. Other parts of the hotel have retained the gorgeous tiled floors and wall panelling of yesteryear, there's free Wi-Fi throughout, and the bar is decorated with large photos of famous French pilots.

Le Mermoz
50 rue Matabiau (05.61.63.04.04/www.hotel-mermoz.com). €€.
One of three aviation-tagged Toulouse addresses run by French chain Privilège, this three-star hotel just a hop from the railway station is slightly plain, but smart, comfortable and tranquil, with a pleasant outdoor patio area and inner courtyard under a glass roof. Rooms are on the small side, but done out in warm, complementary colours with unfussy modern furniture, marble bathrooms, TV and free Wi-Fi. And the flying connection? The hotel is named after the pilot Jean Mermoz, whose renown in France is almost as great as that of his colleague Saint-Exupéry: the fob attached to your key is embossed with his portrait – a nice touch.

Factfile

When to go
Toulouse has a temperate climate, with mild winters and comfortable summers. The city hosts big festivals of music, dance and cinema all year round: in June, the largely musical Rio Loco (www.rio-loco.org) dishes up concerts and other events on a theme – North Africa in 2009; in April, the Toulouse International Fair (www.toulousexpo.com) lines up hundreds of purveyors of foodstuffs, crafts and homewares.

Getting there
Toulouse-Blagnac airport (08.25.38.00.00/ www.toulouse.aeroport.fr) is 6km (3.75 miles) north-west of the city and connected by a shuttle bus (www.navette-tisseo-aeroport.com), every 20mins 5am-8.30pm, journey time 25mins, return tickets €6.30 from the driver). A taxi to the city centre costs around €25. By rail from the UK, take the Eurostar to Paris, then the TGV

Atlantique to Bordeaux, and then the regional line to Toulouse. Total journey time is 8-9hrs.

Getting around
Most of the main visitor attractions are in the centre, which is compact enough to explore on foot. Public transport consists of buses and an efficient, recently extended two-line métro network, which uses the same tickets; see the full transport map at www.tisseo-urbain.fr.

Tourist information
Tourist office Donjon du Capitole, sq Charles-de-Gaulle (05.61.11.02.22/ www.toulouse-tourisme.com).

Internet access
Cyber Copie 18 rue des Lois (05.61.21.03.73/ www.cybercopie.fr). Open 9am-7pm Mon-Fri; 10am-noon, 2-6pm Sat.

Coast

Top: St-Martin-en-Ré.
Middle: Passage du Gois.
Bottom: La Rochelle.

The Atlantic Islands & La Rochelle

Stunning beaches, scrumptious seafood.

Midway along the smoothly concave west coast of France, the seaside town of La Rochelle and a strung-out dot-dash-dot of small islands nearby make up one of the best summer holiday areas in the country. Blessed with excellent climatic conditions, thanks in part to the Bennett Current that loops off from the main course of the Gulf Stream and keeps the local waters warm, and rich in history and gastronomic tradition, these places may be pocket-sized, but they pack a big punch in the popularity stakes.

What's more, although the weather is largely uniform from one to the other (lots of sunshine), the scenery is intriguingly varied. Sandy beaches and dunes are common, but you'll also find plenty of pebble beaches, steep rocky cliffs, evergreen plantations, deciduous woodland, craggy inlets and salt marshes. The man-made scenery, meanwhile, is an attractive continuity of whitewashed houses enlivened with terracotta tiles and brightly coloured shutters; in the case of La Rochelle, which has long been a wealthy commune, the architecture in the centre is a mass of classy stone and elegant proportions. Fortresses and citadels here and there bear witness to the islands' historic role as offshore guard posts, initially against assault by Vikings, and later, in the time of Napoleon, against incursions by the Royal Navy.

These days the invaders come from the landward side, and in many cases they're frequent visitors or occasional residents. A high proportion of properties in the destinations listed below – which belong to two adjacent *départements*, Vendée to the north and Charente-Maritime to the south – are second homes, well over half in the case of Ile de Ré and Ile d'Oléron. And who can wonder? With sea air, abundant sunshine, superb fish and seafood, great views, and a wealth of coastal paths to explore on foot or by bike, this is a corner of France you can happily come back to.

Explore

LA ROCHELLE

Trade in salt, cognac and wine made La Rochelle's fortune, and between the 15th and 17th centuries wealthy merchants built fine limestone houses that still predominate in the old quarter around the port. Hundreds of thousands of people flock to the town every year to enjoy its pretty arcaded streets and café-lined quaysides, and to gaze out at a warm, surfless sea.

The gateway to the streets of the old quarter is the Gothic Grosse Horloge clock tower. A short walk north up grande rue des Merciers brings you to the market square, and two of the town's museums nearby, the Musée du Nouveau Monde (10 rue Fleuriau, 05.46.41.46.50) and the Musée des Beaux-Arts. Double back towards the sea and cross the Canal Maubec, and you come to the old fishermen's quarter of St-Nicolas, with narrow streets full of bars and bric-a-brac shops; in the adjacent Le Gabut district are fishermen's sheds that have been converted into bistros, usually a bit cheaper than on the other side of the harbour.

The two most prominent features of the picturesque Vieux Port are the Tour de la Chaîne and Tour St-Nicolas, once linked by a chain across the water to keep out unwanted seaborne visitors. Follow the old sea wall from the Tour de la Chaîne and you come to the 15th-century Tour de la Lanterne, a former lighthouse and prison with wonderful views. A short walk further west of here is the large Parc Charruyer, which has semi-wild parts for picnicking and a small petting zoo.

When it comes to shopping, the 19th-century covered market, which sets up every morning on place du Marché, serves up freshly caught fish and local salt. La Rochelle's long salt-trading history is also apparent in the area's gift shops, where you can buy salt pots, spoons and bath salts. The streets leading south from here have chic boutiques, especially rue St-Yon, grande rue des Merciers and rue du Palais; rue St-Nicolas and place de la Fourche have antique shops, second-hand bookshops and a weekly flea market on Saturday.

Aquarium de La Rochelle

Bassin des Grands Yachts (05.46.34.00.00/ www.aquarium-larochelle.com). Open Apr-June, Sept 9am-8pm daily. July, Aug 9am-11pm daily. Oct-Mar 10am-8pm daily. Admission €13; free-€10 reductions. This huge aquarium is one of Europe's best, its two levels divided into ten sections that replicate a variety of different marine habitats. There's the Atlantic Hall, with its shrimps, rays and sturgeons; the Mediterranean Cave, with its whopping octopi; the Caribbean Room, with menacing moray eels, porcupine fish and parrot fish; and even a Dark Room, where coral luminescence is revealed with ultraviolet light. Children are always excited by a walk along the Jellyfish Tunnel, an all-glass underwater tube, and by the blue sharks in a giant three-storey tank. Most exhibits have labelling in English; allow at least two hours to see it all.

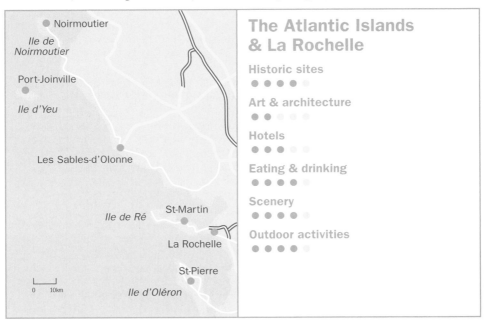

The Atlantic Islands & La Rochelle

Historic sites
● ● ● ● ●

Art & architecture
● ● ● ○ ○

Hotels
● ● ● ○ ○

Eating & drinking
● ● ● ● ○

Scenery
● ● ● ● ○

Outdoor activities
● ● ● ● ○

Musée des Automates
& Musée des Modèles Réduits

Rue de la Désirée (05.46.41.68.08/www.musees larochelle.com). Open Sept-June 10am-noon, 2-6pm daily. July, Aug 9.30am-7pm daily. Admission One museum €7.50; €5 reductions. Two museums €11; €6.50 reductions.

A large, barn-like building is home to these two superior toy museums. The Musée des Automates has the largest collection of antique animated figurines in the country – and what makes them special is that all 300 or so are kept in working order. As well as the hookah-smoking pasha and the Pierrot-style clown with his hat, there are entire moving window displays and, by way of a setting, a reconstruction of a Montmartre street circa 1900. The counterpart to this collection is the Musée des Modèles Réduits, devoted to scale models of cars, boats and trains – each more breathtaking in its detail and craftsmanship than the last.

Musée des Beaux-Arts

28 rue du Gargoulleau (05.46.41.64.65/http://pages perso-orange.fr/musees-la-rochelle). Open Apr-Sept 10am-12.30pm, 2-6pm Mon, Wed-Sat; 2-6pm Sun. Oct-Mar 9.30am-12.30pm, 1.30-5pm Mon, Wed-Sat; 2-6pm Sun. Admission €4; free-€3 reductions.

Modest in size, but pleasantly well lit and airy inside, the town's fine arts museum occupies the 18th-century former bishop's palace. Its collection of paintings spans the 15th to the 20th centuries, and includes works by Corot, Théodore Chassériau, Gustave Doré (notably the powerful *Trois Juges de l'Enfer*) and local boy Eugène Fromentin; there are also pieces by Maillol and Léger.

Muséum d'Histoire Naturelle

28 rue Albert Ier (05.46.41.18.25/www.museum-larochelle.fr). Open Mid May-Sept 10am-7pm Tue-Fri; 2-7pm Sat, Sun. Oct-mid May 9am-6pm Tue-Fri; 2-6pm Sat, Sun. Admission €4; free-€3 reductions.

La Rochelle's renowned natural history museum is a big hitter for a town of this size. It has occupied the very elegant 17th-century Hôtel Jouin de la Tremblaye since 1831, and reopened to the public in 2007 after a ten-year renovation programme that doubled the exhibition space and rearranged the botanical garden. There are five storeys to explore, full of smart, well-lit cases of exotic stuffed animals, larger beasts such as bison, and kangaroo set on central plinths; there's also an ethnology department that exhibits items from Africa and the Pacific islands and a hothouse in the garden. Stars of the show are Zarafa the giraffe, a pygmy Sumatra rhinoceros, and a dodo.

ILE DE NOIRMOUTIER

Noirmoutier is only a part-time island, a club-shaped hunk of land cut off twice a day from the mainland by the tide. It was the site of the first Viking raid on Europe, when the marauding Norsemen attacked a monastery here in 799; today the invaders are largely French, come to enjoy its coastline, characteristic marshland and attractive whitewashed vernacular architecture – in particular, the dozens of former windmills,

a few of which still have their sails. The main commune is Noirmoutier-en-l'Ile, a good-looking harbour town that's dominated by a turreted fourth-century château, now home to a small museum of local artefacts; opposite is the Eglise St-Philibert, a former Benedictine abbatial church that mixes Romanesque and Gothic, notable for its fine 11th-century crypt. In the harbour is the Sealand aquarium (02.51.39.08.11/www. aquariumdenoirmoutier.com), home to 200 species of fish and crustaceans; should viewing them give you an appetite, there are several good waterfront restaurants and cafés nearby.

Noirmoutier is served by two road links from the mainland: a modern bridge and the older, famous Passage du Gois, a four-kilometre (2.5-mile) paved sandbank that the waves wash over at high tide. If you're planning to drive along the Passage, be sure to read the timetables printed on the boards at either end: several cars are stranded by the rising waters every year – and those concrete platforms at intervals along its length are not decorative, but put there to give the cars' occupants a refuge from the flood. Note also that the Passage is closed to vehicle traffic for the popular Foulées du Gois running race (www.lesfouleesdugois.com), when thousands of athletes, professional and amateur, compete against the rising tide and each other. The race is held every year in June.

ILE D'OLERON

Metropolitan France's second largest island after Corsica is nicknamed 'la Lumineuse' for its high sunshine quotient, and is famous among foodies for its superb Marennes-Oléron oysters. It's a largely flat island, reached via a long road bridge from the mainland, with a dramatic rocky coastline to the north and west, and a sandy eastern side. The historic capital is Le Château d'Oléron, on the island's easternmost tip, but the administrative centre is now St-Pierre-d'Oléron, right in the middle. The principal attraction in Le Château is the huge, forbidding citadel, which was built by Vauban in the 17th century and used as a prison during the Revolution; it was so robustly designed that a massive Allied bombing raid in 1945 only partially damaged it.

Between the island and the mainland is the tiny Ile d'Aix (www.iledaix.fr), a day-trip destination accessible by ferry from Boyardville and best known for its Napoleonic associations: this was the last piece of French soil the defeated Napoleon stood on before his exile to St Helena; the small museum contains the stuffed hide of the camel he rode during his Egyptian campaign.

ILE DE RE

A short distance north-west of La Rochelle is Ile de Ré, a long, low island devoted to bivalve farming and salt production. It has lost its true

St-Martin-en-Ré.

island vocation status since a swooping three-kilometre (two-mile) bridge, the longest in France, was built to the mainland in 1988, but an expensive car toll (€9-€16.50, paid on arrival only) keeps it exclusive. The bar and yachting scenes are liveliest around the harbour at St-Martin-en-Ré, the island's fortified capital. Also in the town is Parc de la Barbette, where donkeys wearing traditional blue and white trousers are on hand to give rides to children. Nearby are the pretty villages of La Couarde-sur-Mer, Ars-en-Ré and La Flotte – the latter two of which are so lovely, they've been awarded the Plus Beaux Villages de France label. The Phare des Baleines, on the north-west tip of the island, is a 19th-century lighthouse that affords fantastic 360-degree views. It takes its name from the many whales that used to beach at this spot.

ILE D'YEU

Twenty kilometres (12.5 miles) off the sandy Vendée coast is Ile d'Yeu, a tiny island with fewer than 5,000 residents and an economy based entirely on fishing and tourism. As well as good sea air and a surprising variety of landscapes for such a small patch of land, it's famous for its association with Vichy figurehead Marshal Pétain, who was imprisoned in the citadel here after World War II, and is buried in the island cemetery. His grave has been vandalised on several occasions, most recently in 2007; the citadel, set on a hill in the middle of the island, is now a leisure complex and HQ for the local radio station.

On the north shore is attractive Port Joinville, the main settlement, notable for its cheerful and harmonious whitewashed buildings with terracotta roofs. The town is home to the tourist office, main administrative building, main fishing port, and a good number of restaurants; it's also the arrival point for ferry services from the mainland. Due south of here is the Vieux Château, the romantic remains of a 14th-century castle built on a rocky spur jutting into the sea; it's open to visitors from April to September. The island has some wonderful beaches, but for a few hours away from the dunes there is also a good network of signposted paths; bikes can be hired at various points on the island – contact the tourist office for a full list.

Eat

Fish and seafood – especially langoustines, lobsters and oysters – are the keystones of dining on the Atlantic coast and the nearby islands. Noirmoutier also produces renowned early potatoes, and the Vendée region as a whole is famous for duck, usually served as foie gras or *magret*.

Le Bistrot de Bernard
Ile de Ré *1 quai Criée, Ars-en-Ré (05.46.29.40.26/ www.bistrotdebernard.com). Open 12.30-2pm, 7.30-9.30pm Wed-Sun (July, Aug open daily). Closed Dec & Jan. €€€€.*
The Bernard of the bistro's name is chef Bernard Frigière, who, with his sommelier wife Catherine, has run this establishment in the picturesque port of Ars-en-Ré since 1993. It began life as a railway station café-restaurant between the wars, and has been successively refined and enlarged: it now has two dining rooms and a great waterfront terrace. Start with crab and tomato millefeuille, and follow with lobster and roast pigeon fricassée, or a turbot steak with potatoes grown on the island. There's often live music in the evening, and Bernard's artistry isn't limited to what is visible on your plate: he also did the bronze sculptures and paintings on show inside.

Bô
Ile de Ré *20 cours Vauban, St-Martin-en-Ré (05.46.07.04.04/www.bo-restaurant.com). Open 7-10.30pm Mon, Tue; noon-2pm, 7-10.30pm Thur-Sun (July, Aug open daily). €€€.*
Talented young local chef Maxime Reguin has worked with Alain Ducasse, and he set up on his own at this distinctly *beau* restaurant in 2006. It's arranged around an enormous garden, with a large covered terrace dining area; indoors are polished dark tables, plush chairs and café au lait walls, set off by silver candlesticks and colourful table lights. Reguin cooks precise and refined French dishes with occasional Asian grace notes: starters might include a cod ceviche served with a shot glass of tomato juice, followed by langoustine risotto with asparagus tips and parmesan, or a just-cooked slab of local tuna served with noodles and pleurotte mushrooms. Three bargain lunchtime menus (€18-€34) let you sample his skill without breaking the bank.

Les Embruns
Ile de Ré *6 rue du Chay-Morin, St-Martin-en-Ré (05.46.09.63.23). Open 7.30-10.30pm Mon, Thur; 12.30-2pm, 7.30-10.30pm Tue, Wed, Fri-Sun. €€.*
Run by the friendly Hélène Lefaure, this popular seafood bistro is tucked down a narrow street right behind the tourist office, on the little islet in the middle of St-Martin-de-Ré harbour. The diminutive dining room is bright and unfussy, and oozes pride in the local area, with the names of the island's villages on the tables and maritime accoutrements on the walls – boat propeller, life belt, salt rake, seaside pictures and the like. Lefaure's food makes use of the latest catch and whatever the market has to sell: tasty fish soup, say, or skate wing cooked in raspberry vinegar.

L'Entracte
La Rochelle *35 rue St-Jean-du-Pérot (05.46.52.26.69/ www.lentracte.net). Open 12.30-1.30pm, 7.30-10.30pm daily. €€.*
By its own admission, L'Entracte is the most 'nostalgic' of the three La Rochelle restaurants owned and run by Gregory Coutanceau, son of Richard (*see p222*). Don't expect whimsy, though, either in decor or food: the dining room may have wood panelling and framed vintage posters, but

its lighting, furniture and tableware are all clean and modern, and the wide open kitchen sends out precise and quietly creative fare – a cuttlefish ragoût with two types of sweet pepper, say, or eel chowder made with charentais wine. Alternatively, you could keep things simple and go for the catch of the day, grilled and served whole with local potatoes and *sauce vièrge*.

Les Jardins d'Aliénor

Ile d'Oléron *11 rue du Maréchal-Foch, Le Château d'Oléron (05.46.76.48.30/www.lesjardins dalienor.com). Open Nov-Mar noon-1.30pm, 7-9pm Wed-Sun. Apr-Oct noon-1.30pm, 7-9pm Tue-Sun (July, Aug open daily). €€€.*
Bare stone walls, wicker-backed chairs and crisp white napery on the tables set the tone for a meal at this dapper restaurant looking on to a charming terraced garden. The menu is predominantly fishy, and the beautifully presented dishes skilfully combine French and Italian influences: start with a warm *croustillant* of foie gras served with a pear carpaccio and balsamic reduction, followed by roast sea bass with pesto sauce and an antipasto-style side of preserved peppers; finish up with a sweet mango risotto, or the sublime chocolate and salted caramel millefeuille. And if you feel sleepy after your meal, there are four recently renovated bedrooms upstairs.

La Marine

Ile de Noirmoutier *3 rue Marie-Lemmonier, L'Herbaudière (02.51.39.23.09). Open Sept-June 12.15-1.30pm, 7.15-9pm Mon, Thur-Sat; 12.15-1.30pm Sun. July, Aug 12.15-1.30pm, 7.15-9pm Mon-Sat; 12.15-1.30pm Sun. €€€€.*
At 33, local chef Alexandre Couillon is still relatively young in his profession, but since he took over the family restaurant in 2006 he has won a Michelin star and a prestigious 'rising talent' award from Gault-Millau. In 2008 he had the place completely reworked, and it's now effectively two restaurants that share an open kitchen: at the upper end of the price scale, the striking black and white La Marine; and at the other end, the more traditional bistro La Table d'Elise, which serves an affordable daily market menu. The ingredients are faultlessly fresh on both sides, as in La Marine's sardine crackers, iced cauliflower soup and roast line-caught bass served with shellfish bouillon and orange-scented shallot jam.

Restaurant Richard et Christopher Coutanceau

La Rochelle *Plage de la Concurrence (05.46.41.48.19/www.coutanceaularochelle.com). Open 12.15-1.30pm, 7-9.30pm Mon-Sat. €€€€.*
Considered by many to be the best in the region, this two Michelin-starred restaurant has been run by the Coutanceau family since the 1970s, with chef Richard handing over the kitchen duties to his younger son Christopher in 2007. It's now a Relais & Châteaux address, but the food is no less independent for all that: exquisite confections like frogs' legs in a lemony tempura batter, or lobster salad served with spider crab mousse and asparagus fritters, followed by grilled red snapper with stuffed courgettes and tomato

chutney. The wine list, overseen by sommelier Nicolas Brossard, is just as superb, and twice-yearly wine tasting extravaganzas bring in some of France's top producers. The dining room itself is right on the beach, with large windows on all sides to maximise the view.

Stay

Atlantic Hôtel

Ile d'Yeu *Quai Carnot, Port Joinville (02.51.58.38.80/ www.hotel-yeu.com). €€*
This pleasant three-star hotel stands right on the harbour front in Ile d'Yeu's capital, Port Joinville, and like most of its neighbours has a bracing nautical frontage of white walls and jolly blue shutters. Eight of its bedrooms enjoy a good view of the harbour, and the remaining ten look inland over a small garden and neighbouring houses; the decor is somewhat basic, but the rooms are clean and have bath, WC, satellite TV and Wi-Fi.

Hostellerie Les Cleunes

Ile d'Oléron *25 bd de la Plage, St-Trojan-les-Bains (05.46.76.03.08/www.hotel-les-cleunes.com). €€.*
Towards the southern end of Ile d'Oléron is this low, terracotta-roofed, villa-style hotel arranged around a heated outdoor swimming pool. It's a welcoming, spacious place, with 40 comfortable rooms done out in cheerful yellows and crimsons; some have a sea view and balcony large enough to have breakfast on, whereas others have a view of the pool; two are adapted for disabled travellers. There's a tennis court, billiard room, bikes for the use of guests, a bar with open fireplace, and an elegant restaurant.

Hôtel les Brises

La Rochelle *1 chemin de la Digue Richelieu (05.46.43.89.37/www.hotellesbrises.com). €€.*
The five-storey Hôtel les Brises cuts quite a dash on the seafront, with its vaguely colonial balconies and railing shutters, and superb views out over the Atlantic. From here it's a 20-minute walk into the town centre, or just five minutes to the pleasant Parc Franck-Delmas. The rooms and their bathrooms are functional rather than pretty, and rooms with sea view cost slightly more than those with views inland – but that small extra outlay is well worth it for the chance to sit on the balcony and watch the sun slide down into the sea.

Hôtel Champlain France-Angleterre

La Rochelle *30 rue Rambaud (05.46.41.23.99/ www.hotelchamplain.com). €€€.*
The Champlain France-Angleterre is a three-storey, three-star hotel managed by the Best Western chain. It occupies two neighbouring 18th-century mansions, and has upmarket looks that usually command a much higher price tag: tall windows, swagged curtains, antique furniture, chandeliers and flowers in the common areas, and a lofty main staircase held up by fluted limestone columns. There's a lounge done out like an 18th-century salon, with polished wooden floors, gilded mirrors and moulded doors, and a

Restaurant Richard et
Christopher Coutanceau.

Top: Les Prateaux.
Bottom: Hôtel les Brises.

trim garden. The spacious, high-ceilinged rooms are decorated in the same country house style, and equipped with high-backed velvet armchairs and neat bathrooms.

Hôtel de Toiras
Ile de Ré *1 quai Job-Foran, St-Martin-de-Ré (05.46.35.40.32/www.hotel-de-toiras.com). €€€€.*
Instantly recognisable by its three-storey tower, this lovely address in Ile de Ré's capital St-Martin-de-Ré is a grand 17th-century shipbuilder's mansion right on the harbour. It was extensively restored in 2003, and the 11 bedrooms are individually appointed with tasteful colour schemes and antique furniture. But the suites are better still, with wooden floors, exposed beams, huge oak wardrobes, embroidered bedspreads and open fireplaces. Even if you're not staying here, book a meal at the excellent restaurant.

Les Prateaux
Ile de Noirmoutier *8 allée du Tambourin, Bois de la Chaize (02.51.39.12.52/www.lesprateaux.com). €€.*
Set in the village of Bois de la Chaize, just a couple of kilometres north-east of Noirmoutier-en-l'Ile, this sprawling terracotta-roofed hotel complex looks more Bahamas than coastal France – an impression strengthened by a long first-floor balcony and the almost tropical vegetation in the surrounding park. It's incredibly tranquil – so much so that you may well spot rabbits in the grass outside your window. The curtains and covers in the bedrooms are perhaps a little too chintzy for their own good, but the rooms themselves

are quite generously sized, and some are in outbuildings that increase the sense of retreat. The staff are friendly, and a short path leads right down to the beach.

Résidence de France
La Rochelle *43 rue Minage (05.46.28.06.00/ www.hotel-larochelle.com). €€€.*
The town's only four-star hotel occupies a 16th-century building, but its interior has an uncompromisingly modern, all-white colour scheme that extends to much of the furniture; judicious use of coloured lampshades and the occasional antique mahogany or marble-topped chest of drawers keeps it feeling well bred rather than merely sterile. The 'Résidence' in the name indicates that there are actually more apartments here (36 in all) than traditional hotel rooms and suites (five and 11 respectively). There's an airy lounge with an open fireplace, a piano bar, and a good restaurant.

Richelieu
Ile de Ré *44 av de la Plage, La Flotte (05.46.09.60.70/www.hotel-le-richelieu.com). €€€.*
The four-star Richelieu is a Relais & Châteaux beachfront hotel in the village of La Flotte. It's a modern building – which means, on the one hand, a certain lack of architectural distinction, and on the other, a layout that maximises the number of rooms with sea views. As well as the rooms in the main building, you can stay in one of the wooden chalets in the hotel grounds; there's a heated outdoor pool, a plush thalassotherapy centre, and the Bon Cadeau restaurant.

Factfile

When to go
The climate on this stretch of the Atlantic coast is very pleasant, with mild winters and summers that rarely get too scorchingly hot. The Charente-Maritime shoreline and nearby islands are popular destinations for French holidaymakers, with peak attendance in August; low season is from January to April.

Getting there
La Rochelle airport (05.46.42.30.26/www. larochelle.aeroport.fr) is served by Ryanair, Easyjet and Flybe from several major airports in the UK. High-speed TGV rail services run from Paris direct to La Rochelle (3hrs).

Getting around
Once you're here, hiring a car is the easiest way to get around, although there's a good bus service (www.rtcr.fr). Ile de Noirmoutier, Ile d'Oléron and Ile de Ré are all linked to the mainland by road; Ile d'Yeu is linked by ferry. Getting around La Rochelle is straightforward. Most sights are within walking distance, there's an efficient bus service, and bikes can be hired from place de Verdun (ID and deposit required).

Tourist information
Ile de Noirmoutier Rue du Général Passaga, Noirmoutier-en-l'Ile (02.51.39.12.42/www.ile-noirmoutier.com). Open 9.30am-12.30pm, 2-6pm daily (July, Aug 9.30am-7pm daily).
Ile d'Oléron Rte du Viaduc, Bourcefranc-le-Chapus (05.46.85.65.23/www.ile-oleron-marennes.com). Open 9am-noon, 2-5pm Mon-Fri.
Ile de Ré 3 rue du Père-Ignace, St-Martin-de-Ré (05.46.09.00.55/www.iledere.com). Open 9.15am-noon, 2-5.30pm Mon-Fri (July, Aug also open 11am-1pm, 2-5.30pm Sat).
Ile d'Yeu 1 pl du Marché, Port Joinville (02.51.58.32.58/www.ile-yeu.fr). Open 9am-12.30pm, 2-6pm Mon-Sat; 9.30am-12.30pm Sun (July, Aug 9am-1pm, 2-7pm Mon-Sat; 9.30am-1pm Sun).
La Rochelle 2 quai Georges-Simenon, Le Gabut (05.46.41.14.68/www.larochelle-tourisme.com). Open Oct-May 9am-6pm Mon-Sat; 10am-1pm Sun. June-Sept 9am-7pm Mon-Sat; 10am-5pm Sun.

Internet access
La Rochelle Aquacyber, 10 quai Senac-de-Melhan (05.46.50.29.21). Open 10am-10pm Mon-Wed; 10am-1am Thur-Sat; 3-10pm Sun.

Top: Cliffs around
Etretat. Bottom left:
Rouen Cathedral.
Bottom right: Honfleur.

The Normandy Coast & Rouen

An Impressionist's dream of sculpted cliffs and gentle hills.

For many Britons, Normandy is the part of France with which they're most familiar, perhaps because, being so close to the UK, it's the part they visit first and most often – and also, no doubt, because of the busy two-way traffic across the Channel in centuries past, from the Norman Conquest to D-Day. What's more, much of the Norman landscape, especially the *bocage* to the west, is strongly reminiscent of classic English countryside, with lush woodland, abundant hedgerows and gently undulating fields. In this chapter, however, we've concentrated almost entirely on the coast, where the air is salty and the light has a magical, constantly changing quality that so fascinated Turner, Courbet, Boudin and the Impressionists.

We've focused on a thin ribbon of land, but it's one with refreshing variations of scenery, as indicated in the names given to the different stretches of the coast. Cabourg, Deauville and Honfleur are part of the Côte Fleurie, the floral coast, so called for the rich vegetation that comes down almost to the water's edge; Etretat is on the Côte d'Albâtre, the alabaster coast, named after the famous white chalk cliffs. Then there are the beaches, especially those at Deauville and Cabourg, and any number of coastal paths that climb to grassy flats high above the waves.

There's a plentiful amount of manmade beauty, too. This chapter's sole inland destination, Rouen, has some of the most astonishing Gothic buildings anywhere in the world, and even the small coastal towns we've covered are rich in vernacular architecture, seen in particular in traditional half-timbered houses and wooden markets. A good proportion of the great paintings that were done on the Normandy coast are now on display in its museums; and the local cuisine is rich and delicious, drawing on a vast array of first-class produce from land and sea. All this, and right on the UK's doorstep.

Explore

ROUEN

Normandy's capital city is by no means a homogenous ensemble. Its architectural and historic glories are hemmed in on all sides by an awful lot of modern dross, and the monuments and ancient half-timbered buildings for which it's famous are, as often as not, liberally coated with the muck of ages. Granted, the city was very badly damaged by bombing raids in World War II; but the gaps didn't need to be filled with concrete eyesores. Stand facing the main entrance to the iconic cathedral, and there on the left, just metres away, is a 1960s shopping block so hideous and so inappropriately sited that it makes one dream of a prison sentence for the architects and town planners responsible.

Fortunately, Rouen's main sights – all of which are in the oldest part of the city on the north bank of the Seine – are more than enough compensation. For anyone with an interest in churches, the place is a marvel: as well as the cathedral, there's the Gothic gem that is the 15th-century Eglise St-Maclou (3 pl Barthélemy, 02.35.71.71.72) a short walk to the east, and north of that, the Flamboyant Gothic abbatial church of St-Ouen (pl du Général-de-Gaulle, 02.32.08.31.01), which is as large as the cathedral. Even more impressive than these, perhaps, is the Palais de Justice (rue aux Juifs,

02.32.08.32.40), which once housed the Parliament of Normandy, and is one of the only surviving examples of medieval secular architecture in France. It's a breathtakingly ornate piece of stone lacework that's all the more impressive for having been cleaned in a recent renovation programme lasting several years. Below the expansive courtyard are the remains of France's oldest Jewish monument, the Maison Sublime (www.lamaisonsublime.fr), currently closed to the public.

A block south of the Palais, pedestrianised rue du Gros-Horloge is notable for an archway bearing a glorious old clock, which has a 14th-century movement and a lavishly decorated gilt face. The street leads into place du Vieux-Marché, where Joan of Arc was burned at the stake in 1431; a commemorative cross marks the spot. The centrepiece of the down-at-heel square is the spectacularly hideous Eglise Ste-Jeanne-d'Arc, built in 1979 to look like a fish and a Viking longship. Just south of here, on place de la Pucelle-d'Orléans, is the beautiful 16th-century mansion Hôtel de Bourgtheroulde; as this book went to press, it was in the process of being transformed into the city's first four-star hotel, due to open in late 2009.

Cathédrale Notre-Dame
Pl de la Cathédrale (02.35.71.85.65/www.cathedrale-rouen.net). Open 2-6pm Mon; 7.45am-7pm Tue-Sat; 8am-6pm Sun. Admission free.

Normandy Coast & Rouen

Historic sites
● ● ● ● ○

Art & architecture
● ● ○ ○ ○

Hotels
● ● ● ○ ○

Eating & drinking
● ● ● ● ○

Scenery
● ● ● ● ○

Outdoor activities
● ● ● ● ○

0   10km

Etretat

Honfleur

Rouen

Deauville

Cabourg

Deauville.

Rouen Cathedral.

The cathedral beloved of Monet (he painted it nearly 30 times) is copiously besmirched with the airborne grime of the industrial age, but it's still an awe-inspiring achievement. Built for the most part between the 11th and 16th centuries (although the final additions weren't made until the 1880s, and there have been major repair jobs carried out since then), it's a compendium of different Gothic styles topped with a stunning 19th-century openwork lantern tower. Other notable features – and there are many – include some fine Renaissance stained glass, and a tomb said to contain the heart of Richard the Lionheart. At 11pm every evening from 1 July to 31 August, a free light show projects Monet's paintings on to the cathedral.

Musée des Beaux-Arts
Esplanade Marcel-Duchamp (02.35.71.28.40/ www.rouen-musees.com). Open 10am-6pm Mon, Wed-Sun. Admission €3; free-€2 reductions.
Appropriately for the capital of such a painterly region, Rouen has one of the best fine arts museums in the country. It's strong on the Impressionists, especially the works of Monet and Sisley, but also has major canvases by Caravaggio, Velasquez, Delacroix and Modigliani. There's a large sculpture department, featuring pieces by Géricault and Bourdelle; and a drawing department that holds over 8,000 works by Watteau, Ingres, Degas and more.

CABOURG

The affluent resort of Cabourg is relatively unknown among British holidaymakers, although it has a strong standing among the French – not least for its association with Marcel Proust: the great writer spent eight consecutive summers here, and the town features in *A la Recherche du Temps Perdu* under the name of Balbec. Luxury was important to Proust, and Cabourg is still popular with rich French holidaymakers, who come for its long sandy beach (nicknamed '*la plage aux romantiques*'), four-star hotels, swish villas and well-maintained, flower-planted streets laid out in an easily navigated, fan-shaped grid. The fan's focal point is the smart main square just back from the seafront, home to the Grand Hôtel and the casino, both impressive examples of belle époque architecture.

As the geometric street plan suggests, the Cabourg you see now is a recent creation. It was just a village until two Paris financiers discovered it in the 1850s, and decided to turn it into a luxury resort to rival Deauville and Dieppe. The town has no major monuments or museums, but it's an ideal place to bring small children to: the beach is considered to be one of the best on the Norman coast, the streets are clean, quiet and dotted with pretty gardens, and the atmosphere is one of well-off *bonhomie*. For more active types, there's a good range of seaside sports to take part in, including sailing, land yachting and kite surfing; and in the summer, the modern, recently renovated hippodrome (av Michel d'Ornano, 02.31.91.27.12) hosts trotting races

and concerts. Just across the Dives estuary is the village of Dives-sur-Mer, famous as William the Conqueror's port of departure in 1066; it has a picturesque pleasure harbour, a lovely medieval market hall, and a busy artistic community.

DEAUVILLE

Deauville is one of the swankiest seaside resorts in the country, and, like Cabourg, it got its big break in the 19th century from the fashion for saltwater holidays among aristocrats and the mercantile rich. As well as one of France's best kept beaches, with its famous beach huts and wooden-planked promenade, Deauville has a wealth of listed belle époque buildings, a famous racecourse, posh yachting harbours, and two major international film festivals every year – the Festival du Cinéma Américain in September (www.festival-deauville.com), which brings in US stars such as George Clooney and Sharon Stone, and the Festival du Film Asiatique in April (www.deauvilleasia.com), which showcases the best of cinematic output from the Far East.

The main square, place de Morny, has an attractive fountain and a good covered market. A five-minute walk to the south is the racecourse (45 av Hocquart de Turtot, 02.31.14.20.00/www.france-galop.fr), host of fashionable flat racing events in summer and winter; the area around Deauville produces more thoroughbreds than anywhere else in France. The neighbouring village of Trouville-sur-Mer, to the east across the Touques estuary, was a modish seaside resort some years before Deauville, and until the early part of the 20th century was considered the superior of the two. It has a fine sandy beach and planked promenade of its own, and a harbour lined with some good-looking 19th-century fishermen's houses and an imposing red-roofed fish market, built in 1936.

ETRETAT

Etretat has a big reputation for such a small town, thanks largely to the Impressionists, whose paintings of its vertical chalk cliffs and their three natural arches made it one of the most significant locations in western art. The pretty town itself lies in a depression between two lines of cliffs, with a sandy beach and an abundance of woods and greenery on the outskirts. There are stunning clifftop paths to explore, and some interesting buildings to see: the handsome 19th-century brick-and-stone Château d'Aygues (rte de Fécamp, 02.35.28.92.77) at the edge of town, once home to two queens of Spain and now open to the public in summer; and, in the centre, the wood-framed covered market and the enormous half-timbered Manoir de la Salamandre, which has jetties and elaborate carvings, and now houses the characterful Hôtel de la Résidence (4 bd René Coty, 02.35.27.02.87).

Etretat is home to two museums: Le Clos Arsène Lupin (15 rue Guy de Maupassant, 02.35.10.59.53/www.arsene-lupin.com), devoted to the fictional detective and his creator Maurice Leblanc, whose home this was; and the Musée Nungesser et Coli (Falaise d'Amont, 02.35.27.07.47), which honours two pioneering French aviators who disappeared trying to cross the Atlantic in 1927.

HONFLEUR

Honfleur has to be the prettiest port in Normandy, renowned for its ancient slate-roofed houses, church and abundant artistic heritage. Baudelaire wrote some of the most famous poems of Les Fleurs du Mal here, and the Ecole de Honfleur, whose members included Boudin, Courbet and Jongkind, was the forerunner of Impressionism.

Today, the town is a well-kept and attractive knot of narrow cobbled streets full of small boutiques, food shops and restaurants. Hard by the port, the Eglise Ste-Catherine (pl Ste-Catherine, 02.31.89.11.83), with its separate bell tower, is the largest wooden church in France; the roof over its oldest, 15th-century part was made using the same techniques used in shipbuilding, and looks like an upturned boat. Opposite the church, at the entrance to the old harbour, stands the 17th-century Lieutenance, sole remnant of the town's historic fortifications, built to protect Honfleur from the English. There are a number of small museums in the town, including two devoted to local-born Erik Satie (67 bd Charles V, 02.31.89.11.11) and Eugène Boudin (pl Erik Satie, 02.31.89.54.00); and a five-minute drive away is the iconic Pont de Normandie, a cable-stayed bridge that was the longest in the world when it opened in 1995.

Eat

Norman cuisine is often unrepentantly rich, making extensive use of butter and cream. The region produces some fine cheeses, notably camembert, livarot, and the oldest Norman cheese still in production, pont l'évêque; more oysters are produced here than anywhere else in France; and then there are the famous apples, used widely in cooking and to make the celebrated ciders and calvados.

L'Absinthe

Honfleur 10 quai de la Quarantaine (02.31.89.39.00/ www.absinthe.fr). Open noon-2.45pm, 7.15-9.45pm daily. €€€€.
Looking right out on to the port, L'Absinthe is a hotel, restaurant and bistro, all housed in a centuries-old set of walls. The restaurant side of the operation was once a bar frequented by local fishermen, and now serves delicious contemporary fare in two beautiful dining areas, one dating from the 15th century, the other from the 17th century – both with bare stone walls and wooden beams. The food is fresh and impeccably done: terrine of bass and langoustine on a bed of leeks with a truffle-scented vinaigrette, say, followed by lobster pan-fried in rosemary butter. There are 12 tastefully decorated rooms upstairs, and brasserie La Grenouille serves simpler fare (02.31.89.04.24).

Augusto Chez Laurent

Deauville 27 rue Désiré Le Hoc (02.31.88.28.46/ www.restaurant-augusto.com). Open noon-2pm, 7.30-9.30pm Mon-Fri; noon-2pm, 7.30-10pm Sat, Sun. €€€€.
Augusto was a Deauville institution, having been in business for 35 years, but it recently passed into new hands and gained the 'Chez Laurent'; the decor in its two dining rooms is new as well, with padded navy blue benches and wood-trimmed arches reminiscent of the cabin of a luxury yacht. However, the changes of look and name aside, the place clearly intends to steer the same happy course – which means maintaining its reputation for fantastic lobster and caviar, and sending out sublime fish such as a starter of 'half-cooked, half-smoked' salmon with sautéed ratte potatoes and vinaigrette, or a main of grilled bass with an oyster and butter sauce.

Brasserie Paul

Rouen 1 pl de la Cathédrale (02.35.71.86.07/ www.brasserie-paul.com). Open 9am-11pm daily. €€.
The town's oldest brasserie has a strategic position facing the cathedral, and a large terrace that's much in demand on summer evenings. The dining room was renovated in 2006, and looks every inch the classic French brasserie: lots of wood, brass and glass lamps, paper tablecloths and red bench seating. The menu is a classic too, running to such well-executed and attractively priced dishes as preserved aubergines with a tomato fondue, excellent steak tartare made in the Norman style (with calvados), Offranville chicken with a tarragon sauce, crème brûlée, and a large apple tarte fine. The young Simone de Beauvoir used to come here regularly to eat and work; other famous customers included Apollinaire and Marcel Duchamp.

Chez le Bougnat

Cabourg 27 rue Gaston-Manneville, Dives-sur-Mer, 2 km E of town centre (02.31.91.06.13/www.chez lebougnat.fr). Open noon-2.45pm Mon-Wed, Sun; noon-2.45pm, 7.30-10pm Thur-Sat. €€.
On the other side of the Dives estuary, in the town of Dives-sur-Mer, this convivial 1930s-style bistro is set in what used to be a hardware shop – and there's a whiff of that former function in the copper pans, bric-a-brac and old posters that make up the decor. Chef-owner François Teissonnière draws up his robust, traditional menu according to what's in Caen's big food market that day, but typical dishes might include a three-fish 'choucroute', poularde stuffed with foie gras, roast guinea hen, pan-fried red snapper with a saffron sauce, or lighter fare such as a salad of frisée lettuce with lardons and poached eggs. It's wildly popular, so be sure to book ahead.

Honfleur.

Le Galion

Etretat *Rue René-Coty (02.35.29.48.74). Open noon-2pm, 7-9pm daily. €€.*

This galleon doesn't float, but the 14th-century property just a few metres from the beach is eminently shipshape – by which we mean well run, and also that its rather well-worn dining room, with its line of low windows and carved dark wood pillars like bulkheads, feels not unlike the hold of some venerable sailing vessel. A culinary voyage here might start with foie gras coated in spiced breadcrumbs and fried, or oysters poached in champagne, and continue with veal kidneys with mushrooms or hearty and delicious beef cheeks served with puréed purple Vitelotte potatoes; if it's available, finish off with the eminently Norman parcel of apples and camembert in filo pastry.

Les Nymphéas

Rouen *9 rue de la Pie (02.35.89.26.69/www.les nympheas-rouen.com). Open 12.15-2.15pm, 7.30-10pm Tue-Sat. €€€.*

In this handsome half-timbered 17th-century building, its timbers visible inside as well as out, owner-chef Patrice Kukurudz has been sending out first-class traditional French food to a jewel-box of a dining room for nearly two decades. A lofty ceiling, lamps with smart black shades, long, swagged yellow curtains, large mirrors and elegantly laid tables set the scene for seasonal food that's at once sophisticated and simple: fried scallops with a citrus and spice vinaigrette, say, or roast venison shoulder with a pepper sauce. Duck and lobster are specialities here, notably a fine *canard à la Rouennaise* (pressed duck with a blood and liver sauce) and a *civet* of lobster made with Sauternes wine. The cheese board is excellent.

Restaurant Gill

Rouen *8 quai de la Bourse (02.35.71.16.14/www.gill.fr). Open 12.30-2.30pm, 7-10.30pm Tue-Sat. €€€€.*

Gill is the only two-star restaurant in Normandy. A meal here might start with a salad of fried langoustines with tomato and red pepper chutney. Follow with a perfectly cooked fillet of turbot or Rouen-style pigeon served with fried foie gras and mushroom tartare, and (because the chef, local-born Gilles Tournadre, started his career in pâtisserie) conclude with a sumptuous millefeuille made with Madagascar vanilla. Tournadre has worked at some very prestigious addresses, including Taillevent in Paris, and it certainly shows in the food: the small, modish dining rooms have rather too much pale grey for our liking, but the presentation and flavours are all brightness and colour.

La Terrasse et l'Assiette

Honfleur *8 pl Ste-Catherine (02.31.89.31.33/www.laterrasseetlassiette.com). Open 12.15-2pm, 7.15-9pm daily. €€€€.*

La Terrasse et l'Assiette is one of Honfleur's top restaurants, housed in a classic Norman affair of brick and stone in the old part of the town. The T part of the name alludes to the nice little terrace opposite Honfleur's famous church; as for the *assiette* (plate), the restaurant's Michelin star gives you an idea of the standard of fare you can expect. While his wife Anne-Marie keeps things running smoothly in the

dining room, chef-owner Gérard Bonnefoy assembles super-fresh local ingredients in creations such as a tartare of bream and scallops with ginger and an onion and passion fruit mousse, lobster omelette, a filo parcel of camembert with peppered caramel, or an orange-scented *île flottante*.

Stay

81 L'Hôtel

Deauville *81 av de la République (02.31.14.01.50/www.81lhotel.com). €€€.*

A happy marriage of old and new, and some careful attention to interior detail, make this attractive independent three-star stand out from the crowd. The building is a 1900s townhouse in Anglo-Norman style, with a front door at the top of an elegant flight of canopied steps; inside, the look is worthy of a style magazine, with the old, ornate structures of the building playing off nicely against armchairs and drapery in modish browns and purples. The 21 bedrooms are a real treat, with sumptuous bedding and classy old chairs and tables sprayed shiny silver. The same management also rents out similarly sleek apartments in a 19th-century villa just a short walk away.

D House

Rouen *52 rue de la République (02.35.36.91.51/www.d-house.fr). €€.*

D House is a beautifully decorated *chambre d'hôte* in a classic old apartment building in the heart of historic Rouen: at the rear, it looks right out on to the Gothic Eglise St-Maclou. The friendly owners live in a separate apartment upstairs, and guests have their own lavishly appointed private bathroom, so you could almost convince yourself that you have your own pied à terre in the city. Thoughtful touches abound, from the lion-footed tub, thick towels and L'Occitane toiletries in the bathroom to the exotic decor and Moorish four-poster in the bedroom.

Domaine Saint-Clair

Etretat *Chemin de St-Clair (02.35.27.08.23/www.hoteletretat.com). €€€.*

The Domaine Saint-Clair is a hotel well outside the ordinary: an ivy-clad 19th-century château half a kilometre back from the waterfront, with a conical-roofed tower, an adjoining Anglo-Norman villa and lush surrounding parkland. The individually decorated bedrooms and junior suites are, for the most part, a successful mix of bold yet tasteful wallpapers and linens, with original features like high ceilings and exposed beams; some have lovely four-poster beds and a few have sea views. There are a number of small salons for relaxing in, a library, and an upmarket restaurant; in good weather, breakfast is taken on the terrace.

Dormy House

Etretat *Rte du Havre (02.35.27.07.88/www.dormy-house.com). €€.*

Wake up to one of the most famous views in Western art: this three-star hotel in its own park high up above Etretat enjoys panoramic views of the town, the sea and, of course,

Crowning glory

Granted, it can feel touristy at times, but with credentials like this you would hardly expect it to be any other way. For Rouen's glorious half-timbered restaurant La Couronne (31 pl du Vieux-Marché, 02.35.71.40.90, www.lacouronne.com.fr) is France's oldest inn – so old, in fact, that it had already been in business for 86 years when Joan of Arc was burned in the square in front of it. The 'Crown' is a hostelry that's older than some of the city's best-known monuments, including the Palais de Justice, the Gros Horloge and the Eglise St-Maclou; little wonder it attracts so much attention.

Even if you don't mean to dine here, the building – superbly preserved for a 664-year-old – is worth a look. Its five-storey frontage is made colourful with a dozen flower-filled window boxes capped with an ornate, steep-sided gable that looks like something of a crown itself; and the interior is a warren of variously sized dining rooms with lovely romantic lighting, luxurious table settings and antique structural woodwork galore. Depending on the availability of tables, you might eat in the Salon des Rôtisseurs, with its oak beams and pillars, the Salle Jeanne d'Arc, with its elegant royal blue chairs and table linen, or

the Salon d'Honneur, where Haile Selassie hosted a lavish banquet in 1936.

Still, appearances are one thing – but many a good-looking historic hostelry proves a disappointment when it comes to the food. Happily, that's not the case at La Couronne: this is upmarket classic French cuisine done with considerable aplomb. Talented young chef Vincent Taillefer balances the line-up of year-round classics like grilled sole and superb Normandy steaks with a seasonal menu that changes monthly: a melon gazpacho or a kebab of marinated monkfish in summer, perhaps, or a sauté of veal with olives and tomatoes. A speciality is the duck à la Rouennaise, which is pressed, cut and served at the table by the restaurant's *maître-canardier*, an elaborate ritual that uses a silver press the size and shape of a medieval knight's helmet.

Dine here and you'll be part of a band of former guests that includes Dalí (a regular), Bardot, Sartre, Malraux, Georges Pompidou, Jacques Chirac, John Wayne, Ingrid Bergman, Grace Kelly and royalty from all over the world. And when night falls, the Couronne's windows and gable are picked out with lines of yellow neon – a curiously raffish touch that seems to say: you're only as old as you feel.

Hôtel le Cheval Blanc.

the much-painted cliffs. The bedrooms are mostly large (as are their bathrooms) and have been renovated recently, although not all face the sea – and you'll need to like floral fabrics. Elsewhere in the hotel, there's a swish panoramic restaurant serving luxurious French cuisine, a billiard room, and the Rayon Vert bar.

La Ferme St-Siméon

Honfleur *Rue Adolphe-Marais (02.31.81.78.00/ www.fermesaintsimeon.fr). €€€€.*
The rustic name belies the unquestionable style and luxury of this wonderfully tranquil 'farm', although it's very much to the owners' credit that none of the modern fixtures and fittings is out of keeping with the lovely 17th-century building: antique furniture on terracotta tiled floors, and sumptuous 21st-century upholstery and bedding set off by scrubbed wooden panels on the walls. Try to book a room in the main building: those in the annexe have less character. The main haute cuisine restaurant looks like a dream, all bare beams and half-timbered walls, and is very popular with wealthy locals; a second, more modestly priced dining room, La Table Toutain, opened in 2007. There's a nice little spa with a very attractive indoor pool.

Grand Hôtel

Cabourg *Promenade Marcel Proust (02.31.91.01.79/www.mercure.com). €€€€.*
Cabourg's top seafront hotel is grand in every respect, from its slate roof and arcaded balconies to its lofty lobby with marble pillars, grand piano and enormous chandeliers. Proust was a regular guest, and the room he always stayed in has been recreated in loving period detail (although the writer's bronze bust in the reception area looks absolutely nothing like him); the other bedrooms are determinedly

contemporary, with cutting-edge bathrooms and bold patterned wallpaper. The Balbec restaurant does high-end fish and seafood, and the luxurious Belle Epoque bar looks like it belongs in a stately home.

Hôtel le Cheval Blanc

Honfleur *2 quai des Passagers (02.31.81.65.00/ www.hotel-honfleur.com). €€.*
With its commanding position right on the harbour front, the centuries-old hotel was recently renovated Cheval Blanc – the name refers not to a foamy sea horse, but to the quadrupeds that hauled the mail back in the day when this was a coaching inn – is an excellent place in which to appreciate Honfleur's maritime charms. Inside, the look is that of a family house, with individually decorated, understated but classy bedrooms (all facing the sea) and a cheerful breakfast room with wood panels and warm red carpet. Previous guests have included Victor Hugo and Monet.

Royal-Barrière

Deauville *Bd Cornuché (02.31.98.66.33/ www.lucienbarriere.com). €€€€*
The Royal is one of the luxury Barrière group's three big four-star hotels in Deauville, the others being the Normandy-Barrière (38 rue Jean-Mermoz, 02.31.98.66.22) and the Hôtel du Golf-Barrière (New Golf, 02.31.14.24.00). The standard of accommodation and services is the same across the board, but this one has the culinary edge on its two siblings, with the one Michelin-starred dining room L'Etrier and the gorgeously appointed Côté Royal restaurant. The hotel has the looks, too, having been decorated by Jacques Garcia from head to foot in a modern take on full-bore belle époque: gold-striped wallpapers, and tassels and brass galore. Little wonder the place is so popular with film stars and the jet set.

Factfile

When to go

Normandy has a temperate climate, with temperatures slightly warmer than those in southern England. Rain is common at all times of the year; the warmest months are July, August and September, although the heat is almost never oppressive, especially on the coast.

Getting there

The nearest airport with flights from the UK is Cherbourg (02.33.88.57.60/www.aeroport-cherbourg.com). Regular ferry services sail from Portsmouth to Cherbourg, Caen-Ouistreham and Le Havre. Rail links are reasonably good: there are direct services from Paris to Rouen (1hr 20mins), Le Havre (2hrs 15mins) and Caen (2hrs).

Getting around

Many British visitors like to come to the area by ferry and bring their own car, which has

obvious advantages in terms of sightseeing. The local rail network is good, and regular and well-priced bus services connect the main towns.

Tourist information

Cabourg Jardins de l'Hôtel de Ville, av de la Mer (02.31.06.20.00/ www.cabourg.net).
Deauville pl de la Mairie (02.31.14.40.00/ www.deauville.org).
Etretat Pl Maurice-Guillard (02.35.27.05.21/ www.etretat.net).
Honfleur Quai Lepaulmier (02.31.89.23.30/ www.ot-honfleur.fr).
Rouen 25 pl de la Cathédrale (02.32.08.32.40/ www.rouentourisme.com).

Internet access

Rouen Cyber@Net, 47 pl du Vieux-Marché (02.35.70.73.02).

Top: Côte de Granit Rose. Below left: St-Malo. Below right: Quimper.

Northern Brittany

Wild, wet and wonderful.

The coast of Brittany is often portrayed as a rugged and untamed place – a windswept, saw-toothed succession of fretted headlands, roaring foamy inlets and craggy cliffs. But the reality is a great deal more nuanced. For sure, there's an abundance of wild, dramatic scenery. But the area in general, and its coast in particular, is welcoming, mild in climate and blessed with a great variety of landscapes – often beautiful, never bleak.

The song of the sea is ever present in this proudly maritime region, even at the furthest point from the coast; but conversely, its lush inland greenery extends all the way to the water's edge – and on one famous stretch of Brittany's northern coastline, the Côte d'Emeraude, even the water takes on an emerald tint. Another famous Breton landscape colour is the pink of the rocks along the Côte de Granit Rose, less than an hour's drive from Roscoff; and then, of course, there's the gold of the many wonderful sandy beaches.

The lifestyle here is as colourful as the landscape. Bretons have a strong sense of identity expressed, among other ways, in the staunchly defended local language. The Breton love of good food and carousing is clear to see in the historic coastal towns, where you'll find no end of lively, family-run bars and restaurants serving delicious local cider, seafood, galettes and (here's regional patriotism for you) Breizh Cola. And because the locals are an active bunch, you'll be spoiled for choice when it comes to throwing yourself in the drink, with dinghies, kayaks, windsurfs and full-blown yachts all waiting to get you seaborne. This truly is an invigorating place to visit.

Explore

BREST

This historic naval city stands just a few kilometres east of the craggy Pointe de Coursen, continental France's most westerly point. It's more than a millennium since Brest's wonderful natural harbour first put the town on the map as a fishing port, trading centre and military bastion – and it's still all three today. Yet the town's story isn't one of cosy continuity.

A three-way tug-of-war between France, Brittany and England ended in 1532, when Brittany lost its independence by becoming part of France, which brought military conscription, taxes and the installation of the French navy in the harbour; Brest's economy thereafter was based heavily on shipbuilding, and during the Napoleonic wars the town was the main focus of England's naval blockade. Allied bombing in World War II reduced Brest to a pile of bricks; but the subsequent grid-by-grid rebuilding, economic regeneration and TGV link to Paris restored its fortunes, and a combination of Breton-language schooling and the liberal use of the Breton flag have fostered a recent growth in regional pride.

The most impressive remnant of old Brest is the rambling and beautifully preserved 15th-century château, which houses the Musée de la Marine; it's at its most atmospheric on after-dark tours in July and August. Across the Penfeld river, the picturesque, conical-roofed 14th-century Tour Tanguy contains the Musée du Vieux-Brest (02.98.44.24.96), where large dioramas and photos depict the town before the war. The Conservatoire Botanique de Brest (52 allée du Bot, 02.98.41.88.95/www.cbnbrest.fr) and the Jardin des Explorateurs on rue de l'Eglise are legacies of Brest's many explorers, who brought back exotic plants from their voyages.

Brest is small and easily navigated on foot. The town has a wealth of cheap and cheerful crêperies in addition to the more elaborate sit-down options listed below; for drinks, the quays, the bottom end of rue de Siam and the area around place St-Louis are always good places at which to start.

Musée des Beaux-Arts

24 rue Traverse (02.98.00.87.96/www.mairie-brest.fr). Open 10am-noon, 2-6pm Tue-Sat; 2-6pm Sun. Admission €4; free-€2.50 reductions.

Brest's fine arts museum was destroyed during World War II, and rebuilt from scratch in the 1960s. Although the building is undistinguished, the paintings it holds are varied and interesting, grouped in three broad categories: on the upper floor, 16th- and 17th-century works from France, Italy and Holland (notably Pietro della Vecchia's gloomy study of Isabella of Portugal in her coffin); on the ground floor, a survey of 19th-century artistic schools through the works of minor painters; and further on, the museum's strongest suit, a fine array of Symbolist painters including artists of the Pont-Aven group.

Northern Brittany

Historic sites
● ● ● ● ●

Art & architecture
● ● ● ● ◌

Hotels
● ● ● ◌ ◌

Eating & drinking
● ● ● ● ◌

Scenery
● ● ● ● ●

Outdoor activities
● ● ● ● ●

Ile de Batz
Roscoff
Dinard St-Malo
St-Lunaire
Brest
Quimper
Rennes

0   10km

Musée de la Marine

Rue du Château (02.98.22.12.39/www.musee-marine.fr). Open Apr-Sept 10am-6.30pm daily. Oct-Mar 1.30-6.30pm daily. Last ticket sold at 5.30pm. Admission €5; free-€4 reductions.

Brest has been an important naval shipyard for centuries (France's current flagship, the aircraft carrier *Charles de Gaulle*, was built here), and its castle is home to this offshoot of the national naval museum: here you'll find a formidable and evocative collection of model ships, marine paintings and navigational equipment in vaulted, stone-walled rooms. There's another naval connection, too: the castle also houses the operations room for France's Atlantic Command, which makes it the oldest active military site in the world.

Océanopolis

Port de Plaisance du Moulin-Blanc, 3km E of Brest on D165 (02.98/www.oceanopolis.com). Open times vary. Admission €16.20; free-€11 reductions.

Brest's main attraction is this huge aquarium in a windy location between the Port de Plaisance and the Plage du Moulin-Blanc, with the main entrance in a building shaped to look like a crab. As well as being a serious research facility, Océanopolis is home to a vast variety of marine life – over 10,000 animals in all – housed in 50 tanks in the appropriate tropical, temperate and polar sections. As well as an amazing array of fish – sharks, moray eels, swordfish, octopi – there are a dozen playful seals, and the largest penguin enclosure in Europe.

DINARD

Opposite St-Malo on the other side of the Rance estuary, Dinard is a relaxed town that rarely hits top gear. Most visitors are content to while away the hours on its coastal paths and scented trails, or on one of its three great beaches: the Plage de l'Ecluse, in the centre of town, is wide and sandy, and has a nice playground; Plage du Prieuré, on the east side of town, is a little less pretty, but it's just across the road from the lovely, leafy Parc Port Breton; and Plage de St-Enogat, along the top coast, is superb for a quieter day out.

The statue of Alfred Hitchcock you see as you approach the Plage de l'Ecluse – the master of suspense is perched on a huge egg, with a seagull on each shoulder – celebrates the British film festival (02.99.88.19.04/www.festivaldufilm-dinard.fr) that's held every October. Another big annual event, the Dinard International Music Festival (www.festival-music-dinard.com), brings choirs, vocalists and solo instrumentalists to the town in the first three weeks of August.

The roughly 100-year British influence can be glimpsed on the quaint waterfront, where villas give way to picturesque blue- and white-striped changing cabins; indeed, it was a Scotsman who founded the classy Dinard golf club (at St-Briac-sur-Mer, 02.99.88.32.07/www.dinardgolf.com) in 1887. Dinard also offers gentle cliff-top walks around the Pointe de la Malouine and Pointe du Décollé, which wind down to a lovely seafront via

the romantically named Promenade du Clair de Lune ('moonlight promenade'). Visitors who prefer horseback can opt for a gentle trot around the headland or a gallop on a stallion courtesy of the Centre Hippique de Dinard (at La Val Porée, 02.99.46.23.57/www.dinard-equitation.com).

QUIMPER

The historic capital of Cornouaille, the area settled in the early Middle Ages by migrants from Cornwall (hence the name), is not a coastal town – but it does have a tidal river, and merits inclusion in this chapter for its very distinctive character, due partly to the strong local pride in its Celtic heritage, and partly to the almost rustic look of the attractive old quarter, with its plethora of flowers, ancient half-timbered buildings, narrow streets, and pretty footbridges over the Odet.

The earliest settlement on this spot was founded in Roman times. After centuries of fluctuating fortunes, determined by its successive allegiances to the Duchy of Brittany and the House of Montfort, Quimper began its rise to international renown in the late 17th century when it started making faïence pottery; *faïence de Quimper* is still produced in the historic Locmaria quarter on the southern bank of the river, and is sold widely in the town. There's a faïence museum (14 rue Jean-Baptiste-Bousquet, 02.98.90.12.72/www.quimper-faiences.com), and the workshops of manufacturer HB Henriot (rue Haute, 02.98.90.09.36/www.hb-henriot.com) are open to visitors.

Although Quimper was a hotbed of Resistance activity during World War II, it was spared the destruction meted out to so many other French towns, and the streets around its focal monument, the soaring Gothic St-Corentin cathedral, are a maze of well-preserved wooden-framed houses painted in jolly colours. The cathedral itself is notable for the unusual bend in its middle, and is looking superb after recently emerging from a 20-year restoration programme. Other visitor attractions include a small fine arts museum (40 pl St-Corentin, 02.98.95.45.20/www.musee-beauxarts.quimper.fr) that's strong on paintings of Breton scenes; and, in Quimper's many restaurants, some of the best cider and crêpes in Brittany.

ROSCOFF

On the upper coast of Brittany, the quiet and homely little town of Roscoff has some fine beaches, and a lovely 16th-century church, Notre-Dame de Croas Batz (rue Albert-Mun, 02.98.69.70.17), which has an extraordinarily ornate steeple that looks like a minaret. Although Roscoff is one of France's busiest ferry ports, and so processes large numbers of British tourists every year, it's historically better known in the UK for a particular export, the local pink onion: this was the main departure point for the traditional 'Onion Johnnies', with their berets and stripey jerseys, in the 19th and 20th centuries. A small museum, the Maison des Johnnies (48 rue Brizeux, 02.98.61.25.48), recalls the heyday of this colourful trade.

From Roscoff, you can take a ferry to the Ile de Batz, a long-standing favourite with isolationist campers. A 45-minute drive west of the town brings you to the village of Plestin-les-Grèves, westernmost point of the famously picturesque Côte de Granit Rose, which stretches as far as Louannec. It's one of only three pink granite coastlines in the world.

ST-MALO

Built on a massive granite protuberance ringed by sandy beaches, the imposing citadel of St-Malo looks out to sea over walls that are several metres thick. This is one of the most popular attractions in Brittany, a treasure trove of nooks and crannies and castle turrets; the ancient streets are packed to the gills with restaurants, boutiques and bars, and in the summer they heave with holidaymakers, especially from the UK. St-Malo was the home base for privateers in the 18th and 19th centuries, and the town is still known by the nickname 'la cité corsaire' today.

The first fortifications were built in the 14th century, but the citadel as it stands today was largely the work of military architectural genius Vauban in the 18th century. Large sections of the town (including parts of the cathedral and château) were destroyed by Allied bombing during World War II – but were rebuilt mainly to the original designs after 1944, so the historic character of the old quarter is still very much in evidence today. The centrepiece is the Romanesque and Gothic St-Vincent cathedral (12 rue St-Benoist, 02.99.40.82.31), whose towering steeple provides a convenient landmark. The circuit around the citadel ramparts lasts between half an hour and an hour, depending on how long you pause to savour the stunning views.

Less than a kilometre south of the citadel, on another rocky outcrop, is the standalone 14th-century castle keep known as the Tour Solidor, now home to a museum (02.99.40.71.58) tracing the history of navigation around Cape Horn. A few kilometres east of St-Malo, at the village of Rothéneuf, are the stunning Rochers Sculptés: between 1893 and 1909, the hermit priest Abbé Fouré lived in the rocks here, carving fabulous monsters and pirates into the stone.

Le Château
Rue Châteaubriand (02.99.40.71.57/www.saint-malo.fr). Open Apr-Sept 10am-12.30pm, 2-6pm daily. Oct-Mar 10am-noon, 2-6pm Tue-Sun. Admission €5.40; free-€2.70 reductions.

Built in the 15th century for the Duchy of Brittany, and later modified by a disciple of Vauban, the forbidding castle on the north-east corner of the walled town is now home to the municipal council and, in its keep, a small museum on the history of St-Malo and the local area. The museum is of scant interest to visitors, but the castle itself is well worth seeing, as much for its military architecture as for its commanding views of the citadel and the bay.

Grand Aquarium
Av du Général-Patton, 4km S of St-Malo on D137 (02.99.21.19.00/www.aquarium-st-malo.com). Open times vary. Admission €15.50; free-€9.50 reductions.

This is one of the largest aquariums in the country. It's a modern, well laid-out attraction that draws more visitors than any other privately run tourist site in the region. Notable attractions include a galleon wreck swarming with sharks; a 3D cinema; a petting tank where you can touch spider crabs, starfish and rays; and the Nautibus – which is not, as it might sound, a conveyance for misbehaving children, but a cleverly arranged submarine simulator whose portholes look out on to the activities of real fish.

Eat

Sweet crêpes and savoury galettes are the Breton counterparts to fish and chips, albeit rather healthier. Brittany is also famous for its cider, lobsters, monkfish and oysters – and, of course, *moules-frites*, which differ from the Belgian version in the sauce and type of mussels.

Crêperie Margaux
St-Malo *3 pl du Marché-aux-Légumes (02.99.20.26.02/ www.creperie-margaux.com). Open noon-9pm Mon, Thur-Sun. €.*

This convivial establishment in the middle of the old town is one of St-Malo's best crêperies. In keeping with the no-fuss nature of its focal dish, the recently redone dining area is a straightforward set-up of green vinyl bench seating and plastic chairs at stone-topped tables; in summer, tables are set on the terrace out the front. All the ingredients are fresh, and the dark wheat crêpes (named after the owners' friends) are made to order: choose from classic versions or something more elaborate – scallops flambéed in whisky (the Jeff), or smoked ham, goat's cheese and fig jam (the Manu). A sign on the wall reads 'You're allowed to lick the plate' – and a lot of people do.

Le Décollé
5km W of Dinard *1 pointe du Décollé, St-Lunaire (02.99.46.01.70/www.restaurantdudecolle.com). Open Feb, Mar 12.15-2pm, 7.15-9pm Fri, Sat; 12.15-2pm Sun. Apr-June, Sept-mid Nov 12.15-2pm, 7.15-9pm Wed-Sun. July, Aug 12.15-2pm, 7.15-9pm Tue-Sun. €€€.*

This is a terrific place for a seaside lunch, especially when the sun is shining. Its dining room is unremarkable, but its position on the headland of the same name more than

Quimper.

Côte de Granit Rose.

compensates. When you're not looking at your plate, you'll be looking out at the fabulous view of the bay and St-Malo in the distance; in summer, the floor-to-ceiling windows slide open and tables spill out on to a terrace that's nothing less than glorious. The menu varies with what's in the nets and the market, but is predominantly fishy: choose from a classic line-up of fresh bivalves and shellfish, or a delicious grilled sole in seaweed butter; finish off with a traditional *kouing amman*, a flaky Breton galette served here with buttermilk sorbet.

A la Duchesse Anne

St-Malo *5 pl Guy-la-Chambre (02.99.40.85.33). Open 7.15-9.15pm Mon; noon-1.30pm, 7.15-9.15pm Tue, Thur-Sun. Closed Dec, Jan. €€€€.*
Duchesse Anne is a St-Malo gourmet institution: indeed, it's rooted in the very fabric of the place, hunkered right into the old citadel wall near the château. Locals and visitors have been flocking here since 1945, soaking up the atmosphere of the dining room with its elegant coffered ceiling, wood panelling, jolly mosaic walls and tiled floor, and tucking into some of the town's finest cuisine. Signature dishes include a gratin of langoustines and tarragon, grilled turbot with *beurre blanc*, lobster *à l'armoricaine* (in a rich, brandy-spiked sauce) and *tarte tatin*. In the summer they unfurl the huge canopy, and put tables and flowerpots on the cobbles out front.

L'Ecume des Jours

Roscoff *Quai d'Auxerre (02.98.61.22.83/www. ecume-roscoff.fr). Open noon-1.30pm, 7-9pm Mon, Thur-Sun. €€€.*
Named after a Boris Vian novel, this welcoming, recently renovated waterfront establishment has a commanding location in the bay, and a menu of creative seasonal Breton fare. The walls were put up in the 16th century to house a wealthy shipbuilder, and the chunky bare stonework and exposed beams of the rear dining area give it real character; the front room is more modern, and has big windows through which to enjoy the view of the waves. Start with oysters or a sautée of queen scallops, smoked duck and potatoes, followed by the likes of monkfish medallions in an oyster jus or pork cheeks with pink onion jam.

La Fleur de Sel

Brest *15bis rue de Lyon (02.98.44.38.35/www. lafleurdesel.com). Open noon-2pm, 7.30-9.45pm Mon-Fri; 7.30-9.45pm Sat. €€€€.*
Brest's most elegant restaurant, run by local-born chef Yann Plassard and his wife Caroline, has been a steady local success since they took it on more than ten years ago. Yann selects his fish and seafood in person, just after it's landed, and works these immaculately fresh ingredients into hugely imaginative dishes such as a miniature 'shepherd's pie' made with lobster and truffle reduction, or warm oysters served with a sautée of green potatoes and cider *sabayon*. Meaty mains might include tender fillet steak or a millefeuille of roast young partridge with chestnut cream. The wine list is excellent, and the dining room a pleasing combination of wood, white linens and warm-coloured walls.

Fleur de Sel

Quimper *1 quai Neuf (02.98.55.04.71/www.fleur-de-sel-quimper.com). Open 12.15-1.30pm, 7.30-9pm Mon-Fri; 7.30-9pm Sat. €€.*
No relation to the Fleur listed above, this waterfront address on the north bank of the Odet is a modern, merry-looking red and white affair that specialises in fish and seafood. The dining room looks out over the river, and the watery attractions on the plates include marinated salmon with the eponymous hand-harvested sea salt, grilled fillet of bass with rosemary butter, or catch of the day prepared to the chef's fancy. The prix fixe is a bargain.

Le M

Brest *22 rue du Commandant-Drogou (02.98.47.90.00/ www.le-m.fr). Open noon-2pm, 7.30-9.30pm Mon-Sat. €€€€.*
Behind tall iron gates a very short drive north of Brest's historic centre, the former Nouveau Rossini passed to new owners in 2008, and is now Le M. The grand, grey-stoned Breton house has been entirely redecorated, and the resulting look is bright and modern with dashes of belle époque and art deco: boxy 1930s-style red leather armchairs in the high-ceilinged bar area, and large panels of decadent-looking damask on the pristine white walls of the dining room. Young chef Philippe Le Bigot has worked in London, Paris and the Caribbean, and puts a globetrotting spin on elegant French classics: thin-sliced monkfish with turmeric, perhaps, or medallion of veal rolled in the seeds of blue Himalayan poppies and served with alfalfa shoots.

Maison de l'Océan

Brest *2 quai de la Douane (02.98.80.44.84/ www.maisondelocean.com). Open noon-2pm, 7-11pm daily. €€.*
With a name like that, you know what to expect: a sea view and plenty of fish on the menu. What the name doesn't tell you, though, is just how pretty this shipshape and very popular restaurant looks, nor how reasonable its prices are. Jolly yellow tablecloths, brass seagoing lamps, nautical scenes on the walls and wooden deck-style floors all whet the appetite, as does the showpiece six-sided lobster tank. The fish on your plate will have been landed that very morning, and with three course menus starting at €16.50, it's no wonder the place is always buzzing.

Restaurant Delaunay

St-Malo *6 rue Ste-Barbe (02.99.40.92.46/ www.restaurant-delaunay.com). Open Apr-Sept 6.30-10.30pm Mon-Sat. Oct-Mar 6.30-10.30pm Tue-Sat. Closed 1 Dec-12 Feb. €€€€.*
Behind an inviting purple frontage is one of the best of the many restaurants in this part of town, run by a husband and wife team. Its recently renovated dining room is a cheerful assembly of red and orange velvet chairs, colourful tableware, and gilt-framed oil paintings on the yellow or lilac walls; a handful of tables are set in a brasserie-style glazed area that pushes out on to the pavement. Didier Delaunay's appealing market menu might start with a shellfish cappuccino with parmesan, or tart of langoustines and seaweed served with preserved pears. Mains might

include traditional Breton *cotriade* (fish stew) or roast Mont St-Michel salt marsh lamb in a thyme and garlic jus. The long wine list is strong on Burgundies and Bordeaux.

Le Temps de Vivre

Roscoff *19 pl Lacaze-Duthiers (02.98.61.27.28/ www.letempsdevivre.net). Open noon-1pm Tue, Sun; noon-1pm, 7.30-9pm Wed-Sat.* €€€€.

At the tip of the headland west of the port, this spacious, modern dining room has a Michelin star and an all-glass frontage to let in the view of the English Channel. Chef-owner Jean-Yves Crenn sends out classic and resolutely luxurious fish dishes, such as sea bass served with differently textured artichokes, or warm oysters with a foie gras and lettuce coulis; on the landward side, you might have fried foie gras with summer fruits or roast pigeon with prunes and girolle mushrooms. The adjacent 16th-century hotel (02.98.61.27.28), under the same management, has 15 large and tasteful bedrooms in former pirate's cottages.

Stay

Le Brittany

Roscoff *Bd Ste-Barbe (02.98.69.70.78/ www.hotel-brittany.com).* €€€.

This imposing, granite-walled manor was built for a wealthy merchant in the 17th century, and rebuilt from the ground up in the 1970s. It's now a Relais & Châteaux establishment with a superb waterfront prospect and an unobstructed view out to the Ile de Batz. There's a luxurious spa, bar, Wi-Fi throughout, and several categories of bedroom, from the cosy Petite Tradition with glossy wooden panels and floor to the capacious Apartement Prestige with sea view; all have tasteful decor and old-fashioned furniture. The restaurant, Le Yachtman, with its bare stone walls, Gothic windows, exposed oak beams and huge open fireplace, is worth booking even if you're not staying at the hotel.

Le Continental

Brest *41 rue Emile-Zola (02.98.80.50.40/ www.oceaniahotels.com).* €€.

The Continental is a grand 1930s-style building on a leafy square in the heart of old Brest, and the impression fostered by its external dimensions is maintained by its huge, theatrical lobby, marked out by wood-panelled pillars and encircled by the smart iron railings of a first-floor balcony. This is where you'll find the bar, and an open lounge area kitted out with billiard table, striped armchairs and a large wall map of the local coastline – the overall effect being to conjure up a bygone era when travel was a sophisticated affair. The bedrooms don't have quite the same character, but they're airy and equipped with the usual mod cons.

Grand Hôtel Barrière

Dinard *46 av George V (02.99.88.26.26/ www.lucienbarriere.com).* €€€€.

Given its enviable waterfront location midway along the Promenade du Clair de Lune and the luxurious appurtenances of the 19th-century granite building itself,

it's no surprise that this is where the stars stay when they're in town for the annual film festival. The rooms are stylish, whatever their category, and have a penchant for tastefully striped bed covers, curtains and wallpaper; many have their own balcony, some with head-on sea views, and all have TV and internet connection. There's a children's play area, spa and generously sized indoor pool; and as well as the full menu in the hotel's beautiful belle époque restaurant, a menu of light food is served on the café terrace in summer.

Grand Hôtel des Thermes

St-Malo *100 bd Hébert (02.99.40.75.75/www. thalassotherapie.com).* €€€.

On the outside, the 'Grand' bit is certainly accurate: this 1880s stone edifice is enormous, big enough to contain 169 rooms and suites as well as the large thalassotherapy centre – equipped with six seawater pools and a host of sybaritic spa facilities – that gives it the second part of its name. Indoors, though, it's just a little faceless, the bedrooms fitted out with corporate carpets, and bedcovers and curtains louder than one might expect. Still, the hotel has a great situation, with the Plage du Sillon right on the doorstep.

> **"The dining room has an all-glass frontage to let in the view of the English Channel. Chef-owner Jean-Yves Crenn sends out resolutely luxurious fish dishes, such as sea bass with differently textured artichokes."**

Hôtel Gradlon

Quimper *30 rue de Brest (02.98.95.04.39/ www.hotel-gradlon.fr).* €€.

There's a wonderfully homely feel to this very tasteful little hotel. Individually decorated rooms, in romantic or art deco style, look on to a little courtyard resplendent with flowers and a fountain. The Paul Sérusier junior suite has a polished metal bedstead, floral curtains and leafy wallpaper, while the Gradlon has more of a 1930s look. The hotel was recently renovated throughout, and there's a cosy salon bar in Scottish hunting lodge style, complete with open fireplace.

Hôtel de la Paix

Brest *32 rue Algésiras (02.98.80.12.97/www.hotel delapaix-brest.com).* €€.

Handily located on the northern edge of Brest's historic centre, this recently renovated hotel has a pure, 'zen' interior decoration scheme and soundproofed, well-equipped

St-Malo.

Top and below right: Crêperie Margaux. Below left: Hôtel Gradlon.

bedrooms: large flatscreen TV, free high-speed internet and Wi-Fi. Unusually, there are also a number of small rooms for single travellers. The buffet breakfast is generous, and the swish restaurant (02.98.43.63.63) serves an affordable array of modern seafood dishes – including sushi and sashimi – in the evenings.

Hôtel San Pedro
St-Malo *1 rue Ste-Anne (02.99.40.88.57/ www.sanpedro-hotel.com). €.*
Standing just inside the citadel's western rampart, this pocket-sized hotel with 12 pocket-sized rooms is convenient, inexpensive and very friendly. Owner-manager Mireille Morice has had the whole place done out in a nautical theme, with dark wood details and blue upholstery evoking something of the below-deck feel of a sailing yacht; and there's an abundance of pleasing details that speak of careful attention, like the room numbers painted on little sailboats affixed to the doors. Some of the rooms have sea views, and all have en suite facilities, Wi-Fi and TV with English channels.

Hôtel aux Tamaris
Roscoff *49 rue Edouard-Corbière (02.98.61.22.99/ www.hotel-aux-tamaris.com). €.*
Looking west across the water from its headland location on the edge of town, the 26-room Tamaris is housed in a four-storey residence that was built in the 1930s and is now, with its white shutters and scrubbed stone walls, spick and span and as attractive inside as out. Considerable thought and refinement has gone into the bedrooms, and no two look alike: one might have a headboard that looks like a sail and rigging, another might have a lighthouse painted on to the wall. Many have sea views and prices are very reasonable.

Manoir-Hôtel des Indes
3km W of Quimper *On D765, 1 allée de Prad ar C'hras (02.98.55.48.40/www.manoir-hoteldesindes.com). €€.*
The hotel's name and the exotic thread that runs through its decor pays tribute to the first owner, an adventure-seeking mariner who plied routes to India in the 18th century. Although it looks like the model of a Breton manor house from the outside, its interior is liberally sprinkled with carved Indian panelling and sculptures, and lamps that nod to the Far East; the rooms all have lovely teak floors, some have exposed beams and Moorish-looking four-poster beds. There's a restaurant serving gourmet French fare with eastern influences; and to promote the appropriate feeling of inner peace, there's a gorgeous little indoor pool under bare stone arches, sauna and massage service.

Villa Reine Hortense
Dinard *19 rue Malouine (02.99.46.54.31/ www.villa-reine-hortense.com). €€€.*
This hotel is situated right on the western edge of Plage de l'Ecluse (to which it has its own private pathway) and occupies a typical Côte d'Emeraude villa, with red terracotta roof and pale grey stone walls. It looks stylish enough from the outside, but the interior is truly gorgeous, a riot of refined belle époque furniture, lamps and tableware in tall rooms with tall windows. All but one of its eight luxurious, individually decorated rooms look over the beach; three have a private veranda. The building has a romantic history, too: it was built in 1860 by a Russian prince, former courtier of Napoléon III's mother, Queen Hortense de Beauharnais – and, incredible though it seems, if you book into room four you can splash around in her beautiful silver-plated bath.

Factfile

When to go
Brittany has a warm, temperate climate; rainfall is common, but not excessively so; thanks to the Gulf Stream, weather and water on the south coast are warmer than on the wilder north coast. The region is a popular holiday destination for the French, and August is the busiest month; Quimper and St-Malo, in particular, can get very crowded.

Getting there
Dinard-Pleurtuit-Saint-Malo airport (08.25.08.35.09/www.saint-malo.aeroport.fr) is served by daily flights from London Stansted. Brittany Ferries (0871 244 0744/www.brittany ferries.com) sails from Portsmouth to St-Malo, and Plymouth to Roscoff. The main railway interchange is at Rennes, which can be reached by TGV from Paris (2hrs 15mins); there are also TGV services to St-Malo (3hrs) and Quimper (4hrs 25mins).

Getting around
The best way to see this part of France is to hire a car, although there are regular coach services between the main towns.

Tourist information
Brest Pl de la Liberté (02.98.44.24.96/ www.brest-metropole-tourisme.fr).
Dinard 2 bd Féart (02.99.46.94.12/ www.ot-dinard.com).
Roscoff Quai d'Auxerre (02.98.61.12.13/ www.roscoff-tourisme.com).
Quimper Pl de la Résistance (02.98.53.04.05/ www.quimper-tourisme.com).
St-Malo Esplanade St-Vincent (08.25.13.52.00/ www.saint-malo-tourisme.com).

Internet access
Brest Izee, 38 quai de la Douane (02.98.46.45.59/www.izee.biz). Open 9.30am-7.30pm Mon-Sat.

Top: Bastia.
Bottom: Cap Corse.

Northern Corsica

Maquis, mountains and glorious Mediterranean coastline.

Like an unruly relative, Corsica broods stubbornly a few hours off the French coast. As sweet as the mainland is, this island is the spice that fires the senses. Centuries of strife and emigration have left it gloriously underpopulated, its scenery pristine. Rivers brim with fish while eagles and hawks patrol the hills along the coast, itself a Bahama-blue ribbon lapping on to deserted beaches or crashing against the ochre-coloured shore. Corsicans are justly proud of their environment and do all they can to protect it. The same goes for their culture and language: don't be surprised to see the island's bilingual road signs painted over or peppered with shotgun holes.

The truth is that Corsica has never been truly tamed. Although it was squabbled over by the Greeks and Romans, Arabs and Lombards, then Pisans and Genoese, these invaders never succeeded in occupying more than a few coastal strips. More canny were the British who allied themselves with republican leader Pasquale Paoli in the 18th century. This soldier statesman presided over an Anglo-Corsican republic under George III, Corsica's one true period of independence. But if Paoli's name adorns every avenue, it's the *maquis* who sum up the island's fighting spirit. These irregular World War II troops, named after the thick scented undergrowth which they melted into, ensured that Corsica was France's first liberated province.

Nowadays those *maquis* herbs are used to season sea bass, lamb and brocciu cheese served up to wide-eyed holidaymakers. Fortunately this yearly invasion never becomes a flood. There's always sunbathing space on Northern Corsica's 30 or so beaches, which range from the chi-chi in St-Florent to the hauntingly picturesque in the Désert des Agriates. The region's main towns offer contrasts of a culinary kind. You can dine on sushi with *bobos* in historic Calvi, or tear apart a lobster in Bastia's working port. Algajola, meanwhile, is the ultimate in post-work comedown spots, with beach bars, snorkelling and, if you fancy it, nude bathing. Cap Corse is a jolt back to Corsican reality. This feral spit of terrain punching out into the Mediterranean is a land of butterflies and wildflowers, of ocean panoramas and no-through roads.

Explore

By air or by sea, Bastia and Calvi serve as the twin gateways to Northern Corsica, at once the most varied and accessible part of the island. Fabulous beaches ring both towns and all points in between. A fleet of trains runs between them, touching Algajola but ignoring the wilds of the Désert des Agriates and chic St-Florent. Cap Corse sees plenty of motorcyclists, a fine way to take in the wilderness of the peninsula.

CALVI

Few towns can rival Calvi's aesthetic perfection. The 15th-century citadel dominates the broad bay, looming over the new town. Christopher Columbus was born within its walls, or so claims the proudly displayed plaque marking the foundations of his home. Below, ferries from the mainland glide in and out of the working port, dwarfing traditional fishing boats as they heave their catch on to quai Adolphe Landry. Shouts and raucous laughter permeate the café terraces along this strip, as locals exchange their daily gossip. Set back from the seafront, rue Clémenceau, boulevard Wilson and avenue de la République are lined with traditional brasseries and designer boutiques. Clamber down the crumbling steps round the western side of the citadel and choose one of the sun-bleached boulders: the panoramic seascapes will be yours

alone. Divers can plunge the Med's depths for a peek at the submerged World War II B-17 bomber nearby. Arcing southwards out of town, miles of white sand beaches back on to busy hotels and a rambling, elevated adventure park. Trains depart regularly from Calvi station to the secluded beaches, including Plage de l'Arinella and Plage de la Restitude, further along the bay.

ALGAJOLA

Nothing much happens in Algajola, which is the source of its soothing charm. The five or so simple hotels are set close to the long sandy stretch of Aregno Plage. These are matched by a few simple restaurants inside the walled village centre, a few minutes away. Each dishes up hearty set menus for €20 a throw. Such effortless brilliance is hard to emulate, making Algajola a very attractive base for any Corsican trip. The tiny tourist office inside the equally cute train station (Calvi one way, Bastia the other) dispenses all you need to know about the area, from the artisans' trail up to Pigna to local diving schools. The area's striking coastal paths need no such instruction, although they can be hairy in places. They stretch all the way to Calvi and start from the beach, but with the cheap toes-in-the-sand beach bars and volleyball nets, it's easy to get waylaid. The easternmost part of the beach is reserved for naturists. Go snorkelling here – the water is crystal clear – and you may get more than you bargained for.

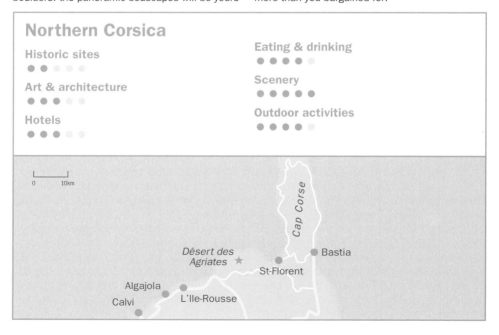

Northern Corsica

Historic sites
● ● ○ ○ ○

Art & architecture
● ● ● ● ○

Hotels
● ● ● ○ ○

Eating & drinking
● ● ● ● ○

Scenery
● ● ● ● ●

Outdoor activities
● ● ● ● ○

0   10km

Cap Corse

Désert des Agriates ★

Bastia

St-Florent

Algajola
Calvi   L'Ile-Rousse

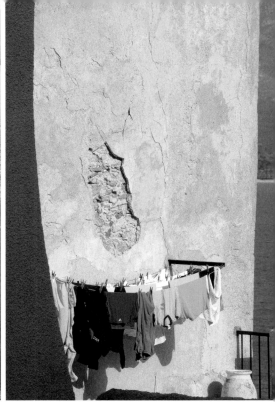

Top: Calvi.
Bottom: St-Florent.

DESERT DES AGRIATES

Spanning the Balagne's *maquis*-covered mountains from Ile-Rousse to St-Florent, the Désert des Agriates is a UNESCO World Heritage site. The 35 kilometres (22 miles) of pristine coastline is backed by craggy cliffs. Inland, the terrain is arid, redolent with lavender and sage; you'd be hard pressed to guess that this shrubland was once the island's most fertile. Towards the end of the 19th century, over-experimentation with slash and burn farming techniques sucked the nutrient-rich soil dry. Thankfully rejected years later as a potential nuclear testing ground, the area was declared a nature reserve by the French government in 1989. Visitors can hop on the ferry from St-Florent to Plage du Lotu and hike the Sentier du Littoral to Ostricioni. The desert hosts just two spots to bed down for the night: Camping U Paradisu (www.camping-uparadisu.com), backing on to the stunning Plage de Saleccia and home to the reserve's only water fountain, and the rustic Refuge de Ghignu (book through the St-Florent tourist office, 04.95.37.06.04).

ST-FLORENT

Sexy and showy, this is Corsica's answer to the Côte d'Azur. Like a mini St-Tropez, St-Florent manages to balance a harbour full of Sunseekers and an age-old *pétanque* culture on its main place des Portes. By day, most desert the cobbled lanes around the small town centre, heading off instead on a boat trip to Plage du Lotu in the Désert des Agriates. Much closer to home, and correspondingly popular, is the soft sand and aquamarine water of Plage de la Roya, three kilometres (two miles) around the bay. Come the evening all are back in town and glammed up in a beachy South of France style: suntans, strappy heels and heaps of Lacoste. One of the town's infrequent British visitors was Lord Nelson, who bombarded St-Florent's Genoese citadel in his pre-Trafalgar days. This fortification – the town's only real 'sight' – is five minutes up pretty rue du Centre. The panorama here is sublime, bettered only by the odd swimming spot that you can hike down to. The two or three laid-back seafood restaurants perched over the water are as accomplished as they are informal.

CAP CORSE

Never more than 14 kilometres (nine miles) across, the Cap Corse peninsula pokes 40 kilometres (25 miles) into the Mediterranean, like a giant finger pointing directly at Genoa. A narrow ridge of mountains sweeps down its centre: with a little elevation, panoramic views can take in the island of Elba on a clear day. While Napoleon was exiled on the latter, he claimed to be able to smell his native Corsica. Head north and the villages grow more sporadic. Giant wind turbines

perch on the peninsula's tip, their laboured spinning casting a shadow over Centuri's picturesque fishing port. Nonza, further to the south, is home to a west-facing, black sand beach; at sunset it's one of the island's most stunning. For the adventurous, the best form of transport for exploring Cap Corse is a motorbike, and you can expect to see bikers by the dozen looping the twisting coastal roads.

BASTIA

For centuries Bastia was Corsica's window on the world, trading with, and being battered by, ships from Pisa, Genoa, Britain and France. Nowadays it's still the first port of call for most visitors. Corsica Ferries' canary yellow fleet pours out passengers: some in jeeps, some on Harleys, some shouldering mountain bikes. The wealth of several centuries, combined with a lack of beach, has left Bastia both handsome and authentic, far removed from the island's more southerly seasonal resorts. And as capital of the northern Haute-Corse region, it has all the associated trappings. The first of these is the massive place St-Nicolas, palm-lined and backed with elegant apartments built for the local bourgeoisie. It's a café-strewn parade ground for promenading couples or mobile-wielding *mademoiselles*. A flea market is held here on Sundays. The tourist office on the square has a map of the town's churches. Pick of these are the Ste-Marie cathedral and the Chapelle Ste-Croix – both Baroque gems – and the Eglise St-Jean Baptiste, Corsica's largest.

A block south, place de l'Hôtel de Ville hosts a colourful market every Saturday and Sunday. Miss it and you can still load up on local jams, cheeses, wines and liqueurs, including local Cap Corse firewater, in the surrounding streets. These lanes are a provençal pastiche of ochre apartments, sky-blue shutters and window boxes. Heading south again through the old ramparts is the Vieux Port. This is Bastia at its most majestic, with rows of waterside restaurants serving up fish, langoustine and crab brought in by the fishing boats bobbing by the quay.

Eat

Corsican dining tends to be a casual affair, even at the island's most elegant tables. From Easter to late September, staff turn out plate after plate to a permanently full house. Opening hours are liable to be elastic: lunch is normally served between noon and 2.30pm, dinner between 7.30pm and 10.30pm. However, you'll find there's more than a spoonful of island attitude: families with children will be served at 6.30pm; a certain venue may not open at all, the owners opting to host a cousin's private birthday party

Castaway Corsica

With some 1,000km (600 miles) of coastline and nearly 200 beaches to choose from, beach bums are spoiled when it comes to spreading out their towel on the island. The best 50 or so beaches have been photographed from the air by local paper *Corse Matin* then compiled into a bilingual glossy, *Plages de Corse*. Available from most of the island's newsagents for €10, it's the ultimate holiday tease to show friends back home.

During the summer months the stretches of sand near the main resorts are a seething mass of umbrellas and deckchairs, but with a little effort it's still easy to escape the sunseekers. Many of the island's beaches are relatively inaccessible, and can only be reached by boat or a stiff hike, which means that visitors can still stumble upon Eden-like stretches of sand.

One of Northern Corsica's most isolated beaches is Plage de Saleccia, a huge sweep of soft white sand and turquoise sea that was used as a location for the invasion sequences in the film *The Longest Day*. It's a windswept spot, punctuated only by lean-tos made out of sarongs, driftwood and other bits of flotsam by the odd passing tourist. Getting here requires some considerable effort – a bumpy 12km (7.5-mile) drive or mountain bike ride down a 4x4-only track off the main D81 highway, or a 45-minute hike through the wilderness of the Désert des Agriates from the similarly stunning Plage du Lotu. In summer, the latter is linked to St-Florent's harbour every hour by Agriate Marittima (06.17.50.65.58/

www.agriate-marittima.com, €14 return) and the good ship *Popeye* (06.62.16.23.76/www.lepopeye.com, €14 return). If you fancy staying on a few nights at Saleccia, then bring a tent – the simple, seasonal U Paradisu campsite (www.camping-uparadisu.com) backs right on to the blissful beach.

For the ultimate castaway experience, though, you'll need to ditch the 4x4 and head even further into the wilderness of Corsica's back country on foot. Plage de Ghignu, the seldom-visited little cousin of Lotu and Saleccia, is for hardcore beach bums only. Visit and you will most likely have the beach to yourself – unsurprisingly as it can only be taken in by way of a two- to three-day coastal trail from Ostriconi to St-Florent. A map of this *sentier littoral* route can be downloaded from the St-Florent tourist office website (www.corsica-saintflorent.com). Just remember that this is a 'desert' and the only drinking holes are at Saleccia and Ghignu – in between you need to carry plenty of water with you.

If that all sounds like too much hassle for a decent spot of sand, then two additional beaches between Calvi and Algajola are well worth hunting down. Both are accessible via the coastal train and are just 100m or so long. A hike down from the Ondari-Arinella stop is Plage de l'Arinella, a hip beach backed by the Asian-inspired Matahari restaurant (*see p257*). Next stop on the line is Ste-Restitude, home of the Plage de la Restitude. This spot is even more laid-back, complete with beach bar and superb snorkelling.

Casa Musicale.

instead. Be prepared to roll with the punches – more often than not, this flexibility yields pleasant surprises. During the winter season, many places close down for six months.

A Casarella
9km SE of Algajola *Pigna (04.95.61.78.08). Open Apr, Sept, Oct 11am-6pm Mon-Fri, Sun; 11am-9pm Sat. May-Aug 11am-9.30pm daily. No credit cards. €.*
Perched 500m (1,650ft) above sea level, this enchanting village is just the place to escape to on a summer afternoon. Entirely pedestrianised, with periwinkle shutters that offset the town's stone buildings, Pigna couldn't be cuter. Amble back to the north-west corner of the village, where grapevines shelter A Casarella's handful of tables and perfect Mediterranean vistas. Start with a glass of organic wine, then linger over the lengthy tapas menu. Unlike most of the restaurants along the coast, this spot takes advantage of more mountainous bounty, including Calenzana-reared goat's cheese, cured pork *figatellu* and chestnut biscuits.

Caveau du Marin
Bastia *14 quai Martyrs Libération (04.95.31.62.31). Open June-Sept noon-2pm Mon-Wed; noon-2pm, 7-11pm Fri-Sun. Oct-May noon-2pm Tue; noon-2pm, 7-11pm Wed-Sun. €€.*
Almost hidden among the restaurants rimming Bastia's port, tiny Caveau du Marin has a handsome terrace and a short menu starring excellent home-style Corsican cuisine. Highlights include ravioli filled with brocciu, a tangy sheep's milk cheese, or grilled stuffed sardines. Be sure to book in advance – this spot may look laid-back, but its local reputation, paired with its diminutive size, means you've got almost no chance of a table without a reservation.

E.A.T. (Épicurien Avant Tout)
Calvi *15 rue Clémenceau (04.95.38.21.87). Open mid Apr-mid Oct lunch & dinner Mon, Tue, Thur-Sun. Mid Oct-mid Apr lunch & dinner Thur-Sun. €€€.*
Loosely translated as 'epicurean above all else', E.A.T. delivers on its promise. Contemporary plates pair flavours and textures, such as chunks of sea bass sizzling on a hot slab of granite. The quay's morning haul, just around the corner, provides fresh fish for the mixed sushi spreads. Owner Rémi trained in London, and has succeeded in bringing a dose of urban sophistication to the island. Lunch menus start at €23; big appetites can upgrade to L or XL.

Le Jardin
Calvi *Hôtel Le Magnolia, rue Alsace Lorraine (04.95.65.08.02/www.hotel-le-magnolia.com). Open Apr-Oct 7-10pm Mon; noon-1.30pm, 7-10pm Tue-Sun. €€.*
Le Jardin has been an institution on the Calvi scene since 1929. Tucked into the city's weaving back streets, outdoor tables are sprinkled in the shade of Hôtel Le Magnolia's 100-year-old leafy namesake. Expect a mix of traditional French cuisine and Corsican specialities – sea bream sautéed with wild marjoram, boar and myrtle stew, plates of Corsican charcuterie. Keep an eye out for the bargain three-course Menu Corse (€28), tweaked daily to feature the market's freshest pickings.

Le Matahari
10km E of Calvi *Plage de l'Arinella (04.95.60.78.47/www.lematahari.com). Open Apr-mid June, mid-end Sept 8am-5pm daily. Mid June-mid Sept 4pm-2am Tue-Sun. €€.*
Better suited to Koh Pha Ngan than Calvi, Le Matahari is no less than a tropical dream. A beach bar on the white sands of Plage de l'Arinella, this delectable spot has the fortune to be the beach's exclusive trader, blessedly off the beaten path. Dig your toes into the sand while dining on Tahitian coconut and shrimp curry or calamari tempura. Inside, the South-east Asian decor matches the cuisine, centred on a wooden sculpted Buddha. Come late afternoon, Calvi's citadel is silhouetted across the bay.

Le Pirate
Cap Corse *Erbalunga, 10km N of Bastia (04.95.33.24.20/www.restaurantlepirate.com). Open Mar-May, Oct-Dec noon-2pm, 7.30-10pm Wed-Sun. June-Sept noon-2pm, 7.30-10pm daily. €€€€.*
In the prettiest seaside restaurant stakes, Le Pirate wins hands down – not an easy achievement when you're one of hundreds on the island. Tables spill from an old stone building in Erbalunga's harbour, balanced on a terrace above the water or positioned on the adjacent patio. What Le Pirate achieves aesthetically, it doubles gastronomically. Chef Jean-Pierre Ricci wears his Michelin star on his sleeve, matching organic local veal, for instance, with a tower of wild mushrooms and scallops. Best value are the set menus (€29-€35 lunch, €65-€90 dinner), which offer the option of pairing local wines with each specific dish.

Restaurant de l'Europe
St-Florent *Quai du Port de Plaisance (04.95.35.32.91/www.hotel-europe2.com). Open Mar-May, Sept-Nov noon-3pm, 7-11.30pm daily. June-Aug noon-3pm, 7pm-1am daily. €€€.*
At first Restaurant de l'Europe, set on the ground floor of St-Florent's most down-to-earth hotel, stands out only for its simplicity. Carefully tended flower boxes line the terrace and plain white tablecloths mirror the sails on boats berthed over the road. But it's the cuisine – not the decor – that's the star here. Tuna tartare is served on a bed of ratatouille; oven-baked *rascasse* is married with lemon and black olives; barbecued lamb chops are doused with a garlic cream marinade. Set at the foot of Patrimonio, Corsica's wine country, it's no surprise that the restaurant also boasts an excellent range of local vintages.

U Castellu
Algajola *10 pl du Château (04.95.60.78.75). Open Apr-mid Oct noon-2pm, 7-10pm Mon, Wed-Sun; 7-10pm Tue. €€*
There's no need for ornate lighting at U Castellu: set just inside Algajola's illuminated château walls, the restaurant's terrace benefits from plenty of flattering, golden light. Take a table on the pretty patio, sit back and enjoy the simple, yet innovative, Corsican cuisine. Vegetable tarts mix roasted peppers with fresh goat's cheese; honey and thyme flavour the lamb. Set menus start at €20, lending the evening even more of a rosy glow.

U Lampione

Cap Corse *Marina, Macinaggio, 25km N of Bastia (04.95.35.45.55). Open Apr-Sept noon-3pm, 7-10.30pm daily. €€.*

Not quite a shack on the beach (but pretty close), U Lampione is a lazy little spot just north of Macinaggio's port. Bypass the town's more upscale eateries, and pick a table on U Lampione's shady terrace, or indoors under one of the wonky ceiling fans. The friendly owners serve up fresh fish – check their daily specials – grilled meats and crispy pizzas, along with *pichets* of local wine. A popular place for hikers to fuel up before setting off on the 19km (12-mile) Sentier des Douaniers around the Cap Corse headland.

Stay

You can count Corsica's business hotels on one hand. Instead of Best Westerns and five-star retreats, the island is blessed with scores of smaller, more homely options, from beachside campsites to boutique guesthouses. Although most shut up shop from October to March, they are jam-packed during high season.

Camping de la Plage

Algajola *Aregno Plage (04.95.60.71.76/www.camping-de-la-plage-en-balagne.com). Closed Mid Nov-mid Mar. No credit cards. €.*

A beachside campground that does exactly what it says on the tin, only better. Camping de la Plage even has its own train platform, from which you can rattle all the way along the coast to Calvi or Bastia. The tracks separate Algajola's golden sands from the main campsite area. A European union of holidaymakers set up shop here from spring onwards; Germans with ritzy mobile homes, Swedes with electric BBQs, Polish walkers with gas stoves and Brits with vast dome tents. The attraction is obvious: a choice between shady and sunny pitches, a spotless stack of showers and loos, and an open-all-hours shop selling roast chickens. A notch up are the wooden chalets and studios, each with a patio, kitchen and bathroom. The splurge option are the air-conditioned Tonga and Morea beach huts, advertised as *pied dans l'eau*. They need to be reserved way in advance.

Casa Musicale

5km SE of Algajola *Pigna (04.95.61.77.31/www.casa-musicale.org). Closed Dec-Feb. €€.*

This hilltop redoubt manages to smash every Corsican stereotype: sun, sea and seafood are deftly replaced with music, mountains and country cooking. Casa Musicale began as a commune in the 1980s, slowly developing into a music school, artists' residency and centre for culinary exploration. Now it's way more highbrow – yet still kooky and friendly – with seven boutique bedrooms. The Bassa (the rooms are all named after Corsican vocal harmonies) boasts vaulted ceilings and a sea view, while petite Mezzana is the most romantic. Bird song (plus the odd rifle crack) awakens guests. Breakfast is dished up on the motley assortment of chairs and tables perched on the terrace.

Castel Brando

Cap Corse *Erbalunga, 10km N of Bastia (04.95.30.10.30/www.castelbrando.com). €€.*

Hidden by a sandy cove on Cap Corse, the venerable Castel Brando revels in glorious isolation. Its location behind bougainvillaea-covered walls was originally for security, not privacy: when it was constructed in the late 19th century, this was one of several *maisons américaines* – palaces built by newly rich Corsicans returning from the Americas. All but the standard rooms have a patio or balcony, while the suites offer a glimpse of the Med. The sea itself is a skip over the road. Masks, snorkels and kayaks are available from the foyer. If taking one of the hotel's bikes, grab a map beforehand: as civilised as Castel Brando is, the surrounding hills are pretty remote.

Clos des Amandiers

Calvi *Rte de Pietramaggiore (04.95.65.08.32/www.clos-des-amandiers.com). €€.*

Clos des Amandiers is a rambling collection of bungalows set in an orchard, 15 minutes on foot from Calvi's historic centre and beach. Guests could be forgiven for not leaving the tranquil confines of the Clos all day. Semi-organised groups into hiking, birdwatching and the like disappear from dawn until dusk, freeing up the whacking great swimming pool, tennis courts, *pétanque* run and ample grounds. The bar and reception is charmingly haphazard, run as it is by a sturdy octogenarian. This multilingual hostess rules over the muddle of dining areas and anterooms. Accommodation is unfussy, and those yearning for more than a comfy bed with a table and chair underneath an olive tree are advised to look elsewhere.

La Dolce Notte

St-Florent *Rte de Bastia (04.95.37.06.65/www.hotel-dolce-notte.com). Closed Nov-Feb. €€.*

This well-run, 20-room hotel fills up fast, so turning up on spec is not an option. It's just a ten-minute walk from St-Florent's chic main drag, but many guests don't make it further than the few metres to the sea before aperitif time. (A decent Atlantic roller would flood the place, but St-Florent is blessed with invariably calm turquoise waters.) Guestrooms are a little stuck in the 1990s, overly flowery with heavy tiles, although the pricier *grand terrace* rooms offer more modern provençal chic.

Le Grand Hôtel

Calvi *3 bd Wilson (04.95.65.09.74/www.grand-hotel-calvi.com). €€.*

Perched outside the old city walls, the Grand is just above the marina: even if you arrive by ferry rather than yacht, you can still be peeking out of your hotel window five minutes after stepping ashore. Not all of the guestrooms have a sea view – ask for one of the suites if you want to be sure – but fine linen and antique furniture are the norm all round. A few of the staff fall into the antique category too, but they polish and dust the Grand's faded glory relentlessly. It's a five-minute stroll back out to the ramparts, train station or to Calvi's town beach. Both evening cocktails and the €9 continental breakfast can be taken in the sun-dappled garden.

Le Jardin.

Castel Brando.

Hôtel Central

Bastia *3 rue Miot (04.95.31.71.12/ www.centralhotel.fr). €€.*
The Hôtel Central has been around a long time and is an accomplished place to stay. Guestrooms are large and perfectly laid out. Eighteen of the antique key fobs open ruby red double rooms on the first or second floor, each a sexy Parisian design transported to downtown Bastia. Antique tiles mix with polished wood furniture and the occasional chair or balcony. The six apartments on the top floor couldn't be more different: each one is light, white and overlooks Bastia's slate rooftops. Elaborately equipped, they can sleep a family of five and have enough plates for a family of 15.

Hôtel Le Splendid

8km NE of Algajola *Rue Comte Valery, Ile-Rousse (04.95.60.00.24/www.le-splendid-hotel.com). €€.*
In days of yore the Splendid was a detached art deco masterpiece lording it over Ile-Rousse. Now painted pink and part of a terrace a few roads back from the harbour, it still gives off a sedentary *Miami Vice* charm. The kidney-shaped pool is lined with sunloungers and shaded by tropical trees. Indoors, showy touches like sexy key fobs, marble stairs and iron balustrades remain. Heading upstairs, the 50 or so rooms are resolutely modern with trendy bathrooms and Wi-Fi access. With free breakfast, €5 a day parking and moderate room rates, it makes a great base for exploring the area.

Hôtel Stella Mare

Algajola *Chemin Santa Lucia (04.95.60.71.18/ www.stellamarehotel.com). Closed Nov-Apr. €€.*
The Stella Mare is a step up in refinement from Algajola's beach cabins, but not much more expensive. The shared outdoor areas are akin to those of a Greek villa: lots of urns, pot plants, scattered seats, loungers, patios and flowers. The terraced gardens roll down to the beach and tiny town centre. Half of the 16 rooms open on to this view, the others on to the steep mountains behind. All are connected with Wi-Fi. The bedrooms themselves are very slick, with light colours and new bathrooms. The fill-your-boots breakfast (€10 per person) is best taken on the hotel's sea view terrace.

U Libecciu

Cap Corse *Macinaggio, 25km N of Bastia (04.95.35.43.22/www.u-libecciu.com). €€.*
This is one of only a handful of hotels on the island's wildest spit of land, and those lapping the Cap by car or bike would be wise to bed down here. There's ample parking and you can freshen up in the pool. What looks like a motel building (albeit in provençal pink and blue) actually houses a series of newish apartments, massive inside and featuring a terrace or balcony apiece. The restaurant serves up decent fare, although there are several eateries near Macinaggio's public beach a few minutes' walk away. Those spending longer (and special rates are available if you plan to) can take in the local tennis courts or diving school, or simply hit the *pétanque* run with a can of Pietra chestnut lager.

Factfile

When to go

May, June and September are the best months to visit, with warm seas and hot sun. High summer can get hectic on the highways, but with an advance hotel booking a trip any time is fine. Aside from January and February, the rest of the year is often mild and sunny, although it can be a little too quiet for some.

Getting there

Bastia Poretta Airport (04.95.54.54.54/www. bastia.aeroport.fr) is 20km (12.5 miles) out of town. A taxi to Bastia should cost just less than €40, while the regular shuttle bus costs €8. Taxis wait outside Calvi's Ste-Catherine Airport (04.95.54.54.54/www.calvi.aeroport.fr). The ten-minute drive downtown costs around €15.

Corsica Ferries (www.corsica-ferries.co.uk) and SNCM (www.sncm.fr) operate ferries from Nice, Toulon and Marseille to Northern Corsica. Crossing times vary from four hours to overnight.

Getting around

Chemins de Fer de Corse operates Corsica's rail service (04.95.32.80.57/www.train-corse.com), which chugs slowly along the scenic coastline from Calvi to Bastia four times daily. More frequent are the superannuated Renault trains, which serve every beach and village between Calvi and Ile-Rousse. Corsicar buses run between Bastia and Calvi (www.corsicar.com; three times daily; 2hrs; €16). Buses between Bastia and St-Florent are run by Transports Santini (04.95.37.02.98; twice daily; 45mins; €5).

Most visitors arrive with their own car or motorbike, although both are available for hire on the island. You need your own transport to explore the D80, which runs around Cap Corse.

Tourist information

Bastia Pl St-Nicolas (04.95.54.20.40/ www.bastia-tourisme.com). Open July-Aug 8am-8pm Mon-Sat; 9am-noon, 4-7pm Sun. Sept-June 8.30am-noon, 2-6pm Mon-Sat; 9am-1pm Sun.
Calvi Port de Plaisance (04.95.65.16.67/www. bastia-tourisme.com). Open July-Aug 9am-7.30pm daily; Sept-June 8.45am-noon, 2-6pm Mon-Sat.

Internet access

Bastia Five Café, 5 bd Giraud (04.95.32.30.12). Open Winter 7am-2am Mon-Fri; 1pm-2am Sat, Sun. Summer 4pm-4am daily.
Calvi L'Orient, rue Clémenceau (04.95.65.00.16). Open 9am-2am daily.

St-Tropez.

St-Tropez & Around

Take your pick – celeb-filled beach clubs or charming *villages perchés*.

Welcome to a land of high-octane glamour, where A-list celebs arrive on Vespas and doormen don't bat an eyelid as the evening's fifth Lamborghini cruises on up. But behind the glitz and the €15,000 per square metre real estate of St-Tropez, a very real coastal region awaits, with lively street markets, gorgeous *villages perchés*, vast chestnut forests and ancient mountain fortresses.

On the St-Tropez peninsula, the idyllic villages of Ramatuelle and Gassin perch amid verdant vineyards and parasol pine-shaded hills, while white sandy beaches (and champagne-fuelled private beach clubs) stretch along the shoreline. This is God's own country – provided He could afford it, of course. Head further back from the coast and the crowds quickly thin out as as the sombre Maures mountains take over from the brightly coloured villas and yacht-filled bay of St-Tropez, and laid-back villages such as La Garde-Freinet restore your faith in French provincial life.

Given St-Tropez's reputation for hedonism, it's fitting that arch-hedonist Nero should have put the place on the map. In the first century AD, the emperor had a Christian centurion, Torpes, beheaded in Pisa. His headless trunk was then set adrift in a boat, with a rooster and a dog. When the boat washed up on the beach that was later named after the hapless centurion, the starving dog hadn't taken so much as a nibble of the corpse – a sure sign of sainthood.

Explore

ST-TROPEZ

In the Middle Ages, the small fishing community at St-Tropez was harried by Saracens until the 15th century, when 21 Genoese families were imported to show the pirates who was who. The place was still a tiny backwater in 1880, when writer Guy de Maupassant sailed his boat in to give the locals their first taste of bohemian eccentricity.

A decade later, post-Impressionist painter Paul Signac, driven into port by a storm, fell in love with St-Tropez and promptly moved in. He opened the famed Salon des Indépendants, and invited his friends (then unknowns, including Matisse, Derain, Vlaminck and Dufy) to exhibit. Wealthy holidaying Parisians stopped by to purchase works by the up-and-coming artists, and soon began buying homes of their own.

Another wave of personalities washed up in 1956 after Roger Vadim and his young protégée Brigitte Bardot arrived to make *And God Created Woman*. In no time at all, St-Tropez became the world's most famous playboy haunt.

The millionaires and superstars are still there, but not all come out to play in the high season madness, remaining bolt-holed in their luxury sea-view abodes. When they do venture out, they are often whisked to an ultra-discreet HIP (Highly Important Person) room. Bardot herself, who alternates between her house in the hills and her seafront home-cum-animal-rights-HQ at La Madrague, is unlikely to be found mooching round the market these days. Instead, star-spotters must make do with a boat tour of the headland's A-list abodes.

St-Tropez is built on a slope, with all the action sliding inexorably towards the Vieux Port. Here, the super-rich wine and dine on their enormous luxury yachts, in full view of the crowded café terraces. East of the Vieux Port, the Château de Suffren (closed to the public) dates back to 972, and is the oldest building in town. Back from quai Jean Jaurès myriad little galleries line the side streets, while place aux Herbes is home to a small but lively daily market – get there around midday to lunch on fresh oysters, sea urchins and white wine. Steep rue de la Citadelle leads to a swarm of tourist-trap restaurants and the impressively walled 17th-century Citadelle (04.94.97.59.43), perched at the top of the village and with spectacular views from its ramparts. Below here, Roger Vadim is buried in the seaside Cimetière Marin. Butterfly enthusiasts should also stop by the Maison de Papillons (04.94.97.63.45), comprising over 4,500 carefully catalogued species.

Behind the Vieux Port, St-Tropez's *pétanque*-playing fraternity hangs out on plane tree-lined place des Lices. The square is also home to a market on Tuesday and Saturday, where fruit, vegetables, *charcuterie*, honey and wine fill the

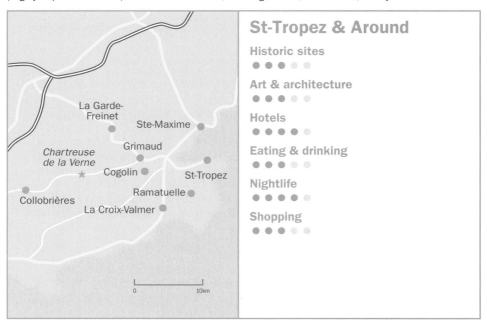

St-Tropez & Around

Historic sites
● ● ● ● ○

Art & architecture
● ● ● ● ○

Hotels
● ● ● ● ○

Eating & drinking
● ● ● ○ ○

Nightlife
● ● ● ● ○

Shopping
● ● ● ● ○

La Garde-Freinet
Ste-Maxime
Chartreuse de la Verne
Grimaud
Cogolin
St-Tropez
Collobrières
Ramatuelle
La Croix-Valmer

0   10km

stalls and traders exchange gossip. On the hill, a kilometre south of town, the pretty Chapelle Ste-Anne (open only on 26 July) commands glorious views over the bay and southern Alps.

Musée de l'Annonciade

Pl Georges Gramont (04.94.17.84.10). Open June-Sept 10am-2pm, 3-7pm daily. Oct-May 10am-noon, 2-6pm Mon, Wed-Sun. Closed Nov. Admission June-Sept €6; free-€4 reductions. Oct-May €4; free-€3 reductions. No credit cards.

Between the Vieux Port and the Nouveau Port, the Musée de l'Annonciade is a superb museum of early 20th-century art, housed in a handsome 16th-century chapel; the collection includes works by Vuillard, Bonnard, Matisse, Braque and Vlaminck.

ST-TROPEZ PENINSULA

Dotted with parasol pines and vineyards, with views down to pristine blue coves, the hills above town seem a world away from the chaos of the port. When the truly chic or truly rich airily talk about summering in St-Trop, often as not they actually mean hiding out in the hill villages in Garbo-esque seclusion, well away from the wannabes who frequent the old port.

Ramatuelle began life as a Saracen stronghold; razed in 1592 during the Wars of Religion, it was rebuilt in 1620. It still has a fortified feel, as tightly knit houses climb around the hill. A gateway by the church leads through to the partly pedestrianised old town, filled with leafy squares, olive oil shops and galleries. The street market on Thursdays and Sundays makes a popular day trip from St-Tropez, and it's packed out during its jazz and theatre festivals in July and August.

Ramatuelle is also just a short distance away from the plage de Pampelonne – five kilometres (three miles) of sand, popular with the glitterati and naturist bathers alike. Among the chi-chi beach clubs, the famed Club 55 was Brigitte Bardot's venue of choice to celebrate her retirement from films in 1974.

Smaller Gassin, where Mick and Bianca Jagger honeymooned in the '70s, offers an incredible view of the peninsula. Squeezing through ancient streets to its medieval fortress and church, it's easy to understand why Gassin has been named one of France's most beautiful villages. Surrounding vineyards all offer complimentary tastings – Château Minuty (04.94.56.12.09), with its chapel and Napoléon III-era mansion to nose around, is particularly recommended.

Slightly back from the coast, La Croix-Valmer is a residential town with fine views across cliffs dotted with the holiday villas of well-heeled French families. From here, there's easy access to the lovely plage de Gigaro and stunning coastal conservation area on the Cap Lardier. The golden sand beaches in the area are a world away from the hoi polloi of plage de Pampelonne.

PORT GRIMAUD & STE-MAXIME

In the bay west of St-Tropez, Port Grimaud was designed in the late 1960s to look like a miniature slice of the Venice lagoon. It's kitschly pretty – and wonderfully surreal. Visitors must park their cars and take in the watery lanes of townhouses on foot or by boat. Kids will love the electric boats that can be hired for a putter around (cheekily, they are €25 per hour by the car park, €20 per hour inside the city walls).

Ste-Maxime has lost the allure it exuded in 1930s posters, but is not without charm. Its wide walkways and clean sandy beaches appeal to families, and it's also an excellent base for those who can't afford the rates in St-Tropez: boats connect the two for €12 return.

MASSIF DES MAURES

Head inland towards Collobrières and you'll soon find yourself in a surprisingly feral mountain area. The heart of the Massif, dotted with remote chapels and neolithic menhirs, can only be reached on foot. It is crossed east–west by the GR9 and GR51 footpaths and north–south by the GR90. For the less ambitious, two short waymarked discovery footpaths leave from near the Office de Tourisme in Collobrières, which also organises themed guided walks.

Surrounded by massive chestnut trees and the cork oak trees from which cork is hewn, Collobrières is Provence's chestnut capital. The Confiserie Azuréenne (bd Général Koenig, 04.94.48.07.20) sells *marrons glacés* and everything imaginable made with chestnuts, including soup, tea and ice-cream. Around 1850, Collobrières was an important logging centre, and 19th-century wood barons' houses contrast with higgledy-piggledy medieval streets. A ten-minute drive back along the D14 to Cogolin leads to the isolated Chartreuse de La Verne (04.94.43.45.41), which looms like a fortress halfway up a remote hillside. Founded by Carthusian monks in 1170, it was burned down on several occasions in the Wars of Religion, and rebuilt each time in local stone.

Join tourists from a dozen different nations in the picture-perfect *village perché* of Grimaud. Window boxes and pavement cafés render this former Saracen and Templar stronghold more beautiful still, while arrows mark the route around its best sights. From the ruins of the 11th-century château that crowns it, there are panoramic views over a starkly contrasting landscape.

Reached through the cork woods north of here, La Garde-Freinet is a lively stopping-off point where the main street, rue St-Jacques, and place Vieille abound with bistros, *brocantes* and designer gifts, and a superb old-fashioned *quincaillerie* (hardware store). Beyond the solid 15th- to 18th-century church, rue de la Planète is the start of an energetic climb to the ruins of the

Port Grimaud.

abandoned original village, inhabited until the 15th century and built on the foundations of a Saracen stronghold. At the same address as the tourist office, the Conservatoire du Patrimoine (04.94.43.08.57, www.conservatoiredufreinet.org) has displays on the fortress and local heritage.

A busy crossroads between the Maures and St-Tropez, Cogolin wins no prizes for beauty, but it does qualify as a real town with an economy based around the manufacture of corks, briar pipes, bamboo furniture and carpet-making (the latter introduced by Armenian immigrants in the 1920s). Its claim to fame is the invention of the *tarte tropézienne*, a sweet brioche filled with cream that's now ubiquitous throughout the region. The Tarte Tropézienne (510 av des Narcisses, 04.94.43.41.20) still prepares it according to the original recipe, patented in the 1950s by Polish baker Alexandre Micka. Also worth a peek is the 11th-century church of St-Sauveur, with a lovely altarpiece by Hurlupin. The market is on Wednesday and Saturday mornings, plus Monday and Friday in summer.

Eat & Drink

Banh-Hoi
St-Tropez *12 rue Petit St-Jean (04.94.97.36.29). Open Late Mar-mid Oct 7.30-11.30pm daily. Closed mid Oct-late Mar. €€€€.*
One of a cluster of unassuming-looking eateries along rue Petit St-Jean, this place is prized by East Asian food fanatics. The critically acclaimed creations from chef Pham Van Ut include delights such as five-spice pork brochettes and Thai-style tuna tartare.

Le Café
St-Tropez *5 pl des Lices (04.94.97.44.69/ www.lecafe.fr). Open 8am-midnight daily. €€€.*
The terrace outside Le Café doubles as a stadium for watching the endless boules matches on place des Lices. There's hearty provençal dining in the evening, but most are happy to sink a *pression* of lager and tuck into a steak tartare or *hamburger-frites*.

Café de Paris
St-Tropez *15 quai Suffren (04.94.97.00.56). Open 7am-3am daily. €€€€.*
An unremarkable terrace gives little indication of the plush, romantic interior of the Café de Paris. Designed by Philippe Starck, the sushi bar and French diner exudes glamour with its backlit white drapes, chandeliers and red velvet banquettes. If you can afford the quayside prices, it's the place to be seen.

Au Caprice des Deux
St-Tropez *40 rue Portail Neuf (04.94.97.76.78/ www.aucapricedesdeux.com). Open Mid Feb-Nov 8pm-midnight daily. Closed Dec-mid Feb. €€€€.*

Au Caprice des Deux serves up contemporary French cuisine at its best, infused with a hint of new world flavour. The beef in the salad is piquant, the cannelloni is stuffed with crab, and you won't find cod with truffle emulsion on many menus in St-Tropez. There's an excellent wine list too.

L'Escale Joseph
St-Tropez *9 quai Jean Jaurès (04.94.97.00.63/ www.joseph-saint-tropez.com). Open noon-3pm, 7pm-midnight daily. €€€€.*
A portside table at L'Escale Joseph means showmanship with style. Incredibly flashy, it epitomises St-Tropez chic. The menu is a real delight, with only the finest cuts to suit a demanding clientele: châteaubriand beef, monkfish cheeks and tournedos Rossini.

"This Franco-Japanese eaterie is owned by Joseph, a character who is as synonymous with St-Tropez as Rick Stein is with Cornwall's Padstow."

Le Gorille
St-Tropez *1 quai Suffren (04.94.97.03.93/ www.legorille.com). Open July, Aug 24hrs daily. Sept-Dec, Feb-June 8am-1am daily. Closed Jan. €€. No credit cards.*
This place has been a portside favourite for the past 50 years or so. Simple, inexpensive dishes predominate on the blackboard menu: think steak-frites, salade niçoise and seafood salads. The friendly, energetic staff keep the place open 24 hours a day in summer for St-Trop's party animals.

Grand Joseph
St-Tropez *1 pl de l'Hôtel du Ville (04.94.97.01.66/ www.joseph-saint-tropez.com). Open noon-3pm, 7.30pm-midnight daily. €€€€.*
This Franco-Japanese eaterie is a recent addition to the fleet of restaurants owned by the eponymous Joseph, a character as synonymous with St-Tropez as Rick Stein is with Cornwall's Padstow. Simple lunch options include tuna and beef carpaccios, with more elaborate truffle and sashimi dishes on the evening menu.

L'Hermitage
Ste-Maxime *118 av de Gaulle (04.94.96.04.05). Open noon-3pm, 7.30pm-midnight daily. €€€.*
The seafront at Ste-Maxime is lined with touristy brasseries and ice-cream parlours, but the menu at L'Hermitage is a departure from the norm, with innovative dishes such as swordfish carpaccio and duck with peaches.

La Ponche

St-Tropez *Pl du Revelin (04.94.97.09.29/*
www.laponche.com). Open Mid Feb-Oct noon-2.30pm,
7-11pm daily. Closed Nov-mid Feb. €€€.
Nestled by the plage de la Ponche, this place serves high-
end cuisine with an innovative twist. The filet mignon is
pork, not beef, while cod arrives with 'tagliatelled'
vegetables. More classic provençal dishes find their way on
to the €40 *menu gastronomique*. The adjoining Hôtel La
Ponche has 18 stunning rooms.

Nightlife

Les Caves du Roi

St-Tropez *Hôtel Byblos, av Paul Signac*
(04.94.65.68.00/www.lescavesduroy.com). Open Easter-
May, Sept 11pm-5am Fri, Sat. June-Aug 11pm-5am
daily. Closed mid Oct-Easter. Admission free.
The paparazzi-free basement club at Hôtel Byblos is one of
the Côte d'Azur's most exclusive clubs. Virtually impossible
to get into unless you arrive early or reserve a table in
advance, Les Caves du Roi has hosted private evenings for
such luminaries as Elton John, and so always attracts a star-
studded clientele.

Le Papagayo

St-Tropez *Résidences du Nouveau Port*
(04.94.97.07.56). Open Mar-May, Sept, Oct 11.30pm-
5am Fri, Sat. June-Aug 11.30pm-5am daily. Closed mid
Nov-Feb. Admission free.
With its port-side location and terrace, Le Papagayo is the
perfect spot for people-watching (A-listers like P Diddy and
Bono have been known to stop by for a drink). Younger and
more energetic than St-Trop's other nightspots, the two-
floor club also stages fashion shows.

Stay

B-Lodge

St-Tropez *23 rue de l'Aïoli (04.94.97.06.57/*
www.hotel-b-lodge.com). €€€.
Located right at the foot of the Citadelle, this freshly
renovated hotel has style in spades. Minimalist rooms
feature four-poster beds, sharp lines and black and white
linen. The pricier guestrooms have balconies and terraces,
and are good value in low season.

Château de Valmer

St-Tropez Peninsula *Rte de Gigaro (04.94.55.15.15/*
www.chateau-valmer.com). Closed mid Oct-mid Apr.
€€€€.
The 19th-century Château de Valmer, south-east of La
Croix-Valmer, offers pure escapism. The pool is set amid
vines and fruit trees, while a palm-lined path leads to the
private beach, shared with sister hotel La Pinède Plage
(04.94.55.16.16, www.pinede-plage.com). The latter has a
fine seafood restaurant looking out over the Med.

Les Girelles

St-Tropez Peninsula *18 bd Patch, Plage de*
Pampelonne, Ramatuelle (04.94.79.86.69).
Closed mid Oct-Easter. €€.
This wonderfully laid-back place is just a stone's throw
from the shoreline, with a tranquil garden to the rear if the
Pampelonne becomes too much. Book ahead, as beach bums
often reserve the 14 rooms many months in advance.

Hôtel le Beauvallon

Ste-Maxime *Bd des Collines (04.94.55.78.88/*
www.lebeauvallon.com). Closed Nov-mid Apr. €€€€.
Set out by the golf club, Hôtel le Beauvallon is a plush
establishment where guests can lounge on the private
beach, gaze out from the infinity pool or whizz into
St-Tropez on the private speedboat. It has two restaurants
to choose from: Les Colonnades (menus €65-€85) and a
cheaper beachfront eaterie (mains €35-€65).

Hôtel Byblos

St-Tropez *Av Paul Signac (04.94.56.68.00/*
www.byblos.com). Closed mid Oct-mid Apr. €€€€.
Opened by Brigitte Bardot in 1967, and the location of
Mick Jagger's proposal to Bianca, the perennially trendy
Hôtel Byblos has rooms and suites that emulate a
Mediterranean village. With its swimming pool, fountain-
filled gardens and restaurants – including Alain Ducasse's
Spoon Byblos – guests in search of a bit of St-Tropez luxury
won't be disappointed.

Hôtel Longo Mai

Massif des Maures *14 rte Nationale, La Garde-*
Freinet (04.94.55.59.60/www.hotel-longomai.com). €€.
Set in the beautiful hill village of La Garde-Freinet, the
Longo Mai oozes rustic chic, with its parquet-floored,
wooden-beamed guestrooms, some of which feature large
terraces. The fine *carte* includes wild boar stew, rack of
lamb and local duck.

Hôtel Lou Cagnard

St-Tropez *18 av Paul Roussel (04.94.97.04.24/*
www.hotel-lou-cagnard.com). Closed Nov-late Dec. €€.
A superb, inexpensive little option with a leafy garden for
alfresco breakfasting. The provençal-themed rooms are
clean and comfortable, although the first floor can get a little
stuffy in summer. A one-week minimum stay policy
operates in high season.

Mas des Oliviers

Ste-Maxime *Quartier de la Croisette (04.94.96.13.31/*
www.hotellemasdesoliviers.com). €€.
West of the centre, Mas des Oliviers has 20 rooms plus
studio apartments to let on a weekly basis, as well as a pool,
tennis courts and well-tended grounds.

Les Moulins

St-Tropez Peninsula *Rte des Plages, Ramatuelle*
(04.94.97.91.91/ www.christophe-leroy.com).
Closed Oct-late Apr. €€€.
Heading out of Ramatuelle, a few hundred metres from
Pampelonne beach, Christophe Leroy's Les Moulins is a

Life's a beach

Each morning in summer, an armada of mega-yachts set off from their €50,000 per week berths in St-Tropez: arriving on a chartered Sunseeker is leagues cooler than parking up behind the plage de Pampelonne's colourful cabanas. The shoreline here is lined with beach clubs, some purveying such rampant excess that even a Rolling Stone might blink with incredulity.

While some may find the sight of banking scions, Saudi princes and Ukrainian oligarchs running up €25,000 tabs in Krug champagne a tad excessive, for others it's a sure sign that it's party time. For a mere mortal to nuzzle into this world of fake boobs, booze and billionaires, it's best to act nonchalant but friendly. Arrive with a big smile, even bigger sunglasses and a very deep suntan.

A celeb-tastic experience necessitates your blacked-out AmEx card and a day at Club 55 (04.94.55.55.55, www.leclub55.com, sun lounger €17/day). It's the glammest club on the strip, so go for slinky, skin-hugging D&G rather than anything gypsy or boho. A-listers such as Paris Hilton and Bono have been known to soak up the elegant yet extravagant atmosphere.

A five-minute cut inland, Nikki Beach (04.94.79.82.04, www.nikkibeach.com, sun lounger €30/day) is a champagne-swigging hotspot for the young and beautiful. Board shorts are the thing here (lunchbox trunks are so passé). Disco music pounds all day long as the designer-clad euro crowd, who spend their winters at the original Nikki Beach in Miami, test out their best chat-up lines.

The birthplace of topless sunbathing, La Voile Rouge (04.94.79.84.34, sun lounger €25/day) is truly bacchanalian. If your idea of naughtiness is buying your partner a pair of sexy knickers, you'll be in for a wide-eyed wake-up call at this cocktail-fuelled, semi-naked orgy of a beach bar. Strip down and try not to gawp: expect your field of vision to include sights like string-clad beauties licking champagne off the odd (older) tummy.

Neptune Plage (04.94.79.81.52, www.plage neptune.com, sun lounger €25-€40/day) is one of Pampelonne's top naturist beach clubs. It remains ever popular with an all-ages crowd, eating, sunbathing and playing beach tennis as naked as nature intended. The public stretch of sand to the south of here is like a Spencer Tunick art installation.

Further down is Tikki Hutte (04.94.55.96.96, www.tiki-hutte.com), with its rows of beachside

cabanas. Although not a beach club as such, the complex features inexpensive bars and eateries that stay open in the evening, when the rest of plage de Pampelonne drifts back to St-Tropez central. This stretch is also a popular haunt for the metal-detecting fraternity, who appear at sundown in search of buried coins, lost engagement rings and a Swiss timepiece or two.

On the beach's southern shores, Aqua Club (04.94.79.84.35, www.aqua-club.fr, sun lounger from €16/day) is effortlessly chilled. It's frequented by St-Trop locals and more discreet A-listers, kids aren't banned and boob jobs are restrained. Sport a pair of washed-out Baywatch boxers or a sun-bleached T-shirt to fit in with the regulars.

Hôtel Byblos.

country inn with five cottage-type rooms. The provençal restaurant blends a few Thai and tempura dishes (mains €28-€38) into the mix.

Pan Deï Palais

St-Tropez *52 rue Gambetta (04.94.17.71.71/ www.pandei.com). €€€.*
Walk through the nondescript wooden entrance to find a foyer that resembles an avant-garde gentlemen's club, with club chairs, colourful vases and Persian rugs. Rooms are effortlessly stylish (cream walls, rich woods), while the mosaic-bottomed pool is an oasis of calm.

Pastis

St-Tropez *61 av du Général Leclerc (04.98.12.56.50/ www.pastis-st-tropez.com). €€€€.*
Petite and perfectly formed, this harbourside hotel is owned by two former designers. Rooms are wonderfully soothing, with pleasing attention to detail (including top-quality linen and bath products). With just nine rooms, often as not you'll have the funky lobby and outdoor pool all to yourself.

Le Sube

St-Tropez *15 quai Suffren (04.94.97.30.04/ www.hotel-sube.com). Closed 3wks Jan. €€€.*

Smack in the centre of the old port, the woody Sube is a favourite with yachties. A fire burns in winter in the chesterfield-filled bar, and regulars vie for seats on its minuscule balcony overlooking the port.

La Villa Marie

St-Tropez Peninsula *Chemin Val Rian, rte des Plages (04.94.97.40.22/www.villamarie.fr). Closed Oct-Apr. €€€€.*
The four-star Villa Marie is a glorious countryside retreat, with its own spa and lush, cypress-dotted gardens. The 42 pastel-perfect bedrooms are luxuriously appointed, with great views towards the Mediterranean. The dining terrace looks out towards the distant plage de Pampelonne and serves up indulgent platters of lobster and Alaskan pincer crab claws.

Le Yaca

St-Tropez *1 rue Aumale (04.94.55.81.00/ www.hotel-le-yaca.fr). €€€€.*
This beautiful hotel makes an immediate impact, thanks to its contemporary art-filled foyer. A tranquil swimming pool forms the central oasis of the little complex, while the provençal-meets-Moorish guestrooms will break a few hearts on departure.

Factfile

When to go
St-Tropez and the surrounding villages are at their most hectic and bacchanalian from June to August. Once the in-crowd has moved on to its next season fixture, the area becomes more family-oriented; in winter, it's pretty deserted.

Getting there
Toulon-Hyères is the nearest airport to the region. St-Raphaël and Toulon are easily accessible by TGV from Paris (and therefore from the UK via Eurostar). The journey to St-Raphaël takes just under five hours. Sodétrav (08.25.00.06.50, www.sodetrav.fr) runs daily buses between St-Tropez and Toulon via Hyères, and between St-Tropez and St-Raphaël, via Grimaud, Cogolin and Ste-Maxime.

Getting around
Les Bateaux Verts (04.94.49.29.39, www.bateauxverts.com) runs hourly boat services from Ste-Maxime to St-Tropez from Feb to Oct, and every 20 minutes at peak times. Sodétrav runs four buses a day between St-Tropez, Ramatuelle and Gassin in July and Aug, and on Thur, Sat and Sun in Sept and June.

Tourist information
La Croix-Valmer Esplanade de la Gare (04.94.55.12.12/www.lacroixvalmer.fr).

Open Mid June-Sept 9.30am-12.30pm, 2.30-7pm Mon-Sat; 9.15am-1.30pm Sun. Oct-mid June 9am-noon, 2-6pm Mon-Fri; 9.15am-noon Sat, Sun.
Port Grimaud 1 bd Aliziers (04.94.55.43.83/ www.grimaud-provence.com). Open June-Sept 9am-12.30pm, 3-7pm Mon-Sat; 10am-1pm Sun. Closed Oct-May.
Ramatuelle Pl de l'Ormeau (04.98.12.64.00/ www.ramatuelle-tourisme.com). Open July-Aug 9am-1pm, 3-7.30pm daily. May, June, Sept-mid Oct 9am-1pm, 3-7pm Mon-Sat. Mid Oct-Apr 9am-12.30pm, 2-6pm Mon-Fri.
Ste-Maxime Promenade Simon Lorière (04.94.55.75.55/www.ste-maxime.com). Open 9am-12.30pm, 2.30-7pm Mon-Sat; 10am-noon, 4-7pm Sun.
St-Tropez Quai Jean Jaurès (08.92.68.48.28/ www.ot-saint-tropez.com). Open Apr-June, Sept, Oct 9am-12.30pm, 2-7pm daily. July, Aug 9.30am-8pm daily. Nov 9.30am-noon, 2-6pm Mon-Sat; 2-6pm Sun. Dec-Mar 9.30am-noon, 2-6pm daily.

Internet access
Ste-Maxime Kreatik Café, 22 rue Pierre Curie (04.94.49.20.14/www.kreatik.com). Open 10am-10pm Tue-Sun.
St-Tropez Kreatik Café, 19 av Général Leclerc (04.94.97.40.61/www.kreatik.com). Open 10am-10pm Tue-Sun.

Small Gems

Top: Pavillon Noir.
Left: Musée Granet.
Right: Jas de Bouffan.

Aix-en-Provence

The Côte d'Azur's cultured cousin.

There's something almost cinematic about Aix. Its stately mansions, leafy streets and bubbling fountains are unreal in their prettiness, and the elegant cafés of cours Mirabeau have all the manicured appeal of a film set. The people, too, look as if they might have spent an hour or two in wardrobe before stepping out of their houses. In short, this is a graceful, cultured city, more urbane than urban; it is a nursery for new artistic talent but also a refuge for wealthy, healthy retirees who enjoy the finer things in life. It is in stark contrast, in other words, to its rougher southern rival Marseille. Yet despite its reputation as the haughty bastion of the bourgeoisie, Aix is also a surprisingly young city, with some 40,000 students, a thriving café society, and daring cultural projects such as the Pavillon Noir dance centre.

Aix's origins go back to Roman times. Aquae Sextiae was founded in 122 BC by Roman consul Sextius after he had defeated the Celto-Ligurian Oppidium at Entremont, the remains of which lie outside the city. In 1409 the university was founded by Louis II of Anjou, and the city flourished under his artistically inclined son, Good King René, its court drawing artists such as Nicolas Froment and Barthélemy Van Eyck. The city boomed again in the 1600s as its newly prosperous merchant class built stylish townhouses, modelled on the Parisian fashions of the day. A new district, the Quartier Mazarin, sprang up to the south of the medieval town, virtually doubling the city's size. In the past 20 years, Aix has again expanded rapidly as modern housing and business districts have swallowed up rural villages and the grandiose *bastides* built by the nobility outside the city.

Just outside town, Montagne Ste-Victoire is famed for its Cézanne connection, its triangular contours oddly familiar from his paintings. Hiking trails cross its wooded slopes, while the sheer cliffs are best left to climbers.

Explore

Pedestrian-friendly central Aix divides neatly into Vieil Aix (the old town) and the later Quartier Mazarin. The two are set on either side of the stately cours Mirabeau, and encircled by a string of boulevards that trace the line of the old city ramparts; beyond lies the modern city.

VIEIL AIX & COURS MIRABEAU

At the heart of the city, cours Mirabeau is a handsome, plane tree-lined avenue. Laid out in 1649, it soon became the favoured spot for local nobility to construct their mansions, and remains the epicentre of Aix's café society. At No.53 the legendary Deux Garçons, a hangout of Cézanne and Zola's, remains an artistic and intellectual meeting place. Next door at No.55 was the hat shop where Paul Cézanne lived as a child.

North of cours Mirabeau lies the remarkably well preserved maze of Vieil Aix, buzzing with small bistros, cafés and shops. Graceful squares and smart mansions alternate with more secretive, winding *ruelles*, while statues peer from niches and fountains dot the squares.

Busy shopping streets rue Aude and rue Maréchal Foch lead to place Richelme, which comes alive every morning with fruit and vegetable stalls. On Maréchal Foch, note the doorway of the late 17th-century Hôtel Arbaud at No.7, framed by two muscular male slaves.

On beautiful place de l'Hôtel de Ville, the Gothic belfry with astrological clock and rotating figures was once a town gateway, while the 17th-century Hôtel de Ville (04.42.91.90.00, closed Sat, Sun) was the historic Provençal assembly. At the back, a double stairway leads up to the regional assembly room, adorned with portraits and mythological subjects; it was here that Cézanne finally married his long-time companion Hortense Fiquet in 1886.

Running north, rue Gaston de Saporta contains some of Aix's finest *hôtels particuliers*. Hôtel Etienne de St-Jean (No.17) houses the Musée du Vieil Aix; Hôtel de Châteaurenard (No.19), where Louis XIV stayed in 1660, has a staircase painted with trompe l'oeils by Daret (you can only visit the entrance hall); Hôtel Maynier d'Oppedé (No.23), with a fine 1757 façade, is now the Institute of French Studies. The street leads into the historic core of the university, and to the Cathédrale St-Sauveur, with its sculpted portals and fortified towers. Next door, the baroque archbishop's palace contains the Musée des Tapisseries; its courtyard hosts opera productions during the Festival International d'Art Lyrique (*see p391*).

West of the town hall, place des Cardeurs is lined with ethnic restaurants. From here, narrow streets lead to the Thermes Sextius, along with some fragments of medieval city wall on rue des Etuves and the last surviving tower on boulevard Jean Jaurès. West of the baths, the Pavillon Vendôme stands amid its formal gardens.

Aix-en-Provence

Historic sites
● ● ● ○ ○

Art & architecture
● ● ● ● ○

Hotels
● ● ● ● ○

Eating & drinking
● ● ● ● ○

Nightlife
● ● ● ○ ○

Shopping
● ● ● ● ○

Cours Mirabeau.

South-east of the town hall, the colonnaded Palais de Justice was built in the 1820s. In front of it, place de Verdun fills with bric-a-brac and book stalls on Tuesday, Thursday and Saturday mornings. It continues into place des Prêcheurs and place de la Madeleine, which resound to the city's main food market on the same days, in the shadow of the Eglise de la Madeleine. Further east lies the Villeneuve *quartier*, which replaced the royal gardens in the late 16th century.

Cathédrale St-Sauveur

Rue Gaston de Saporta (04.42.23.45.65). Open 8am-noon, 2-6pm Mon-Sat; 9am-noon, 2-6pm Sun (closed during services). Cloister 9.30am-noon, 2-6pm Mon-Sat. Admission free.

With its semi-fortified exterior and Gothic central door, Aix cathedral is a hotchpotch of Romanesque, Gothic, Renaissance and Baroque – reflecting its on-off construction from the fifth to 18th centuries. At first sight the interior looks unremarkable, but it has two jewels. The first is off the right-hand nave: a polygonal, fifth-century Merovingian baptistery, with crisply carved capitals and traces of frescoes (the hole in the ground is a throwback to the days of total immersion baptism). The second gem is in the central nave: Nicolas Froment's 15th-century triptych *Mary in the Burning Bush*, with King René and Queen Jeanne praying in the wings. In the left nave, the 17th-century Corpus Domini chapel has a fine wrought-iron grille and a painting by Jean Daret.

Eglise de la Madeleine

Pl des Prêcheurs. Open 8-11.30am, 3-5.30pm daily. Admission free.

This former Dominican convent was rebuilt in the 1690s in the baroque style; its neoclassical façade, busy with swags and garlands, is a 19th-century addition. Inside are several handsome altarpieces by Carlos Van Loo, as well as a 15th-century Annunciation attributed to Flemish painter Barthélemy Van Eyck.

Musée des Tapisseries

Pl des Martyrs de la Résistance (04.42.23.09.91). Open 15 Apr-15 Oct 10am-6pm Mon, Wed-Sun. 16 Oct-14 Apr 1.30-5pm Mon, Wed-Sun. Closed Jan. Admission free-€2.50. No credit cards.

On the first floor of the former bishop's palace, the tapestry museum displays 17th- and 18th-century tapestries that were discovered in the 19th century. There's a particularly lively series of scenes from *Don Quixote*, woven in northern France between 1735 and 1744, along with costumes and model sets from opera productions at the Aix festival.

Musée du Vieil Aix

17 rue Gaston de Saporta (04.42.21.43.55). Open Apr-Oct 10am-1pm, 2-6pm Tue-Sun. Nov-Mar 10am-noon, 2-5pm Tue-Sun. Admission €4; free-€2.50 reductions. No credit cards.

The collection focuses on folk art and popular traditions, with *santons* (Christmas crib figures) and crèche puppets, plus some fine lacquered furniture and faïence. The house,

with its stately entrance hall, frescoes and tiny *cabinet* (antechamber), with an ornately carved and gilded domed ceiling, gives a glimpse of 17th-century aristocratic life.

Muséum d'Histoire Naturelle

6 rue Espariat (04.42.27.91.27/www.museum-aix-en-provence.org). Open 10am-noon, 1-5pm daily. Admission free-€2.50. No credit cards.

Mineralogy, ornithology and palaeontology collections, including dinosaur skeletons and hundreds of dinosaur eggs discovered on the Montagne Ste-Victoire, are displayed against painted backdrops, in this fine 17th-century *hôtel*.

Pavillon Vendôme

32 rue Celony or 13 rue de la Molle (04.42.91.88.75). Open Mid Apr-mid Oct 10am-6pm Mon, Wed-Sun. Mid Oct-mid Apr 1.30-5.30pm Mon, Wed-Sun. Admission free-€2.50. No credit cards.

Built in 1665 by Pierre Pavillon, this mini-pleasure palace, set in formal gardens, was where the Duc de Vendôme hid away with his mistress, Lucrèce de Forbin Solliès: the mascaron over the entrance is said to be her portrait. Giant atlantes hold up the balcony and the interior is adorned with 17th- and 18th-century furniture and portraits.

Thermes Sextius

55 cours Sextius (08.00.63.96.99/www.thermes-sextius.com). Open 8.30am-7.30pm Mon-Fri; 8.30am-1.30pm, 2.30-6.30pm Sat.

Behind wrought-iron railings and a classical façade, the Thermes now houses the glass and marble pyramids of an ultra-modern health spa. A small fountain still marks the warm spring of the original 18th-century bathing establishment, while to the right of the entrance is evidence of even earlier bathers – the remains of first century BC Roman baths, fed by the Source Imperatrice.

QUARTIER MAZARIN

Laid out on a strict rectilinear grid plan in 1646, the Quartier Mazarin was conceived as a speculative venture and sold off in lots, masterminded by Mazarin, Archbishop of Aix and brother of Louis XIV's powerful minister Cardinal Mazarin. It gradually became the aristocratic quarter, and still feels very refined. There are few shops or restaurants, other than classy *antiquaires* and select designer fashion names, but plenty of fine doorways, balustrades and wrought-iron balconies. At the far end of rue Cardinale stands the Eglise St-Jean-de-Malte, built by the Knights of Malta at the end of the 13th century. Stark and almost unadorned, it was one of the earliest Gothic structures in Provence, with a broad nave and side chapels but no transept. Beside it, the Commanderie of the Knights of Malta now houses the Musée Granet, the city's fine art and archaeology collection.

Musée Arbaud

2A rue du 4 Septembre (04.42.38.38.95). Open 2-5pm Mon-Sat. Admission €3; free under-10s. No credit cards.

Musée Granet.

Old masters that belonged to the Mirabeau family hang amid provençal earthenware and manuscripts collected by scholar Paul Arbaud. Fine pieces of Marseille and Moustiers faïence are light years away from most of the tourist fodder made today.

Musée Granet
Pl St-Jean-de-Malte (04.42.52.88.32/www.museegranet-aixenprovence.fr). Open June-Sept 11am-7pm Tue-Sun. Oct-May noon-6pm Tue-Sun. Admission €4.
Housed in the 17th-century Palais de Malte, Aix's newly refurbished fine art museum has quadrupled in size. The impressive collection includes Italian and Flemish primitives, Dutch interiors and Flemish masters (among them a pair of portraits by Rubens), a motley crew of Italian Baroque paintings and works by the weird Lubin Baugin. Don't miss some splendidly pompous 18th-century portraits by Hyacinthe Rigaud, or Ingres's magnificently malevolent *Jupiter and Thetis*. At the time of Cézanne's death, curator Henri Pontier haughtily refused to accept any of his works – an embarrassing omission now made up for by a room of seven small oil paintings, including a portrait of Cézanne's mother and a tiny study for *The Bathers*. Here, too, is the recent Philippe Meyer donation, which includes works by Bonnard, Mondrian, Picasso, Klee and Tal Coat, along with a room of Giacometti bronzes and oils. The basement houses an interesting display of archaeological finds from the Oppidium d'Entremont, with pottery, bronze tools and some extraordinary carved heads and fragments from a series of sculpted warriors.

BEYOND THE CENTRE
South of La Rotonde fountain, a new business, residential and shopping district, Quartier Sextius Mirabeau, forms a bridge between old and new Aix. The allées de Provence, a pedestrianised shopping street in provençal hues, leads to the stepped, pink stone-clad terraces of the new Grand Théâtre de Provence. Behind it are the striking black concrete Ballet Preljocaj – Pavillon Noir and the Cité du Livre arts centre, which together form a dynamic new cultural hub.

Further out, the suburbs are dotted with former country villas and *bastides*, built in the 17th and 18th centuries by the nobles and parliamentarians of Aix. These include the Château de la Pioline, now a hotel, and the Jas de Bouffon, bought by Cézanne's father in 1859; here, too, is the Fondation Vasarely. At Les Milles, the refectory of the prison camp where numerous intellectuals were interned during World War II is now the Mémorial National des Milles. Towards Marseille, beneath the perched village of Bouc-Bel-Air, are the romantic, Italian-influenced Jardins d'Albertas, dotted with statues.

North of Vieil Aix, past the pyramidal Mausoleum of Joseph Sec – a rare example of Revolutionary architecture dating from 1792, a time when there were more pressing things to do than build – a steep hill climbs to the Lauves. It's here that Cézanne built his last studio, the Atelier

Cézanne. If you continue climbing, you'll come to a roundabout with the remains of an ancient city gate. Follow the signs along avenue Paul Cézanne to the spot where the artist painted many of his famous scenes of Montagne Ste-Victoire: a bit of a hike, but the view is worth it. The remains of the Celto-Ligurian Oppidium d'Entremont, site of Sextius's victory in the second century AD, lie just outside the city to the north-west.

Atelier Cézanne
9 av Paul Cézanne (04.42.21.06.53/www.atelier-cezanne.com). Open Apr-June, Sept 10am-noon, 2-6pm daily. July-Aug 10am-6pm daily. Oct-Mar 10am-noon, 2-5pm daily. Admission €5.50; free-€2 reductions.
Cézanne built this studio in 1902, and worked here until his death in 1906. Then outside the town, with views of the triangular silhouette of Montagne Ste-Victoire, it now overlooks post-war housing developments. Preserved just as it was in the artist's lifetime, the first-floor studio is an artistic clutter of easels and palettes, along with many of the props – fruit, vases, a broken cherub statue – that are familiar from his still lifes. Visitors are advised to book in advance with the tourist office.

Ballet Preljocaj – Pavillon Noir
8-10 rue des Allumettes/530 av Mozart (04.42.93.48.00/www.preljocaj.org). Tickets €6-€22.
This dramatic spider's web of black concrete and glass, designed by architect Rudy Ricciotti, is home to the Ballet Preljocaj and visiting dance companies. Four rehearsal studios on the upper storeys are illuminated after dark so that passers-by can glimpse works in progress, while the 378-seat auditorium is buried underground. The programme includes public rehearsals and *apéro-danses*, where you can meet the dancers over a drink after the performance.

Cité du Livre
8-10 rue des Allumettes (04.42.91.98.88/www.cite dulivre-aix.com). Open noon-6pm Tue, Thur, Fri; 10am-6pm Wed, Sat. Admission free.
Marked by a gigantic book at the entrance, this converted 19th-century match factory houses the historic Bibliothèque Méjanes (a public library and collection of rare manuscripts), the archives of Albert Camus and the Fondation St-John Perse, which includes a permanent display of manuscripts by the Nobel prize-winning poet. A busy programme of events includes an annual literary festival in October and December's short film festival.

Fondation Vasarely
1 av Marcel Pagnol, Jas de Bouffan (04.42.20.01.09/ www.fondationvasarely.fr). Open 10am-1pm, 2-6pm Tue-Sat. Admission €7; free-€4 reductions.
At this 'centre architectonique', Hungarian-born abstract artist Victor Vasarely (1906-97) put his theories about geometrical abstraction and kinetic art into practice on a grand scale. The building itself is composed of hexagonal structures of black and white squares and circles that reflect off the water. Inside are large-scale paintings, tapestries and reliefs.

Jardins d'Albertas

N8, Bouc-Bel-Air (04.91.59.84.94/www.jardinsalbertas. com). Open May, Sept, Oct 2-6pm Sat, Sun, public holidays. June-Aug 3-7pm daily. Closed Nov-Apr. Admission €6; free under-16s. No credit cards.
Earlier on in the 18th century, the Marquis d'Albertas dreamed of constructing a lavish rural retreat – but then came the Revolution, and he was assassinated on 14 July 1790. The grand château was never built and only the formal gardens, laid out with magnificent terraces and pools, were ever completed. During the last weekend in May, an annual plant sale (along with talks and events) transforms the gardens into a burst of colour.

Jas de Bouffan

3km E of Aix centre. Reservation advised (04.42.16.10.08/information 04.42.16.11.61/www.aix enprovencetourisme.com). Open 11.30am-5pm daily. Admission €5.50; free-€2 reductions.
This 18th-century country house, bought by the Cézanne family in 1859, marked the social ascension of Cézanne's father from hatmaker to banker. At last accepting his son's desire to be an artist, he had a studio constructed under the eaves. Here Cézanne produced many of his most celebrated works, painting the avenue of chestnut trees, the pond and the two gardeners who posed for *The Card Players*. A multimedia presentation explores Cézanne's life and the history of the house.

Oppidium d'Entremont

3km NW of Vieux Aix via av Solari (D14), direction Puyricard (04.42.21.97.33/www.entremont.culture. gouv.fr). Open 9am-noon, 2-5.30pm Mon, Wed-Sun. Admission free.
This Celto-Ligurian hilltop settlement developed around the second century BC on the site of an earlier sanctuary, and was destroyed by Romans in the second century AD at the behest of the land-hungry Marseillais. Excavated sections reveal a grid plan, plus traces of shops, warehouses and workshops.

Site Mémorial des Milles

Les Milles (04.42.24.34.68). Open 9am-12.15pm, 1-5pm Mon-Thur; 9am-12.15pm, 1-4pm Fri. Admission free.
Requisitioned as early as 1939 (before the German occupation), in a period of growing xenophobia and nationalism, this brick and tile factory became an internment camp for 'enemy subjects' in France. Prisoners were refugees from the Spanish Civil War and German and Austrian intellectuals, many of them Jewish, who had fled the Nazi regime. Among them were two Nobel prize-winners and the Surrealist painters Max Ernst and Hans Bellmer. After June 1940, Les Milles became a transit camp; nearly 2,000 Jews were deported from here to Auschwitz via Drancy. In the entrance, documents and archive photos tell the story of Les Milles, but it is the refectory that is the most telling witness, decorated with murals by prisoners that take a subtly satiric slant in the row of caricatured warders painted in a parody of Leonardo's *Last Supper*. Across the road, at the former Gare des Milles, a railway wagon is a reminder of those sent to Auschwitz.

MONTAGNE STE-VICTOIRE

Looming over the plain a few kilometres outside Aix, the triangular form of Montagne Ste-Victoire is inextricably linked to Paul Cézanne. At once both familiar and far larger than in his paintings, the mountain also offers rugged villages, wild landscapes and the changing colours that so obsessed Cézanne. He began going on long walks on the mountain when he was a schoolboy, and painted it in over 60 canvases and countless watercolours. The best way to approach it is in a loop along the D17 to the south of the mountain and the D10 to the north. Cézanne rented a room to paint in at the Château Noir, just before Le Tholonet, from 1887, and later a hut at the Carrières de Bibémus quarry. Later he built his own *atelier* on the Lauves hill, with a view of the mountain. At Le Tholonet, the Moulin Cézanne (04.42.66.90.41, closed Sept-Apr) has an exhibition on local history and the friendship between Cézanne and Zola, with temporary painting and sculpture exhibitions upstairs.

Picasso is buried in the grounds of the privately owned Château de Vauvenarges under the mountain's northern flank, where he lived from 1959 to 1965. The château is open to the public by appointment during the summer; call the Aix tourist office for details.

If you're planning to do some hiking, it's simpler to approach the mountain from its wooded, sheltered northern side than the more barren southern route, with its limestone cliffs. The GR9 climbs to the Croix de Provence at the western end of the ridge from Vauvenargues, and is also joined by a footpath from the attractive Col des Portes just further east, running along the top of the ridge to the highest point, the Pic des Mouches (1,011m/3,317ft).

Eat

Antoine Côté Cour

Cours Mirabeau *19 cours Mirabeau (04.42.93.12.51). Open 7.30pm-midnight Mon; 12.30-2.30pm, 7.30pm-midnight Tue-Sat. €€.*
The fashionable folk of Aix flock to this Italianate restaurant, set in an 18th-century townhouse near place Rotonde, which serves up wonderful gnocchi and pasta creations. An ornate entrance off the cours Mirabeau leads to a beautiful courtyard, perfect for al fresco dining.

Bistro Latin

Vieil Aix *18 rue de la Couronne (04.42.38.22.88). Open noon-2.30pm, 7.30-10.30pm Tue-Sat. €€.*
After 20 years of service, this charming, pared-down little bistro is still going strong. The decently priced prix fixe menu includes such delights as baby red peppers stuffed with brousse cheese served with tapenade, or herby *daube d'agneau*. There's a reasonable wine list too.

L'Orienthé.

Brasserie des Deux Garçons

Cours Mirabeau *53 cours Mirabeau (04.42.26.00.51).*
Open 7am-2am daily (meals noon-3pm, 7-11.30pm daily). €€.
Alias 'les 2 G', the legendary Deux Garçons is named after the two waiters who bought it in 1840, and has welcomed the likes of Cézanne, Picasso and Truffaut over the years. Its interior is a delight, with tall mirrors, chandeliers, an old-fashioned cashier's desk and a salon to the side where you can read the papers or write your novel. There are two dining sections, one serving brasserie fare, the other a more ambitious restaurant. Food is unexceptional, but the atmosphere is hard to beat.

Café Bastide du Cours

Cours Mirabeau *43-47 cours Mirabeau (04.42.26.10.06/www.cafebastideducours.com).*
Open noon-1am daily. €€€.
One of the most charming restaurants in Aix, the Bastide du Cours has a sumptuous dining room and lovely heated terrace, with tables arranged around an enormous plane tree. The sophisticated cooking is rooted in provençal tradition: chavignol goat's cheese in lavender honey and thyme pastry, and slow-roasted lamb shank with wild thyme are out of this world. Make sure you leave space for the brioche hamburger with fresh fruits, mango and raspberry coulis. There's a bargain €15 lunch menu on offer during the week.

Les Deux Frères

Beyond the Centre *4 av Reine Astrid (04.42.27.90.32/ www.les2freres.com). Open noon-2pm, 8-9.30pm Mon-Fri; noon-2pm, 8-10.30pm Sat, Sun.* €€€.
The Benchérif brothers – Stéphane in the kitchen, Olivier front of house – are behind this acclaimed eaterie, a ten-minute walk from the town centre. Modern Med cuisine is served in a chic minimalist setting, with video screens transmitting what's going on in the kitchen, and a spectacularly lit terrace. The Benchérif brothers also run Le 37 (04.42.12.39.68) on place des Tanneurs, which serves more traditional cuisine.

Le Formal

Vieil Aix *32 rue Espariat (04.42.27.08.31).*
Open noon-1.30pm, 8-9.30pm Tue-Sat. €€.
Chef Jean-Luc Formal delivers beautifully presented, modern cuisine in his eponymous restaurant. Sample a summery starter of seasonal vegetables, edible flowers and red mullet fillets, or go for lamb in filo pastry with a shot of carrot juice. The barrel-vaulted cellars, with exposed stone, pale wood and modern paintings, are a welcome respite from the summer heat and tourist hordes. You'll need to book well ahead.

L'Orienthé

Vieil Aix *32 rue Espariat (04.42.27.08.31).*
Open noon-1.30pm, 8-9pm Tue-Sat. €€.
Leave your shoes at the door and relax over one of 50 varieties of tea and a delectable pastry at this exotic salon. Customers sit on pillows at low tables amid candles and incense, and the vibe is supremely mellow.

Le Passage

Quartier Mazarin *10 rue Villars (04.42.37.09.00/ www.le-passage.fr). Open 10am-midnight daily.* €€.
Reine Sammut of La Fénière in the Lubéron is the *éminence grise* behind this stylishly converted sweet factory, which now contains a galleried restaurant, *salon de thé*, wine boutique and cookery school. A trio of young chefs keeps up her culinary vision in a pan-Mediterranean menu that takes in the likes of grilled fish with ratatouille, tartares and a superb lobster risotto. There's a handsome wine list, and service is excellent.

Pierre Reboul

Vieil Aix *11 petite rue St-Jean (04.42.27.08.31).*
Open noon-1.30pm, 7.30-9.30pm Tue-Sat. €€€€.
Michelin-starred chef Pierre Reboul moved here only recently from St-Rémy, and has been stirring up some debate with his avant-garde cooking style. This is as close as you'll get to molecular experimentation in largely traditional Aix, with modern decor to match. The *menu dégustation* features quirky treats such as pan-seared foie gras with apple and passion fruit or quail burger with gherkin sorbet and spicy juice.

La Rotonde

Vieil Aix *2A pl Jeanne d'Arc (04.42.91.61.70/ www.larotonde-aix.com). Open 8am-2am daily.* €€.
Overlooking the fountain, this stylish address has a sleek terrace and boudoir-style interior. As the day goes on it morphs from breakfast and lunchtime gaff to clubby nightspot, with a DJ and a large array of champagnes, whiskies and cocktails (try the house Rotonde with vodka, rum, lime and raspberries).

Yamato (Koji & Yuriko)

Beyond the Centre *21 av des Belges (04.42.38.00.20/ www.restaurant-yamato.com). Open 7-10pm Tue; noon-2pm, 7-10pm Wed-Sun.* €€€€.
Occupying an elegant 1930s house set in a Japanese garden, Yamato serves up what is probably the most authentic Japanese cuisine in southern France. As well as excellent sushi and sashimi and crisp, light tempura, you'll find good grilled fish and specialities like *uoroke* and *sukiyaki* (strips of beef simmered at the table over a flame).

Stay

Hôtel Aquabella

Vieil Aix *2 rue des Etuves (04.42.99.15.00/ www.aquabella.fr).* €€€.
This large, modern hotel adjoining the Thermes Sextius may lack the character of some of Aix's older hotels, but it more than compensates with its spacious, comfortable rooms and prime location. The 110 air-conditioned rooms are elegantly simple, and this clean, minimalist aesthetic runs through the rest of the hotel too. Facilities include a glass-walled restaurant and a heated outdoor swimming pool. There is also direct access from the hotel to the ultra-modern Thermes Sextius health spa.

Hôtel des Augustins

Vieil Aix *3 rue de la Masse (04.42.27.28.59/ www.hotel-augustins.com). €€.*

This appealing three-star hotel occupies part of an Augustine monastery where Martin Luther stayed on his way back from Rome. It became a hotel in the 1890s; the reception is set in a spectacular vaulted space and the 29 air-conditioned bedrooms are comfortable enough, though the provençal decor doesn't quite live up to the lobby's promise. Two of the rooms feature private terraces. There's no restaurant on site, but there are countless options within a couple of minutes' walk.

Hôtel Cardinal

Quartier Mazarin *24 rue Cardinale (04.42.38.32.30/ www.hotel-cardinal-aix.com). €€.*

Beloved by festival-going writers, artists and musicians, this little two-star hotel has bags of charm. Several of the 29 handsome rooms have stucco mouldings, a couple have 18th-century painted overdoor panels, and all are decorated with high-quality fabrics, paintings and new bathrooms. There are also six suites with kitchenettes. If you're looking for a bargain near the town centre, this place is hard to beat.

Hôtel Cézanne

Beyond the Centre *40 av Victor Hugo (04.42.91.11.11/www.hotelaix.com). €€€.*

The 55-room Hôtel Cézanne oozes boutique chic and has become the hippest hotel in town. The bar features scarlet banquettes and cool artwork, while the bedrooms are decorated with a mix of modern and vintage furniture: some have stainless-steel four-posters, others are dolled up in gold or candy pink; all feature high-quality beds and great showers. And in true boutique style, breakfast carries on till noon.

Hôtel Le Pigonnet

Beyond the Centre *5 av du Pigonnet (04.42.59.02.90/ www.hotelpigonnet.com). €€€.*

Cézanne once painted the Montagne Ste-Victoire from the shady garden of this civilised 18th-century mansion, about a kilometre outside town. The current owners bought the *bastide* in 1924 and opened up a four-room hotel. The Pigonnet now has four stars and some 50 rooms in all, and the atmosphere is akin to a posh country house party, with wonderful gardens to explore, an outdoor pool, and comfortably floral rooms. Breakfast is served on the veranda and there's a very good restaurant on site too.

Hôtel des Quatre Dauphins

Quartier Mazarin *54 rue Roux Alphéran (04.42.38.16.39/www.lesquatredauphins.fr). €€.*

The Four Dolphins is a simple two-star hotel in a 17th-century *maison bourgeoise* on one of the nicest streets in the Quartier Mazarin. The 13 small but tastefully decorated – think pale pastel shades and provençal prints – and air-conditioned rooms are set over three floors (no lift). There's no restaurant on site, but there are countless eating options within a few minutes' walk. This place is a real bargain for central Aix, so you need to book well ahead.

Factfile

When to go

The weather is pretty mild and dry year round, except for late autumn which can be blustery, cold and wet. Beware summer temperatures which can become oppressive during the middle of the day. The annual Festival International d'Art Lyrique (*see p391*) takes place during July.

Getting there

Aix TGV station is 10km (6 miles) west of the city and served by regular shuttle buses from the *gare routière*. There are roughly nine trains a day from Paris (2hrs 57mins). The old Aix station is on the Marseille-Sisteron line, with trains roughly every hour from Marseille-St-Charles. Aéroport Marseille-Provence (04.42.14.14.14) is 25km (15 miles) away. It has two terminals, one for international (www.marseille.aeroport.fr) and one for low-cost (www.mp2.aeroport.fr) carriers.

Getting around

Aix's municipal bike hire system (www.vhello.fr) allows you to pick up a bike from one of 16 points around town and deposit it at another. The Navette Aix-Marseille (www.navetteaix

marseille.com) is a high-speed (30mins) shuttle service between Aix *gare routière* on av de l'Europe (04.42.91.26.80) and the Porte d'Aix in Marseille, with buses every five minutes at peak times. Aix is also served by six to ten buses daily from Avignon and an hourly shuttle from Marseille airport. La Diabline is an electric minibus; there's an information and ticket desk (04.42.26.37.28) at the Office du Tourisme. Take the No.1 for Atelier Cézanne, No.20 for the Oppidium d'Entremont, No.16 for La Pioline and Les Milles, and No.4 from the old casino to the Fondation Vasarely.

Tourist information

Tourist office 2 pl du Général de Gaulle (04.42.16.11.61/www.aixenprovencetourism. com). Open Sept-Apr 8.30am-7pm Mon-Sat; 10am-1pm, 2-6pm Sun. July, Aug 8.30am-9pm Mon-Sat; 10am-1pm, 2-6pm Sun.

Internet access

Virtualis Pl de l'Hôtel de Ville (04.42.26.02.30/ www.virtualis.fr). Open 9am-midnight Mon-Fri; noon-midnight Sun.

Top: Avignon Festival. Left: Collection Lambert. Right: Palais des Papes. Bottom right: Rue Joseph Vernet.

Avignon

This papal stronghold is the new gateway to Provence.

Avignon is a town of many faces. Home to the papacy for most of the 14th century, it is crowned by the awe-inspiring medieval Palais des Papes, and still holds a wealth of artistic treasures. Modern times have brought a lively student life, thriving gay community and troubled suburban sprawl – though the city centre's ancient walls protect tourists from its grittier side. The annual performing arts festival is a vibrant artistic free-for-all, with a lively fringe scene (Avignon Off) to rival that of Edinburgh.

When approaching the city along the banks of the Rhône, the Rocher des Doms – with its gleaming virgin on top of the Cathédrale Notre-Dame-des-Doms – makes an imposing sight. Four kilometres (2.5 miles) of beautifully preserved ramparts add to the effect; sadly, ubiquitous 19th-century architect and 'improver' Viollet-le-Duc didn't stop at adding frilly crenellated tops to the sturdy walls, but also filled in the moat. Just outside the walls stands the city's other top tourist attraction: the celebrated bridge. Only four arches of the original 22 remain, together with a tiny Romanesque chapel, but the 12th-century Pont St-Bénezet still exerts a peculiar fascination. To set enquiring minds at rest: nobody ever dances on the *pont* of nursery rhyme fame, save for a few hapless tourists.

In 2001 a sleek new TGV station suddenly put Avignon within easy reach of Paris. For stressed urbanites, the dream of leaving the capital and opening an upmarket B&B or a chic designer gallery became a glorious possibility. An influx of skips and scaffolding followed, along with a surge of new bars, hotels, shops and restaurants – and a rise in house prices. The festival over, Avignon used to revert to being a sleepy provincial town. Now the artistic adventure continues year round, thanks to a busy programme of student-led theatre, music and exhibitions.

Explore

Collection Lambert

*Hôtel de Caumont, 5 rue Violette (04.90.16.56.20/
www.collectionlambert.com). Open July, Aug 11am-
7pm daily. Sept-June 11am-6pm Tue-Sun. Admission
€9.50; free-€8 reductions.*

Housed in a stately 18th-century *hôtel particulier*, this
formidable collection, on extended loan from Parisian art
dealer Yvon Lambert, spans the 1960s to the present. Three
annual temporary exhibitions and site-specific commissions
keep things fresh, while the main collection is strong on
conceptual and minimalist art, taking in painting, sculpture,
installation, video and photography by heavyweights such
as Nan Goldin, Jean-Michel Basquiat and Cy Twombly.

Eglise St-Didier

*Pl St-Didier (04.90.86.20.17). Open 8am-6.30pm daily.
Admission free.*

This pretty example of provençal Gothic has delicate
14th-century Italian frescoes in the north chapel. In the
Chapelle St-Bénezet are relics of the bridge-building saint
himself, or his skull at least.

Fondation Angladon-Dubrujeaud

*5 rue Laboureur (04.90.82.29.03/www.angladon.com).
Open 1-6pm Tue-Sun (closed Tue in winter). Admission
€6; free-€4 reductions. No credit cards.*

The marvellous collection displayed in this 18th-century
mansion was amassed by the 19th-century Paris *couturier*
Jacques Doucet. It was eventually inherited by his great-
nephew and his wife, Jean and Paulette Angladon-
Dubrujeaud, who bequeathed it to the museum. On the
ground floor, a remarkable line-up of paintings includes
works by Degas, Picasso, Cézanne and Modigliani – as
well as the only Van Gogh in Provence. Upstairs, a series
of rooms display paintings, antiques and *objets d'art*
to lavish effect.

Musée Calvet

*65 rue Joseph Vernet (04.90.86.33.84/www.fondation-
calvet.org). Open 10am-1pm, 2-6pm Mon, Wed-Sun.
Admission €6; free-€3 reductions. No credit cards.*

This beautiful fine art museum displays its collection in
elegant, colonnaded rooms built around a central courtyard.
The ground floor has Gobelins tapestries and medieval
sculpture, while its 18th- and 19th-century French paintings
include works by the Avignon-based Vernet family and
David's *La mort de Bara*. A good modern section showcases
works by Bonnard, Vuillard, Sisley, Manet and Dufy; look
out, too, for Camille Claudel's sculpture of her brother Paul,
who had her incarcerated in a nearby mental asylum when
her relationship with Rodin became too scandalous.

Musée du Petit Palais

*Pl du Palais (04.90.86.44.58/www.petit-palais.org).
Open June-Sept 10am-6pm Mon, Wed-Sun. Oct-May
10am-1pm, 2-6pm Mon, Wed-Sun. Admission €6;
free-€3 reductions. No credit cards.*

Several lesser habitations were razed to the ground to make
way for the Petit Palais, built in 1317 for Cardinal Berenger
Fredoli. Subsequent inhabitants each made their mark on the
palace: in the late 15th century, its Renaissance façade and

Avignon

Historic sites
● ● ● ● ○

Art & architecture
● ● ● ● ○

Hotels
● ● ● ● ○

Eating & drinking
● ● ● ● ○

Nightlife
● ● ● ● ○

Shopping
● ● ● ○ ○

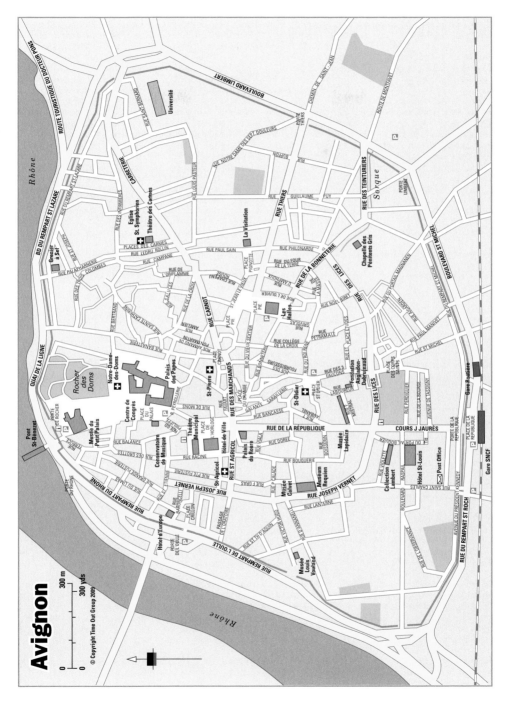

tower were added by Cardinal Giuliano della Rovere, the future Pope Julius II. It now houses medieval paintings, frescoes and sculptures, many rescued from churches destroyed in the Revolution. Don't miss the sarcophagus of Cardinal Jean de Lagrange, with its anatomically realistic depiction of a decaying corpse, and his mutilated tomb effigy.

Musée Lapidaire

27 rue de la République (04.90.85.75.38/www.musee-lapidaire.org). Open June-Sept 10am-6pm Mon, Wed-Sun. Oct-May 10am-1pm, 2-6pm Mon, Wed-Sun. Admission €2; free-€1 reductions. No credit cards.
Avignon's archaeological collection is superbly displayed in this 17th-century Jesuit chapel as part of the Fondation Calvet. As well as Greek, Gallo-Roman and Etruscan sculpture, mosaics and glass, it is rich in Egyptian sculpture, *stelae* (inscribed slabs) and *shabtis* (small statues of servants, buried with the dead to serve them in the afterlife). The Gallo-Roman selection has a depiction of the Tarasque of Noves, the local man-eating monster.

Musée Louis Vouland

17 rue Victor Hugo (04.90.86.03.79/www.vouland.com). Open July-Sept noon-6pm Tue-Sun. Oct-June 2-6pm Tue-Sun. Closed Feb. Admission €6; free under-12s. No credit cards.
A 19th-century *hôtel particulier* with trompe l'oeil ceilings houses the largely 18th-century decorative arts collection of former resident Louis Vouland. A preserved meat salesman, Vouland spent 50 years acquiring furniture and porcelain, including faïence from Les Moustiers, Montpellier and Marseille, and Ming porcelain. Among the 19th-century paintings are works by Avignon artists Claude Firmin, Clément Brun and Pierre Grivolas.

Muséum Requien d'Histoire Naturelle

67 rue Joseph Vernet (04.90.82.43.51/www.museum-requien.org). Open 9am-noon, 2-6pm Tue-Sat. Admission free.
Founded in 1840, this old-fashioned natural history museum is packed with rocks, minerals, stuffed animals and fossils. Buried in the archives is John Stuart Mill's collection of dried flowers and herbs, while temporary exhibitions have focused on everything from crystals to local insect life.

Palais des Papes

Pl du Palais (04.90.27.50.73/www.palais-des-papes.com). Open Mar-June, mid Sept-Nov 9am-7pm daily. July-mid Sept 9am-8pm daily (9pm during festival). Nov-Feb 9.30am-5.45pm daily. Admission Mid Mar-Oct €10.50; free-€8.50 reductions. Nov-early Mar €8.50; free-€7 reductions.
More like a fortress than a palace, the labyrinthine Palais des Papes is an unmistakable power statement. The interior is strangely empty after the devastation wreaked during the Revolution, when it was used as a prison and barracks; soldiers chipped off bits of fresco to sell, but exquisite fragments remain. The Palais comprises two interlocking parts: the forbidding Palais Vieux, built in the 1330s for Pope Benedict XII, and the more showy Palais Neuf, tacked on a decade later by Clement VI. Wander at will (an

audioguide is included in the entry fee) or join a guided tour. Across the main courtyard from the ticket office is the Salle de Jésus, the antechamber of the papal council room, where frescoes from the cathedral are displayed. Next door, the Chapelle St-Jean has delightful frescoes (c1346) by Matteo Giovanetti, Clement VI's court painter. Upstairs, the ceiling of the Grand Tinel banqueting hall was once coloured blue and studded with gold stars to resemble the sky, while the kitchens, with their huge pyramid-shaped chimney, could cater for 3,000 guests. There are more Giovanetti frescoes, lavish with lapis lazuli and gold, in the Chapelle St-Martial.

Beyond the Salle de Parement (robing room), Benedict XII's tiled study was only discovered in 1963. The papal bedchamber is followed by the Chambre du Cerf, Clement VI's study, where some charming frescoes exude the spirit of courtly love. Next is the vast Chapelle Clémentine, which was barely large enough to hold the college of cardinals when it gathered in conclave to elect a new pope. Through the Chamberlain's Room, whose raised stone slabs mark the spot where papal treasure was discovered, stairs lead up to the battlements, with dramatic views over the city. Back on the ground floor, the Grande Audience hall has a bevy of biblical prophets frescoed by Giovanetti.

Palais du Roure

3 rue Collège du Roure (04.90.80.80.88). Open Guided tour 3pm Tue or by appointment. Library (open for research) 9am-noon, 2-5.30pm Mon-Fri. Admission €4.60; €2.30 reductions. No credit cards.
The birthplace of Marquis Folco de Baroncelli-Javon, who devoted his life to writing poetry, breeding bulls and preserving Camarguais traditions, has a charming courtyard with fragments of frescoes and a splendid carved doorway. It is now a literary archive and library, museum of local culture, and headquarters of the Festival Provençal, an autumn festival of theatre and music in the Provençal language (for details contact the tourist office).

Pont St-Bénezet

Rue Ferruce (04.90.27.51.16/www.palais-des-papes.com). Open Mar-June, mid-Sept-Nov 9am-7pm daily. July-mid Sept 9am-8pm daily (9pm during festival). Nov-Feb 9.30am-5.45pm daily. Admission Mid Mar-Oct €4.50; €3-€3.50 reductions. Nov-mid Mar 3.50; €2-€3 reductions. Combined ticket (Palais & bridge) €11-€13; €8.50-€10 reductions.
Construction of the original pont d'Avignon was begun in 1185 by a shepherd boy from the Ardèche, who later became St Bénezet. Divinely inspired to build a bridge, he lifted the first massive stone, convincing the sceptical populace that it was possible. When completed, the bridge had 22 arches and was nearly a kilometre long. It played a key role in the town's development, although in 1660, after a huge flood, the Avignonnais finally gave up the unequal maintenance struggle. Today, only four arches and a tiny fisherman's chapel remain; a small museum in the reception area explains the history. Despite the song, it seems unlikely that anyone ever danced on the narrow, busy structure. It's more likely that locals danced *sous le pont* (under the bridge): the Ile de la Barthelasse, which the bridge used to cross, was a favourite R&R spot during the Middle Ages.

Eat

Les 5 Sens

18 rue Joseph Vernet (04.90.85.26.51/www.restaurant les5sens.com). Open 11.30am-2.30pm, 7.30-11pm Tue-Sat. €€€€.

The sleek, Indian-influenced interior may be a touch too modern for some tastes, but the courtyard is delightful – and there's no doubting the quality of chef Thierry Baucher's beautifully presented contemporary cuisine. Leave space for the wonderful cheeseboard.

Au Tout Petit

4 rue d'Amphoux (04.90.82.38.86/www.autoutpetit.fr). Open noon-2pm, 7-10.30pm Mon, Tue, Thur-Sat; noon-2pm Wed. €.

The chef at this teeny restaurant offers inventive, modestly priced 'cuisine ré-créative', introducing modern accents to classic dishes. The team are also firm believers in the beneficial properties of a good home-made soup, which can be bought to take away. The two-course €11 lunchtime deal is an absolute bargain.

Café de la Comédie

15 pl Crillon (04.90.85.74.85). Open 7am-1am (7am-3am during festival) Mon-Sat. €.

In a calm, spacious square that's liberally dotted with restaurants, Café de la Comédie attracts a fascinatingly mixed clientele – including celeb chef Keith Floyd, who once claimed it as his local caff. Sit back under a plane tree and gaze upon the Renaissance façade of Avignon's first theatre.

Caves Breysse

41 rue des Teinturiers (04.32.74.25.86). Open Restaurant noon-2.30pm Tue-Fri. Bar 6am-11pm daily. €€.

A relaxed wine bar on the fashionable rue des Teinturiers, Caves Breysse invites you to explore the wines of the region by the glass. An excellent pit stop for a lunchtime *plat du jour*, it's equally well suited to early-evening aperitifs.

Christian Etienne

10 rue de Mons (04.90.86.16.50/www.christian-etienne.fr). Open noon-2pm, 7-9.30pm Tue-Sat. €€€€.

In the shadow of the Palais des Papes, this is one of Avignon's most ambitious restaurants. Etienne's cuisine is sophisticated and seasonal: summer might bring a menu devoted to the humble tomato, featuring such delights as braised lamb with baby fennel and dried tomatoes, and tomato mousse with aubergine caviar. If you're on a budget, book in for the modestly priced lunchtime menu.

La Fourchette

17 rue Racine (04.90.85.20.93). Open 12.15-1.45pm, 7.15-9.45pm Mon-Fri. €€.

La Fourchette's reasonable prices and excellent cuisine have won a diehard local following – so it's always best to book ahead. The menu combines classic dishes (including a very good *daube de boeuf*, served with macaroni) with lighter, more modern combinations.

Le Grand Café

La Manutention, 4 rue des Escaliers Ste-Anne (04.90.86.86.77/www.legrandcafe-avignon.com). Open noon-midnight Tue-Sat. €€.

Set in a converted army supplies depot this place attracts a lively, bohemian crowd. Glimmering candles and huge mirrors make it an atmospheric spot for dinner, while the menu is unpretentious and inviting, concentrating on classic provençal dishes with a twist.

Hiély Lucullus

5 rue de la République (04.90.86.17.07/www.hiely-lucullus.com). Open noon-2pm, 7-10pm Mon-Fri; 7-10pm Sat. Closed 1wk Jan. €€€€.

The stately, wood-panelled dining room at Hiély Lucullus is where the buttoned-up bourgeoisie of the town head for a traditional feast. Quality food is assured, and the wine list is equally smart – just don't go there expecting a boisterous crowd or cutting-edge cuisine.

La Mirande

4 pl de la Mirande (04.90.85.93.93/www.la-mirande.fr). Open 12.30-2pm, 7.30-10pm Mon, Thur-Sun. €€€€.

Under hotshot young chef Julien Allano, La Mirande is a quietly luxurious place to dine, whether you eat in the rose garden or the 15th-century dining room; save room for artful desserts from pastry chef Gaëtan Orlando. Tuesday and Wednesday nights bring an informal *table d'hôte* (€92), where a feast is whipped up before your eyes in the 19th-century kitchens.

Numéro 75

75 rue Guillaume Puy (04.90.27.16.00/www.numero75.com). Open noon-2.15pm, 8-10pm Mon-Sat. €€€.

Set inside a beautifully converted former *hôtel particulier* that once belonged to the Pernod family, Numéro 75 also has a lush walled garden. Its Mediterranean menu might not be the finest cuisine in town, but it's a wonderfully romantic spot for dinner.

Piedoie

26 rue des Trois Faucons (04.90.86.51.53). Open July 12.30-3pm, 7.15-10.30pm daily. Aug-June 12.30-3pm, 7.15-10.30pm Mon, Thur-Sun. €€€.

Thierry Piedoie's cluttered, intimate restaurant has an enticing menu of regional favourites to choose from, all cooked with a light, modern hand. Produce is fresh and carefully sourced, and this is the place to enjoy a spectacular white truffle salad in season.

Woolloomooloo

16bis rue des Teinturiers (04.90.85.28.44/www.woolloo.com). Open 11.45am-2pm, 7.30pm-midnight daily. €€.

The honorary HQ of Avignon's arty crowd buzzes with a fascinating selection of brooding students and neophyte playwrights, who fuel their inner creativity with plates of 'world food' (tandoori chicken, North African lamb, courgette and leek soufflé, chicken tagine) and veggie platters. Eat indoors or out on the convivial terrace, cluttered with mix and match seating and ethnic souvenirs.

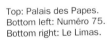

Top: Palais des Papes.
Bottom left: Numéro 75.
Bottom right: Le Limas.

Stay

La Banasterie
11 rue de la Banasterie (04.32.76.30.78/ www.labanasterie.com). €€.
Set in a charming 16th-century house, this upmarket B&B is on one of the old town's most atmospheric streets. Its rooms are named after great chocolates of the world, and decorated in rich, welcoming hues.

Hôtel Boquier
6 rue du Portail Boquier (04.90.82.34.43/ www.hotel-boquier.com). €.
Not far from the tourist office, this 18th-century building has been sympathetically transformed into a budget hotel. Its airy bedrooms are sparsely furnished, but the agreeable public spaces and hospitable owners make this a competitive choice.

Hôtel Cloître St-Louis
20 rue Portail Boquier (04.90.27.55.55/ www.cloitre-saint-louis.com). €€€.
The 16th-century cloister, chapel wing and fountain courtyard of a former monastery make an imposing setting for this smart hotel – along with a contemporary steel and glass extension by Jean Nouvel. The bedrooms are less impressive than the exterior, but there's a nice walled garden and small rooftop swimming pool.

Hôtel d'Europe
14 pl Crillon (04.90.14.76.76/www.hotel-d-europe.fr). €€€€.
Picasso, Charles Dickens, Tennessee Williams and Jackie Onassis are some of the past guests at this 16th-century mansion, which opened as a hotel in 1799. Rooms are traditional but not too fussy, while the suites have their own private terraces. The hotel has its own smart bar and restaurant and cookery lessons can be arranged with in-house chef Bruno d'Angelis.

Hôtel Le Médiéval
15 rue Petite Saunerie (04.90.86.11.06/www. hotelmedieval.com). €€.
A fine 17th-century mansion has been converted into this charming small hotel, with an attractive flower-filled courtyard and impressive sweeping staircase. Some of the simply furnished rooms are studios, which include a useful kitchenette for longer stays.

Hôtel de la Mirande
4 pl de la Mirande (04.90.14.20.20/www.la-mirande.fr). €€€€.
Hôtel de la Mirande, situated on a peaceful square just a short walk from the Palais des Papes, is a very smart affair, with 20 handsome, spacious rooms. Aubusson tapestries, antique furniture, Pierre Frey fabrics and Venetian chandeliers transport you back in time at this 18th-century cardinals' palace, although plenty of 21st-century luxuries abound too. The hotel restaurant, La Mirande (*see p291*), is highly regarded.

Le Limas
51 rue du Limas (04.90.14.67.19/www.le-limas-avignon.com). €€. No credit cards.
Starck bathroom fittings and Le Corbusier furniture contrast with the period features in this lovely 18th-century mansion, now a *chambre d'hôte*. Breakfast is served on the roof terrace in summer, with superb views over Avignon and the Palais des Papes.

Factfile

When to go
The weather is pretty mild and dry year round, except for late autumn which can be blustery, cold and wet. Summer temperatures can become oppressive in the middle of the day. The annual Festival d'Avignon (*see p391*) takes place over three weeks in July.

Getting there
From July to September, a weekly Eurostar (www.eurostar.com) service connects London to Avignon direct in 6hrs 30mins. At other times of the year you must change in Lille or Paris. The Gare TGV (08.92.35.35.35, www.tgv.com) is 4km (2.5 miles) south of Avignon. A bus service (*navette*), taking passengers to the Gare Centre Ville, meets every train and leaves from the centre for the Gare TGV every 15mins. Avignon airport (www.avignon.aeroport.fr) is 8km (5 miles) outside the city; Jet2 and Flybe operate scheduled flights from the UK. The main bus station is on av Montclar (04.90.82.07.35).

Getting around
Avignon is easy to get around by foot. Information about local buses and car hire can be found at the tourist office. For taxis, contact Taxis Radio Avignonnais (pl Pie, 04.90.82.20.20); long waits are common during the festival.

Tourist information
Tourist office 41 cours Jean Jaurès (04.32.74.32.74/www.ot-avignon.fr). Open Apr-June, Aug-Oct 9am-6pm Mon-Sat; 10am-5pm Sun. July 9am-7pm Mon-Sat; 10am-5pm Sun. Nov-Mar 9am-6pm Mon-Fri; 9am-5pm Sat; 10am-noon Sun.

Internet access
L'Opéra Café 24 pl de l'Horloge (04.90.86.17.43). Open 9am-1am daily.

The Cité and Pont Vieux.

Carcassonne

Join the crowds in the stunning capital of Cathar country.

Few words in the guidebook lexicon are as likely to raise a sceptical eyebrow as 'fairytale', but Carcassonne richly deserves the accolade. Come at it by road from the south or east, and you're met by something straight out of a book of romances: a proud medieval citadel of turrets, conical roofs, arrow slits and crenellated walls, all apparently resting on a thick cushion of trees. Whether you see it in the warm glow of summer or the clearer, bleaker light of midwinter, the self-appointed capital of Cathar country is a marvel to behold.

That's the town's most photographed, most conspicuously historic face. But come at Carcassonne from one of the other directions, and you realise that it is, in effect, two towns for the price of one, separated by the Aude river: opposite the aforementioned medieval Cité is the lower town known as the Bastide St-Louis, a good six centuries younger. For visitors, the best route between the two is the long, 14th-century Pont Vieux, now reserved for pedestrians only; and indeed, Bastide and Cité are both walker's territory *par excellence*, two warrens of narrow streets (many cobbled) and ancient stonework that brim with surprises.

How you feel about Carcassonne will almost certainly depend on the timing of your trip. The citadel is France's second most visited site after Mont St-Michel and in high season the whole town can get oppressively crowded. Your best bet is to visit in the spring or late autumn, when good rooms are easier to come by and the charm of the town is at its most apparent. Two or three days are enough to get to know Carcassonne itself; after that, if time permits, you can use it as the base for a series of daytrips into the surrounding area. Within an easy drive, you can enjoy Cathar castles, vineyards, horse riding – and, of course, the Mediterranean.

Explore

THE CITÉ

Carcassonne's star attraction stands less than a kilometre to the south-east of the Bastide St-Louis, 150 metres (500 feet) higher on a small plateau that was first fortified in the fourth century AD. The citadel is compact enough for you to be able to roam at random without losing your bearings, but there are also a number of guided tours, including some in English; enquire at the tourist office just inside the main entrance. However, bear in mind that in peak season the Cité is by far the busiest part of the town, and the combination of large crowds and narrow streets can make for a rather tiring tour. You'll get a much stronger feel for the history and atmosphere of the place if you time your visit for late spring or late autumn.

Although military defences were erected on the plateau at some time around 300 AD, the first settlers came to Carcassonne some 900 years earlier. It became a major Roman agglomeration in the second century AD, but with the collapse of the Roman empire the town passed into the hands of the Moors in the eighth century; and for centuries after that, Carcassonne was the front line between France and Aragon – hence the piecemeal construction of the monumental defences visitors see today. The result was the largest fortress ever built in Europe, shielded by a double wall three kilometres (two miles) around, a barrier strengthened by 52 turrets capped with conical slate roofs that reach high above the Aude valley. In its heyday, the fortress was so redoubtable that a mere 1,400-strong garrison was sufficient to defend it; now only 120 people live here, and the gates are open in welcome.

Still, as attractive as the citadel looks today, it had fallen into such disrepair by the first half of the 19th century that there were plans to demolish it altogether. Happily, the writer Prosper Mérimée, in his capacity as inspector of national monuments, was co-opted into a campaign to save it, and Napoléon III gave imperial approval to the scheme in 1853. Architect Eugène Viollet-le-Duc was put in charge of what was to be one of the largest restoration projects in Europe, and he devoted much of his time and energy to the citadel until his death in 1879; work continued under different supervisors until 1913.

Viollet-le-Duc's intervention was not unanimously welcomed, however. Detractors pointed out that the use of slate in the roofs was inauthentic, and criticised his over-Gothic remodelling; some have even had a bad word to say about the excessively perfect condition of some of the structures. Nowadays, though, most people are content to revel in what is a strikingly coherent restoration – and one whose importance has been recognised by inclusion on UNESCO's World Heritage list, however strictly faithful to the historical facts it may or may not be.

Carcassonne

Historic sites
● ● ● ● ●

Art & architecture
● ● ● ○ ○

Hotels
● ● ● ○ ○

Eating & drinking
● ● ● ○ ○

Nightlife
● ○ ○ ○ ○

Shopping
● ● ○ ○ ○

Basilique St-Nazaire.

The main way into the Cité is through the Porte Narbonnaise on its eastern side, so called because it faces in the direction of the town of Narbonne. Just inside it, on the right, you'll find a branch of the tourist office that can supply maps, audio guides and advice. A walk along the gap between the two defensive walls, the *lices* (lists), makes a good general introduction to the citadel, as it lets you get a feel for its layout and affords some superb photo opportunities. Not allowing for stops to admire and record the views, the walk takes about an hour.

Once you've completed that *tour d'horizon*, you can storm the Cité's interior. The narrow streets are well supplied with small restaurants, and shops selling a variety of antiques and curios, including replica weaponry. Two museums give an overview of medieval life inside the massive walls, both with an emphasis on the military side: the Musée Mémoires du Moyen-Age by the tourist office, and the Musée de la Chevalerie next to the Château Comtal. After the imposing Château Comtal and the St-Nazaire basilica, the largest attraction is the Grand Théâtre, a semicircular open-air auditorium that hosts the headline acts in the annual Festival des Deux Cités, one of France's largest summer arts festivals and nearly entirely free. The programme of rock, jazz, opera, theatre and dance dishes up the likes of Depeche Mode, Lenny Kravitz and the Orchestre National du Capitole de Toulouse – and the venue, surrounded on either side by a medieval stone wall, is as atmospheric as anyone could possibly wish for.

Basilique St-Nazaire

Pl Auguste-Pierre Pont. Open Summer 9am-noon, 2-7pm daily. Winter 9am-noon, 2-5pm daily. Admission free.

The Gothic St-Nazaire basilica is the Cité's main sacred building, but its oldest portion is Romanesque and dates from the 11th century. It was much enlarged in the 13th and 14th centuries, and although Viollet-le-Duc refashioned the exterior in the 1850s, it's not all that spectacular to look at from the outside. The real interest lies within, in its sculpture and, in particular, some of the finest stained glass in the south of France – the oldest of which is over 700 years old. Mass is held here every Sunday at 11am; decorous dress is de rigueur at all times.

Château Comtal

1 rue Viollet-le-Duc (04.68.11.70.70/www.carcassonne. monuments-nationaux.fr). Open Apr-Sept 9.30am-6.30pm daily. Oct-Mar 9.30am-5pm daily. Admission €8; free-€5 reductions.

This imposing château dates from the 12th and 13th centuries, and was home to the Trencavel family, hereditary counts of Carcassonne. It stands against the Cité's western inner wall, a fortress within a fortress, protected by a ditch, curtain wall, turrets, forbidding gatehouse and barbican. From here, visitors can get access to a section of the Cité

ramparts; the château also has an architecture museum and a permanent exhibition on the citadel's restoration in the 19th century.

BASTIDE ST-LOUIS

The Bastide St-Louis, or *basse ville* (lower town), is a relative newcomer beside the Cité: begun in 1247 by order of King Louis XI (later St Louis), it was the first major expansion of Carcassonne outside the citadel. Its largely grid-based plan is not, as you might think, a modern arrangement, but is as old as the Bastide itself: it was designed to allow reinforcements to gallop quickly to the rescue in the event of attacks on the Cité, and it makes for easy crossings even today.

A century after the fortified town was founded, it was sacked by England's Black Prince, Edward Plantagenet, and the residents beefed up its defences with a wall as long as the one surrounding the citadel (although few traces of it remain today). Today the Bastide is the commercial and residential heart of Carcassonne, and although you're best off tackling it on foot – either simply following your nose or a map, or using one of the audio guides in English available from the tourist office – a handful of free electric minibuses, called 'Toucs', are available to take the strain at peak shopping times.

The centrepiece of the lower town is the bustling place Carnot, site of the thrice-weekly open-air market and the second main venue for the Deux Cités summer arts festival; it's lined by café terraces and makes a convenient place for a refreshment stop. A block south of here is the rue de Verdun, one of the quarter's two main shopping arteries. As well as boutiques, it also has the small Musée des Beaux-Arts, which has a collection of largely second-rate paintings, and the rather more interesting Halle au Grains (covered wheat market), an attractive, recently restored 18th-century stone building with exposed wooden roof supports. A short stroll to the south brings you to the dour Cathédrale St-Michel, a 13th-century construction extensively modified by Viollet-le-Duc; and a stone's throw due east stands the monumental Porte des Jacobins, sole survivor of four fortified gateways built at the four points of the compass in the 18th century.

As this brief summary suggests, the Bastide is short on big-hitting visitor attractions, but there are plenty of historic townhouses to admire (from the outside), and many of the streets themselves are atmospheric in their own right – especially those that have been closed to vehicle traffic; traffic jams are a recurring problem in some parts of the town. And if you venture a short distance outside the Bastide to the north or north-west, you come to the Canal du Midi, which, like the Cité, has UNESCO World Heritage status. You can hire boats for up to 12 people from Société Nautic on quai Riquet (04.68.71.88.95).

Canal du Midi.

Eat

Restaurants and cafés are not lacking in Carcassonne, with the Bastide especially well supplied with options. Southern French cuisine is all about robust flavours and chunky portions – and you shouldn't come to Carcassonne without having cassoulet, the region's signature stew of pork, duck, sausage and haricot beans, served in an earthenware pot. Many a venue, especially in the Cité, claims to serve the best; but frankly, it's hard to go wrong with such a simple, hearty dish.

Auberge de Dame Carcas

The Cité *3 pl du Château (04.68.71.23.23/ www.damecarcas.com). Open noon-2pm, 7-10pm Mon, Tue, Thur-Sun. €€.*
The lady of the name, shown carrying a piglet on this rustic restaurant's sign, is the heroine of a local legend. The town was under siege and close to starvation, but the canny wench used the last of the food to fatten a young porker, threw it to the enemy – and thereby tricked them into thinking the town had ample supplies and lifting the seige. Pork features fairly prominently on the menu of this cheerful and unpretentious spot, in the guise of, say, andouillette sausage or grilled suckling pig in a honey sauce; other typical dishes include pan-fried foie gras with a red-fruit sauce, and a generous salad made with duck gizzards. An open kitchen, endearing decorative pigs and a small pavement terrace are further attractions.

Brasserie le Donjon

The Cité *4 rue Porte d'Aude (04.68.25.95.72/ www.brasserie-donjon.fr). Open noon-2pm, 7.30-10pm daily. €€.*
Affiliated to the nearby Best Western hotel of the same name, the Donjon brasserie is located smack bang in the heart of the Cité sightseeing action, opposite the Château Comtal. It has a stylish contemporary interior that sets warm orange walls against charcoal tabletops and designer chairs, and a menu based largely on traditional fare – like the ubiquitous cassoulet, a plate of three types of foie gras, or a chunky steak served with potatoes fried with chopped bacon. There's also a run of more inventive modern dishes such as coppa sausage and beetroot millefeuille, or breaded medallions of monkfish with a parmesan risotto. By way of an aperitif, order a glass of *hypocras* – spiced red wine that was popular throughout medieval Europe – or the local liqueur Or Kina, made from a secret concoction of plants and herbs.

Brasserie le Longchamp

Bastide St-Louis *Pl Carnot (04.68.25.15.22). Open noon-2.30pm, 7-9.30pm daily. €.*
This lively spot is not, perhaps, the prettiest place in town, but it's conveniently set on the Bastide's place Carnot, and very good for people-watching, inside and out. It draws in plenty of tourists, and just as many locals – many of whom are here to discuss racing form and have their daily flutter:

the Longchamp is part brasserie, part branch of the state-managed betting organisation. The food is unpretentious and reasonably priced: an artichoke and chorizo salad, perhaps, and a no-nonsense, affordable cassoulet. Finish off with a delicious raspberry tart.

La Cotte de Mailles

The Cité *2 rue St-Jean (04.68.72.36.24/www. cottedemailles.com). Open June-Sept noon-3pm, 7-9.30pm daily. Oct-May noon-3pm, 7-9.30pm Mon, Fri-Sun. €€.*
With all the medieval things to marvel at in Carcassonne, it seems only logical to eat medieval as well. Happily, 'the Coat of Mail' is not some kitsch theme restaurant; rather, it's a convivial, family-run establishment that specialises in recipes from Carcassonne's distant past. The menu is written in gothic script, and alongside traditional dishes like the cassoulet made with lamb (more authentic than other kinds, or so they claim) are tasty things like venison stew with seasonal vegetables, and perch in a liquorice and orange sauce. Portions are generous and, to complete the time-travel feel, served on wooden plates; spiced wines made to centuries-old recipes are available to start or conclude a meal.

> # "You shouldn't come to Carcassonne without having cassoulet, the region's signature stew of pork, duck, sausage and haricot beans, served in an earthenware pot."

Le Parc Franck Putelat

The Cité *80 chemin des Anglais (04.68.71.80.80/ www.leparcfranckputelat.com). Open noon-2pm, 7.30-9.30pm Tue-Sat. €€€€.*
Owner-chef Franck Putelat's one Michelin-starred restaurant is a short *trebuchet* lob to the south of the Cité ramparts and just a few hundred metres from his previous fiefdom, the Barbacane at the Hôtel de la Cité (where he also won a Michelin star). His seasonal, modern-meets-traditional menu features such succulent delights as an award-winning *timbale* of beef fillet and truffles, superb versions of classics like *poularde de Bresse*, and a sprinkling of exotic numbers like roast slipper lobster scented with herbs. Three thematic set menus let Putelat completely unbottle his inventive genie, and the €29 lunchtime menu – three courses, plus wine and coffee – is a fantastic bargain; book well ahead. The wine list is particularly strong on Languedoc bottles.

Le Saint-Jean

The Cité *1 pl St-Jean (04.68.47.42.43/www.le-saint-jean.fr). Open Summer 9am-2am daily. Winter 9am-2pm, 6pm-2am Mon, Wed-Sun. Closed Jan. €€.*

This restaurant-bar-ice cream parlour looks as though it has been airlifted from some resort on the coast, and is slightly on the small side; but it enjoys unbeatable views of the Château Comtal from its outside dining area, an especially dramatic sight when lit up after dark. Outside is all smart wooden furniture and parasols, the interior a sleeker, cool-toned and modern affair, with a brushed metal bar counter and shiny metal stools. But the food is good whether eaten in or out, and all made with faultlessly fresh ingredients: try one of the huge salads that are a meal in themselves – like the 'Visigoth', made with goat's cheese, roquefort and tomme from the Pyrenees, or the roast duck stuffed with foie gras. If you have any room left, wind up with some of their own-made ice-cream.

Shop

Carcassonne isn't what you'd call a retail destination, but the Cité has a fair number of boutiques selling antiques and medieval-style trinkets. For food and gifts to take home, it's the Bastide you need: the north–south rue Georges-Clémenceau is the main shopping drag, but you'll find more of interest on the east–west rue de Verdun. The town's main market is held on Tuesday, Thursday and Saturday mornings on place Carnot; it's a colourful affair and strong on local produce. The recently refurbished Halle au Grains, on place Eggenfelden, is home to the town's covered food market.

Comptoir des Vins et Terroirs

The Cité *2 rue Comte-Roger (04.68.26.44.76/ www.comptoir-vins.fr). Open Sept-June 11am-3pm, 7-9pm daily. July, Aug 11am-3pm, 7pm-midnight daily.*

Part wine bar, part wine shop, the Comptoir des Vins et Terroirs is housed in a stone-walled annexe of the Donjon hotel, and specialises in local bottles: it has over 100 fine Languedoc wines in stock. You can try before you buy, too, either in an organised tasting session (phone in advance) or at one of the bar's outside tables; they also serve good plates of cheese and charcuterie.

Esprit de Sel

The Cité *10 rue de la République (04.68.72.03.01). Open 10am-12.30pm, 2-7pm Tue-Sat.*

This smart but offbeat gift shop has an impressive variety of stock, and four separate rooms in which you could easily spend an hour. The compendious range includes things like affordable and interesting silver jewellery, furniture, funky tableware, clocks, lamps, clothes made entirely from natural fibres, L'Occitane soaps and cosmetic products, and even attractive leather-bound notebooks.

Stay

Unsurprisingly, room rates tend to go up the closer a hotel is to the picture-postcard turrets of the Cité – with (relatively speaking) the highest rates of all inside its ramparts. They also fluctuate with the season, with July and August commanding a premium.

Château St-Martin

3km N of Carcassonne *Hameau de Montredon (04.68.47.44.41/www.chateausaintmartin.net). Closed Jan, Feb. €€.*

This hotel is 3km (2 miles) outside the centre, in the hamlet of Montredon: near enough to be convenient, far enough to be tranquil. The recently built accommodation, set in parkland, has been done in the style of a sprawling Languedoc country house, with terracotta roofs, large veranda and open-air swimming pool. Decor-wise, the 15 rooms are simple almost to the point of monastic, but they all have air-conditioning, Wi-Fi and fully equipped bathrooms. The on-site restaurant, housed in a building flanked by a five-storey octagonal tower dating from the 12th century, serves classic regional cuisine made with seasonal, local ingredients.

Citéa Carcassonne La Barbacane

The Cité *Rte de St-Hilaire (04.68.77.27.00/ www.citea.com). €€.*

If you plan to spend more than a couple of days in Carcassonne – to use it, say, as base camp for a series of excursions along the canal and into the surrounding area – the convenience of a small apartment might win out over the cosseting of a hotel. This brand new building is short on character, but it's right next to the Cité, and spotlessly clean. Its 70 apartments range from doubles to family size, all with small kitchen area, and amenities include air-conditioning, free high-speed internet, a small fitness room and reception staff who can help with reservations and other basic hotel-style services.

Le Domaine d'Auriac

2km S of Carcassonne *Rte de St-Hilaire (04.68.25.72.22/www.domaine-d-auriac.com). €€€.*

A five-minute drive to the south of the town brings you to this distinctly aristocratic-looking 19th-century stone beauty, once a private manor house and now a 24-room Relais & Châteaux hotel. The place couldn't be more peaceful: it's insulated from the outside world by private grounds so extensive they even have an 18-hole golf course. Rooms are large and done out in cheerful yellows and floral designs; there are also three stand-alone villas with lofty, wood-beamed roofs a short distance from the main building. There are two restaurants: the main dining room, and the Bistrot d'Auriac in the club house; the excellent food runs from choice cuts of beef or lamb to game (in season), and artful creations such as roast langoustines served with stuffed courgette flower. The hotel's other amenities include a billiard room in what used to be an abbatial cellar, a swimming pool and a tennis court.

Hôtel de la Cité.

Hôtel du Château

The Cité *2 rue Camille-St-Saëns (04.68.11.38.38/ www.lemontmorency.com). €€.*
This is the flagship address in a three-hotel chain just outside the Cité; it's also the nearest to the ramparts, and enjoys superb point-blank views of the ancient stonework. It's an extremely stylish place in which to stay, its 16 rooms decorated in a classy modern assembly of warm-coloured leather, dark wood and fine linens; waist-high panelling, exposed stonework and curved ceilings add a historic feel, and CD players and flatscreen TVs keep it anchored in the 21st century. There's a suite, a heated outdoor pool and jacuzzi, a cosy bar and an outdoor dining area – and all in all, it's decent value for money, especially in low season. Its sister establishment on the other side of the street, the Hôtel Montmorency (04.68.11.96.70), serves as an annexe; the third sibling, the Hôtel l'Octroi (106 av Général-Leclerc, 04.68.25.29.08), is more basic, but also much cheaper.

Hôtel de la Cité

The Cité *Pl Auguste-Pierre-Pont (04.68.71.98.71/ www.hoteldelacite.com). €€€€.*
The four-star Hôtel de la Cité is, without a doubt, Carcassonne's top hotel. It occupies an attractive medieval stone building high up in the old quarter, and, as you'd expect from an Orient Express establishment, it oozes luxury. No two rooms and suites look the same, but all are decorated with consummate panache: marble bathrooms, luxurious fabrics and bed linen – and, in a few cases, floor-to-ceiling, Gothic-style wooden panelling; several rooms also have their own balcony or terrace. The hotel has the only swimming pool (heated, summer only) inside the Cité walls, and two excellent restaurants that are worth booking into even if you're not staying here: the Barbacane (dinner only), and the more affordable brasserie Chez Saskia.

Hôtel du Pont Vieux

The Cité *32 rue Trivalle (04.68.25.24.99/ www.lacitedecarcassonne.fr). €.*
This cheerful, family-run budget address certainly won't win any prizes for decor, but its bedrooms are clean and all have air-conditioning and private bathrooms. The third-floor terrace is open to all guests and enjoys good views of the Cité, and there's a pleasant courtyard at ground level in which to have breakfast. In off-season, the Pont Vieux offers a four-day tour package that includes accommodation at the hotel, car hire, daily picnic hampers, and a portfolio of scenic attractions, vineyards and restaurants in the region.

Maison Coste

Bastide St-Louis *40 rue Coste Reboulh (04.68.77.12.15/www.maison-coste.com). €€.*
Pretty but inconspicuous doors lead to this unexpectedly gracious private house, filled with light and decorated with a style and eye for detail that most boutique hotels would envy. The proprietors run a design shop on the premises for which this is a wonderful showcase, with beautiful old furniture, handsome fabrics and generosity in every proportion. Of the three rooms and two suites, our favourite is the large Lied d'Ossian, its lack of bathroom resulting in a lower price and a short walk to a private claw-foot tub down the hall. There's a tiny garden with sunbathing area.

Factfile

When to go

The Languedoc-Roussillon region has the second hottest climate in France. May, June and September are Carcassonne's most comfortable months; July can be very hot, as can August, when the town heaves with tourists. Hotel rates drop significantly in low season (broadly speaking, October to April); winters are mild. The Festival des Deux Cités (www.festivaldecarcassonne.com) is held during July, and dishes up major theatre, opera and music of all kinds throughout the town. For six weeks in July and August, the Cité is awash with daily jousting, troubadours, parades and street entertainment.

Getting there

Carcassonne airport (04.68.71.79.14/ www.carcassonne.aeroport.fr) is situated by rte Montréal, 5km (3 miles) east of the town centre. The Agglobus shuttle service serves the railway station and the town centre; the journey takes about 15mins and costs €5 (pay on bus). The mainline railway station is a short walk north of the lower town, on av du Maréchal-Joffre (04.68.71.79.68/www.sncf.com), and is served by regular direct trains from Montpellier and Toulouse.

Getting around

Local buses are cheap and frequent, but Carcassonne is a town best negotiated on foot. If you fancy a waterborne excursion, there are plenty of cruises along the Canal du Midi; Hélios & Lou Gabaret (27 rue des Trois-Couronnes, 04.68.71.61.26/www.carcassonne-croisiere.com) does excursions with commentary in English as well as French. For information about cycle hire, contact the tourist office.

Tourist information

Tourist office 28 rue de Verdun (04.68.10.24.30/www.carcassonne.org). Open 9am-6pm Mon-Sat; 9am-noon Sun.

Internet access

L'Alerte Rouge 73 rue de Verdun (04.68.25.20.39). Open 9.30am-10pm Mon-Sat.

Top: Musée des Beaux-Arts. Bottom left: Palais des Ducs. Bottom right: Hostellerie du Chapeau Rouge.

Dijon

Hold the mustard – this cultured city has so much else to relish.

Dijon is more than mere mustard – in fact, the city's condiment connections are increasingly tenuous these days, with seeds being shipped in from North America, production shifting to the countryside and the closure of the Mustard Museum in 2006. Yet the diminishing influence of the yellow sauce doesn't mean Dijon's days are over. On the contrary, the thinning of its mustard mantle serves to reveal a city rich in other aspects, from a wealth of eye-popping architecture and fascinating noble history to a relaxed, modern ambience and proximity to some of France's most enchanting countryside and world-renowned vineyards.

After starting life as a second-rate Roman settlement (Divio) on the military route from Lyon to Mainz, it wasn't until the 11th century that Dijon gained major kudos thanks to Robert I, who established the city as a capital of his newly founded duchy in 1032. Thus began the era of the notorious Dukes of Burgundy. The dukes went on to forge their own mini empire and Dijon was transformed from mercantile node to hub of wealth, power and education. Though the dukes didn't spend much time in the city, it remained an important base.

Following immersion into France in the 15th century the Burgundy Parliament was transferred from Beaune to Dijon, which continued to serve as administrative centre and capital. Dijon underwent significant urban development in the 17th and 18th centuries, and today stands out as a winsome, bustling university town, mixing up modernist motifs with its bourgeois roots.

If all that history and culture isn't enough to get you on the next TGV, then think of the food. Aside from familiar classics such as *boeuf bourguignon*, snails and *coq au vin*, there are wonderful lesser-known local dishes like *oeufs en meurette* (eggs in red wine). The city is also famous for crème de cassis and the ubiquitous *pain d'épices* (gingerbread), as well as mustard, of course. And with the vines of Nuits-St-Georges and Gevrey-Chambertin just a few kilometres outside town, the possibilities for epicurean exploration are legendary.

Explore

Dijon's centre is easy to explore on foot. Pretty much everything you'll want to see is within the vaguely pentagonal 'downtown' area. North-west is place Darcy, home to the tourist office, the handsome Jardin Darcy and the distinctive Porte Guillaume; east lies the lively rue Musette, the distinctive Poste Grangier and the covered food market (Les Halles); south-east you'll find Dijon's high street, rue de la Liberté, which leads to the Palais des Ducs, Notre-Dame church and a cute concentration of medieval lanes, coloured roofs and limestone architecture. Further south are rue Berbisey, place Emile Zola and rue Monge – the best area for restaurants, bars and cafés. You'll stumble across most of Dijon's key attractions without even trying, but an organised route exists in the Owl Trail. Brochures for this, as well as Dijon visitor cards and more, are available from the tourist office.

Hôtel de Vogüé
8-12 rue de la Chouette (03.80.74.51.51). Open 9am-8pm daily. Admission free.
The 17th-century Hôtel de Vogüé is one of Dijon's most prominent *hôtels particuliers* – private houses used principally by the aristocracy. Located near Notre-Dame church, this was one of Dijon's first parliamentary buildings and is renowned for its handsome Renaissance-style portico, traditional varnished tile roof and exquisite detailing. You can't enter the house itself, but the exterior architecture is worth the visit. Other *hôtels particuliers* can be found in and around rue Verrerie, rue Vannerie, rue des Forges and rue Chaudronnière. Ask at the tourist office for information.

Musée des Beaux-Arts
Place de la Libération (03.80.74.52.09/www.dijon.fr). Open May-Oct 9.30am-6pm Mon, Wed-Sun. Nov-Apr 10am-5pm Mon, Wed-Sun. Admission free.
Located within the Palais des Ducs, Dijon's Museum of Fine Arts contains a collection of European paintings that mainly covers early Renaissance to Impressionism. There's a room dedicated to 16th-century designer and architect Hugues Sambin, while other floors house modern and contemporary galleries. Given the duke's philandering in Flanders it's little surprise to find an emphasis on Flemish painters, but there are French and Italian works too, including some by Manet and Monet. The museum also hosts major international exhibitions from time to time.

Musée Magnin
4 rue des Bons-Enfants (03.80.67.11.10/www. musee-magnin.fr). Open 10am-noon, 2-6pm Tue-Sun (1st Tue of mth until 8pm). Admission €3.50; free-€2.50 reductions.
The Musée Magnin is housed in the 17th-century Hôtel de Lantin, former home of Jeanne and Maurice Magnin, an arts-loving couple and members of the *grande bourgeoisie*. The museum has been assembled from the prodigious collection of paintings, drawings and objects that they donated to the city in 1938. In fact the whole house has pretty much been kept as it was, elegant furnishings, impressive antiques and all.

Dijon

Historic sites
● ● ● ○ ○

Art & architecture
● ● ● ● ○

Hotels
● ● ● ● ○

Eating & drinking
● ● ● ● ○

Nightlife
● ● ● ○ ○

Shopping
● ● ● ○ ○

Top: Le Chabrot.
Bottom: Hôtel Wilson.

Musée de la Vie Bourguignonne

17 rue Ste-Anne (03.80.48.80.90/www.dijon.fr).
Open 9am-12.30pm, 1.30-6pm Mon, Wed-Sun.
Admission free.

The Musée de la Vie Bourguignonne is set in a 17th-century Cistercian convent (the Monastère des Bernardines) and explores historical life in Burgundy over three floors. On the ground floor are waxworks in glass cases that illustrate the customs, dress and craft-based existence of Burgundians at the end of the 19th century. The second floor is given over to a grand re-creation of a 19th-century shopping street, while a less dynamic top floor explores local life through natural elements such as wood and stone. Information is in French but an English catalogue is available free from the reception. The Museum of Sacred Art is located in the church next door.

Notre-Dame de Dijon

Rue de la Préfecture (03.80.28.84.91). Open 7.30am-7pm Mon-Sat; 9am-7pm Sun. Admission free.

Situated directly behind the Palais des Ducs, the 13th-century Notre-Dame church is a sight to behold with its glorious façade, skinny colonettes and gaping gargoyles. The famous Jacquemart clock tower on top was built in 1382. Inside is one of the oldest statues of the Virgin Mary in France, said to date from the 11th century. The gap in her arms where a baby Jesus should be is down to rampaging revolutionaries, as are the missing statues on the church's façade. At the back of the church, in rue de la Chouette, you'll find a small stone owl: to maintain tradition, rub it and make a wish.

Palais des Ducs et des Etats de Bourgogne

Pl de la Libération (03.80.74.52.70). Open May-Oct 10am-5pm Mon, Wed-Sun. Nov-Apr 9.30am-6pm Mon, Wed-Sun. Admission free.

Originally built in the 11th century as a fortress, this imposing building was rebuilt in the 13th century and became the official palace of the Dukes of Burgundy via the first Duke of Valois, Philippe the Bold. Today the capacious building functions as the town hall and also hosts the Musée des Beaux-Arts. You need to take a guided tour (arranged through the tourist office; available only in French) to see the interior of the palace, which houses the impressive 15th-century ducal kitchens, the tombs of some of the former dukes and various elegant salons. The Philippe le Bon tower (€2.30 adults, €1.20 reductions; check with tourist office for opening times) affords visitors who brave its 316 steps incredible views of the city.

Eat

Foodies will be happy to know that Dijon boasts several three Michelin-starred restaurants, and many eateries offer good lunchtime deals. The 19th-century Les Halles covered market on rue Ramey (open Tue, Thur & Fri morn, all day Sat) is a great place for local produce. Rue Monge and place Emile Zola have the best concentration of restaurants, while rue Berbisey is good for bars. A tour of the nearby Côte d'Or region is a must for wine enthusiasts: Alter and Go (06.45.73.31.35) offers insightful half- and full-day tours, and other tours are available through the tourist office.

Le Bistrot des Halles

10 rue Bannelier (03.80.49.94.15). Open noon-2pm, 7-10.30pm Tue-Sat. €€.

This less formal offshoot of Jean Pierre Billoux's Le Pré aux Clercs is situated on the south side of Les Halles food market. It offers a provocative mix of Burgundian classics and inventive modern fare in a classic 1930s bistro setting – all bulging art deco lamps, checked tablecloths and ornate mirrors. Efficient staff clad in traditional black-and-white uniforms zip around with steaming *escargots*, carafes of wine and shapely glasses containing things like pumpkin cappuccino. The food is first-class and reasonably priced, and the ever-changing daily specials make this a deservedly popular stop for those who like a long, lazy lunch.

Le Chabrot

36 rue Monge (03.80.30.69.61). Open noon-2.30pm, 7-10.30pm Mon-Sat. €€.

This colourful space represents one of Dijon's more vibrant dining spots. The red, yellow and green walls, punctuated with undulating mirrors and designer lamps, draw a young and trendy crowd who love the upbeat interior (even the original wood-beamed ceiling has been painted canary yellow) and chef Jean-François Vachez's consistently good food. There's a great range of terrines, as well as salads and mischievous takes on classics (*coq au vin* served on a bed of tagliatelle). Le Chabrot also boasts over 200 wines.

La Dame d'Aquitaine

23 pl Bossuet (03.80.30.45.65/www.ladame daquitaine.fr). Open 7-10.30pm Mon, Sun; noon-1.30pm, 7-10.30pm Tue-Sat. €€€.

La Dame d'Aquitaine can be found tucked away in a 13th-century medieval crypt off rue Bossuet. The vaulted ceiling, ancient stone walls and intimate, candlelit atmosphere make the place popular with couples, especially at weekends. The menu features Burgundy classics (snails, duck cooked in cassis) alongside a broader range of fish, meat and vegetarian dishes from south-west France. As well as decent à la carte options, there are some good value set menus (€29-€42).

Hostellerie du Chapeau Rouge

5 rue Michelet (03.80.50.88.88/www.chapeau-rouge.fr). Open noon-2pm, 7.30-10pm daily. €€€€.

Hostellerie du Chapeau Rouge is situated within the hotel of the same name. This swish, upmarket four-star is one of the best spots in town, and the same can be said for its Michelin-starred restaurant. The menu reflects the modernist interior – Philippe Starck furnishings, trees arranged behind glass walls – as chef William Frachot creates impressive fusion dishes that nod vaguely to French tradition but feature such incongruous ingredients as bok choi, turnip chips and salami.

La Petite Marche

27-29 rue Musette (03.80.30.15.10). Open noon-2.30pm Mon-Sat. €€.

Vegetarians often get a poor deal when it comes to eating out in France. So the Petite Marche, a dedicated organic/vegetarian café located upstairs from the (very good) bio supermarket on rue Musette, will come as a welcome relief. It's a spacious place with sparse, down-to-earth decoration (simple wooden tables and iron chairs) and a menu that focuses on healthy, artery-friendly recipes such as salads, snacks, Indian starters and quiches.

Le Pré aux Clercs

13 pl de la Libération (03.80.38.05.05/www.bourgogne-restaurants.com/lepreauxclercs).Open noon-1.30pm, 7.30-9.30pm Tue-Sat; noon-1.30pm Sun. €€€€.

Le Pré aux Clercs, the grand dame of the Dijon dinner scene, has been serving food since 1833. For the last 35 years it's been under the watchful eye of chef-owner Jean-Pierre Billoux and his wife Marie Françoise. Set in an 18th-century building just across from the Palais des Ducs, this classy establishment's gastronomic delights include roast duck with gingerbread stuffing, and *meurette d'escargots*. The wine list is impressive and service is charming.

Stéphane Derbord

10 rue Wilson (03.80.67.74.64/www.restaurant stephanederbord.fr). Open noon-1.45pm, 7.30-9.15pm Tue-Sat. €€€€.

Stéphane Derbord's Michelin-starred restaurant is a much-loved place in Dijon. Perhaps the cosiest and friendliest of the city's high-end eateries, the dining room of this 17th-century *relais de poste* sports wood-panelled walls, modern etchings and lemon-coloured tablecloths. Stéphane's wife, Isabelle, presides over the main room, helping guests steer their way through the varied menu. There's plenty of seafood (pike dumplings, sea bass lasagne), as well as meat and game, and though you'll find evidence of local traditions they've mostly been playfully subverted.

Shop

The main shopping street in Dijon is rue de la Liberté, which extends east from place Darcy to the Palais des Ducs. You'll mostly find brands and chains here; more independent clothes stores and boutiques can be found along rue du Bourg and rue Piron, while rue de la Verrerie is known as the antiques quarter.

Aux Grands Crus

22 rue Verrerie (03.80.31.68.71/www.auxgrands crus.com). Open 9am-noon, 2-7pm Tue-Sat.

As the name implies, only the best local wines are sold at this small but dedicated wine shop on rue Verrerie. The focus is on regional specialities, meaning you can find wines and vintages here from many of the best Burgundy vineyards – which in turn means a lot of world-class wine. Regular tastings are held in the *cave* below.

Babylone Bazaar

23 rue des Forges (no phone). Open 2-7pm Mon; 9.30am-12.15pm, 2-7pm Tue-Sat.

This cute little store is a great stop-off for women seeking something fresh and trendy. The clothes and accessories here are designed for hip young *femmes* with brands such as Angel, Biscotte and Tequila Solo. There are jeans, shirts and tops, as well as scarves, belts and bracelets.

Boutique Maille

32 rue de la Liberté (03.80.30.41.02/www.maille.com). Open 9am-noon, 2.15-7pm Mon-Sat.

Boutique Maille is Dijon's most famous outlet for all things mustard. It's not the only shop – and certainly not the cheapest – but it is the oldest (it opened in 1777) and is the only place in town where you can get *moutarde fine* delivered straight from a pump. There's also a range of pre-packaged flavours and colours to choose from, and a smattering of mustard pots and other accoutrements.

Chapellerie Bruyas

65 rue des Godrans (03.80.30.49.23). Open 9am-noon Mon; 9am-noon, 2-7pm Tue-Sat.

Chapellerie Bruyas caters for all cranial whims with a wide stock of flat caps, fedoras, trilbies, toques – even ear-muffs – all crammed on to shelves that are stacked right up to the ceiling. There's headgear here for all sexes and ages, and the amiable staff are only too happy to answer any questions you may have.

Mulot et Petitjean

13 pl Bossuet (03.80.30.07.10/www.mulotpetitjean.fr). Open 9am-noon, 2-7pm Tue-Sat.

Mulot et Petitjean specialises mainly in *pain d'épice*, famously tasty gingerbread. The shop opened back in 1796 and is still run by members of the original Petitjean family. Aside from *pain d'épice* you can find everything from mustards and bonbons to crème de cassis and *nonnettes*, all beautifully presented. Perfect for gifts.

La Rose de Vergy

1 rue de la Chouette (03.80.61.42.22/www.rose devergy.com). Open 9.30am-7pm Tue-Sat.

This lovely shop is one of Dijon's best known – and best loved. It's supremely cute, piled high with all kinds of treats and sweets – bonbons, biscuits, mustards and *pain d'épice*. The whole experience is enhanced by the friendliness of owners Annette and Marc Planchard, who make most of the goods in a workshop below. A small collection of tables and chairs allows you to sample some of the wares on site.

Stay

Dijon's accommodation options aren't quite as varied – or consistent – as its restaurants, but there are a few decent spots to choose from. As a general rule the chain hotels are a little outside the centre, while 'downtown' is where you'll find hotels with more history and character.

Hôtel de Vogüé.

Hostellerie du Chapeau Rouge

5 rue Michelet (03.80.50.88.88/www.chapeau-rouge.fr). €€€.

Don't be put off by the Best Western symbol – this is no bland business hotel. On the contrary, it's the slickest four-star in town, featuring 30 rooms that vary in style from Asian minimalist chic to 19th-century trad, though all come with swish marble bathrooms, comfy beds, TVs and writing desks. The four deluxe rooms are the largest and some have jacuzzis too, but one or two of the standards are almost the same size so it's worth checking first if you can. As well as the Michelin-starred restaurant there's a pleasant bar and the hotel is near all the main sights.

Hôtel de la Cloche (Sofitel Dijon)

14 pl Darcy (03.80.30.12.32/www.hotel-lacloche.com). €€€.

Dominating one corner of place Darcy, Dijon's grandest hotel is still one of its best. Built in 1884, it has retained its grandiose 19th-century feel, particularly in the expansive lobby with its marble floors and chandeliers. Grace Kelly, Napoleon III and Rodin have all laid their heads here. Standard rooms are comfortable and sleek, with big beds, spacious bathrooms, desks and minibars, while the club, privilege and fifth-floor suites improve incrementally in terms of space, comfort and features. The hotel's restaurant is reassuringly refined (and expensive), the bar inevitably luxurious and there's a pretty, secluded garden for summer.

Hôtel du Palais

23 rue du Palais (03.80.67.16.26/www.hoteldupalais-dijon.com). €.

Located on a quiet side street round the corner from the sweeping place de la Libération, this fantastic little two-star – set in an historic 18th-century *hôtel particulier* – lays claim to being the very first hotel in Dijon. The entrance hall, reception and breakfast room (which boasts an original painted ceiling) lend the place the impression of a refined private house, though the 14 rooms are much simpler, with standard furnishings and smallish bathrooms. They're cheerfully decorated, though, and often generously proportioned (except those on the attic floor), and many have great views. There's also free Wi-Fi, friendly service and a breakfast for €7.

Hôtel Le Sauvage

64 rue Monge (03.80.41.31.21/www.hotel lesauvage.com). €€.

Situated in a 15th-century *relais de poste*, this quirky, slightly ramshackle two-star lies through a stone arch in a medieval cobbled courtyard just off buzzing rue Monge. The stables have been transformed into garages, the exterior stone walls are covered in ivy and the rooms are decorated in faux 17th-century style. Pseudo-antique furnishings, high ceilings and thick wooden beams create the requisite nostalgia vibe. The rooms overlooking the courtyard are splendid in summer, and there's a small library, breakfast room and very good restaurant next door.

Hôtel Wilson

Pl Wilson (03.80.66.82.50/www.wilson-hotel.com). €€.

This former 17th-century coaching inn has been restored and modernised but has retained many of its original features. The vintage vibe is apparent when you enter the spacious reception area, with its antique stone-and-wood feel and original fireplace. Rooms are similarly tasteful and old-fashioned, with quaint furnishings but free Wi-Fi and modern bathrooms (some have tubs). Though not as centrally located as other hotels, the Wilson is still within walking distance of most key sights. There's safe parking for €9 a night, a breakfast for €12 and the Michelin-starred restaurant Stéphane Derbord a few paces away.

Factfile

When to go

Weather-wise, May to September is the best time to visit the city – winter can be pretty cold but is usually dry. The major Fêtes de la Vigne (www.fetesdelavigne.com), which celebrated its 60th anniversary in 2009, takes place in August.

Getting there

Dijon is easily accessible by rail and bus from all major French cities. The train station (rue du Docteur Rémy) is linked with Lyon, Nice, Paris and Strasbourg. Journey time from Paris on the TGV is approx 1hr 40mins. Train tickets can be bought at the SNCF Boutique (55 rue du Bourg; 12.30-7pm Mon, 10am-7pm Tue-Sat). Eurolines (08.92.89.90.91; 9.30am-12.30pm, 2-6.30pm Tue-Fri, 10am-noon Sat) can be found at 53 rue Guillaume Tell. The closest airport is Dijon-Bourgogne (open June-Sept).

Getting around

The best way to get around Dijon is on foot, but there is also a free shuttle service called Diviaciti, which serves the town centre (7am-8pm Mon-Sat), as well as the Velodi municipal bike hire scheme with several pick-up points in the city centre. If you'd like to explore the surrounding countryside and vineyards, you can book a tour via the tourist office or rent a car at the main train station.

Tourist information

Tourist office 11 rue des Forges (08.92.70.05.58/ www.dijon-tourism.com). Open Apr-Sept 9.30am-6.30pm Mon-Sat; 10am-6pm Sun. Oct-Mar 9.30am-1pm, 2-6pm Mon-Sat; 10am-4pm Sun.

Internet access

Cybersp@ce21 46 rue Monge (03.80.30.57.43). Open 11am-midnight Mon-Sat; 2pm-midnight Sun.

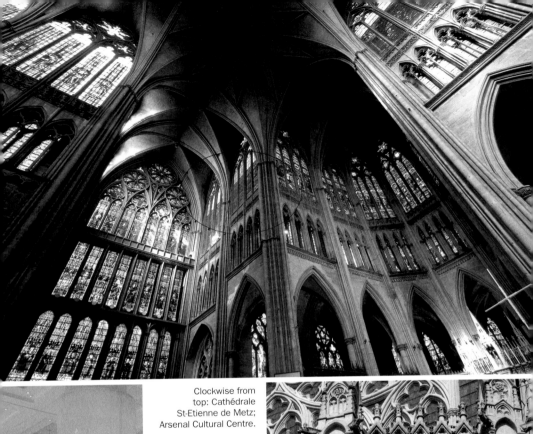

Clockwise from top: Cathédrale St-Etienne de Metz; Arsenal Cultural Centre.

Metz

This honey-coloured gem has a bright future and a fascinating past.

Single-handedly giving the lie to the idea that everything in northern France is insipid and industrial, this handsome capital of the Lorraine region is a genuine delight, wooing visitors with an array of French and Prussian architecture, an award-winning commitment to green, natural spaces and a convivial yet cosmopolitan atmosphere. The city naturally divides into two key areas: the Centre Ville, with its distinctive *pierre de Jaumont* (honey-yellow limestone) buildings and winding, medieval streets; and the newer Ville Allemande (German quarter) – home to hotels, residences and grandiloquent Prussian buildings.

In Roman times the city went by the tortuous title of Divodurum Mediomatricorum; it was popular for having the fourth largest amphitheatre in the world. By the Middle Ages the name had been mercifully shortened to the more manageable 'Metz' and the city was enjoying its advantageous position in the centre of Europe. Fortunes changed in the 19th century when a tug-of-war was inaugurated between France and Germany for the Alsace-Lorraine region. In 1870 Napoleon III's armies surrendered to Kaiser Wilhelm I and Metz was ceded to Germany until the end of World War I. It was then re-annexed by the Nazis in 1940, before being liberated by Allied troops in 1944.

Now, more than half a century later, Metz's star is most definitely on the rise once again. In 2007, the TGV Est line opened, slashing journey times in half: the 320kph (200mph) trip from the capital now takes just 82 minutes. The city's other landmark project, the new Pompidou Centre, also began its journey in Paris, although the speed with which it has reached its destination has been considerably slower. The dramatic showpiece building is finally set to open its doors in 2010, seven years after the plan was first agreed. But coupled with existing venues such as the Arsenal and Les Trinitaires, it is set to place Metz squarely at the heart of France's cultural radar.

Explore

The city's centrepoint is the majestic St-Etienne cathedral, located on place d'Armes, which also hosts the main tourist office; the covered market and Cour d'Or museums are nearby. It's a short stroll north to the Moselle, the charming Ile du Saulcy and the striking Temple Neuf. South lie the city's labyrinthine lanes, which will bring you to the Ville Allemande and its various landmarks: the Porte des Allemands, the train station, and the red sandstone post office. The Pompidou Centre site lies behind the train station.

Arsenal Cultural Centre

Av Ney (03.87.39.92.00/www.mairie-metz.fr/arsenal). Open times vary. Admission varies.

In Prussian times, this building was used for storing armaments. Now its capacious interior hosts everything from concerts and conferences to art exhibitions, theatre performances and trade fairs – indeed, some 200 events per year take place here. The site also manages the 12th-century Templars' Chapel and the fourth-century St-Pierre-aux-Nonnains church, both of which are nearby.

Cathédrale St-Etienne de Metz

Pl d'Armes (03.87.75.54.61). Open Oct-Mar 8am-6pm daily. Apr-Sept 8am-7pm daily. Admission free.

All roads lead inexorably to the glitzy 42m (138ft) nave of the Cathédrale St-Etienne, the third tallest cathedral in France (behind Beauvais and Amiens) and Metz's most striking attraction. Despite its prodigious height, the cathedral (built between 1220 and 1522) is famed mainly for its stained glass – allegedly the largest expanse in the world. It was installed between the 13th and 20th centuries, including latter-day additions from Chagall. Illuminated naturally by day and artificially by night, the windows provide visitors with a kaleidoscopic visual feast. Down below is a 15th-century Romanesque crypt with religious documents and a sculpture of the Graoully, the mythical dragon that terrorised the town in the third century.

Musées de la Cour d'Or

2 rue du Haut Poirier (03.87.68.25.00/http://musees. ca2m.com). Open 9am-5pm Mon, Wed-Fri; 10am-5pm Sat, Sun. Admission €4.60; free-€3.30 reductions.

Formerly a granary and a convent, the Cour d'Or today houses Metz's key museums. It's a vast space with more than 60 rooms built atop ancient Roman baths excavated in the 1930s, the vestiges of which make up the Musée d'Art et d'Histoire on the lower floor. Other permanent exhibits explore the region's architecture and fine art scenes, including a wealth of paintings from the 16th century to the 20th century. There's much to explore here, though the sprawling layout can get confusing. Allow a minimum of two hours to see everything.

Les Trinitaires

12 rue des Trinitaires (03.87.20.03.03/www.les trinitaires.com). Open times vary. Admission varies.

This stunning concert venue, with its sandstone hues and rhythmic arcades, was a convent in a previous life, founded by the religious order of Les Trinitaires. Since 1965 it has

Metz

Historic sites
● ● ● ● ●

Art & architecture
● ● ● ● ●

Hotels
● ● ● ● ●

Eating & drinking
● ● ● ● ●

Nightlife
● ● ● ● ●

Shopping
● ● ● ● ●

been entertaining the city with a range of jazz, rock, *chanson*, hip hop, traditional and classical sounds. There are three refurbished concert spaces: down in the crypt, sit-down events in the theatre, and the large Robert Ochs hall, a former chapel now used mainly for band worship. The venue also helps to host the annual Musiques Volantes and Zikametz festivals.

Eat

Perhaps unsurprisingly for a city with connections to Rabelais, there are many good restaurants here. Most are located in the Centre Ville, but one or two lovely surprises are hidden away in the Ville Allemande. Lorraine's cuisine, like that of neighbouring Alsace, tends towards the hearty – sauerkraut, pork, sausages and beer – as well as quiches and tarts (quiche lorraine and *tarte flambée* are menu staples).

You can buy local produce at the wonderful covered market, formerly the bishops' palace, opposite St-Etienne cathedral (8am-7pm Mon-Sat); look out for the Chez Mauricette stall. Night owls can find excellent wines and local food at Le Strapontin (15 place de Chambre) and Bar à Vins (8 rue des Piques), funky decor and decent cocktails in BSM (2 rue Sainte Marie), and an artsy ambience in tiny, quaint Le Mathis (72 rue En-Fournirue).

"At the helm is chef-musician Christophe Dufossé, whose cuisine eschews regionalism and tradition in favour of innovative fusions."

Au Pampre d'Or
31 pl de Chambre (03.87.74.12.46). Open 7-10.30pm Mon; noon-2.30pm, 7-10.30pm Wed-Sat; noon-2.30pm Sun. €€€€.
Located slap bang in front of the cathedral, Au Pampre d'Or is one of Metz's finest restaurants – and one of the few to have earned a coveted Michelin star. Located in a 17th-century private mansion, it's also a formal affair, with neutral-coloured walls, smartly dressed staff and circular tables decorated with crisp white tablecloths. Chef Jean-Claude Lamaze creates correspondingly classic dishes – truffles, foie gras, game and fish – all cooked to perfection and served with fresh, seasonal accompaniments. In summer dine alfresco and enjoy the great food and impeccable service alongside peerless views of the cathedral.

A la Ville de Lyon
7 rue des Piques (03.87.36.07.01/www.alavilledelyon.com). Open noon-2pm, 7-10pm Tue-Sat. €€€.
A la Ville de Lyon specialises in traditional Lyonnais cooking. Chef Georges Viklovszki serves up impressive dishes such as *quenelles* (dumplings), tripe, and ham with lentils along with superior Côtes du Rhône and Beaujolais wines in two historic, old-fashioned rooms. Romantics will love the smaller room, a 14th-century chapel with a superb vaulted roof. Staff are relaxed but it's definitely a place for dressing up.

La Baraka
25 rue de Chambre (03.87.36.33.92). Open noon-2pm, 7-10pm Mon, Tue, Thur-Sun. €€€.
If you're more in the mood for couscous than quiche, La Baraka is a good option. Adjoining the wonderful Hôtel de la Cathédrale (*see p319*), it enjoys a slightly less refined, more down-to-earth ambience, but serves up Metz's finest Moroccan and Algerian dishes. They're reasonably priced too, and if mint tea's not your thing there are some decent North African wines on the list as well.

Le Bouche à Oreille
46 pl St-Louis (03.87.15.14.66). Open 7-10.30pm Mon; noon-1.30pm, 7-10.30pm Tue-Sat. €€.
Cheese rules supreme at this cheap and cheerful restaurant on charming place St-Louis, with fondues, *tartiflettes* and omelettes all available. The restaurant itself has a ramshackle charm, its walls and ceiling plastered in archaic paraphernalia – saucepans, rustic baskets, even baby clothes. The tables and chairs are simple and wooden, the portions are large, and the staff can be friendly or brusque depending on how busy it is. An unpretentious and inexpensive option.

L'Etude
11 av Robert Schuman (03.87.36.35.32/www.l-etude.com). Open 11.30am-2pm, 7-10pm Mon-Sat. €€€.
L'Etude is one of a handful of swish restaurants situated out in the Ville Allemande. As the name suggests, the place has scholarly pretensions: one wall is lined with books, there's live jazz and *chanson* some weekends, and you'll also find leather armchairs to recline in with a *digestif*. The menu is bursting with edifying options, mostly imaginative takes on traditional French dishes – everything, needless to say, is cooked to perfection and immaculately presented. Impressively, the staff know not only their wines but what's on the bookshelves too. Highly recommended.

Magasin aux Vivres
5 av Ney (03.87.17.17.17/www.citadelle-metz.com). Open noon-2pm, 7.30-10pm Tue-Fri; 7.30-10pm Sat; noon-2pm Sun. €€€€.
Tucked within the plush Citadelle hotel, Magasin aux Vivres opened to rapturous applause in 2005 and almost immediately earned itself a Michelin star. At the helm is chef-musician Christophe Dufossé, whose cuisine eschews staunch regionalism and tradition in favour of innovative fusions. Set in a modern, minimal space that's entirely in keeping with the neighbouring hotel's slick decor, you're

just as likely to find Asian ingredients here as French, though remixes of local classics often appear too. Foodies will enjoy exploring the two *dégustation* options (€85 for seven dishes; €105 for ten). The wine list and service are both immaculate.

Restaurant Maire
1 rue du Pont des Morts (03.87.32.43.12/www. restaurant-maire.com). Open 9am-3pm, 7-10pm Mon, Thur-Sun; 6-10pm Wed. €€€.
Restaurant Maire is one of Metz's more established high-end restaurants, with wonderful riverside views from the terrace and sumptuous food. Yves Maire's dishes tend towards the simple but classic, all lovingly made with fresh, seasonal ingredients. Signature dishes include slow-cooked lamb, and fillet of beef cooked in pinot noir.

Restaurant Thierry
5 rue des Piques (03.87.74.01.23/www.restaurant-thierry.fr). Open noon-3pm, 7-11pm Mon, Tue, Thur-Sat. €€€.
Adventurous diners will enjoy eating here. The Caribbean, Louisiana, South-east Asia – no place is too exotic for chef Thierry Krompholtz, who loves to blend far-flung cuisines in ever more original ways. Green tea soup, seafood tagine, tempura and caramelised piglet cheeks are all utterly delicious. The setting is pleasant too: a 16th-century townhouse that holds on to some traditional bistro elements (exposed brickwork, an open fireplace) while updating with splashes of Asian chic.

Shop

The bustling, pedestrianised rue des Jardins, rue Serpenoise and rue des Clercs (where you'll find Galeries Lafayette) are the places to head to for brand names, as is the sprawling St-Jacques shopping centre. Smaller streets such as pretty rue Taison, rue Ste-Marie and rue de la Chèvre tend towards more independent outlets, while there are crafts and antiques shops aplenty in the Outre-Seille area.

Les Ames Galantes
26 rue Taison (03.87.74.55.22). Open 10am-1pm, 2-7pm Tue-Sat.
This gorgeous boutique on attractive rue Taison stocks a cute yet sophisticated collection of women's clothing that runs the gamut from dresses, coats and blouses to jewellery, belts and hats. Choose from locally made pieces or imported items from independent designers in Paris, Marseille and Lyon.

Antiquités de Treyvy Frédéric
10 rue Tête d'Or (03.87.76.28.27). Open 2.15-7pm Mon-Fri; 10am-noon, 2-7pm Sat.
Located near the train station, this charming antiques shop sells all kinds of trinkets, gewgaws and large furniture pieces. Look out for armoires, ornate full-length mirrors,

elegant crystal, glass and silverware, sculptures, paintings and more. It's a clean and well-lit space, and the owners buy as well as sell.

Le Boite à Chapeaux
19 rue Fontaine (03.87.17.46.58). Open 2.30-7pm Mon; 10am-noon, 2-7pm Tue-Fri; 9.30am-noon, 2-7pm Sat.
If its headgear you're after, the 'Box of Hats' – set in a large room on rue Fontaine – should be able to oblige. Posters of cowboys sporting stetsons squint ruggedly at shoppers as they browse the shop's healthy range of leather Kangols, riding hats, sleek panamas and fancy boaters.

Les Domaines Hennequin
28 rue Tête d'Or (03.87.36.22.50). Open 10am-12.30pm, 2.30-7pm Tue-Fri; 10am-7pm Sat.
Germany may be more renowned for its Mosel wines than France, but the vines grow equally well in parts of Alsace-Lorraine. Not much is produced, though, and even less is exported. But Les Domaines Hennequin is one of the few places you can get clued up on the local grape scene, and the shop also does a good line in champagne and whiskies. There's also a larger retail outlet at 33 bd André Maginot (03.87.75.30.37).

La Ferme Lorraine
2 pl Raymond Mondon (03.87.63.09.09). Open 3.30-7pm Mon; 9am-1pm, 2.30-9pm Tue-Thur; 9am-7pm Fri; 8.30am-6pm Sat.
This bucolic little shop, which is located on a rather busy roundabout near the train station, works on a co-operative basis, stocking fresh local goods from six Lorraine producers. It packs a lot into its small space: cheese, fruit, meat, vegetables, jam, wine and cider, much of it organic. There are fresh quiches and tarts on offer too. If you're planning a bike ride or walk, this is the perfect spot to pick up some picnic ingredients.

Gibus
5 rue des Jardins (no phone). Open 10am-12.30pm, 2.30-7pm Mon-Fri; 10am-7pm Sat.
This smart, attractive store on rue des Jardins stocks a great range of men's and women's fashion, as well as vintage homewares (analog radios, kitsch lamps, funky chairs). The clothes range from seductive blouses and stylish handbags to smart-casual shirts and hip T-shirts. Prices are reasonable, staff are affable.

Stay

There's a fairly good selection of hotels and budget accommodation in Metz, ranging from a flashy four-star to cosy two-stars, spread between the Ville Allemande (which has the advantage of being near the train station) and Centre Ville (which is closer to the shops and key sights). During the summer rooms fill up fast, so book well ahead.

Top left: L'Etude.
Bottom left: Hôtel de
la Cathédrale. Right:
Le Bouche à Oreille.

Pompidou leaves Paris

Since its completion in 1977, the 'inside-out' Centre Pompidou has been a huge success, and its primary colours, exposed pipes and air ducts make it one of the best-known sights in Paris. But it's what's inside that matters too – the museum now holds the largest collection of modern art in Europe, rivalled only in its breadth and quality by MoMA in New York. And herein lies the problem: its vaults contain some 50,000 works by 5,000 artists, but only a fraction – about 600 works – can be displayed at any one time.

The obvious solution was to build another gallery, and on 9 January 2003 the Centre Pompidou and the City of Metz, in conjunction with the Ministry of Culture and Communication, agreed to set up the first decentralised branch of the Pompidou in Metz. The aim was to develop a space with the same *raison d'être* as the original Centre Pompidou, which is namely 'to present and help discover all forms of artistic expression, raise public awareness of the major works of the 20th and 21st century, and take part in Europe's cultural landscape'. And, presumably, to shift some of that stock sitting in the basement in Paris.

So, why Metz? Well, there are several factors involved. The city happened to have a former Roman amphitheatre to offer as a foundation;

it is now only 82 minutes from Paris on the new TGV Est line (it previously took nearly three hours to get between the two); and its position as a European 'crossroads' means excellent access by rail, road and air and a huge cultural catchment area. Since being officially announced the project has moved at an inevitably slow pace, with an initial wildly optimistic completion date of 2007. But Pompidou Metz is now finally set to open its doors in May 2010.

Designed by Shigeru Ban and Jean de Gastines – whose designs were chosen from 157 original competing entries – the building is every bit as architecturally groundbreaking as you'd expect, featuring undulating translucent 'membranes' made from Teflon-coated fibreglass that are intended to emulate the simplicity and flexibility of a Chinese hat. Like its big brother in Beaubourg, the Pompidou Metz will be an adaptable, multi-disciplinary space with three massive tunnel-style galleries, criss-crossed and stacked atop each other like Lego blocks, with huge windows at the ends offering natural light and views of the city. There will also be a separate space for live concerts, plus a shop and restaurant. With a new Louvre outpost due to open in Lens in 2012, it seems that France's cultural compass is firmly stuck on north.

La Citadelle
5 av Ney (03.87.17.17.17/www.citadelle-metz.com). €€€.
Metz's only four-star hotel is located in a refurbished former military supplies depot that dates back to the 16th century. Inside its imposing, linear bulk lurks an incredibly slick hotel that's all deluxe decor and minimalist chic. The 79 rooms are spacious and tastefully decorated with Asian-inspired reds, mauves and blacks. The beds are incredibly comfortable and the expansive bathrooms come complete with rain showers and Anne Sémonin products. There are pleasant views across the promenade de l'Esplanade from the front rooms, and the hotel is right next door to the Arsenal cultural centre. Factor in a swish piano bar, a first-class breakfast and one of the finest restaurants in town (the Magasin aux Vivres, *see p315*), and you have one of Metz's best accommodation options.

Grand Hôtel de Metz
3 rue des Clercs (03.87.36.16.33/www.hotel-metz.com). €€.
This centrally located 62-room hotel has recently been upgraded to a three-star. Set in an 18th-century building, the place feels rather old-fashioned, though there are pleasant surprises such as oversized bathtubs in the mini-suites and free Wi-Fi. Rooms are comfy and roomy enough (especially the prestige rooms, which are immense), though some have better views than others. There's a breakfast buffet included in the rate.

Hotel All Seasons Metz
23 av Foch (03.87.66.81.11/www.accorhotels.com). €€.
This three-star hotel occupies a large 19th-century belle époque building on busy avenue Foch. Its formal interior has been given a zingy, corporate makeover: swirling, patterned carpets, dark brown woods and rowdy splashes of colour in the public areas. Rooms are similarly contemporary, with red, brown and black colour schemes. The suites offer the best views. César's restaurant is downstairs, as is the trendy relaxation salon, which comes complete with square chairs and fireplace. Wi-Fi and breakfast are included in the room price.

Hôtel de la Cathédrale
25 pl de Chambre (03.87.75.00.02/www.hotel cathedrale-metz.fr). €€.
The Hôtel de la Cathédrale, ensconced partly in a 17th-century post office and partly in a medieval house, is a lovely three-star run with pride and passion by a Berber couple who have spent a great deal of time refurbishing both properties. Flush with original features like stone fireplaces and 300-year-old floorboards, the rooms are thoughtfully appointed with matching antiques and collectibles, and embellished with hand-crafted bedlinen, curtains and oriental rugs. Several offer stunning views of the cathedral.

Hôtel Métropole
5 pl du Général de Gaulle (03.87.66.26.22/www.hotelmetropole-metz.com). €.
Close to the main train station, Hôtel Métropole is one of the city's more consistent two-stars. The building dates back to the early 1900s, but the interior is thoroughly modern – positively pseudo-tropical in fact, with cascading waterfalls, chirping budgies and hanging plants in the foyer. The rooms are equally chirpy, with orange and yellow colour schemes. Staff are friendly, the simple rooms are reasonably sized and there's free internet access, underground parking and a pleasant breakfast area. A decent, inexpensive option.

Hôtel du Théâtre
1-3 rue du Pont St-Marcel (03.87.31.10.10/www.hotel-du-theatre-metz.abcsalles.com). €€.
Part hotel, part museum, the Hôtel du Théâtre is a genuine step back into history. Originally an 18th-century home, it has been reconstructed with a wonderful eye for detail. The impressive reception has exposed beams, a stone fireplace and an olde worlde restaurant area, where staff serve in traditional Lorraine uniform. This nostalgic effect is echoed throughout the 66 rooms and suites, which differ in size and shape but contain varying degrees of period detailing (floral curtains, antique furniture, creaking floorboards). Some rooms offer enchanting views of the Moselle and historic parts of the city. Counter-balancing all this heady history are a jacuzzi, sauna, hammam and outdoor pool.

Factfile

When to go
The best time to visit is between April and October, when you can catch the Metz en Fête summer events and the Mirabelle Festival. There are also some charming Christmas markets during late November and early December.

Getting there
The TGV takes just 82mins to get from Paris to Metz. By car, the A31 (Luxembourg to Nancy) and the A4 (Paris to Germany) both pass close to the city. There are five airports less than two hours from Metz (Metz-Nancy-Lorraine, Luxembourg, Saarbrücken, Frankfurt-Hahn and Zweibrücken).

Getting around
Metz is easy to get around on foot. Information about local buses and car hire can be found at the tourist office.

Tourist information
Tourist office 2 pl d'Armes (03.87.55.53.76/http://tourisme.mairie-metz.fr). Open Apr-Sept 9am-7pm Mon-Sat; 10am-5pm Sun. Oct-Mar 9am-7pm Mon-Sat; 10am-3pm Sun.

Internet access
Net C@mpus 8 rue de Paris (03.87.50.39.24). Open 10am-8pm Mon-Fri; 10am-7pm Sat.

Mountains

Auvergne Volcanoes

Feel the earth move under your feet.

The Volcans d'Auvergne is France's largest Parc Naturel Régional, with 395,000 hectares (almost a million acres) of majestic landscape within its boundaries, all created by volcanic eruptions between five and a half million and six and a half thousand years ago. If you love Scotland, you'll love this: vast swathes of raw countryside bursting in summer with butterflies and rare plants, and covered in winter with a picturesque veil of snow. The area is also France's third biggest winter sports destination, with two main ski resorts and hundreds of kilometres of cross-country skiing on offer.

The park is divided into five main areas, four of which are volcanic. The bite-sized Chaîne des Puys, a range of 75 volcanic peaks and craters laid out across a high-altitude plateau, makes a fascinating introduction to volcanology with day or half-day walks leading to volcanic summits where you can peer inside the craters. The Mont-Dore region is home to France's very own Lake District and the Auvergne's main ski area, which revolves around the 1,886-metre (6,186 feet) Puy de Sancy. Further south, the Artense is a granite plateau that borders the Dordogne river, while the Cézalier region is a vast area of lava flow that has given rise to a plateau punctuated with lakes and peat bogs. Last but by no means least, the Monts du Cantal together form Europe's largest volcano, whose multiple eruptions and glacial movements have created the deep valleys that run down from the peak of Puy Mary.

A Parc Naturel Régional, as opposed to a Parc National, is an inhabited area and its purpose is not only to protect natural species but also to promote sustainable development. To this worthy end, a forward-thinking approach to tourism has resulted in some marvellous places to stay and ways to visit the region that make less of an imprint on the landscape, while allowing you to experience the Auvergne's precarious and fascinating ecology.

Explore

CLERMONT-FERRAND & THE CHAINE DES PUYS

Built on a long-extinct volcano, and the only major city within the Massif Central, Clermont-Ferrand is a surprisingly cultivated place with an illustrious past. Local hero Vercingétorix put up a brave resistance to the Romans in 52 BC, and thereafter it became an important Gallo-Roman trading city on the Via Aggrippa. From this heritage comes the beautiful Romanesque basilica of Notre-Dame-du-Port, a UNESCO World Heritage site that has just reopened after major renovation. The tourist office houses a Romanesque art centre exhibiting pieces from this and the five other important Romanesque churches in the area.

Looming over the city is the black Gothic cathedral of Notre-Dame, built in the 13th century from pierre de Volvic, a black stone whose breeze block-like consistency testifies to its volcanic past. Leading up to the cathedral, the old town has winding cobbled streets lined with medieval, Renaissance and art nouveau buildings that now house art galleries, wine bars and restaurants. Underneath are cellars three or four storeys deep that have been used for st-nectaire ripening, resistance activity and refuge when the Michelin tyre factory was bombed in 1944. Michelin is still synonymous with the city, and a brand new attraction charts its history, inventions and iconography. Clermont-Ferrand's other claim to fame is as the birthplace of philosopher Blaise Pascal, though the house, near the cathedral, no longer exists.

After visiting nearby Vulcania, the no-expense-spared science park built right into the heart of the volcanic chain and well worth a visit, you can explore the neighbouring volcanoes for yourself on well-signposted walks such as Le Pariou (start from the Aire des Goules car park on the D941B about eight kilometres/five miles from Clermont-Ferrand), a two-hour hike up and down a volcanic peak with a view into the crater from the top. The south-east side of Le Pariou has been protected by a wooden staircase that makes climbing easier; descending by the other side to make a circular route is not advisable before mid April as it can be icy.

Le Puy des Goules is a slightly longer walk (2.5hrs) from the same car park, while the summit of Puy de Dôme only takes 45 minutes from its viewpoint off the D941A (inaccessible in winter, but a breathtaking view in summer). There are medieval villages to explore too, such as Montfermy (12 kilometres/7.5 miles north-west of Vulcania) with its 12th-century frescoed church and a summer restaurant, and Montpeyroux (17 kilometres/10.5 miles south of Clermont-Ferrand just off the A75), a fortified village with a dungeon tower, Romanesque church and fabulous views.

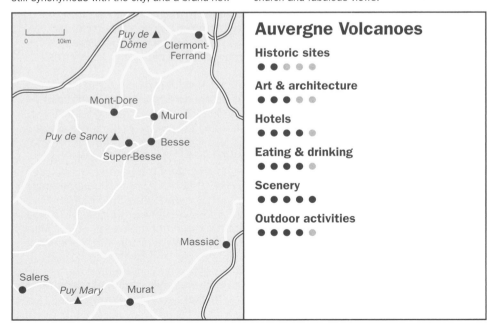

Auvergne Volcanoes

Historic sites
● ● ○ ○ ○

Art & architecture
● ● ● ○ ○

Hotels
● ● ● ● ○

Eating & drinking
● ● ● ● ○

Scenery
● ● ● ● ●

Outdoor activities
● ● ● ● ○

L'Aventure Michelin

Clermont-Ferrand *32 rue du Clos Four (04.73.98.60.60/www.laventuremichelin.com). Open 10am-6pm Tue-Sun (till 7pm July, Aug). Admission €8; €5 reductions.*
This exhibition combines digital technology with vintage vehicles, advertisements and maps to explore the world of the roly-poly Michelin man. Exhibits include the 1944 *Michelin Guide* used for the Normandy Landings.

Volcan de Lemptégy

15km N of Clermont-Ferrand *St-Ours-les-Roches (04.73.62.23.25/www.auvergne-volcan.com). Open times vary. Closed Nov-Feb. Admission €9; €7 reductions.*
A good follow-on from Vulcania, this open-air mining museum allows you to see, touch and climb on the different types of volcanic rock you've just learned about. Walk the site with a knowledgeable guide, or visit on a little train, followed by a 3D film to thrill the kids.

Vulcania

15km N of Clermont-Ferrand *St-Ours-les-Roches (08.20.82.78.28/www.vulcania.com). Open times vary. Closed mid Nov-mid Mar. Admission €21; €15 reductions.*
Don't listen to locals who say that Vulcania was a waste of money: they just hate the fact that it was Valéry Giscard d'Estaing's project. This is perhaps Europe's finest science museum. The visit takes you deep into the bowels of the earth with imaginative, interactive exhibits bringing volcanology to life. You'll stare into a foaming, fiery volcanic crater; be pelted with water, air, heat and vibrations as you experience a hypothetical re-eruption of the Auvergne's volcanoes; and be strapped into your cinema seat for a 3D ride through mankind's mythological interpretations of the monsters that cause the earth to move. More intellectual souls will be delighted by the first edition of Sir William Hamilton's 1776 account of the eruption of Mt Etna. If one day's eruption is not enough you can enter again for €2 any day for a week; just pick up a free leaflet at the entrance.

LES MONTS-DORE

This ski area has two main resorts, Super-Besse and Mont-Dore, plus the little family resort of Chastreix-Sancy. From Super-Besse (1,350 metres-1,850 metres/4,500 feet-6,000 feet), you can ski over the mountain to Mont-Dore, and the two resorts offer a fairly impressive combined total of 86 kilometres (54 miles) of downhill skiing, including no less than six black runs. A host of more unusual winter sports are on offer too, from husky driving to speed riding (a ski-paragliding hybrid) and skijöring. On the way up the mountain stop off at Besse, a pretty little country town with a thriving market. This area is also a well-known centre for thermal health treatments, and the 19th-century *thermes* at Mont-Dore are magnificent. The ski lifts operate all year round, in summer taking mountain bikes up the pistes.

The Massif du Sancy is France's very own Lake District, with the surrounding mountains and forests reflected in the glassy waters. On the D996 between Besse and Mont-Dore, the mirror-like Lac Chambon is a great place for swimming, fishing or messing around on boats. In summer you can sunbathe on its two beaches, and the nearby village of Murol is worth a detour for its dramatic medieval castle. The perfectly circular Lac Pavin near Super-Besse is a rare meromictic lake (where two layers of water never mix) located in the crater of a volcano that could potentially erupt again. At 1,244 metres (4,100 feet), Lac de Guéry, on the D993 north of Mont-Dore, is frozen over during winter. But at the beginning of March (dates differ according to weather conditions) an armada of fishermen descend with shovels and rods for the opening of the *pêche blanche* season – fishing, Inuit-style, through holes in the thick ice – which goes on for two to three weeks.

Musée de la Toinette

6km NE of Mont-Dore *Murat-le-Quaire (04.73.81.12.28/www.toinette.com). Open Sept-mid Nov, mid Dec-Easter 10am-noon, 2-6pm daily. Easter-Aug 10am-noon, 2-7pm daily. Closed mid Nov-mid Dec. Admission €5.60; €3.30 reductions.*
This museum of rural life in an old farmhouse near the spa town of La Bourboule evokes an emotional response. As you move through the authentic room sets replete with images, sounds and smells, you are guided by the voice of Toinette, the 19th-century peasant who lived here.

CANTAL

Once you get to Cantal you may regret that you didn't spend your entire holiday here – the wild countryside is truly majestic. To get here from Clermont-Ferrand you can speed down the motorway (1.5hrs), getting off at Massiac, after which it's a pretty drive through a sweeping landscape of hillsides, small villages and drystone-walled fields where Salers cattle graze. En route, stop off at the Maison de la Pinatelle in Chalinargues (off the N122, 15 kilometres/ ten miles before Murat), an eco-museum that provides an educational introduction to the Cantal. The gastronomic Le Jarrousset restaurant (*see p326*) just before Murat makes a fine lunch stop. Alternatively, the cross-country route to the Cantal from Besse takes you across the Cézalier plateau, where you can visit La Godivelle, the Volcans d'Auvergne's highest and tiniest community with just 22 inhabitants. The village is sandwiched between two beautiful lakes and surrounded by a nature reserve containing some 80 protected species.

The whole of the Cantal is a massive volcano, 70 kilometres (45 miles) in diameter, whose seven steep valleys were carved out by glaciers. In the centre is the 1,783-metre (5,848 feet) peak of Puy Mary. Inaccessible from November to May, in summer the roads are clogged by more than half a million visitors who come to marvel at the incredible view, which stretches as far as Mont Blanc on a clear day. By 2010, however, the jams should have eased. Four new visitor centres are being converted out of old rural buildings in Mandailles, Dienne, Le Falgoux and Le Claux. Minibuses will then link the different sites and allow visitors to appreciate the views without clogging up the roads.

If the fashionable Salers burger has not yet reached a gastropub near you, you can taste one in the medieval town of Salers where a statue of the man who saved this rare breed and revived a community presides over the main square. Several attractive hotels and restaurants now inhabit its ancient buildings. Salers is just a 30-kilometre (20 miles) hop across a mountain pass from Dienne in summer, but in winter it involves a 100-kilometre (60 miles) detour via the bustling Cantal capital of Aurillac, a great place to stock up on local wine and cheese.

Eat

The Auvergne is the belly of France, with its gutsy *cuisine de terroir* that makes the most of the richly flavoured local produce. Immerse yourself in the five AOC cheeses of the region – cantal, salers, st-nectaire, bleu d'auvergne and fourme d'ambert – by following the Route des Fromages (www.fromages-aoc-auvergne.com). Brown road signs point you in the direction of 40 farms and dairies ready to show you how the cheeses are made and give you a tasting. In addition, the Parc Naturel Régional des Volcans d'Auvergne label has been awarded to several products that are made within the park: Salers beef, Avèze gentian liqueur, three types of honey, and three types of pâtisserie.

The staple dishes of Auvergne cooking – *pounti* (a savoury cake made with pork, swiss chard and prunes), *tripoux* (tripe), *truffade* (a rich gratin of potatoes, bacon and cheese), and *potée* (a stew of pork leg, sausage and cabbage) – make their way on to just about every menu in the region, ranging from farmhouse fare to refined interpretations. The lively, fruity and reasonably priced Côtes d'Auvergne wines are a real discovery: don't miss out on a visit to Desprat Vins in Aurillac (10 av JB Veyre, 04.71.48.58.44, www.vin-passion.com).

Auberge de la Golmotte
Monts-Dore *Le Barbier, 2.5km from Mont-Dore on the Clermont-Ferrand road (04.73.65.05.77/www.auberge lagolmotte.com). Open noon-2.30pm, 7-9pm Wed-Sat; noon-2.30pm Sun.* €€.

One of the most charming things about this roadside *auberge* with its rustic interior is the fresh *ombleu* fish swimming in a trough outside. Each day chef Michel Longuet catches them with his bare hands to cook up for his clients. Reasonably priced menus start at €16, but it's worth splashing out on the gourmet €34 menu with delicacies such as crayfish salad with chestnuts, warm quail with honey and vinegar, and venison with red fruits.

Le Boeuf dans l'Assiette
Monts-Dore *Av Michel Bertrand, Mont-Dore (04.73.65.01.23). Open noon-2pm, 7-9.30pm Tue-Sun.* €€.
Great steaks cooked on an open fire in the centre of the room, accompanied by lashings of fresh green salad and *frites*, all washed down with a glass of local Côtes d'Auvergne. This simple formula makes the restaurant a hit with locals and tourists alike. Portions are copious: the *salade auvergnate* starter with cantal cheese, cured ham and walnuts would constitute a main in most other restaurants.

> "The Auvergne is the belly of France, with its gutsy *cuisine de terroir* that makes the most of the richly flavoured local produce."

Le Chardonnay
Clermont-Ferrand *1 pl Philippe Marcombes (04.73.90.18.28). Open noon-2pm, 7.30-10pm Mon-Fri; 7.30-10pm Sat.* €€.
Le Chardonnay is a very decent wine bar and restaurant with seriously good food and a buzzing atmosphere. A black interior gives it a trendy feel, and you can choose between sitting at the bar for a glass of wine from one of the 500 bottles in the cellar, or table seating for a bistro meal. The menu concentrates on meat (several variations on pork and duck), though you can also try locally fished *ombleu* here, and of course AOC cheeses. Reserve in advance.

Le Jarrousset
Cantal *RN122, 2km E of Murat (04.71.20.10.69/ www.restaurant-le-jarrousset.com). Open call for details.* €€€.
Chef Jérôme Cazanave is bringing it all back home. After stints with Bocuse, Bras and Westermann, he has set up his own gastronomic restaurant in his native Auvergne, where he sources the best local produce. What looks like a roadside *relais* in the middle of nowhere hides a smart dining room with modern art on the walls and a panoramic view of the mountains. Expect crisp white tablecloths and elegant service as you enjoy Salers beef with ginger and cardamom or a neat cabbage parcel of pig's foot and ear with foie gras

Top: Vulcania.
Bottom: Le Jarrousset.

and white lentils. After this rich fare, the 'wink at the Massiac countryside', a concoction of apple, sorbets and calvados, comes as a refreshing stroke of genius.

L'Oustagou

Clermont-Ferrand *1 rue du Terrail (04.73.90.72.01/ www.oustagou.fr). Open noon-2.30pm, 7-11pm Mon-Fri; noon-2.30pm, 7-11.30pm Sat; noon-2.30pm, 7-10.30pm Sun. €€.*
L'Oustagou, set across three floors right beside the cathedral, is the ideal place to sample some Auvergne specialities. The best thing of all is the *plateau de fromages*: for just €3 you can take your pick from six AOC cheeses from a wooden board that is generously left on the table, accompanied by crusty bread. Try gaperon, a garlic-flavoured cheese that is so strong it rarely makes it out of the region. The carafe wine at €3.50 for 25cl is very drinkable, and the energetic young waitress who speeds up and down the stairs deserves a medal.

Relais du Col de la Moréno

Chaîne des Puys *Col de la Moréno (on the D942), 10km W of Clermont-Ferrand (04.73.87.16.46/ www.aubergemoreno.com). Open noon-1.30pm Mon, Tue; noon-1.30pm, 7.30-9pm Thur-Sat; 7.15-8.30pm Sun. €€.*
Enjoy one of best *truffades* in the region, made to Raphael's grandmother's recipe with lashings of cheese and tasty pork morsels in the potato mix. It comes with salad and charcuterie, or can be served as a side dish to accompany Salers beef, boned pig's foot or the excellent perch fillet cooked in lard with a vinegar jus and mushrooms. Book early to reserve a table in the room with the roaring log fire; the other one is not quite so cosy. There are also six slightly spartan but very clean rooms and a self-contained family apartment on site.

Stay

Alta Terra

Cantal *Lavigerie (on the D680), 14km NE of Murat (04.71.20.83.03/www.altaterra-cantal.com). €.*
This old roadside *relais* has been done up by a young Franco-Swiss couple in eco-friendly style. There are two double and two family rooms with pine panelling, feather wall insulation and pretty *brocante* finds, plus a sauna, hammam and outdoor hot tub. The restaurant part of the *relais*, decorated with 1960s kitsch and old maps, is now a *café gourmande* serving herbal teas, cakes and quiches. A very sweet children's corner includes a tiny bed for weary toddlers.

Auberge Ayjean

Cantal *La Gandilhon, Lavigerie (on the D680), 14km NE of Murat (04.71.20.83.43/www.auberge-puy-mary.com). €.*
Auberge Ayjean is the last house before you reach the Col du Pas de Peyrol, and is a beautifully converted barn where owner Valérie Fabre's father used to house his calves. Its six spacious rooms have a natural feel, with beams, stone walls and neutral linen fabrics. Most guests take the half-board package as the chef serves up wonderful *cuisine de terroir*, and wine buffs are in heaven browsing the 500-plus bottles in the walk-in *cave*. A limited number of tables are available for non-residents but reserve in advance, especially in summer.

Auberge de Mazayes

Chaîne des Puys *Mazayes-Basses, 25km W of Clermont-Ferrand (04.73.88.93.30/www.auberge-mazayes.com). €€.*
A drowsy cat rolls in the grass, Targus the boxer slopes under a table and Tony (one of the owners) walks in with armfuls of the freshly picked flowers he arranges week by week. A perfect hideaway with superb *cuisine du terroir*, the Auberge de Mazayes is the kind of place you could hole up in for a week just to chill out. But if you're feeling energetic there are a host of signposted walks starting from this sleepy hollow. The 15 rooms in the converted farm building have antiques, original art, floral bedspreads, beams and volcanic stone walls, with modern white bathrooms. Breakfast (€9) is served outside in summer.

Auberge des Montagnes

Cantal *Pailherols, 30km E of Aurillac (04.71.47.57.01/ www.auberge-des-montagnes.com). €.*
This magical place has been in the same family for five generations, having started life as a hunters' lodge in 1880. The Cambourien family now own half the village, with one of their twin daughters running pâtisserie courses in a second hotel overlooking its own trout-filled lake (you can fish and she will cook it up for you). With tartan fabrics, club chairs, a roaring fire and umbrella stands filled with ancient walking sticks, the *auberge* feels like a trip back to the 1920s, and the fantasy continues with rides in Monsieur Cambourien's horse-drawn sled or *calèche*. The other twin daughter married a talented chef, who now cooks up imaginative, beautifully presented dishes (menus from €21).

Le Bailliage

Cantal *rue Notre-Dame, Salers (04.71.40.71.95/ www.salers-hotel-bailliage.com). €€.*
Le Bailliage is both grand and great fun, as Madame Gouzon, its bubbly owner, has given free rein to her interior decorating fantasy. Thus, in this traditional Auvergnat village, you can book into the sexy Marilyn suite, the Zen suite, or the Nature and Mountain suites with walls of wood and pebbles. Husband Jean-Michel is the award-winning chef in Le Bailliage's restaurant, the perfect place to enjoy Salers beef with a *forestière* sauce, *foie gras poêlée* and AOC cheeses in a dressed-up setting with impeccable service.

Datcha Anastasia

Monts-Dore *St-Anastaise, 8km S of Besse (04.73.71.21.84/chambres-d-hotes-auvergne. blogspot.com). No credit cards. €.*
Joel Charbonnel and Gérard Lombardi offer a gay-friendly welcome in their gorgeously restored farmhouse in this tiny hamlet near Besse. Not for nothing is it called a *datcha* – the couple lived in Moscow for three years, and have filled the three-floor house with exquisite objects from their travels,

Landscape portraits

What links the following – a huge barcode spread out on a mountainside, giant letters spelling MAINTENANT floating across a lake, a hillside like a cow's flank whose spots have been munched into the landscape by the cows themselves, and bamboo instruments played by the wind? The answer is they were all massive open-air installations that transformed the summer landscape of the Massif du Sancy for the first time in 2007 as part of the annual Horizons festival of art and nature (www.horizons-sancy.com), which is fast establishing a reputation as an international rendezvous for land art.

'It was an ambitious idea,' says Luc Stelly of the Sancy Tourist Office. 'We wanted to show that the Massif du Sancy is not just a winter destination, and to do something modern and daring in the Auvergne. It's all credit to the mayors of the 11 different *communes* that they saw its potential.'

Each *commune* gives €8,000 to an artist to create a work each summer, which is not a lot when you consider the scale of the works on show. The whole community gets involved, putting up the artists and helping to create the work. For Laeticia Carlotti's *Ondes et Cible* (2008) schoolchildren collected some 15,000 spent gun cartridges left by hunters and formed a huge target on the landscape. For Jean-Paul Ganem's *Projet Pré Vache Clôture* (2007) local farmers lent their cows to graze circular patches into the hillside. On the opening day of the festival a fleet of coaches take the artists, judges and locals on a magical mystery tour of the 11 artworks.

The works have an environmental theme, commenting on the fragility of the planet and nature's amazing ability to reclaim. After green turns to brown these ephemeral works start to disappear into the landscape, and by the following summer a blank canvas awaits a new group of artists.

Left: Auberge des Montagnes. Right: Datcha Anastasia.

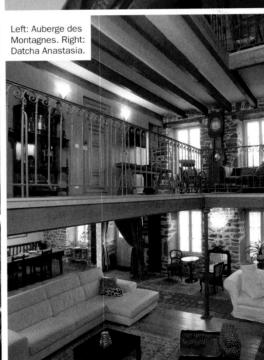

together with 20th-century design classics. Choose from the Japanese room with two futons and geisha pillows, the art deco yellow room or the funky African room in the eaves. Bathrooms are shared, but there are plans to add an en suite shower to the African room. Joel will also cook you a delicious evening meal for an additional €17.

Fortuniès 1864
Cantal *Fortuniès, 2.5km NE of Dienne (04.71.20.83.01). No credit cards. €€.*
This old house is a passion for Jean-Baptiste, Samuel and Marie-Julie, childhood friends who discovered the place while out mountain biking and dreamed of restoring it. Their concept is brilliantly thought out: two fully furnished *eco-gîtes* where you can have as little or as much autonomy as you want. A computer screen in the wall holds all their secrets and tips about local markets, biking routes and the like, or you can opt for a full *traiteur* service. The decor combines contemporary design (a steel-clad shower) with remnants of the past (a curtained bed in a cubby-hole, volcanic stone walls). The setting, with a churchyard overlooking a ravine, is pure magic.

Hôtel Saluces
Cantal *rue de la Martille, Salers (04.71.40.70.82/ www.hotel-salers.fr). €€.*
The 16th-century residence of the governor of Salers is now a tasteful hotel with eight individually decorated rooms in nuanced fabrics, with marble and slate tiles in the bathrooms. An adjoining property is being added to the ensemble containing a queenly suite. Though it is classed as a hotel this feels more like a home, and you can pop down any time to the tearoom with its piano on the ground floor. In summer, breakfast is in the flower-filled courtyard garden.

La Roussière
Cantal *St Clément, Pailherols, 30km E of Aurillac (04.71.49.67.34/www.laroussiere.fr). No credit cards. €€.*
At the foot of the Plomb du Cantal, this old farmhouse has been transformed into a spacious and welcoming *chambre d'hôte*. There are three en suite bedrooms and an attic dormitory for kids. As it is isolated most guests opt for the *table d'hôte*, where you eat an evening meal with your host – a chance to enjoy Monsieur Gregoir's organic vegetables from the garden and tap his amazing knowledge of local history and walking routes.

Le Sancy
Monts-Dore *Pl Alfred Pipet, Besse (04.73.79.50.13/ www.hotel-sancy-besse.com). €.*
This family-run hotel in the village of Besse doubles as a popular local brasserie and *tabac* where skiers and locals crowd in for no-nonsense *steak-frites* and carafes of red at lunchtime. Above, there are nine sunny rooms with the same simple style: checked fabric, pine furniture and old photographs from the mountains, with clean white bathrooms. Most of the rooms can sleep four. Friendly owner Madame Sapchat only adds to the charm factor.

Factfile

When to go
The Auvergne is a year-round destination, with the exception of November and early December when most hotels and restaurants close. Its exposed position gives weather conditions at 1,500m (5,000ft) similar to those much higher up in the Alps, providing downhill and cross-country skiing from late November through to the end of April. The small peaks of the Chaîne des Puys can be walked in boots even in winter, but the main tourist attraction, Vulcania, is closed from mid November to mid March. In the Cantal, Puy Mary and its roads are closed by snow all winter. After the snow melts, the rich and rare flora and fauna of this natural park burst back into life, and the ski lifts transform into walkers' lifts to the high plateau. The park is criss-crossed by both GR routes and short signposted walks. There is fabulous mountain biking and horse riding in the Cantal, and signposted cycle touring too.

Getting there
The Auvergne is increasingly accessible from Britain by flights to Limoges and Rodez (Ryanair). Direct TGV trains from Paris to Clermont-Ferrand take 3.5hrs.

Getting around
Buses from the train station in Clermont-Ferrand will take you to Super-Besse, and Mont-Dore has a train station. A train route from Clermont travels through the Cantal from Massiac through Murat and Vic-sur-Cère to Aurillac (following the N122). You could feasibly arrange a pick-up to take you to any of the accommodation near this route (Pailherols, Fortuniès) and spend the rest of your holiday exploring on foot, horse or bike. But a car allows you to discover a lot more. You can rent one from Clermont, Aurillac or the airports.

Tourist information
Auvergne region Comité Regional de Tourisme de l'Auvergne (www.auvergne-tourisme.info).
Besse (04.73.79.52.84/www.sancy.com).
Cantal (04.71.60.58.21/www.cantaltourisme.fr).
Clermont-Ferrand Pl de la Victoire (04.73.98.65.00/www.clermont-fd.com).
Mont-Dore (04.73.65.20.21/www.sancy.com).

Internet access
Clermont-Ferrand Atlanteam, 11 av Carnot (04.73.14.99.76/www.atlanteam.com).
Open 10am-midnight Mon-Sat; 2-10pm Sun.

Aiguille du Midi; Chamonix town centre.

Chamonix Valley

Whether you're hiking or boarding, this is as tough as it gets.

Like Hawaii's North Shore among surfers, Chamonix's name echoes with a mythological resonance for skiers the world over, many of whom speak intimately about descents they've never laid eyes upon, let alone skied. Nor do the mammoth peaks disappoint when devotees finally wind their way to this mountain mecca; from the slumped cone of Mont Blanc to the jagged spine of Brévent, the overwhelming scale of Chamonix's surroundings mean that newcomers tend to wander around with eyes on the skies and jaws firmly on the floor.

For all that, Chamonix is a year-round destination as popular with climbers, hikers and cyclists in summer as it is with skiers and snowboarders in winter. Nor does it feel like a 'resort' in the conventional sense; a working town with a distinct local identity, Chamonix is both self-contained and culturally expansive, with traditional Savoyard eateries nestling up to Michelin-starred restaurants, boutique eco-hotels, internationally renowned cocktail bars and clubs kicking into the small hours.

For most, however, a holiday in Chamonix is so physically demanding that even mustering the energy to sip a beer after dinner can require a massive effort. Those who do go out will often settle on a quieter bar a short walk from the clamorous town square, where they can sit by the fireside and relate stories of the day's adventures – be they skiing the off-piste powder of the Vallée Blanche, hiking immortal Mont Blanc, climbing the south-east face of Brévent or negotiating the steep, technical mountain biking trails of Flégère.

And while there are as few posers as there are complete beginners when it comes to outdoor sports in Chamonix – the mountains are seldom easy going for either – those simply seeking a stunning location in which to rest and rekindle their relationship with nature need look no further than this most sublime and inspirational of valleys.

Explore

CENTRAL & WESTERN CHAMONIX

Chamonix's main square, place Balmat, is a bustling spot beside the rushing Arve river, its numerous café terraces perfect for watching lazy summer afternoons fade into evening over a bottle or two. The centre of attention is a dramatic statue of Horace-Bénédict de Saussure, the 18th-century Swiss physicist widely regarded as the founding father of alpinism, and Chamonix-born Jacques Balmat, part of the first team to successfully ascend Mont Blanc; the latter's stone effigy points excitedly at its slumped snowcap to this day.

The majority of bars and restaurants crammed into the square are tourist-friendly – from pizza places to big-screen sports bars. Yet it's neighbouring rue des Moulins that locals once bitterly referred to as the 'rue d'Anglais' for its transient population of Brits. Several of the British-owned bars aggravating Anglo-French tensions – including the likes of Cybar and Dicks Tea Bar – were destroyed by fire in early 2006, and those venues that have risen in their place are decidedly more continental; best of the bunch is Soul Food, a diminutive sweatbox plastered with funk album covers and owned by dreadlocked vinyl junkies who beat bongos when not serving cocktails to a largely French crowd.

The surrounding streets are peppered with a mix of chocolate-box stores plying tourists with hard-carved Savoyard trinkets, upmarket fashion retailers satisfying local cravings for fur coats and, not surprisingly, adventure shops selling and hiring ski and hiking equipment.

The tourist office is a good place to pick up information on local events and lift closures. The latter often sees disgruntled skiers cross the road to the three-screen Cinéma Vox, which shows films in both French and English, and hosts extra screenings in extended periods of bad weather. Those with money to burn may also lighten their mood (and their wallets) at the local casino on place de Saussure, home to a smart restaurant and tables hosting roulette, blackjack and poker.

Further west, the pedestrianised promenade du Fori winds around a cluster of modern buildings with endearing rounded roofs: covered in snow the impression is of an alien city; in summer a serene Teletubby village. First among these is the grand municipal library (route de la Patinoire, 04.50.53.34.82, www.bibliomontblanc.com), site of regular cultural exhibitions; nearby is the Richard Bozon sports centre (214 avenue de la Plage, 04.50.53.23.70), which boasts swimming, sauna and steam facilities, tennis courts covered and otherwise, a roofed ice rink and a crash-matted indoor climbing wall.

Many of those practising their monkey moves at the latter can be found putting them to the test at the Gaillands rock face on the far western side of

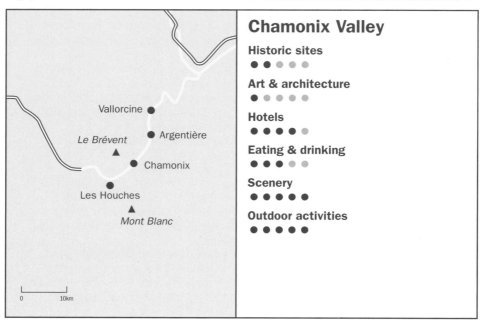

Chamonix Valley

Historic sites
● ● ● ● ●

Art & architecture
● ● ● ● ●

Hotels
● ● ● ● ○

Eating & drinking
● ● ● ● ○

Scenery
● ● ● ● ●

Outdoor activities
● ● ● ● ●

Vallorcine

Le Brévent
▲

Argentière ●

Chamonix ●

Les Houches ●
▲
Mont Blanc

0   10km

Aiguille du Midi.

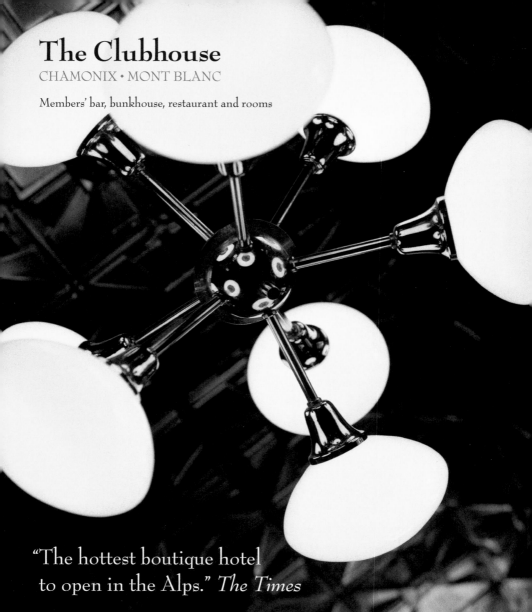

The Clubhouse
CHAMONIX · MONT BLANC

Members' bar, bunkhouse, restaurant and rooms

"The hottest boutique hotel
to open in the Alps." *The Times*

"One of the 25 coolest places on earth" *Arena*
"The restaurant is *the* place to dine." *Elle*
"Part Bond lair, part world-class cocktail bar, part ski hub." *The Observer*

Bookings, membership and dinner reservations: please see our website (clubhouse.fr),
visit in person or call us on +33 4 50 90 96 56.

the resort, the routes of which are regularly discussed over a few cold beers at hip hotel Le Vert (see p345), a short walk away on route des Gaillands.

The closest lift to the town centre is the recently refurbished Planpraz gondola, from the top of which the vertiginous cable car to the jagged 2,525-metre (8,300 feet) spire of Brévent accesses a steep and unsettling black run that regularly gets the better of unwary intermediates. In summer it makes for a fantastic walk, the path curling as it does around various stone outcrops popular with serious climbers. The neighbouring area of La Flégère is better suited to intermediate skiers, with a host of challenging reds winding their way down from the peaks of 2,415-metre (7,900 feet) Col Cornu and 2,395-metre (7,850 feet) L'Index respectively.

Musée Alpin

89 av Michel Croz (04.50.53.25.93). Open 2-7pm daily. Admission €5.50; free-€4.30 reductions.
Chamonix's Musée Alpin, on the south side of the river, expounds the history of the surrounding mountains as well as the development of the world's most famous ski resort, with wonderful vintage posters, maps and photographs sitting alongside geological exhibits, not all of them adequately signed in English.

CHAMONIX SUD & L'AIGUILLE DU MIDI

South-west of the centre lies the peripheral party town of Chamonix Sud, a cluster of bars and eateries with more character and fewer crowds than many of their central peers. Cham Sud's proximity to the cable car accessing the 3,840-metre (12,600 feet) Aiguille du Midi makes it popular with powder hounds as well as party animals – Chamonix's soft stuff is as famous for its depth as for the speed with which it is tracked out after a heavy snowfall, which makes every minute count when it comes to being first in line the next morning. And there are few mountains worldwide with a reputation quite like the Aiguille du Midi (the name means 'needle of midday', a reference to the way the sun hovers over the peak at noon), which nestles up to the intimidating cone of 4,807-metre (15,770 feet) Mont Blanc.

A quick glance at the piste map reveals no colourful network of groomed runs, but rather a single dotted red line snaking around the back of the uppermost lift station and winding its way a full 24 kilometres (15 miles) down the majestic white face. This is the famous Vallée Blanche, an off-piste route known for its length and staggering glacial beauty rather than its steepness per se (snowboarders will struggle on the flatter sections), but a notoriously perilous path all the same thanks to the number of crevasses lying unseen on all sides, which regularly claim the lives of unguided and inexperienced skiers.

It's also the spot where Mary Shelley, who visited Chamonix in 1816 while writing *Frankenstein*, set the final showdown between monster and maker.

Not that a trip to the top of the Aiguille need be so potentially risky a pursuit; plenty of visitors make the ascent without equipment of any kind. The thrill of the cable car ride itself is enough to tempt many, while others relish the opportunity of dining at the topmost café – reputed to be Europe's highest eaterie. Most, however, come simply for the views, which are breathtaking in the extreme.

LES HOUCHES

Its relative distance from Chamonix (six kilometres/3.75 miles) means that visitor numbers to Les Houches are significantly fewer than in the main resort. But its cheaper accommodation pulls in plenty of travellers on a budget (although many of the town's modern developments are themselves a fair slog from the picturesque centre), and the abundance of uncrowded, authentically French eating and drinking options appeals to those keen to avoid the British hordes.

Beside the central Baroque Saint Jean-Baptiste chapel, a small museum, the Musée Montagnard, illuminates the development of the village with vintage photographs, art and artefacts, with changing exhibitions highlighting the often harsh life faced by settlers through the ages. There are also several guided tours operating in summer, including one exploring Les Houches's churches and another focusing on the 1930s construction of its awesome 25-metre (82 feet) statue of Christ – overlooking a local forest and floodlit at night, this white stone redeemer recalls Rio de Janeiro's, unveiled around the same time.

A third tour centres on the engineering of the Les Houches lift system, which today constitutes the shuddering Bellevue cable car, queue-plagued at peak times, and the recently renovated Prarion bubble lift, which ascends the far side of the same mountain. Both are open throughout the summer, making for pleasant downhill hikes, although there are some similarly lovely walks leading from Les Houches itself. One such wander accesses the Merlet Animal Park (04.50.53.47.89, www.parcdemerlet.com, open May-Sept), where ibex, chamois, marmots and deer roam freely around a restaurant and exhibition centre. Another trail leads to the Carlaveyron Nature Reserve (04.50.54.02.24), with its uppermost glacial terrain overlooking lush forest and the dramatic waterfalls of the Gorges de la Diosaz (04.50.47.21.13, www.gorgesdeladiosaz.com, open June-Sept).

Such surroundings naturally lend themselves to the pursuit of outdoor activities, with paragliding, white water rafting and mountain biking all organised during summer by Cham Aventure

(04.50.53.55.70, www.cham-aventure.com). There are also two separate outdoor climbing areas – one at Les Chavants and another in the neighbouring village of Plaine St Jean – plus a good indoor wall, the regionally renowned Mont Blanc Escalade (04.50.54.76.48, www. montblancescalade.com). Clamberers can also make use of a handful of Tyrolean treetop walkways, including one at Indiana Ventures (2185 Route de Coupeau, 04.50.49.48.60, www.indianaventures.com).

If Les Houches is a less popular winter destination, that's partly due to its relatively low altitude and the lingering problem of its lifts being left off the standard Chamonix pass (you'll need either a local pass or the pricier Mont Blanc Unlimited card). That said, the low altitude issue comes into its own when Chamonix proper is assailed by bad weather (the Les Houches lifts are often working when everything in Chamonix shuts down, in which case they become included on the standard pass). The lift system struggles to support the entire valley's skiers and boarders simultaneously, but visibility is seldom a problem on its wonderful tree runs, including some hairy off-piste lines beneath the cable car and some long reds and blues under the bubble. The uppermost slopes also boast some of the region's few decent beginner runs, which combine with the lack of crowds to make Les Houches a better bet for first-timers than central Chamonix.

Its on-slope eating options are also a cut above the average; many consider Les Vieilles Luges, on the Aillouds piste, among the best in the valley thanks to a charming 250-year-old chalet setting, rustic wooden decor and panoramic valley views.

ARGENTIERE & AROUND

Like Les Houches, Argentière makes up for its relatively far-flung location (seven kilometres/ four miles from Chamonix) with plenty of affordable accommodation and a more relaxed atmosphere than the main resort. Unlike Les Houches, however, the vibe is decidedly British here; Argentière has over the years developed as a popular outpost for UK seasonaires, with fry-ups appearing on menus almost as frequently as fondues.

Argentière is a quieter spot in the summer months, when tourists tend to be families and couples making the most of the area's hiking potential. Countless walks await, from a leisurely trot along the Arve to central Chamonix, to a more demanding ascent through stream-scarred woodland and around the sublime Argentière glacier to the top of the Grand Montets cable car; both are roughly eight kilometres (five miles) long.

The cable car is also what attracts so many skiers and snowboarders to Argentière; soaring as it does over 2,000 metres (6,500 feet) to the top of the 3,275-metre (10,750 feet) Grands Montets, the lift opens up some of Chamonix's longest and most exhilarating black and red runs. Nor is this an experts-only affair: Argentière's proximity to the extensive blue slopes of nearby Le Tour – a charming hamlet linked to the village of Vallorcine in the neighbouring valley – makes it similarly popular with families and first-timers.

Eat & Drink

Alan Peru
Chamonix *Av l'Aiguille du Midi (04.50.53.16.04/ www.alanperu-chamonix.com). Open Summer noon-3pm, 7-11pm daily. Winter 7-11pm daily. €€.*
This diminutive Asian fusion restaurant has won over locals and tourists alike since opening in 2006. Its innovative menu straddles culinary borders aplenty: starters of Japanese dumplings might be followed by the likes of Thai duck curry, a creamy aubergine massala, or a chilli-spiked Malaysian laksa, the latter particularly pleasing after a cold day on the slopes. Owners Joshua Brock and Warren Sullivan are also renowned for their experimental desserts, including a mouth-watering brioche with white chocolate and rhubarb compôte. The affordable prices, contemporary decor and chilled sounds suit the largely youthful clientele to a T, but be prepared to wait for a table at peak times.

Atmosphère
Chamonix *123 pl Balmat (04.50.55.97.97/ www.restaurant-atmosphere.com). Open noon-2pm, 7-11pm daily. €€€.*
From the outside, the covered terrace of Atmosphère looks a little like a houseboat – partly thanks to the extended floral display, partly thanks to the fact that it's suspended over the rushing Arve river. The nautical theme seems equally applicable indoors, where tables dressed in white linen nestle a little too closely together. For all that, Atmosphère's modern French menu has sparked countless culinary love affairs with both visitors and locals: there's a monthly changing three-course set dinner (dishes might include millefeuille of aubergine with ricotta and tapenade, or roast pollack with carrots and thyme), plus a pricier à la carte.

Le Bartavel
Chamonix *26 cour du Bartavel (04.50.53.97.19). Open 11.30am-11.30pm Tue-Sun. €€.*
The cheapness, cheer and town square centrality of this excellent pizzeria make it a hit with tourists. The sparsely decorated dining room tends to be packed with English-speaking customers splitting gargantuan salad starters (try the goat's cheese and walnut variety), or tearing into wood-fired pizzas – including a calabrese mixing anchovies with spicy Italian sausage, and a gut-busting chamoniarde loaded with ham, potatoes and local raclette cheese. Service is swift and occasionally unsmiling, and the lighting harsh and sanitised. But for an affordable, easy and satisfying feed, Le Bartavel can't be beat.

La Calèche.

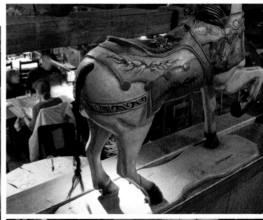

Offset your
flight with
Trees for Cities
and make your
trip mean
something for
years to come

www.treesforcities.org/offset

Trees for Cities
Charity registration number 1032154

Brasserie de L'M

Chamonix *81 rue Joseph Vallot (04.50.53.58.30).*
Open 9am-11pm daily. €€€.
Fancy lamps spewing jets of flame guard the doors to
Brasserie de L'M, a recent addition to Chamonix's
restaurant roster and a fine place to come for modern
European fare with flair. Its interior recalls the Savoyard-
by-numbers design scheme that graces countless
restaurants in the centre – a nondescript mix of wooden
beams, red curtains with gingham trim and the occasional
sled nailed to the wall – but it's spacious and less cluttered
than most. Smart starters include oysters (€8 for six) served
with shallot vinegar, while mains include mammoth
portions of mushroom risotto and superb fillet steaks, the
latter served on black slates and accompanied by roasted
onions and glass jars of chunky chips.

"The steel tanks and winking interfaces of this Canadian-owned microbrewery don't just look pretty; they also turn out some of the finest beers in the Alps, including a superb Granite Pale Ale."

La Calèche

Chamonix *18 rue du Docteur Paccard
(04.50.55.94.68/www.restaurant-caleche.com).
Open noon-2pm, 7-11pm daily.* €€.
No local restaurant does Savoyard kitsch with quite the
conviction of La Calèche, its maze-like interior a clutter of
eccentric alpine ephemera: rows of copper pots hang from
the timber-beamed ceiling; corridors are lined with antique
sewing machines and prams housing china dolls; and the
glazed eyes of stuffed animals overlook proceedings from
high shelves. There's also live music in the form of a
traditional yodeller and accordionist. The menu sticks
largely to regional specialities: many of them are cheese-
based (*tartiflette* and box-roasted mont d'or come with
green salad or potatoes and vegetables respectively), but
dedicated carnivores can grill their own slices of beef,
turkey or duck on a traditional *pierrade* (hot stone).

Le Caveau

Chamonix *13 rue du Docteur Paccard
(04.50.55.86.18). Open 6pm-2am daily.* €€.
Le Caveau's subterranean interior is suitably cavernous;
it's also dark and slightly cold. But it certainly looks the
part, a long stone tunnel separated into booth-style seating

on both sides, and with a central aisle lending it the
atmosphere of an old-fashioned train. Despite this, there's
a homely glow to the place and staff are friendly and
efficient, cheerfully leaning over to relight candles when
they blow out (which they do regularly), and happy to
recommend pizzas. Those seeking more substantial fare can
choose from starters such as battered calamari, and mains
including Swedish meatballs or salmon with mushrooms
in crayfish sauce.

La Crèmerie du Glacier

Argentière *333 rte des Rives, Les Bossons
(04.50.55.90.10/www.lacremerieduglacier.com).
Open 7-10pm daily. Closed mid May-mid June.* €€.
Chamonix's mountain restaurants are renowned for being
short on character, which makes this enigmatic eaterie at
the base of the Argentière glacier a real find. Starting life
as a hut serving drinks to hikers in the early 20th century,
the Crèmerie has since expanded its menu to include the
usual Savoyard specialities – fondues, raclettes, *tartiflettes*
and *croûtes au fromage* (even the salads tend to have cheese
in them). The chalet's intimate timber interior is decorated
with framed vintage photographs and typically kitsch
curtains, and there's a charming garden with sweeping
views up to Mont Blanc. Six simple rooms cater to those
who have drunk too much to ski down.

L'Impossible

Chamonix *9 chemin du Cry (04.50.53.20.36/
www.restaurant-impossible.com). Open 7-11pm daily.
Closed mid Apr-mid May & mid Sept-mid Dec.* €€€.
Long one of the region's most famous restaurants,
L'Impossible's 18th-century farmhouse is an effortlessly
romantic spot in which to dine locally, intimate and
atmospherically lit by candles and chandeliers. There's a
homely air lent by supportive timber beams, a floating brick
fireplace and some eccentric decorative touches (a stag's
head, a replica of the *Mona Lisa*), all of which contrast
pleasantly with the smartly upholstered chairs, crisp linen
and gleaming wine glasses. Inventive starters include the
likes of pheasant terrine and smoked salmon with avocado
mousse; mains include herb-encrusted rack of lamb and
quail stuffed with foie gras. The wine list is among
Chamonix's finest.

Micro Brasserie de Chamonix

0.5km N of Chamonix *320 rte de Bouchet
(04.50.53.61.59/www.mbchx.com). Open 4pm-
2am daily.* €€.
The steel tanks and winking interfaces of this Canadian-
owned microbrewery don't just look pretty; they also turn
out some of the finest beers in the Alps, including a superb
Granite Pale Ale and a Blonde de Chamonix to blow the
head off a demi of Kronenbourg. The bar is large and laid-
back, its walls peppered with modern mountain paintings
and its scattering of wooden tables perfect for indulging in
decent snacks (including mammoth portions of nachos) or,
later in the evening, an excellent Asian-influenced dinner
menu. Occasional live music turns up the volume, but a
slightly out-of-the-way location makes the MBC more
peaceful than most.

Office Bar

Argentière *274 rue Charlet Straton (04.50.54.15.46/ www.the-office-bar.eu). Open 3pm-1am daily. €€.*
Foremost among Argentière's drinking spots is the Office Bar, which was given something of a gastro makeover in recent years and now serves up the likes of game pies and vegetarian tagines alongside the burgers and fish and chips; parties remain decidedly madcap, however, with costumes and colourful après ski antics aplenty.

La Terrasse

Chamonix *43 pl Balmat (04.50.53.09.95/ www.laterrassechamonix.com). Open Summer 10am-1am daily. Winter 4pm-2am daily. €.*
This boisterous café and bar is set in a stylish conservatory-style building; expect horny tourists dancing to live bands and DJs on the ground floor, and a more relaxed atmosphere upstairs where cocktails are sipped beneath the looming fronds of a central palm tree.

Stay

Les Chalets de Philippe

3km E of Argentière *Le Lavancher (06.07.23.17.26/ www.chaletsphilippe.com). €€€€.*
The amiable Philippe oversees a cluster of traditional chalets dating in parts back to the 17th century, and joined by rickety wooden walkways to form a hamlet straight out of *The Lord of the Rings*. Excuses to leave the compound are hard to come by: amenities include a cinema room with comfy sofas, a spa complex with two outdoor jacuzzis, and a large dining room overseen by a resident gourmet chef (who also delivers). Chalets range from a honeymoon hideaway decorated with Baroque-style carvings to the traditional Les Trolles, furnished with antiques and a grand fireplace, and with private use of the spa after 6.30pm.

Clubhouse

Chamonix *74 promenade des Sonnailles (04.50.90.96.56/www.clubhouse.fr). €€€.*
This members' bar and boutique hotel, set in a stylishly converted art deco townhouse, is run by the people behind London and New York's Milk & Honey. As such, the mission statement reads like a glossy glamour magazine, but prices are surprisingly low for the rooms, which range from simple bunk cells to more extensive suites, all decorated with muted chocolate hues, artful spot lighting and minimal modern furnishings, plus flatscreen TVs and DVD players. Breakfast and dinner is included, and the fireside bar features an extensive range of cocktails. There's also a small treatment room with trained masseurs.

Grand Hôtel des Alpes

Chamonix *75 rue du Docteur Paccard (04.50.55.37.80/www.grandhoteldesalpes.com). €€€€.*
This tower-spiked behemoth of a building was closed for 12 years before recently reopening as the glamorous, Italian-run Grand Hôtel des Alpes. Basic rooms overlook either Brévent or, for a few dollars more, Mont Blanc, while indulgent options include the Ancient Tower and Honeymoon suites, the former featuring a private jacuzzi, the latter a prismatic ceiling of criss-crossing wooden beams; all rooms feature DVD players, with films available from reception. Communal spaces are also a cut above average, teeming with fireside sofas and terraces with gorgeous mountain views, while the library is bursting with books in various languages. There's also a spa with jacuzzi, sauna, steam room and pool.

Les Granges d'en Haut

Les Houches *Rte des Chavants (04.50.54.65.36/ www.grangesdenhaut.com). €€€€.*
This fairytale hamlet of 14 wooden chalets is tucked away in the pine forests of Les Houches. Each building at Les Granges d'en Haut features four bedrooms, four bathrooms (three en-suite), a private sauna, a modern kitchen and an open-plan living and dining room ranged around an open fire. Staying here isn't cheap, but the mix of rustic elegance and high-end indulgence is hard to beat: artful building materials include oak, stone and polished slate, services range from free Wi-Fi to firewood provided daily, and there's both a panoramic restaurant and a smart spa featuring an indoor pool, gym, sauna and steam room, plus treatment cabins. There's also a private shuttle whisking guests to and from the slopes.

> **"Philippe oversees a cluster of chalets dating in parts back to the 17th century, and joined by rickety wooden walkways to form a hamlet straight out of *The Lord of the Rings*."**

Hameau Albert 1er

Chamonix *38 route du Bouchet (04.50.53.05.09/ www.hameaualbert.fr). €€€€.*
With an international reputation and prices to match, the Hameau Albert 1er boasts expansive rooms decorated with luxurious modern furnishings (glass tables, chunky space-age chairs, floating fireplaces), while those seeking personal space can book the sumptuous Chalet Soli, which sleeps six and boasts a timber-beamed lounge and private sauna. Eating options are split between an artful gastro palace with the feel of a 1950s cruise liner and a re-created farmhouse serving informal Savoyard specialities; a trip to the gleaming Quartz Bar is akin to drinking in an oversized diamond, with live lounge music several nights a week. There are also heated indoor and outdoor pools and a treatment spa.

Micro Brasserie de Chamonix.

Les Chalets de Philippe.

Hôtel Le Labrador

Chamonix *101 rte du Golf (04.50.55.90.09/ www.hotel-labrador.com). €€.*
The three-star Labrador's position on Chamonix's 18-hole golf course makes it as popular with summer visitors as with skiers making use of the nearby lift to Flégère. Facilities can vary from room to room: those with views of Mont Blanc cost more, but suffer from slightly outdated interior design, while some cheaper rooms have been recently redecorated. The hotel bar and lounge is a cosy wooden space of worn leather chairs set around a traditional fireplace, and the timbered breakfast room is spacious and refreshingly bright. There's also a spa with sauna, steam room and jacuzzi, while the adjoining Chalet Le Labrador offers a cosy alternative for those seeking more isolation.

Hôtel Le Morgane

Chamonix *145 av de l'Aiguille du Midi (04.50.53.57.15/ www.morgane-hotel-chamonix.com). €€€.*
Set in the relative peace of Chamonix Sud, the four-star Morgane is a sleek, contemporary establishment. Recent refurbishment has left the place a far cry from traditional Savoyard shacks: the modern lobby mixes granite and rough-hewn timber to impressive effect, while the 56 rooms feature furnishings from the likes of Starck and Eames, and slate floors dressed with furs. There's also a treatment spa with pool, sauna and steam room, while the restaurant uses only ingredients sourced from the region – all part of the Morgane's vocal commitment to ecological sustainability.

Hôtel L'Oustalet

Chamonix *330 rue Lyret (04.50.55.54.99/ www.hotel-oustalet.com). €€.*
Easily one of the quaintest and most characterful hotels in Chamonix, L'Oustalet is run by two cheerful sisters, Agnès and Véronique Durban, and conveniently located near the Aiguille du Midi lift station. The 15 comfortable rooms are warm and traditionally furnished with single or double beds in spacious, wood-panelled surroundings (family suites offer separate rooms with bunks for little ones); en suite bathrooms are gleaming and modern. The airy downstairs café specialises in a range of artisanal teas, and offers hearty lunches; guest breakfasts are also superb. There's an outdoor swimming pool for summer visitors.

Le Vert

1km S of Chamonix *964 rte des Gaillands (04.50.53.13.58/www.verthotel.com). €€.*
The Vert is increasingly popular with young travellers thanks to its adventurous spirit and colourful approach to partying. Skiers and snowboarders relish the on-site shop selling, hiring and repairing hardware, while staff organise all manner of activities in summer – from biking and rafting to rock climbing and canyoning. The bar is a popular meeting place thanks to its pool table, film screenings and music nights (DJs in winter, live bands in summer). Rooms aren't the most glamorous – clean and perfectly comfortable wood-panelled cabins – but after all that action, you'll just be happy to have somewhere to collapse.

Factfile

When to go

Winter is the most popular time to visit Chamonix; recent years have seen as many poor as epic seasons in terms of snowfall, but levels tend to be better than in other European resorts. Early spring provides reliable snow coverage, albeit slushier and over a less extensive area, while summers offer a pastoral wonderland of lush woodland paths and gorgeous mountain trails for hikers and bikers, plus challenging rock climbs aplenty.

Getting there

Chamonix is 88km (55 miles) from Geneva Airport, from where regular daily coach services run direct to the resort (04.50.53.01.15/ www.sat-montblanc.com); Cham-Van organises private transfers for groups and individuals (06.32.24.03.94/www.chamvan.com). Geneva Airport is also home to a full complement of car hire companies, with the A40 motorway providing an easy direct route to Chamonix.

Getting around

The Chamonix Bus Company runs a comprehensive service around the valley, and is free to lift pass holders, but bear in mind that waiting times can be lengthy at the end of a day's skiing. The Chamo'Nuit nightbus runs from Chamonix to Les Houches or Argentière from around 8pm to midnight between December and April, while the Mulets eco-buses circulate the town centre every day between late June and September. Maps and timetables for all routes are posted at stops, or can be picked up at the tourist office. Those with cars will find plenty of parking at or around major lift stations, but a shortage in the centre of town, especially during peak season.

Tourist information

Argentière 24 rte du Village (04.50.54.02.14). Open Dec-Mar 8.30am-noon, 3-6.30pm daily. **Chamonix** 85 pl du Triangle de l'Amitié (04.50.53.00.24/www.chamonix.com). Open Jan-mid Apr 8.30am-7pm daily; mid Apr-Dec 9am-12.30pm, 2-6.30pm daily.

Internet access

Le Lapin Agile 11 rue Whymper, Chamonix (04.50.53.33.25/www.lelapinagile.fr). **Mojo's** pl Balmat, Chamonix (04.50.89.12.26).

Clockwise from top:
La Plagne; Le Chabichou.

Courchevel to Val d'Isère

Welcome to the world's finest winter playground.

After an awesome season in 2008-09, when the Alps saw the best snowfall for a quarter of a century, skiing is back on the agenda for many people, who have been put off in recent years by rising prices, diminishing snowlines and a weakening pound. Prices remain high, of course, with ski passes now topping out at around €200 a week in the big resorts and *croque-monsieurs* coming in at more than a fiver a throw. But there are ways to keep costs down, such as hiring an apartment independently, loading up the car with a hypermarket haul en route to the resort and picking a week outside the main school holidays if at all possible.

France remains the number one destination for package and independent skiers, with more than a third of UK skiers opting to head to their nearest neighbour for their annual fix of the white stuff, and new developments by companies such as Canadian giant Intrawest and Pierre et Vacances mean that the rabbit hutch regime of old is slowly being phased out. Gone are the days when erecting a pull-out bed in the living room meant you couldn't open the fridge. Most new apartment blocks feature spacious reception areas, well-equipped kitchens and in-house swimming pools.

So, where to go? For endless piste networks, state-of-the-art lifts, guaranteed snow and easy access from the UK, the mega resorts of the Tarentaise – La Plagne, Les Arcs, Val d'Isère and the Trois Vallées – are quite simply top of the pile. Whereas close competitors such as Zermatt, St Anton and Verbier all have their flaws, the Tarentaise is the ultimate ski destination. The figures speak for themselves. Spread across some 30 kilometres (19 miles) of high mountainside, there are more than 1,300 kilometres (800 miles) of piste and 450 lifts – enough to keep even the busiest piste basher happy for a lifetime or two. And while some of the purpose-built architecture is more concrete block than cuckoo clock, the resorts are fighting back with sensitive new development to repair the damage that was done decades ago.

If you simply can't bear to be among the modern apartment blocks, don't despair – each resort featured in this chapter is blessed with efficient lift-served access to one or more charming low-level villages. The perfect mix of charm and convenience.

Explore

COURCHEVEL

In Courchevel, social status rises with altitude and Courchevel 1850 is firmly at the top of the pile. As the Côte d'Azur's spiritual winter home, Courchevel's highest outpost is the last word in *luxe* and, with its very own *altiport*, you can avoid the hairpins and fly directly into this luxury winter wonderland, where the pistes are perfectly groomed, the champagne is perfectly chilled and the jet-set are perfectly manicured.

Many celebs have been linked with Courchevel 1850 in the last few years, with everyone from Roman Abramovich and Charles Aznavour to David and Victoria Beckham taking a turn in the snow. So, why do they come? For the same reason that so many cash-rich French and Brits choose to come – namely that it offers supremely pampered skiing in the world's biggest ski area, and nightlife, restaurants and accommodation to beat most other resorts hands down.

If you're put off by the thought of sharing a gondola with a magnate or two, don't be. If you know where to go (or not to go), it is possible to stick to some kind of budget. Alternatively, a social nosedive will bring you first to Courchevel 1650, a quiet base with a pretty village centre and decent home slopes. Further down again is Courchevel 1550, a long way below 1850 both physically and financially but linked by a gondola,

and a good budget base. Finally, at the bottom of the heap but better-looking than some of its ugly sisters above, is the old village of Le Praz 1300, surrounded by forests and a million miles from the glitz above.

Courchevel sits at one end of intermediate heaven, the vast Trois Vallées. The area also encompasses Brit-friendly Méribel, which vies with Val d'Isère for the title of most popular destination in Europe for British skiers; the highest resort in Europe, Val Thorens, where the apartments are at a breathless 2,300 metres (7,500 feet); and the French-dominated destination of Les Menuires. But it is Courchevel that usually provides the best snow. This is skiing on a truly gargantuan scale, with 600 kilometres (375 miles) of runs, nearly 200 lifts and some 1,500 snow cannons. From 1850, pistes and spacious gondolas spread out in all directions, providing gentle posing territory for the perfectly groomed clientele on the relaxed greens that meander through the woods above the resort.

For more vertical challenges, you need to head up to the valley's highest point, Saulire, reached by a giant cable-car from the top of the main Verdons gondola. If you've got nerves of steel, turn right at the top and, after edging along a frighteningly narrow path, you'll find yourself at the top of the infamous Couloirs. This series of short, sharp chutes is a rite of passage for any good skier, but it looks tougher than it is. Once all three chutes were black pistes, but in these more

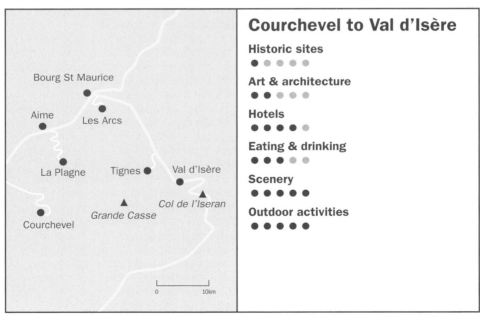

Courchevel to Val d'Isère

Historic sites
● ● ● ● ●

Art & architecture
● ● ● ● ●

Hotels
● ● ● ● ●

Eating & drinking
● ● ● ● ●

Scenery
● ● ● ● ●

Outdoor activities
● ● ● ● ●

Val d'Isère.

Whatever your carbon footprint, we can reduce it

For over a decade we've been leading the way in carbon offsetting and carbon management.

In that time we've purchased carbon credits from over 200 projects spread across 6 continents. We work with over 300 major commercial clients and thousands of small and medium sized businesses, which rely upon our market-leading quality assurance programme, our experience and absolute commitment to deliver the right solution for each client.

Why not give us a call?

T: London (020) 7833 6000

cautious times only one, the grand couloir, remains a marked run. Time your descent right and you can enjoy a captive audience in the cable-car overhead. If vertigo gets the better of you, turn left and you can join the hordes heading over to Méribel or back down towards 1850.

Courchevel is also a great boarding destination, with three funparks and plenty of underused off-piste. On the Verdons piste, rolling curves provide the perfect practice zone for budding freestylers, while more experienced boarders will want to head for the Plantrey snowpark, with an obstacle course and half-pipe. There's also a third park at the 'Hoops of Biollay'.

Unsurprisingly, Courchevel is very well endowed with off-slope diversions too, including swimming, ice-skating, bowling and climbing. Oh, and there are also plenty of boutiques for the likes of David and Victoria, of course. Back outdoors, there's an ice-climbing wall, snowmobiling, paragliding, a floodlit sledge run from 1850 down to 1550 and 20 kilometres (12.5 miles) of hiking trails. So whether it's shopping or schussing you're after, if you've got the money Courchevel has the goods.

VAL D'ISERE

If you're looking to keep all the people happy all the time, then Val d'Isère, spread out along a remote valley on the road up to the 2,770-metre (9,080 feet) Col de l'Iseran, France's highest mountain pass, is probably your best bet. Families will love the superb Children's Village at the base of the slopes; piste-bashers will love the seemingly endless intermediate ski area and seriously smart lift system; boarders will love the snowpark with its half-pipe, double bowl, boardercross course and several rails, plus a dearth of dreaded draglifts; gastronomes will enjoy the 50-odd eateries dotted around town; party people will enjoy the best après ski this side of Austria; and powder fanatics will enjoy some of the finest lift-served off-piste in the world. Even aesthetes will be happy – the town has managed to retain a fair amount of character (although the satellite resort of La Daille is fabulously ugly), and there are plenty of old chalets and hotels to rest your head in. So why don't we all go there? Well, the main reason to stay away is the cost: ski passes, hotel rooms and cafés au lait all come at a premium in 'the world's best ski resort'. But if your pockets are deep enough, this place is hard to beat.

With Brits making up a third of Val's visitors, it can sometimes feel a bit like you're skiing on the Fulham Road, but with more than 300 kilometres (190 miles) of piste shared between Val and next-door neighbour Tignes, there's plenty of room to escape. Val's skiing divides into three areas – the two main mountains of Bellevarde and Solaise, and the isolated Col de l'Iseran, which feeds the highest lift-served pistes and offers limited summer glacier skiing. Access to the mountains is from either Val itself, the satellite village of La Daille or the charming hamlet of Le Fornet. Fastest access to Bellevarde is by the state-of-the-art Olympique cable-car/gondola hybrid, which takes as many as 2,600 people up the 1,000-metre (3,300 feet) Face de Bellevarde in just five minutes, or the high-speed Funival underground funicular from La Daille. Solaise and the Col de l'Iseran are both served by cable-cars.

One of Val's USPs is an exceptional snow record and testament to this is the fact that the resort opens for business in November every year and hosts the opening men's World Cup downhill in December. Those looking to ape Jean Claude Killy should point their skis in the direction of the red OK World Cup downhill run or the black bumps of the daunting Face descent. If you're not quite ready for the downhill, then the appropriately named Verte is Val's longest run, five green kilometres (three miles) from Bellevarde down to La Daille and the perfect place to find your ski legs.

Despite its macho image, Val is essentially an intermediates' paradise, with the really tough stuff taking place beyond the piste markers. There are some wonderful blue runs in the area, especially down from the Col de l'Iseran towards Le Fornet and from the Tovière ridge down into the Tignes bowl. The only real negatives of Val's skiing are the homeward runs at the end of the day – a combination of overcrowding and icy conditions means that sometimes it works out easier to take the lift back down instead.

Off the slopes, there's loads to do. Rev heads can burn round the ice-driving circuit (04.79.06.21.40); more natural highs include a skating rink, indoor swimming pool and health centre (04.79.06.05.90) with pool, sauna, Turkish bath and gym. Budding chefs, meanwhile, might prefer to book on to one of the pâtisserie classes at the Adroit bakery (04.79.06.16.09, €28).

TIGNES

It may not be pretty, but Tignes is about as snowsure as it gets. From a resort level of 2,100 metres (6,900 feet) to a ceiling of 3,450 metres (11,350 feet) at the top of the Grande Motte cable car, this purpose-built high-rise project from the 1950s and 1960s offers year-round white stuff and easy access to the delights of Val d'Isère over the Tovière ridge and the Col de Fresse. But it's much more than just a high-altitude satellite of its glamorous neighbour: Tignes contributes plenty to the world-famous Espace Killy area. There's patrolled off-piste with dedicated lift access, chutes and drops to test the nerve of any freerider or boarder, and enough fine cruising pistes to keep the high-mileage majority happy.

Top: Val d'Isère. Above: La Plagne. Below and left: Champagny-en-Vanoise.

The architectural history of Tignes makes fairly bleak reading. Originally built from 1956 onwards by architect Raymond Pantz as a 'liner on a sea of snow', it quickly came to be known as a titanic eyesore of the Alps. In the 1970s the slightly more stylish Val Claret was added a kilometre up the valley, although the kindest words that could be used about it remain 'modern' and 'functional'. Now every effort is being made to get the cars underground, the concrete behind wood cladding and the old reputation buried once and for all – but there's still some work to do. When the sun's out, the resort is high if not handsome. In bad weather it can feel as if you're stranded on the moon. But Tignes isn't about alpine charm and cutesy chalets, rather it is a triumph of function over form; this is as guaranteed as snow gets.

If you truly can't bear the thought of a week in a concrete liner, then stop off at the traditional village of Tignes Les Brévières, which is linked into the main lift system. This is the only surviving village to predate the vast hydroelectric dam that dominates the valley – the original village of Tignes was lost beneath the waters of the newly created Lac du Chevril. The dam was completed in 1952, after many years of resistance from locals, and damages paid by the government to the local community helped to build the first ski lifts and buildings of today's mega resort.

"Used as a stunt double for the Andes in Luc Besson's cult film *The Big Blue*, the icy depths of Lac de Tignes are open to all-comers to experience the big chill of ice diving."

There are four main sectors to Tignes' skiing – Grande Motte, Tovière, Palet and Aiguille Percée – all interlinked and mostly perfect intermediate cruising territory. The jewel in the crown is the Grande Motte underground funicular, which whizzes skiers from Val Claret 1,000 metres (3,300 feet) skywards in just seven minutes and deposits them at the base of the summer ski area and the Grande Motte cable-car, which goes up to Tignes' highest point. The snow conditions up on the glacier are almost always exquisite, a fact not lost on the crowds queuing for the cable-car.

The busy Tovière sector divides Tignes from Val d'Isère and sees a lot of cross-border traffic, but it's a necessary evil if you want to explore Val's tougher skiing. Its lower reaches are home to Tignes' nursery slopes, just above Le Lac.

On the opposite side of the bowl from Tovière, a series of more antiquated lifts leads up to Tignes' highest non-glacier skiing from the Col des Ves and some of the area's toughest runs. From here you can zigzag your way along the mountainside to the Aiguille Percée, local natural landmark and the starting point for the famous Sache black run – and various off-piste variations – down to Tignes Les Brévières.

Away from the pistes, Tignes also offers some of the best lift-served off-piste in the world, with legendary descents such as the north face of the Grande Motte, with a 900-metre (2,950 feet) vertical drop and crevasses, ice towers and rocks littered all around, the Tour de Pramecou and the Vallon de la Sache, a stunning 1,200-metre (3,900 feet) descent in the heart of the National Park. These off-piste treats should only be enjoyed in the company of a guide. Contact the Bureau des Guides (04.79.06.42.76). Tignes is also a very popular boarding spot, with guaranteed snow and an excellent snowpark. Situated above Val Claret, it has a vertical drop of 120 metres (400 feet) and includes a half-pipe, quarter-pipe and rails. There's also a Snowpass pass that gives access to the snowpark and 20 other lifts.

Off the slopes, Tignes is pretty much a non-starter; neighbouring Val d'Isère is a much better option. If you do find yourself stuck here without skis, head for the Bains du Montana, at the Hôtel Village Montana in Tignes Le Lac, replete with outdoor pool, jacuzzi, sauna, Turkish bath and fitness centre. Up at Val Claret, the Val Claret Spa has thermal baths and hot water jets galore. Back outside, the coolest activity has to be ice diving in Tignes' frozen lake. Used as a stunt double for the Andes in Luc Besson's cult film *The Big Blue*, the icy depths of Lac de Tignes are open to all-comers to experience the big chill. The water hovers around the freezing mark as you're lowered through a hole in the ice kitted out in a full dry suit (don't worry – you're tethered to the surface and accompanied by a guide). Once you've taken the plunge, you can swim under the ice and check out the kaleidoscopic light show above as the sun beats down and the peaks appear in distorted glimpses through the openings in the surface. First-time dives cost approx €75 and no experience is necessary. Book through Evolution 2 (www.evolution2.com).

LA PLAGNE

Of the 134 runs in La Plagne's massive Grand Domaine, 79 are blue and 11 are green. Flattery, it seems, will get you everywhere, and the resort is these days the most skied in Europe.

La Plagne's mass appeal is plain to see, with snowsure pistes, doorstep skiing, acres of gentle off-piste, snowmaking galore and a lift system as smooth as the motorway skiing it serves. Success has bred a raft of lift improvements in recent years, including the €15 million link to Les Arcs across the Ponthurin Gorge and a real effort to harmonise new lifts and buildings with the natural surroundings.

Twas not always thus, of course. Bringing skiing to the masses in the 1960s led to a rabbit hutch building mentality and the resort's reputation as one of the least attractive on the circuit is still borne out by the concrete behemoths of Plagne Centre and Plagne Bellecôte, results of an era of alpine skiing now, fortunately, slowly being buried under wood cladding. But even at resort level things are changing, with sensitive mini-villages cropping up at Plagne Soleil and Plagne Villages. The other major drawback about La Plagne's ten 'villages' is an almost uniformly disappointing après ski scene. With most of La Plagne's kid-carrying clientele happy to ski all day and sleep all night, nightlife teeters on the edge of terrible in most of the resorts, although Plagne Centre just about passes muster. But with 225 kilometres (140 miles) of daytime cruising to explore, an early night is probably just what you need.

The main skiing, above Plagne Centre and Plagne Bellecôte, is all between 2,000 metres (6,500 feet) and 2,700 metres (8,850 feet). Main access from Plagne Centre is via the Grande Rochette Funiplagne cable-car, which whisks skiers up to 2,500 metres (8,200 feet) in just four minutes, wind or no wind. From the top the options are endless – some steepish, often mogulled reds back down to Plagne Centre, a great underused blue across to Plagne Bellecôte, or a descent into the Champagny sector via the five-kilometre (three-mile) blue Geisha, which is as attractive as its name suggests – wide, scenic and south-facing.

The other main lift out of Plagne Centre is the Becoin chair up to Biolley. This gives access to a superb, steep competition red back to Plagne Centre or, off the back, a couple of blacks – including the daunting Morbleu, which is sometimes icy, usually bumpy and always tricky. It also leads, via another chair, to Plagne Montalbert's gentle but rather isolated tree-lined ski area, which bottoms out at the village at 1,350 metres (4,400 feet) and is covered by snow cannons.

La Plagne's other main area is above Bellecôte and the much more attractive chalet-style Belle Plagne. Main access is by the Roche de Mio gondola. Starting in Bellecôte, the lift goes via Belle Plagne and finishes up at Roche de Mio at 2,700 metres (8,850 feet). From Roche de Mio, you can go further up to the Glacier de Bellecôte.

The glacier is steeper than most and, when it's open, the snow is almost guaranteed to be in prime condition.

Back at Roche de Mio, reds and blues head down to Belle Plagne or into the Champagny sector, while it is also possible to ski all the way down to the villages of Montchavin and Les Coches, a descent of some 1,500 metres (4,900 feet) and with some great off-piste along the way (especially in the trees above Les Bauches). From here, you can either hop on the Vanoise Express double-decker cable-car across the valley to Les Arcs or head back home for a well-earned rest.

For a high-altitude resort there's plenty to do in La Plagne apart from skiing, and the high-altitude resorts are all linked by lift or bus until 1am. In Belle Plagne there's a fitness centre with sauna, Turkish bath, mudwraps and manicures to soothe away your aches and pains, plus a four-lane bowling alley if you'd prefer to strike out. Down in Bellecôte there's a heated outdoor pool, reached by a tunnel from the changing rooms, while over in Plagne Centre there's a cinema showing English-language movies twice a week. Back outside, eager thrill-seekers should head for the bobsleigh run, which was built for the Albertville Winter Olympics. If you want to hear your screams echoing around the valley, climb into the 90km/h (56mph) self-steering mono bob, lie back and think of England as you shoot down the track. Alternatively put your faith in French driving skills and climb into the taxi bob, which reaches speeds of up to 100km/h (62mph).

LES ARCS

Like its identical twin, La Plagne, across the Ponthurin Gorge, which is now spanned by the much-vaunted Vanoise Express cable-car, Les Arcs is a classic French example of the victory of function over form. Look up from the original ribbon of three developments that make up Les Arcs (1600, 1800 and 2000) and you will be greeted by the wonderful sight of 200 kilometres (125 miles) of perfect intermediate cruising territory with a west-facing aspect, modern lift system and oodles of snowmaking to counteract the sun's rays. So far, so good. But look back down from the top of the mountain and you'll be greeted by another fine chapter out of the French Ski Handbook circa 1970: How not to build a ski resort. The vast apartment buildings were supposed to mimic and blend in with the mountains through their design, but the lines don't quite work and the effect is one of irritation rather than imitation.

Okay, so it's no chocolate box, but as already mentioned Les Arcs is first and foremost about function, and it's got that in spades. From the UK, the Eurostar ski train leaves St Pancras and stops in the valley town of Bourg St Maurice. From there a stroll round the back of the station

La Plagne.

LE TUNNEL
15

Bags packed, milk cancelled, house raised on stilts.

You've packed the suntan lotion, the snorkel set, the stay-pressed shirts. Just one more thing left to do — your bit for climate change. In some of the world's poorest countries, changing weather patterns are destroying lives.

You can help people to deal with the extreme effects of climate change. Raising houses in flood-prone regions is just one life-saving solution.

**Climate change costs lives.
Give £5 and let's sort it *Here & Now***

www.oxfam.org.uk/climate-change

Be Humankind ⊗ **Oxfam**

connects you with the seven-minute funicular ride up to Arc 1600. Having already bought your ski passes online via the website, you can check into your ski-in, ski-out apartment and check straight back out the back door and on to the slopes. After cruising Les Arcs' pistes using your hands-free lift pass, you can slip across to La Plagne on the double-decker cable-car, which crosses nearly 400 metres (1,300 feet) above the valley floor without the help of a single pylon along the way. Minimum hassle, maximum vertical. Now that's function for you.

If you're after chocolate box, go to Austria. Or, alternatively, try out the faux-Savoyard surroundings of Arc 1950, put together by ski resort giant Intrawest. This enclave of wooden chalet-style apartments and cute cafés is akin to visiting an alpine theme park, but in the case of Les Arcs, it beats the real thing.

"The big hitter at the Cap Horn is the seafood platter at €130 for two, but if you have to ask the price then you're probably better off skiing straight on by."

Stretching like a sunbather across a sunny, west-facing mountainside, Les Arcs' slopes are an easy target for the vagaries of global warming. But the area does have height on its side, with a top height of 3,200 metres (10,500 feet) at the summit of the Aiguille Rouge cable-car. This is where Les Arcs' jewel lies – some very steep piste skiing, including the sublime seven-kilometre (four-mile) Aiguille Rouge run from the summit of the resort down to the valley village of Le Pré, and some fairly decent off-piste on the steep pitches below the summit.

The rest of the ski area is a sea of blue and red, with main mountain access from Arc 1800 via the two-stage Transarc gondola, which lifts the masses slowly up to the Aiguille Grive at 2,600 metres (8,500 feet). From here the world is your oyster, with access to Arc 2000 and the Aiguille Rouge, an endless choice of tree-lined runs back down to Arc 1600 and Arc 1800 ending in specially designated 'quiet zones', or a traverse over to the former backwater of Vallandry, now thrust into the limelight as the starting point for the Vanoise Express to La Plagne. Even if you don't decide to hop across the gorge (which requires a supplement), it's

worth heading over in this direction to escape the crowds above 1800 and enjoy some wonderfully gentle off-piste through the trees.

Local legend Régis Rolland is known as the godfather of European snowboarding and, fittingly enough, his home town is still a big boarding destination. The Apocalypse Park, just down from Arpette and served by the Clair Blanc chairlift, changes features throughout the season. There's a boardercross course, plus hips, jumps and rails, with three different levels – green, red and black. Special snowpark passes give access to the park. There's also a floodlit half-pipe at Arc 2000 and acres of tree-lined off-piste wherever you look, although there are also plenty of flattish blues dotted around, so look before you leap.

Les Arcs was designed as a ski resort, so anything non-ski related, such as a public pool or half-decent shopping, will involve a ride down to Bourg St Maurice in the funicular. There's an ice grotto above 1800, plus snowshoeing and dog sledding, but the general message is: if you don't want to play in the white stuff, head elsewhere.

Eat & Drink

Belliou La Fumée
Les Arcs *Pré St Esprit (04.79.07.29.13).*
Open Dec-Apr, July, Aug noon-4pm daily. €€€.
Les Arcs' main slopes are dotted with self-service standards. For a gourmet lunch with a rustic touch, you need to head down the mountain to the outlying villages. Pré St Esprit is home to the enchanting 500-year-old Belliou La Fumée, named after a Jack London novel.

Le Cap Horn
Courchevel *1850 (04.79.08.33.10/www.le-cap-horn.com). Open mid Dec-mid Apr 8.30am-6pm. €€€€.*
If you want to feast in your furs and mix with the Muscovites, then the Cap Horn, perched just above the town at 2,100m (6,900ft), is the ideal spot – you don't even have to strap your skis on to get there. The main draw is the vast piste-side sun terrace, the perfect place to catch some rays and check out the swanky clientele. On the menu, the big hitter is the seafood platter at €130 for two, but if you have to ask the price then you're probably better off skiing straight on by. Most other mains are around €30-€40, and there's a 900-bottle wine cellar to help you wave goodbye to any afternoon sporting action.

Le Chabichou
Courchevel *1850 (04.79.08.00.55/www.chabichou-courchevel.com). Open Dec-Apr, July, Aug 12.30-1.30pm, 7.30-9.30pm daily. €€€€.*
Michel Rochedy's two Michelin-starred alpine gastronomic temple still reigns supreme in the Tarentaise, with menus topping out at a truly high-altitude €200. But with dishes such as line-caught sea bass confit in mountain hay bouillon with lightly smoke-flavoured single cream, or pan-seared

foie gras with carrot and bitter orange confit, it's worth every euro. Every Thursday morning you can pick up some tips from the master in the Chabichou's kitchens for €75.

Dick's T-Bar
Val d'Isère *(04.79.06.14.87/www.dicksteabar.com). Open Dec-Apr 9am-4am daily. €€.*
At Val's most famous bar/nightclub, the action kicks off at 9am with a full English breakfast and develops, with the help of live bands and DJs, into the most crowded venue in this high-octane party town right up until closing time at 4am. If you can still move after a day on the slopes, then it's definitely worth stopping in for some dirty dancing and cocktails. You'll find offspring in Méribel and Val Thorens.

La Folie Douce
Val d'Isère *Above La Daille (04.79.06.01.47/ www.lafoliedouce.com). Open Dec-Apr during skiing hours. €€.*
Next door to La Fruitière (*see below*), and run by the same people, this is where afternoon skiing and après ski blur into one, a real rarity in France. The action kicks off mid-afternoon, with thumping beats and open-air dancing in a sort of Ibiza-on-snow vibe. The party wraps up at 5pm, and then it's a hazy slalom back down to La Daille. One of the best on-piste parties in the French Alps.

La Fruitière
Val d'Isère *Above La Daille (04.79.06.07.17/ www.lafoliedouce.com). Open Dec-Apr 11.30am-3.30pm daily. €€.*
Val d'Isère's best on-mountain restaurant, at the top of the La Daille gondola, is an old dairy reassembled halfway up the mountain. The look is very *authentique* – all distressed wood, blue tiles, and waiters decked out in blue aprons. The menu is pretty special too, with wonderful mountain sausages, and, unsurprisingly given the building's past incarnation, a cheeseboard to die for. There's also a great sun terrace outside.

La Grande Rochette
La Plagne *Above Plagne Centre (04.79.09.09.08). Open Dec-Apr during skiing hours. €€.*
Perched at the top of the Grande Rochette lift at 2,500m (8,200ft), this restaurant-cum-snack bar won't win any awards for its standard fare but its south-facing terrace is a sunseeker's paradise and makes the ideal spot for a sundowner, with wonderful views across to Courchevel 1850 – don't have too many, though, as it's a gruelling 600m (2,000ft) of vertical back down to Plagne Centre.

Le Jump Bar
Courchevel *1850 (04.79.08.09.00). Open Dec-Apr 9.30am-1am daily. €€.*
The heaving Jump Bar, part of the Hôtel de la Croisette, is a perenially popular watering hole where you'll find big wooden tables, live sports on the TV and plenty of fellow Brits drinking plenty of beer. Its position, just a few metres from the piste and main lift station, goes some way to explaining its popularity. There's a small, traffic-choked terrace out the front, but the real fun is indoors.

Perdrix Blanche
Val d'Isère *(04.79.06.12.09). Open Dec-Apr 8am-1am daily. €€€.*
Ideally positioned in the centre of town, this long-standing restaurant is a piscine oasis in a sea of cheese, with all manner of crustacean delights, from oysters to sea snails, delivered daily up the mountain, plus sushi platters in the evening. The rest of the menu is a mountain mish-mash, with salads, pizzas, stir-fries, fondues and grills all on offer. For a meaty treat, the châteaubriand (€68 for two) is superb. There's an extensive wine list too.

La Soucoupe
Courchevel *Above 1850 (04.79.08.21.34). Open Dec-Apr during skiing hours. €€.*
For tasty mountain fare and top-of-the-world views, head down to the bottom of the giant Saulire cable-car, where La Soucoupe dishes up traditional Savoyarde specials in cosy, unpretentious surroundings – if it's snowing outside, there's a vast open fire to warm up by. Downstairs is simple self-service and a handsome terrace, while upstairs the food and prices are decidedly more *haute*.

La Tête Inn
La Plagne *Belle Plagne (04.79.55.10.85). Open Dec-Apr, July, Aug 8am-2am daily. €€.*
Unlike anything else in purpose-built La Plagne, the Tête Inn dates back to 1830. Historically it stood alone on the hillside, but is now the focus of Belle Plagne's main street after dark. The decor is unrepentant cowshed wood, with barrels for tables and hay rakes on the walls. Formerly called Mat's Pub, La Tête still recognises the importance of the Brit market and serves up a decent selection of beers and live music several times a week.

Stay

Les Barmes de l'Ours
Val d'Isère *(04.79.41.37.00/www.hotel-les-barmes.com). Open Dec-Apr. €€€€.*
If you're looking for some serious pampering, then this hotel at the foot of the pistes in Val is the place to put your feet up. The four-star luxe building contains 49 rooms and 26 suites done out in four different styles – loft, chalet, Nordic and lodge. The vast spa area contains an indoor pool, jacuzzi, sauna, hammam and fitness centre, the perfect spot to build up an appetite for dinner in one of the hotel's three restaurants. If you really want to blow the budget, book the Lours suite with its own fireplace, projector screen and jacuzzi.

Les Grandes Alpes
Courchevel *1850 (04.79.00.00.00/www.lesgrandesalpes.com). Open Dec-Apr. €€€€.*
Nothing much comes cheap in 1850 and accommodation is no exception. But if you're determined to splash out, then the four-star, chalet-style Grandes Alpes is a decent bet: it's expensive enough but the welcome is friendly and the interior is handsomely decked out, with 33 supremely comfy

Le Chabichou.

Les Barmes de l'Ours.

rooms and 12 luxurious suites. The building is well positioned right beside the Jardin Alpin piste and there's a fitness centre, pool and restaurant on site.

Hôtel La Cachette
Les Arcs *1600 (04.79.08.10.10/www.hotelcachette. com). Open Dec-Apr, July, Aug. €€.*
The low-key resort of Arc 1600 is home to one of the best family hotels in the Alps. Don't be put off by the rather austere exterior – the Hôtel la Cachette is about as kid-friendly as you can get, from the excellent in-house nursery to the buffet-style restaurant. Food is a typical all-inclusive affair with little choice, but the rest of the place has been done well with comfy rooms, friendly staff and an excellent piste-side position. For the ultimate hassle-free holiday, catch the Eurostar direct to Bourg St Maurice and change on to the seven-minute funicular which brings you pretty much straight to the hotel door.

Hôtel Les Glières
La Plagne *Champagny-en-Vanoise (04.79.55.05.52/ www.hotel-glieres.com). Open Jan-Apr, July-Sept. €€.*
If you'd prefer to escape the concrete chaos of high-altitude La Plagne but still benefit from one of the finest ski areas in the world, then Hôtel Les Glières could be the perfect solution. Set in the charming old village of Champagny-en-Vanoise, at a height of 1,250m (4,100ft), this rustic two-star is linked into the main ski area by a thoroughly modern seven-minute gondola ride, and in good snow conditions skiing is possible to within a snowball's throw of the front door. The decor and dishes are simple Savoyard fare, but you'll be sleeping in one of the most attractive ski villages in the French Alps.

Hôtel Terra Nova
La Plagne *Plagne Centre (04.79.55.79.00/www.hotel-terranova.com). Open Dec-Apr. €€.*
Decent hotel options are few and far between in La Plagne, which is dominated by apartment blocks, so the three-star Terra Nova is a welcome arrival in Plagne Centre. Set on the piste a couple of minutes' walk from the main resort complex, the 120 rooms are spacious and well presented, and many have balconies overlooking the slopes. There is a bar and buffet-style restaurant on site, and facilities include a kids' club, sauna and covered parking. Check the Crystal website (www.crystalski.co.uk) for some brilliant low-season bargains.

Les Suites du Montana
Tignes *Le Lac (04.79.40.01.44/www.vmontana.com). Open Dec-Apr. €€€€.*
Tignes Le Lac is home to plenty of hotels, many of which place function above form. But the four-star Suites du Montana are a cut above the competition, with vast duplex suites, two restaurants and a spa complex with indoor pool, sauna and hammam to soothe aching limbs. If you can't afford the suites, there are also some three-star hotel rooms on site.

Factfile

When to go
The ski season runs from early December to mid April (dates depend on resort). Christmas/New Year is very busy and the snow can be unreliable, although the last couple of seasons have seen great early snow. January is very quiet (and the cheapest time of the season) with generally good snow, but can be very cold. February usually has the best snow but most crowds (French half term). March and early April are ideal, with plenty of snow and sunshine, and longer days.

Getting there
Geneva and Chambéry are the nearest airports to the resorts. Val d'Isère and Tignes involve the longest transfer, and if you rent a car at the airport, remember that the final road up to the resorts may require snowchains if the weather's bad (you can hire them at the airport). There are also frequent bus services from both airports to the resorts (www.altibus.com). TGV high-speed trains and the weekly Eurostar ski train stop at the valley towns of Moutiers, Aime and Bourg St Maurice, with buses up to the resorts (or a funicular up to Arc 1600).

Getting around
Somebody has got to pay for all the fancy lifts, and ski passes in each resort cost around €200 for a six-day adult pass, with reductions for children. Within the different resorts, there are usually free ski buses that circulate between the various accommodation 'villages'.

Tourist information
Les Arcs (04.79.07.12.57/www.lesarcs.com).
La Plagne (04.79.09.79.79/www.la-plagne.com).
Courchevel (04.79.08.00.29/www.courchevel.com).
Tignes (04.79.40.04.40/www.tignes.net).
Val d'Isère (04.79.06.06.60/www.valdisere.com).

Internet access
Courchevel 1850 Prends Ta Luge et Tire Toi (04.79.08.78.68/www.laluge.com).
Plagne Centre Le Cyber Centre (www.lecybercentre.com).
Les Arcs 1800 Chez Boubou (04.79.07.40.86).
Val d'Isère Powdermonkey Internet (04.79.41.66.09/www.powdermonkey.co.uk).
Tignes Le Lavachet TC's Bar (04.79.06.46.46/www.tcsbar.com).

Top (left to right): Foix; Mirepoix. Middle: Hautes Pyrénées. Bottom (left to right): The Ariège; Foix.

The Pyrenees

High, wide and handsome.

The Pyrenees, which stretch some 450 kilometres (280 miles) from the Basque Country to the shores of the Mediterranean and count no less than 35 peaks over 3,000 metres (9,850 feet) along the way, are older than the Alps, and through the centuries the chain's high summits and deep valleys have harboured everyone from religious heretics and *résistants* to Spanish Civil War exiles.

Covering five French *départements*, the landscape of this vast region varies radically on its journey from west to east, ranging from the ski resorts, spa towns and *transhumance* routes of the Hautes Pyrénées, through the gentler, greener Ariège with its strong Cathar history, to the Pyrénées Orientales which combine serious skiing with Romanesque architecture and Catalan cuisine.

The Pyrenees' thermal waters have been exploited since at least Roman times, and Louis XIV sent his soldiers here to be healed, but the 19th century was the great era of spa travel. Royals, rich aristocrats and bohemians made the annual pilgrimage to 'take the waters', preferring the temperate climate here to the harsher Alps, and with the relaxing influence of the sulphuric waters came a certain loosening of morals. As well as the cavortings of writers George Sand, Alfred de Vigny, Victor Hugo and François-René Chateaubriand, Napoleon's step-daughter Hortense de Beauharnais visited in 1807 – without her husband Louis, King of Holland. Nine months later the future Emperor Napoleon III was born, said to have been conceived in a mountain refuge near Cauterets either by an aristocratic lover or by one of the shepherds who worked as masseurs in the thermal baths. Nowadays the Pyrenees are more popular for summer hiking and winter skiing than thermal bathing, but a host of handsome new spas mean that modern-day visitors can combine exertion and relaxation in one of the most stunning regions of Europe.

Explore

HAUTES PYRENEES

The Hautes Pyrénées' jagged snowy peaks form a seemingly impenetrable border with Spain, and the dead-end vibe of the area's towns and villages – many roads end in the mountains and the Bielsa tunnel is the only means of getting into Spain in winter – means this feels less like border country and more like a kingdom of its own. Traditional ways of life, including shepherding, live on, and in summer the high pastures are grazed by thousands of sheep and ginger-coated Bazadaise cattle.

The reintroduction of bears – about 20 of them now roam the National Park – and a burgeoning vulture population have not been welcomed by local farmers, who claim that both attack their flocks, and many now use the gigantic Pyrenean mountain dog, known as the 'Pastou', to guard their flocks. While you're unlikely to see a bear, you'll almost certainly spot the Pyrenees' own version of the chamois, the izard, with its perky horns, as well as marmots when they emerge from their winter hibernation in April. Pyrenean lilies and irises, moss campion, sweet poppy and Irat saxifrage contribute to the colourful landscape once the snows have melted.

The small but elegant spa town of Bagnères-de-Bigorre makes a great place to base yourself. With its esplanade, squares of pollarded trees, fountains, botanical gardens and 19th-century bourgeois houses, it is simply delightful and offers the area's only real cultural highlights through its four museums: the fine art Musée Saliès, the folk art Musée du Vieux Moulin, the Musée d'Histoire Naturel and the Musée du Marbre (Bagnères was an important marble quarrying area).

A few kilometres from Bagnères-de-Bigorre is the dramatic Pic du Midi Observatory (08.25.00.28.77/www.picdumidi.com). Perched at 2,877 metres (9,450 feet), and reached by a 15-minute cable car ride from the ski station at La Mongie, this early 20th-century fortress in the clouds is a wonderful feat of engineering. Its dome houses a telescope whose power is such that if the earth wasn't round you could read the time on Big Ben through its lens, together with a NASA telescope used for the Apollo missions and a Bernard Lyot coronagraph. Visits to the dome are only on days when the telescope's not in use, but there's an excellent astrological museum that tells the story of the Pic's pioneers. If you book in advance you can even stay the night in clean but basic rooms, star-gaze with an astronomer and watch the dawn rise over the peaks. An incredible off-piste descent on skis (winter) or by mountain bike (summer) is also possible.

From Bagnères head to Luz-St-Sauveur, where at the *thermes* you can see Empress Eugénie's marble bath and lounge in the thermal pools. Luz also hosts a well-known jazz festival in mid July,

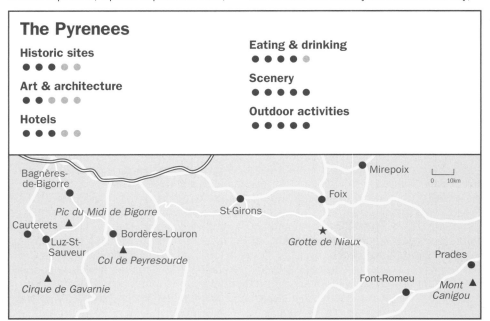

The Pyrenees

Historic sites
● ● ● ● ○

Art & architecture
● ● ● ○ ○

Hotels
● ● ● ○ ○

Eating & drinking
● ● ● ● ○

Scenery
● ● ● ● ●

Outdoor activities
● ● ● ● ●

Mirepoix

0   10km

Bagnères-de-Bigorre

Foix

Pic du Midi de Bigorre

St-Girons

Cauterets ▲

Luz-St-Sauveur

Bordères-Louron

Grotte de Niaux

Prades

Col de Peyresourde

Font-Romeu

Mont ▲ Canigou

Cirque de Gavarnie

Pic du Midi Observatory.

Top: Mirepoix. Middle (left to right): Foix; Mirepoix. Bottom (left to right): Mirepoix; Foix.

and at the end of September the shepherds' return from the high pastures is celebrated with a sheep auction and meat-fest when everybody has the right to buy their lamb chop and have it cooked by local restaurants.

From Luz it's 20 kilometres (12.5 miles) to the famous Cirque de Gavarnie, the semi-circular wall of mountains that Victor Hugo called 'the colosseum of Nature'. This glacial amphitheatre includes 15 peaks over 3,000 metres (9,850 feet), the highest of which is the Pic de Marboré at 3,248 metres (10,650 feet). In the centre is the 422-metre (1,380 feet) Cascade de Gavarnie, a waterfall that freezes in winter. The Cirque is the most graphic representation of a border you could ever hope to see: right behind it is Spain, though it is hard to imagine anything beyond. In summer, though, walkers can cross from one country to another through the Brèche de Roland, a dramatic break in the rock face that gets its name from Charlemagne's nephew who, in Arthurian-type legend, smote the mountain with his sword. The Brèche is also the crossing-point for 1,000 Aragon cattle that still have the rights to summer pasture on the lusher, French side of the range. Short walks around the bottom of the Cirque can be done in boots or snow shoes (hire from La Cordie, Gavarnie, 05.62.92.47.61). If you want to lunch here, go through the village of Gavarnie and stop at La Chaumière (05.62.92.48.08), a pretty café serving simple food with an unbeatable view of the Cirque.

The nearby spa town of Cauterets is an equally good base, with a fancy new leisure spa opening in summer 2010. Remnants of its 1900 heyday – the wooden train station transplanted here from the 1900 Paris Great Exhibition, caryatids and masks on the façades of buildings, and a Russian princess's folly – give it all the charm of a belle époque poster. A few kilometres up the mountain is the Pont d'Espagne beauty spot – a picturesque waterfall and bridge where Spanish and French peasants used to exchange goods. Further up lies the ski area of Cirque du Lys, reached by a 12-minute cable-car ride from the town centre.

Aquensis

Rue du Pont d'Arras, Bagnères-de-Bigorre (05.62.95.86.95/www.aquensis.fr). Open 10.30am-8pm Mon, Wed-Sat; 1-8pm Tue, Sun. Admission €22 (3hrs incl towel & bathrobe).
In 2003 Bagnères made the smart move of adding this leisure spa to its thermal offerings. Beneath a structure of soaring wooden beams that ascend to the glass roof, where you can see the starfish silhouettes of bathers lounging in the outdoor *lit d'eau*, is a magnificent pool with cascades, jets and currents, a musical pool with surreal underwater sounds and a Moroccan hammam. On the first floor are pine cabins for beauty treatments and the outdoor space with two jacuzzis and saunas.

Musée Salies

Pl des Thermes, Bagnères-de-Bigorre (05.62.91.07.26/ www.museesbagneres.fr). Open June, Sept, Oct 10am-noon, 4-6pm Wed-Fri; 3-6pm Sat, Sun. July, Aug 10am-noon, 4-6pm Tue-Fri; 3-6pm Sat, Sun. Admission €4; free-€3 reductions.
Situated above Bagnères' 1783 thermal baths, the Musée Salies is home to a decent collection of works by Orientalists (Chasseriau, Vigneron), Barbizon landscape painters and local flower painter Blanche Odin. The museum also hosts temporary exhibitions.

THE LOURON VALLEY

Still in the Hautes Pyrénées *département*, the Louron Valley has long been left in the shade by its showier neighbours to the west, giving it the feel of a forgotten valley. To reach it, head down the main trunk road to the Bielsa tunnel and veer off in the direction of the Col de Peyresourde, one of the most challenging mountain stages of the Tour de France. The valley's treasure lies in its frescoed churches, strung out along the river. Most were built in the 11th century, when after centuries of pillaging by the Saracens the valley was finally won back. In the 16th century they were decorated by itinerant artists from Aragon, notably Maître Rodrigis, and their painted walls and ceilings tell the graphic story of local martyrs Calixte and Mercurial, as well as more familiar Biblical themes, in amazing colour and detail.

The keys to the churches are held by an army of volunteers; to visit, ask at the tourist office in Loudenvielle (05.62.99.95.35) or Bordères-Louron (05.62.99.92.00). There are eight churches, the most important being St Calixte in Cazaux-Fréchet, Saint-Barthélemy in Mont, St Félix in Armenteule and the amazing St Mercurial in Vielle-Louron. In Loudenvielle, the L'Arixo visitor centre (05.62.99.97.70) has an exhibition about the churches, and its manager, Yoann Lemonnier, is also a mountain guide (06.01.92.37.58/ www.pachamama-pyrenees.com).

Balnéa

On the D25 just outside Loudenvielle, 5km S of Bordères-Louron (08.91.70.19.19/www.balnea.fr). Open 2-7.30pm Mon-Fri; 10.30am-8pm Sat, Sun (school hols 10am-9pm daily). Admission €12.50 Mon-Fri; €15 Sat, Sun & hols; free-€10 reductions.
Balnéa emulates a Roman baths with its caldarium, frigidarium and tepidarium. A second space for families has a tropical vibe with waterfalls and jets, and there is a floor dedicated to massages and beauty treatments. It doesn't quite live up to Aquensis, and the changing rooms are rather bleak, but it still makes for a relaxing day.

THE ARIEGE

In springtime, driving or cycling over the mountain passes that take you eastwards into the Ariège feels like travelling from one season to another. Behind you are the snows and thick forests, and suddenly a lush landscape of green fields and rushing rivers opens up. St-Girons and Foix are the main towns, and centuries of feudal battles and religious persecution have left their mark. A new Regional Natural Park has just been created in the area to promote its natural beauty and safeguard its heritage and traditions.

St-Girons is a quiet market town with an esplanade, a great bookshop and Philippe Faur's famous gourmet ice-cream empire (www.philippe faur.com). Above the town, the village of St-Lizier was the seat of powerful bishops, two of whom were canonised. Lanes climb ever upwards to the 11th-century cathedral and 17th-century bishop's palace at the top; the complex is being restored and will reopen in 2010 with a museum, luxury hotel and restaurant. About halfway up the village there is a second, vast church, the Eglise St-Lizier (05.61.96.77.77, www.ariege.com/st-lizier), with a beautiful Romanesque cloister. A former hospital created by Bishop Ossun in the 16th century is now an old people's home, but you can still visit the astonishing pharmacy, completely intact with its pots and bottles of unguents with labels like 'Elixir longue vie' and 'Huile de chien' (boiled puppies, meant to be good for sciatica).

Dominated by the triple towers of Gaston Phoébus's castle, Foix is the administrative capital of the *département*. But this town and the surrounding region has a long anti-establishment tradition, with Cathars, Demoiselles (19th-century peasant rebels who disguised themselves as women) and Spanish Republicans all putting up resistance. This is why the Résistances film festival (www.cine-resistances.fr) takes place here annually in July, with a programme of provocative features and documentaries.

The country between Foix and Mirepoix was a Cathar stronghold in the 13th century, under the protection of Mirepoix's ruler Raymond Péreille. The subject is taken very seriously around here, and rightly so – the persecution of these pacifist nonconformists by the Albigensian Crusade managed to obliterate an entire religion. The Château de Montségur (05.61.01.06.94, www.montsegur.fr) was where the last 220 Cathars were burned alive, after a ten-month siege. To get the full story you can't do better than to climb the ruins with historian Fabrice Chambon (06.18.28.62.80). A small museum in the village of Montségur shows archaeological finds from the château and the village of 6,000 inhabitants that clung to its slopes.

Mirepoix is an attractive town rebuilt on a medieval grid after a flood in 1289. Around the covered market square sit brightly coloured half-timbered houses. You will hear a lot of English spoken on the café terraces, and it's a great centre for antiques hunters, with several *brocantes* and a *dépôt-vente* just out of town.

Grotte de Niaux

Niaux, 12km S of Foix (05.61.05.10.10/www.sesta.fr). Open daily, guided tours only (closed Mon Nov-Mar). Tours in English Apr-Sept. Admission €9.40; free-€7.50 reductions.
South of Foix near Tarascon, the Grotte de Niaux houses one of France's most important examples of prehistoric cave art. The visit by torchlight gives a vivid impression of what Cro-Magnon man himself would have seen by the light of his tallow candles. There's an 800m (2,600ft) walk on sometimes slippery ground before you arrive in the Salon Noir, where an amazing 54 bison, 29 horses and 15 ibex were painted on the walls some 13,000 years ago, together with mysterious red symbols.

Parc de la Préhistoire

10km S of Foix (05.61.05.10.10/www.grands-sites-ariege.fr). Open Apr-June, Sept, Oct 10am-6pm Mon-Fri (closed Mon May, Sept & Oct); 10am-7pm Sat, Sun. July, Aug 10am-8pm daily . Admission €9.70; free-€7.40 reductions.
At the Parc de la Préhistoire you'll find an exciting museum space that takes you on a voyage of time and scale (from huge blow-ups of cave paintings to tiny tools). It starts with representations of the horse from Cro-Magnon to Picasso, and the art of today's indigenous people is examined alongside the Niaux cave paintings. There's also an ultraviolet facsimile of the Salon Noir showing how it would have looked 13,000 years ago. In the grounds, landscaped with waterfalls and caves, actors teach prehistoric skills, such as lighting a fire from flint.

PYRENEES ORIENTALES

The Eastern part of the Pyrenees is firmly Catalan and you can hop in and out of Spain – as locals do to get cheap petrol – especially at Llivia, a peculiar island of Spanish territory surrounded by France. Font-Romeu is the most important ski resort in the Pyrenees, with 40 runs, 23 ski lifts and 500 snow cannons. It's also a centre for high altitude training. Paula Radcliffe lives here year-round, and other international athletes come to take advantage of its training complex, built to prepare competitors for the 1968 Mexico Olympics. In summer, the cable cars take hikers and mountain bikers up to the high peaks.

Heading further east, the last mountain before the Mediterranean is 2,785-metre (9,150 feet) Mont Canigou, dominating the town of Prades and the surrounding villages and orchards. It takes around five hours to reach the summit from Vernet-les-Bains or Casteil, and there are *refuges* along the way. The weather can be highly unpredictable, so midsummer is the best time to climb. Casteil is also the starting point for the 40-minute climb to the dramatic 11th-century Abbaye St Martin du Canigou (04.68.05.50.03, http://stmartinducanigou.org), perched at more than 1,000 metres (3,300 feet) and home to a silent religious community. Visits are by guided

The little engine that could

It may be *petit*, and as cute as can be, but the Train Jaune in the Pyrénées Orientales is one of the great heroes of railway evolution. In the early 1900s it took two days to reach Perpignan from the high villages of the Cerdagne – a journey of little over an hour by car today – and from the first snowfall they were completely cut off from the world. But by 1927, this 63km (40-mile) line running from Villefranche to La Tour-de-Carol Enveitg on the border with Spain had saved these dying villages and opened up a whole new industry that brought prosperity to the region: skiing. Along the way, it produced an amazing 650 feats of engineering, more than one per kilometre. Soaring viaducts, audacious tunnels and France's highest station at Bolquère (1,593m/5,225ft) make it one of the most breathtaking train rides in the world. And what makes it all the more impressive is that it was never steam-powered. A barrage and nine hydroelectric stations along the Têt river were created to power the electric traction line.

These days the 'Canary', proudly bearing the Catalan colours of yellow and red, carries mainly tourists and it's the finest way to discover the Catalan Pyrenees Regional Natural Park. From Villefranche, an attractive but touristy medieval garrison town enclosed by Vauban ramparts, the train winds through the gorges of the Têt to Fontpédrouse with its hot springs. It then climbs ever onwards to Mont-Louis (another military village modelled by Vauban) and heads over the Perche pass to Font-Romeu before descending, with some incredible twists and turns, across the Cerdagne plateau.

At an average 35km/h (22mph) it's a gentle shunt, giving you plenty of time to admire the snow-topped mountains, river valleys and Romanesque churches on the two-hour journey. Over half of the line's 22 stops are request, so you have to tell the driver your destination when you get on – many marked walks start from the various stops, and there are a host of historical sights to see. There are around five trains a day and tickets cost €3.50 to €18.10 one-way, depending on how far you go. Visit www.trains touristiques-ter.com for a full timetable.

tour only. Far more accessible is the nearby Abbaye St-Michel-de-Cuixa (04.68.96.15.35) with its beautiful rose marble cloister.

Prades is a friendly, down-to-earth Catalan town, proud of its adopted son, the cellist Pablo Casals, who was exiled here during the Spanish Civil War and began the international chamber music festival that takes place in the area's Romanesque churches from late July to mid August (www.prades-festival-casals.com). Do take the time to explore the pretty villages around Prades, such as Taurinya and Eus.

Les Bains de Llo
Rte des Gorges, Llo, 8km S of Font-Romeu (04.68.04.74.55/www.lesbainsdello.com). Open 10am-7.30pm daily. Closed 6 Nov-19 Dec & 1st 2wks June. Admission €9; free-€7.50 reductions.
The Cerdagne mountain range's thermal waters have long been used for alfresco bathing, and Les Bains de Llo has a lovely outdoor pool where you can lounge in the hot water with a snowy backdrop. There's also an attractive spa offering relaxation and beauty treatments. For bathing *au naturel* head for the hot springs just south of Fontpédrouse on the N116 towards Prades.

Solar Furnace
7 rue du Font Solaire, Font-Romeu (04.68.30.77.86/ www.promes.cnrs.fr). Open Sept-June 10-11.30am, 2-6pm daily; July, Aug 10am-6.30pm daily. Admission €6; free-€3.50 reductions.
Approaching Font-Romeu from the west, you can't miss the Solar Furnace. This astonishing piece of engineering consists of 11,340 mirrors arranged like an audience on the hillside to reflect sunlight on to a vast concave mirrored wall. This directs the rays into a single point, creating a temperature of 3,500°C. The facility is used by the CNRS (National Scientific Research Centre) to test materials, develop solar energy and find ways of recycling industrial waste. The small science museum inside has a film on the Solar Furnace and exhibits on light and renewable energy.

Eat

Auberge d'Antan
The Ariège *Domaine de Beauregard, av de la Résistance, St-Girons (05.61.66.66.64/www.ariege. com/aubergedantan). Open 7.30-10.30pm Mon-Fri; noon-2pm, 7.30-10.30pm Sat, Sun. Closed Mon Oct-May, 2wks Mar & 2wks Nov. €€.*
A word of advice: don't eat anything for a day before coming here because the portions are vast. Paul Fontvieille's idea is to evoke the generosity of olden times in this barn-like restaurant on the château estate, its beamed interior hung with hams, and with a suckling pig fresh from the fire lying prostrate on the counter. It's useless to try to resist: the price of the two-course menu is not much less than the full four-course Rabelaisian experience, with amuse-bouches, pâtés, pork meat, steaks or salt cod, and calorific desserts to follow.

Bistrot de Pays El Taller
Pyrénées Orientales *2 pl Verdaguer, Taurinya, 6km S of Prades (04.68.05.63.35/www.eltaller.fr). Open 10am-midnight Mon, Tue, Thur; 10am-2am Fri-Sun. €€.*
'Bistrot de Pays' is a new label for restaurants whose aim is to keep village culture alive – a brilliant initiative that has spawned hundreds of café-bistros that have become the life and soul of small villages around France. El Taller is a marvellous example of the trend. Run by four energetic young men, it offers free concerts, film screenings and art exhibitions, as well as a delicious menu in a contemporary glass-and-iron building. Local lamb, *magret de canard*, langoustines and scallops are beautifully presented, and the community spirit means you might finish up playing boules on the forecourt with the locals. Not to be missed.

Bonzom et Fils
Pyrénées Orientales *Av des Contes de Cerdagne, Saillagouse, 9km S of Font-Romeu (04.68.30.14.27/ www.bernard-bonzom.com). Open Sept-June 8am-noon, 3-7.30pm Tue, Thur-Sat; 8am-noon Sun. July, Aug 8am-noon, 3-7.30pm Tue-Sun. Closed Nov. €.*
The downstairs tasting room at this astonishing smokery and delicatessen is designed for sampling the products on sale in the shop, but you could quite happily dine on the large platters of cheese and *charcuterie* if it were open at mealtimes. As it is, a trip here makes for a fantastic aperitif. Monsieur Bonzom's son guides you through a selection of specialist hams and *saucissons*: chorizo, jésu, boudin noir, pa de fetge, tir a buixo, jambon de cerdagne and fouet. As for the cheeses, there are *chèvres* from the Ariège, Catalan tomme and different types of *brebis*. In July and August you can visit the smokery and the Bonzoms' *charcuterie* museum down the road.

La Chaumière
Pyrénées Orientales *96 av Emmanuel Brousse, Font-Romeu (04.68.30.04.40). Open noon-2pm, 7.30-10pm Wed-Sun. Closed 3wks June & 2wks Nov. €€.*
This rustic-chic restaurant in Font-Romeu is just the place to warm up after the ski slopes, with two rooms decked out in wood and stone complete with animal stalls. Locals crowd round the bar, and the Catalan chef produces stylish dishes such as pimentos stuffed with salt cod. The tenderest cuts of beef are served on slate slabs, and desserts – *rhum baba, soupe de chocolat* – are naughty but nice.

Le Ciel d'Or
The Ariège *8 rue de Maréchal Clauzel, Mirepoix (05.61.60.19.19/www.relaisroyal.com). Open 12.30-1.30pm, 7.30-9.30pm Tue-Thur, Sat; 7.30-9.30pm Fri, Sun. Closed Jan, 1st wk Feb & Tue eve Nov-Easter. €€€€.*
Le Ciel d'Or's enchanting location is matched by the sublime cuisine of Robert Abraham. Skewers of spicy *écrevisses* tempered by asparagus tips and a millefeuille salad of goat's cheese, peppers and exotic shoots was a work of art, and the *magret de canard* with blanched spinach, a cake of beetroot purée and a single almond was wonderfully innovative. Three variations on strawberries and a two-tier platter of irresistible macaroons made the perfect finish. Gerwin, one of the Dutch owners, is a wonderful host.

Clockwise from top: Font-Romeu; Fresco, Louron Valley; Aquensis; Cauterets.

Hôtel Le Saint Vincent

Hautes Pyrénées *31 rue du Maréchal Foch,
Bagnères-de-Bigorre (05.62.91.10.00/www.hotel-saint-
vincent.com). Open 12.30-3pm; 7.30-10pm Tue-Sat;
12.30-3pm Sun (July, Aug open daily). Closed Nov. €€.*
The restaurant of this family-run hotel serves up reasonably
priced classic French cuisine in a sunny yellow dining room.
Dishes include the likes of *magret de canard*, lamb shank,
steak or grilled sea bass. Don't bypass the *crème caramel
maison* – one of the best we've ever tasted. This place is a
real locals' favourite, so you need to arrive early.

Logis de Mirepoix

The Ariège *2 cours du Docteur Chabaud, Mirepoix
(05.61.68.21.63/www.logisdemirepoix.com). Open Sept-
June 7.30-10pm Fri; noon-2pm, 7.30-10pm Sat, Sun.
July, Aug 7.30-10pm Tue-Fri; noon-2pm, 7.30-10pm
Sat, Sun. Closed Jan-mid Feb. €€.*
This family-run place is great fun as Eric, Chantal and
Sandra dress up in swashbuckling costumes to serve you,
and you drink out of pewter tankards which you are
encouraged to clink with gusto. The setting is an 18th-
century lodge with beams and brocade. The set menu
includes an aperitif, stuffed mushrooms, cassoulet (which
one diner dubbed better than the famous Hôtel de la Cité's
in Carcassonne) or armagnac-flambéed beef, salad, dessert
and wine, all for €24. Candlelight brings it all alive, either
inside or out in the pretty garden.

Le Phoébus

The Ariège *3 cours Irénée Cros, Foix
(05.61.65.10.42/www.ariege.com/le-phoebus). Open
noon-2pm, 8-10.30pm Tue-Fri; 8-10.30pm Sat;
noon-2pm Sun. Closed 23 July-23 Aug. €€-€€€€.*
In a great location overlooking the river and Gaston
Phoébus's château, Didier Lamotte and his right-hand man
Yan Fauré give all budgets a chance to enjoy some fine
cooking. The six menus run the gamut from €19 to €85, and
only vary in the amount of luxury ingredients they include.
A whole section of the menu is devoted to foie gras 'in all
its states', and *cochonnerie* also gets star billing so the more
adventurous can see whether a talented chef really can
make a silk purse of a pig's ear.

Tentation

The Ariège *8 rue Gambetta, St-Girons (05.61.04.88.60/
www.philippefaur.com). Open Sept-June noon-2pm Tue-
Thur; noon-2pm, 8-11.30pm Fri, Sat. July, Aug noon-
2pm Mon, Sun; noon-2pm, 8-11.30pm Tue-Sat. €€€.*
The last thing you'd expect to find in the market town of
St-Girons is this trendy restaurant with its fruity colours.
But gourmet *glacier* Philippe Faur has brought a touch of
urban chic to the town where three generations of his family
were ice-cream makers before him. What has made Faur a
star in foodie circles is his savoury ice-creams: foie gras,
espelette pepper, and truffles and caviar are his top flavours,
and here Jean-Marc Granger has devised the perfect dishes
to go with them. The *dégustation* menu brings you three
mini-plats on a rectangular plate with spoonfuls of the
accompanying ice-creams – smoked salmon with the caviar,
Bresse chicken with the foie gras, and cod with the peppers.

La Vieille Maison Cerdane

Pyrénées Orientales *Pl de Cerdagne, Saillagouse,
9km S of Font-Romeu (04.68.04.72.08/www.planotel.fr).
Open noon-2pm, 7.30-9pm daily. Closed 1wk Mar
& 1wk Dec. €€€.*
While the rooms in this family-run hotel are quite simple,
the restaurant is an absolute delight. The food bursts with
colour and energy – the *filet de rascasse* was combined with
an amazing array of flavours, including espelette peppers,
ginger, honey and seaweed. During our meal, Eric Planes,
the proprietor and brother of the adventurous chef, showed
us a whole crate of *morilles* that had just been brought to
him by a neighbour out mushrooming in the woods. Game
and pork are other delights here, and the *crème catalane* is
one of the best. There's a great wine list too.

Stay

Las Astrillas

Pyrénées Orientales *12 carrer d'Avall, Taurinya, 6km
S of Prades (04.68.96.17.01/www.gite-prop.com/66). €.*
This *chambres d'hôtes* in a village just outside Foix looked
so pretty we knocked on the door and were warmly
welcomed by the mayor of Taurinya, Bernard Loupien. In
an old Catalan mas, four bedrooms and a suite are arranged
around a lovely garden where you can enjoy a pastis with
your convivial host. Rooms are simply furnished with old
armoires and one has a piano. Bernard is also a keen cook
and will serve you Catalan specialities in the rustic dining
room or alfresco in the summer.

Château de Beauregard

The Ariège *Av de la Résistance, St-Girons
(05.61.66.66.64/www.chateaubeauregard.net). €€€.*
This lovely 19th-century château has everything you need
for a romantic break, and it needn't cost the earth. Eight
rooms, all named after writers and decorated with antiques,
include Victor Hugo with a little conservatory and piano, or
Zola with a day-bed on the terrace, while the two prestige
suites, Colette and George Sand, feature more contemporary
decor, state-of-the-art bathrooms, huge flatscreen TVs and
decks with sunloungers overlooking the pool. The icing on
the cake is the spa: a barn with stone walls, pebble floor and
a real log fire blazing while you relax in the jacuzzi or
hammam after an aromatic massage.

Château de Ludiès

The Ariège *Ludiès, 16km W of Mirepoix
(05.61.69.67.45). €€.*
An eccentric wonderland between the imaginations of the
Brontë sisters and Lewis Carroll is found in this country
manor near Mirepoix, where *brocante* fans will be keen to
explore every room. Every nook and cranny is filled with
cabinets of curiosities, antique toys, apothecary jars and
fresh flowers, while the owner's collection of 19th-century
costumes is displayed on mannequins, spilling over into a
costume museum in a barn. A coterie of animals includes
two cats, a dog, a goose, chickens and frogs. Four rooms in
the main house are joined by two suites in an outhouse.

Le Ciel d'Or.

Clockwise from top:
Logis de Mirepoix;
Tentation; Villa Rose.

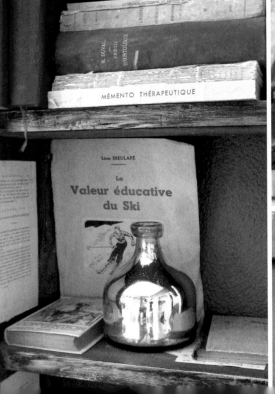

Les Cimes
The Louron Valley *Rte du Col de Peyresourde, Estarvielle, 5km S of Bordères-Louron (05.62.99.67.21/ www.hotel-les-cimes.net).* €.
Set at the foot of the Col de Peyresourde, this old *relais* used to be the scene of feverish telegraphing as sports journalists reported on the notorious mountain stage of the Tour de France. Now avid backpackers Frédéric and Véronique have filled it with the flavours of their world travels via colourful photographs of markets around the world, ethnic souvenirs and global food in the restaurant. All the rooms have views over the valley, some (like the spacious African-themed room) have a balcony, and a Chinese-themed lounge offers TV, books and board games.

Hôtel Le Grand Tetras
Pyrénées Orientales *Av Emmanuel Brousse, Font-Romeu (04.68.30.01.20/www.hotelgrand tetras.free.fr).* €€.
The Grand Tetras is the best ski hotel in Font-Romeu. The simple decor and compact rooms are compensated for by fabulous balcony views and a small pool, sauna and outdoor hot tub on the roof for après ski relaxation. It's comfortable, convivial and well situated in the centre of town. Ask for a 'Plein Sud' room for a balcony with mountain view.

Villa Belisama
The Ariège *Rue Notre-Dame, St-Lizier, 2km N of St-Girons (05.61.02.83.24/www.ariege.com/belisama).* €€.
Marylène runs this exceptional *chambres d'hôtes* in a 16th-century canon's house right at the top of the village of St-Lizier. Two spacious rooms are built into the eaves – Magdala has a private terrace, and Galileo has a roll-top bath open to the bedroom under a glass roof – while the duplex Jabbaren also has a terrace overlooking the large swimming pool. Several walled gardens include a herb garden and one with a hammock, and a third terrace offers a splendid view of the Couserans mountains. Be sure to reserve for dinner as Marylène is an excellent cook, and don't be afraid of the enormous Pyrenean mountain dog Cybel, who is a big softie at heart.

Villa Rose
Hautes Pyrénées *54 rue George Lassalle, Bagnères-de-Bigorre (05.62.34.09.84/www.villarose65.com).* €€€.
In this elegant townhouse, interior designer Marie-Christine Mécoën has paid homage to Bagnères' illustrious spa past, and the ladies who came here to 'take the waters' – George Sand, Princess Eugénie and Napoleon's sister-in-law Reine Hortense. Only three rooms have been made into bedrooms, with subtle colour combinations and handsome antique furniture. The Fontaine des Fées room, with its double shower and window overlooking the garden, is particularly romantic. All the other rooms are salons: the Salon des Tisanes where you can breakfast with the scent of roses coming in from the garden; the Salon du Chocolat where Marie-Christine serves hot chocolate 18th-century style; and the library filled with antiquarian books.

Factfile

When to go
With a clearly defined winter sports season, and summer rambling, the only real off months in the Pyrenees are April and November. Spring comes early or late according to the altitude, but by mid May the meadows are in bloom. If you want to walk on the high mountains, though, you'll have to wait until midsummer. Getting involved in *transhumance* – accompanying flocks to the high pastures in June and celebrating their return at the end of August – is a great way to experience the mountains. Ask at tourist offices for dates.

Getting there
The nearest airport is Tarbes-Lourdes, served by Ryanair, which is right on the doorstep of the Hautes Pyrénées. Pau (Ryanair) and Toulouse (Easyjet) airports are also not far away. The Ariège and Pyrénées Orientales regions are well served by Carcassonne and Perpignan airports (both Ryanair). By train, TGVs from Paris go to Lourdes (5h50mins) and Tarbes (6hrs) with connections to Bagnères-de-Bigorre and La Mongie. TGVs from Paris to Toulouse (5hrs 20mins) link with slow trains to Foix and Tarascon, and coaches to Mirepoix.

Getting around
Getting to one place and staying there is quite easy by public transport, but if you want to tour around then a car is essential. If you're into cycle touring, the Route des Cols is a fabulous, challenging ride taking in many of the highlights of the Tour de France stages, while the Voie Verte in the Ariège is a lowland route created from old railway lines.

Tourist information
The Ariège Rte de Ganac, Foix (05.61.02.30.80/www.ariegepyrenees.com).
Hautes Pyrénées (05.62.56.70.46/ www.tourisme-hautes-pyrenees.com).
Pyrénées Orientales (04.68.51.52.53/ www.cdt-66.com).

Internet access
The Ariège Café Castignolles, 48 pl Général Leclerc, Mirepoix (05.61.68.10.40).
Hautes Pyrénées Maison du Parc National et de la Vallée, pl St-Clément, Luz-St-Sauveur (05.62.92.38.38/www.luz.org).
Pyrénées Orientales Sun Caffé, 48 av Emmanuel Brousse, Font-Romeu (04.68.30.33.49).

Top and middle:
Riquewihr. Bottom:
Haut-Koenigsbourg.

The Vosges

Thick forests, fairy-tale villages and fine wines galore.

Two expansive regional parks, three French *régions* and hundreds of pretty villages fall within the Vosges. While the lush forests and great glacial lakes of the mountains are a hiker's heaven, the vineyards and *winstubs* in the valley attract wine-lovers and gourmands from all over the world. It's no wonder that this has been one of the most fought-over areas in Europe.

Characterised by gently curved peaks and dense evergreen forests, the Vosges offers a verdant, vibrant environment that is explored by few outside France and Germany. Its regional parks contain over 9,000 kilometres (5,600 miles) of hiking trails, 1,000 kilometres (600 miles) of cross-country skiing tracks, and dozens of old fortresses that attest to the region's bloody history. In the south, the Parc Naturel des Ballons des Vosges boasts the highest vantage points and, out of season, you can easily pass hours off the beaten track without meeting another soul.

On the Alsace plain at the eastern foot of the mountains, the Route des Vins produces some of France's most prized white wines. Like so many aspects of life here, the wine has a strong Germanic influence, with the aromatic, fruity gewürztraminer an Alsatian institution. Nestling among the vineyards, you'll find endless story-book villages brimming with gaily painted half-timbered houses and medieval architecture – and frequently populated by large white storks, one of the trademark symbols of the region.

Such charms extend to Colmar, the capital of the wine country. The cobbled streets of its old town could have come straight from the pages of *Hansel and Gretel*, and its cultural and gastronomic offerings make it an ideal base for exploring the Vosges. Eating is both a pleasure and an art here. The region is home to some of the country's most respected chefs, with many kitchens headed by generations of the same family, and their cuisine bears much in common with the Vosges itself. Both are marked by history, yet have an eye turned deftly towards contemporary tastes.

Explore

COLMAR

Colmar boasts the charm of an Alsatian village with the facilities of a bigger town. Its historic centre is packed with narrow cobbled streets and old half-timbered houses painted in striking blues, reds and yellows.

One of Colmar's highlights is the outstanding fine art collection at the Musée d'Unterlinden, with the Isenheim altarpiece its chief crowd-puller. From the museum, you can wander south to the Maison des Têtes, an attractive Renaissance hotel whose high bay windows and façade are decorated with over 100 grimacing stone faces. On top of its grandiose gable sits a statue of a cooper sculpted by Colmar-born Frédéric Auguste Bartholdi, the man who created the Statue of Liberty. Several of his statues are dotted around town, and there is a Musée Bartholdi (03.89.41.90.60, www.musee-bartholdi.com) at 30 rue des Marchands, where he lived.

In the streets around the yellow sandstone Collégiale St-Martin church (known locally as the cathedral), several buildings feature old shop signs lovingly crafted by Colmar-born Jean-Jacques Waltz, who became an Alsatian artistic legend under the pseudonym Hansi. You can see touches of his trademark humour in the butcher's sign at 7 rue des Serruriers, which dates back to 1930. Just south of the cathedral, the Renaissance Maison Pfister boasts an octagonal tower (designed as a fire escape), intricate panel paintings and a superb two-tiered oriel window. From here, it's a short walk to place de l'Ancienne Douane, which is dominated by the 15th-century Koïfhus (old customs house) and its brightly coloured Burgundy-style roof tiles. In the middle of the square, a stream leads south to Colmar's most tourist-friendly area, La Petite Venise. It's picture-book stuff, with colourful half-timbered fishermen's houses rising from the banks of the Lauch river. The bygone feel of the district continues on Petite rue des Tanneurs, where tall black-and-white buildings feature multiple open verandas, formerly used by tanners to dry animal hides.

As well as its sumptuous Christmas market, Colmar hosts two major annual events. The Festival International de Colmar (www.festival-colmar.com) in July is one of Europe's top classical music festivals, while the ten-day Foire aux Vins d'Alsace (www.foire-colmar.com) in August offers a carnival atmosphere for tasting local wines and catching big-name musicians (Leonard Cohen and Simply Red in 2009) at the open-air arena.

Musée d'Unterlinden

1 rue d'Unterlinden (03.89.20.15.50/www.musee-unterlinden.com). Open May-Oct 9am-6pm daily. Nov-Apr 9am-noon, 2-5pm Mon, Wed-Sun. Admission €7; free-€5 reductions.

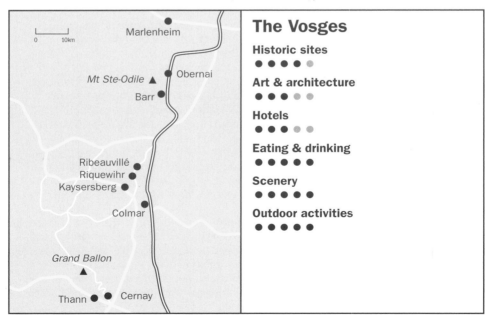

The Vosges

Historic sites
● ● ● ● ○

Art & architecture
● ● ● ○ ○

Hotels
● ● ● ○ ○

Eating & drinking
● ● ● ● ●

Scenery
● ● ● ● ●

Outdoor activities
● ● ● ● ●

Flamme & Co.

Set in a former 13th-century Dominican convent, Colmar's finest museum is best known for Mathias Grünewald's landmark masterpiece of religious art, the Isenheim altarpiece. The work takes the form of a polyptych (c1515) that has been dismantled to display all its different configurations. The most famous depicts Christ on the cross, his overstretched arms emphasising the painful resignation of his frail body. Other highlights include 15th-century engravings by Colmar's Martin Schongauer, plus works by Picasso, Renoir and Poliakoff.

PARC NATUREL DES BALLONS DES VOSGES

The bigger of the area's two regional parks, the Parc Naturel des Ballons des Vosges (www.parc-ballons-vosges.fr) encompasses the Vosges' southern range and includes its highest peaks and most spectacular scenery. Thick pine forests and expansive glacial lakes litter the mountainside, which peaks out into soft, rounded summits known as *ballons*. The Club Vosgien (03.88.32.57.96, www.club-vosgien.com) is France's oldest hiking association and has marked out an astonishing 7,000 kilometres (4,400 miles) of trails within the park, including six long-distance *grandes randonnées*. Cyclists are well catered for thanks to a network of bike paths and signposted routes, and in winter the park is a prime venue for cross-country skiers.

The Route des Crêtes is a spectacular 80-kilometre (50-mile) road that unerringly follows the main ridge of the park's highest mountains via forests, pastures, lakes and farms. Built during World War I to deliver supplies to troops, the trail begins in Cernay and continues north over the high point of the Vosges, the Grand Ballon (1,424 metres/4,700 feet), where a spectacular vista opens out on to the Black Forest and, in clear weather, as far as the Alps. At Vieil Armand (formerly Hartmannswillerkopf), the remains of German bunkers and trenches mark the site of one of World War I's bloodiest battles. A military cemetery stretches out over the hillside, providing a poignant reminder that what is now a peaceful haven was once the deathbed of tens of thousands of young soldiers.

ROUTE DES VINS

Stretching from Marlenheim in the north to Thann in the south, the 170-kilometre (105-mile) Route des Vins meanders lazily through dozens of picture-perfect winegrowing villages at the eastern foot of the Vosges. The area is a flurry of terraced vineyards, ruined châteaux, geranium-filled window boxes and stork's nests. This is the Alsatian countryside at its most lusciously bucolic – even if tour buses frequently threaten to destroy the peace. The most famous sites, such as Riquewihr, Ribeauvillé and Kaysersberg, are blessed with immaculately preserved medieval ramparts, towers, and cobbled streets lined with colourful half-timbered houses. Many of the lesser-known villages (Barr, Mittelbergheim, Andlau) have ample charm and fewer tourists.

All along the Route des Vins, local producers offer free tastings. The most famous of the region's seven grape varieties are the whites – riesling, gewürztraminer, muscat and pinot gris, although a few villages also produce pinot noir red and rosé. The smooth, sparkling crémant d'Alsace is made from pinot blanc. Note that it is possible to navigate between the different villages on foot by following the *sentiers viticoles*.

OBERNAI

Enclosed by 13th-century rampart walls and towers, pretty Obernai is centred on a medieval market square, surrounded by a host of grandiose, steeply gabled buildings. Wander across the cobbled square and you'll hit the Puits à Six Sceaux, an ornately sculpted stone Renaissance well holding six buckets. From Obernai, you can drive or hike the 12 kilometres (7.5 miles) to Mont Ste-Odile, the holy mountain of Alsace. Its 763-metre (2,500 feet) summit houses a former convent (now a hotel) and a chapel containing the remains of Ste Odile, who is credited with curing the blind and sick in the eighth century. From the terrace, there are spectacular views on to the remains of a Celtic wall and the vineyards in the valley below.

RIQUEWIHR

If you didn't know it was the real deal, you could mistake Riquewihr for Disneyland, such is its fairy-tale charm. Set inside tall 16th-century ramparts, its pedestrianised medieval alleys and courtyards abound with idyllic half-timbered and dressed stone houses, many featuring finely sculpted figures lodged into their corners and old-fashioned wrought-iron shop signs designed by Hansi. Climb up the 13th-century Tour du Dolder gatehouse for a splendid view across the village.

Eat

The Vosges is one of France's truly great gastronomic centres and Alsace, on the eastern side, has the highest number of Michelin-starred restaurants outside Paris. The staples of Alsatian cooking are cabbage and pork, offered in all imaginable forms at traditional *winstubs* (literally 'wine rooms').

L'Auberge de l'Ill

17km N of Colmar *2 rue de Collonges au Mont d'Or, Illhaeusern (03.89.71.89.00/www.auberge-de-l-ill.com). Open noon-2.30pm, 7.30-9.30pm Wed-Sun. Closed 1wk Jan & 4wks Feb-Mar. €€€€.*

Castles in the air

With its strategic position at the crossroads of Europe, the Vosges has historically been an important military outpost, and the area's mountainsides are littered with spectacular ruined and restored castles from bygone eras.

The northern Vosges boasts the highest concentration of castles in Europe, many of them precariously balanced on top of pink sandstone cliffs that rise dramatically out of the forest. Parts of the ruined 12th-century Vieux Windstein seem to sit impossibly atop vertical slabs of thin, weathered rock, while the elongated crumbling walls and delicate towers of the Grand et Petit Wasigenstein resemble a stretched-out ocean liner in the middle of the forest.

The most famous of the northern castles is Fleckenstein (www.fleckenstein.fr), built in the Middle Ages on a 43m (140ft) rocky spur by the Emperor Friedrich Barbossa. Deemed to be impenetrable in its day, it eventually fell victim to Louis XIV's destructive spree of the area's fortresses in the 17th century. Today, you can still see an ornate entrance door, a series of troglodyte rooms, and a spectacular staircase cut out of the rock.

Several castles benefited from a strategic 17th-century makeover by the military engineer Vauban, including La Petite Pierre (www.parc-vosges-nord.fr), set in a quaint fortified village, and Lichtenberg (www.chateaudelichtenberg.com). Sitting atop a raised outcrop, Lichtenberg is one of the area's best-preserved castles, featuring a marble mausoleum and splendid views from its towers.

In the southern Vosges, ruined fortresses overlook many of the villages along the Route des Vins, offering the possibility of a pleasant hike away from the summertime crowds. From Ribeauvillé, a 9km (5.5 mile) trail takes you up past three dramatic castles, while Eguisheim is the starting point for a rewarding 12km (7.5 mile) four-castle circuit.

The jewel in the Vosges' fortified crown, however, is the Château du Haut-Koenigsbourg (www.haut-koenigsbourg.fr; *pictured*), nestled 757m (2,500ft) above the Alsace plain. Built in the Middle Ages and subsequently abandoned, the site was given a grandiose restoration after Alsace fell under the German Empire in 1871. For Kaiser Wilhelm II, Haut-Koenigsbourg represented both a link with Germany's glorious Imperial past and a symbol of its new power, and he threw money aplenty into the renovation project. Today, the castle's high fortified walls and radiant pink towers have become a symbol of the Vosges, and a magnet for tourists. A visit takes you across the immaculately restored drawbridge and into a grand courtyard, complete with old-fashioned inn, forge and windmill. Other highlights include an ornate external spiral staircase and the enormous ceramic stoves that fill many of the castle's superbly furnished rooms.

The Auberge de l'Ill is a French gastronomic landmark. It was awarded three Michelin stars in 1967, and has never lost them. The setting is a beautiful 19th-century farmhouse, with interiors given an elegant modernist makeover. In summer, aperitifs are served in the garden overlooking the river Ill. The property has been run by generations of the Haeberlin family, and current chef Marc has added creative flair to his father's exquisite (albeit classical) Alsatian recipes. Subtle contrasts characterise his cuisine, like the *foie d'oie* marinated in sukiyaki or the gently curried lobster stew with citrus fruit. As you'd expect from such a high-class establishment, the presentation is irreproachable. Make sure you reserve well in advance.

Le Bistro des Saveurs

Obernai *35 rue de Sélestat (03.88.49.90.41).*
Open noon-3pm, 7-10pm Wed-Sun. €€€€.
At the Bistro des Saveurs, the decor and cuisine share a similar concept: traditional values given an innovative, modern twist. The classic timber interior and grand fireplace are complemented by elegant furnishings and designer glassware, while typical French dishes are lovingly given new life using local produce and discerning creativity. Chef Thierry Schwartz knows how to reinvent even the simplest ingredients: everyday garden carrots are cooked for several hours in sauce for succulent tenderness, and tomatoes are grilled over a beech fire and delicately filled with their own sorbet. Wife Hélène looks after the clientele, doing the rounds of the tables and carefully explaining how each dish is crafted.

Flamme & Co

Route des Vins *4 rue du Général de Gaulle, Kaysersberg (03.89.47.16.16/www.flammeandco.fr).*
Open 6pm-midnight Tue-Sun. €€.
The medieval village of Kaysersberg makes an unlikely spot for a youth-oriented designer restaurant, but Olivier and Emmanuel Nasti's Flamme & Co has proved a popular hangout since opening in 2006. The concept is simple: reinvigorate the classic Alsatian *flammekueche*. On the menu, you'll find the traditional recipe (baked bread dough covered with crème fraîche, onions and lardons) alongside 30 original variations. Toppings include *magret de canard* seasoned with oranges and cabbage, salmon with roasted mango, and *escargots de la Weiss*, snails prepared in vegetable stock and garlic. There's also a selection of dessert *flammées* (the apple and cinnamon is delicious). Eat up at the bar and you'll see the chef cook your dish in the wood fire. A lounge room upstairs hosts regular events and DJ nights.

Schwendi

Colmar *23 Grand'Rue (03.89.23.66.26).*
Open noon-10.30pm daily. €€.
With a prime location in the heart of Colmar (including a summertime terrace), this traditional *winstub* is extremely popular, so expect to wait for a table. Under the frosted windows, the interior is lined with wooden tables and benches. Protruding wooden beams give the place a nook and cranny feel, and the walls are adorned with enamel advertising plaques for old Alsatian products. The

speciality here is *rösti*, grated potatoes cooked with lardons and served in a metal casserole with anything from munster cheese to Strasbourg sausage. Other staples include *choucroute garnie* and the pizza-like *flammekueche*. Hearty, no-frills food in a lively pub atmosphere.

La Table du Domaine

Route des Vins *30A rte de Molsheim, Soultz-les-Bains, 15km N of Obernai (03.88.47.98.98/www.lucien-doriath.fr). Open noon-2pm Wed, Thur, Sun; noon-2pm, 7-9.30pm Fri, Sat.* €€€.
One of Alsace's many gastronomic specialities is foie gras, and Lucien Doriath has been practising the art since 1987. The homely restaurant on his premises offers up some of the freshest foie gras you're likely to sample: it comes served with chutney, caramelised, fried, with a glass of rhubarb wine, and in a salad with gizzards. For a different take on duck, try the *confit de canard, choucroute de canard* or *magret de canard* (with foie gras sauce). Given the menu, it's a blessing that Doriath's foie gras is soft, velvety and rich – in short, a benchmark for the region. If you're not too ducked out, head for the boutique next door.

La Table du Gourmet

Riquewihr *5 rue 1ère Armée Française (03.89.49.09.09/www.jlbrendel.com). Open 12.15-1.45pm, 7.15-9.15pm Mon, Fri-Sun; 7.15-9.15pm Wed. Closed lunch Nov-Mar & 5wks Jan-Feb.* €€€€.
Chef Jean-Luc Brendel has transformed a 16th-century winegrower's house into a handsome showcase for his creative Franco-Alsatian cuisine. Inside, dark oak beams are complemented by warm red walls for a modern, homely feel. As for the food, Brendel works with fresh produce from local suppliers, favouring wild herbs, berries and floral flavours that follow the seasons. In spring, he crafts a light but crisp tempura asparagus on a bed of prawns and horseradish mousse, while summer ushers in concoctions such as sole with lemon thyme and parmesan. The superb wine cellar includes a selection from neighbouring vineyards.

Stay

Hikers can benefit from cheap, basic rooms and meals at *gîtes d'étape* (www.gites-de-france.com).

Domaine Jean Sipp

Route des Vins *60 rue de la Fraternité, Ribeauvillé (03.89.73.60.02/www.jean-sipp.com).* €.
In the heart of Ribeauvillé's picture-book old town, the wine producer Sipp has two *chambres d'hôte* next to its own 15th-century house. Both rooms are named after one of the estate's vintage wines: the larger Clos Ribeaupierre comes with wood-panelled walls, leather armchairs, TV, private bathroom, and two single beds (which can be pushed together); the Kirchberg, meanwhile, features a double bed, bathroom and TV. Although no breakfast is offered, both rooms include a kitchenette with fridge. Alternatively, there's a host of inviting *boulangeries* and tearooms just a few minutes' walk away on the Grand'Rue.

Hôtel Amiral.

Zinck Hôtel.

Le Grand Hôtel

Parc Naturel des Ballons des Vosges *Pl du Tilleul, Gérardmer, 50km E of Colmar (03.29.63.06.31/ www.grandhotel-gerardmer.com). €€€.*
Known as the 'pearl of the Vosges', Gérardmer is a pretty lakeside town set among evergreen forests. The Grand Hôtel boasts a central location and a site that, as its name suggests, is on the large side. The main building houses 68 clean and comfortable rooms, and all guests have access to three on-site restaurants, indoor and outdoor pools, and a relaxation centre. For real luxury, though, reserve one of the four chalet suites within the hotel grounds. Decked out with wood-panelled interiors and elegant furniture, they feature corner bathtubs and king-size beds, while the two superior suites also boast hydro-massage showers and large terraces.

Hôtel Amiral

Colmar *11B bd du Champs de Mars (03.89.23.26.25/ www.hotel-amiral-colmar.com). €€.*
This 47-room hotel is just a few minutes' walk from Colmar's historic centre. Rooms are calm and modern, although if you ask for room 207 you'll get an insight into the building's former life: from the wood-panelled ceiling and beams hangs a wooden wheel and metal ceiling pulley, used when the complex was a malthouse in the 18th century. Other rooms feature bare stonework, and machinery also decorates the entrance and corridors. A copious buffet breakfast includes cereals, fruit, various breads, and a platter of cheese and ham. There's even an old machine you can use to squeeze fresh orange juice.

Hôtel Gilg

Route des Vins *1 rte des Vins, Mittelbergheim (03.88.08.91.37/www.hotel-gilg.com). Closed Jan & 3wks June-July. €.*
Set in the centre of Mittelbergheim, one of the prettiest villages on the Route des Vins, this homely inn dates back to 1614, making it one of the oldest *winstubs* in Alsace. To get

to the 15 bedrooms, you climb a superb two-storey stone staircase, sculpted by the same stonemasons who worked on Strasbourg cathedral. The wood-panelled rooms offer the charm of the old and the comforts of the new (modern bathrooms, flatscreen TV). The restaurant's Alsatian and French cooking attracts locals as well as hotel guests.

Le Parc

Obernai *169 rte d'Ottrott (03.88.95.50.08/ www.hotel-du-parc.com). Closed 4wks Dec-Jan & 2wks June-July. €€€.*
This luxury complex at the edge of Obernai boasts large landscaped gardens, a spa, three bars, two restaurants, and indoor and outdoor swimming pools. Built in 1954 in Alsace's classic half-timbered style, the hotel houses 62 quiet guestrooms that all come with air conditioning, cable TV and modern furnishings. Although they're not as spacious as in some luxury outfits, many feature their own fireplace, and some offer balcony views of the Vosges, with Mont Ste-Odile nestling directly above. The Asiane Spa centre can get busy at peak times, but it's a haven for pampering, complete with sauna, jacuzzi, hammam, masseurs and gym. The hotel is a 15-minute walk from Obernai's historic centre.

Le Zinck Hôtel

Route des Vins *13 rue de la Marne, Andlau (03.88.08.27.30/www.zinckhotel.com). €€.*
The Zinck family has transformed a 17th-century mill into this colourful hotel on the edge of Andlau's vineyards. The centrepiece of the breakfast room is the mill's original water wheel, and there's also an imposing period fireplace. As for the 18 rooms, they mix rustic charm with urban modernity – and each has been lovingly furnished in a unique style. Choose from the elegant green walls and minimalism of the Chambre Branchée (trendy room), the grandiose 1001 Nuits with its veiled double bed, or the quaint Alsacienne, complete with chequered bed linen, wood-panelled walls and traditional hand-carved chair.

Factfile

When to go

The winter months make high mountain passes inaccessible, but provide excellent skiing potential. The Christmas markets attract bus-loads along the Route des Vins, while the summer months bring sun and more buses. Crowds can be avoided by visiting in spring or autumn – or by lacing up hiking boots and heading into the regional parks.

Getting there

Strasbourg Airport (03.88.64.67.67/www.strasbourg.aeroport.fr) is most convenient for the northern Vosges, while the south is best served by Euroairport (03.89.90.31.11/www.euroairport.com) near Mulhouse. From Paris, TGV trains run directly to both cities and to Colmar (2h50).

Getting around

TER (www.ter-sncf.com) trains connect the region's towns. A car is the easiest way to explore the smaller villages on the Route des Vins, although LK (www.l-k.fr) runs buses from Colmar and Mulhouse to some of the major destinations, as well as into the mountains.

Tourist information

Colmar 4 rue Unterlinden (03.89.20.68.92/ www.ot-colmar.fr). Open Apr-Oct 9am-6pm Mon-Sat; 10am-1pm Sun. Nov-Mar 9am-noon, 2-6pm Mon-Sat; 10am-1pm Sun.

Internet access

Connecte-Toi 24 av Jean de Lattre de Tassigny, Colmar (03.89.23.16.05). Open 10am-midnight Mon-Sat; 2.30pm-midnight Sun.

Need to Know

ACCOMMODATION

CAMPING

Camping à la Ferme www.bienvenue-a-la-ferme.com.

Castels Camping www.les-castels.com.

Federation of Camping & Caravanning www.campingfrance.com.

Yelloh Villages www.yellohvillage.com.

SELF-CATERING

Chez Nous www.cheznous.com.

Clévacances www.clevacances.com.

Erna Low Ski www.ernalow.co.uk.

French Country Cottages www.french-country-cottages.co.uk.

Gîtes de France www.gites-de-france.com.

VFB Holidays www.vfbholidays.co.uk.

AGE RESTRICTIONS

For heterosexuals and homosexuals, the age of consent is 15. You must be 18 to drive, and to consume alcohol in a public place. You must be 16 to buy cigarettes.

AIRLINES

Aer Lingus www.aerlingus.com.

Air France www.airfrance.com.

American Airlines www.americanairlines.com.

bmibaby www.bmibaby.com.

British Airways www.britishairways.com.

British Midland www.flybmi.com.

Continental www.continental.com.

Easyjet www.easyjet.com.

flybe www.flybe.com

Ryanair www.ryanair.com.

United www.united.com.

CHANNEL CROSSINGS

Brittany Ferries www.brittanyferries.com.

Eurotunnel www.eurotunnel.com.

LD Lines www.ldlines.co.uk.

Norfokline www.norfolkline.com.

P&O Ferries www.poferries.com.

SeaFrance www.seafrance.com.

SpeedFerries www.speedferries.com.

EUROSTAR

Eurostar services (www.eurostar.com) to Paris depart from the dedicated terminal at St Pancras International. Thanks to the new high speed track, the journey from London to Paris now takes 2hrs 15mins direct, slightly longer for trains stopping at Ashford and Lille. Eurostar services from the new terminal at Ebbsfleet International, near junction 2 of the M25, take 2hrs 5mins direct. Check in at least 30mins before departure time. Eurostar trains from London St Pancras arrive at Gare du Nord (08.92.35.35.39, www.sncf.fr), with easy access to public transport and taxi ranks. Cycles can be taken as hand luggage if they are dismantled and carried in a bike bag. You can also check them in at the Eurodispatch depot at St Pancras (Esprit Parcel Service, 08705 850 850) or Sernam depot at Gare du Nord (01.55.31.58.40). Check-in must be done 24hrs ahead; a Eurostar ticket must be shown. The service costs £20/€25.

CUSTOMS

Custom declarations are not usually necessary if you arrive from another EU country and are carrying legal goods for personal use. Coming from a non-EU country, you can bring:
• 200 cigarettes, 100 small cigars, 50 cigars or 250g tobacco.
• 1 litre of spirits (more than 22% alcohol) or 2 litres of wine or beer.
• 50g (1.76oz) of perfume.

DISABLED TRAVELLERS

It's always wise to check up on a site's accessibility and provision for disabled access before you visit. There is general information (in French) on the Secrétaire d'Etat aux Personnes Handicapées website (www.handicap.gouv.fr).

DRIVING

If you bring your car to France, you must bring its registration and insurance documents. In peak holiday periods, the organisation Bison Futé hands out brochures at motorway *péages* (toll gates), suggesting less crowded routes. French roads are categorised as Autoroutes (motorways, with an 'A' in front of the number), Routes Nationales (national 'N' roads), Routes Départementales (local, 'D' roads) and rural Routes Communales ('C' roads). Autoroutes are toll roads; some sections, including most of the area around Paris, are free.

BREAKDOWN SERVICES

The AA and RAC do not have reciprocal arrangements with an equivalent organisation in France, so it's advisable to take out additional breakdown insurance cover, for example with a company like Europ Assistance (0870 737 5720/www.europ-assistance.co.uk). If you don't have insurance, you can still use its service (08.10.00.50.50, available 24/7), but it will charge you the full cost.

CAR HIRE

To hire a car, you must be 25 or over and have held a licence for at least a year. Some agencies accept drivers aged 21-24, but a supplement of €20-€25 per day is usual. Take your licence and passport with you. Bargain firms may have an extremely high charge for damage: make sure you read the small print.

Car hire companies

Ada www.ada.fr.

Auto Europe www.auto-europe.co.uk.

Avis www.avis.com.

Budget www.budget.com.

Europcar www.europcar.com.

Hertz www.hertz.com.

Rent-a-Car www.rentacar.fr.

DRUGS

French police have the power to stop and search anyone. It's wise to keep prescription drugs in their original containers and, if possible, to carry copies of the original prescriptions. If you're caught in possession of illegal drugs, you can expect a prison sentence and/or a fine.

ELECTRICITY

Electricity in France runs on 220V. Visitors with British 240V appliances can change the plug or use an adaptor (*adaptateur*). For US 110V appliances, you'll need to use a transformer (transformateur), available at BHV or branches of Fnac and Darty.

EMBASSIES & CONSULATES

Australian Embassy 4 rue Jean-Rey, 15th, Paris (01.40.59.33.00/www.france.embassy. gov.au). M° Bir-Hakeim. Open Consular services 9.15am-noon, 2-4.30pm Mon-Fri; Visas 10am-noon Mon-Fri.

British Embassy 35 rue du Fbg-St-Honoré, 8th, Paris (01.44.51.31.00/www.amb-grande bretagne.fr). M° Concorde. Consular services: 18bis rue d'Anjou, 8th. M° Concorde. Open 9.30am-12.30pm, 2.30-4.30pm Mon-Fri. Visas: 16 rue d'Anjou, 8th (01.44.51.31.01). Open 9.30am-noon by phone; 2.30-4.30pm Mon-Fri.

Canadian Embassy 35 av Montaigne, 8th, Paris (01.44.43.29.00/www.amb-canada.fr). M° Franklin D. Roosevelt. Open 9am-noon, 2-5pm Mon-Fri. Consular services: 01.44.43.29.02. Open 9am-noon Mon-Fri. Visas: 37 av Montaigne, 8th (01.44.43.29.16). Open 8.30-11am Mon-Fri.

Irish Embassy 12 av Foch, 16th, Paris. Consulate 4 rue Rude, 16th (01.44.17.67.00). M° Charles de Gaulle Etoile. Open Consular/visas 9.30am-noon Mon-Fri; by phone 9.30am-1pm, 2.30-5.30pm Mon-Fri.

New Zealand Embassy 7ter rue Léonard-de-Vinci, 16th, Paris (01.45.01.43.43/www.nzembassy. com/france). M° Victor Hugo. Open 9am-1pm, 2-5.30pm Mon-Fri (closes 4pm Fri). July, Aug 9am-1pm, 2-4.30pm Mon-Thur; 9am-2pm Fri. Visas 9am-12.30pm Mon-Fri.

South African Embassy 59 quai d'Orsay, 7th, Paris (01.53.59.23.23/www.afriquesud.net). M° Invalides. Open 8.30am-5.15pm Mon-Fri. Consulate & visas 8.30am-noon Mon-Fri.

US Embassy 2 av Gabriel, 8th, Paris (01.43.12.22.22/http://france.usembassy.gov). M° Concorde. Consulate & visas: 4 av Gabriel, 8th (08.10.26.46.26). M° Concorde. Open Consular services 9am-12.30pm, 1-3pm Mon-Fri. Visas 08.92.23.84.72 or check website for non-immigration visas.

EMERGENCIES

Ambulance (SAMU) 15

Police 17

Fire (Sapeurs-Pompiers) 18

Emergency (from a mobile phone) 112

HEALTH

Nationals of non-EU countries should take out insurance before leaving home. EU nationals residing in France can use the French Social Security system, which refunds up to 70 per cent of medical expenses. UK residents travelling in Europe require a European National Health Insurance Card (EHIC). This allows them to benefit from free or reduced-cost medical care when travelling in a country belonging to the European Economic Area (EEA) or Switzerland. The EHIC replaces the E111 form and is free of charge. For further information, refer to www.dh.gov.uk/travellers.

PHARMACIES

French pharmacies sport a green neon cross. A rota of *pharmacies de garde* operate at night and on Sundays. If closed, a pharmacy will have a sign indicating the nearest one open. Staff can provide basic medical services such as bandaging wounds (for a small fee) and will indicate the nearest doctor on duty. *Parapharmacies* sell almost everything pharmacies do but cannot dispense prescription medication. Toiletries and sanitary products are usually cheaper in supermarkets.

ID

French law requires that some form of ID be carried at all times. Be prepared to produce your passport or EHIC card.

LANGUAGE

GETTING AROUND

where is the métro? où est le métro?; **when is the next train for... ?** c'est quand le prochain train pour... ?; **ticket** un billet; **station** la gare; **platform** le quai; **entrance** entrée; **exit** sortie.

SIGHTSEEING

museum un musée; **church** une église; **exhibition** une exposition; **ticket** (for museum) un billet; (for theatre, concert) une place; **open** ouvert; **closed** fermé; **free** gratuit; **reduced price** un tarif réduit.

ACCOMMODATION

do you have a room for this evening? avez-vous une chambre pour ce soir?; **full** complet; **room** une chambre; **bed** un lit; **double bed** un grand lit; **a room with twin beds** une chambre à deux lits; **with bath(room)/shower** avec (salle de) bain/ douche; **breakfast** le petit déjeuner.

EATING OUT

I'd like to book a table for three people at 8pm je voudrais réserver une table pour trois personnes à vingt heures; **lunch** le déjeuner; **dinner** le dîner; **coffee** un café; **wine** le vin; **beer** une bière; **mineral water** eau minérale; **tap water** une carafe d'eau; **the bill, please** l'addition, s'il vous plaît.

SHOPPING

cheap pas cher; **expensive** cher; **how much?/ how many?** combien?; **have you got change?** avez-vous de la monnaie?; **I'll take it** je le prends; **may I try this on?** est-ce que je pourrais essayer cet article?; **do you have a smaller/ larger size?** auriez-vous la taille en-dessous/ au dessus?; **I'm a size 38** je fais du 38.

MONEY

The amount of currency visitors may carry is not limited. However, sums worth over €7,600 must be declared to customs when entering or leaving the country.

THE EURO

Non-French debit and credit cards can be used to withdraw and pay in euros, and currency withdrawn in France can be used subsequently all over the euro zone. Daylight robbery occurs,

however, if you try to deposit a euro cheque from any country other than France in a French bank: the current charge is around €15 for this service.

ATMS

Withdrawals in euros can be made from bank and post office automatic cash machines. The specific cards accepted are marked on each machine, and most give instructions in English. Credit card companies charge a fee for cash advances, but rates are often better than banks.

CREDIT CARDS

Major international credit cards are widely used in France; Visa (more commonly known in France as Carte Bleue) is the most readily accepted. French-issued credit cards have a security microchip (*puce*) in each card. The card is slotted into a reader, and the holder keys in a PIN to authorise the transaction. Non-French cards work, but generate a credit slip to sign.

Lost/stolen credit cards

Call one of the following 24hr services which have English-speaking staff: **American Express** 01.47.77.70.00. **Diners Club** 01.49.06.17.50. **MasterCard** 01.45.16.65.65. **Visa** 08.92.70.57.05.

OPENING HOURS

Standard opening hours for shops are 9/10am-7/8pm Mon-Sat. Some shops close on Monday. Shops and businesses often close at lunch, usually 12.30-2pm.

SMOKING

Although smoking seems to be an essential part of French life (and death), the French state and public health groups have recently waged war against the cigarette on several fronts. Smoking is now banned in all enclosed public spaces, including bars, cafés, clubs, restaurants, hotel foyers and shops, as well as on public transport. Many bars, cafés and clubs offer smoking gardens or terraces. There are also increasingly strident anti-smoking campaigns. Health warnings on cigarette packets are unignorable, and prices have soared.

TAX

French VAT (*taxe sur la valeur ajoutée* or TVA) is arranged in three bands: 2.1 per cent for items of medication and newspapers; 5.5 per cent for food, books, CDs and DVDs; and 19.6 per cent for all other types of goods and services.

TAX REFUNDS

Non-EU residents can claim a refund or *détaxe* (around 12 per cent) on VAT if they spend over €175 in any one day in one shop and if they live outside the EU for more than six months in the year. At the shop concerned ask for a *bordereau de vente à l'exportation*, and when you leave France have it stamped by customs. Then send the stamped form back to the shop. *Détaxe* does not cover food, drink, antiques, services or works of art.

TELEPHONES

DIALLING & CODES

All French phone numbers have ten digits. Paris and Ile-de-France numbers begin with 01; the rest of France is divided into zones (02-05). Mobile phone numbers start with 06. 08 indicates a special rate; numbers beginning with 08 can only be reached from inside France. If you are calling France from abroad, leave off the 0 at the start of the ten-digit number. The country code is 33. To call abroad from France dial 00, then the country code, then the number. Since 1998 other phone companies have been allowed to enter the market, but France Télécom still has the monopoly on basic service. It has a useful website with information on rates and contracts: www.agence.francetelecom.com.

MOBILE PHONES

A subscription (*abonnement*) will normally get you a free phone if you sign up for at least one year. Two hours' calling time a month costs about €35 per month. International calls are normally charged extra – a lot extra. The three companies that rule the mobile phone market in France are:

Bouyges Télécom www.bouyguestelecom.fr.

France Télécom/Orange www.orange.fr.

SFR www.sfr.fr.

PUBLIC PHONES

Most public telephones in Paris, almost all of which are maintained by France Télécom, use *télécartes* (phonecards). Sold at post offices, *tabacs*, airports and train and métro stations, the phoecards cost €7.50 for 50 units and €15 for 120 units.

TIME & SEASONS

France is one hour ahead of Greenwich Mean Time (GMT). France uses the 24hr system (for example, 18h means 6pm).

TIPPING

A service charge of ten to 15 per cent is legally included in your bill at all restaurants, cafés and bars. However, it is polite to either round up the final amount for drinks, or to leave a cash tip of €1-€2 or more for a meal, depending on the restaurant and, of course, the quality of the service.

TOURIST OFFICE

Maison de la France www.franceguide.com. Official website of the French Tourist Office.

INTERNATIONAL OFFICES

London Lincoln House, 300 High Holborn, WC1V 7JH (0906 824 4123).

New York 825 Third Avenue, 29th Floor, 10022 (1-514 288 1904).

TRAINS

The TGV high-speed train has slashed journey times and is being extended to all the main regions. There are few long-distance bus services. Tickets can be bought at any SNCF station (not just the one from which you'll travel), SNCF shops and travel agents. If you reserve online or by phone, you can pay and pick up your tickets from the station or have them sent to your home. SNCF automatic machines (*billeterie automatique*) only work with French credit/debit cards. Regular trains have full-rate White (peak) and cheaper Blue (off-peak) periods. You can save on TGV fares by buying special cards. The Carte 12/25 gives under-26s a 25-50 per cent reduction; even without it, under-26s are entitled to 25 per cent off. Buy tickets in advance to secure the cheaper fare. Before you board any train, stamp your ticket in the orange *composteur* machines located on the platforms, or you might have to pay a hefty fine. To purchase tickets in advance from the UK, contact Rail Europe.

Rail Europe
08448 484 064/www.raileurope.co.uk.

SNCF reservations & tickets
08.92.35.35.35/www.sncf.com.

VISAS

EU nationals don't need a visa to enter France, nor do US, Canadian, Australian, New Zealand or South African citizens for stays of up to three months. Nationals of other countries should enquire at the nearest French embassy or consulate before leaving home. If they are travelling to France from one of the countries in the Schengen agreement, the visa from that country should be sufficient. EU citizens may stay in France for as long as their passport is valid. For non-EU citizens who wish to stay for longer than three months, they must apply to the French embassy or consulate in their own country for a long-term visa.

WEIGHTS & MEASURES

Remember that all speed limits are in kilometres per hour. One kilometre is equivalent to 0.62 miles (1 mile = 1.6km). Petrol, like other liquids, is measured in litres.

Festivals & Events

JANUARY

Burgundy
St-Vincent Tournante
Saint Vincent is the patron saint of wine production and 22 January is St Vincent's Day, the focus for a celebration of wine that dates back to the Middle Ages. Each year a particular village in Burgundy is selected for a celebration that includes a procession with banners of the 80 wine societies that exist today, followed by copious wine tasting.
www.st-vincent-tournante.fr

Nantes, Brittany
La Folle Journée
This internationally acclaimed classical music marathon hosts around 250 concerts over five days. The event focuses on a different composer and historical period every year.
www.follejournee.fr

FEBRUARY

Nice
Carnaval de Nice
Some of the most fabulous carnival processions in the world saunter down the promenade des Anglais, their satirical intent inspired by *Le Roi des Dupes* (the Lord of Misrule).
www.nicecarnaval.com

Paris
Six Nations
Hordes of Brits and Celts invade Paris and the Stade de France for three big rugby weekends in spring. You'll need to book tickets several months in advance if you want to join them.
www.rbs6nations.com

MARCH

Paris
Banlieues Bleues
Five weeks of quality French and international jazz, blues, R&B and soul in Seine St-Denis.
www.banlieuesbleues.org

APRIL

Paris
Marathon de Paris
Perhaps the world's most picturesque marathon, with 35,000 runners heading from the Champs-Elysées along the Right Bank to the Bois de Vincennes, and back along the Left Bank to the Bois de Boulogne.
www.parismarathon.com

MAY

Across France
La Nuit des Musées
All over France, for one night only, museums open their doors late, accompanied by special events and workshops.
www.nuitdesmusees.culture.fr

Cannes, nr Nice
Cannes Film Festival
The legendary film extravaganza brings a fortnight of deal-brokering and frantic paparazzi activity to Cannes. It's almost impossible to get tickets to Official Selection films, but you can buy tickets for Directors' Fortnight and Critics' Week films.
www.festival-cannes.fr

Coutances, Normandy
Jazz sous les Pommiers
International and local jazz talents perform everything from New Orleans to electro jazz at this festival held over the Ascension weekend.
www.jazzsouslespommiers.com

Mutigny, Champagne
La Fête de la Vigne et du Vin
Every year the town of Mutigny welcomes visitors from far and wide to celebrate wine making in the area with music and, of course, tasting.
www.champagne-tourisme.com

Paris
French Tennis Open
The glitzy Grand Slam tournament, whose tricky clay courts have been the downfall of many a champion, never fails to attract showbiz stars and tennis fans from around the world.
www.frenchopen.org

JUNE

Across France
Fête de la Musique
Celebrated across France, and now in many other parts of the world as well, free concerts (performed by both professional musicians and amateurs) fill the streets in a celebration of the summer solstice and the longest day of the year (21 June). Expect everything from classical and jazz to rock, hip hop, house and electro.
www.fetedelamusique.culture.fr

Bordeaux
Vinexpo
This vast international trade fair is held in Bordeaux every two years for the world's biggest names in the wine and spirits industry. By invitation only.
www.vinexpo.com

Bordeaux
Bordeaux fête le vin
Every even-numbered year the Bordeaux region celebrates with this four-day wine festival that stretches along the banks of the Garonne river. With a tasting pass, visitors can try a range of wines from the region.
www.bordeaux-fete-le-vin.com

Loire Valley
24 heures du Mans
The toughest, most gruelling and most renowned endurance sports car racing event in the world began in 1923 as a competition to test the reliability and durability, as well as speed, of sports cars. Today's opponents still race for a full 24 hours round the Circuit de Sarthe, which incorporates public roads into the racetrack.
www.lemans.org

Lyon
Les Nuits de Fourvière
Held in the two beautiful ancient amphitheatres in the Fourvière district of Lyon, this internationally recognised arts festival offers a wide range of cultural events (theatre dance, music and cinema) throughout June and July. In 2009 there were performances from the likes of Blur, Tracey Chapman and Pete Doherty.
www.nuitsdefourviere.fr

Montpellier
Montpellier Danse
This dance festival, established in 1981, now welcomes some of the most prestigious dance companies from around the world.
www.montpellierdanse.com

Paris
Marche des Fiertés (Gay Pride March)
Outrageous floats and flamboyant costumes parade towards Bastille; then there's an official fête and various nightlife events.
www.inter-lgbt.org

Paris
Paris Jazz Festival
Two months of free weekend jazz concerts in the colourful Parc Floral.
www.parisjazzfestival2009.net

Paris
Prix de Diane Hermès
The French answer to the Derby draws the cream of high society to Chantilly, sporting silly hats and keen to have a flutter.
www.france-galop.com

Paris
Solidays
This three-day, multi-genre music festival, held for the benefit of HIV/AIDS charities, takes place in the Hippodrome de Longchamp in the Bois de Boulogne.
www.solidays.com

Reims
Les Flâneries Musicales de Reims
This famous classical and jazz music festival takes place in many of the city's oldest and most beautiful buildings.
www.flaneriesreims.com

Vienne, nr Lyon
Jazz à Vienne
First held in 1981, Jazz à Vienne is an internationally recognised event and has featured giants such as Miles Davies and Ella Fitzgerald in the past. The main concerts are held in the historic Théâtre Antique, but there is also blues, gospel and Cuban music on offer in the many fringe venues around town.
www.jazzavienne.com

JULY

Across France
Bastille Day
(Le Quatorze Juillet)
Fireworks and *bals des pompiers* (open-air parties at fire stations) commemorate 1789's storming of the Bastille, an event which came to symbolise the rebellion of the French Revolution. At 10am on the 14th, crowds line up along the Champs-Elysées as the President reviews a full military parade.

Aix-en-Provence
Le Festival international d'Art Lyrique d'Aix-en-Provence
Created in 1948, this is one of Europe's major opera festivals and sees performances held throughout July.
www.festival-aix.com

Arles, Nr Avignon
Rencontres d'Arles
With a wealth of exhibitions, curated collections and a lively fringe festival (www.voies-off.com), this is a major event on the contemporary photography scene.
www.rencontres-arles.com

Avignon
Festival d'Avignon
More than 60 years on, Avignon remains a prestigious meeting point for some of the most avant garde names in performing arts. The focal point for activities is the impressive Palais des Papes.
www.festival-avignon.com

Belfort, nr The Vosges

Eurockéennes

One of the most important French rock festivals, Eurockéennes attracts over 100,000 spectators a year and some big-name international acts to a stunning lakeside setting.
www.eurockeennes.fr

Calvi, Corsica

Calvi on the Rocks

This electro festival is held on a beautiful Corsican beach in July. The event is building a strong reputation and is increasingly attracting big-name international DJs.
www.calviontherocks.com

Carhaix, Brittany

Veilles Charrues

This is one of the largest annual musical festivals in France, attracting a 200,000-strong crowd. International headliners during the last few years have included the likes of REM and The Cure.
www.vieillescharrues.asso.fr

Colmar, The Vosges

Festival international de Musique Classique de Colmar

Over the last 20 years this has become one of the top classical musical festivals in Europe, drawing orchestras from around the world. It was originally set up by a German conductor and has been run by Russian violinist and conductor Vladimir Spivakov since 1989.
www.festival-colmar.com

Nice

Nice Jazz Festival

Jazz concerts are staged in the stylish Roman arena at this poppier alternative to Jazz à Juan (www.antibesjuanlespins.com). In recent years, line-ups have included the likes of Rufus Wainwright, Diana Krall and Pink Martini.
www.nicejazzfestival.fr

Paris

Paris-Plage

Palm trees, huts, hammocks and around 2,000 tonnes of fine sand on both banks of the Seine bring a seaside vibe to the city. Not only this – there's a floating pool too.
www.paris.fr

Paris

Paris Cinéma

Premieres, tributes and restored films make up the programme at this popular summer film-going initiative.
www.pariscinema.org

Paris

Le Cinéma en Plein Air

A themed season of films projected under the stars on to Europe's largest inflatable screen.
www.villette.com

Across France

Le Tour de France

The ultimate cycling endurance test climaxes in Paris after some 3,500km (2,175 miles). Blink and you'll miss the winner flying past the finishing line on the Champs-Elysées.
www.letour.fr

Patrimonio, Corsica

Nuit de la Guitare de Patrimonio

This international guitar festival, founded in 1990, has grown over the years to attract some of the world's most renowned guitar players. The event has remained an informal affair and is set in magnificent surroundings.
www.festival-guitare-patrimonio.com

Prades, The Pyrenees

Festival Pablo Casals

Founded in the 1950s by the great Spanish Catalan cellist, this festival in the small town of Prades in the Pyrenees has become one of the world's most important chamber music events.
www.prades-festival-casals.com

La Roque d'Anthéron, nr Aix-en-Provence

Le Festival de La Roque-d'Anthéron

This acclaimed international piano festival takes place during July and August in the grounds of the Château de Florans.
www.festival-piano.com

AUGUST

Aurillac, Auvergne Volcanoes

Le Festival d'Aurillac

An international celebration of street performance and street art held over four days in August.
www.aurillac.net

Bayonne, Basque Country

Fêtes de Bayonne

The main Basque festival in France was founded in 1933, and now attracts over 350,000 people each year. The hectic programme of events includes cow racing, bull fighting, fireworks displays, ballroom dancing and lots of music.
www.fetes.bayonne.fr

Colmar, The Vosges

Foire aux Vins d'Alsace

This regional wine fair dates back to just after World War II and is a good opportunity to taste a wide range of local Alsace wines.
www.foire-colmar.com

Dijon

Fêtes de la Vigne

Dijon's annual celebration of local food and wine is set against a lively backdrop of music and dancing.
www.fetesdelavigne.fr

Paris
Rock en Seine
Three days, three stages and one world-class line-up of rock and indie bands.
www.rockenseine.com

SEPTEMBER

Across France
Journées du Patrimoine
Historic buildings across France open up to the public for this annual architectural heritage weekend.
www.culture.gouv.fr

Deauville, Normandy
Festival de Deauville
This international festival of American cinema includes a competition for independent US films. Since its creation in 1975, it has welcomed many of the biggest stars of American cinema.
www.festival-deauville.com

Lille
Grande Braderie
The biggest flea market in Europe dates back to the 12th century and pulls in over three million visitors each year. Sellers include everyone from professional antiques dealers to individuals keen to clear out their attics.
www.lilletourism.com

Paris
Jazz à la Villette
The first fortnight in September brings one of Paris's best jazz festivals to La Villette.
www.jazzalavillette.com

Paris
Techno Parade
The Saturday parade (which finishes at Bastille) marks the beginning of electro music-fest Rendez-vous Electroniques.
www.technoparade.fr

Paris
Festival d'Automne
A major annual festival of challenging contemporary theatre, dance and modern opera, intent on bringing non-Western culture into the French consciousness. 'Autumn Festival' is a bit of a misnomer, as some exhibitions run over into January.
www.festival-automne.com

OCTOBER

Paris
Nuit Blanche
Culture by moonlight as the city's galleries and museums host special after-dark installations, and swimming pools, bars and clubs stay open late into the night.
www.paris.fr

Paris
Prix de l'Arc de Triomphe
France's most famous – and lucrative, as far as the bookies are concerned – flat race attracts the horse racing elite for a weekend of fun, usually on the first weekend of the month.
www.prixarcdetriomphe.com

Paris
Mondial de l'Automobile
A fortnight of automotive madness with cutting-edge vehicle design from around the world.
www.mondial-automobile.com

Paris
FIAC
The Louvre and the Grand Palais are the two venues for this week-long international contemporary art fair.
www.fiacparis.com

NOVEMBER

Beaune, Nr Dijon
Vente des Vins des Hospices de Beaune
This auction is one of the most famous charity events in the world and sets the trend for the price of Burgundy wine each year. It also coincides with a popular festival in honour of Burgundian wine involving a succession of lively events and tastings in the town.
www.beaune.com/hospices

Les Sables-d'Olonne, nr Ile de Ré
Vendée Globe
Every four years the town celebrates the start of the world's most prestigious solo round-the-world yacht race, which the winner usually takes around 80 to 90 days to complete. The last race took place in 2008.
www.vendeeglobe.org

Paris
Festival des Inrockuptibles
This festival, curated by popular French music magazine *Les Inrockuptibles*, boasts top international indie, rock, techno and trip hop acts.
www.lesinrocks.com

DECEMBER

Paris
Africolor
This month-long African music festival began in 1989 in the northern suburb of St-Denis and now features artists from all over the globe.
www.africolor.com

Strasbourg
Marché de Noel de Strasbourg
The largest and most famous Christmas market in France takes place throughout December.
www.noel-strasbourg.com

Advertisers' Index

Please refer to relevant sections for contact details

Index

Page references in italics indicate illustrations.